P9-DWE-827

RADICAL

MY YEAR WITH A SOCIALIST SENATOR

RADICAL © 2022 SOFIA WARREN

Published by Top Shelf Productions, an imprint of IDW Publishing, a division of Idea and Design Works, LLC. Offices: Top Shelf Productions, c/o Idea & Design Works, LLC, 2765 Truxtun Road, San Diego, CA 92106. Top Shelf Productions®, the Top Shelf logo, Idea and Design Works®, and the IDW logo are registered trademarks of Idea and Design Works, LLC. All Rights Reserved. With the exception of small excerpts of artwork used for review purposes, none of the contents of this publication may be reprinted without the permission of IDW Publishing.

IDW Publishing does not read or accept unsolicited submissions of ideas, stories, or artwork.

Editor-in-Chief: Chris Staros

Edited by Leigh Walton

Design by Nathan Widick

ISBN: 978-1-60309-512-9   25 24 23 22   1 2 3 4

Visit our online catalog at topshelfcomix.com.

Printed in Canada.

RADICAL

MY YEAR WITH A SOCIALIST SENATOR

SOFIA WARREN

To Ana, Gabriel,
and Noah

Julia Salazar,
state senator for NY-18

Boris Santos,
chief of staff

Duncan Bryer,
researcher and
office manager

Gabbi
Zutrau,
digital
comms

Who's Who?
Character Guide

Cea Weaver,
coordinator
of Housing
Justice
for All

Isabel Anreus,
constituent services
manager

Ramón
Pebenito,
organizer

Ramses
Dukes,
organizer

Andresa
Stewart-Cousins,
Senate majority
leader

Alvin Peña,
organizer

Jessica
Ramos
Franco,
organizer

Mark
Mishler,
counsel

Carl Heastie,
Assembly speaker

Guillermo
Martinez,
legislative
director

Andrew
Cuomo,
governor

Melissa Galeano,
constituent services
and scheduler

Michael
Carter,
comms
director

Sofia Warren,
cartoonist

Veronica Cruz,
director of
Albany operations

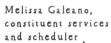

Author's Note

This is a memoir. The scenes depicted herein have been reconstructed from my memory, with the significant help of the many recordings I took along the way: audio, video, photos, notes, and sketches. Dialogue has been edited for clarity and brevity, and some scenes have been reordered or condensed for the same reasons.

Preface

This is Julia Salazar.

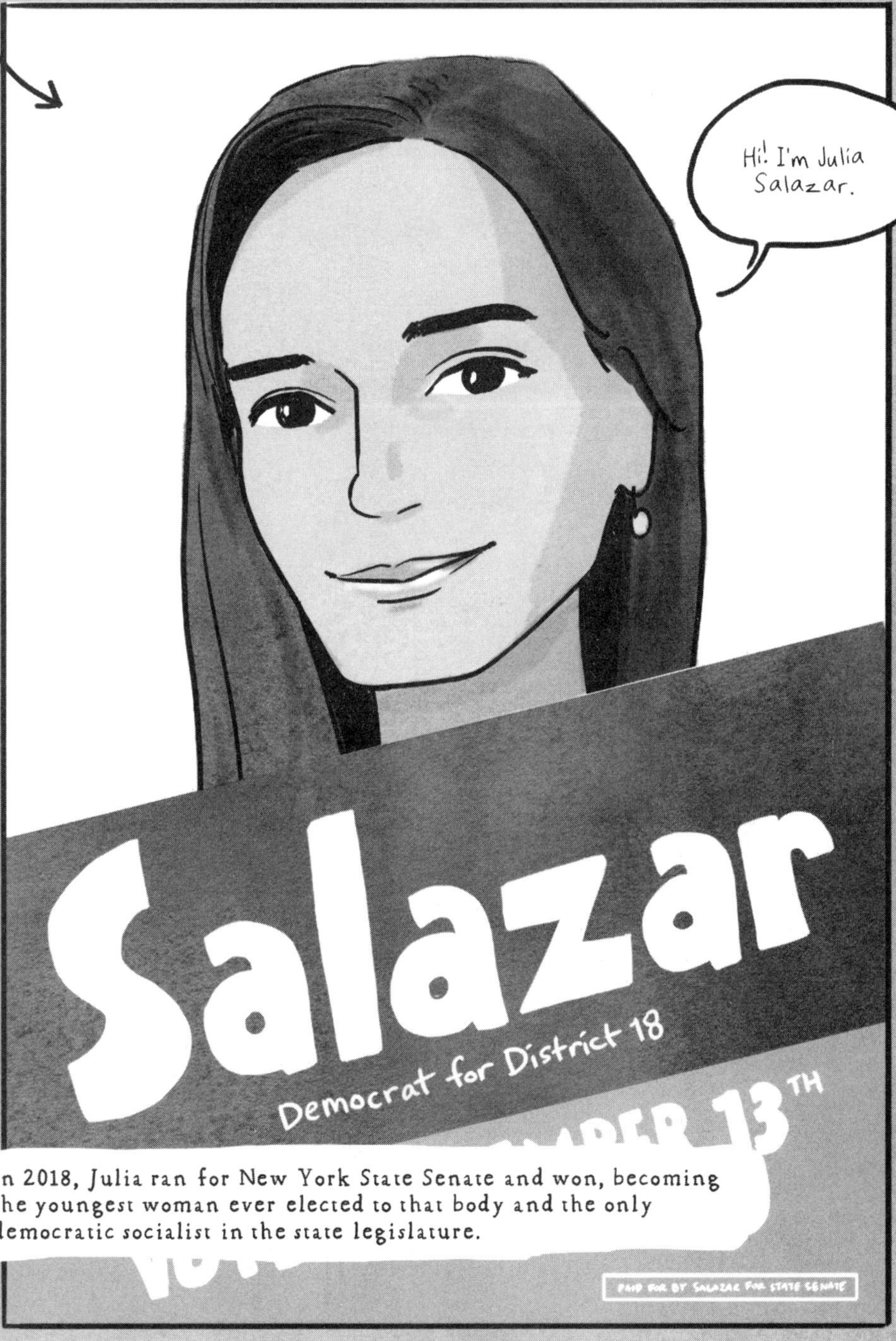
Hi! I'm Julia Salazar.
Salazar
Democrat for District 18
PAID FOR BY SALAZAR FOR STATE SENATE

In 2018, Julia ran for New York State Senate and won, becoming the youngest woman ever elected to that body and the only democratic socialist in the state legislature.

I wrote this book because she would not stop following me.

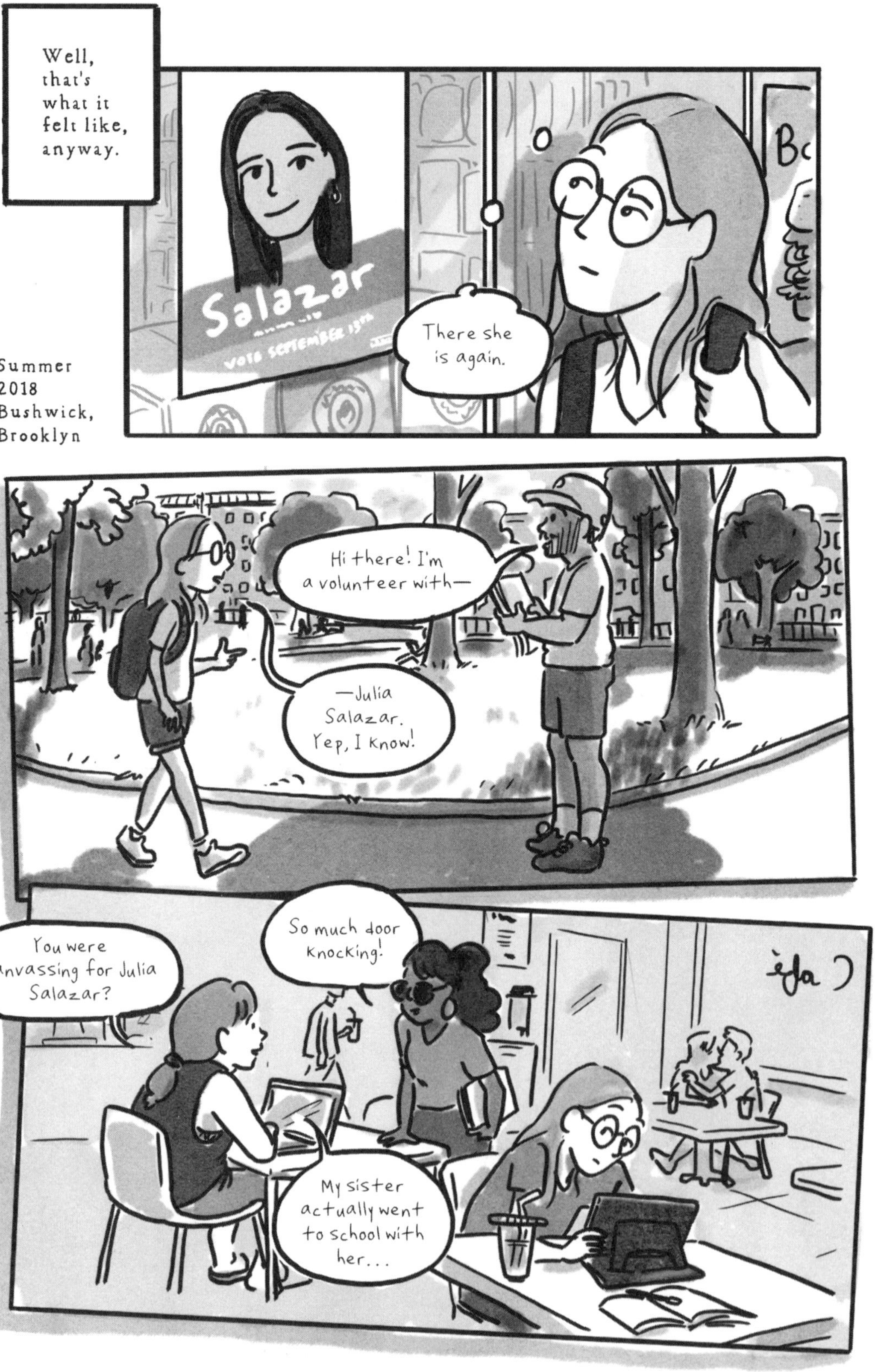
Well, that's what it felt like, anyway.
Salazar
VOTE SEPTEMBER 13TH
There she is again.
Summer 2018 Bushwick, Brooklyn
Hi there! I'm a volunteer with—
—Julia Salazar. Yep, I know!
You were canvassing for Julia Salazar?
So much door knocking!
My sister actually went to school with her...

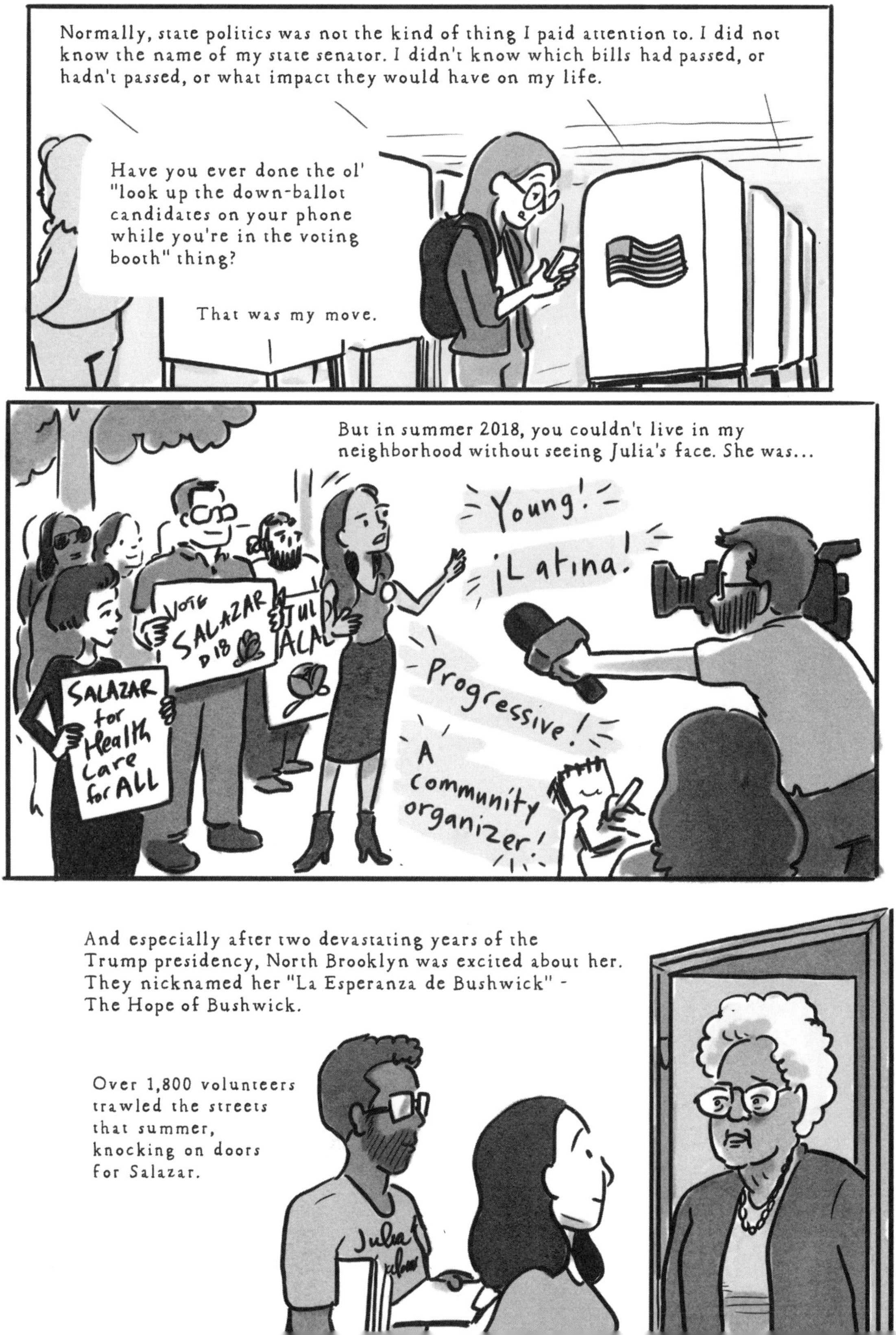
Normally, state politics was not the kind of thing I paid attention to. I did not know the name of my state senator. I didn't know which bills had passed, or hadn't passed, or what impact they would have on my life.
Have you ever done the ol' "look up the down-ballot candidates on your phone while you're in the voting booth" thing?
That was my move.
But in summer 2018, you couldn't live in my neighborhood without seeing Julia's face. She was...
Young!
¡Latina!
Progressive!
A community organizer!
VOTE SALAZAR D18
SALAZAR for Health care for ALL
And especially after two devastating years of the Trump presidency, North Brooklyn was excited about her. They nicknamed her "La Esperanza de Bushwick" - The Hope of Bushwick.
Over 1,800 volunteers trawled the streets that summer, knocking on doors for Salazar.

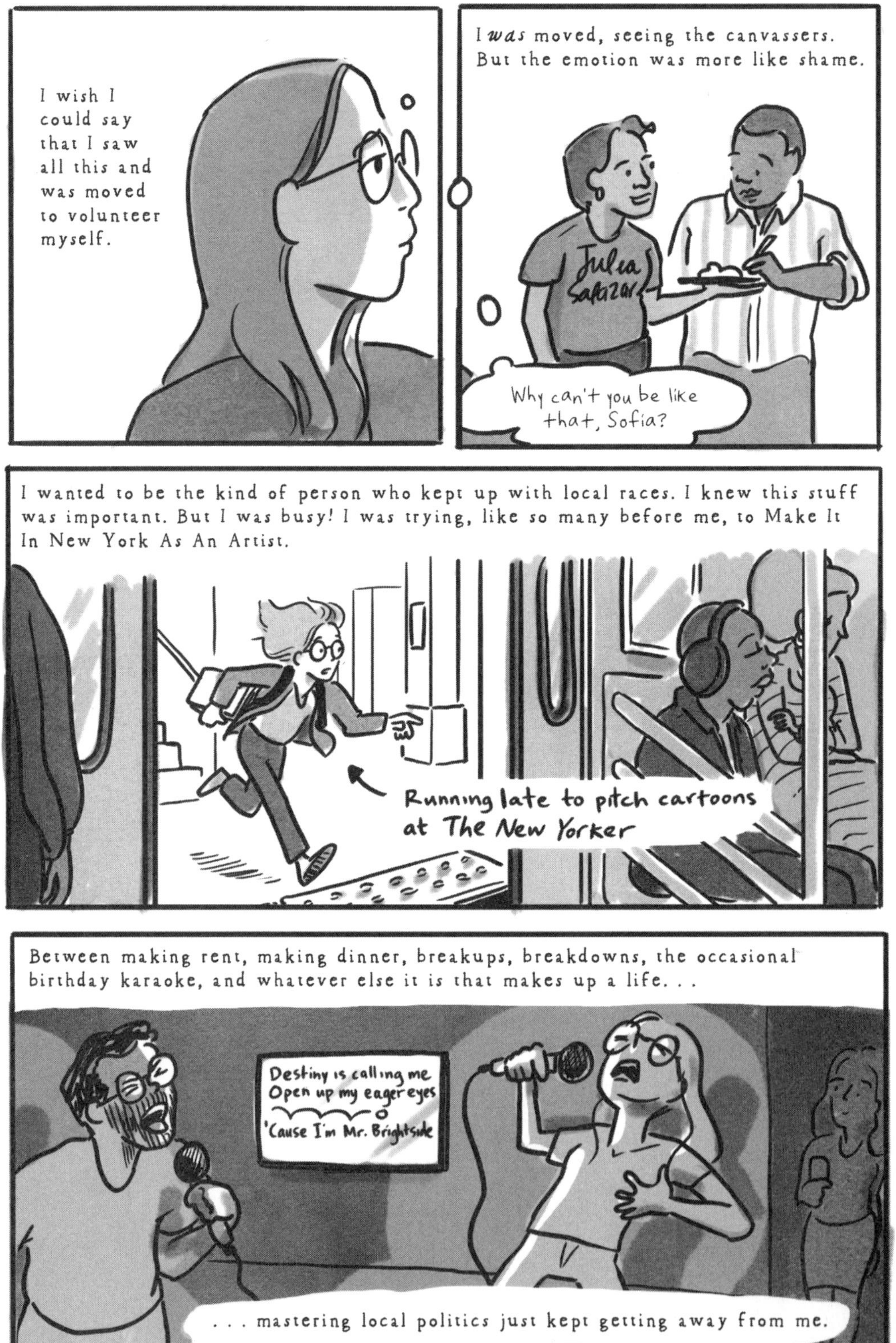
I wish I could say that I saw all this and was moved to volunteer myself.
I *was* moved, seeing the canvassers. But the emotion was more like shame.
Julia Salazar
Why can't you be like that, Sofia?
I wanted to be the kind of person who kept up with local races. I knew this stuff was important. But I was busy! I was trying, like so many before me, to Make It In New York As An Artist.
Running late to pitch cartoons at *The New Yorker*
Between making rent, making dinner, breakups, breakdowns, the occasional birthday karaoke, and whatever else it is that makes up a life. . .
Destiny is calling me
Open up my eager eyes
'Cause I'm Mr. Brightside
. . . mastering local politics just kept getting away from me.

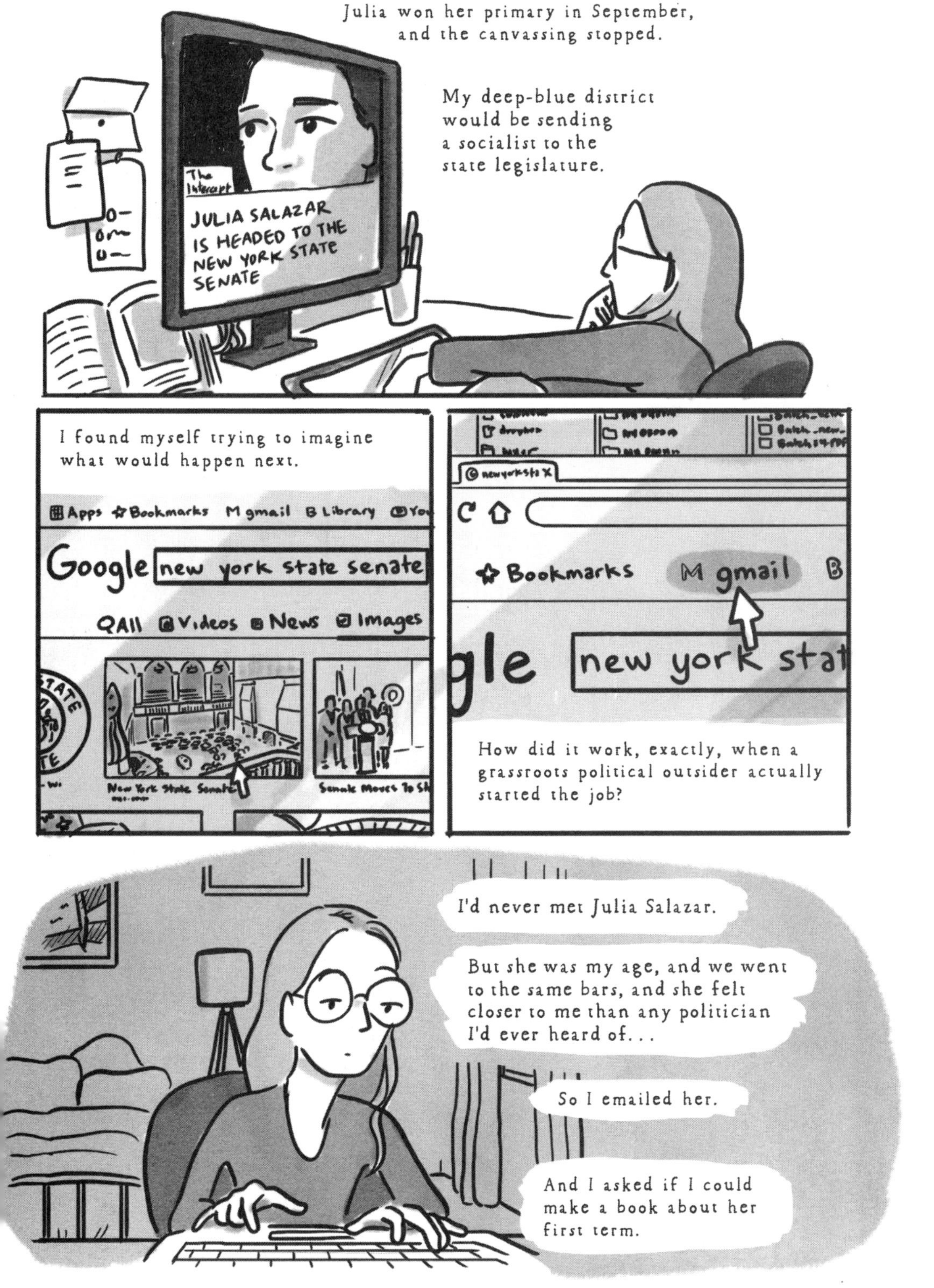
Julia won her primary in September, and the canvassing stopped.
The Intercept
JULIA SALAZAR IS HEADED TO THE NEW YORK STATE SENATE
My deep-blue district would be sending a socialist to the state legislature.
I found myself trying to imagine what would happen next.
Apps Bookmarks gmail Library
Google new york state senate
All Videos News Images
New York State Senate
Senate Moves To St
Bookmarks gmail
new york stat
How did it work, exactly, when a grassroots political outsider actually started the job?
I'd never met Julia Salazar.
But she was my age, and we went to the same bars, and she felt closer to me than any politician I'd ever heard of...
So I emailed her.
And I asked if I could make a book about her first term.

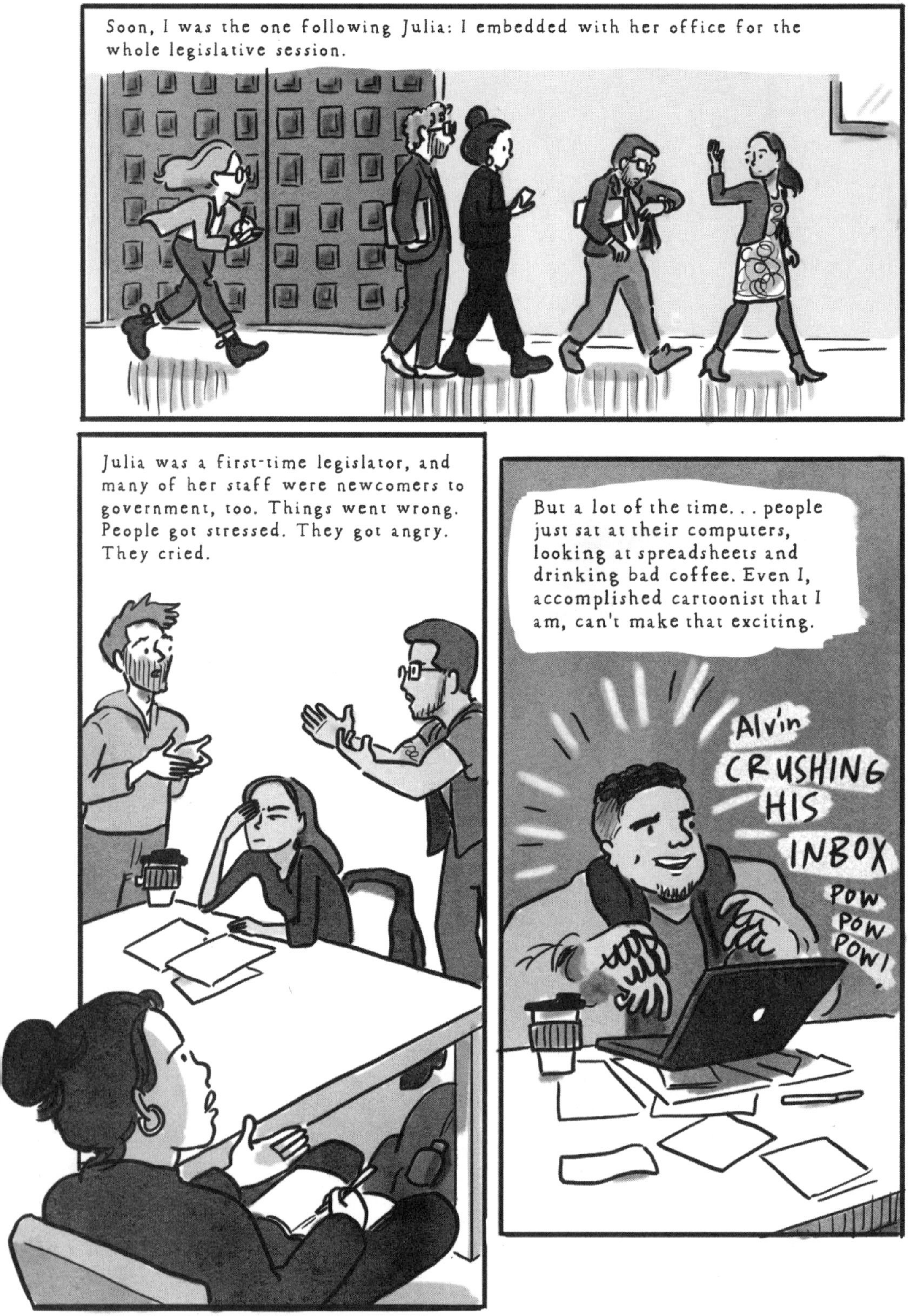
Soon, I was the one following Julia: I embedded with her office for the whole legislative session.
Julia was a first-time legislator, and many of her staff were newcomers to government, too. Things went wrong. People got stressed. They got angry. They cried.
But a lot of the time. . . people just sat at their computers, looking at spreadsheets and drinking bad coffee. Even I, accomplished cartoonist that I am, can't make that exciting.
Alvin CRUSHING HIS INBOX
POW POW POW!

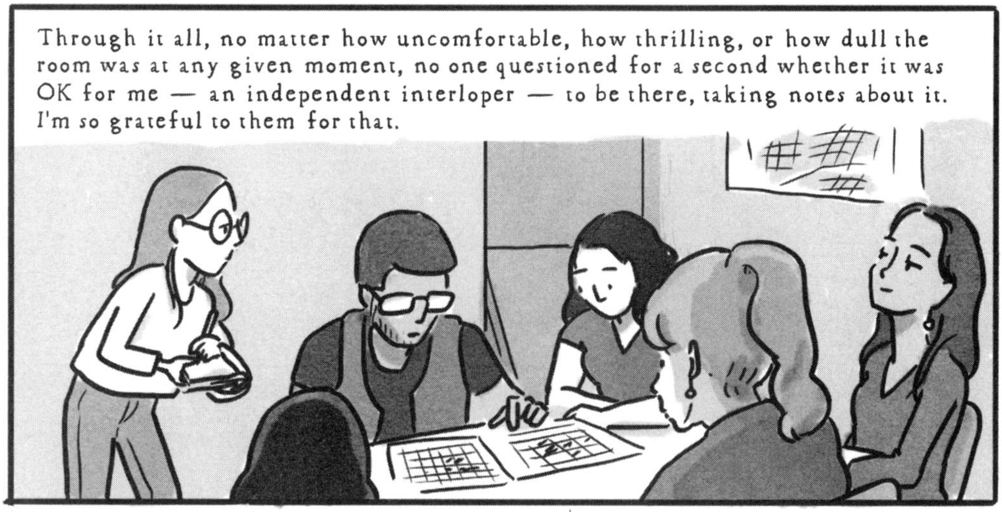
Through it all, no matter how uncomfortable, how thrilling, or how dull the room was at any given moment, no one questioned for a second whether it was OK for me — an independent interloper — to be there, taking notes about it. I'm so grateful to them for that.

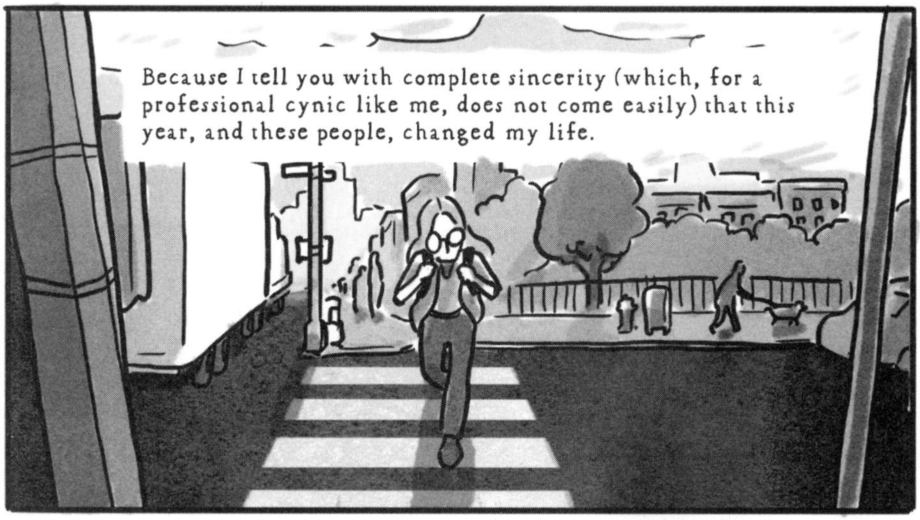
Because I tell you with complete sincerity (which, for a professional cynic like me, does not come easily) that this year, and these people, changed my life.

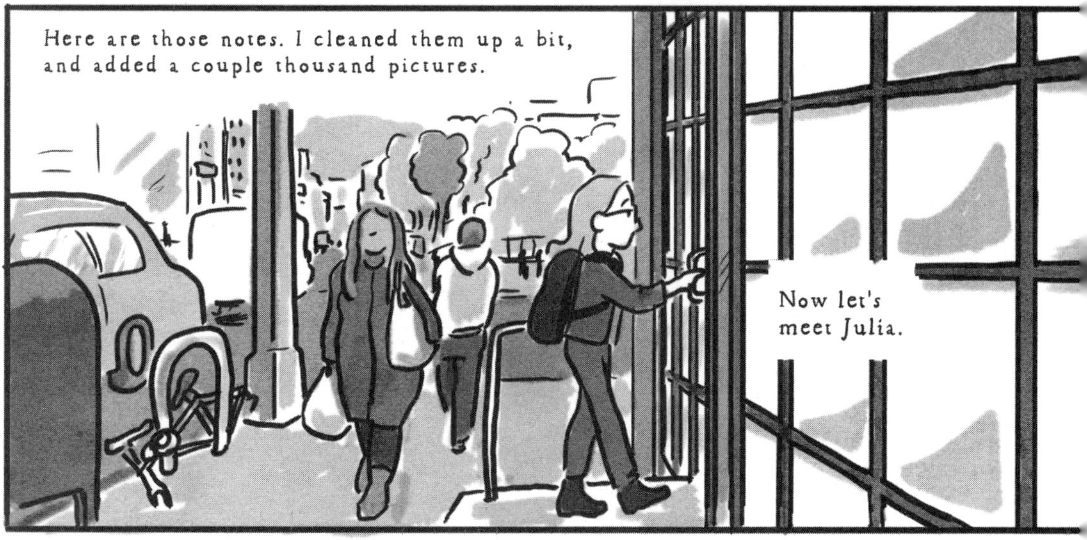
Here are those notes. I cleaned them up a bit, and added a couple thousand pictures.
Now let's meet Julia.

Part I

Chapter One

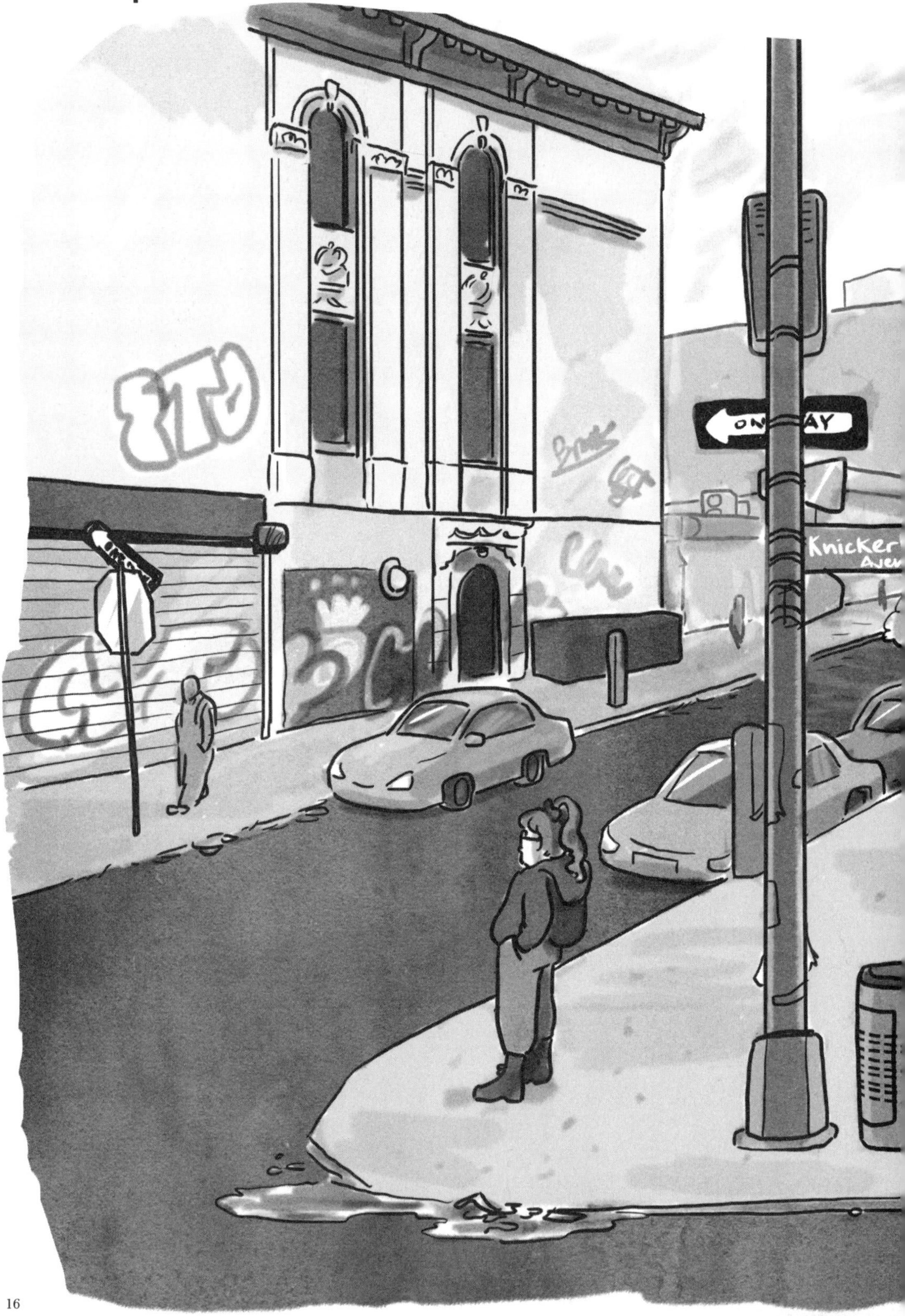
Knicker

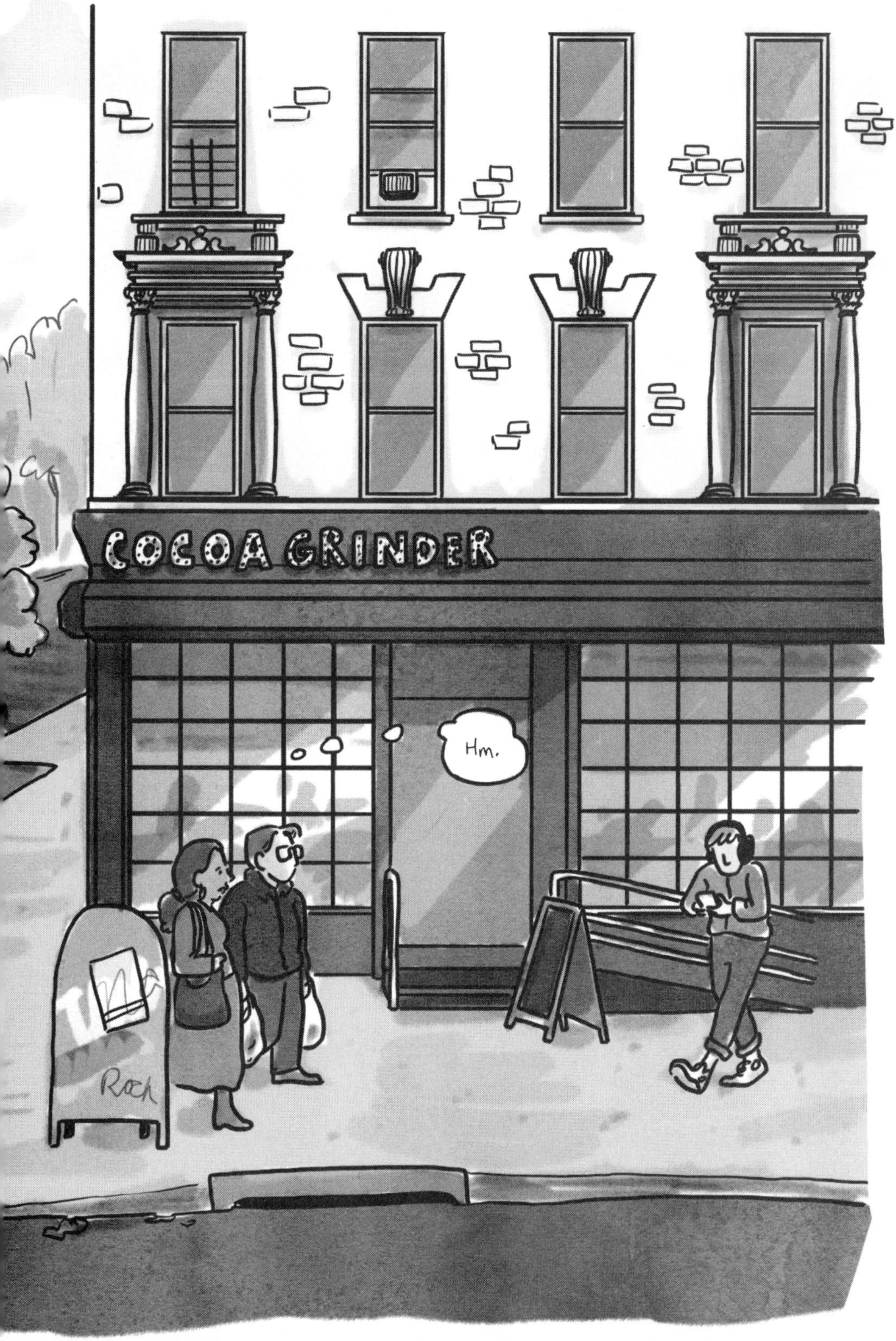
COCOA GRINDER
Hm.

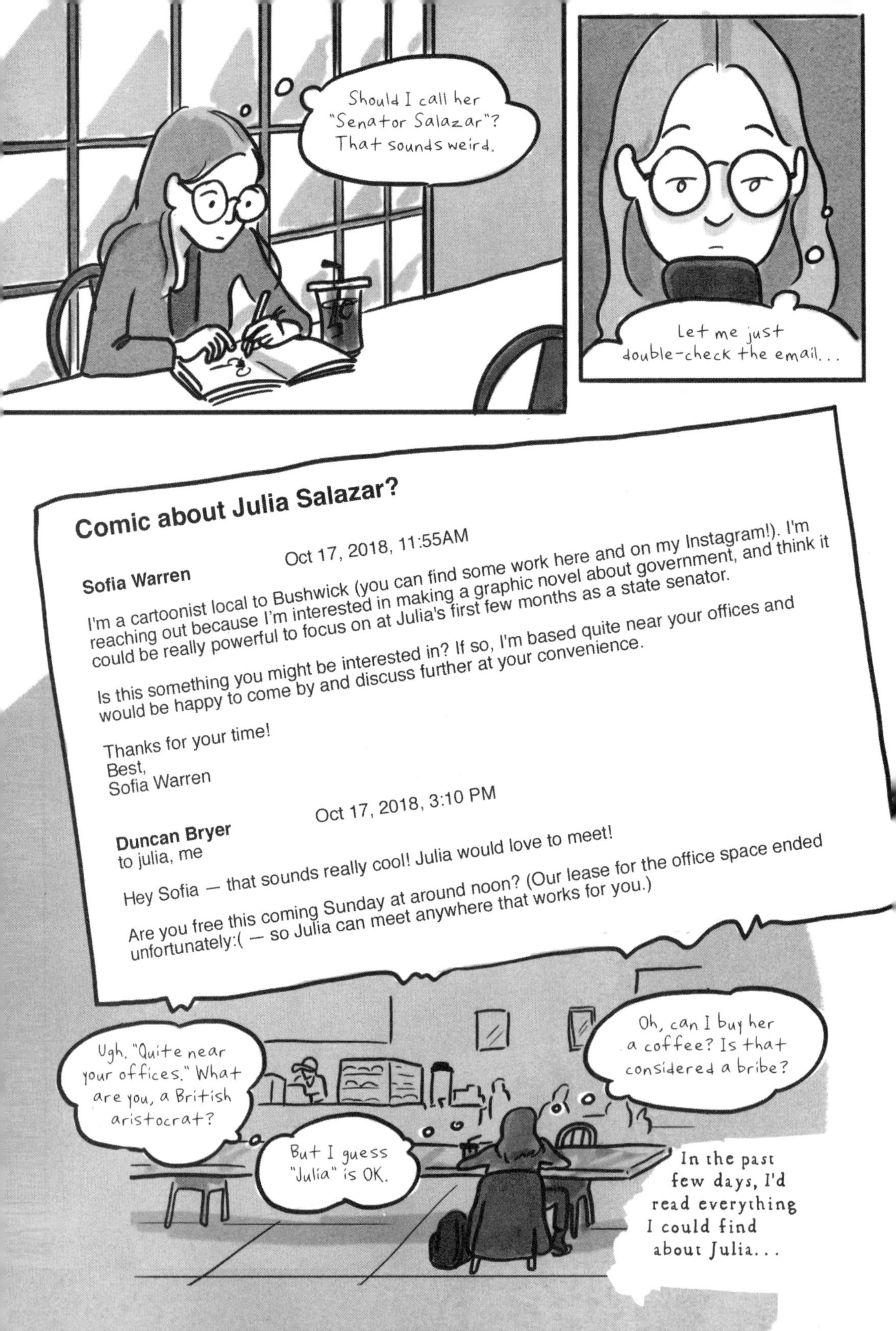

Should I call her "Senator Salazar"? That sounds weird.
Let me just double-check the email...
Comic about Julia Salazar?
Sofia Warren
Oct 17, 2018, 11:55AM
I'm a cartoonist local to Bushwick (you can find some work here and on my Instagram!). I'm reaching out because I'm interested in making a graphic novel about government, and think it could be really powerful to focus on at Julia's first few months as a state senator.
Is this something you might be interested in? If so, I'm based quite near your offices and would be happy to come by and discuss further at your convenience.
Thanks for your time!
Best,
Sofia Warren
Duncan Bryer
Oct 17, 2018, 3:10 PM
to julia, me
Hey Sofia — that sounds really cool! Julia would love to meet!
Are you free this coming Sunday at around noon? (Our lease for the office space ended unfortunately:(— so Julia can meet anywhere that works for you.)
Ugh. "Quite near your offices." What are you, a British aristocrat?
But I guess "Julia" is OK.
Oh, can I buy her a coffee? Is that considered a bribe?
In the past few days, I'd read everything I could find about Julia...

. . . which was no small amount: for a local race, her campaign had received a huge amount of press.

There were so many conflicting claims about her character — I'll get to that in a minute — that it made me very curious who, exactly, would be walking through the door.

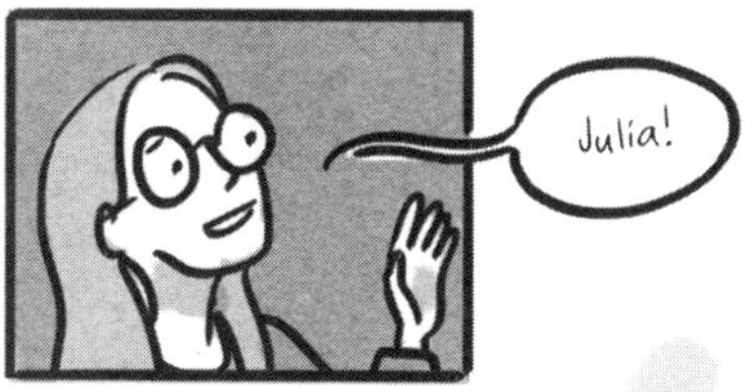
Julia!

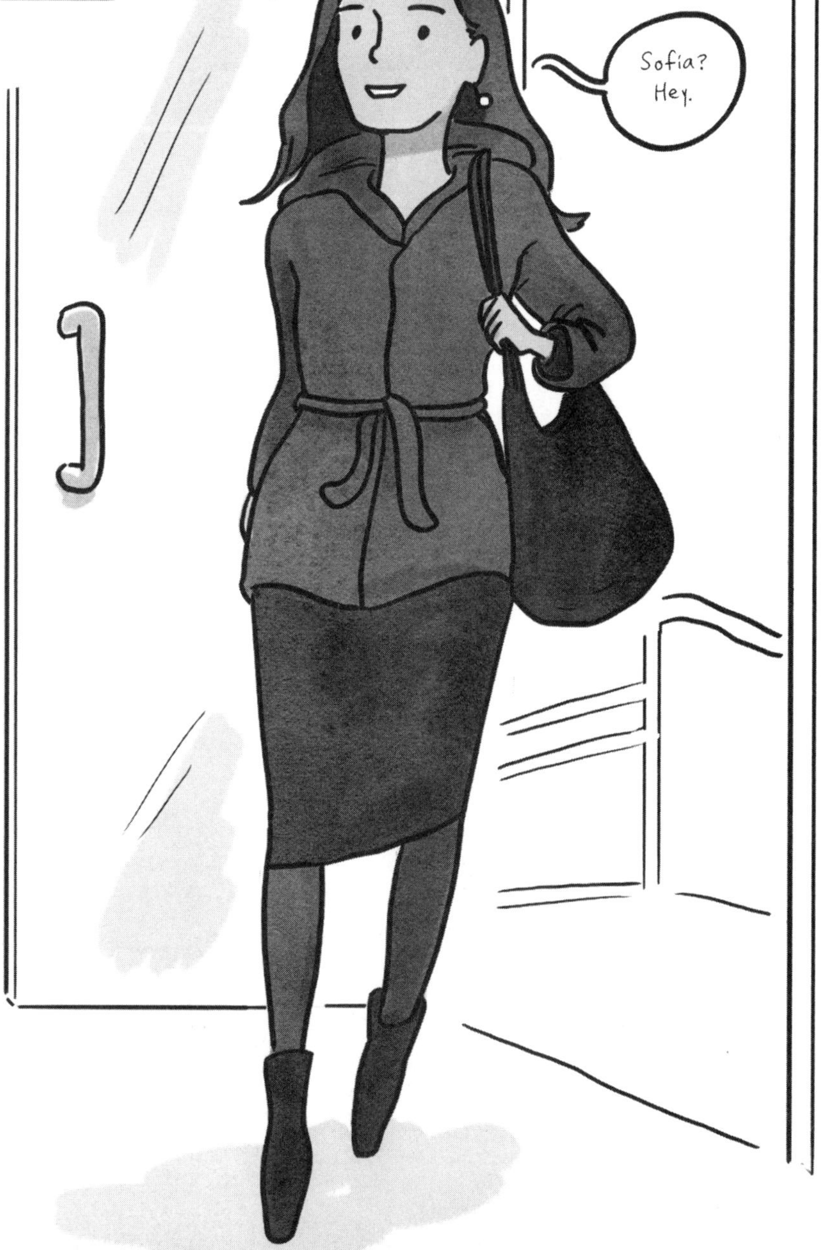
Sofia?
Hey.

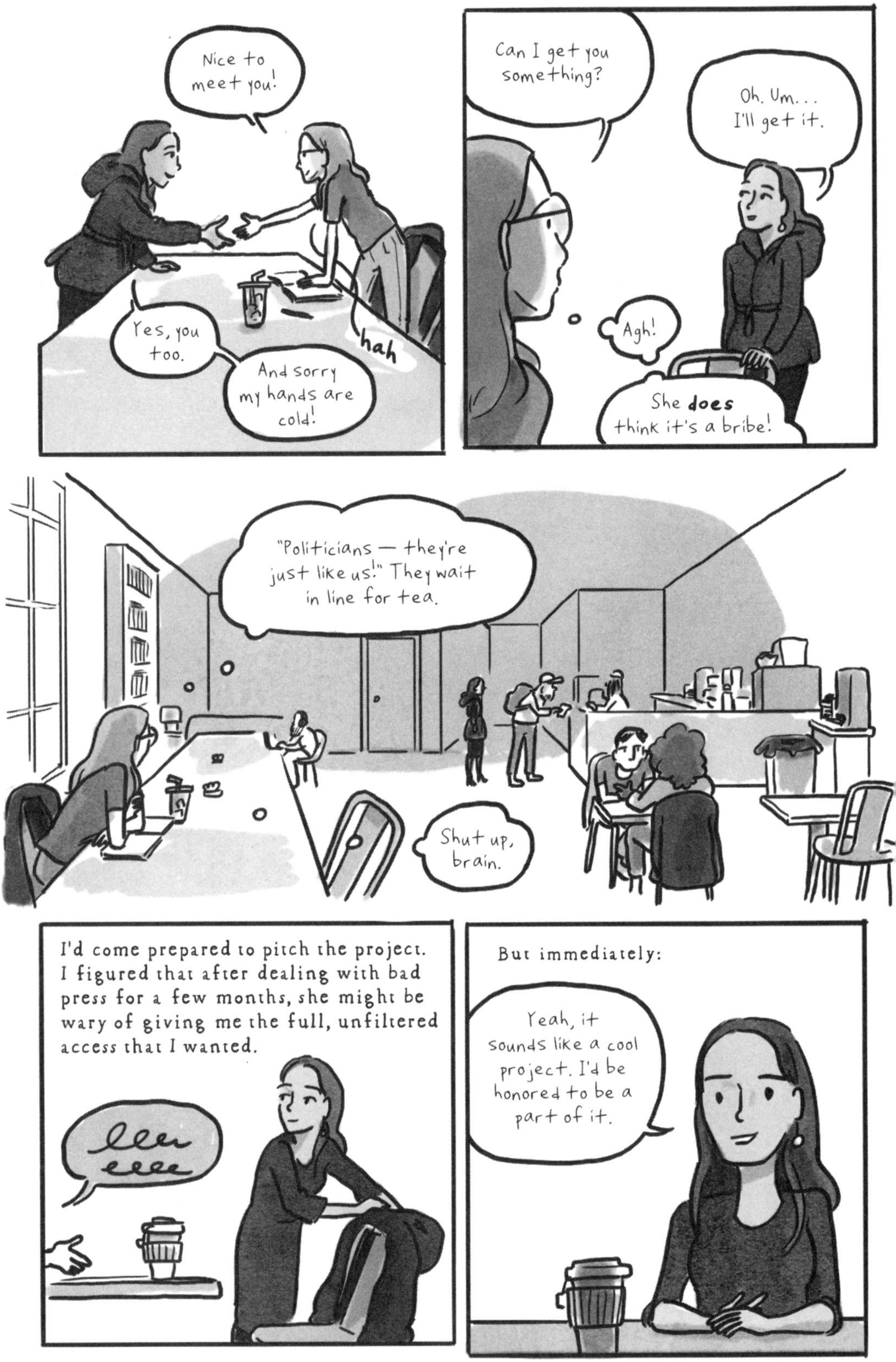
Nice to meet you!
Yes, you too.
And sorry my hands are cold!
hah
Can I get you something?
Oh. Um... I'll get it.
Agh!
She **does** think it's a bribe!
"Politicians — they're just like us!" They wait in line for tea.
Shut up, brain.
I'd come prepared to pitch the project. I figured that after dealing with bad press for a few months, she might be wary of giving me the full, unfiltered access that I wanted.
But immediately:
Yeah, it sounds like a cool project. I'd be honored to be a part of it.

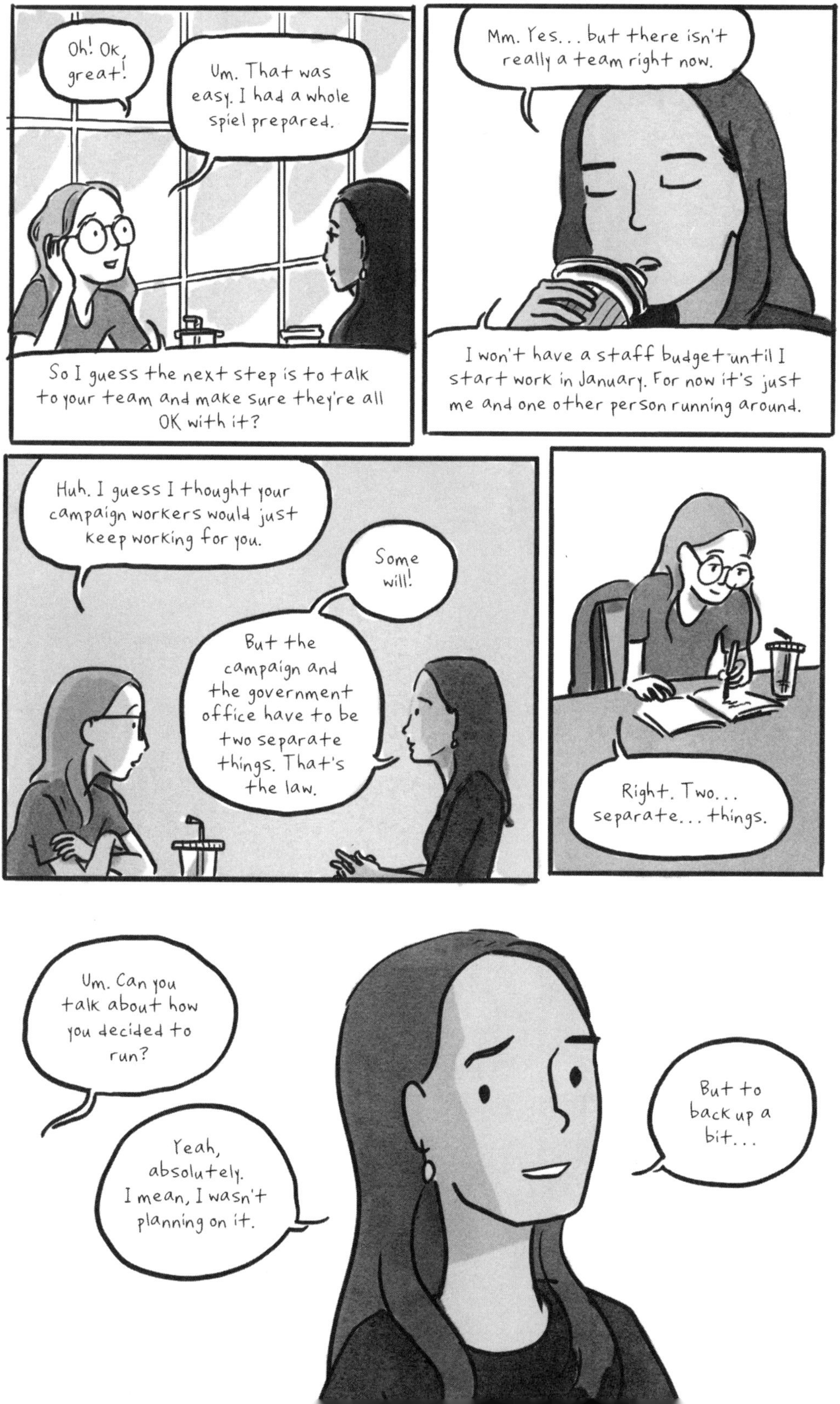
Oh! Ok, great!
Um. That was easy. I had a whole spiel prepared.
So I guess the next step is to talk to your team and make sure they're all OK with it?
Mm. Yes... but there isn't really a team right now.
I won't have a staff budget until I start work in January. For now it's just me and one other person running around.
Huh. I guess I thought your campaign workers would just keep working for you.
Some will!
But the campaign and the government office have to be two separate things. That's the law.
Right. Two... separate... things.
Um. Can you talk about how you decided to run?
Yeah, absolutely. I mean, I wasn't planning on it.
But to back up a bit...

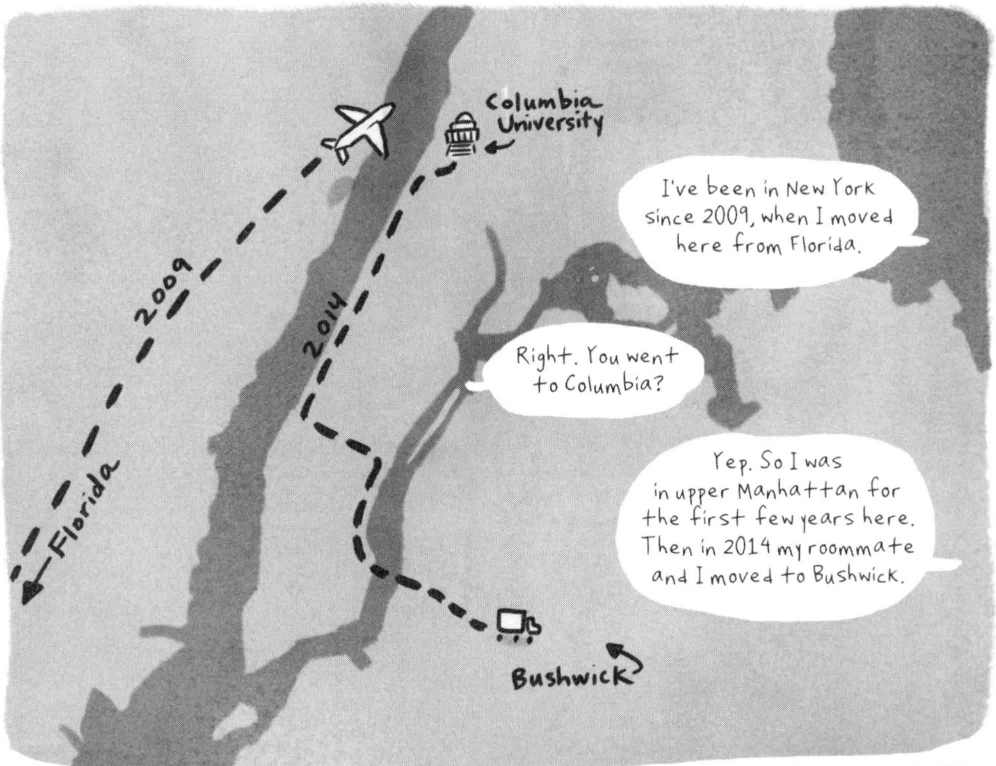
Columbia University
2009
2014
Florida
Bushwick
I've been in New York since 2009, when I moved here from Florida.
Right. You went to Columbia?
Yep. So I was in upper Manhattan for the first few years here. Then in 2014 my roommate and I moved to Bushwick.

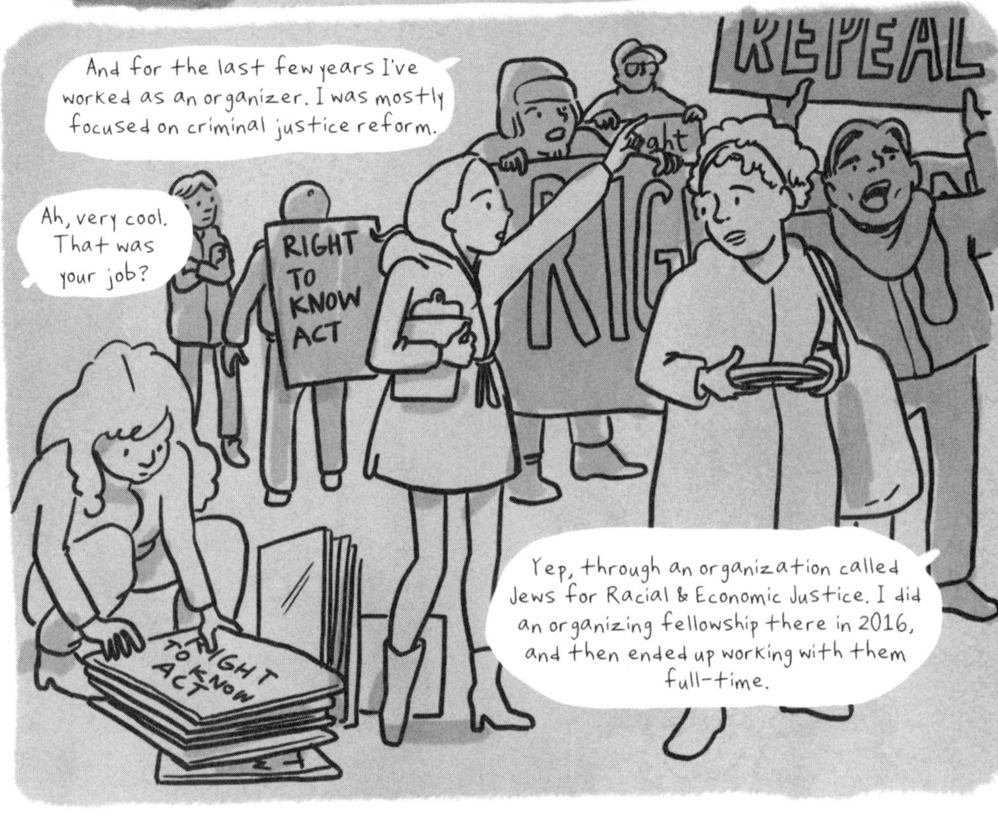
REPEAL
And for the last few years I've worked as an organizer. I was mostly focused on criminal justice reform.
Ah, very cool. That was your job?
RIGHT TO KNOW ACT
RIGHT TO KNOW ACT
Yep, through an organization called Jews for Racial & Economic Justice. I did an organizing fellowship there in 2016, and then ended up working with them full-time.

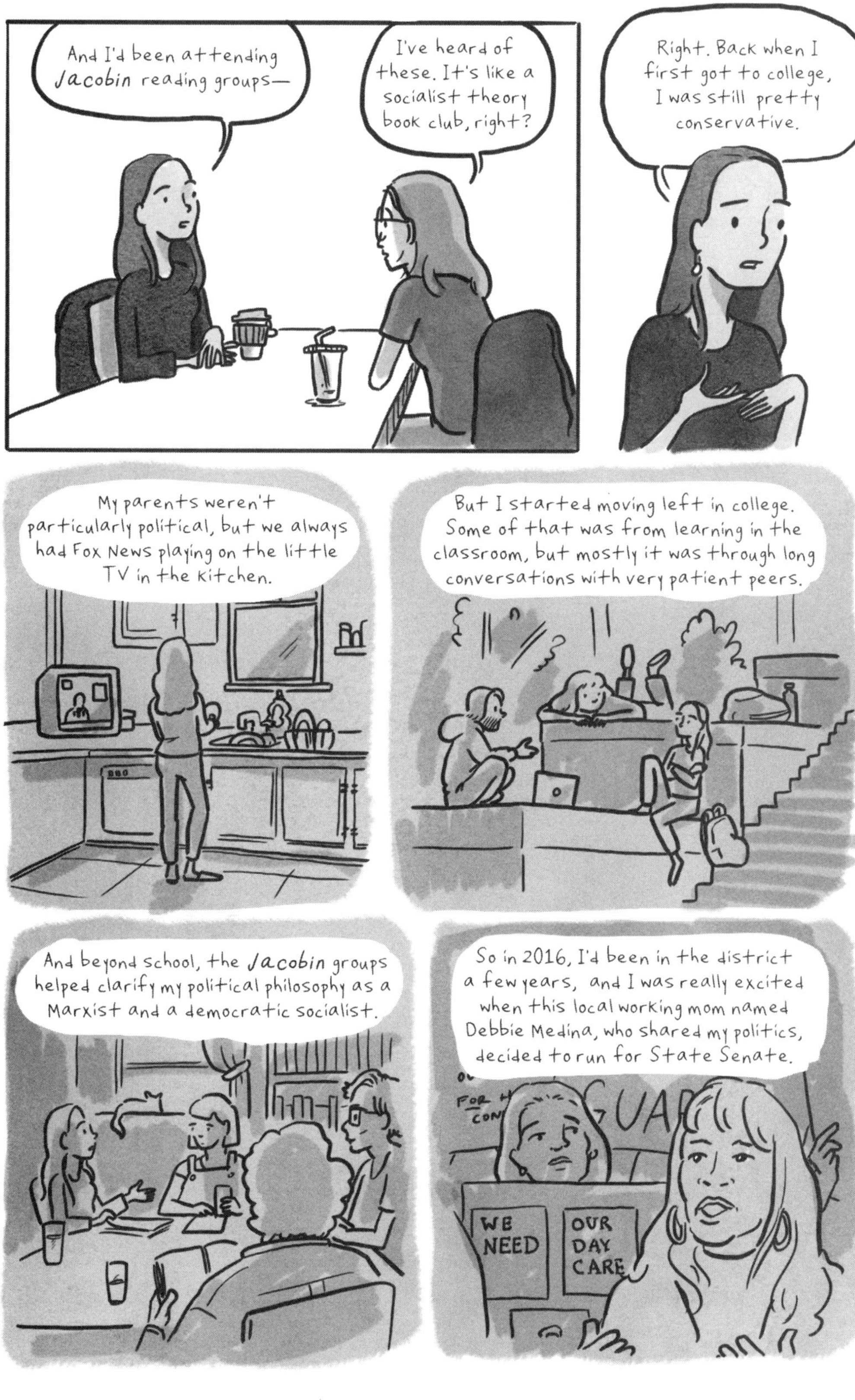
And I'd been attending *Jacobin* reading groups—
I've heard of these. It's like a socialist theory book club, right?
Right. Back when I first got to college, I was still pretty conservative.
My parents weren't particularly political, but we always had Fox News playing on the little TV in the kitchen.
But I started moving left in college. Some of that was from learning in the classroom, but mostly it was through long conversations with very patient peers.
And beyond school, the *Jacobin* groups helped clarify my political philosophy as a Marxist and a democratic socialist.
So in 2016, I'd been in the district a few years, and I was really excited when this local working mom named Debbie Medina, who shared my politics, decided to run for State Senate.
WE NEED
OUR DAY CARE

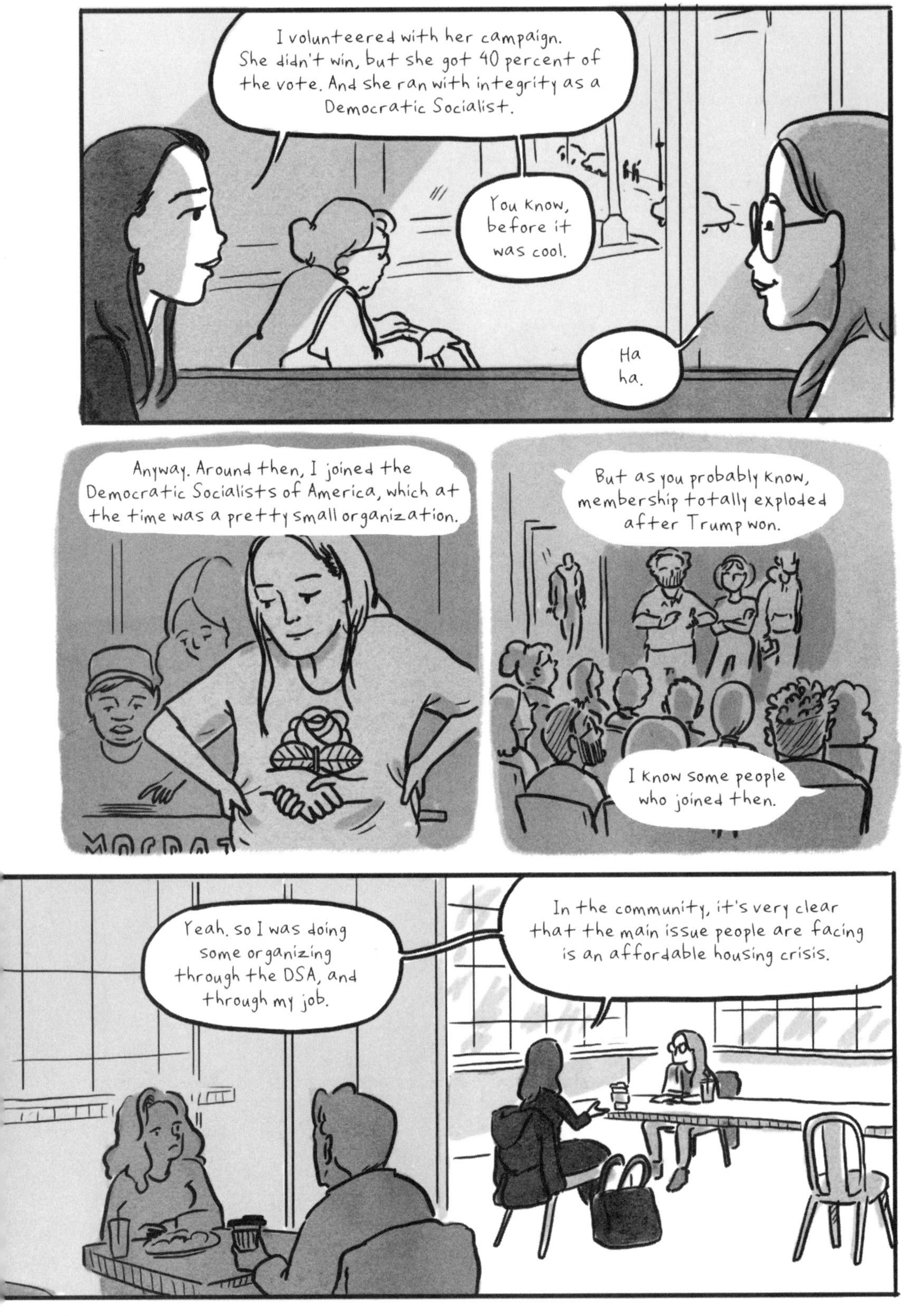
I volunteered with her campaign. She didn't win, but she got 40 percent of the vote. And she ran with integrity as a Democratic Socialist.
You know, before it was cool.
Ha ha.
Anyway. Around then, I joined the Democratic Socialists of America, which at the time was a pretty small organization.
But as you probably know, membership totally exploded after Trump won.
I know some people who joined then.
Yeah. So I was doing some organizing through the DSA, and through my job.
In the community, it's very clear that the main issue people are facing is an affordable housing crisis.

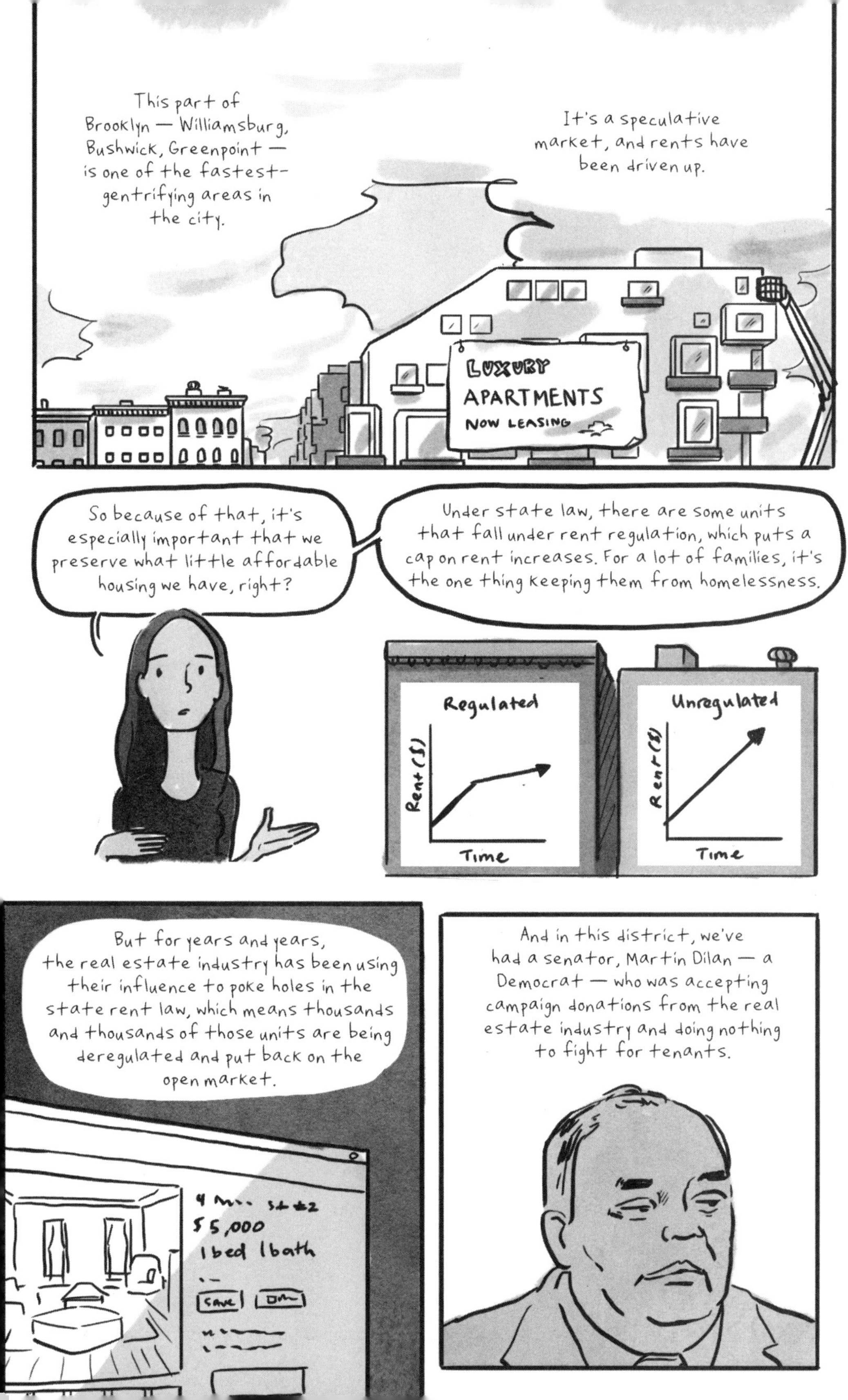
This part of Brooklyn — Williamsburg, Bushwick, Greenpoint — is one of the fastest-gentrifying areas in the city.
It's a speculative market, and rents have been driven up.
LUXURY APARTMENTS NOW LEASING
So because of that, it's especially important that we preserve what little affordable housing we have, right?
Under state law, there are some units that fall under rent regulation, which puts a cap on rent increases. For a lot of families, it's the one thing keeping them from homelessness.
Regulated
Rent ($)
Time
Unregulated
Rent ($)
Time
But for years and years, the real estate industry has been using their influence to poke holes in the state rent law, which means thousands and thousands of those units are being deregulated and put back on the open market.
$5,000
1bed 1bath
Save
And in this district, we've had a senator, Martin Dilan — a Democrat — who was accepting campaign donations from the real estate industry and doing nothing to fight for tenants.

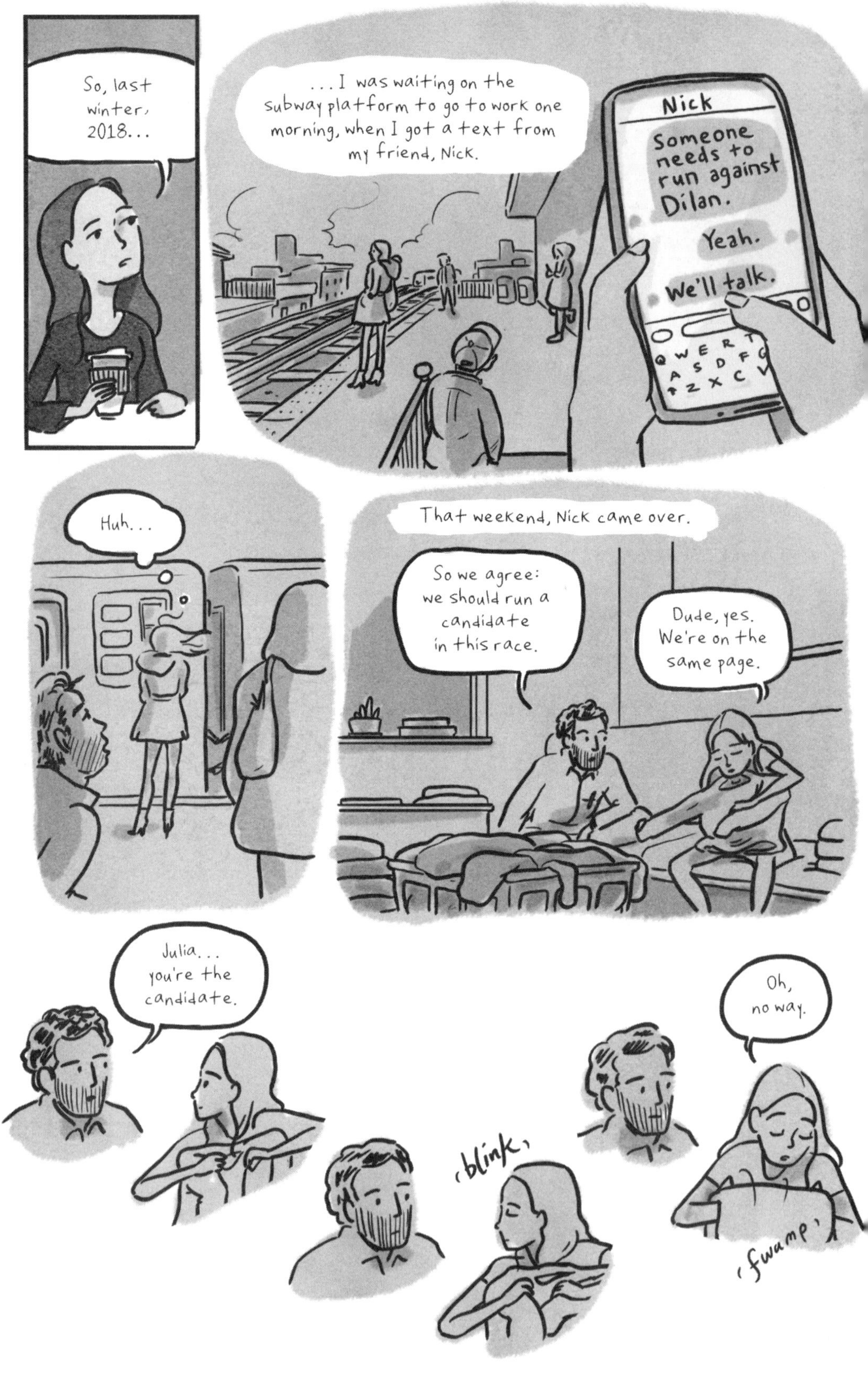
So, last winter, 2018...
...I was waiting on the subway platform to go to work one morning, when I got a text from my friend, Nick.
Nick
Someone needs to run against Dilan.
Yeah.
We'll talk.
Huh...
That weekend, Nick came over.
So we agree: we should run a candidate in this race.
Dude, yes. We're on the same page.
Julia... you're the candidate.
blink
Oh, no way.
fwamp

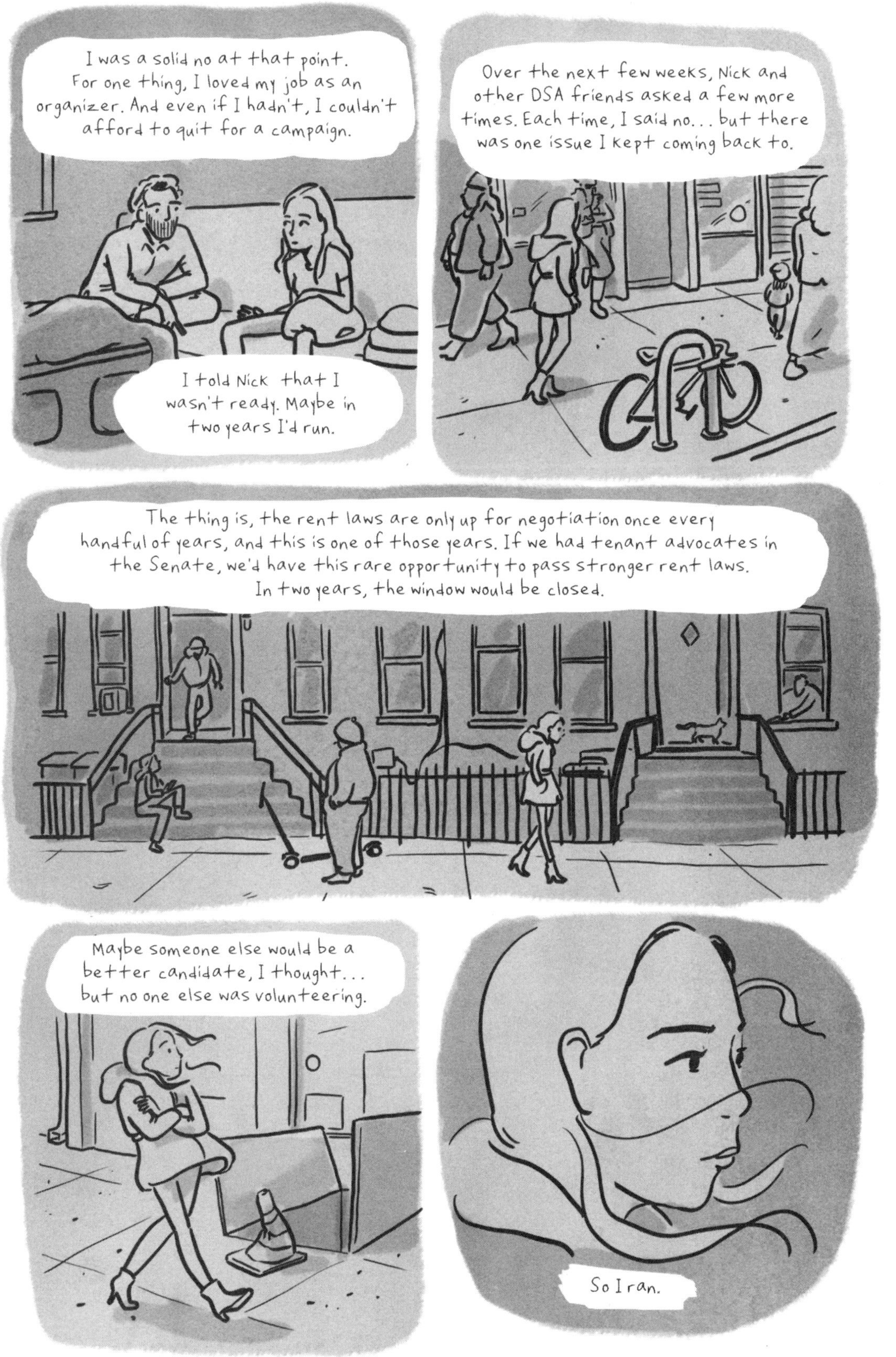
I was a solid no at that point. For one thing, I loved my job as an organizer. And even if I hadn't, I couldn't afford to quit for a campaign.
I told Nick that I wasn't ready. Maybe in two years I'd run.
Over the next few weeks, Nick and other DSA friends asked a few more times. Each time, I said no... but there was one issue I kept coming back to.
The thing is, the rent laws are only up for negotiation once every handful of years, and this is one of those years. If we had tenant advocates in the Senate, we'd have this rare opportunity to pass stronger rent laws. In two years, the window would be closed.
Maybe someone else would be a better candidate, I thought... but no one else was volunteering.
So I ran.

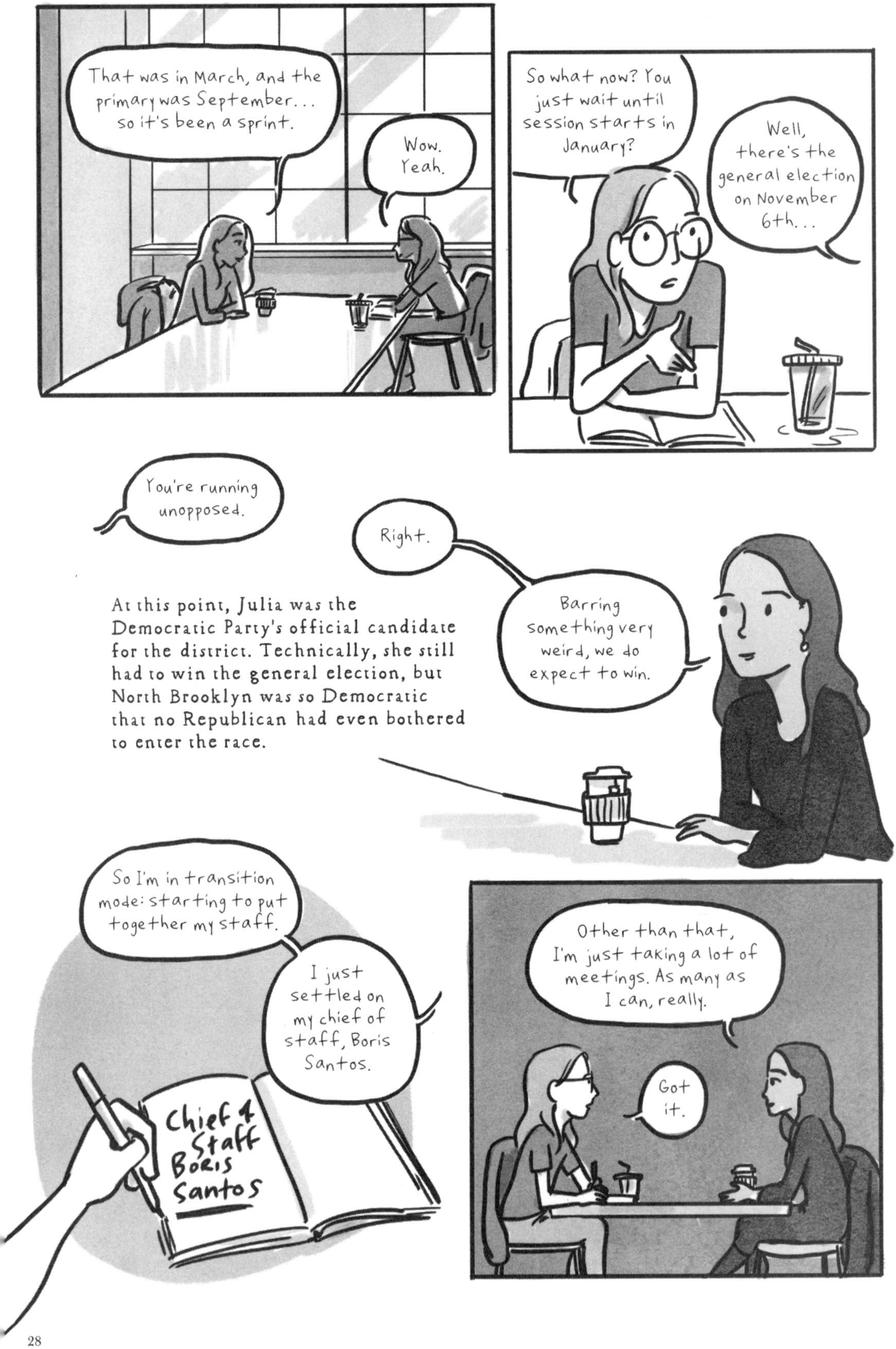
That was in March, and the primary was September... so it's been a sprint.
Wow. Yeah.
So what now? You just wait until session starts in January?
Well, there's the general election on November 6th...
You're running unopposed.
Right.
Barring something very weird, we do expect to win.
At this point, Julia was the Democratic Party's official candidate for the district. Technically, she still had to win the general election, but North Brooklyn was so Democratic that no Republican had even bothered to enter the race.
So I'm in transition mode: starting to put together my staff.
I just settled on my chief of staff, Boris Santos.
Chief of Staff Boris Santos
Other than that, I'm just taking a lot of meetings. As many as I can, really.
Got it.

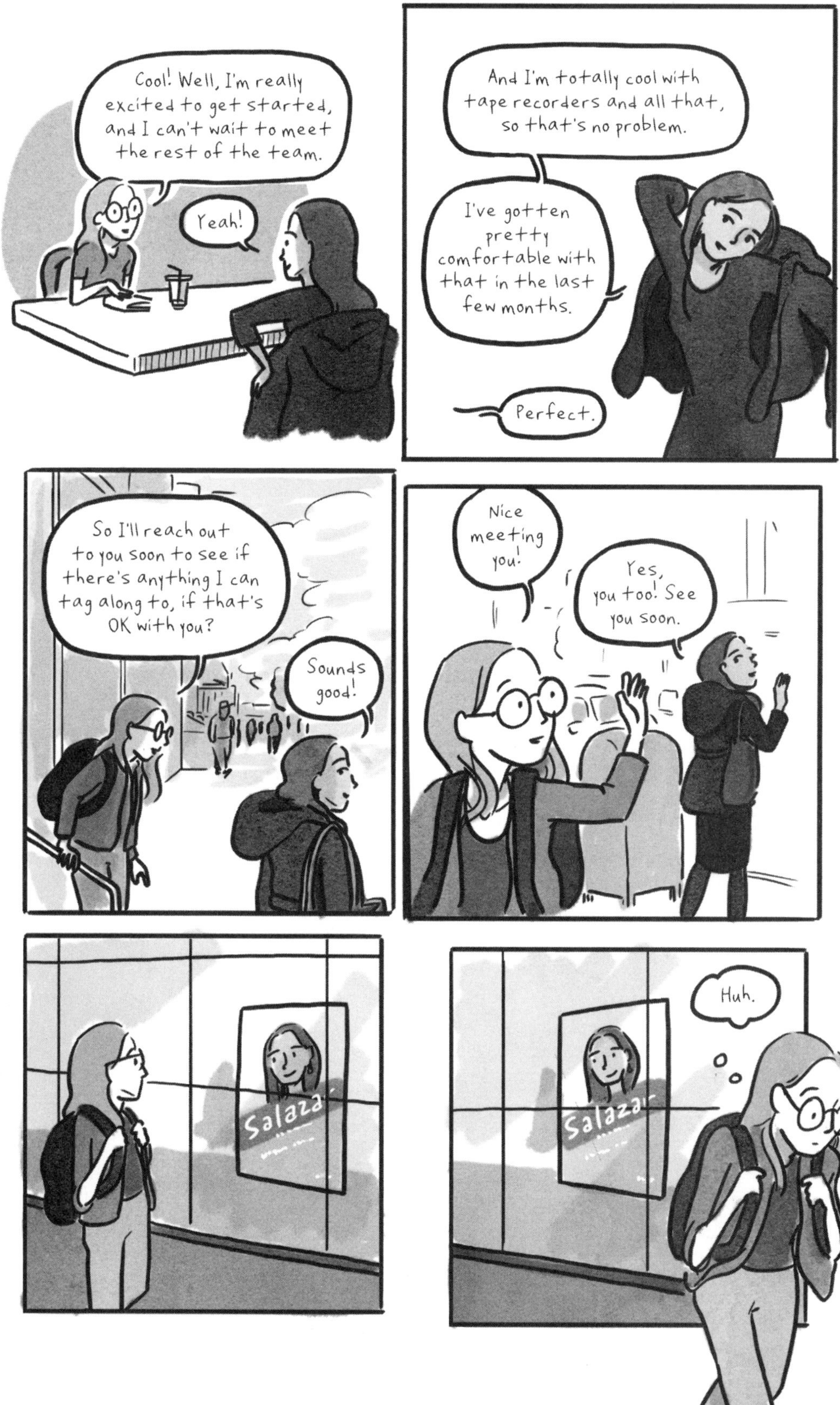
Cool! Well, I'm really excited to get started, and I can't wait to meet the rest of the team.
Yeah!
And I'm totally cool with tape recorders and all that, so that's no problem.
I've gotten pretty comfortable with that in the last few months.
Perfect.
So I'll reach out to you soon to see if there's anything I can tag along to, if that's OK with you?
Sounds good!
Nice meeting you!
Yes, you too! See you soon.
Salaza
Salaza
Huh.

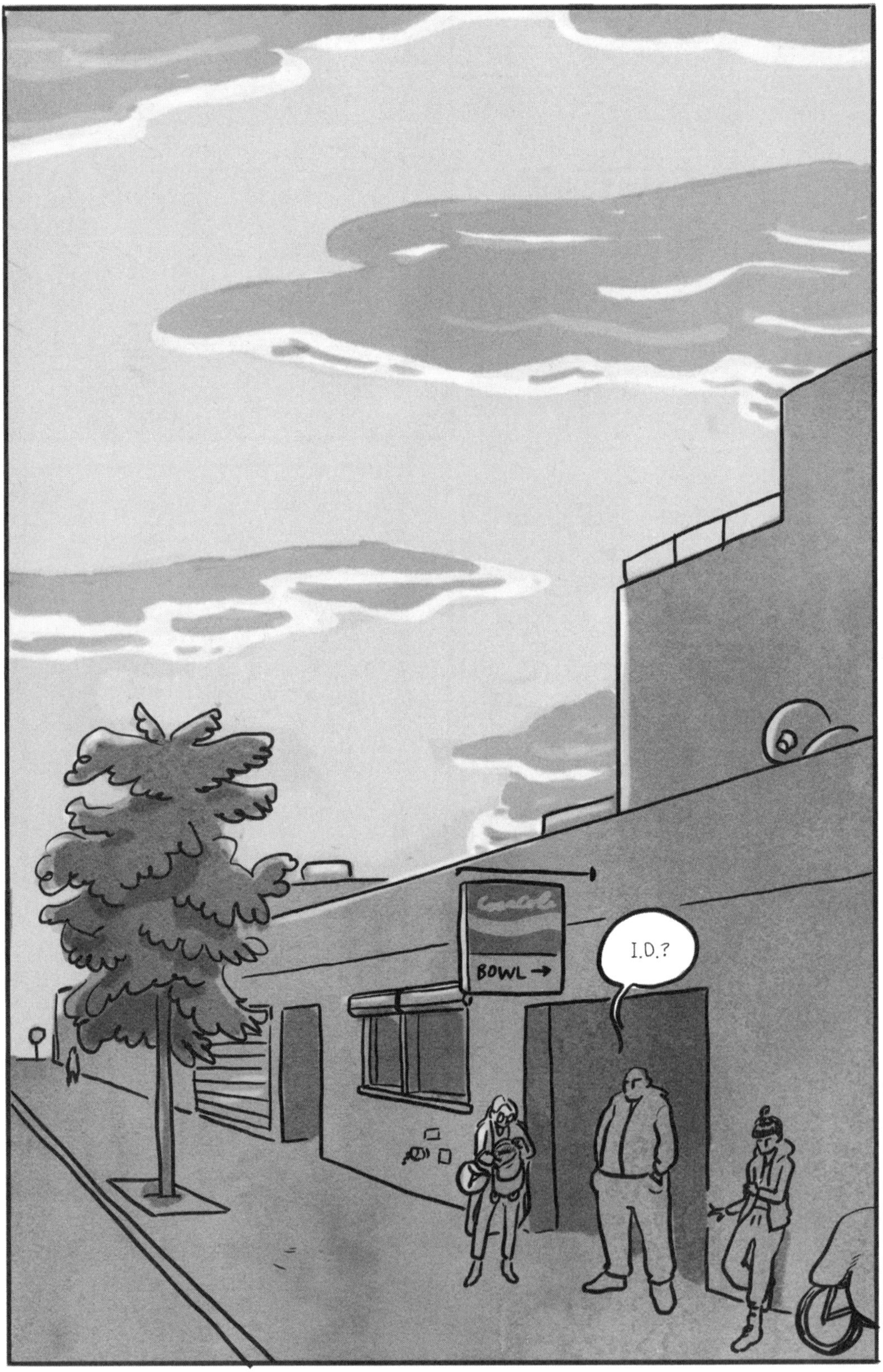
BOWL →
I.D.?

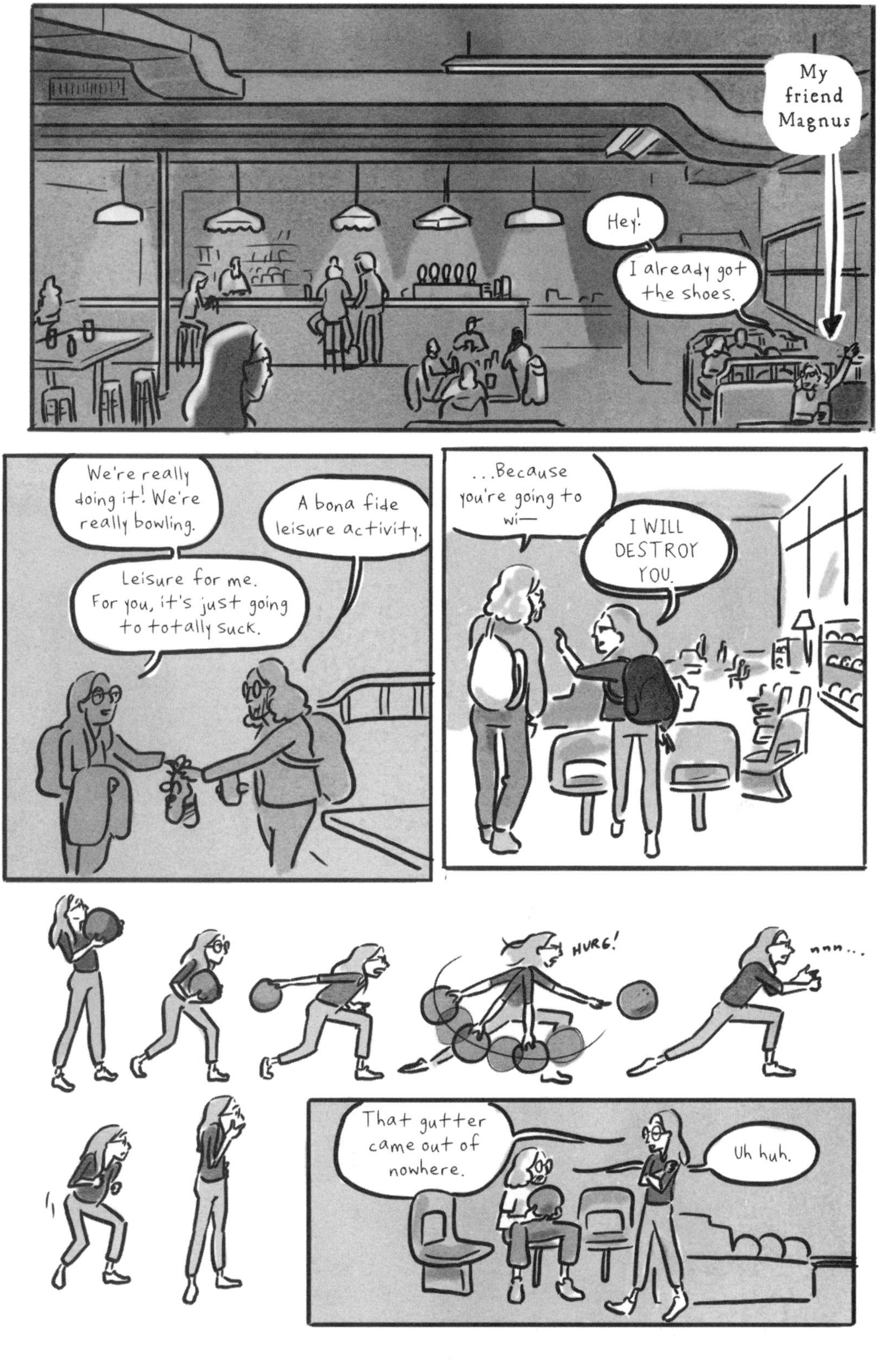
My friend Magnus
Hey!
I already got the shoes.
We're really doing it! We're really bowling.
A bona fide leisure activity.
Leisure for me. For you, it's just going to totally suck.
...Because you're going to wi—
I WILL DESTROY YOU.
HURG!
nnn...
That gutter came out of nowhere.
Uh huh.

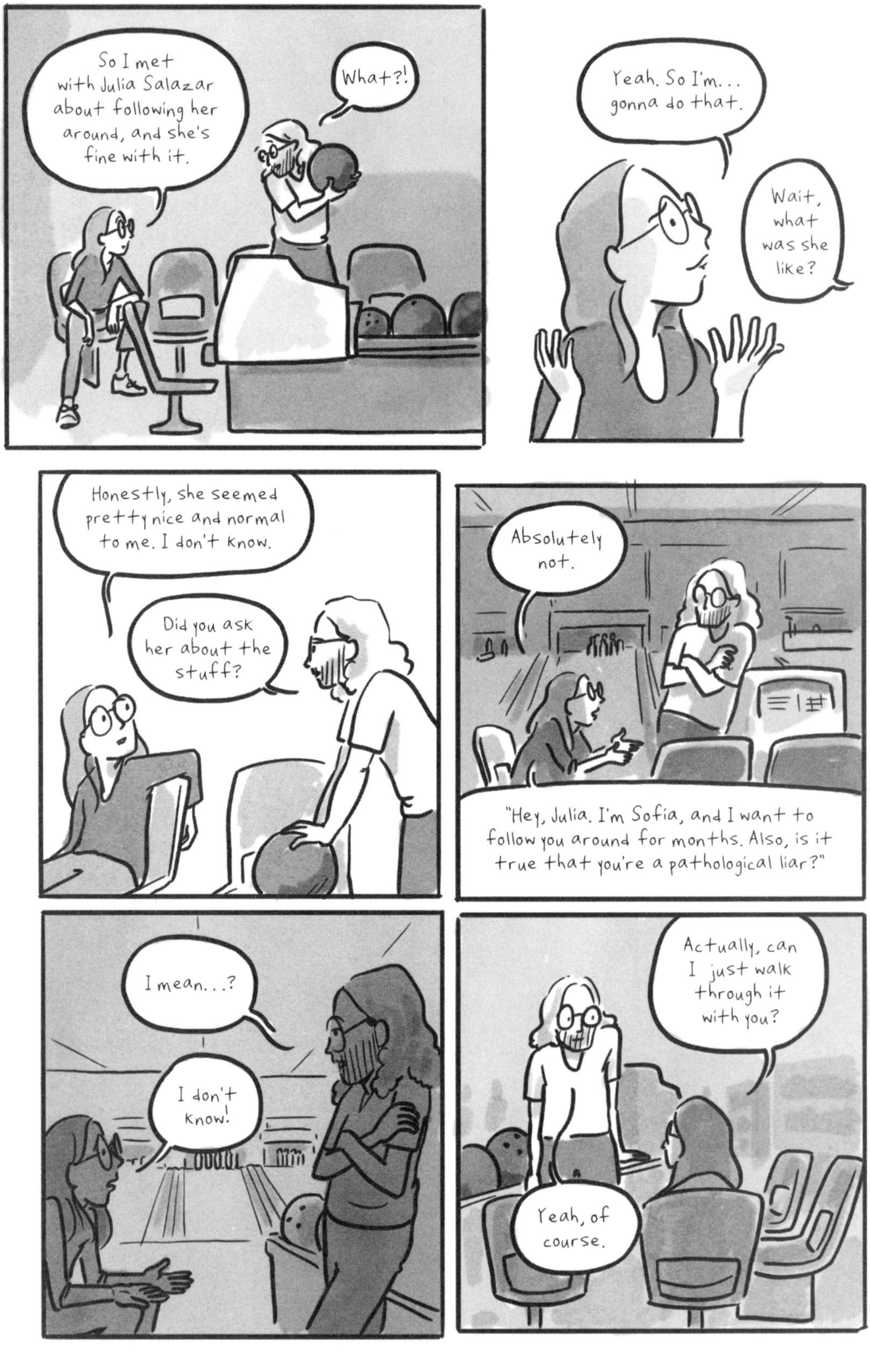

So I met with Julia Salazar about following her around, and she's fine with it.
What?!
Yeah. So I'm... gonna do that.
Wait, what was she like?
Honestly, she seemed pretty nice and normal to me. I don't know.
Did you ask her about the stuff?
Absolutely not.
"Hey, Julia. I'm Sofia, and I want to follow you around for months. Also, is it true that you're a pathological liar?"
I mean...?
I don't know!
Actually, can I just walk through it with you?
Yeah, of course.

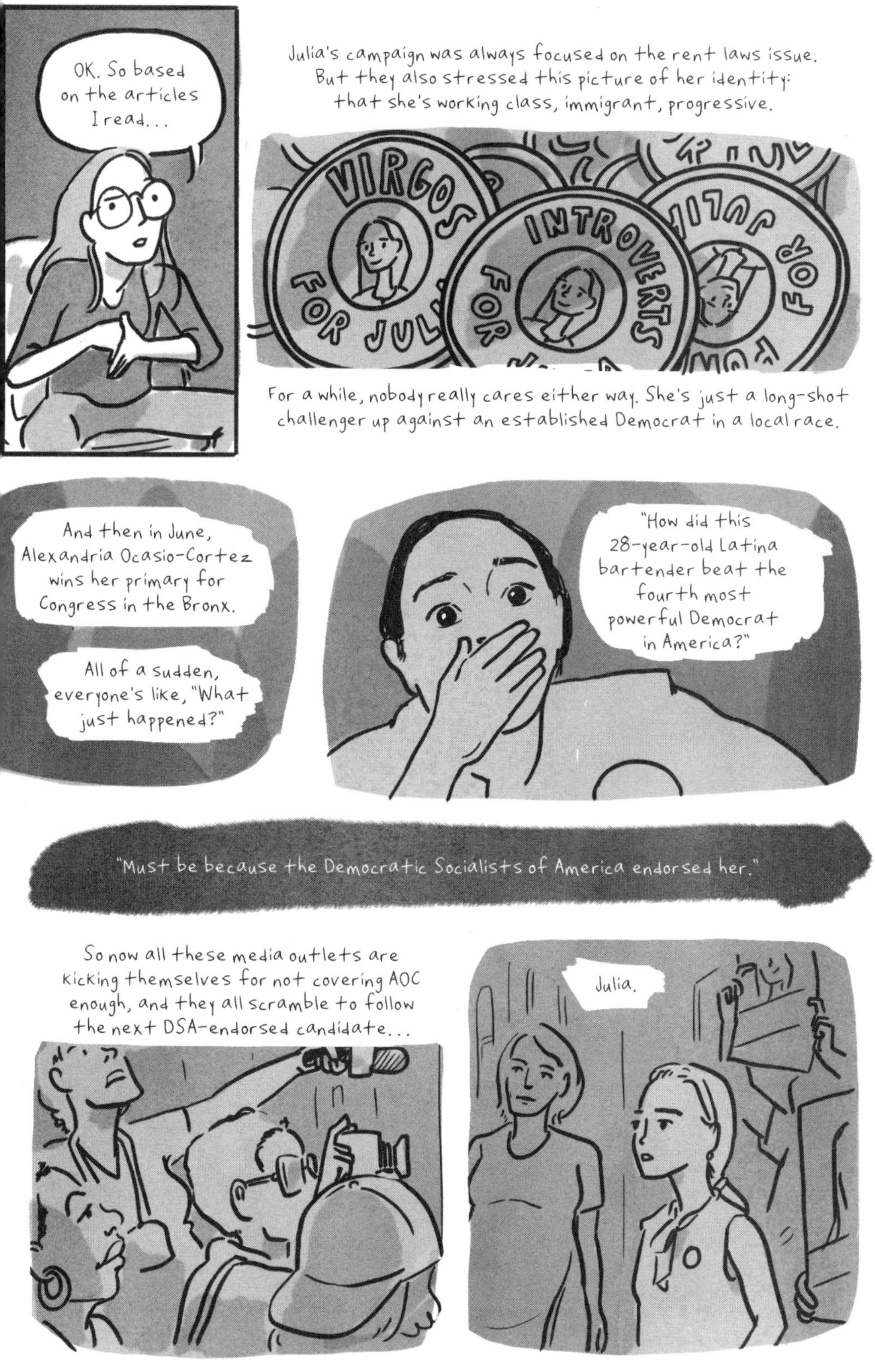
OK. So based on the articles I read...
Julia's campaign was always focused on the rent laws issue. But they also stressed this picture of her identity: that she's working class, immigrant, progressive.
VIRGOS FOR JUL
INTROVERTS FOR
For a while, nobody really cares either way. She's just a long-shot challenger up against an established Democrat in a local race.
And then in June, Alexandria Ocasio-Cortez wins her primary for Congress in the Bronx.
All of a sudden, everyone's like, "What just happened?"
"How did this 28-year-old Latina bartender beat the fourth most powerful Democrat in America?"
"Must be because the Democratic Socialists of America endorsed her."
So now all these media outlets are kicking themselves for not covering AOC enough, and they all scramble to follow the next DSA-endorsed candidate...
Julia.

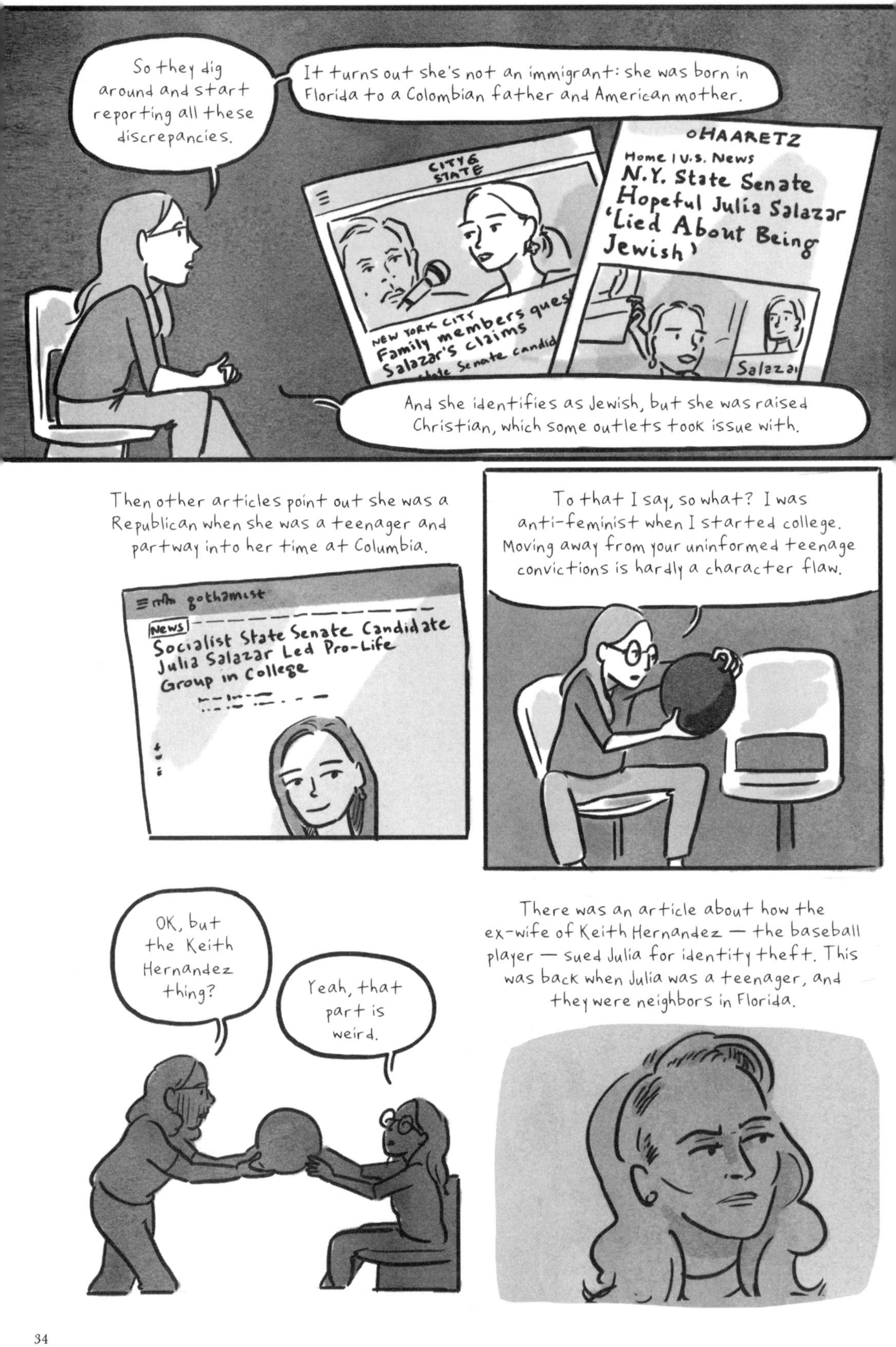

So they dig around and start reporting all these discrepancies.
It turns out she's not an immigrant: she was born in Florida to a Colombian father and American mother.
CITY & STATE
NEW YORK CITY
Family members quest
Salazar's claims
Senate candid
HAARETZ
Home | U.S. News
N.Y. State Senate Hopeful Julia Salazar 'Lied About Being Jewish'
Salaza
And she identifies as Jewish, but she was raised Christian, which some outlets took issue with.
Then other articles point out she was a Republican when she was a teenager and partway into her time at Columbia.
gothamist
News
Socialist State Senate Candidate Julia Salazar Led Pro-Life Group in College
To that I say, so what? I was anti-feminist when I started college. Moving away from your uninformed teenage convictions is hardly a character flaw.
OK, but the Keith Hernandez thing?
Yeah, that part is weird.
There was an article about how the ex-wife of Keith Hernandez — the baseball player — sued Julia for identity theft. This was back when Julia was a teenager, and they were neighbors in Florida.

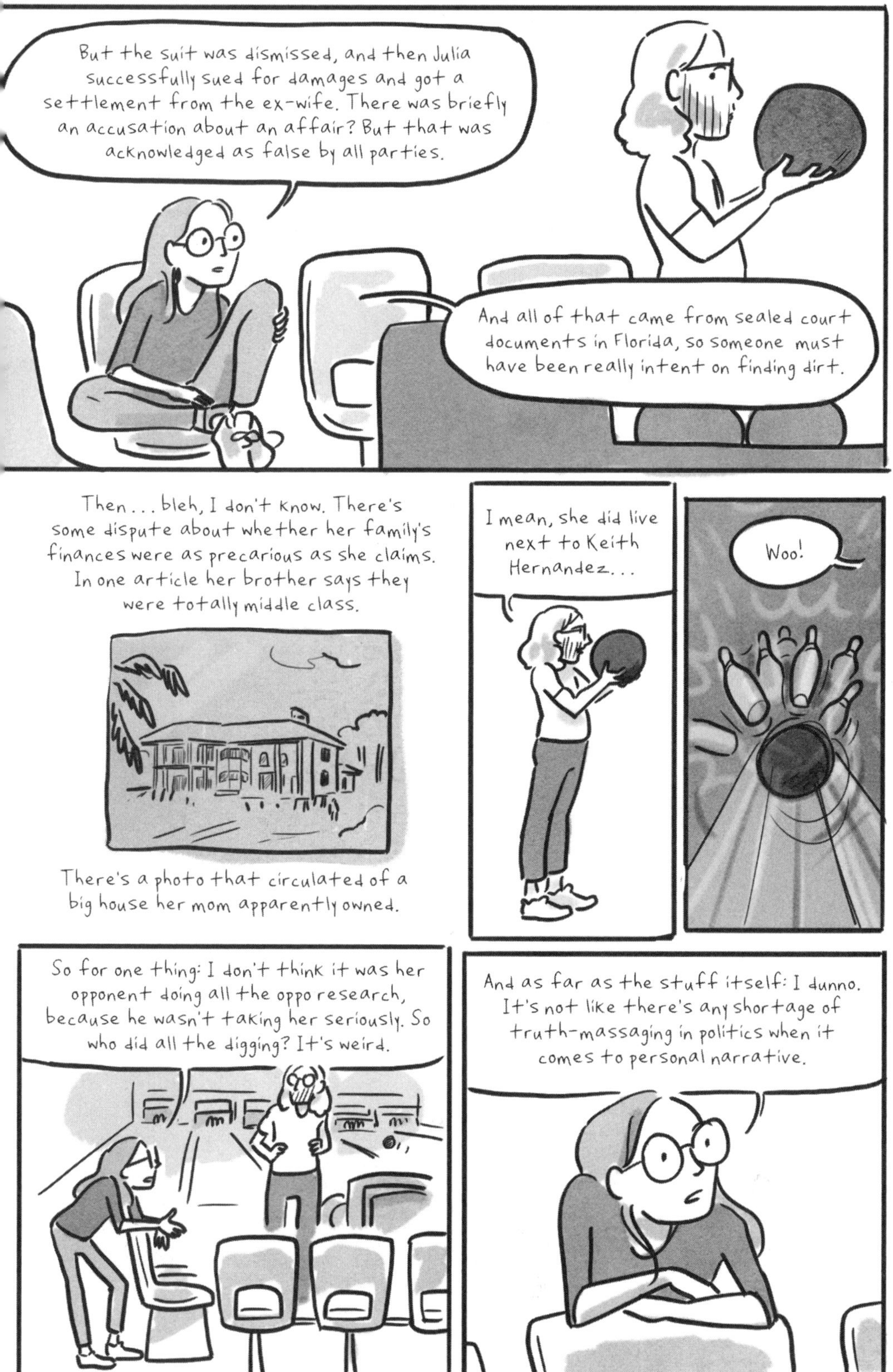

But the suit was dismissed, and then Julia successfully sued for damages and got a settlement from the ex-wife. There was briefly an accusation about an affair? But that was acknowledged as false by all parties.
And all of that came from sealed court documents in Florida, so someone must have been really intent on finding dirt.
Then... bleh, I don't know. There's some dispute about whether her family's finances were as precarious as she claims. In one article her brother says they were totally middle class.
There's a photo that circulated of a big house her mom apparently owned.
I mean, she did live next to Keith Hernandez...
Woo!
So for one thing: I don't think it was her opponent doing all the oppo research, because he wasn't taking her seriously. So who did all the digging? It's weird.
And as far as the stuff itself: I dunno. It's not like there's any shortage of truth-massaging in politics when it comes to personal narrative.

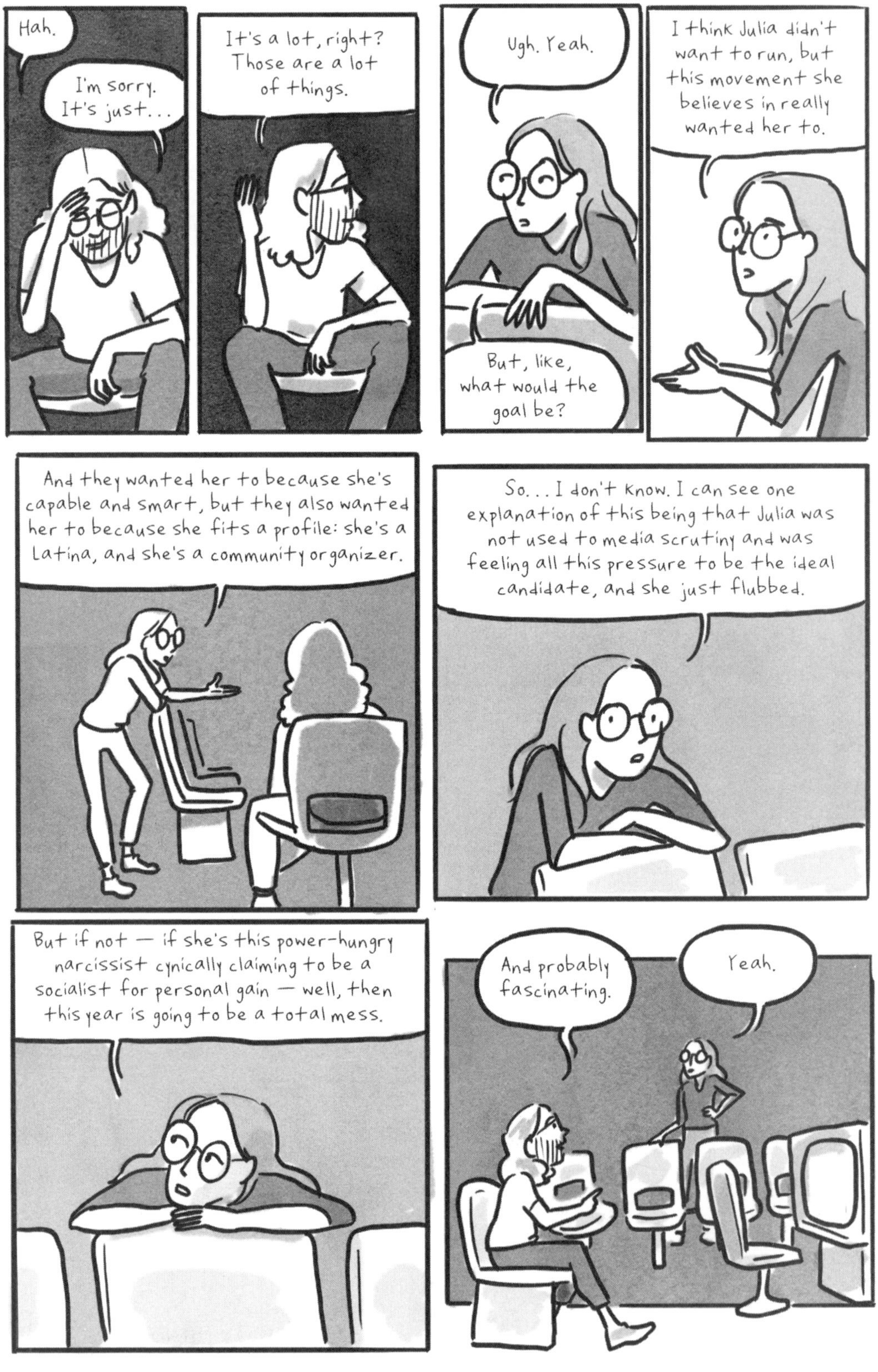
Hah.
I'm sorry. It's just...
It's a lot, right? Those are a lot of things.
Ugh. Yeah.
But, like, what would the goal be?
I think Julia didn't want to run, but this movement she believes in really wanted her to.
And they wanted her to because she's capable and smart, but they also wanted her to because she fits a profile: she's a Latina, and she's a community organizer.
So... I don't know. I can see one explanation of this being that Julia was not used to media scrutiny and was feeling all this pressure to be the ideal candidate, and she just flubbed.
But if not — if she's this power-hungry narcissist cynically claiming to be a socialist for personal gain — well, then this year is going to be a total mess.
And probably fascinating.
Yeah.

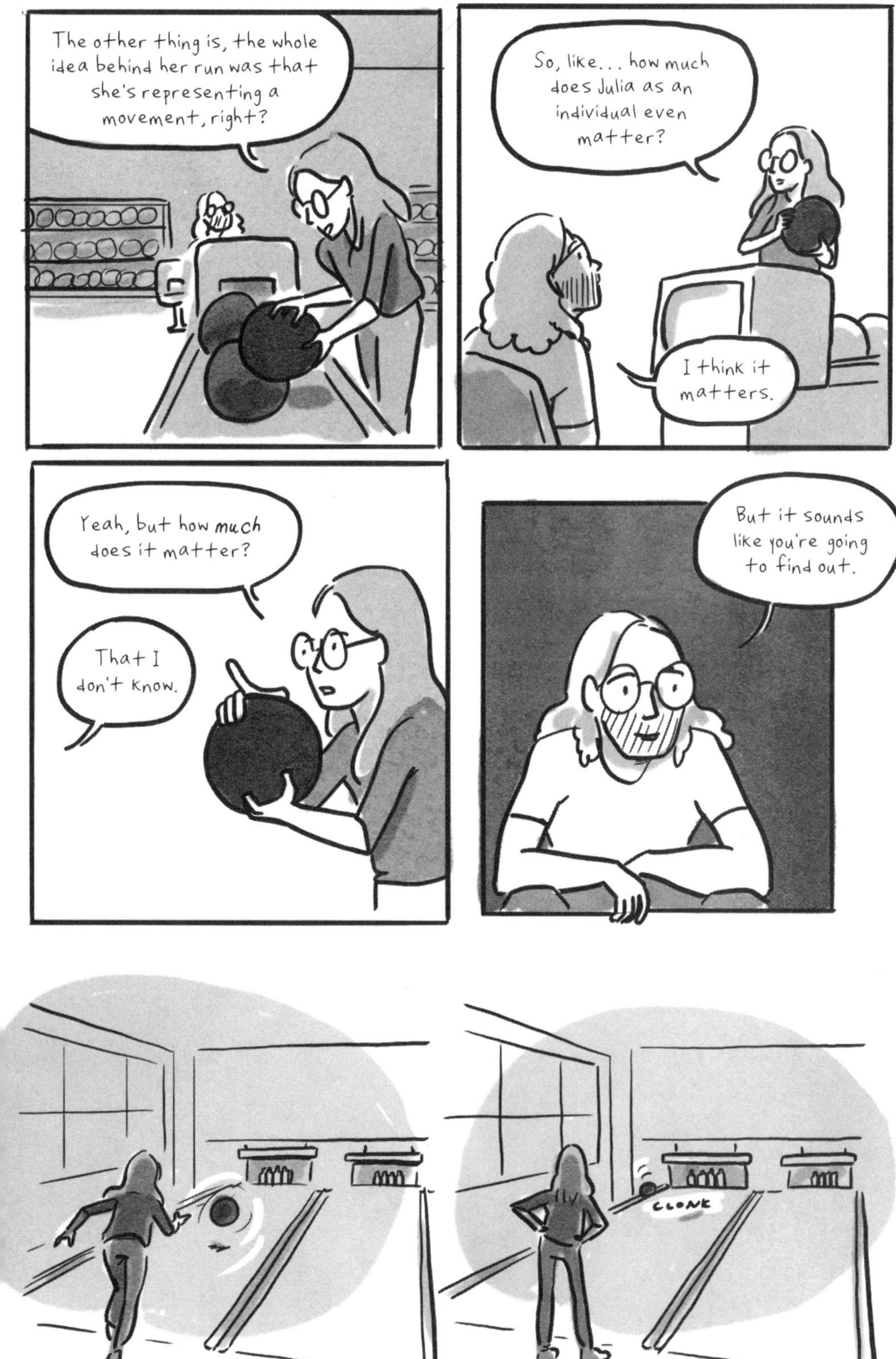
The other thing is, the whole idea behind her run was that she's representing a movement, right?
So, like... how much does Julia as an individual even matter?
I think it matters.
Yeah, but how much does it matter?
That I don't know.
But it sounds like you're going to find out.
CLONK

Chapter Two

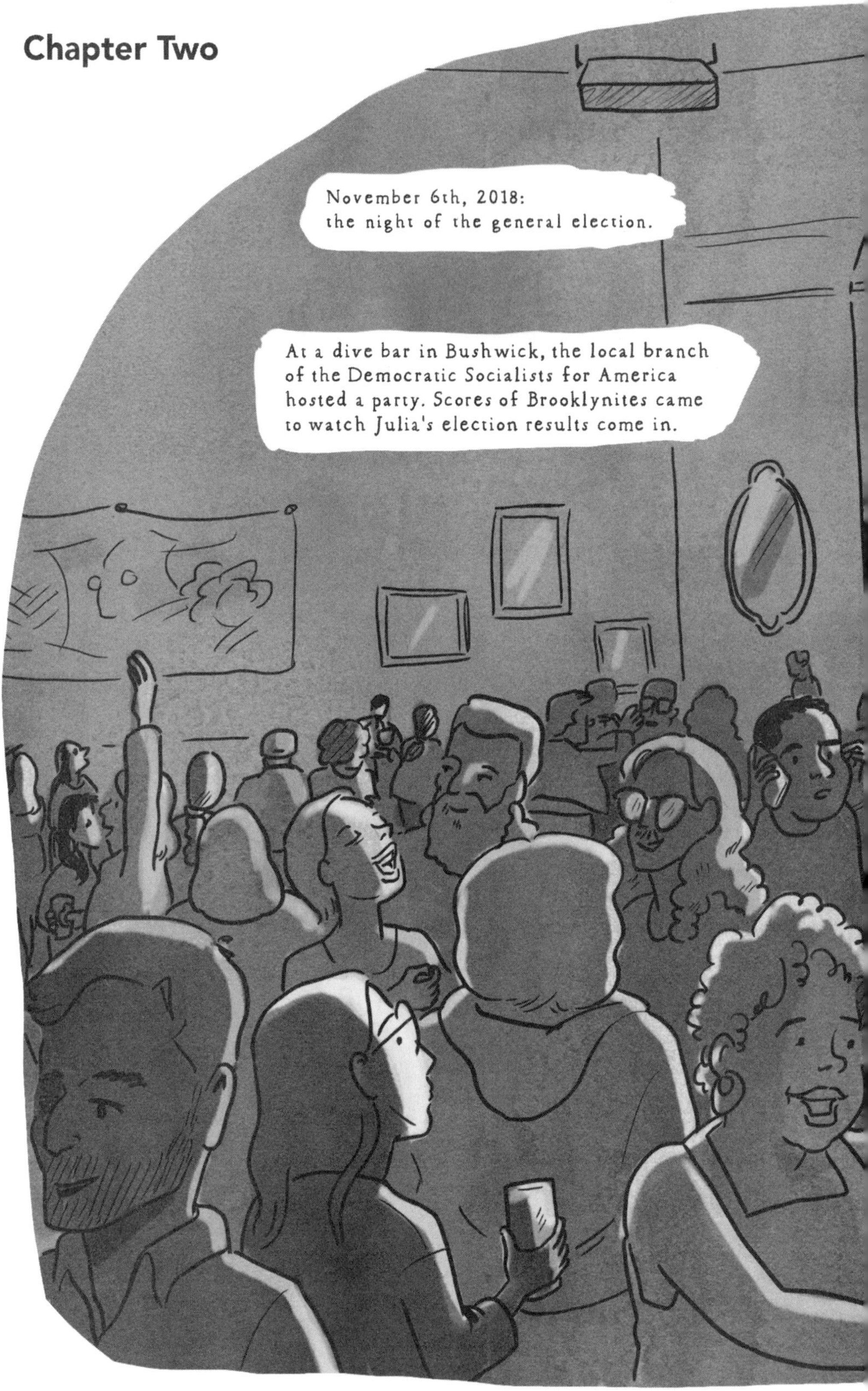
November 6th, 2018:
the night of the general election.
At a dive bar in Bushwick, the local branch of the Democratic Socialists for America hosted a party. Scores of Brooklynites came to watch Julia's election results come in.

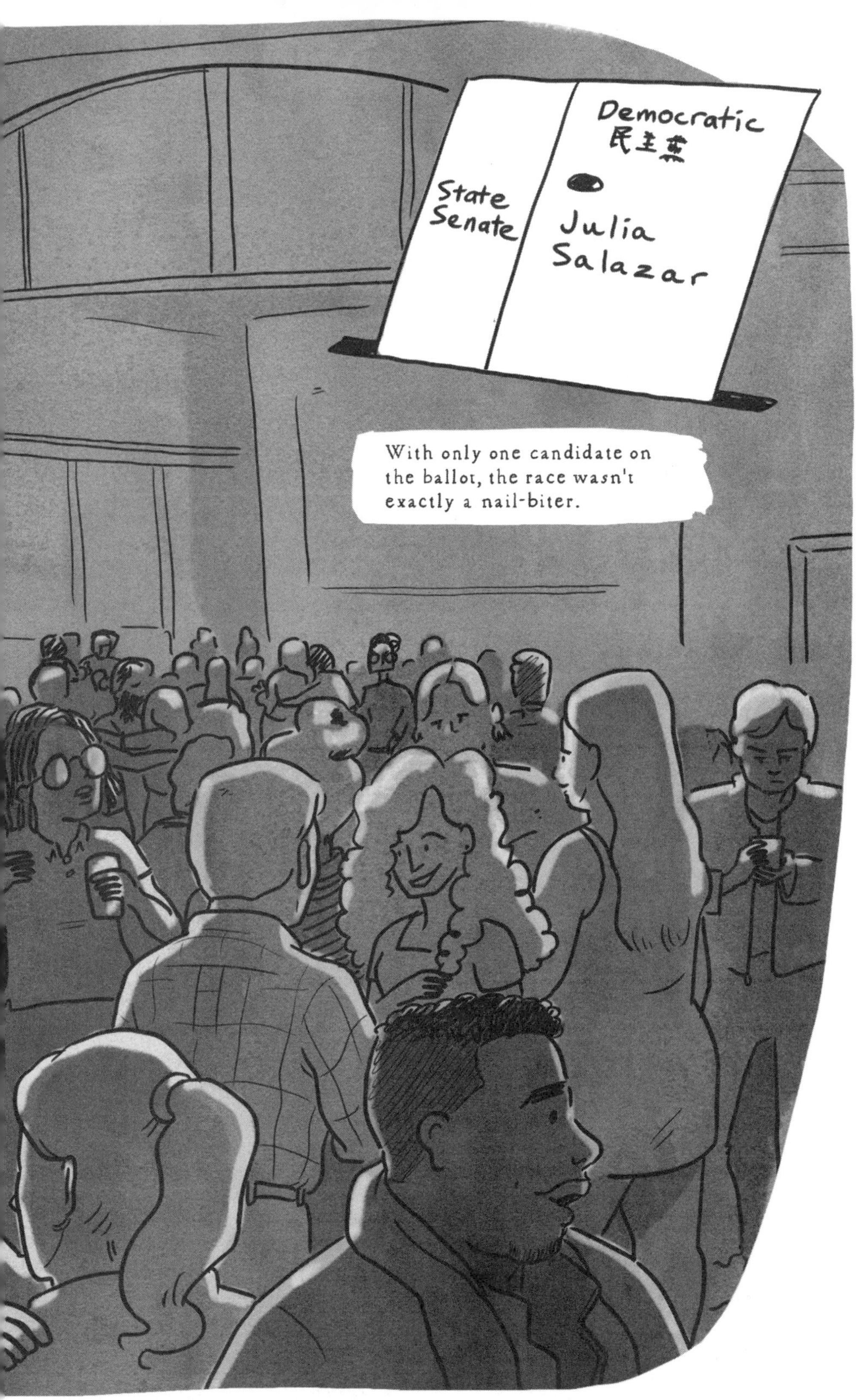
State Senate
Democratic
民主黨
Julia Salazar
With only one candidate on the ballot, the race wasn't exactly a nail-biter.

But there was a lot more to celebrate than Julia's victory...

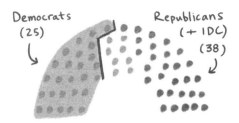 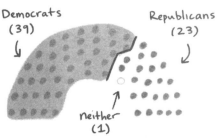

2016 ——————→ 2018

Democrats
(25)

Republicans
(+ IDC)
(38)

Democrats
(39)

Republicans
(23)

neither
(1)

... Because tonight, Democrats won back the Senate from the Republicans, who had been in control for all but a handful of years since World War II.

When I'd learned that the Senate wasn't already Democratic, I'd been surprised. I'd always thought of New York as one of the most solidly Democratic states.

The governor, Andrew Cuomo, was a Democrat.

As was the majority of the State Assembly.

Democrats

Republicans

... was because of a block of Democratic senators who had been voting with the Republicans.

In fact (as my recent Google searches had taught me), the only reason Republicans had maintained their State Senate majority for the last several years...

They called themselves the Independent Democratic Conference, or

IDC.

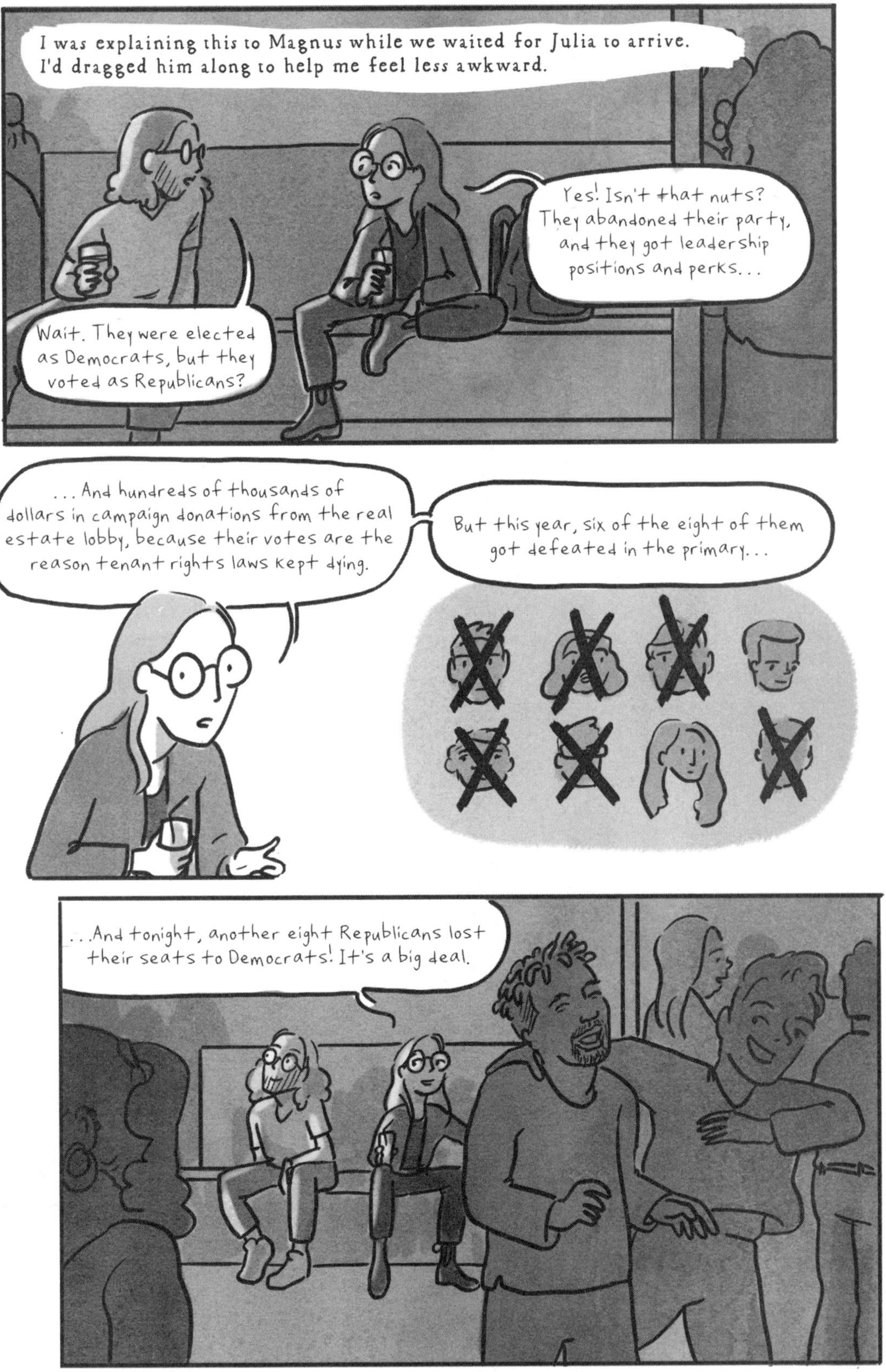
I was explaining this to Magnus while we waited for Julia to arrive. I'd dragged him along to help me feel less awkward.
Yes! Isn't that nuts? They abandoned their party, and they got leadership positions and perks...
Wait. They were elected as Democrats, but they voted as Republicans?
...And hundreds of thousands of dollars in campaign donations from the real estate lobby, because their votes are the reason tenant rights laws kept dying.
But this year, six of the eight of them got defeated in the primary...
...And tonight, another eight Republicans lost their seats to Democrats! It's a big deal.

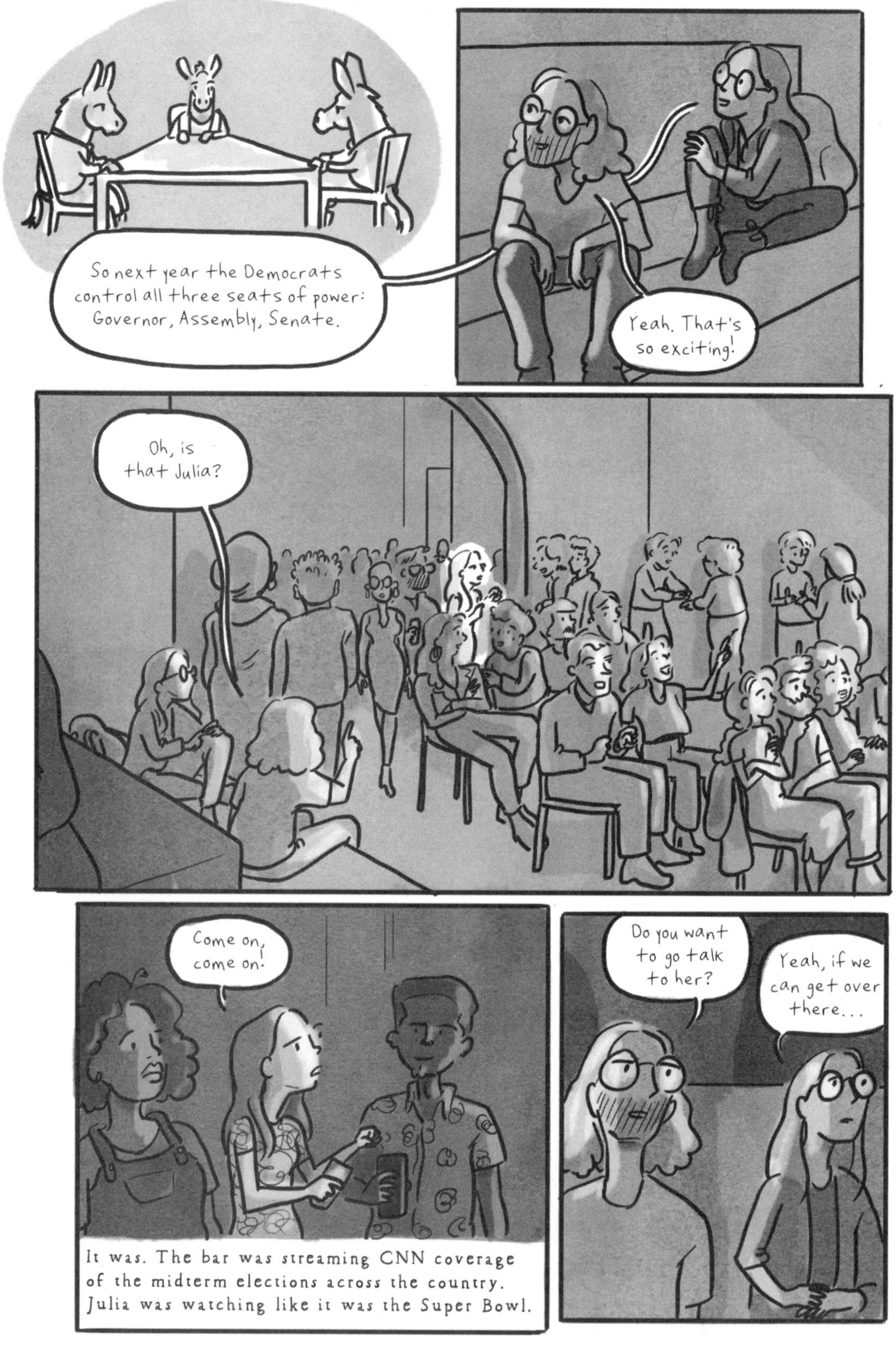
So next year the Democrats control all three seats of power: Governor, Assembly, Senate.
Yeah. That's so exciting!
Oh, is that Julia?
Come on, come on!
It was. The bar was streaming CNN coverage of the midterm elections across the country. Julia was watching like it was the Super Bowl.
Do you want to go talk to her?
Yeah, if we can get over there...

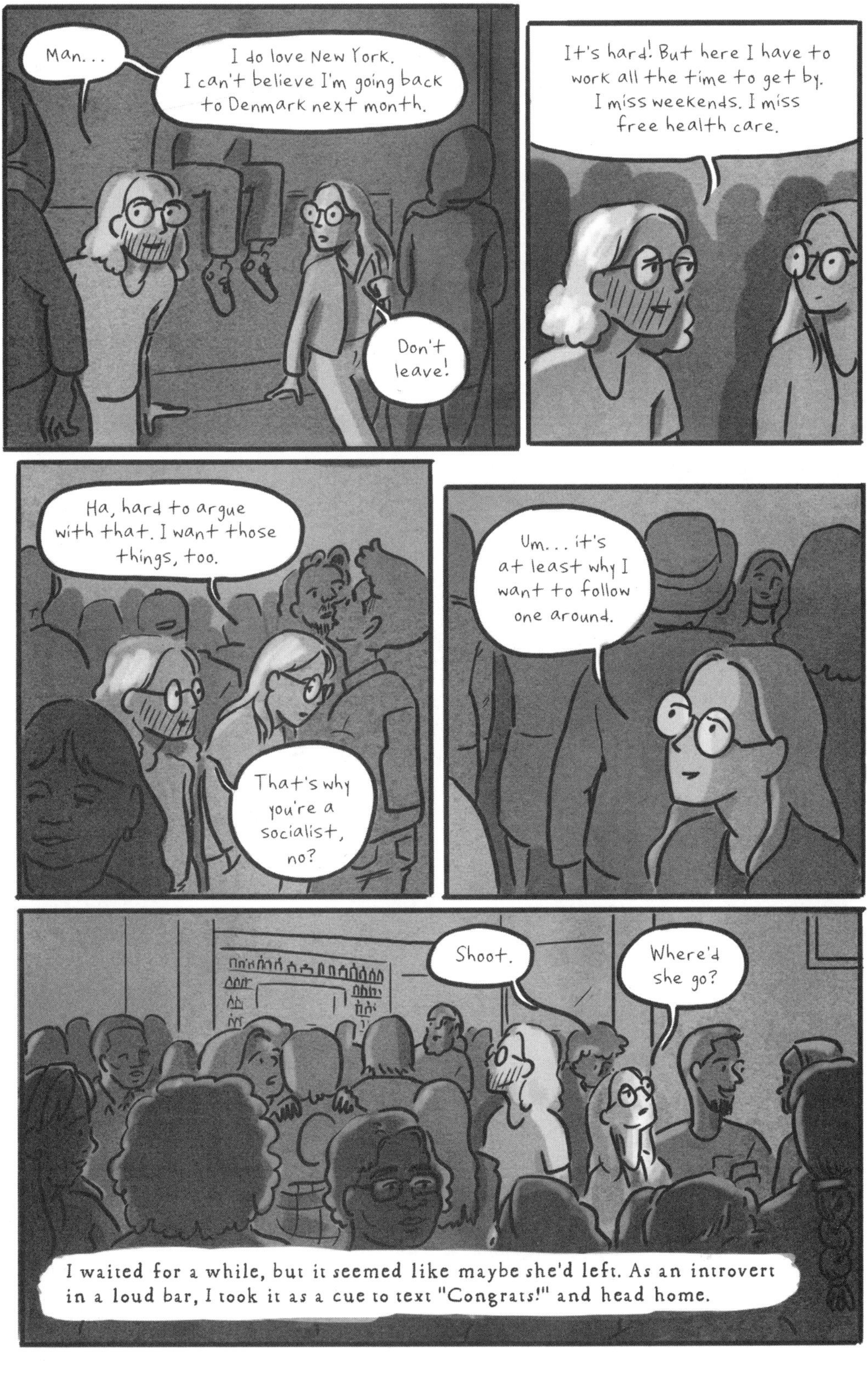

Man...
I do love New York. I can't believe I'm going back to Denmark next month.
Don't leave!
It's hard! But here I have to work all the time to get by. I miss weekends. I miss free health care.
Ha, hard to argue with that. I want those things, too.
That's why you're a socialist, no?
Um... it's at least why I want to follow one around.
Shoot.
Where'd she go?
I waited for a while, but it seemed like maybe she'd left. As an introvert in a loud bar, I took it as a cue to text "Congrats!" and head home.

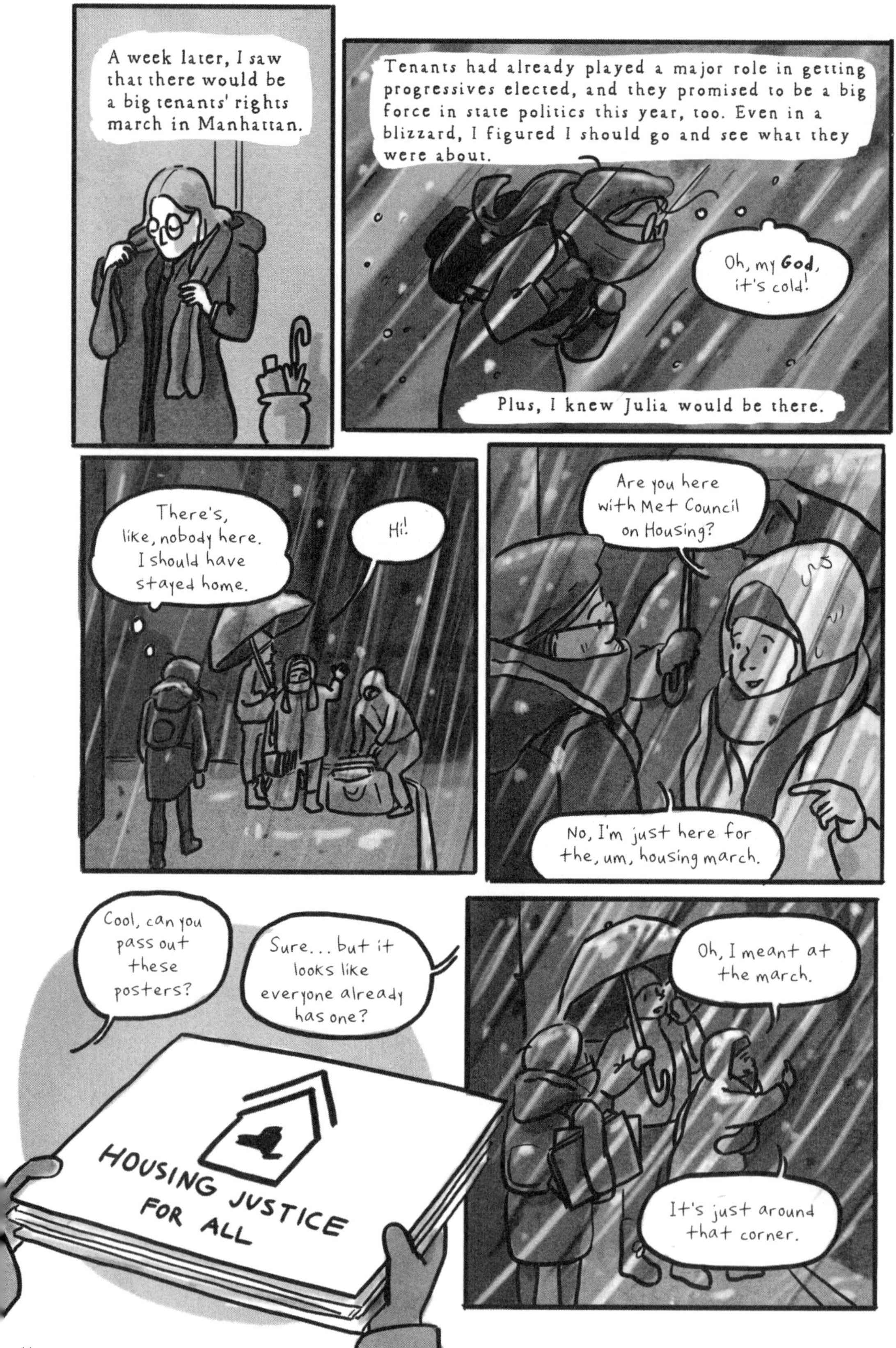
A week later, I saw that there would be a big tenants' rights march in Manhattan.
Tenants had already played a major role in getting progressives elected, and they promised to be a big force in state politics this year, too. Even in a blizzard, I figured I should go and see what they were about.
Oh, my **God**, it's cold!
Plus, I knew Julia would be there.
There's, like, nobody here. I should have stayed home.
Hi!
Are you here with Met Council on Housing?
No, I'm just here for the, um, housing march.
Cool, can you pass out these posters?
Sure... but it looks like everyone already has one?
HOUSING JUSTICE FOR ALL
Oh, I meant at the march.
It's just around that corner.

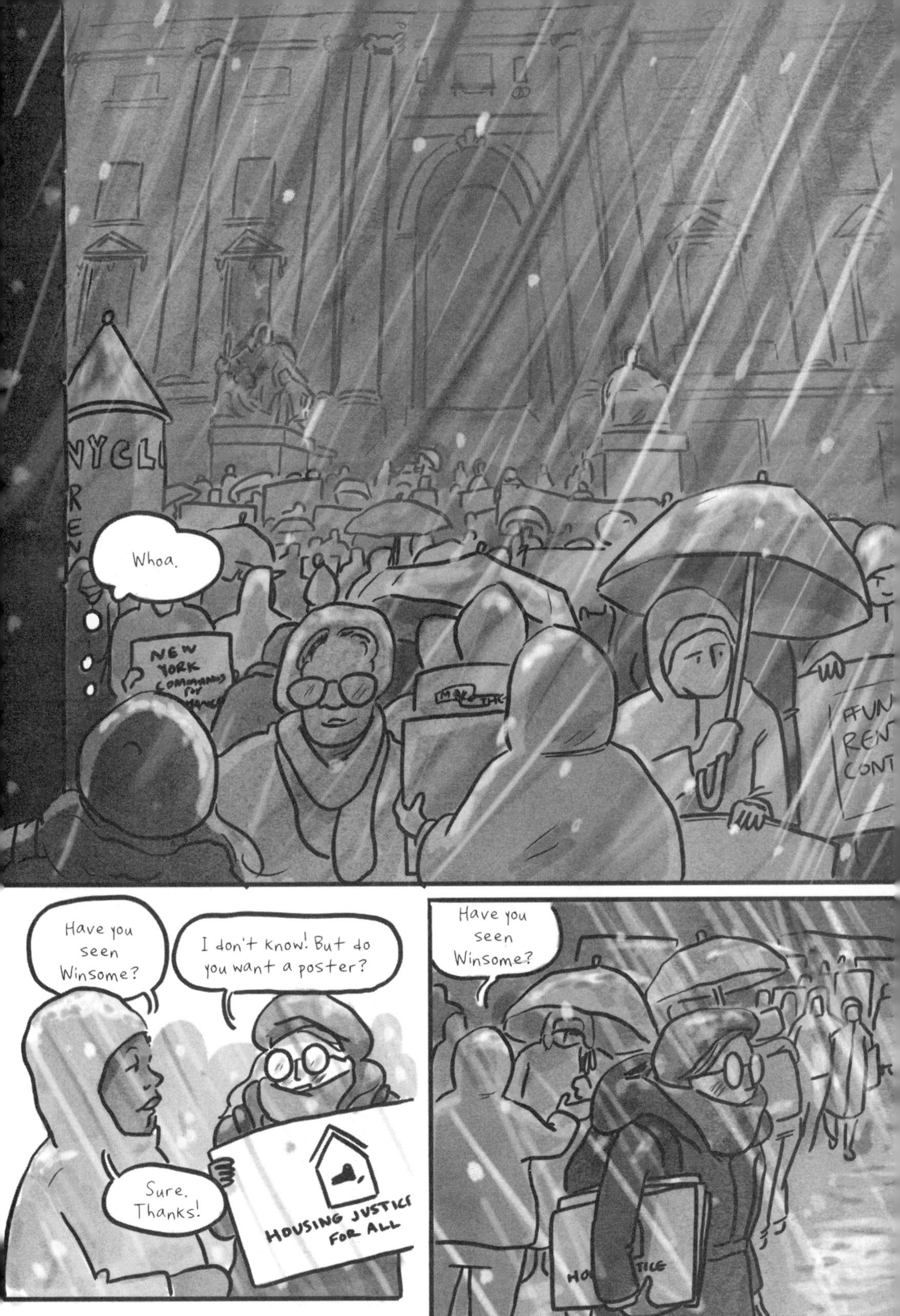
Whoa.
NEW YORK
Have you seen Winsome?
I don't know! But do you want a poster?
Sure. Thanks!
HOUSING JUSTIC
FOR ALL
Have you seen Winsome?

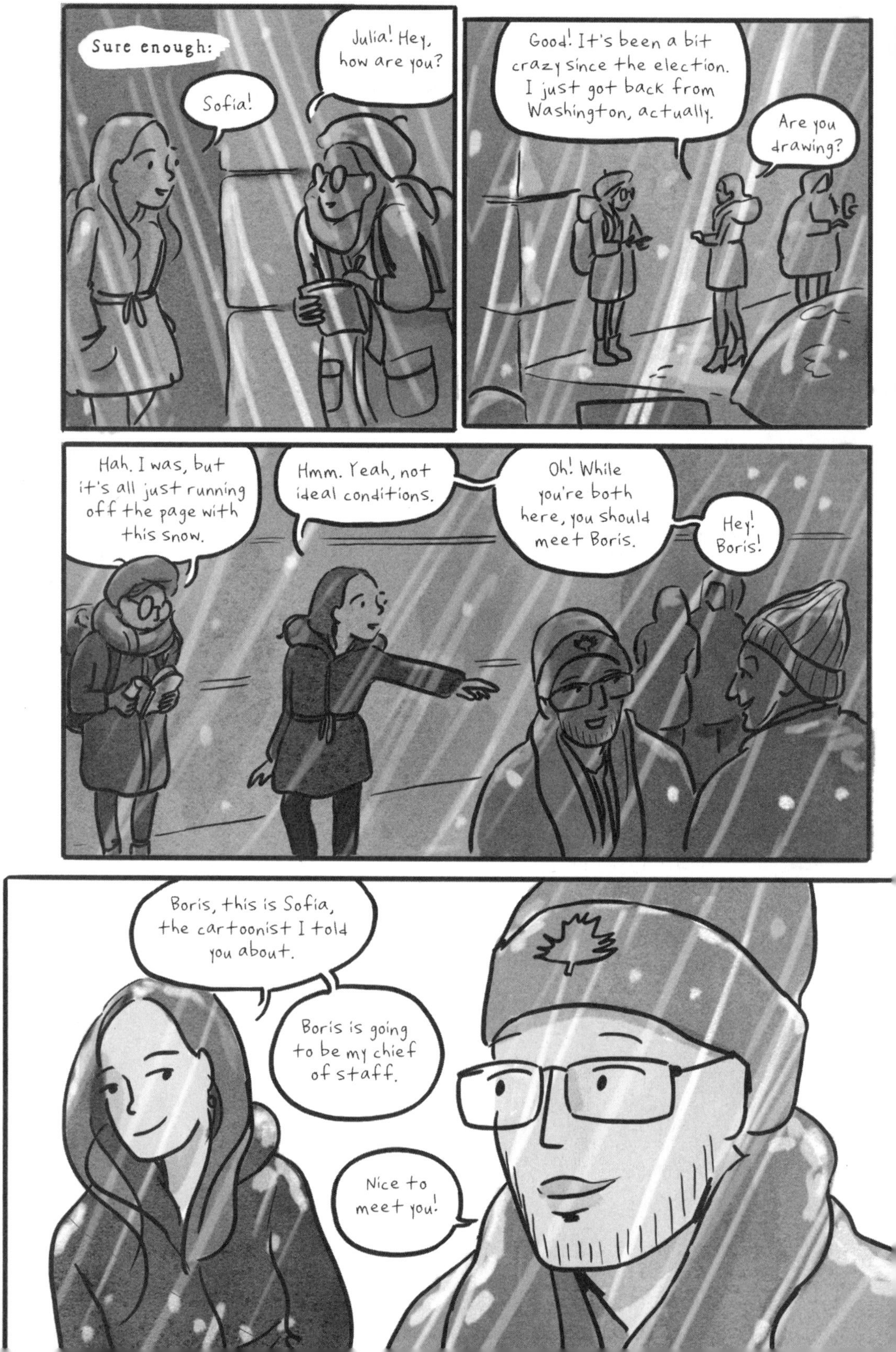
Sure enough:
Sofia!
Julia! Hey, how are you?
Good! It's been a bit crazy since the election. I just got back from Washington, actually.
Are you drawing?
Hah. I was, but it's all just running off the page with this snow.
Hmm. Yeah, not ideal conditions.
Oh! While you're both here, you should meet Boris.
Hey! Boris!
Boris, this is Sofia, the cartoonist I told you about.
Boris is going to be my chief of staff.
Nice to meet you!

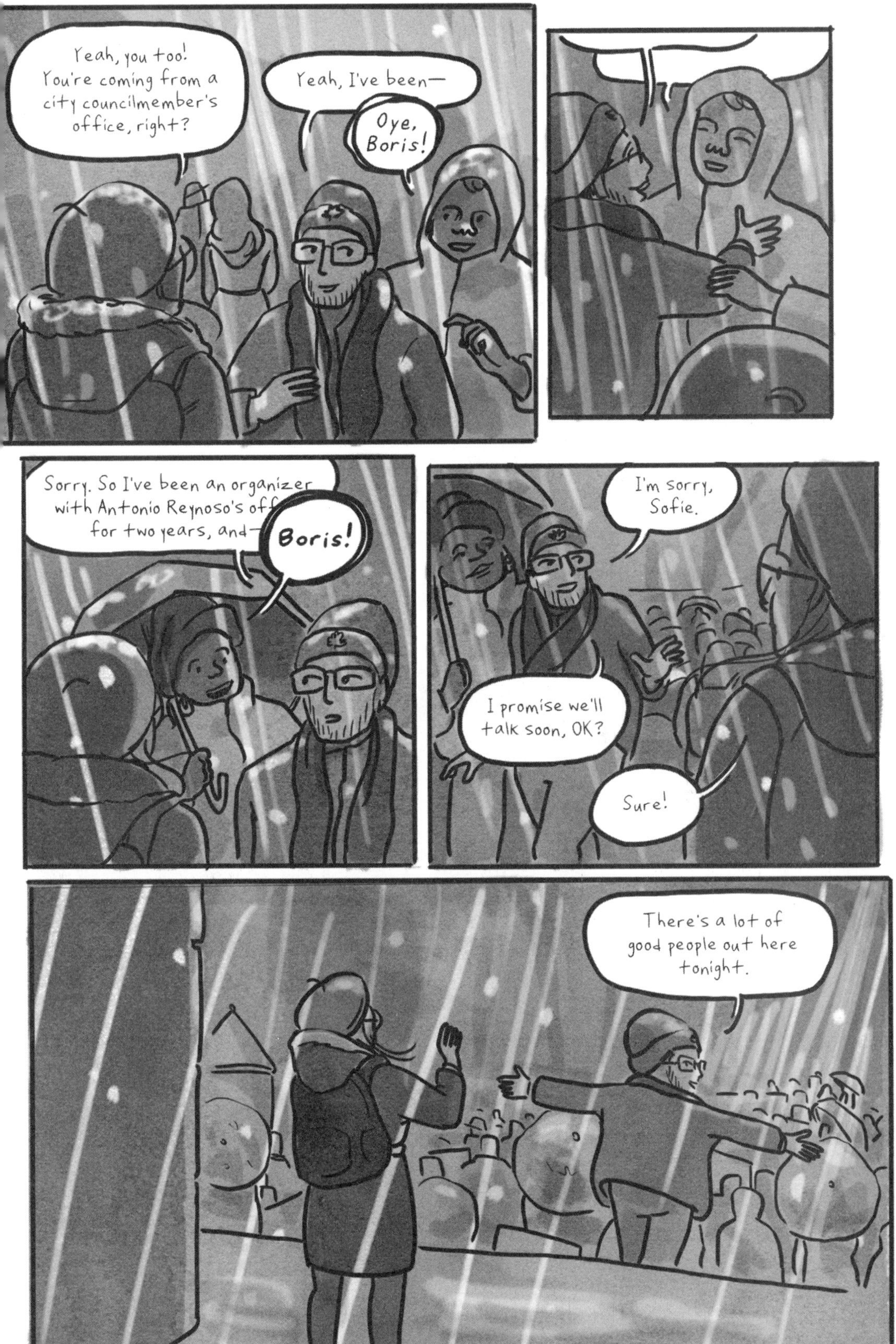

Yeah, you too! You're coming from a city councilmember's office, right?
Yeah, I've been—
Oye, Boris!
Sorry. So I've been an organizer with Antonio Reynoso's off for two years, and—
Boris!
I'm sorry, Sofie.
I promise we'll talk soon, OK?
Sure!
There's a lot of good people out here tonight.

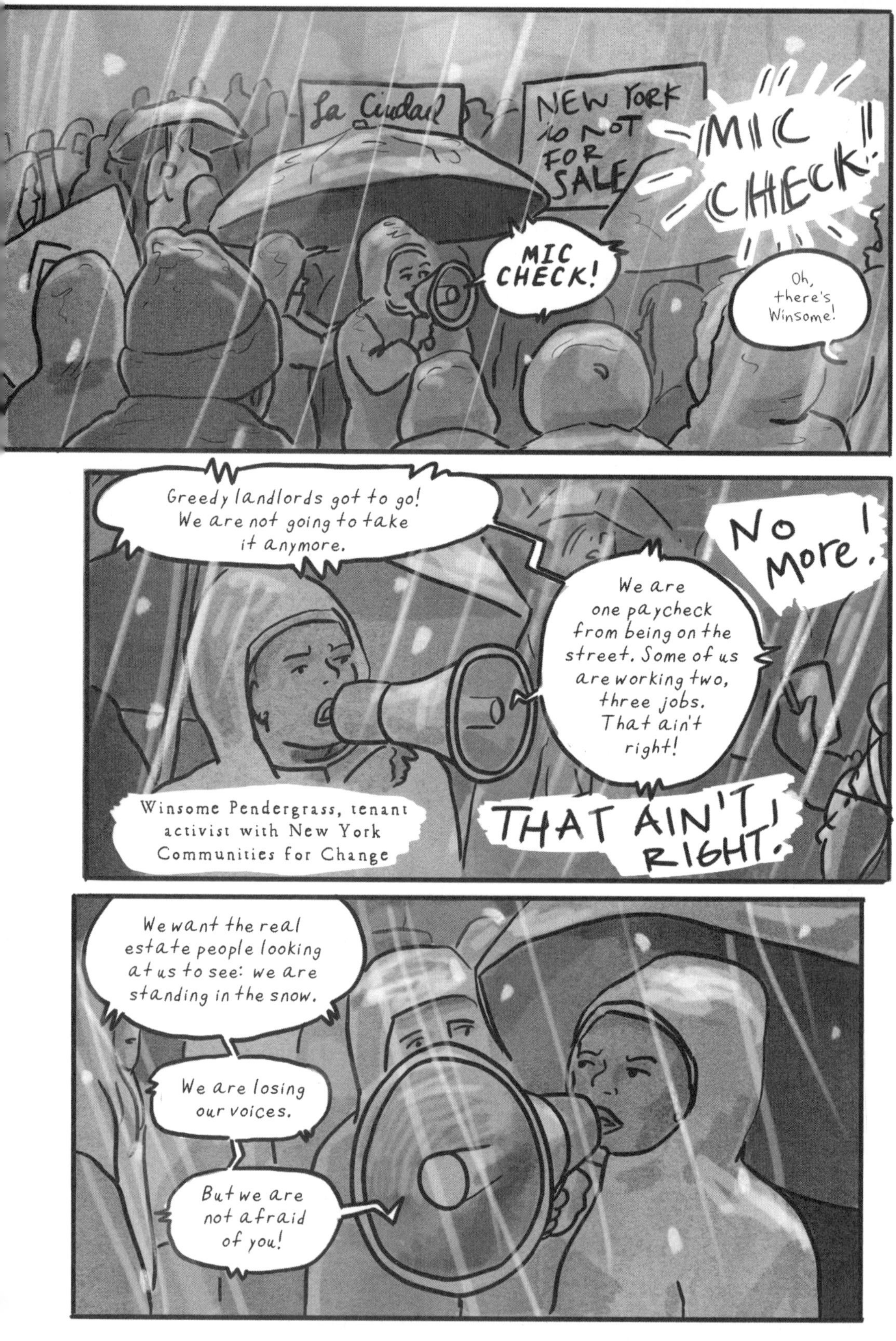
La Ciudad
NEW YORK is NOT FOR SALE
MIC CHECK!
MIC CHECK!
Oh, there's Winsome!
Greedy landlords got to go! We are not going to take it anymore.
No More!
We are one paycheck from being on the street. Some of us are working two, three jobs. That ain't right!
Winsome Pendergrass, tenant activist with New York Communities for Change
THAT AIN'T RIGHT!
We want the real estate people looking at us to see: we are standing in the snow.
We are losing our voices.
But we are not afraid of you!

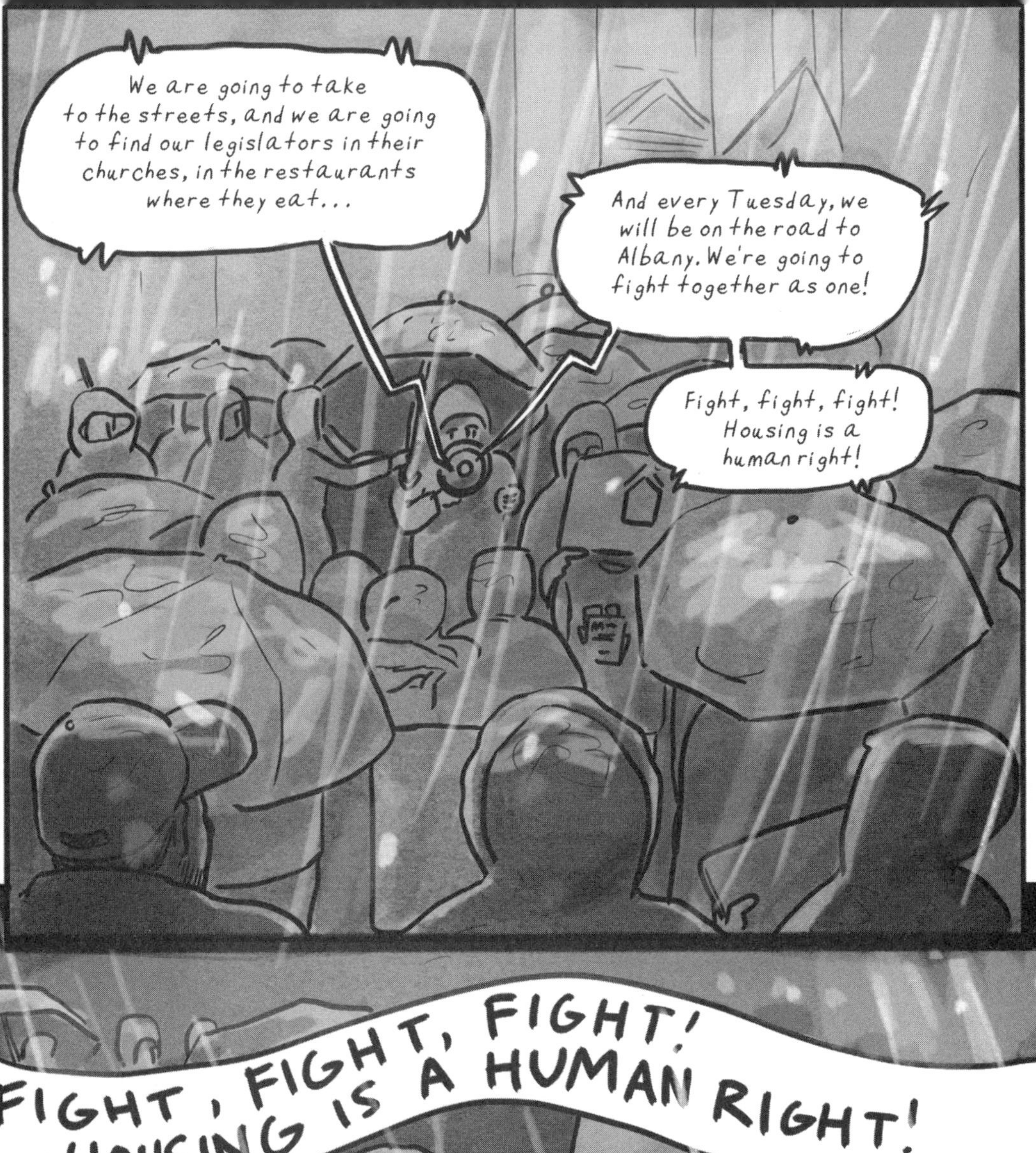
We are going to take to the streets, and we are going to find our legislators in their churches, in the restaurants where they eat...
And every Tuesday, we will be on the road to Albany. We're going to fight together as one!
Fight, fight, fight! Housing is a human right!

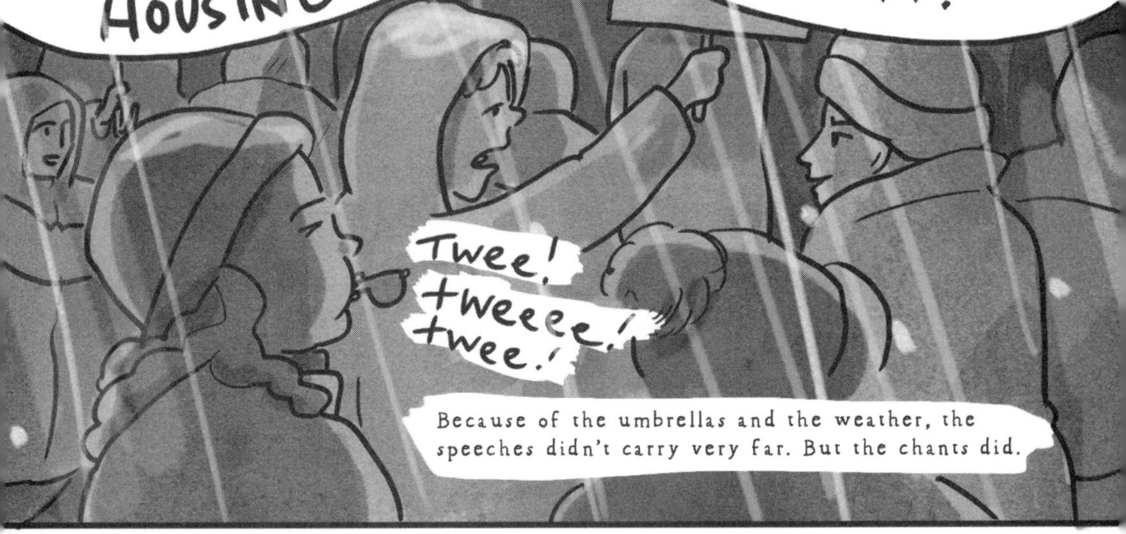
FIGHT, FIGHT, FIGHT! HOUSING IS A HUMAN RIGHT!
Twee! tweeee! twee!
Because of the umbrellas and the weather, the speeches didn't carry very far. But the chants did.

This coalition was called

HOUSING JUSTICE FOR ALL

La Ciudad es Nuestra · MAKE THE ROAD · END THE HOUSING CRISIS

And it was made up of tenant groups from all across the state.
North Brooklyn wasn't the only district with an affordable housing crisis.

There were over five million tenants in New York City, and millions more across the state. New York had a higher percentage of renters than any other state in the country.

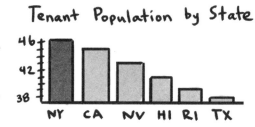

Tenant Population by State

% of Pop. — 46, 42, 38 — NY CA NV HI RI TX

We CAN'T pay RENT increases and EAT TOO

STOP ENDLESS increases for TENANTS

That there was any rent regulation system at all in New York was a testament to the success of past tenant movements. Most states had none whatsoever.

But for one thing, the regulations had been so diluted over time that even protected tenants found themselves facing harrassment, eviction, and rent hikes.

NYC

■ Some rent regulation
☐ No rent regulation

NEW YORK IS NOT FOR SALE

And for another, the system only applied to about half the units in the greater New York City area, and did not apply at all to the millions of tenants living outside those counties.

With market-rate rents skyrocketing and public housing waitlists in the hundreds of thousands, tenants pushed out of rent-regulated homes often had nowhere else to go.

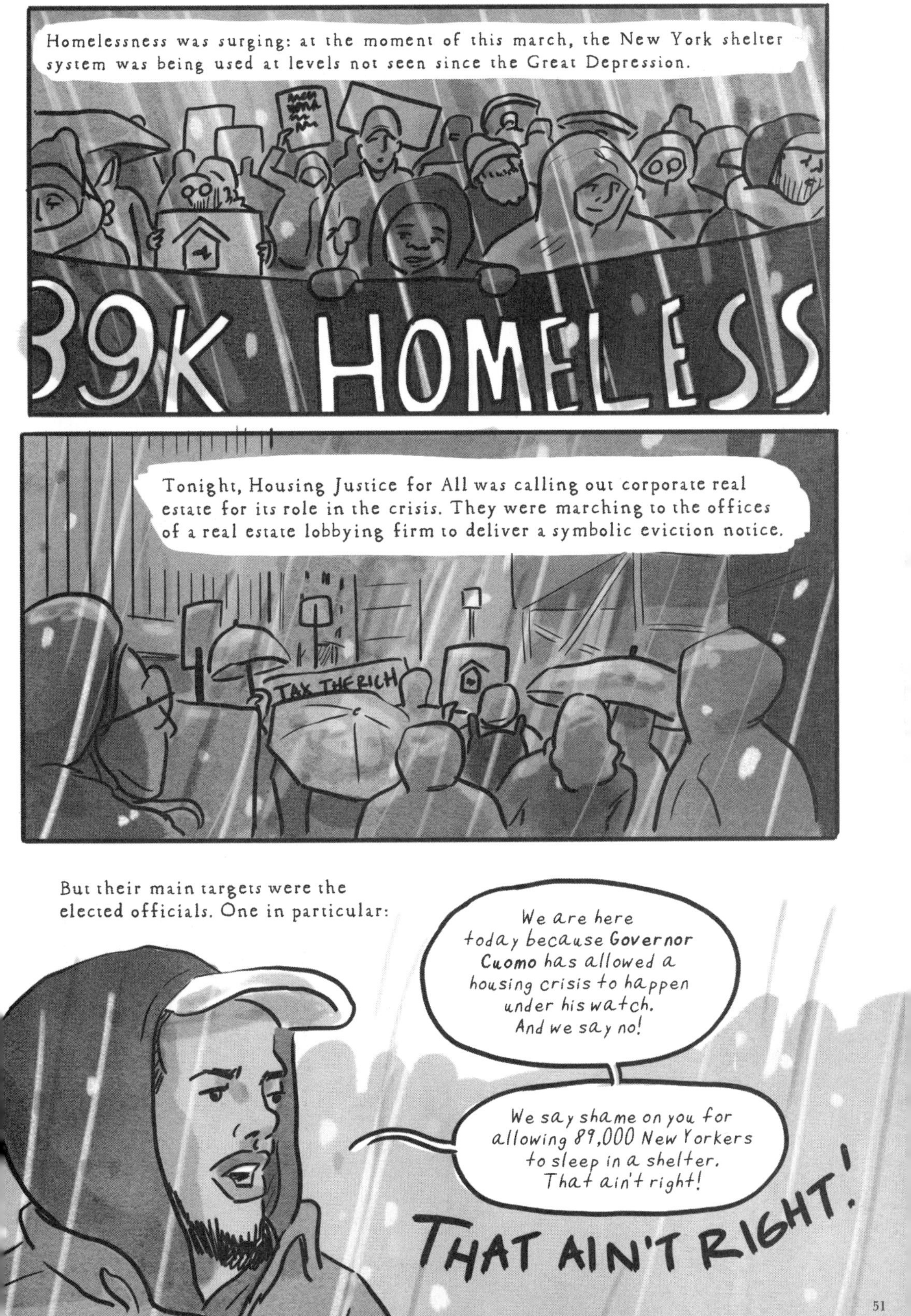

Homelessness was surging: at the moment of this march, the New York shelter system was being used at levels not seen since the Great Depression.
9K HOMELESS
Tonight, Housing Justice for All was calling out corporate real estate for its role in the crisis. They were marching to the offices of a real estate lobbying firm to deliver a symbolic eviction notice.
TAX THE RICH
But their main targets were the elected officials. One in particular:
We are here today because **Governor Cuomo** has allowed a housing crisis to happen under his watch. And we say no!
We say shame on you for allowing 89,000 New Yorkers to sleep in a shelter. That ain't right!
THAT AIN'T RIGHT!

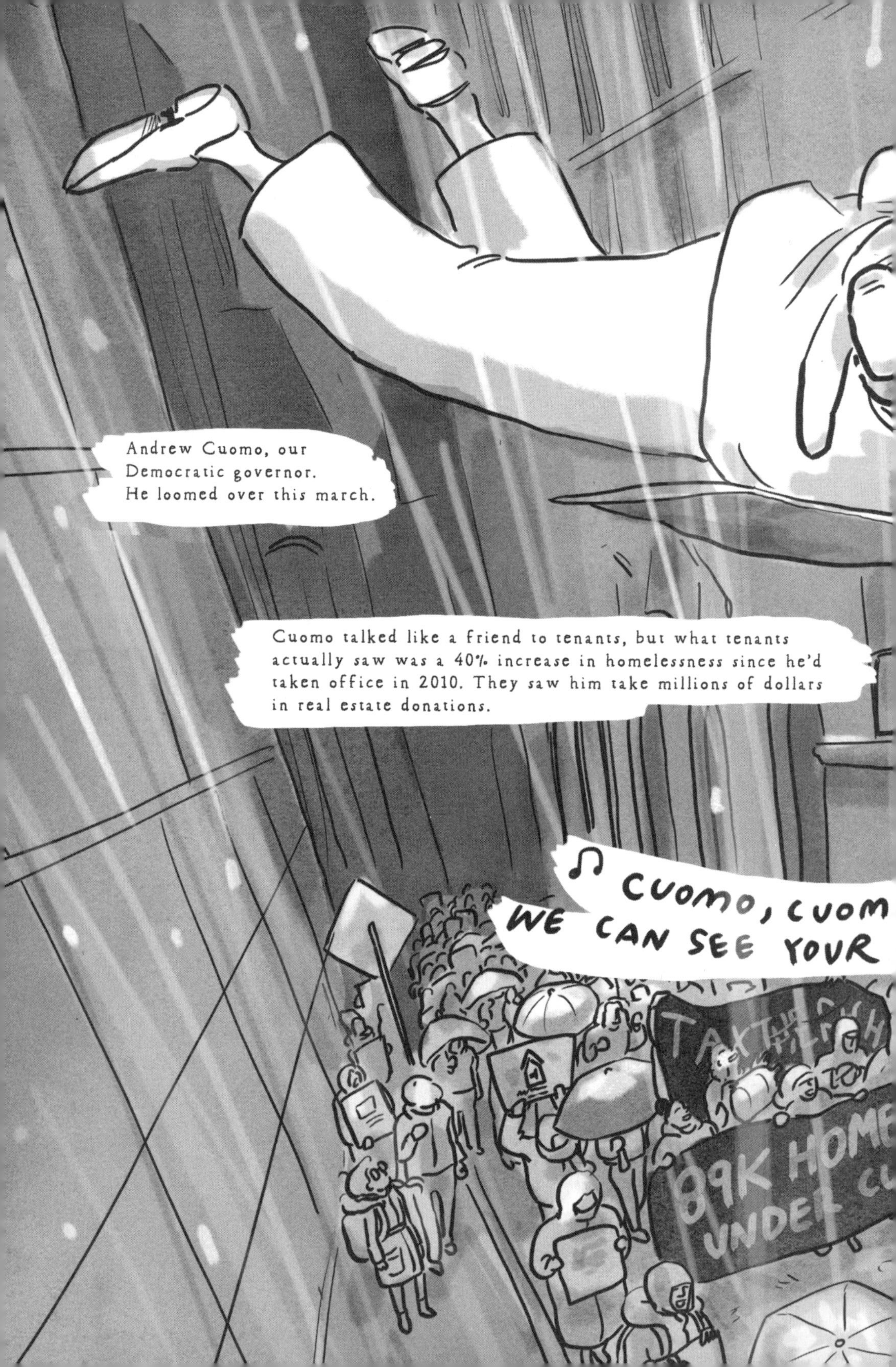
Andrew Cuomo, our Democratic governor. He loomed over this march.
Cuomo talked like a friend to tenants, but what tenants actually saw was a 40% increase in homelessness since he'd taken office in 2010. They saw him take millions of dollars in real estate donations.
♫ CUOMO, CUOM
WE CAN SEE YOUR

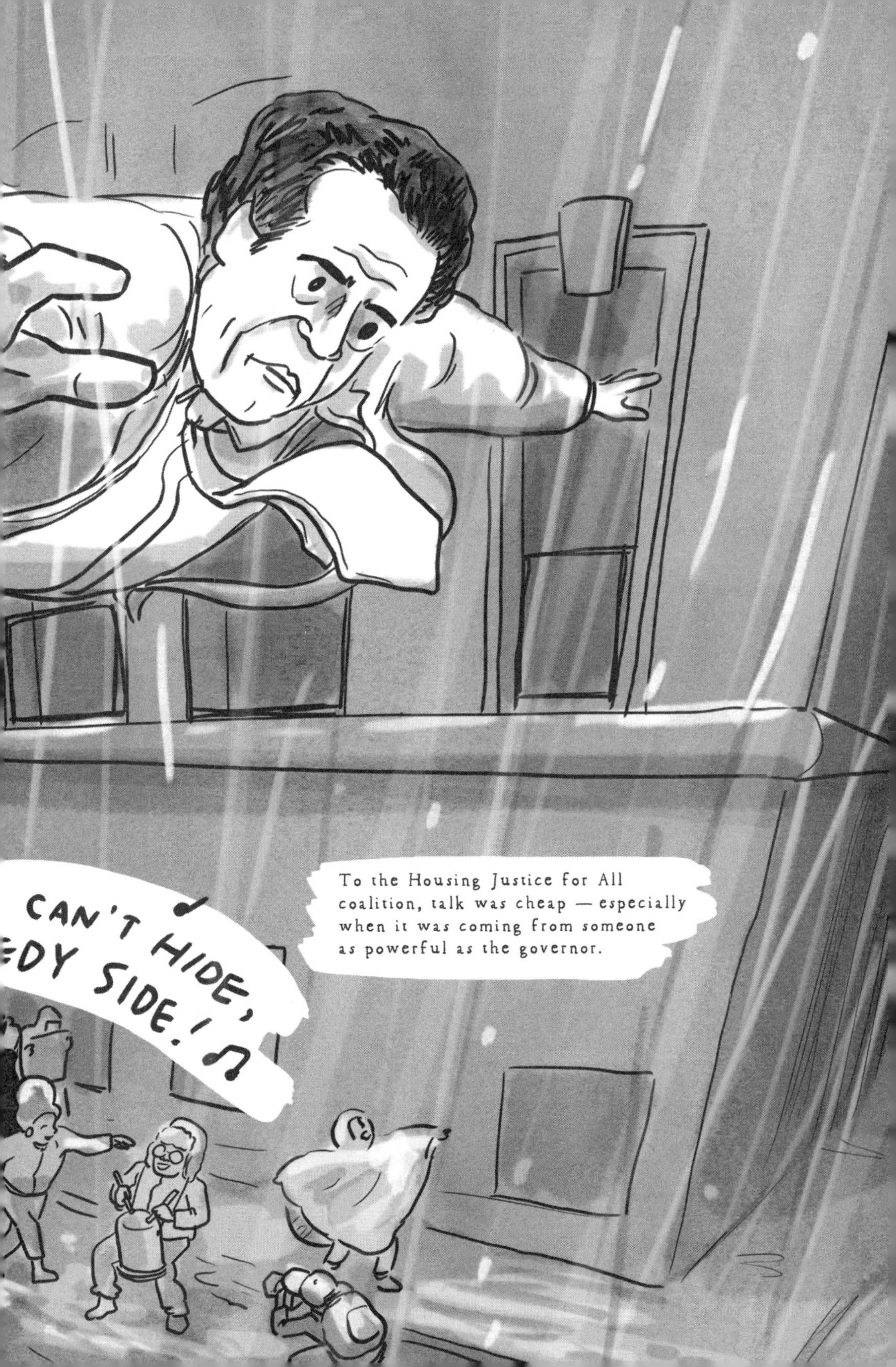
CAN'T HIDE,
EDY SIDE!
To the Housing Justice for All coalition, talk was cheap — especially when it was coming from someone as powerful as the governor.

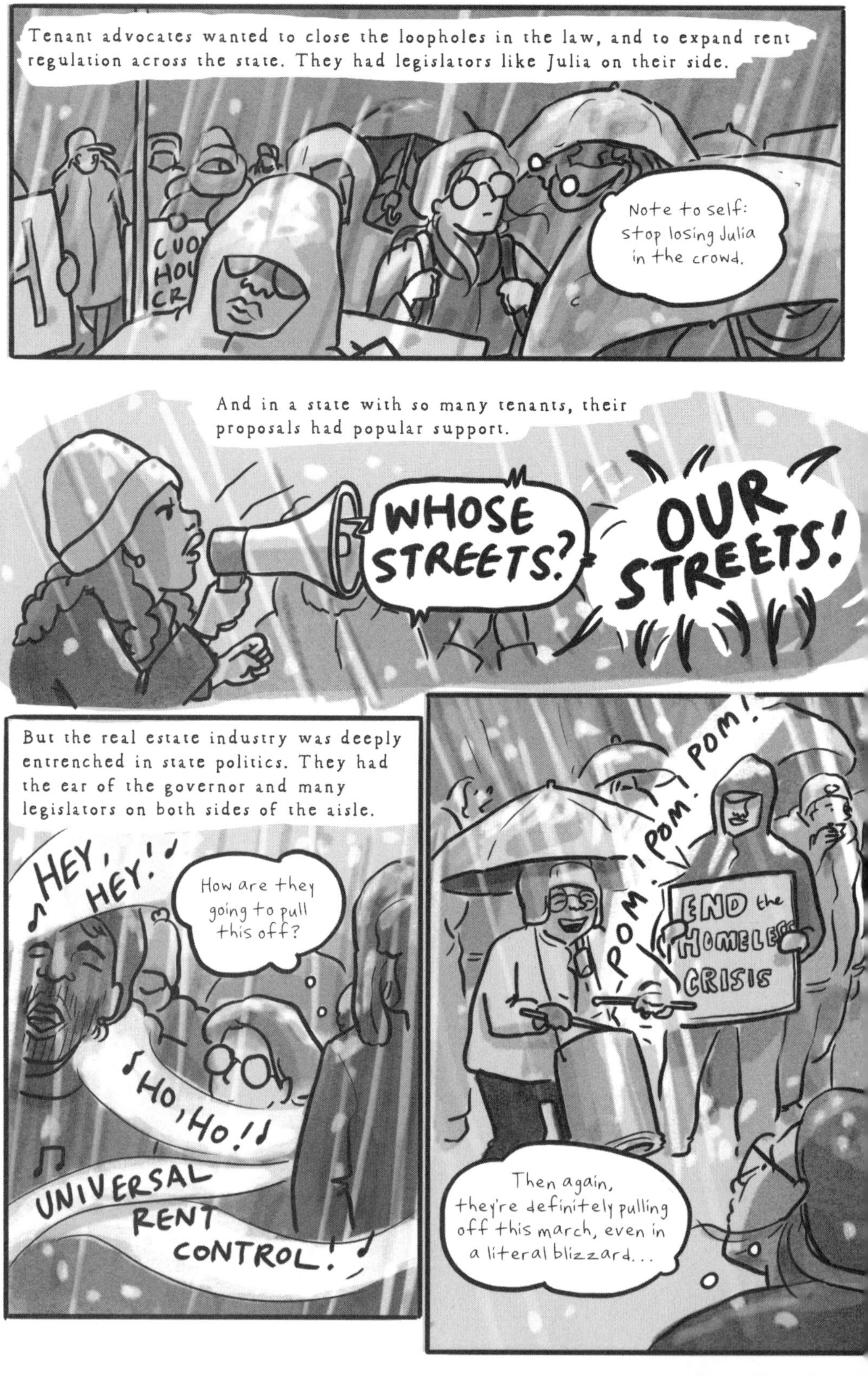
Tenant advocates wanted to close the loopholes in the law, and to expand rent regulation across the state. They had legislators like Julia on their side.
Note to self: stop losing Julia in the crowd.
And in a state with so many tenants, their proposals had popular support.
WHOSE STREETS?
OUR STREETS!
But the real estate industry was deeply entrenched in state politics. They had the ear of the governor and many legislators on both sides of the aisle.
HEY, HEY!
How are they going to pull this off?
HO, HO!
UNIVERSAL RENT CONTROL!
POM! POM! POM! POM!
END the
CRISIS
Then again, they're definitely pulling off this march, even in a literal blizzard...

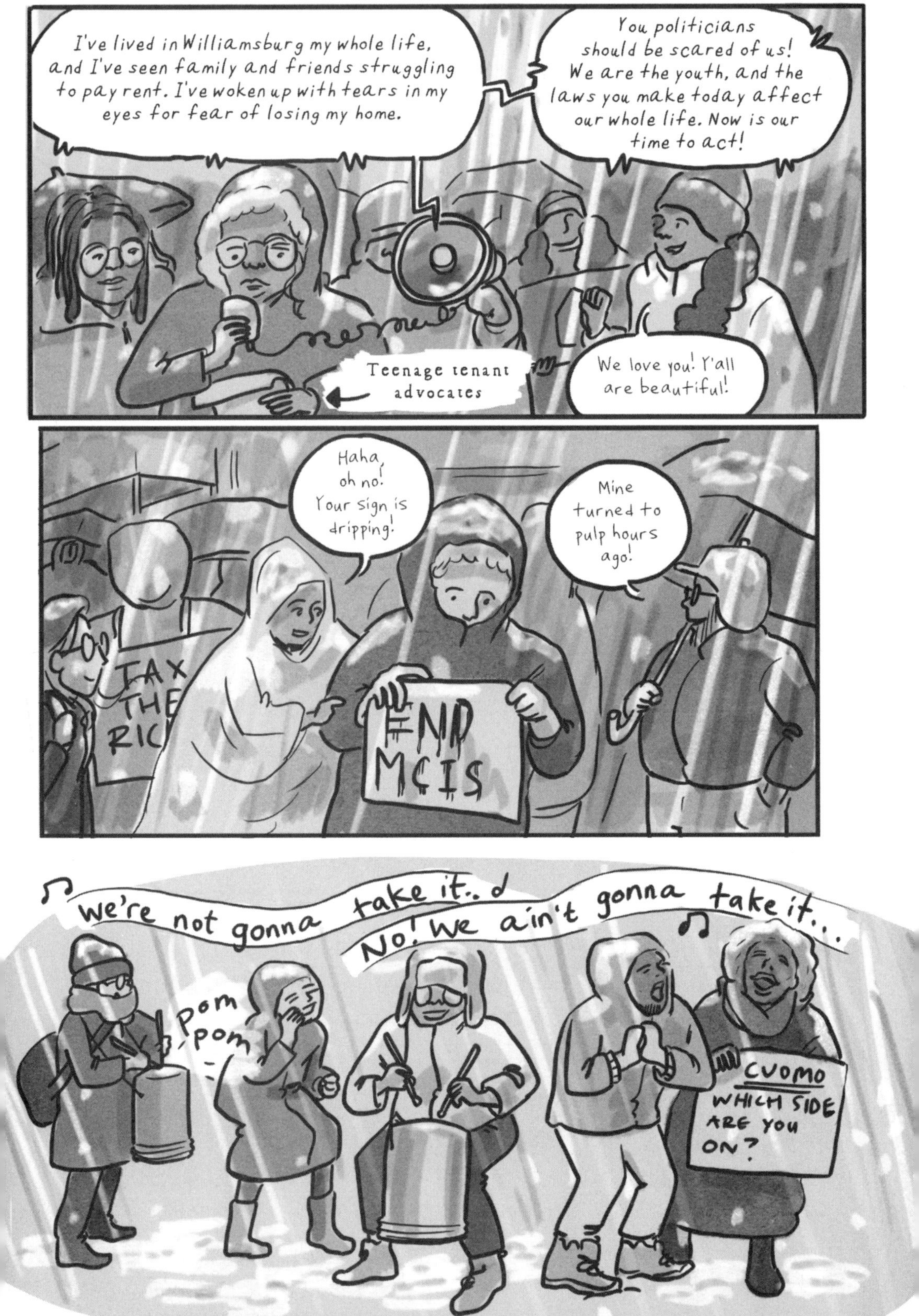
I've lived in Williamsburg my whole life, and I've seen family and friends struggling to pay rent. I've woken up with tears in my eyes for fear of losing my home.
You politicians should be scared of us! We are the youth, and the laws you make today affect our whole life. Now is our time to act!
Teenage tenant advocates
We love you! Y'all are beautiful!
Haha, oh no! Your sign is dripping!
Mine turned to pulp hours ago!
TAX THE RIC
END MCIS
we're not gonna take it..
No! we ain't gonna take it...
pom pom
CUOMO WHICH SIDE ARE YOU ON?

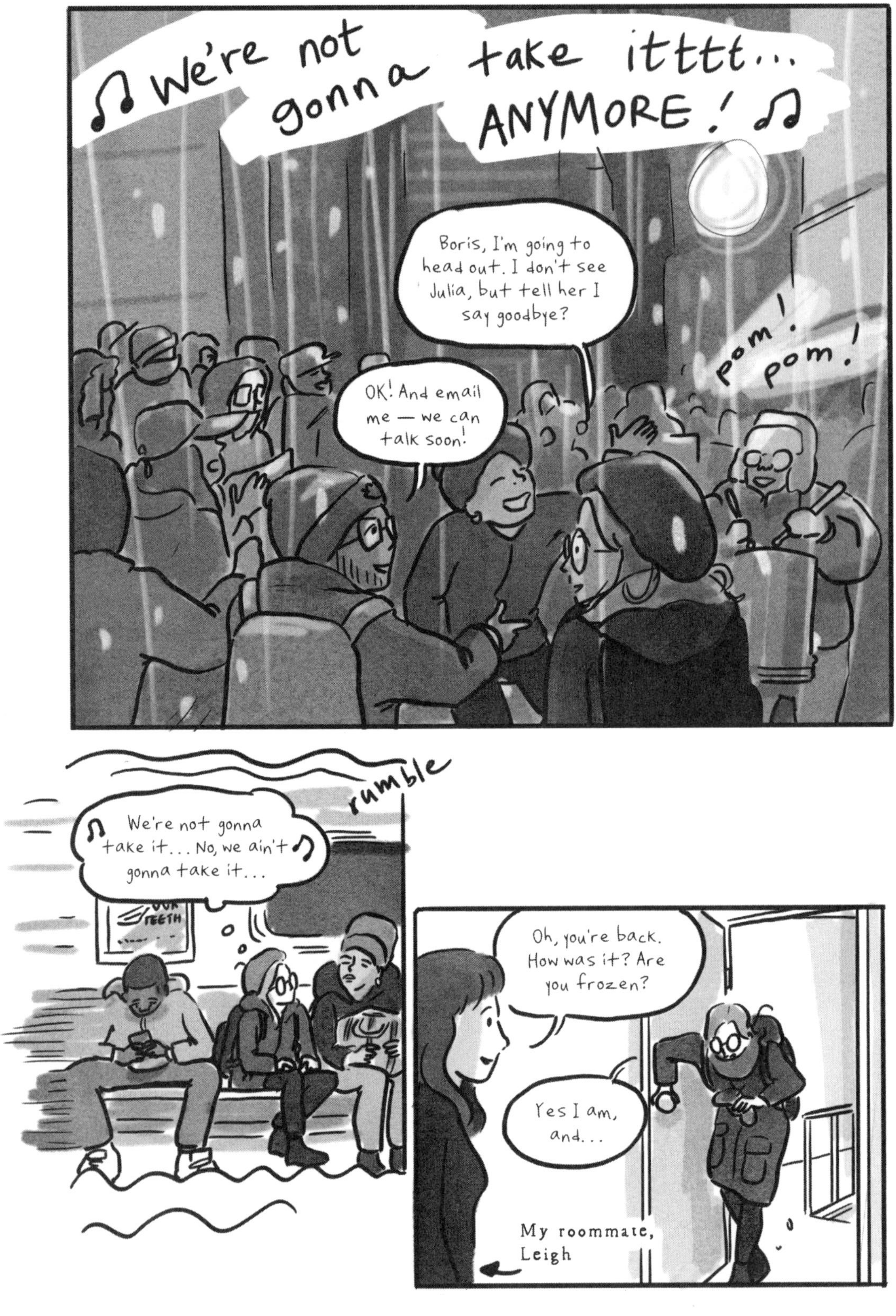
♫ We're not gonna take itttt... ANYMORE! ♫
Boris, I'm going to head out. I don't see Julia, but tell her I say goodbye?
OK! And email me — we can talk soon!
pom! pom!
rumble
♫ We're not gonna take it... No, we ain't gonna take it... ♫
Oh, you're back. How was it? Are you frozen?
Yes I am, and...
My roommate, Leigh

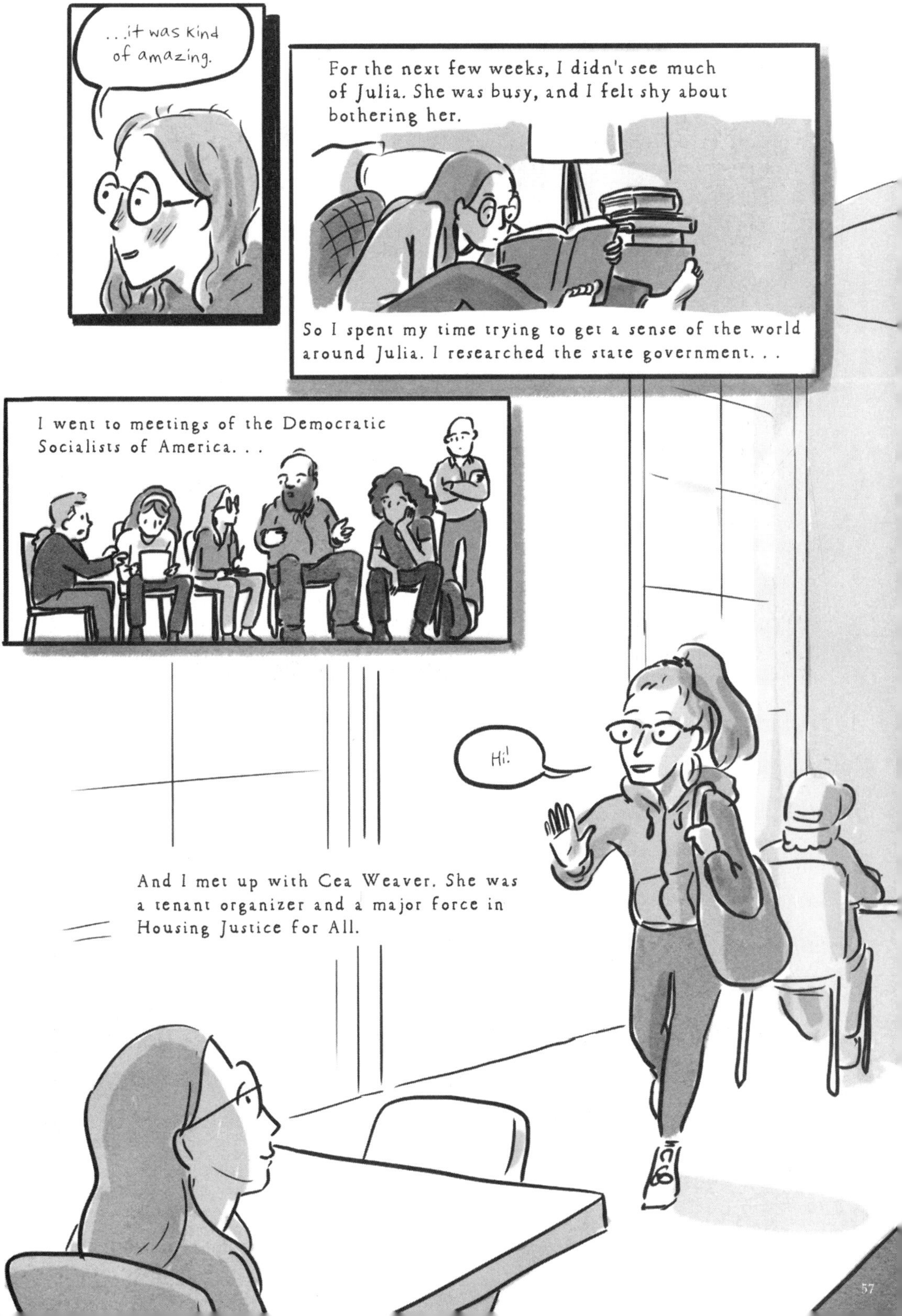
...it was kind of amazing.
For the next few weeks, I didn't see much of Julia. She was busy, and I felt shy about bothering her.
So I spent my time trying to get a sense of the world around Julia. I researched the state government...
I went to meetings of the Democratic Socialists of America...
Hi!
And I met up with Cea Weaver. She was a tenant organizer and a major force in Housing Justice for All.

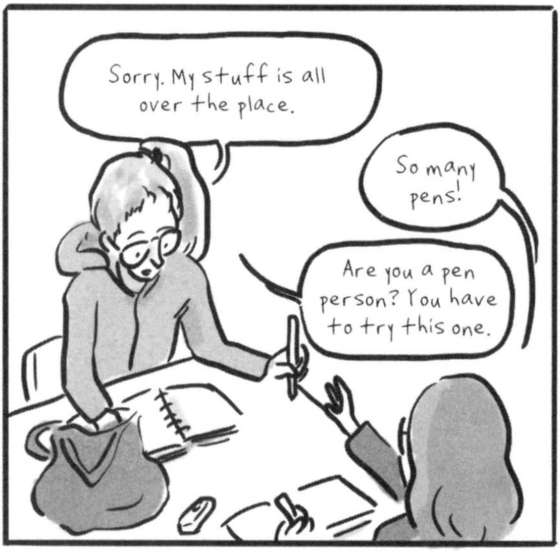
Sorry. My stuff is all over the place.
So many pens!
Are you a pen person? You have to try this one.

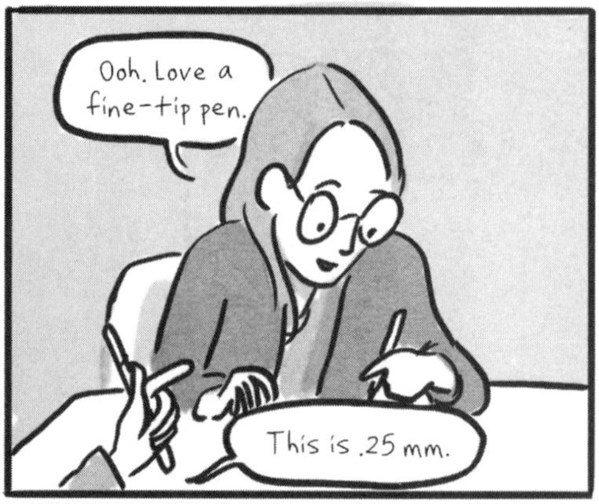
Ooh. Love a fine-tip pen.
This is .25 mm.

We talked about pens for, like, a while. I loved it, but I'll spare you the details.

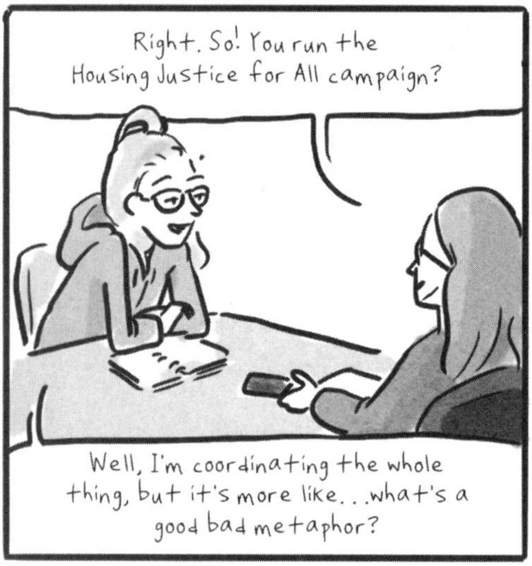
Right. So! You run the Housing Justice for All campaign?
Well, I'm coordinating the whole thing, but it's more like...what's a good bad metaphor?

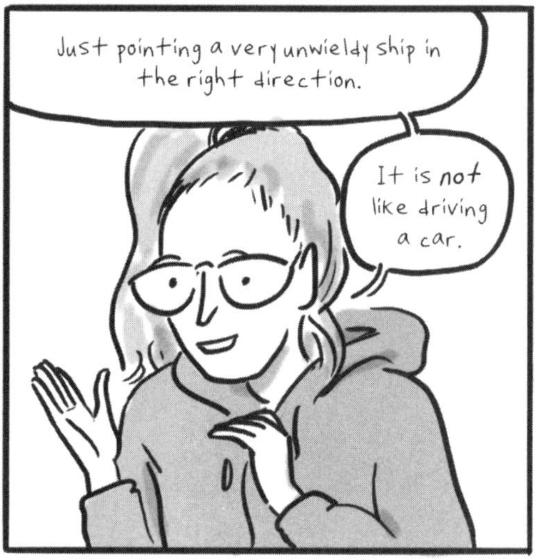
Just pointing a very unwieldy ship in the right direction.
It is *not* like driving a car.

It turns out, getting fifty different tenant organizations from all over the state to work together wasn't always a cakewalk... but we'll return to that later.

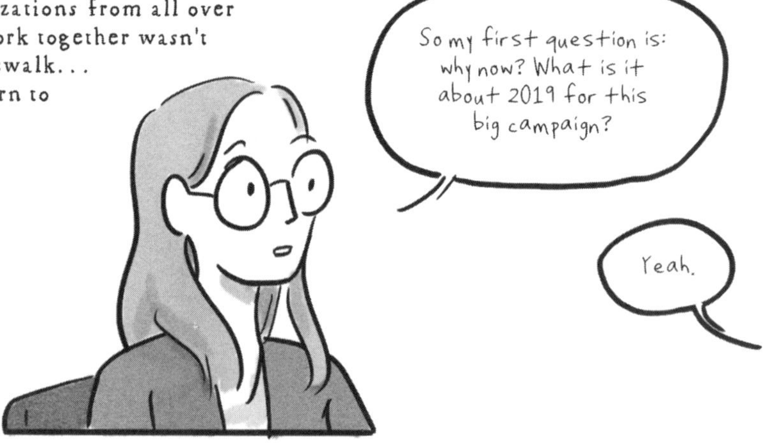
So my first question is: why now? What is it about 2019 for this big campaign?
Yeah.

For decades, we had this Republican State Senate, which was horrible.

In the Senate, you had a handful of good, progressive, on-the-side-of-tenants elected officials... but no one else really wanted to fight for tenants' rights.

And now **everything** is different.

It's been a bit of a whirlwind: now we have all these young advocates in the Senate. It's a total paradigm shift in what we're willing to demand for tenants in Albany.

We've been used to fighting for stronger rent laws with the assumption that we're going to lose for many years.

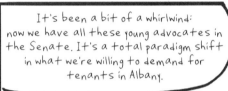

And now we're not just fighting for stronger rent laws. We're fighting to expand tenants' rights across the state.

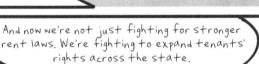

So there are people up in Albany who don't understand that if they support our platform from two years ago, it's not the same as supporting us now.

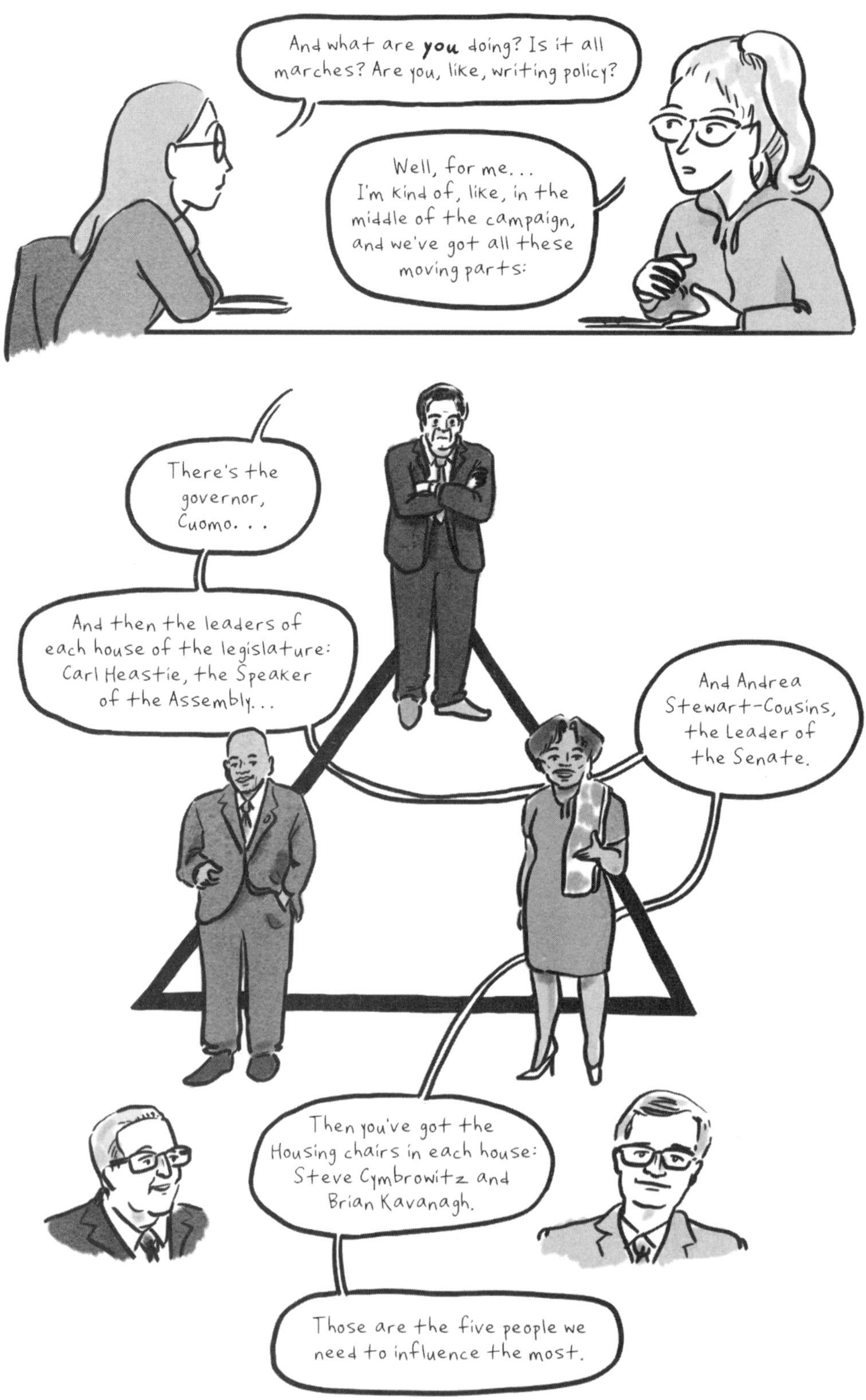

And what are **you** doing? Is it all marches? Are you, like, writing policy?
Well, for me... I'm kind of, like, in the middle of the campaign, and we've got all these moving parts:
There's the governor, Cuomo...
And then the leaders of each house of the legislature: Carl Heastie, the Speaker of the Assembly...
And Andrea Stewart-Cousins, the Leader of the Senate.
Then you've got the Housing chairs in each house: Steve Cymbrowitz and Brian Kavanagh.
Those are the five people we need to influence the most.

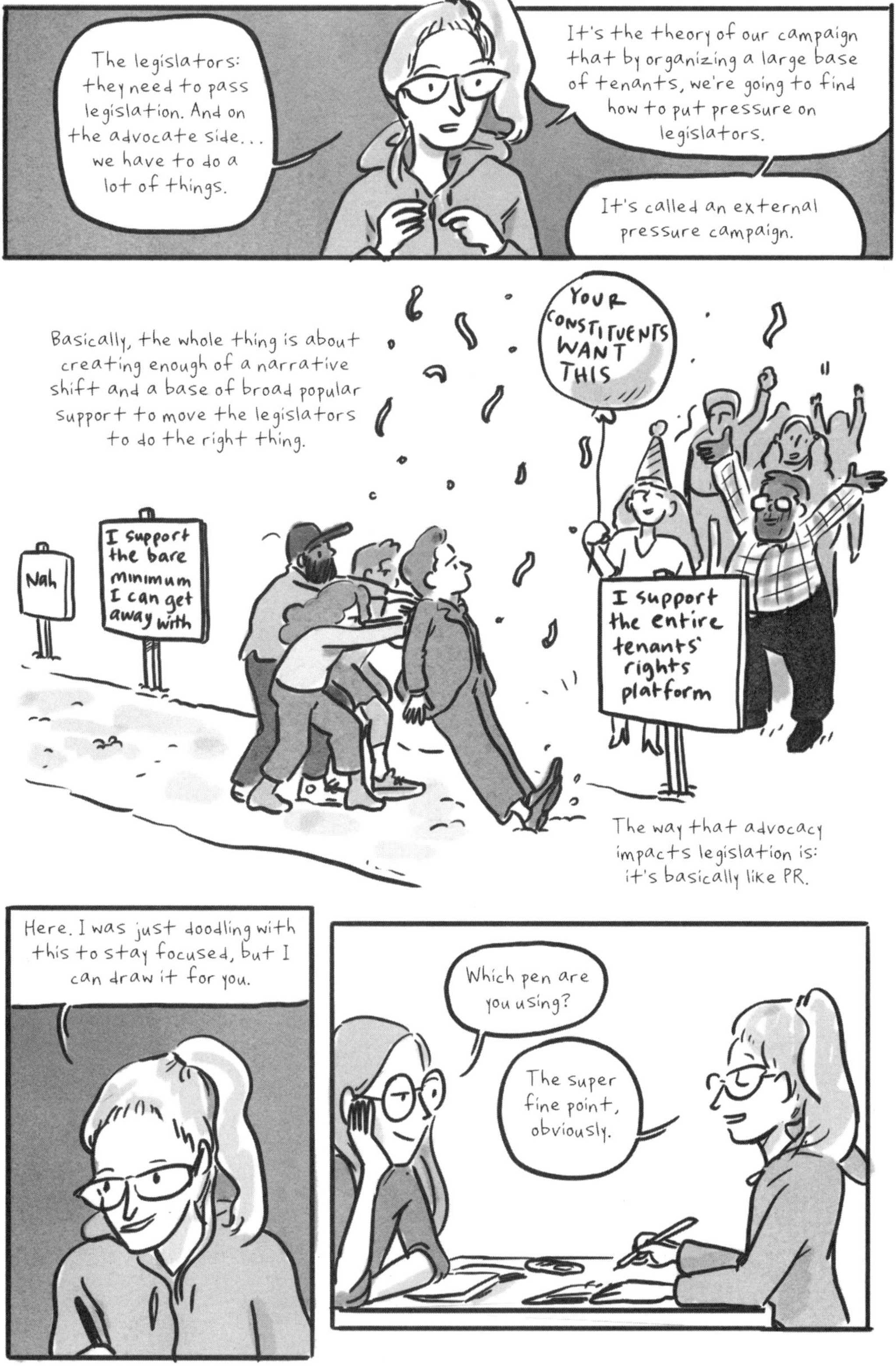
The legislators: they need to pass legislation. And on the advocate side... we have to do a lot of things.
It's the theory of our campaign that by organizing a large base of tenants, we're going to find how to put pressure on legislators.
It's called an external pressure campaign.
Basically, the whole thing is about creating enough of a narrative shift and a base of broad popular support to move the legislators to do the right thing.
YOUR CONSTITUENTS WANT THIS
Nah
I support the bare minimum I can get away with
I support the entire tenants' rights platform
The way that advocacy impacts legislation is: it's basically like PR.
Here. I was just doodling with this to stay focused, but I can draw it for you.
Which pen are you using?
The super fine point, obviously.

So there is this unholy alliance between the elected officials who are writing policy and the real estate industry.
Real estate gives money to electeds, and electeds give them money through tax policy.
scribble~
And down here are tenants.
elected officials
$ tax policy
Real estate
$ donations (+ illegal $)
Tenants
There's this vicious cycle, and a firewall between this elite and us.
elected officials
$ tax policy
Real estate
$ donations (+ illegal $)
Tenants
Our job is to make it impossible for elected officials to stand with the real estate industry. Making the real estate industry toxic.
elected officials
$
donations
Tenants
And at the same time, lifting up the power of tenants and showing that standing up to the real estate industry can actually win you elections.
elected officials
$
donations
Tenants

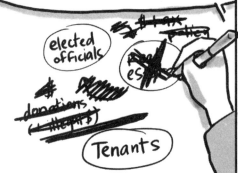

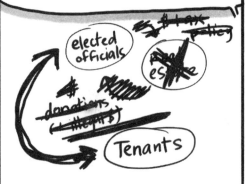

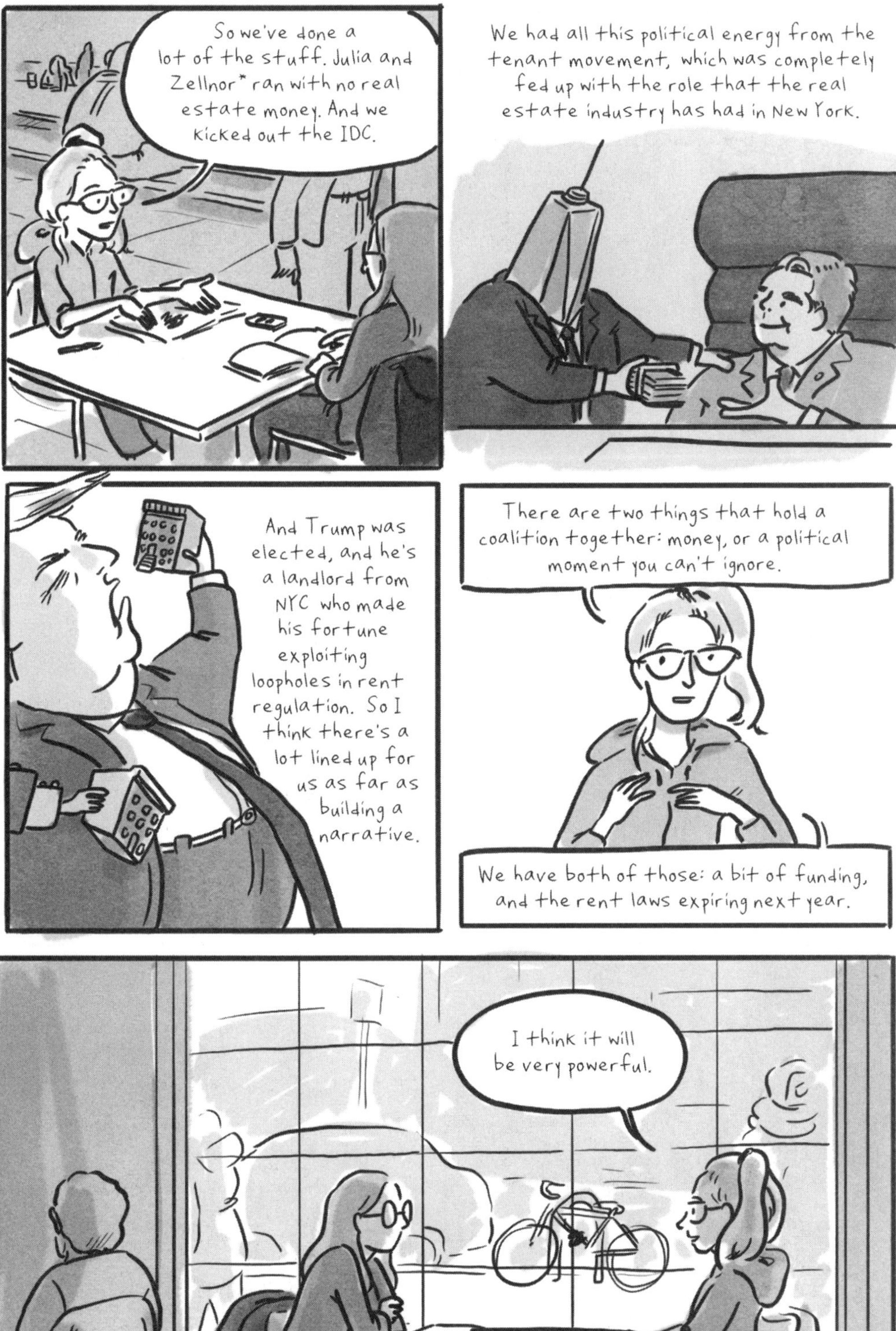
So we've done a lot of the stuff. Julia and Zellnor* ran with no real estate money. And we kicked out the IDC.
We had all this political energy from the tenant movement, which was completely fed up with the role that the real estate industry has had in New York.
And Trump was elected, and he's a landlord from NYC who made his fortune exploiting loopholes in rent regulation. So I think there's a lot lined up for us as far as building a narrative.
There are two things that hold a coalition together: money, or a political moment you can't ignore.
We have both of those: a bit of funding, and the rent laws expiring next year.
I think it will be very powerful.

*Zellnor Myrie, another newly elected state senator from Brooklyn

Chapter Three

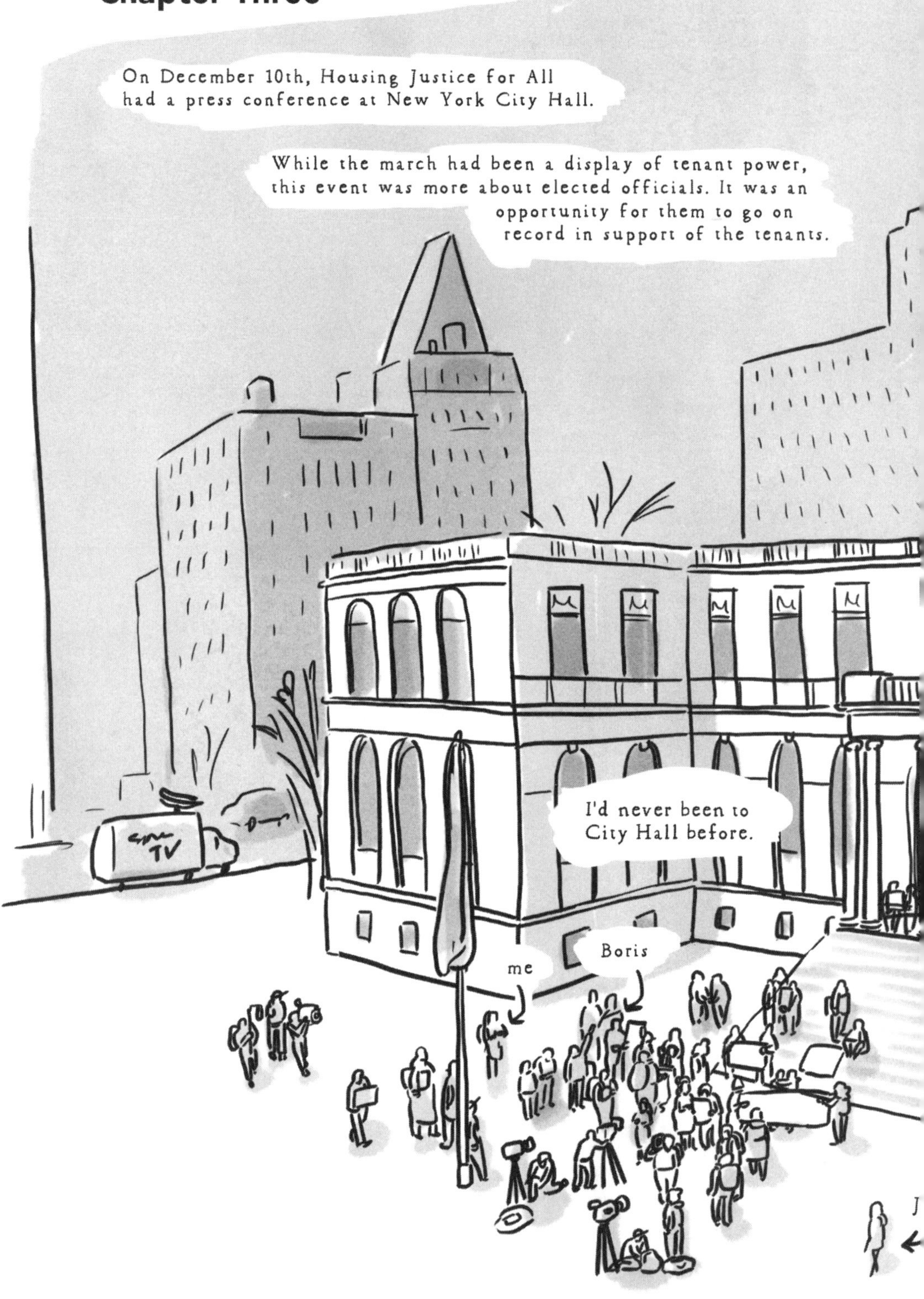

On December 10th, Housing Justice for All had a press conference at New York City Hall.
While the march had been a display of tenant power, this event was more about elected officials. It was an opportunity for them to go on record in support of the tenants.
TV
I'd never been to City Hall before.
me
Boris

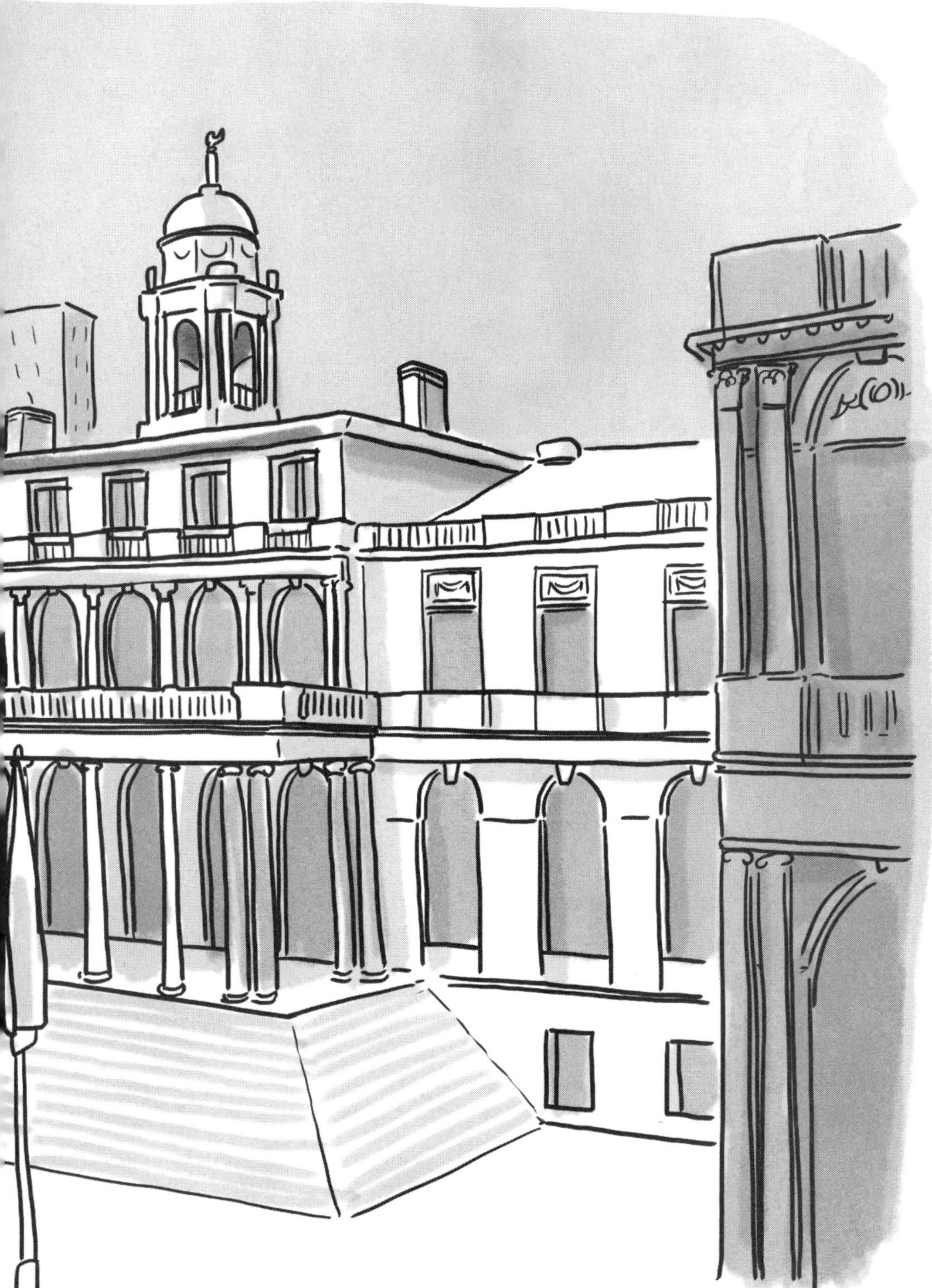

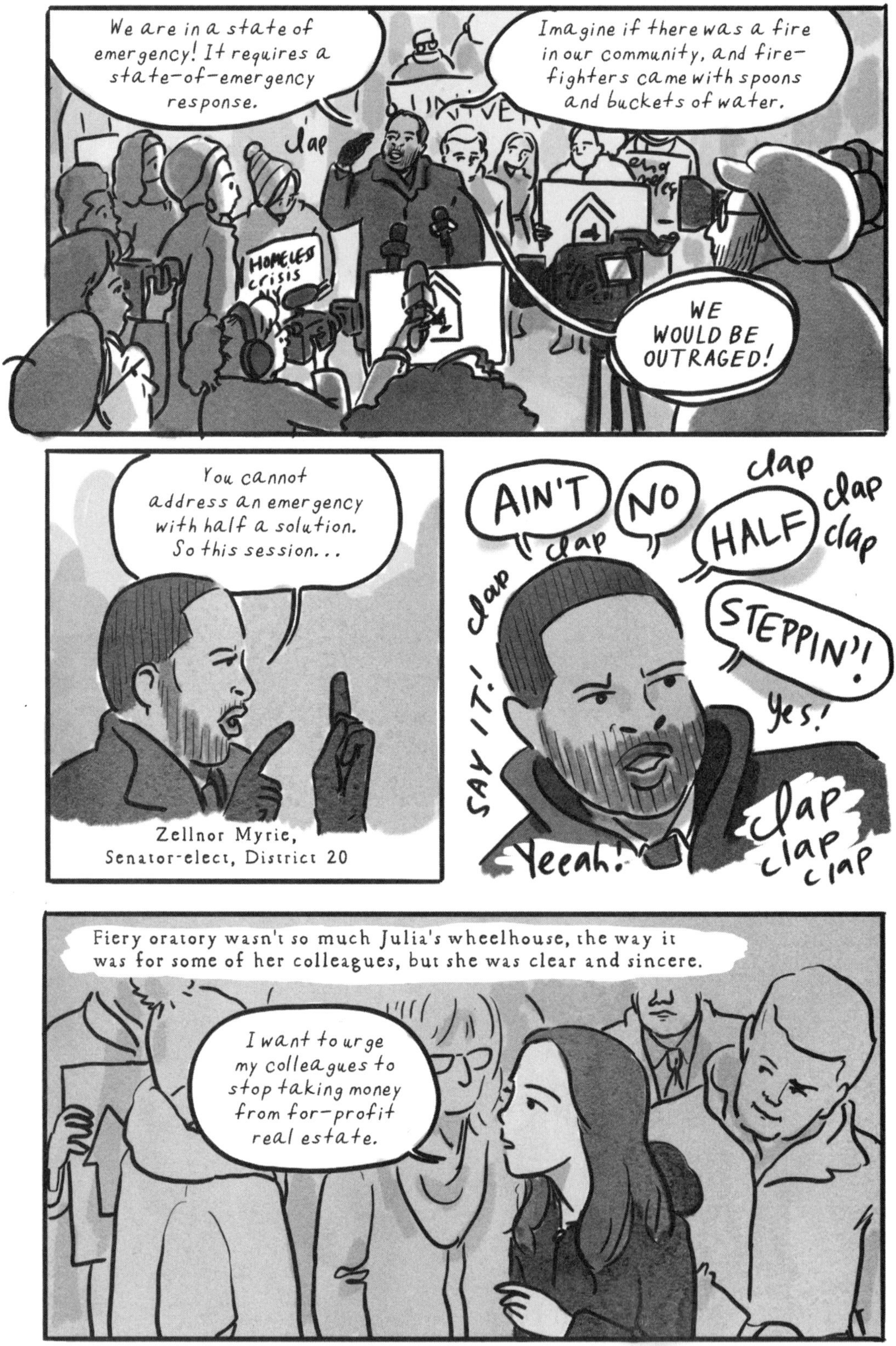

We are in a state of emergency! It requires a state-of-emergency response.
clap
Imagine if there was a fire in our community, and fire-fighters came with spoons and buckets of water.
WE WOULD BE OUTRAGED!
You cannot address an emergency with half a solution. So this session...
Zellnor Myrie,
Senator-elect, District 20
AIN'T
NO
HALF
STEPPIN'!
clap
clap
clap
clap
clap
SAY IT!
Yes!
Yeeah!
clap
clap
clap
Fiery oratory wasn't so much Julia's wheelhouse, the way it was for some of her colleagues, but she was clear and sincere.
I want to urge my colleagues to stop taking money from for-profit real estate.

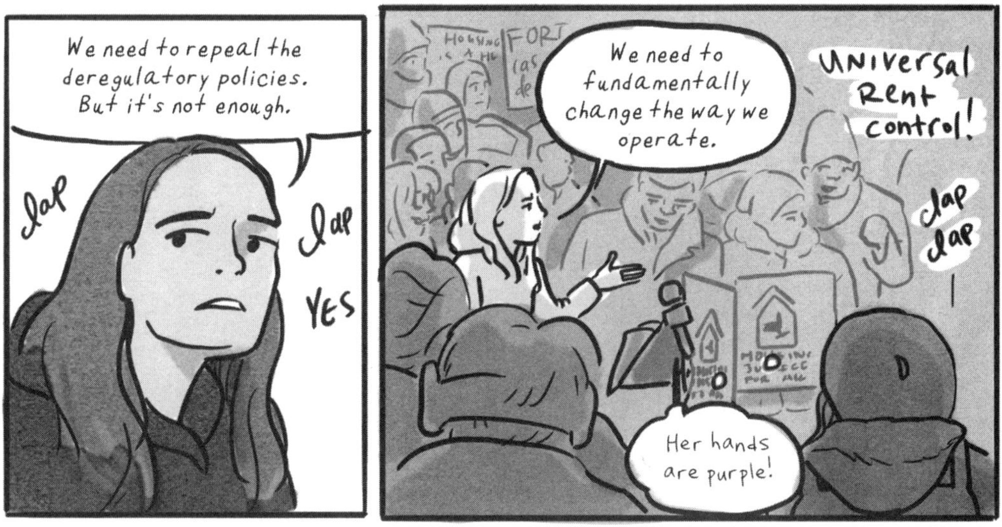
We need to repeal the deregulatory policies. But it's not enough.
clap
clap
YES
We need to fundamentally change the way we operate.
Universal Rent control!
clap clap
Her hands are purple!

Just after:

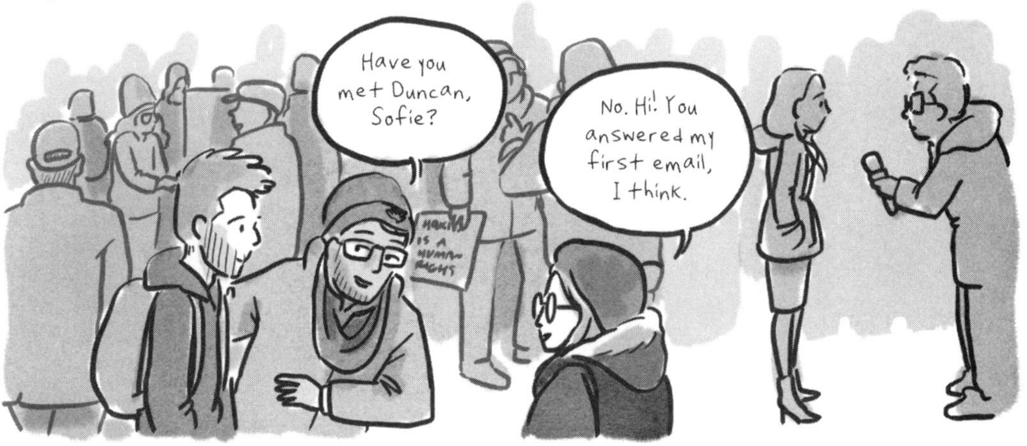
Have you met Duncan, Sofie?
No. Hi! You answered my first email, I think.

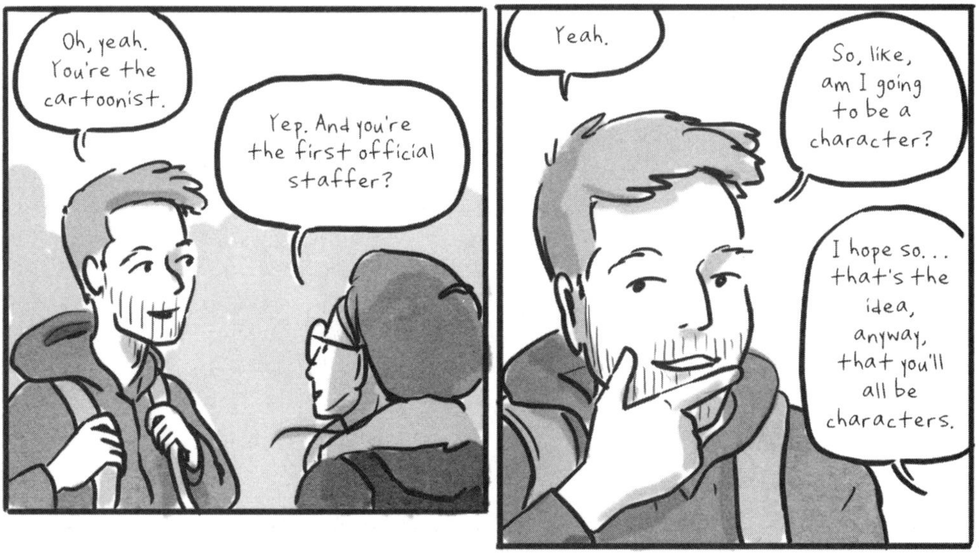
Oh, yeah. You're the cartoonist.
Yep. And you're the first official staffer?
Yeah.
So, like, am I going to be a character?
I hope so... that's the idea, anyway, that you'll all be characters.

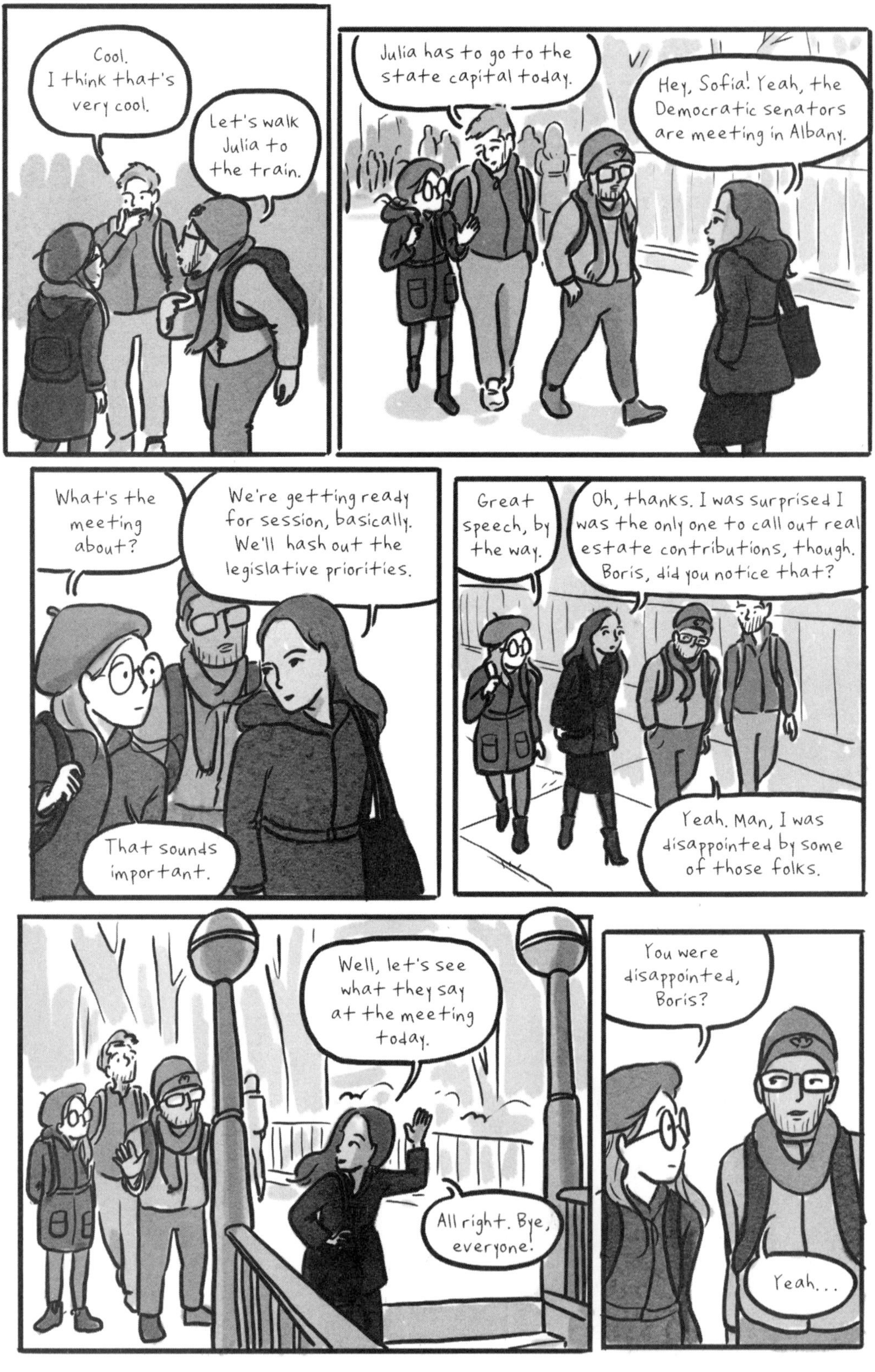
Cool.
I think that's very cool.
Let's walk Julia to the train.
Julia has to go to the state capital today.
Hey, Sofia! Yeah, the Democratic senators are meeting in Albany.
What's the meeting about?
We're getting ready for session, basically. We'll hash out the legislative priorities.
That sounds important.
Great speech, by the way.
Oh, thanks. I was surprised I was the only one to call out real estate contributions, though. Boris, did you notice that?
Yeah. Man, I was disappointed by some of those folks.
Well, let's see what they say at the meeting today.
All right. Bye, everyone!
You were disappointed, Boris?
Yeah...

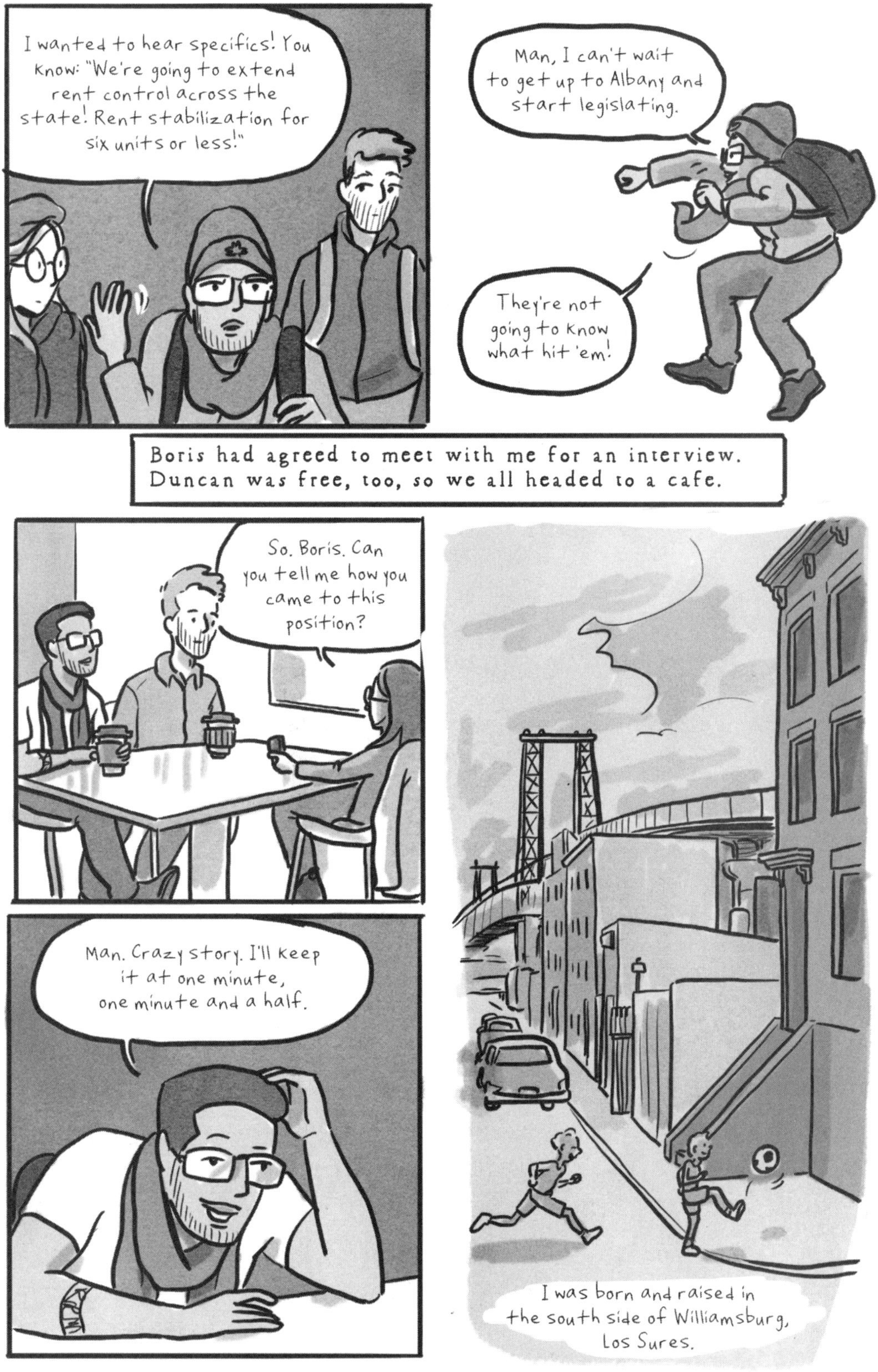
I wanted to hear specifics! You know: "We're going to extend rent control across the state! Rent stabilization for six units or less!"
Man, I can't wait to get up to Albany and start legislating.
They're not going to know what hit 'em!
Boris had agreed to meet with me for an interview. Duncan was free, too, so we all headed to a cafe.
So. Boris. Can you tell me how you came to this position?
Man. Crazy story. I'll keep it at one minute, one minute and a half.
I was born and raised in the south side of Williamsburg, Los Sures.

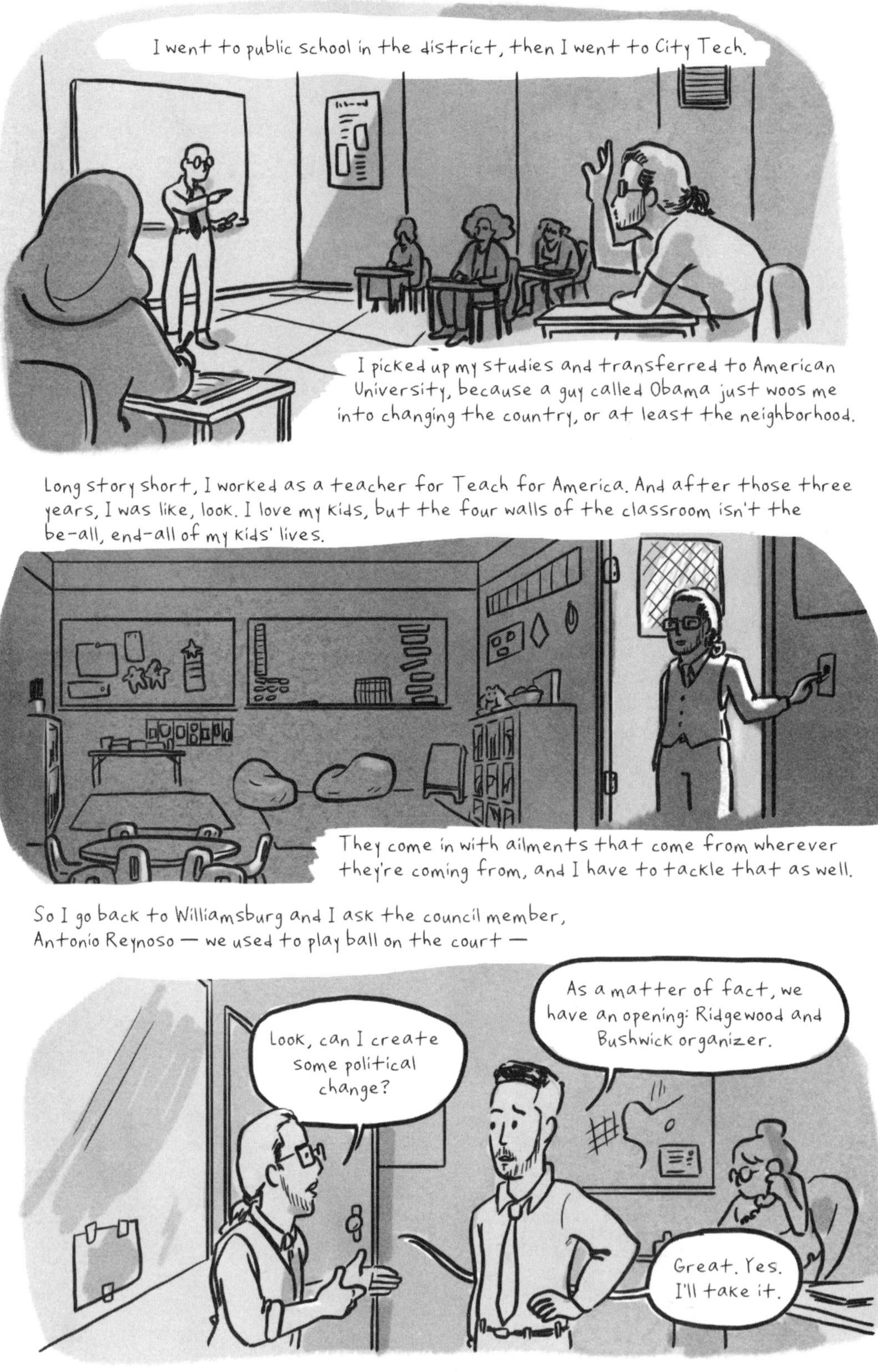
I went to public school in the district, then I went to City Tech.
I picked up my studies and transferred to American University, because a guy called Obama just woos me into changing the country, or at least the neighborhood.
Long story short, I worked as a teacher for Teach for America. And after those three years, I was like, look. I love my kids, but the four walls of the classroom isn't the be-all, end-all of my kids' lives.
They come in with ailments that come from wherever they're coming from, and I have to tackle that as well.
So I go back to Williamsburg and I ask the council member, Antonio Reynoso — we used to play ball on the court —
Look, can I create some political change?
As a matter of fact, we have an opening: Ridgewood and Bushwick organizer.
Great. Yes. I'll take it.

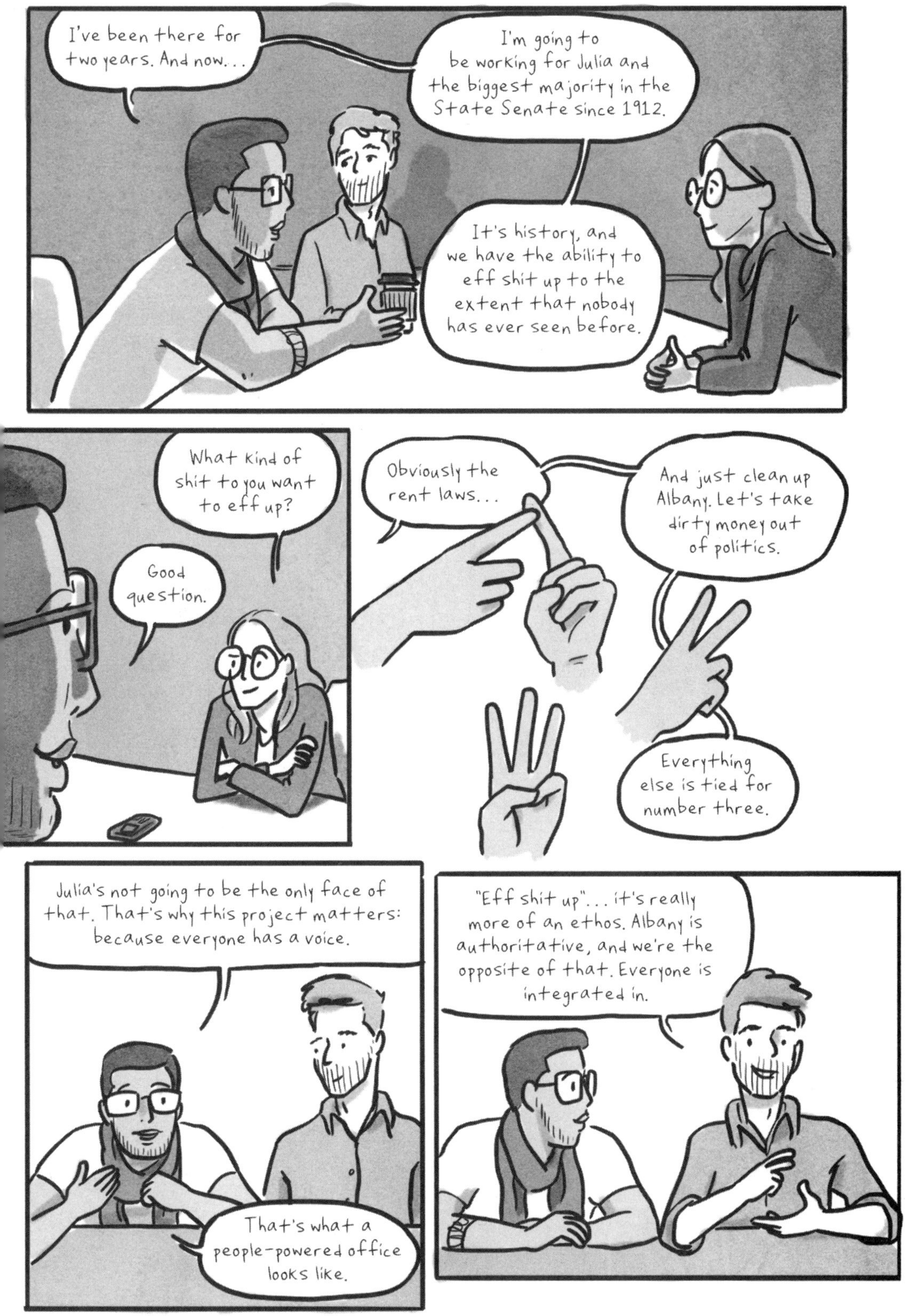
I've been there for two years. And now...
I'm going to be working for Julia and the biggest majority in the State Senate since 1912.
It's history, and we have the ability to eff shit up to the extent that nobody has ever seen before.
What kind of shit to you want to eff up?
Good question.
Obviously the rent laws...
And just clean up Albany. Let's take dirty money out of politics.
Everything else is tied for number three.
Julia's not going to be the only face of that. That's why this project matters: because everyone has a voice.
That's what a people-powered office looks like.
"Eff shit up"... it's really more of an ethos. Albany is authoritative, and we're the opposite of that. Everyone is integrated in.

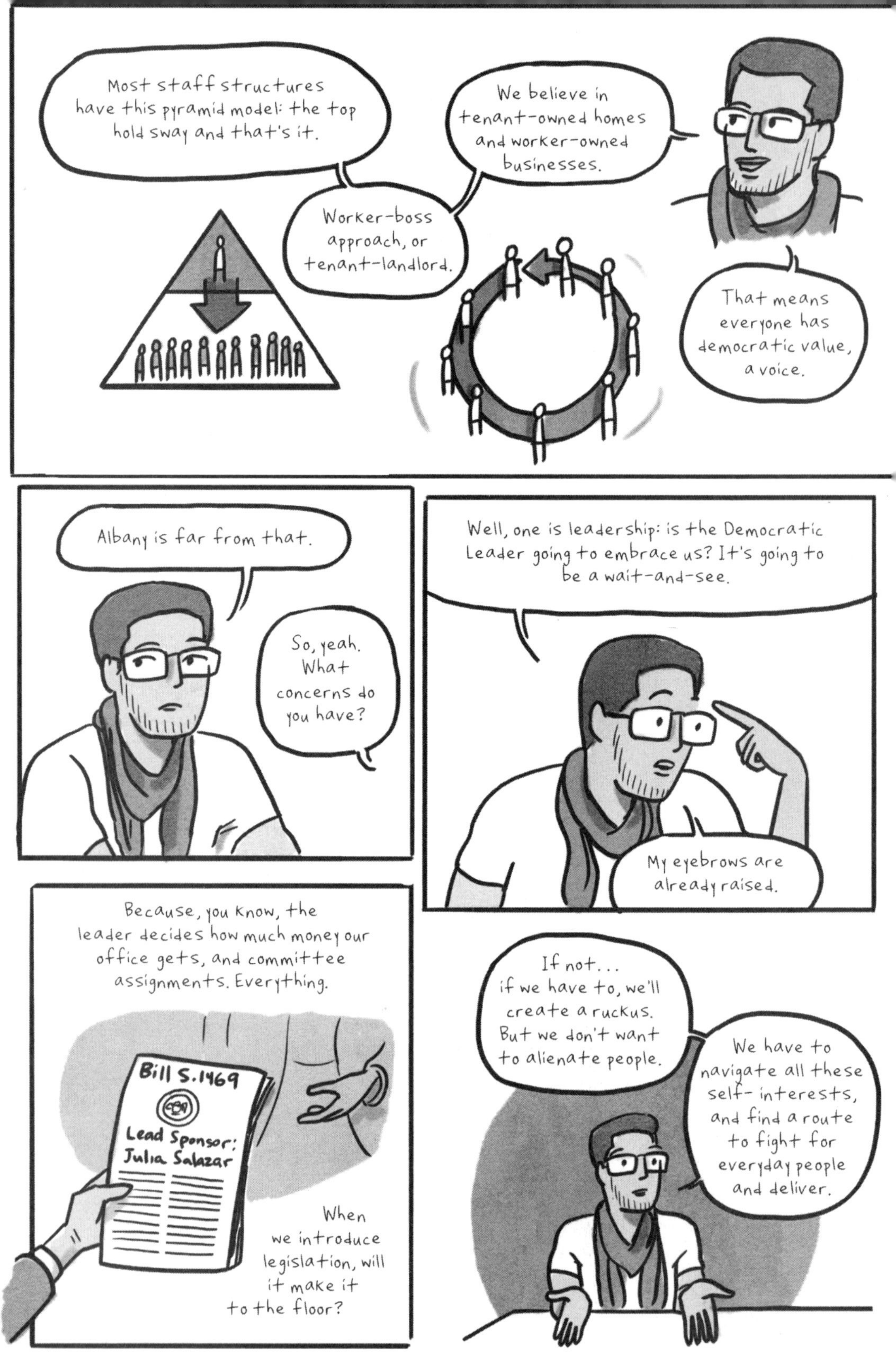
Most staff structures have this pyramid model: the top hold sway and that's it.
Worker-boss approach, or tenant-landlord.
We believe in tenant-owned homes and worker-owned businesses.
That means everyone has democratic value, a voice.
Albany is far from that.
So, yeah. What concerns do you have?
Well, one is leadership: is the Democratic Leader going to embrace us? It's going to be a wait-and-see.
My eyebrows are already raised.
Because, you know, the leader decides how much money our office gets, and committee assignments. Everything.
Bill S.1469
Lead Sponsor: Julia Salazar
When we introduce legislation, will it make it to the floor?
If not... if we have to, we'll create a ruckus. But we don't want to alienate people.
We have to navigate all these self-interests, and find a route to fight for everyday people and deliver.

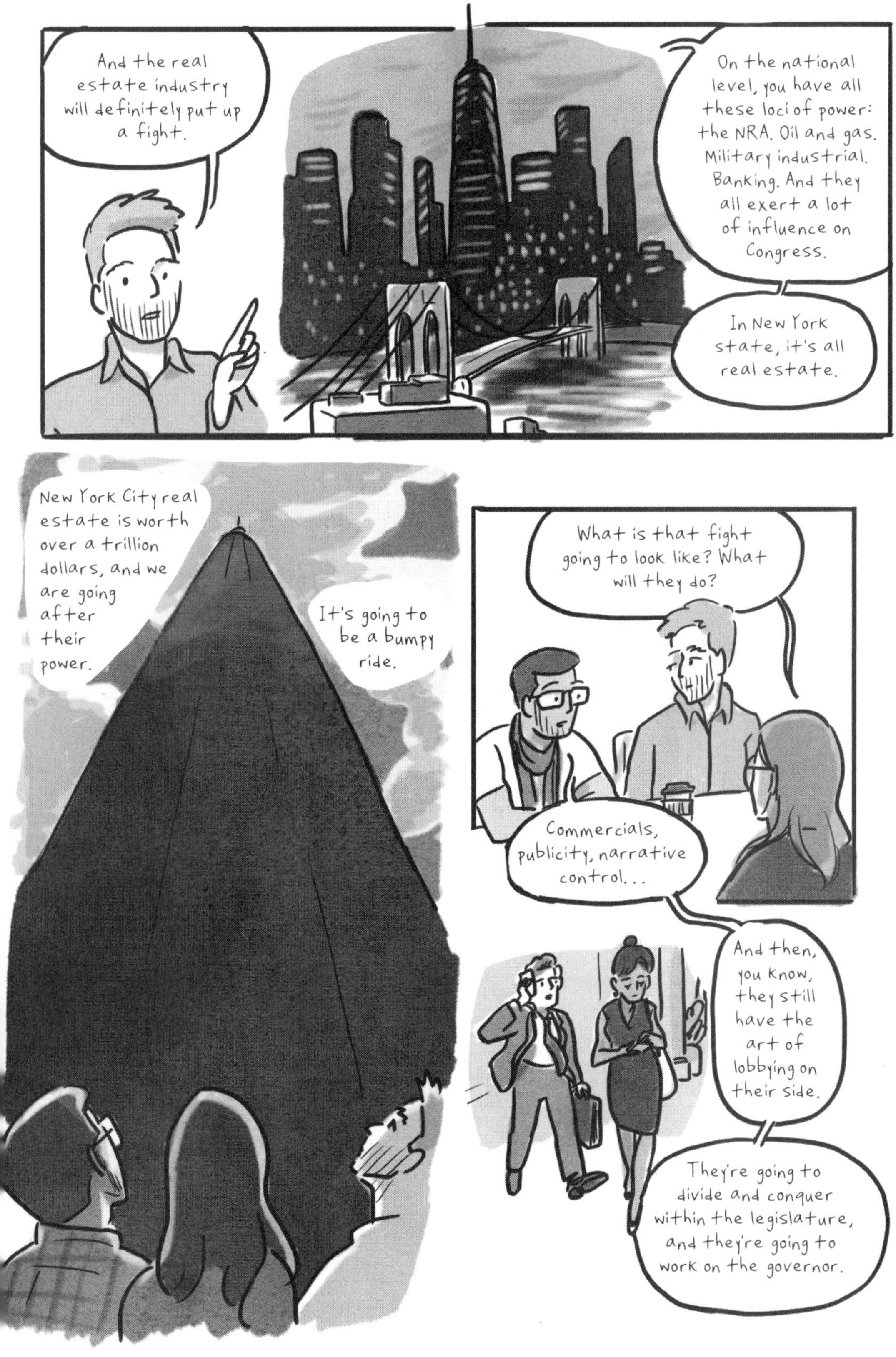
And the real estate industry will definitely put up a fight.
On the national level, you have all these loci of power: the NRA. Oil and gas. Military industrial. Banking. And they all exert a lot of influence on Congress.
In New York state, it's all real estate.
New York City real estate is worth over a trillion dollars, and we are going after their power.
It's going to be a bumpy ride.
What is that fight going to look like? What will they do?
Commercials, publicity, narrative control...
And then, you know, they still have the art of lobbying on their side.
They're going to divide and conquer within the legislature, and they're going to work on the governor.

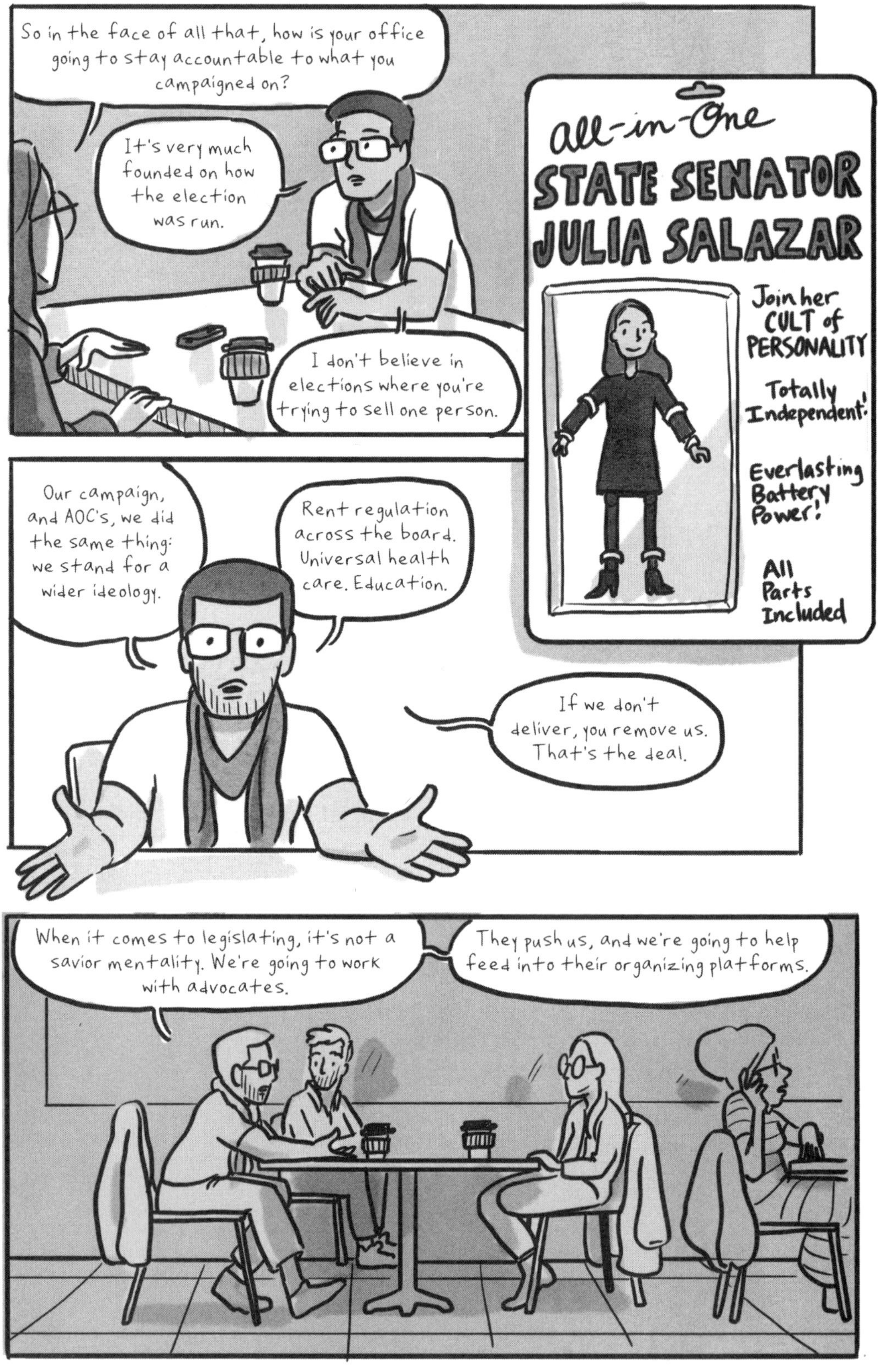

So in the face of all that, how is your office going to stay accountable to what you campaigned on?
It's very much founded on how the election was run.
I don't believe in elections where you're trying to sell one person.
all-in-One
STATE SENATOR JULIA SALAZAR
Join her CULT of PERSONALITY
Totally Independent!
Everlasting Battery Power!
All Parts Included
Our campaign, and AOC's, we did the same thing: we stand for a wider ideology.
Rent regulation across the board. Universal health care. Education.
If we don't deliver, you remove us. That's the deal.
When it comes to legislating, it's not a savior mentality. We're going to work with advocates.
They push us, and we're going to help feed into their organizing platforms.

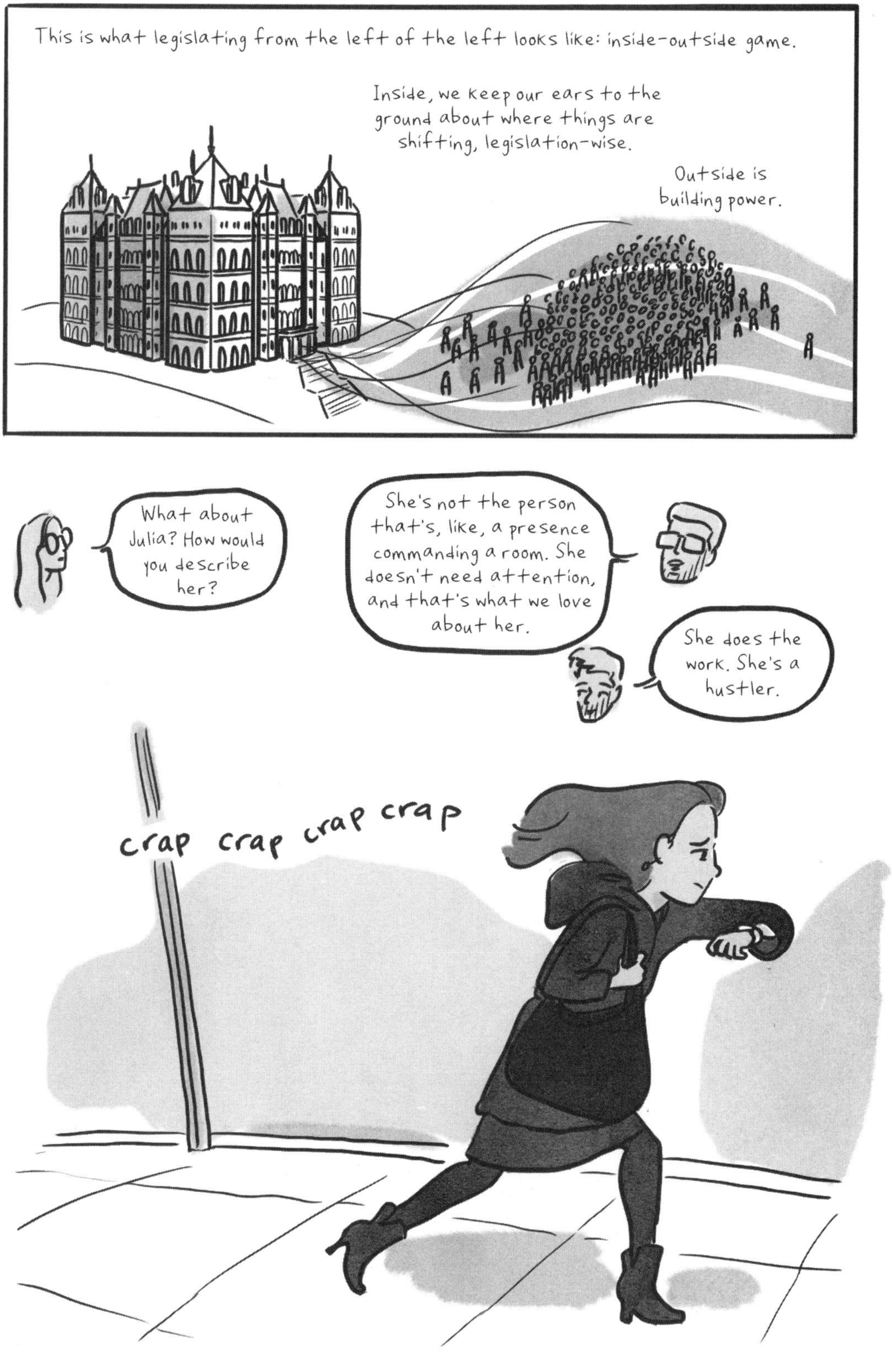
This is what legislating from the left of the left looks like: inside-outside game.
Inside, we keep our ears to the ground about where things are shifting, legislation-wise.
Outside is building power.
What about Julia? How would you describe her?
She's not the person that's, like, a presence commanding a room. She doesn't need attention, and that's what we love about her.
She does the work. She's a hustler.
crap crap crap crap

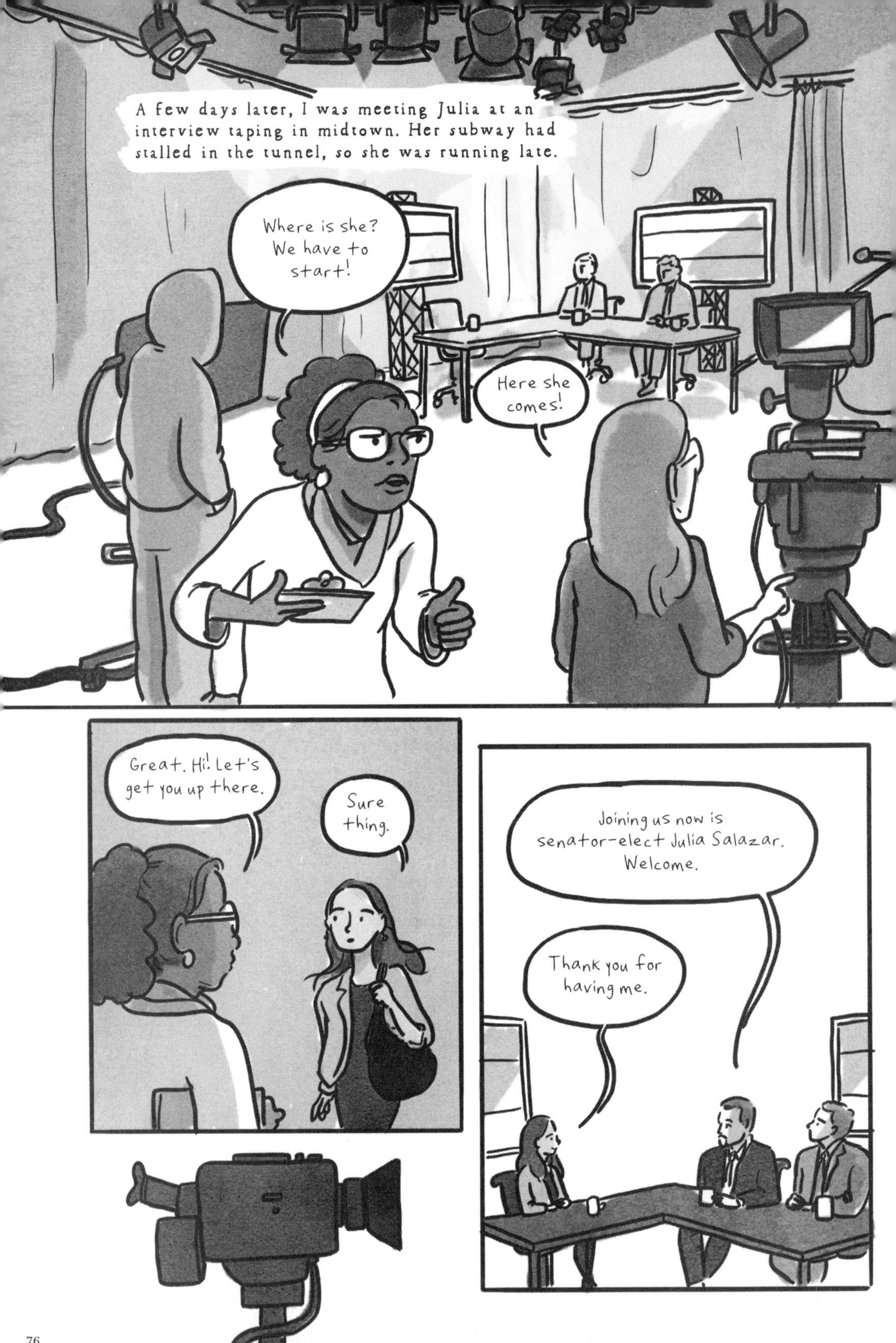
A few days later, I was meeting Julia at an interview taping in midtown. Her subway had stalled in the tunnel, so she was running late.
Where is she? We have to start!
Here she comes!
Great. Hi! Let's get you up there.
Sure thing.
Joining us now is senator-elect Julia Salazar. Welcome.
Thank you for having me.

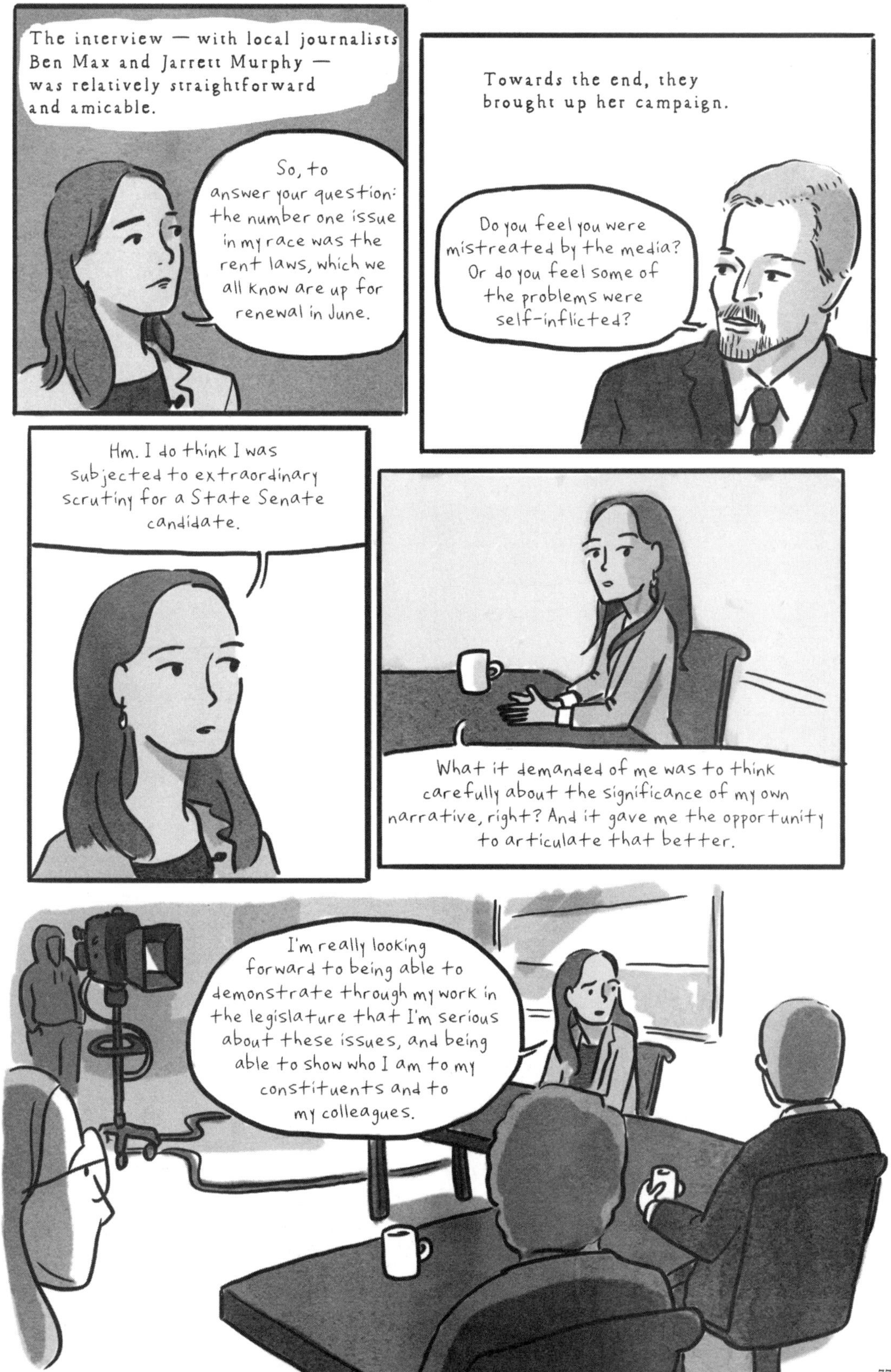
The interview — with local journalists Ben Max and Jarrett Murphy — was relatively straightforward and amicable.
So, to answer your question: the number one issue in my race was the rent laws, which we all know are up for renewal in June.
Towards the end, they brought up her campaign.
Do you feel you were mistreated by the media? Or do you feel some of the problems were self-inflicted?
Hm. I do think I was subjected to extraordinary scrutiny for a State Senate candidate.
What it demanded of me was to think carefully about the significance of my own narrative, right? And it gave me the opportunity to articulate that better.
I'm really looking forward to being able to demonstrate through my work in the legislature that I'm serious about these issues, and being able to show who I am to my constituents and to my colleagues.

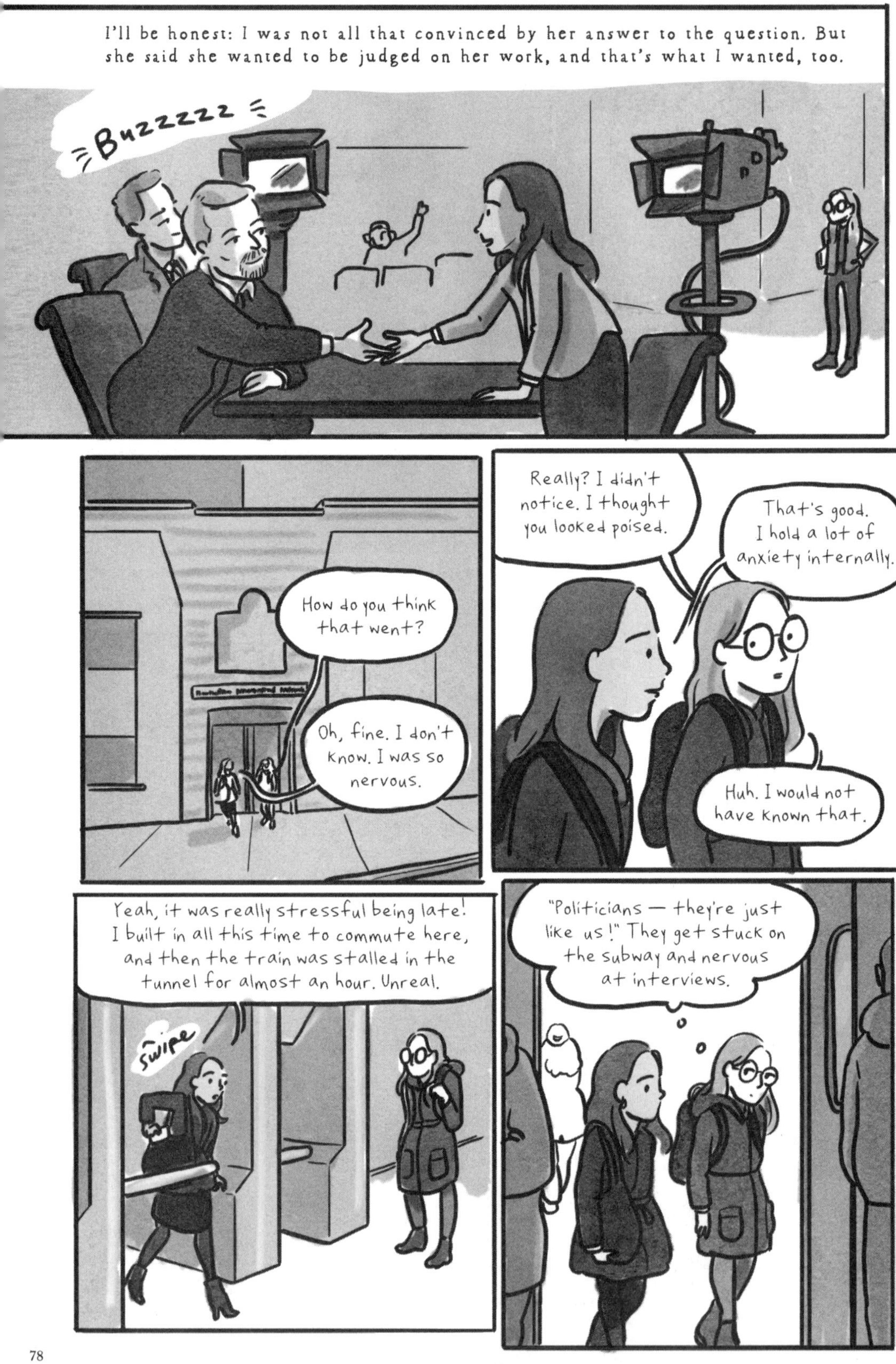
I'll be honest: I was not all that convinced by her answer to the question. But she said she wanted to be judged on her work, and that's what I wanted, too.
Buzzzzz
How do you think that went?
Oh, fine. I don't know. I was so nervous.
Really? I didn't notice. I thought you looked poised.
That's good. I hold a lot of anxiety internally.
Huh. I would not have known that.
Yeah, it was really stressful being late! I built in all this time to commute here, and then the train was stalled in the tunnel for almost an hour. Unreal.
swipe
"Politicians — they're just like us!" They get stuck on the subway and nervous at interviews.

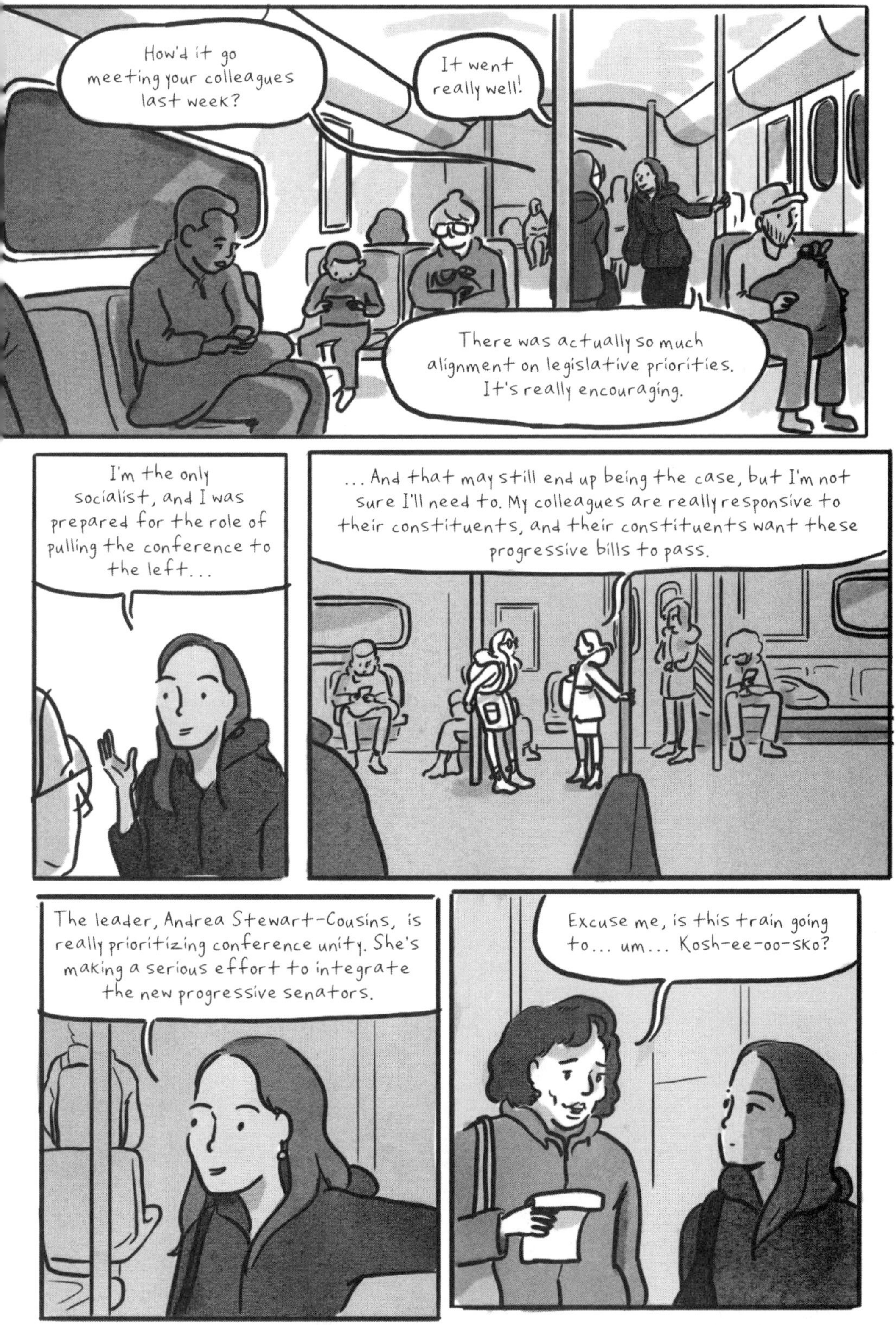

How'd it go meeting your colleagues last week?
It went really well!
There was actually so much alignment on legislative priorities. It's really encouraging.
I'm the only socialist, and I was prepared for the role of pulling the conference to the left...
...And that may still end up being the case, but I'm not sure I'll need to. My colleagues are really responsive to their constituents, and their constituents want these progressive bills to pass.
The leader, Andrea Stewart-Cousins, is really prioritizing conference unity. She's making a serious effort to integrate the new progressive senators.
Excuse me, is this train going to... um... Kosh-ee-oo-sko?

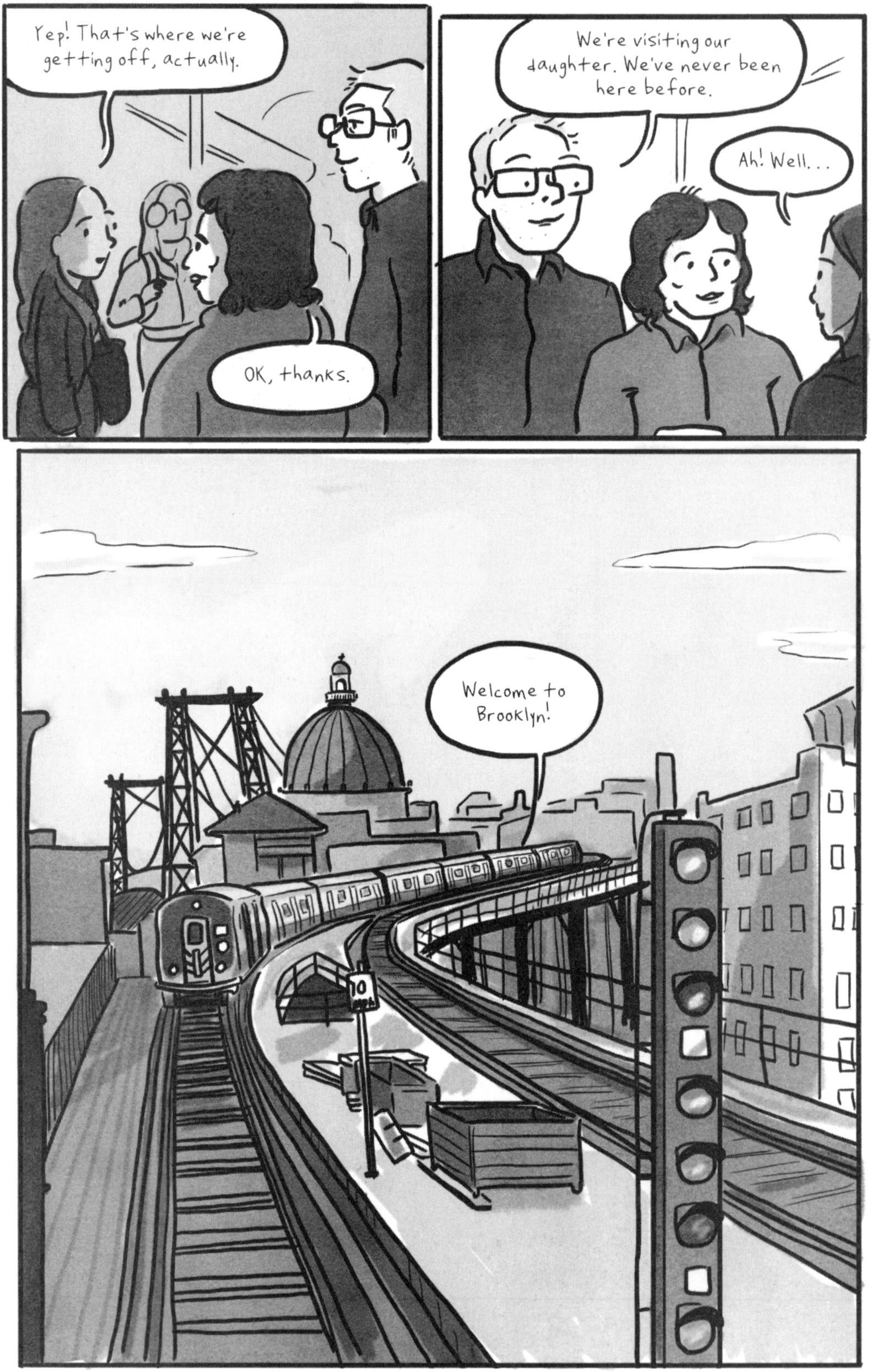
Yep! That's where we're getting off, actually.
OK, thanks.
We're visiting our daughter. We've never been here before.
Ah! Well...
Welcome to Brooklyn!
10

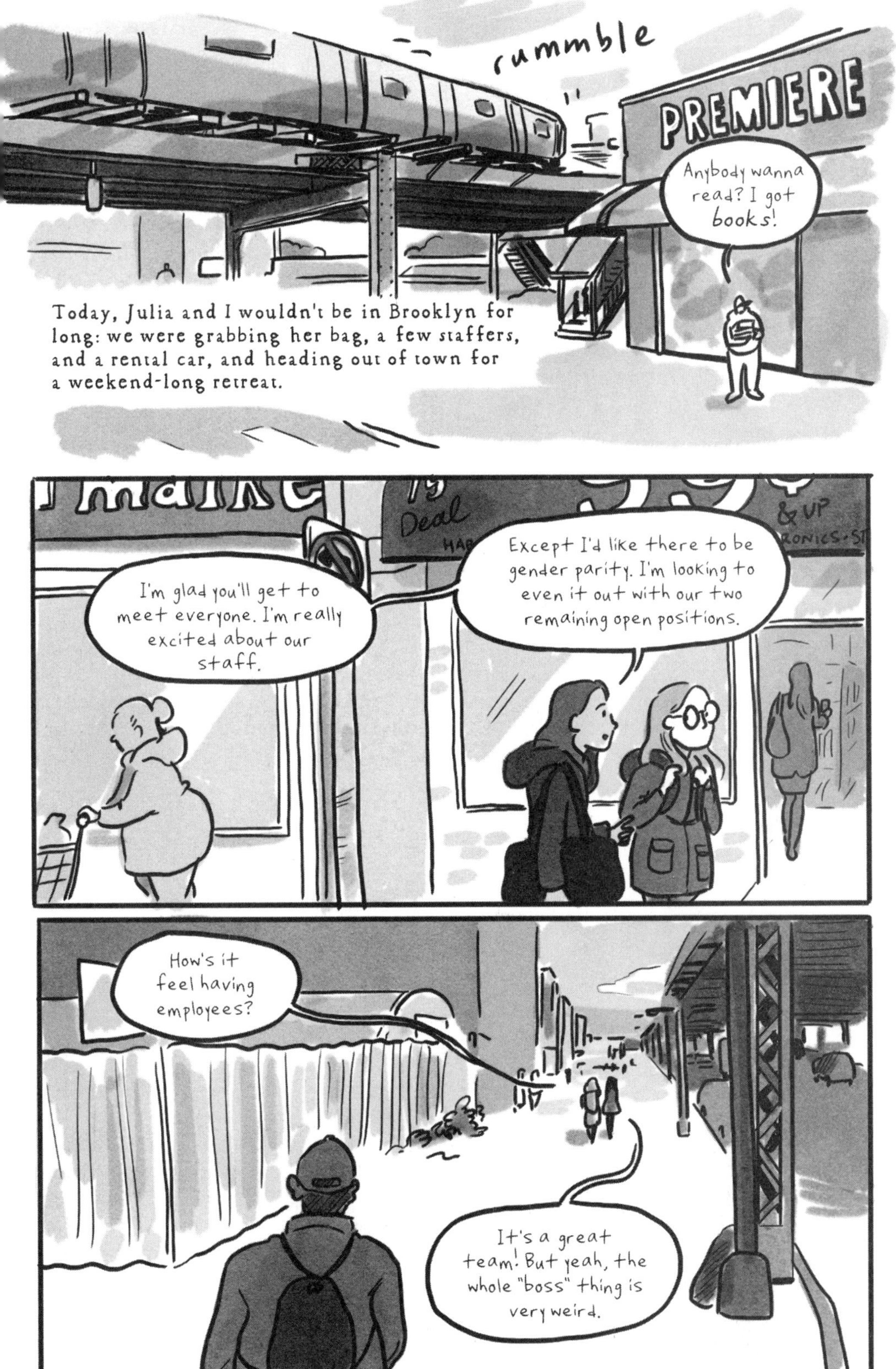
rummble
PREMIERE
Anybody wanna read? I got books!
Today, Julia and I wouldn't be in Brooklyn for long: we were grabbing her bag, a few staffers, and a rental car, and heading out of town for a weekend-long retreat.
Deal
& UP
I'm glad you'll get to meet everyone. I'm really excited about our staff.
Except I'd like there to be gender parity. I'm looking to even it out with our two remaining open positions.
How's it feel having employees?
It's a great team! But yeah, the whole "boss" thing is very weird.

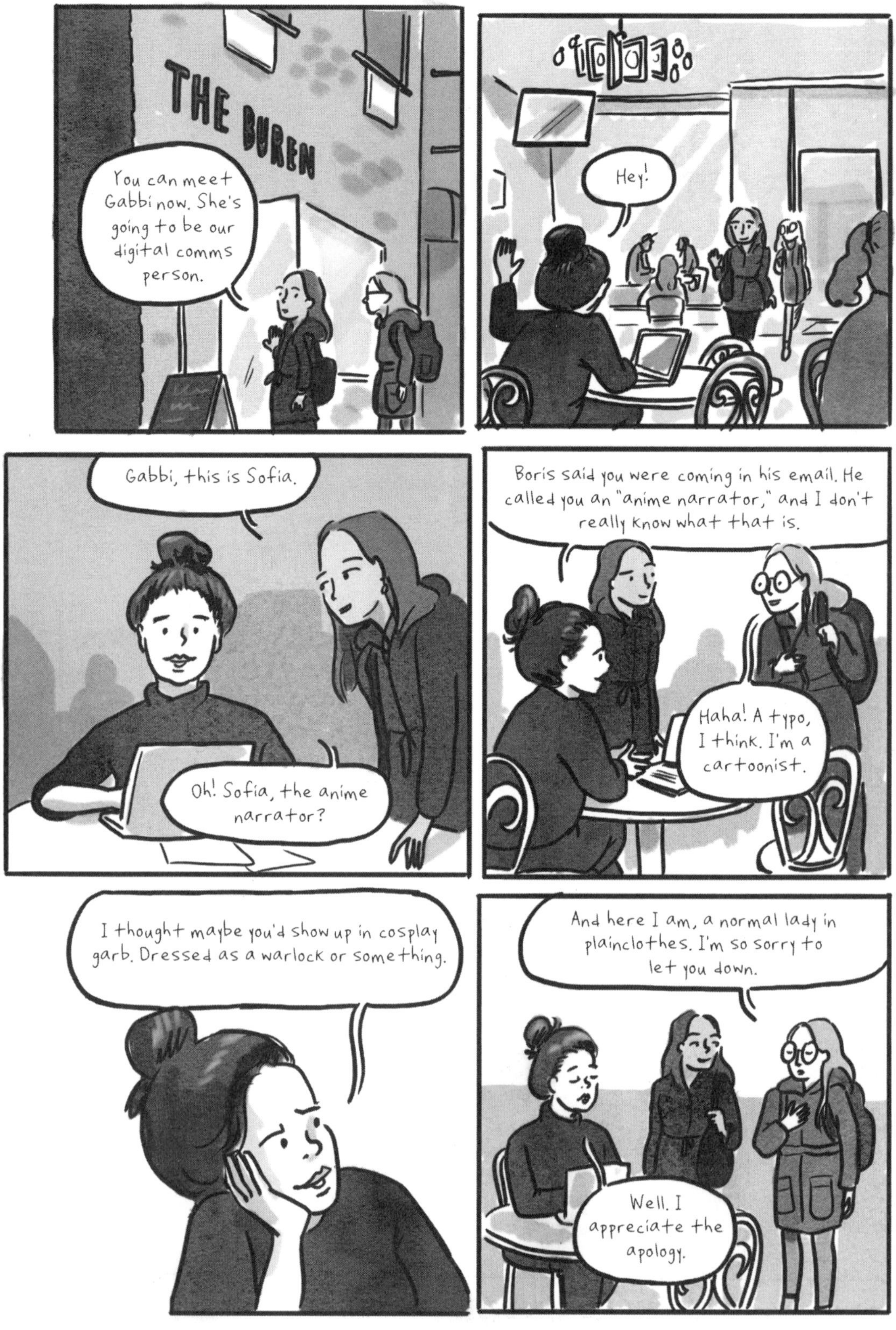
THE BUREN
You can meet Gabbi now. She's going to be our digital comms person.
Hey!
Gabbi, this is Sofia.
Oh! Sofia, the anime narrator?
Boris said you were coming in his email. He called you an "anime narrator," and I don't really know what that is.
Haha! A typo, I think. I'm a cartoonist.
I thought maybe you'd show up in cosplay garb. Dressed as a warlock or something.
And here I am, a normal lady in plainclothes. I'm so sorry to let you down.
Well. I appreciate the apology.

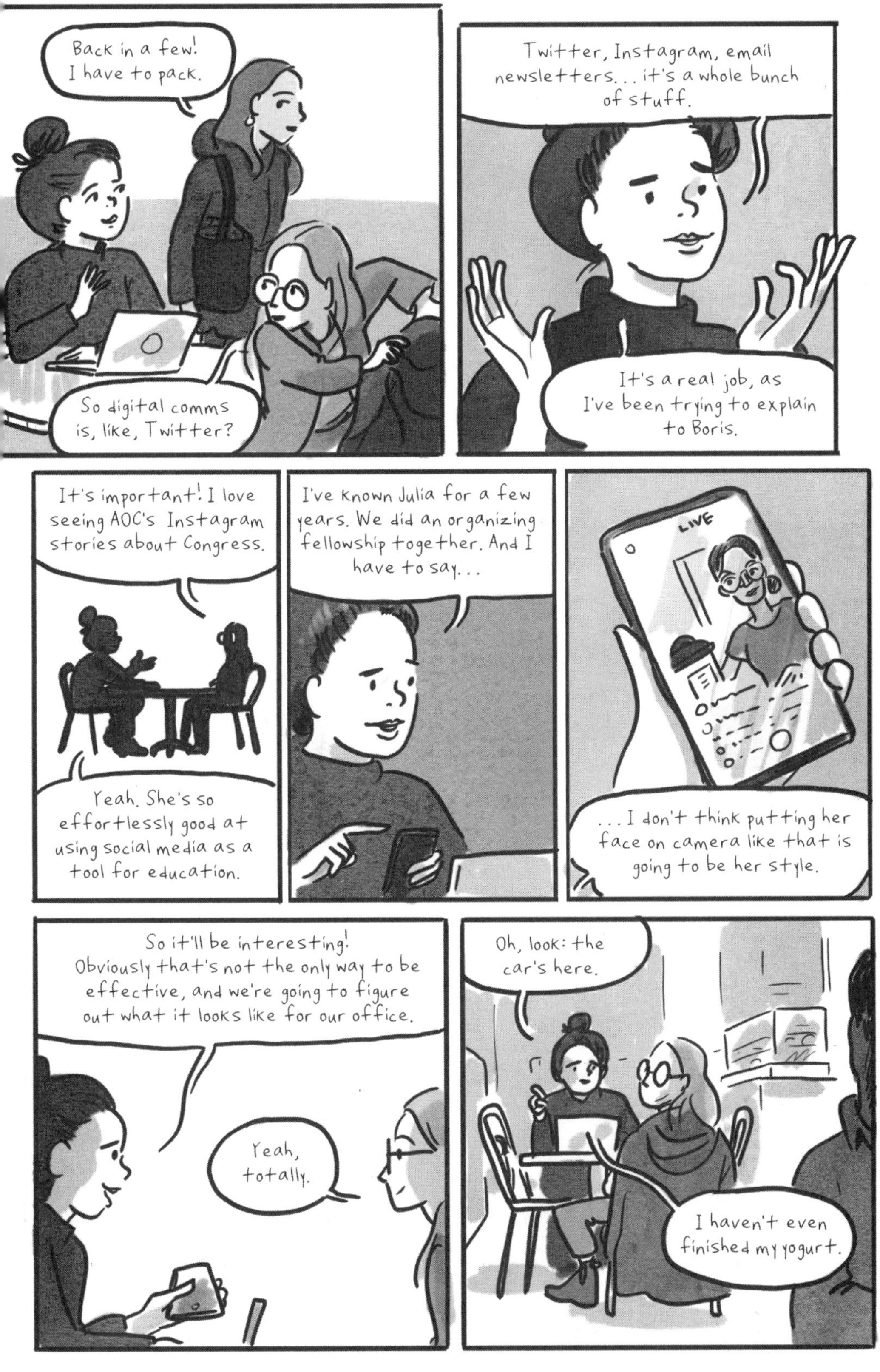
Back in a few! I have to pack.
So digital comms is, like, Twitter?
Twitter, Instagram, email newsletters... it's a whole bunch of stuff.
It's a real job, as I've been trying to explain to Boris.
It's important! I love seeing AOC's Instagram stories about Congress.
Yeah. She's so effortlessly good at using social media as a tool for education.
I've known Julia for a few years. We did an organizing fellowship together. And I have to say...
LIVE
...I don't think putting her face on camera like that is going to be her style.
So it'll be interesting! Obviously that's not the only way to be effective, and we're going to figure out what it looks like for our office.
Yeah, totally.
Oh, look: the car's here.
I haven't even finished my yogurt.

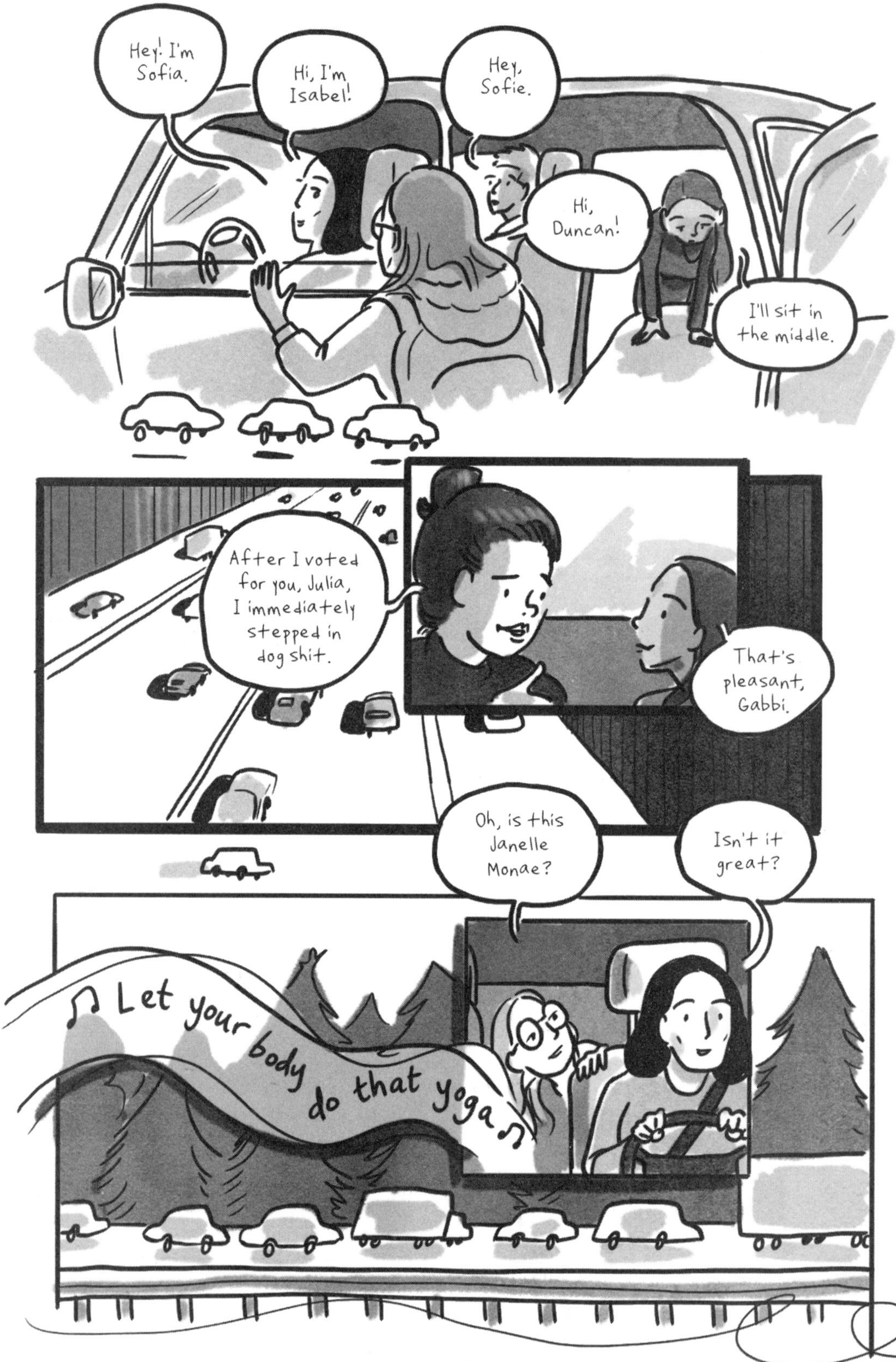

Hey! I'm Sofia.
Hi, I'm Isabel!
Hey, Sofie.
Hi, Duncan!
I'll sit in the middle.
After I voted for you, Julia, I immediately stepped in dog shit.
That's pleasant, Gabbi.
Oh, is this Janelle Monae?
Isn't it great?
♫ Let your body do that yoga ♫

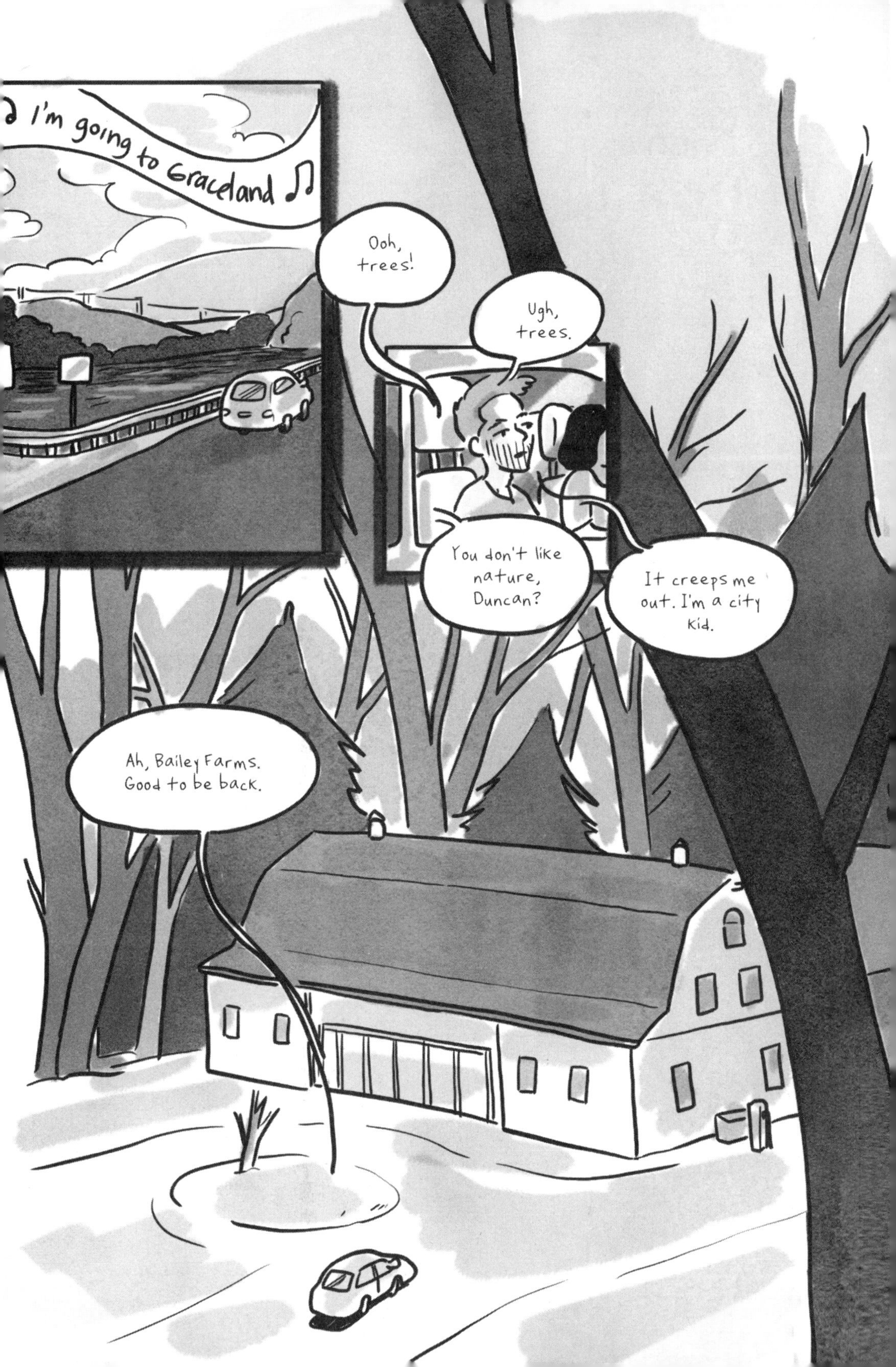
♪ I'm going to Graceland ♫
Ooh, trees!
Ugh, trees.
You don't like nature, Duncan?
It creeps me out. I'm a city kid.
Ah, Bailey Farms. Good to be back.

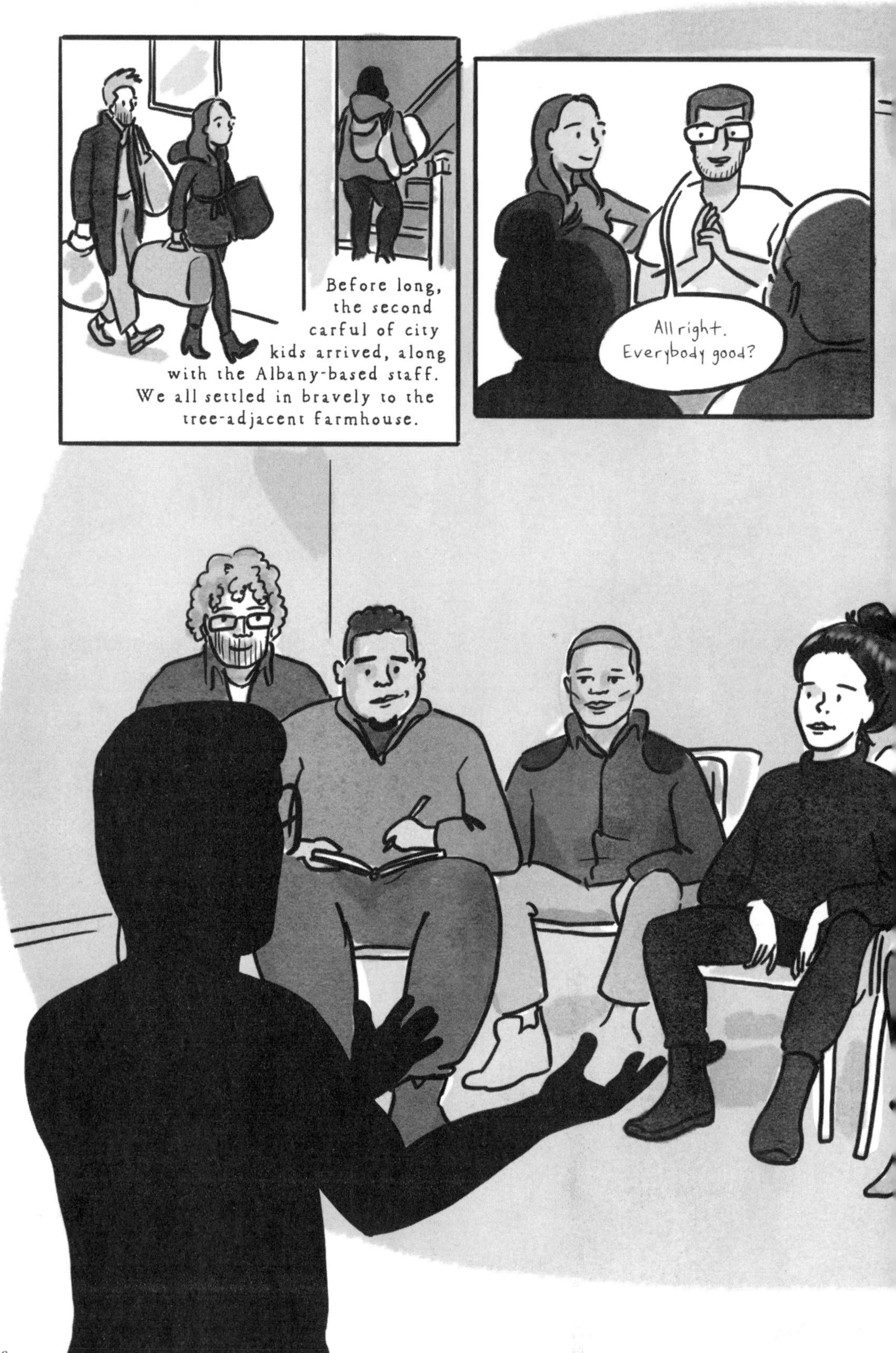
Before long, the second carful of city kids arrived, along with the Albany-based staff. We all settled in bravely to the tree-adjacent farmhouse.
All right. Everybody good?

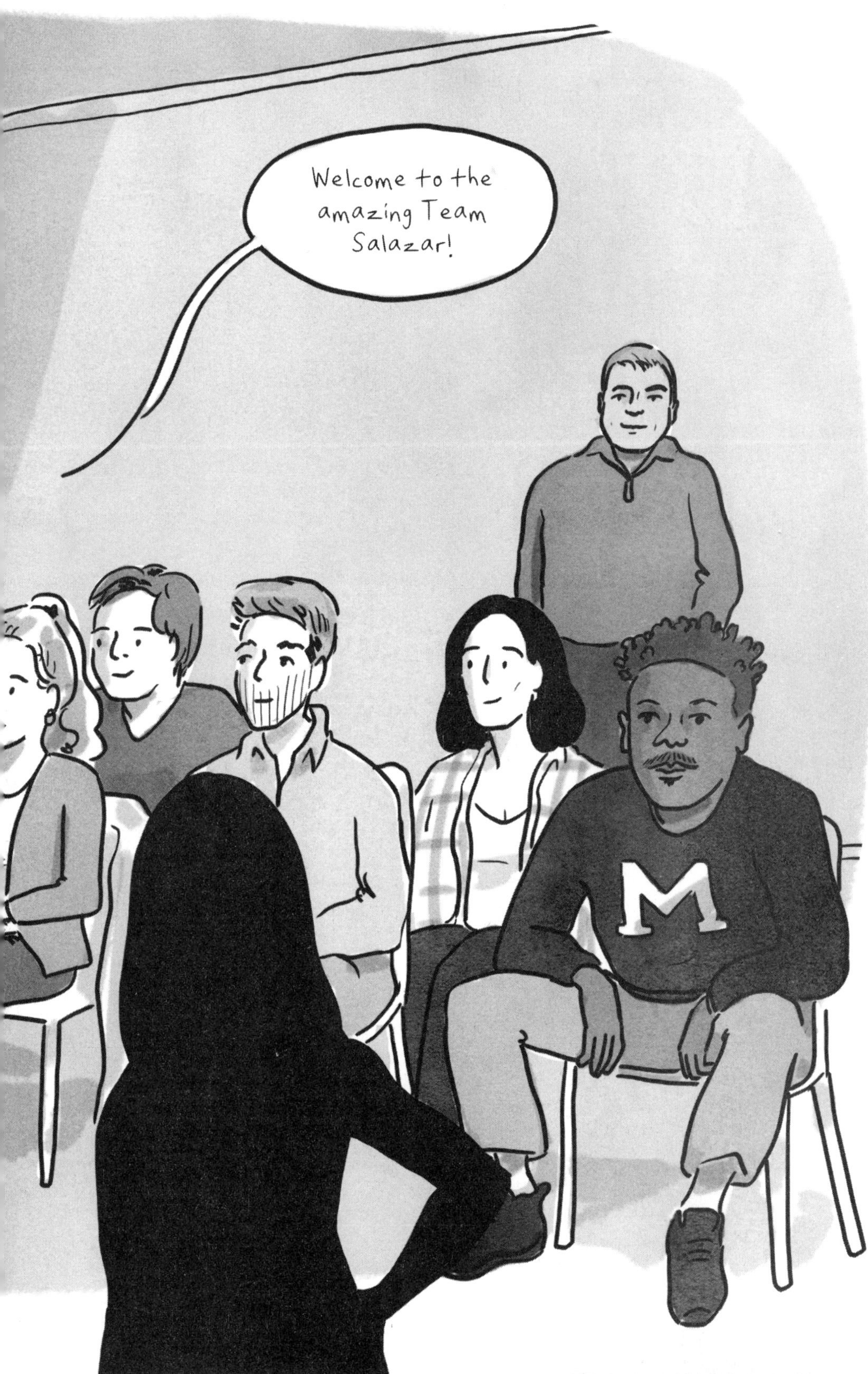
Welcome to the amazing Team Salazar!

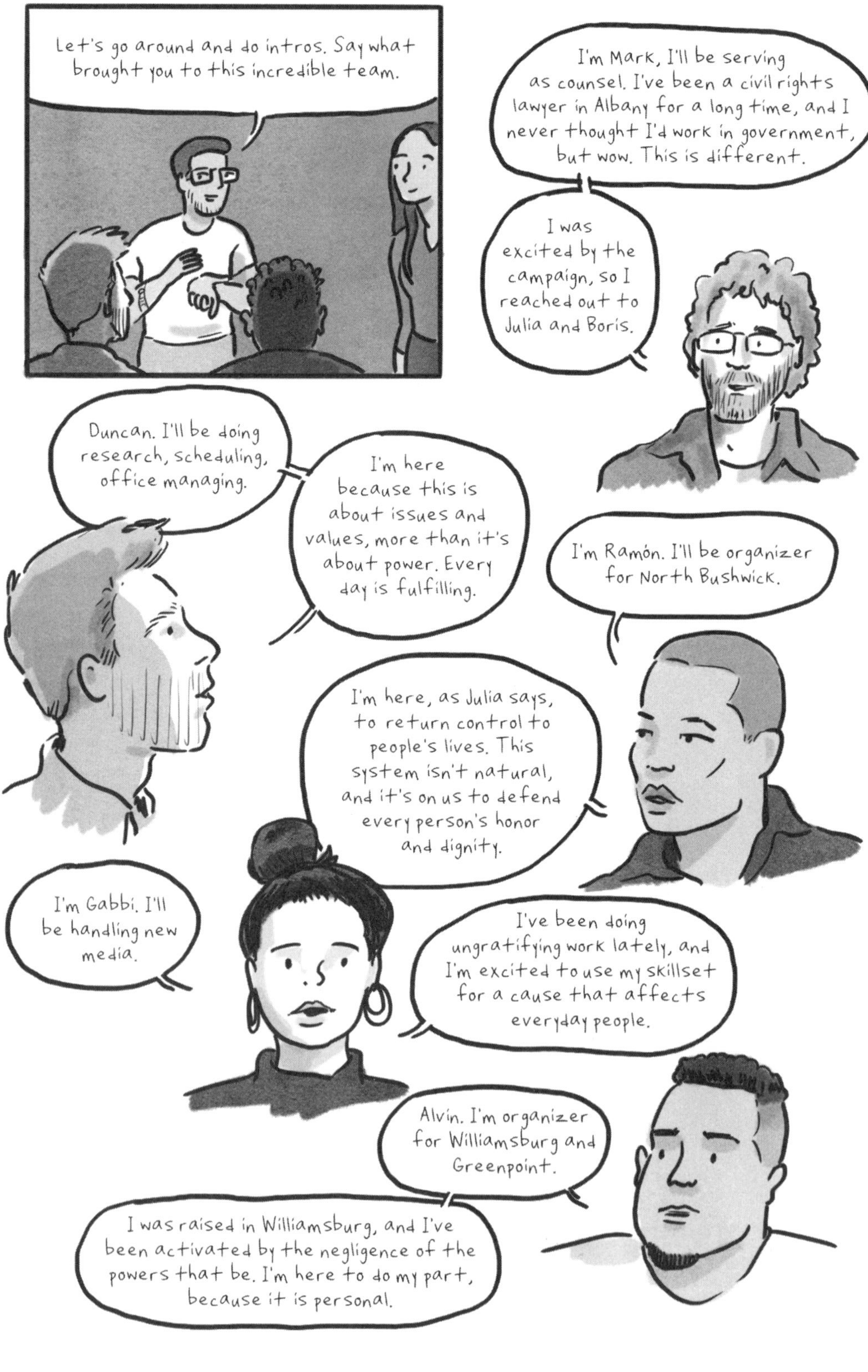
Let's go around and do intros. Say what brought you to this incredible team.
I'm Mark, I'll be serving as counsel. I've been a civil rights lawyer in Albany for a long time, and I never thought I'd work in government, but wow. This is different.
I was excited by the campaign, so I reached out to Julia and Boris.
Duncan. I'll be doing research, scheduling, office managing.
I'm here because this is about issues and values, more than it's about power. Every day is fulfilling.
I'm Ramón. I'll be organizer for North Bushwick.
I'm here, as Julia says, to return control to people's lives. This system isn't natural, and it's on us to defend every person's honor and dignity.
I'm Gabbi. I'll be handling new media.
I've been doing ungratifying work lately, and I'm excited to use my skillset for a cause that affects everyday people.
Alvin. I'm organizer for Williamsburg and Greenpoint.
I was raised in Williamsburg, and I've been activated by the negligence of the powers that be. I'm here to do my part, because it is personal.

Hi! Guillermo. I'll be legislative director.

I've been in the legislature since 1992, and I've seen the corruption: who gives a good speech and then goes home and doesn't care. I'm bringing that institutional history to fight for those values that make people's lives better.

Hey, I'm Michael. I'll be director of communications.

I've seen how New York falls short of its progressive ideals, and I want to make it how people say it is.

Hey, y'all, I'm Ramses. I'll be organizing in South Bushwick and Bed-Stuy.

I've always said, work for someone whose character you trust. We're going to change the fabric of our neighborhood.

I'm Isabel. I'm going to be constituent services manager.

I worked as the field director for the campaign, and I hope we can keep going with the atmosphere we built there. And on a personal level, this was something in my life that I needed. I love being here.

Hey, I'm Jessica. I'll be organizer in Cypress Hills and East New York, where my family and I live.

I grew up in Bushwick. This district is my home, and I'm always going to work to make it better. The opportunity to continue that work with the resources of this office behind me... it's incredible.

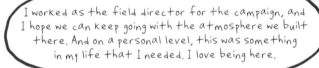

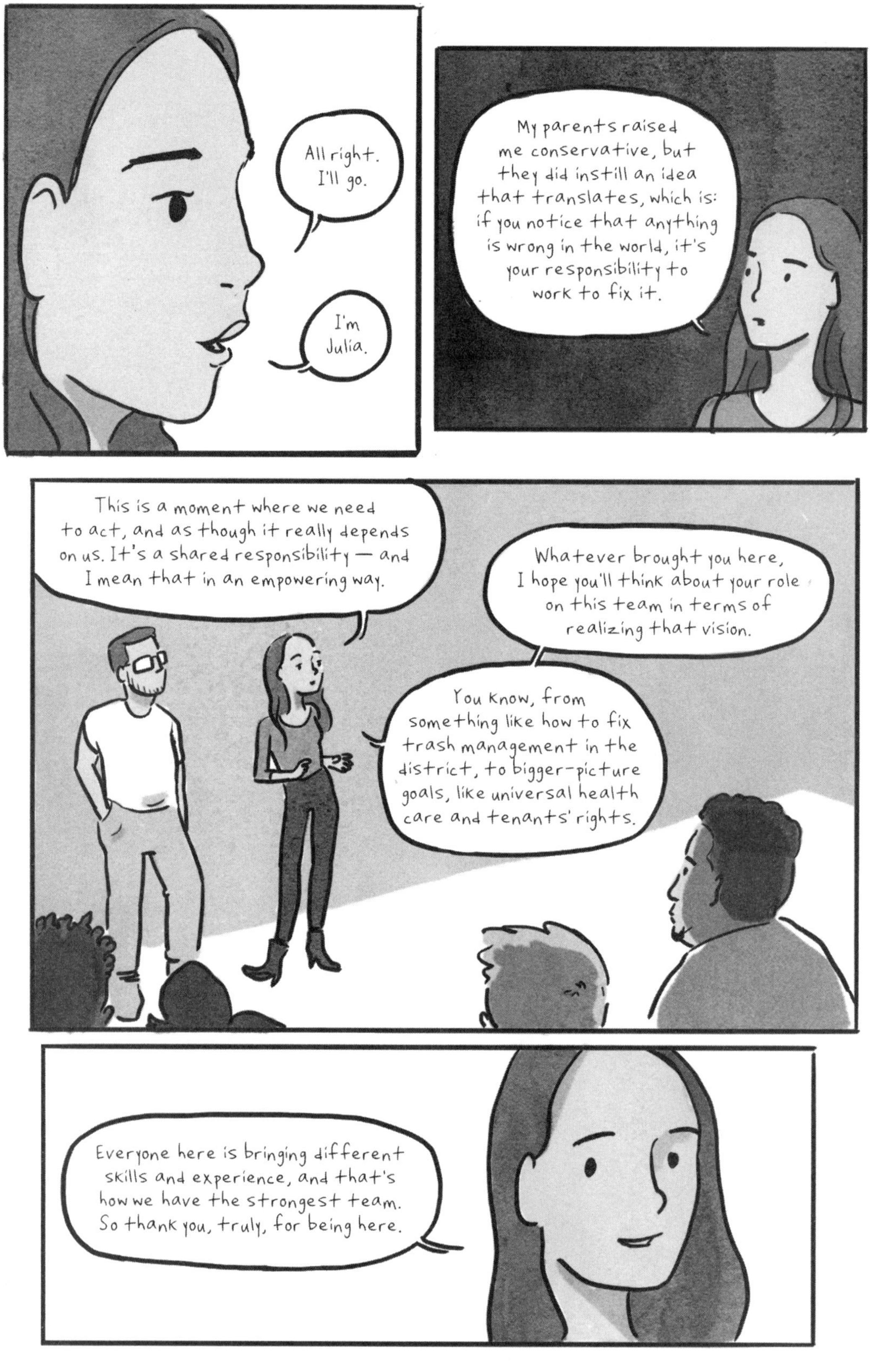
All right. I'll go.
I'm Julia.
My parents raised me conservative, but they did instill an idea that translates, which is: if you notice that anything is wrong in the world, it's your responsibility to work to fix it.
This is a moment where we need to act, and as though it really depends on us. It's a shared responsibility — and I mean that in an empowering way.
Whatever brought you here, I hope you'll think about your role on this team in terms of realizing that vision.
You know, from something like how to fix trash management in the district, to bigger-picture goals, like universal health care and tenants' rights.
Everyone here is bringing different skills and experience, and that's how we have the strongest team. So thank you, truly, for being here.

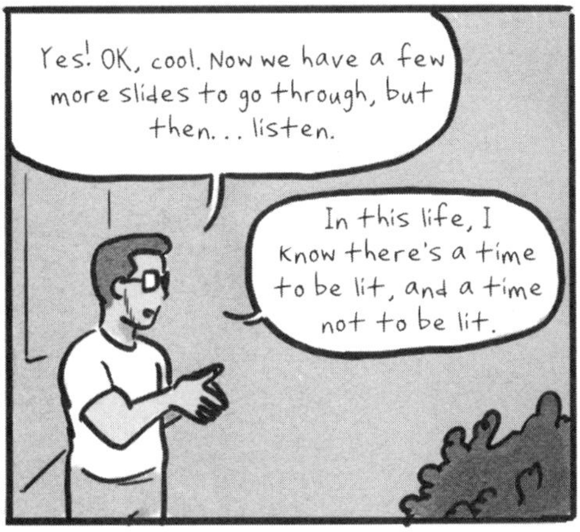
Yes! OK, cool. Now we have a few more slides to go through, but then... listen.
In this life, I know there's a time to be lit, and a time not to be lit.

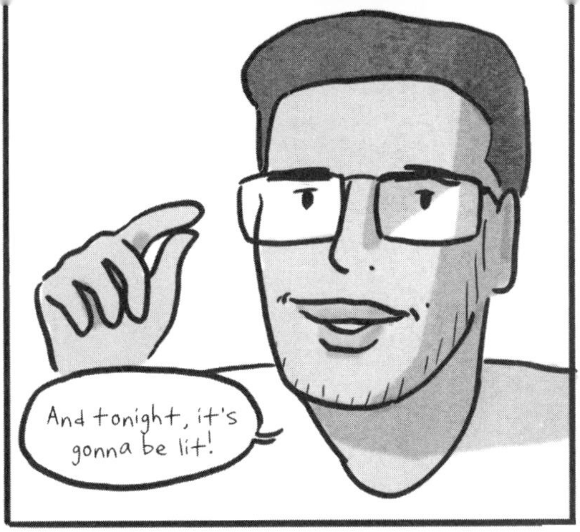
And tonight, it's gonna be lit!

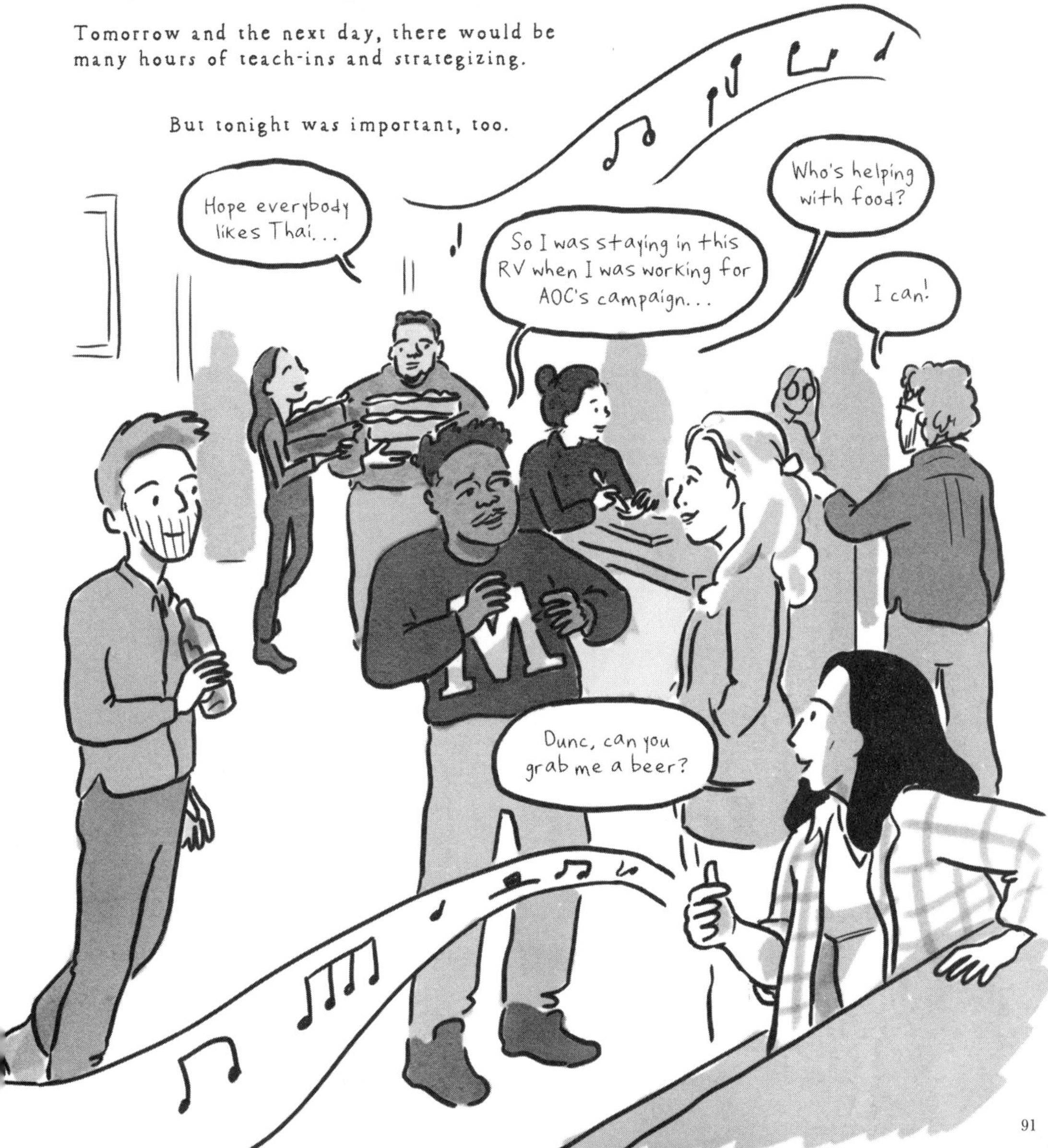
Tomorrow and the next day, there would be many hours of teach-ins and strategizing.
But tonight was important, too.
Hope everybody likes Thai...
So I was staying in this RV when I was working for AOC's campaign...
Who's helping with food?
I can!
Dunc, can you grab me a beer?

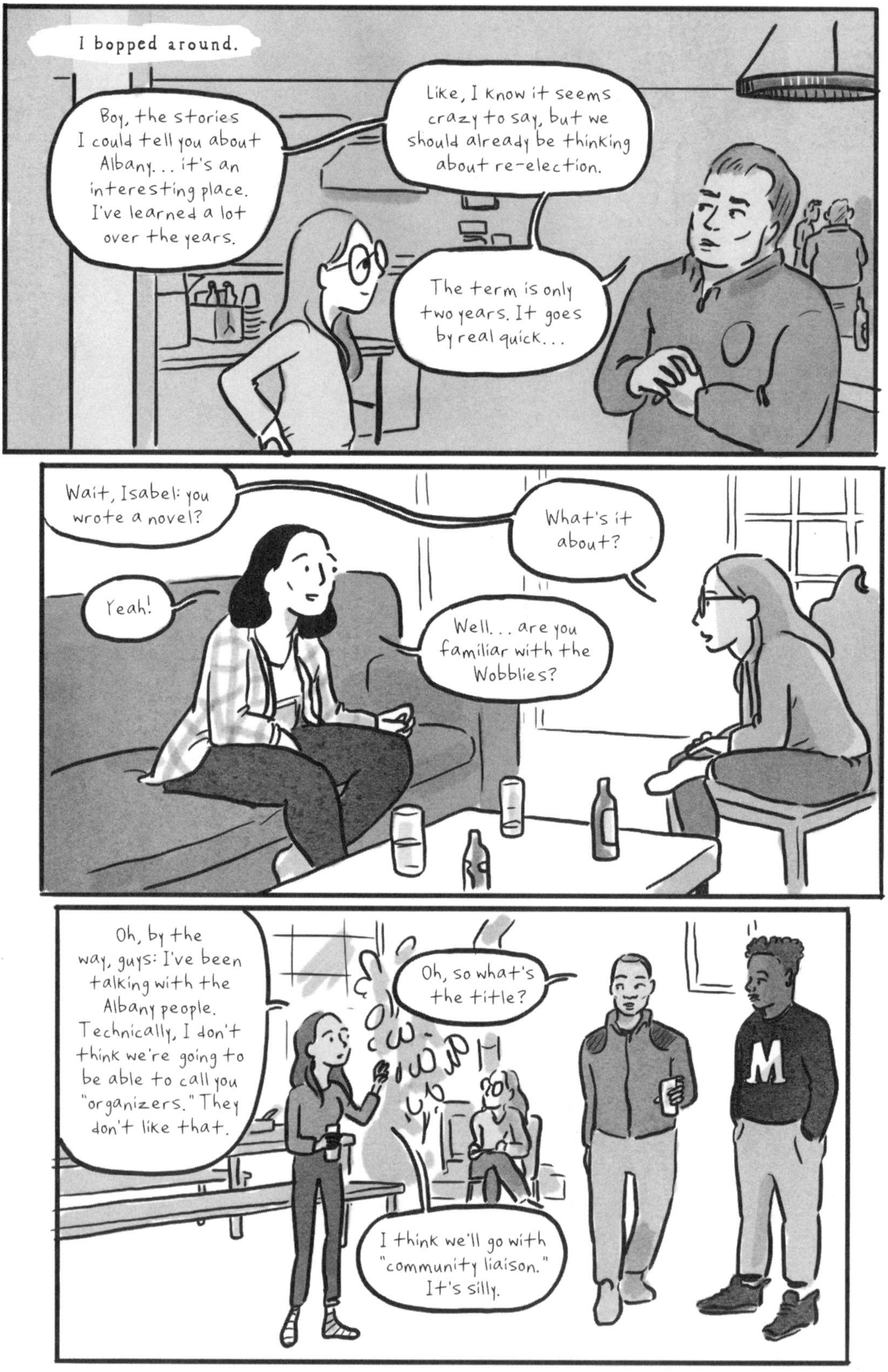
I bopped around.
Boy, the stories I could tell you about Albany... it's an interesting place. I've learned a lot over the years.
Like, I know it seems crazy to say, but we should already be thinking about re-election.
The term is only two years. It goes by real quick...
Wait, Isabel: you wrote a novel?
What's it about?
Yeah!
Well... are you familiar with the Wobblies?
Oh, by the way, guys: I've been talking with the Albany people. Technically, I don't think we're going to be able to call you "organizers." They don't like that.
Oh, so what's the title?
I think we'll go with "community liaison." It's silly.

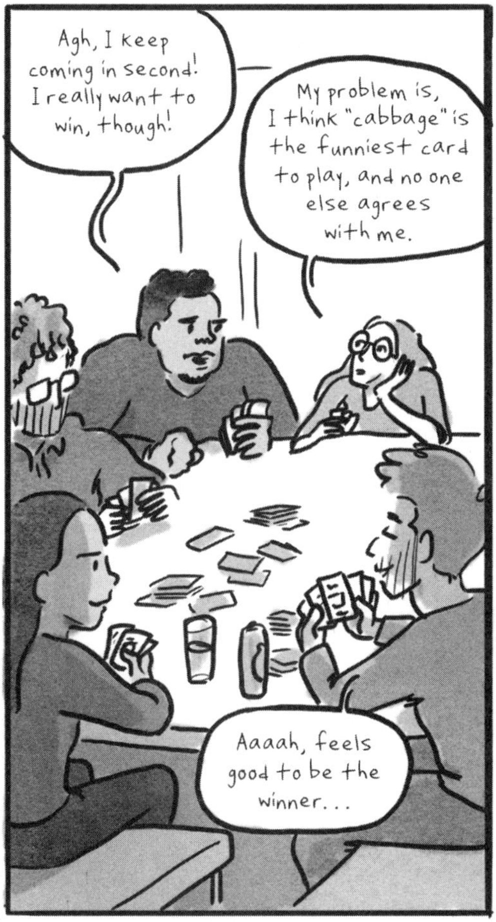
Agh, I keep coming in second! I really want to win, though!
My problem is, I think "cabbage" is the funniest card to play, and no one else agrees with me.
Aaaah, feels good to be the winner...

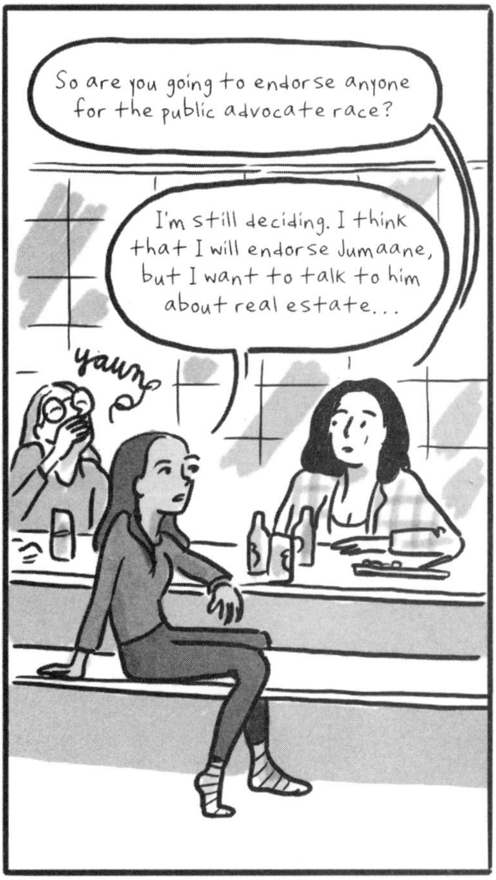
So are you going to endorse anyone for the public advocate race?
I'm still deciding. I think that I will endorse Jumaane, but I want to talk to him about real estate...
yawn

At 2AM, a discussion of the state constitution was still going strong, but I could barely keep my eyes open.

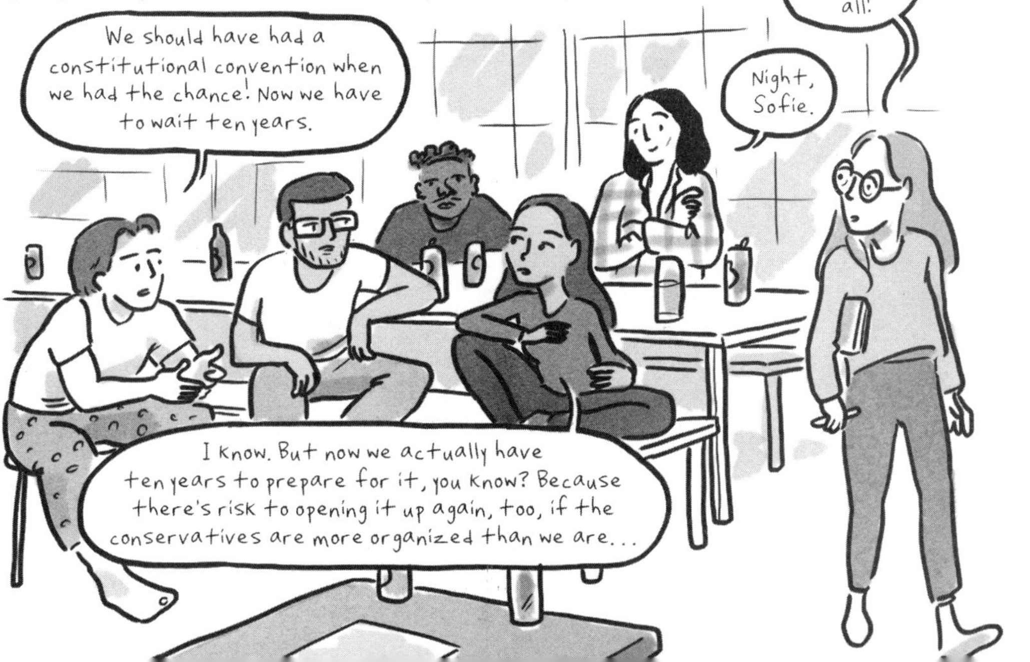
Goodnight, all!
Night, Sofie.
We should have had a constitutional convention when we had the chance! Now we have to wait ten years.
I know. But now we actually have ten years to prepare for it, you know? Because there's risk to opening it up again, too, if the conservatives are more organized than we are...

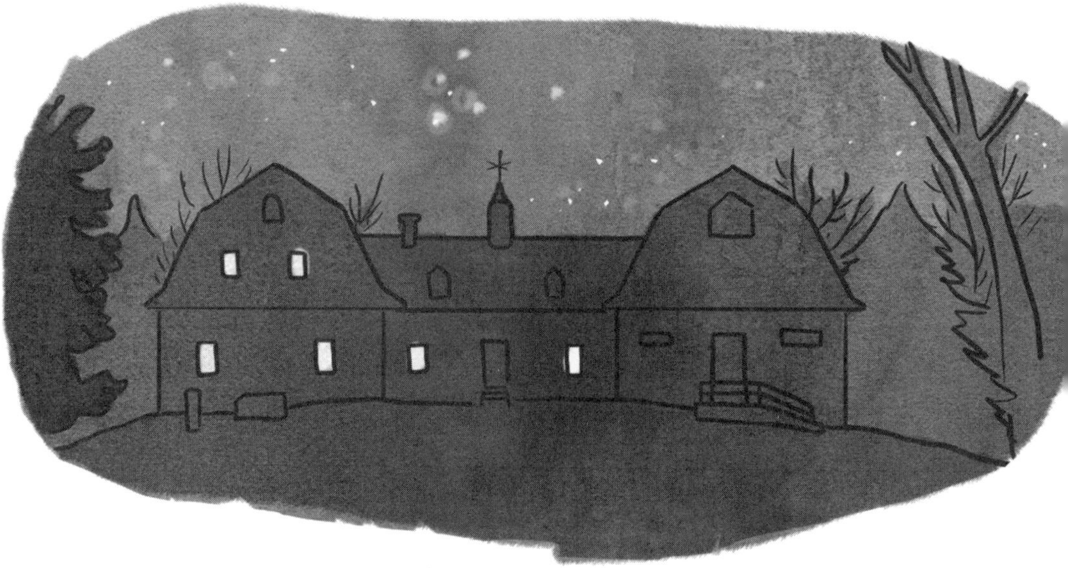
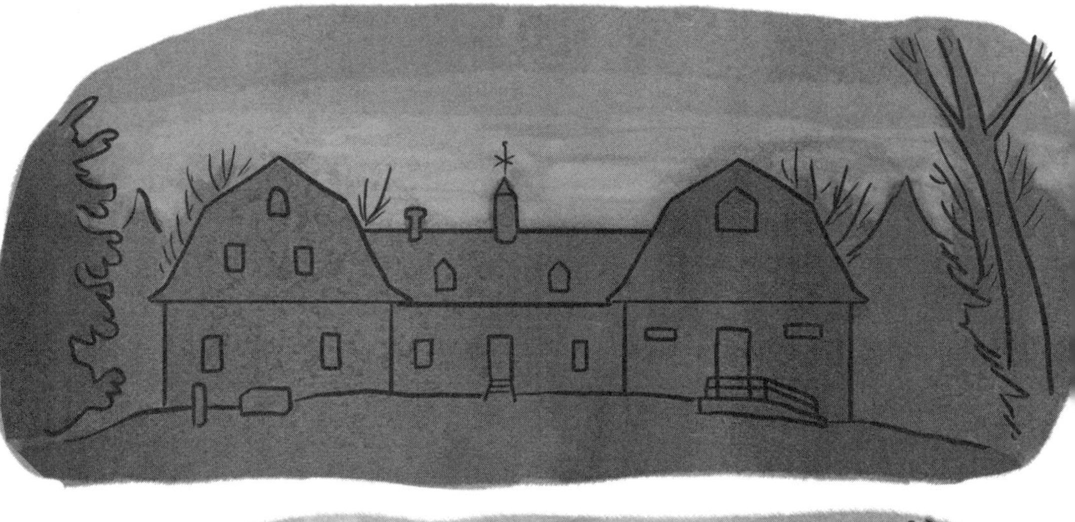
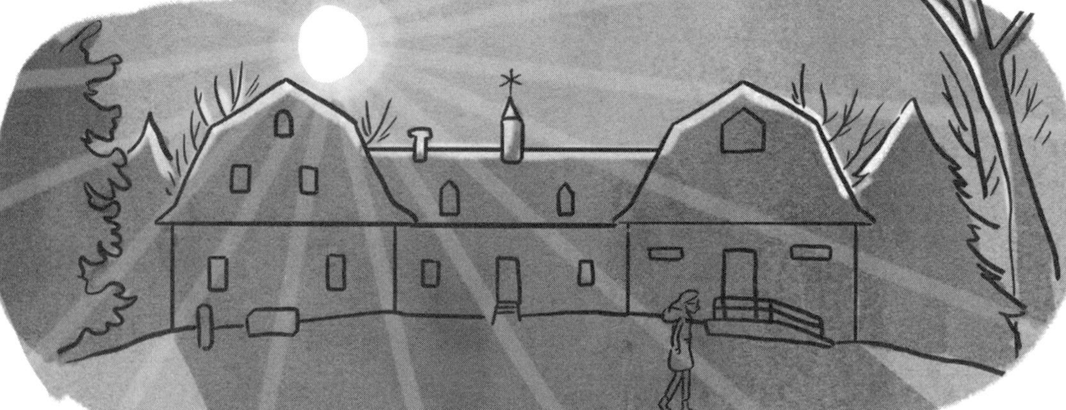

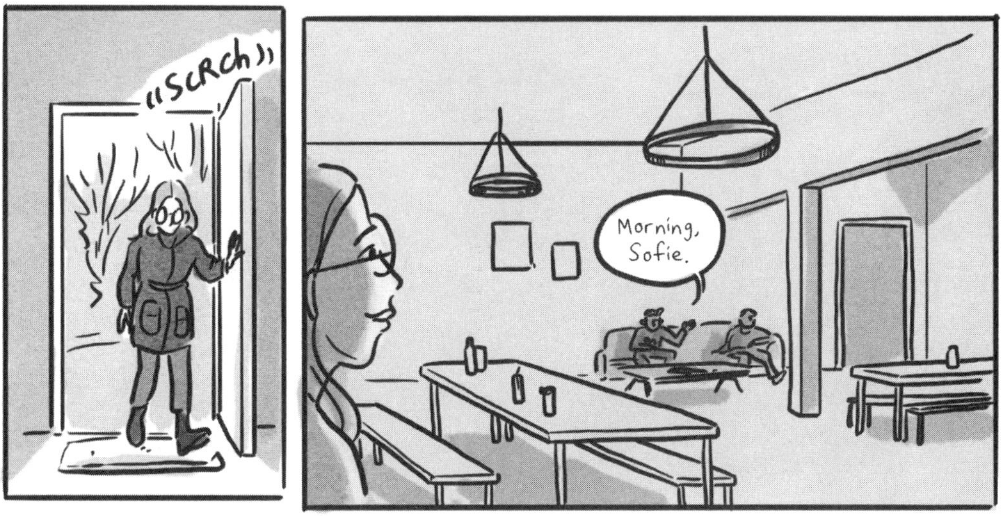
((SCRCh))
Morning, Sofie.

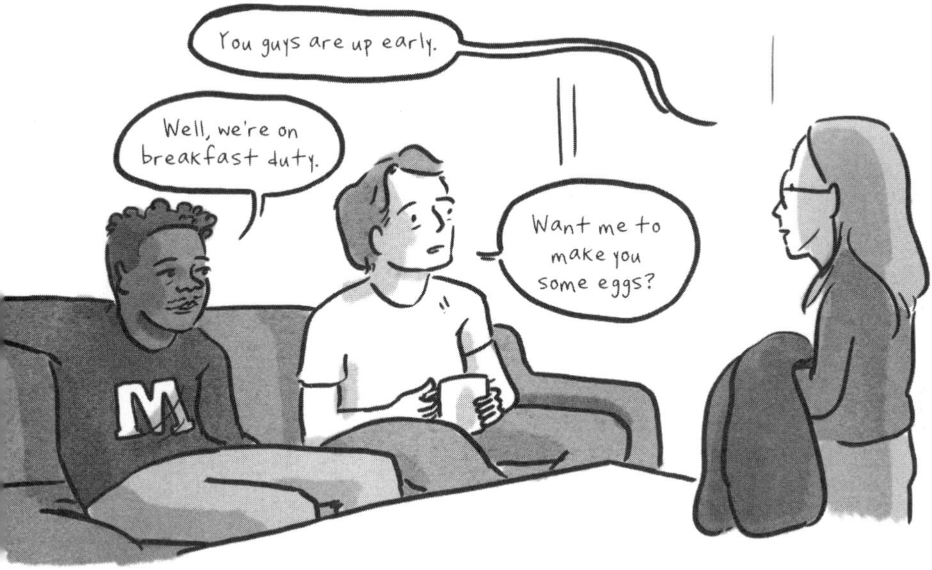
You guys are up early.
Well, we're on breakfast duty.
Want me to make you some eggs?

Some of us were slow getting started.

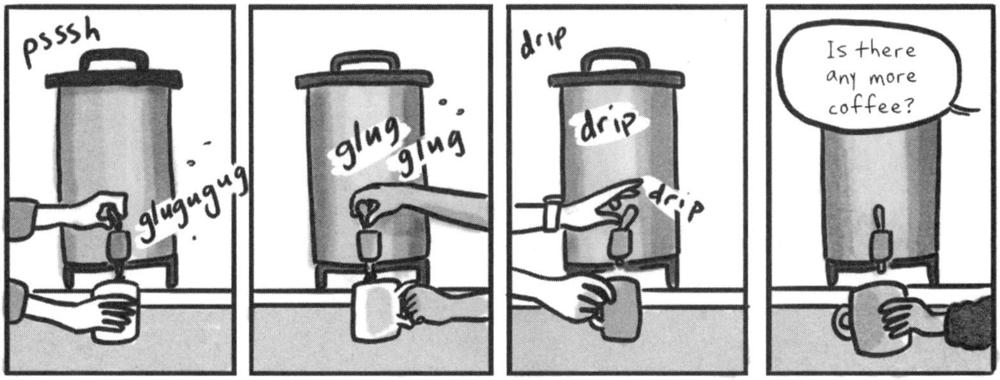
psssh
glugugug
glug glug
drip
drip
drip
Is there any more coffee?

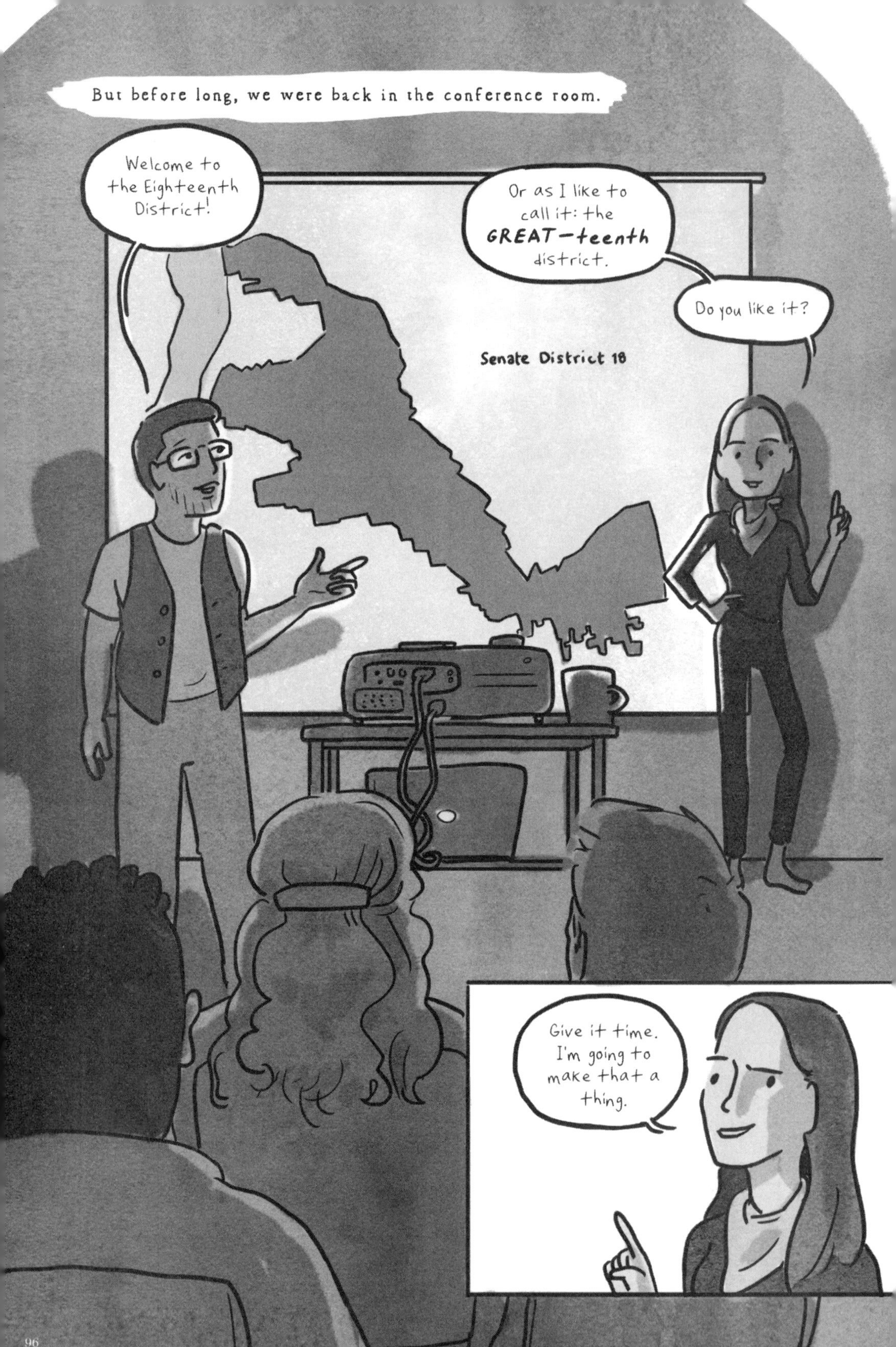
But before long, we were back in the conference room.
Welcome to the Eighteenth District!
Senate District 18
Or as I like to call it: the GREAT-teenth district.
Do you like it?
Give it time. I'm going to make that a thing.

We got into it. Boris walked through the demographics of the district. . .

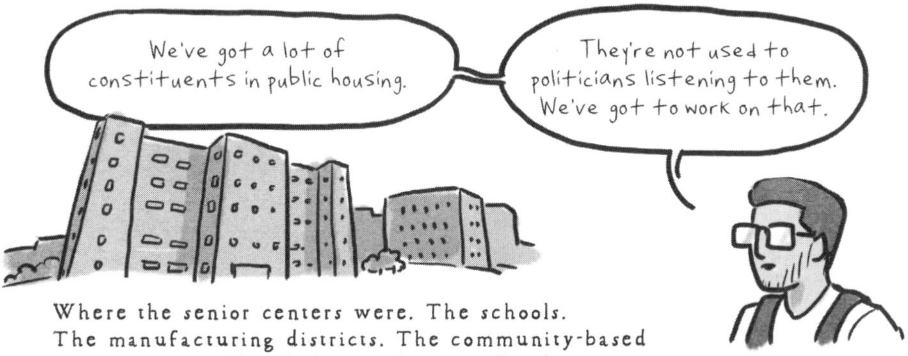
We've got a lot of constituents in public housing.
They're not used to politicians listening to them. We've got to work on that.

Where the senior centers were. The schools. The manufacturing districts. The community-based organizations. The shelters. The superfund sites. The hospitals. The commercial zones.

Local political history, which was dominated for decades by a powerful, bullying politician named Vito Lopez.

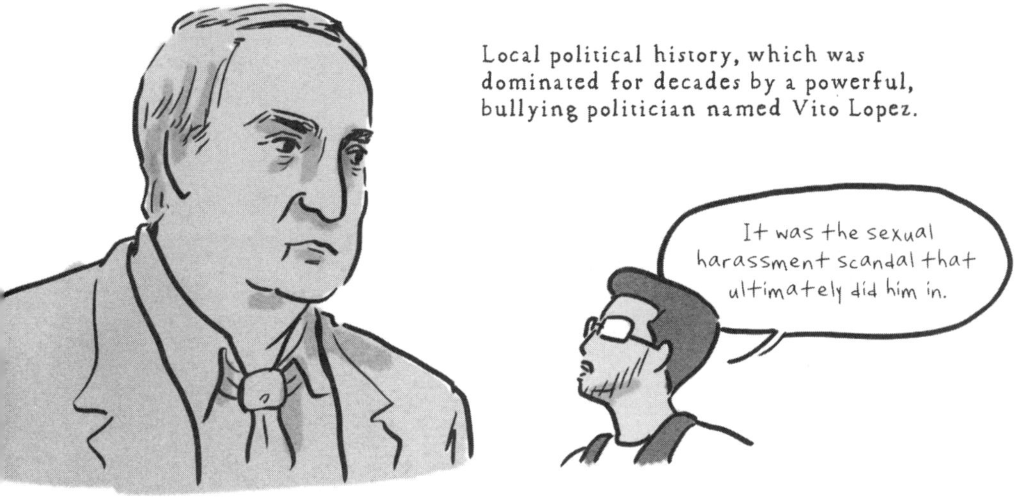
It was the sexual harassment scandal that ultimately did him in.

Most of the staff would be based in the district, dealing with the local, everyday issues that would never make the news.

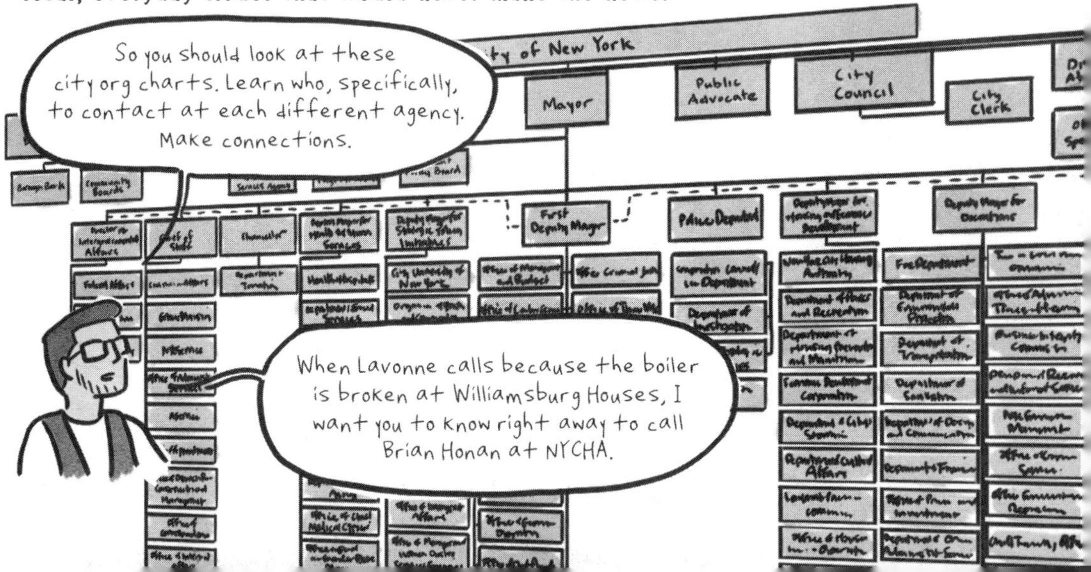
So you should look at these city org charts. Learn who, specifically, to contact at each different agency. Make connections.
ty of New York
Mayor
Public Advocate
City Council
City Clerk
First Deputy Mayor
When Lavonne calls because the boiler is broken at Williamsburg Houses, I want you to know right away to call Brian Honan at NYCHA.

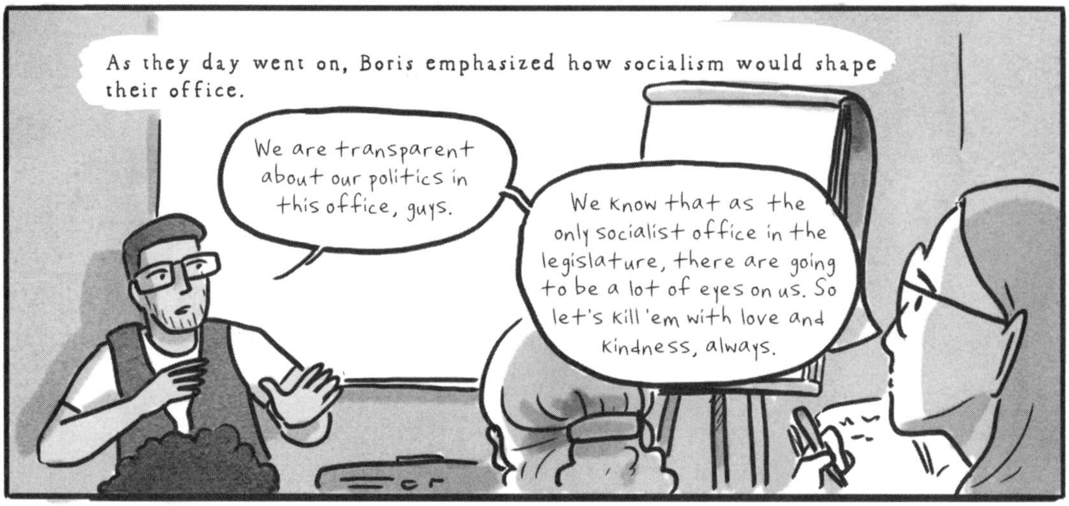
As they day went on, Boris emphasized how socialism would shape their office.
We are transparent about our politics in this office, guys.
We know that as the only socialist office in the legislature, there are going to be a lot of eyes on us. So let's kill 'em with love and kindness, always.

Democratic socialism, as Julia defined it, was a political movement driven by the idea that everyone has the right not only to survive, but to thrive.

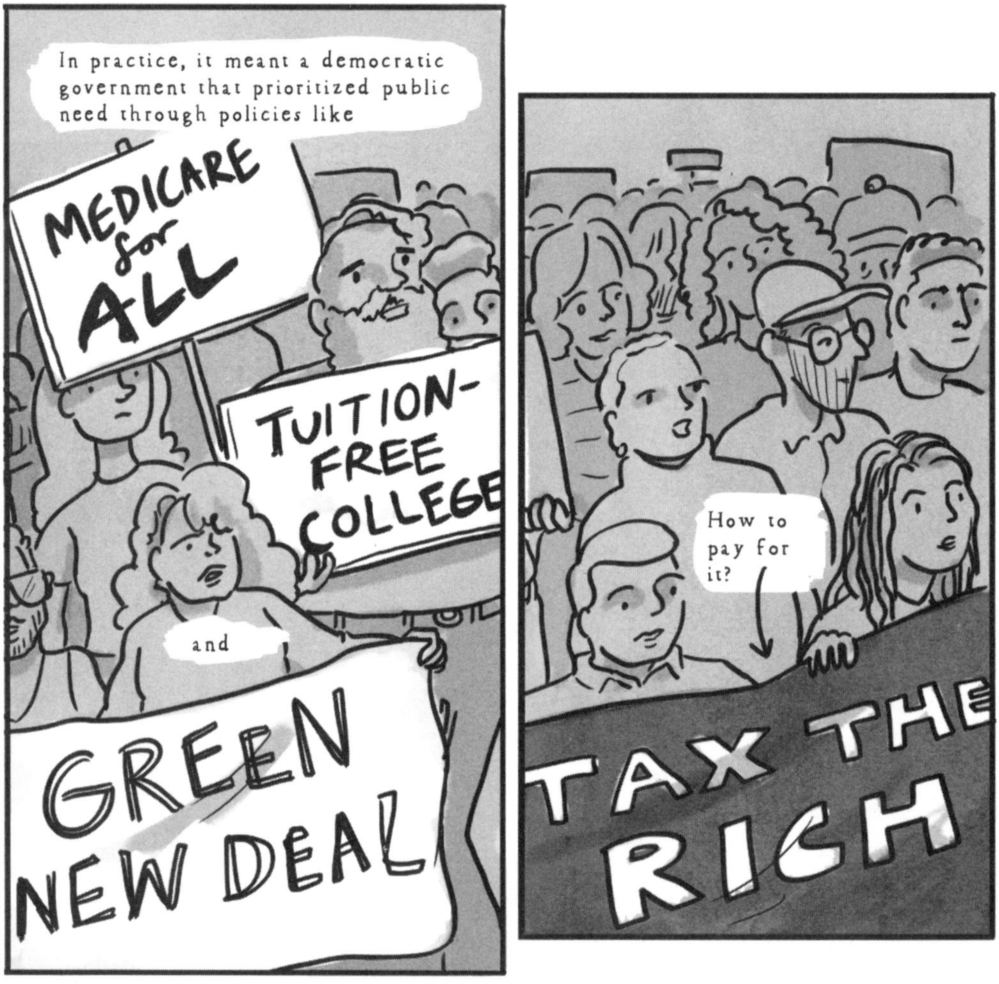
In practice, it meant a democratic government that prioritized public need through policies like
MEDICARE for ALL
TUITION-FREE COLLEGE
and
GREEN NEW DEAL
How to pay for it?
TAX THE RICH

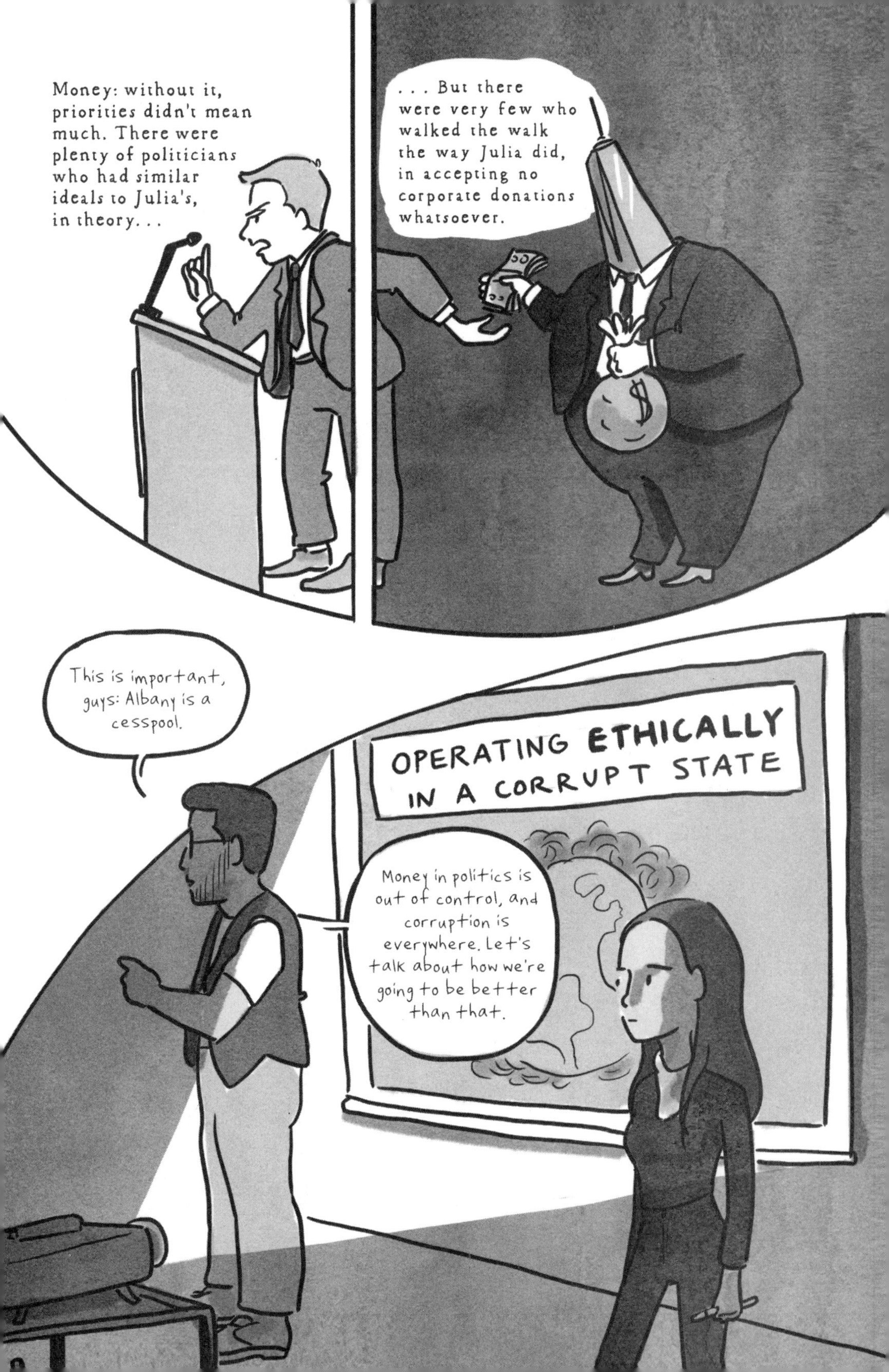
Money: without it, priorities didn't mean much. There were plenty of politicians who had similar ideals to Julia's, in theory. . .
. . . But there were very few who walked the walk the way Julia did, in accepting no corporate donations whatsoever.
This is important, guys: Albany is a cesspool.
OPERATING ETHICALLY IN A CORRUPT STATE
Money in politics is out of control, and corruption is everywhere. Let's talk about how we're going to be better than that.

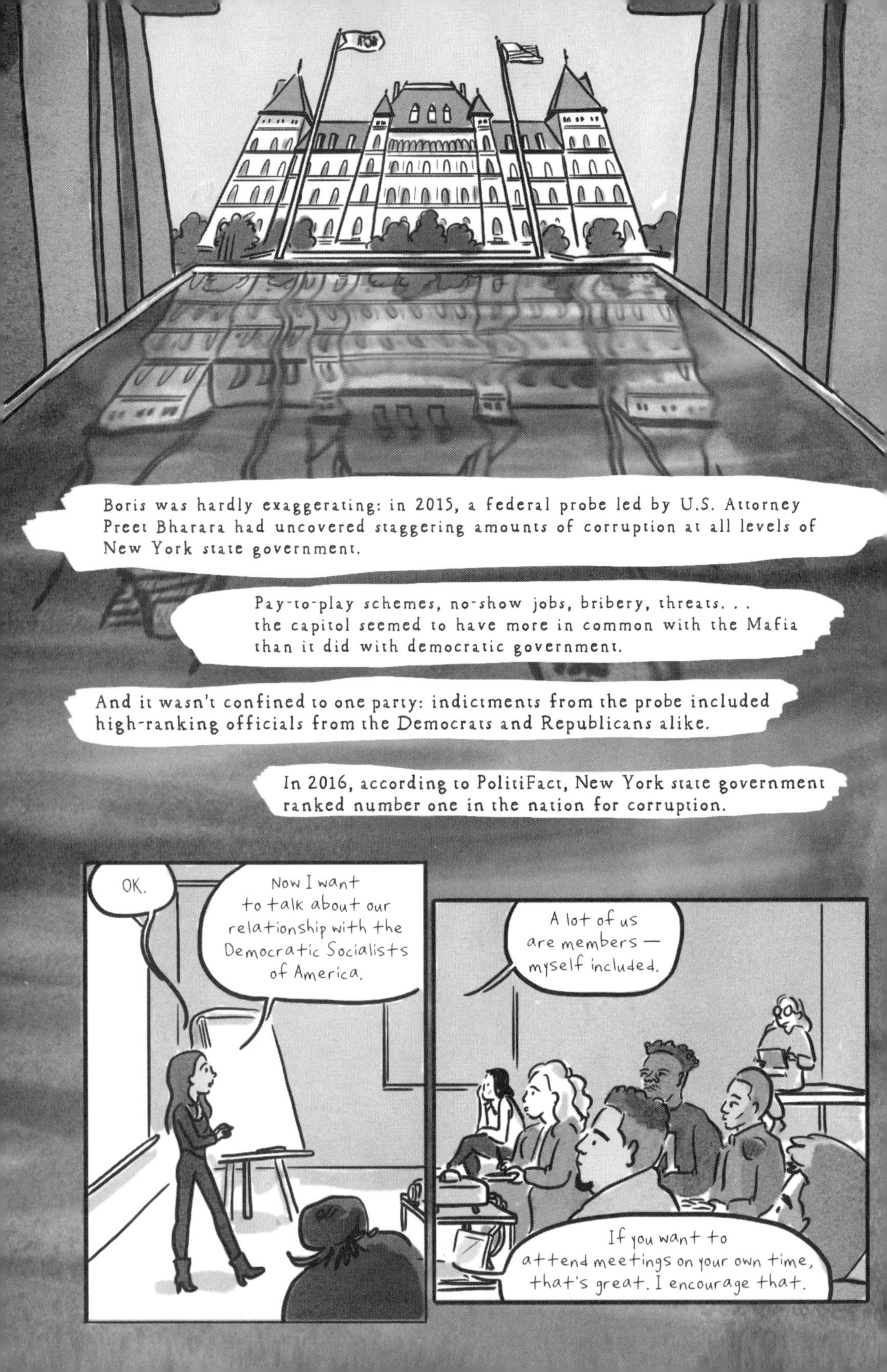
Boris was hardly exaggerating: in 2015, a federal probe led by U.S. Attorney Preet Bharara had uncovered staggering amounts of corruption at all levels of New York state government.
Pay-to-play schemes, no-show jobs, bribery, threats. . . the capitol seemed to have more in common with the Mafia than it did with democratic government.
And it wasn't confined to one party: indictments from the probe included high-ranking officials from the Democrats and Republicans alike.
In 2016, according to PolitiFact, New York state government ranked number one in the nation for corruption.
OK.
Now I want to talk about our relationship with the Democratic Socialists of America.
A lot of us are members — myself included.
If you want to attend meetings on your own time, that's great. I encourage that.

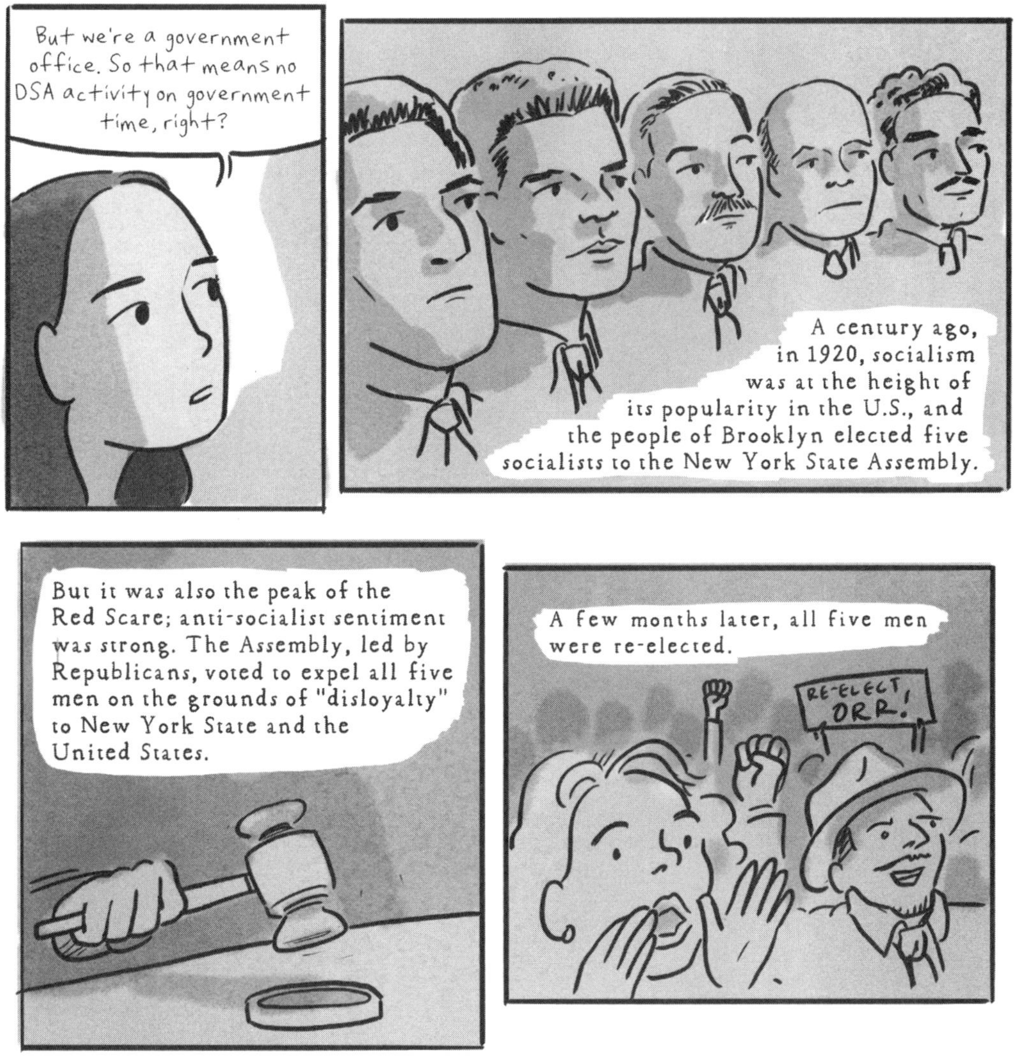
But we're a government office. So that means no DSA activity on government time, right?
A century ago, in 1920, socialism was at the height of its popularity in the U.S., and the people of Brooklyn elected five socialists to the New York State Assembly.
But it was also the peak of the Red Scare; anti-socialist sentiment was strong. The Assembly, led by Republicans, voted to expel all five men on the grounds of "disloyalty" to New York State and the United States.
A few months later, all five men were re-elected.
RE-ELECT ORR!

Again, the Assembly held a vote. Three were expelled, and two would have been allowed to remain, but they resigned in solidarity.

Later, two went on to win back their seats yet again.

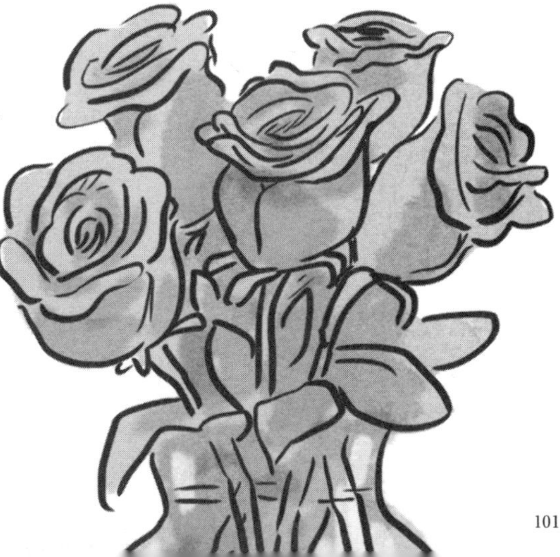

In the hundred years since, there had been no shortage of corrupt politicians, with dozens convicted.

The New York Times

The Many Faces of New York's Political Scandals

In the past decade, more than 30 current or former state officeholders in New York have been convicted of crimes, sanctioned or otherwise accused of wrongdoing. Here are some of them.

But to my knowledge, there had been no other open socialists.

In some ways, Julia would be doing on the state level what AOC would do on the national stage: they would both be freshman lawmakers, representing the left-most pole of their Democratic conference.

President (R)

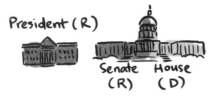

Senate   House
(R)   (D)

But AOC's conference would be fighting against a wall of red in the U.S. Senate and the White House.

Governor (D)

 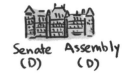

Senate   Assembly
(D)   (D)

Julia would be sitting in the most progressive Senate in New York history, alongside a Democratic Assembly and Governor. This team expected to get things done.

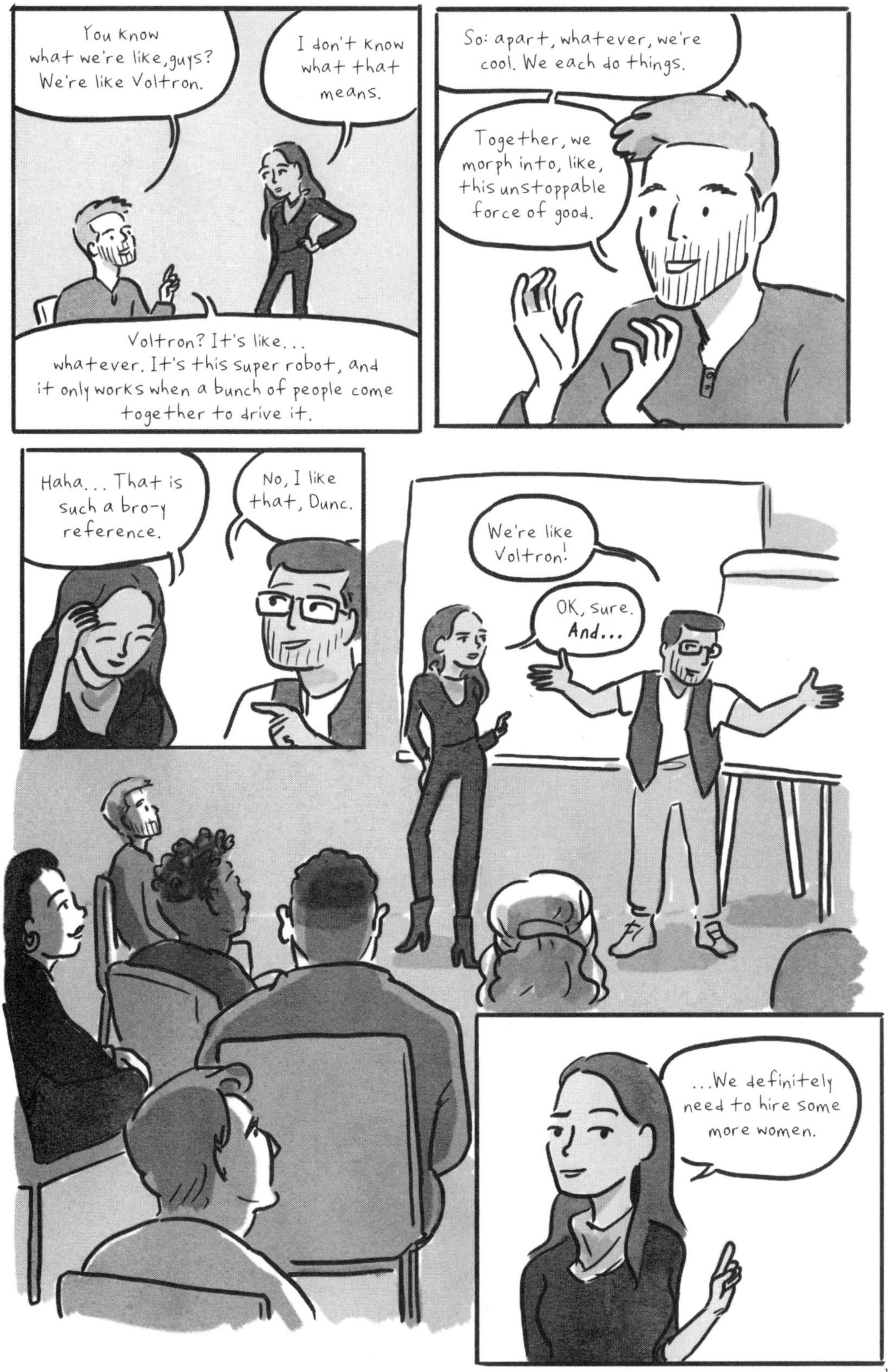
You know what we're like, guys? We're like Voltron.
I don't know what that means.
Voltron? It's like... whatever. It's this super robot, and it only works when a bunch of people come together to drive it.
So: apart, whatever, we're cool. We each do things.
Together, we morph into, like, this unstoppable force of good.
Haha... That is such a bro-y reference.
No, I like that, Dunc.
We're like Voltron!
OK, sure. **And...**
...We definitely need to hire some more women.

Part II

Chapter Four

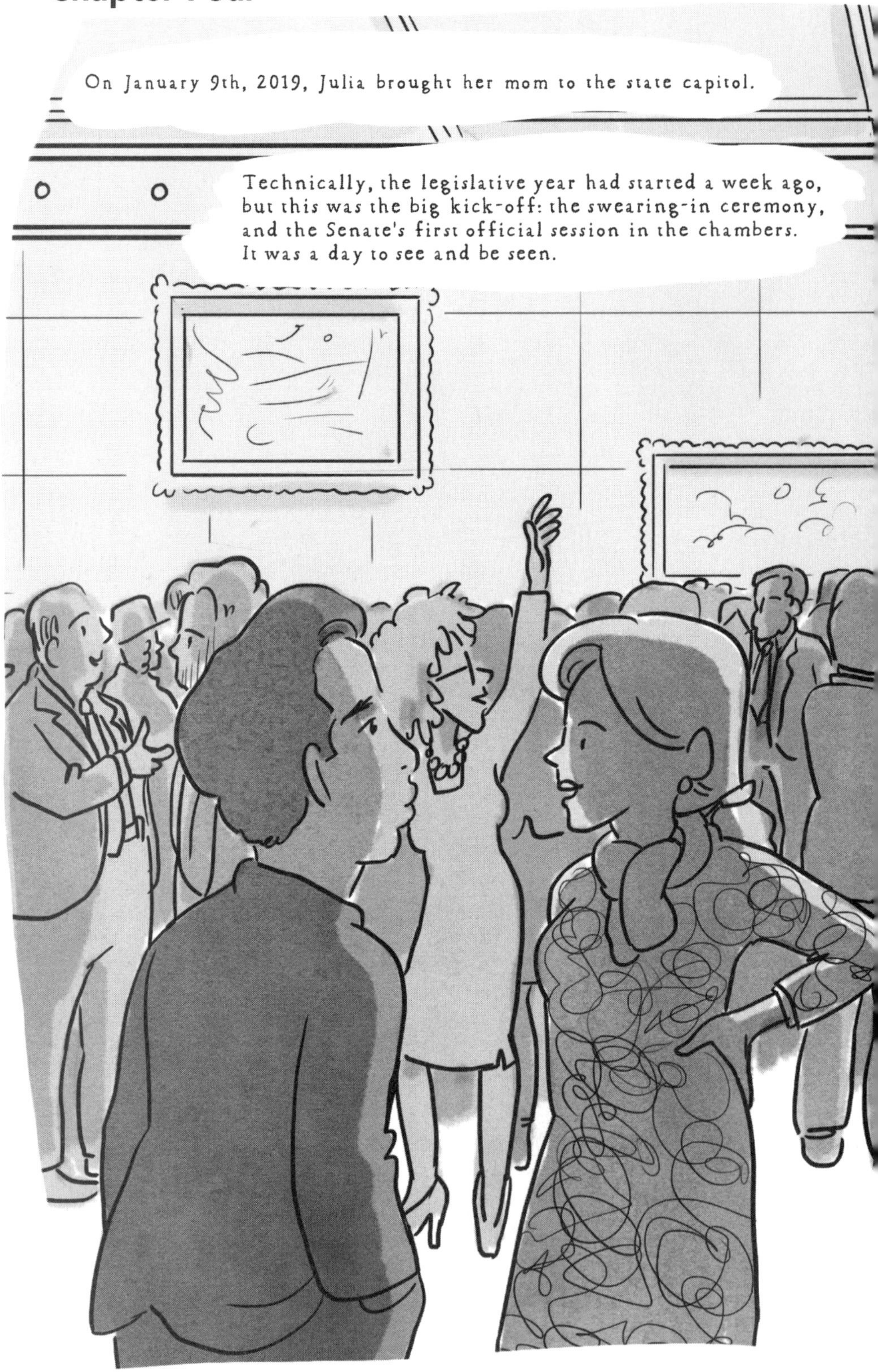
On January 9th, 2019, Julia brought her mom to the state capitol.
Technically, the legislative year had started a week ago, but this was the big kick-off: the swearing-in ceremony, and the Senate's first official session in the chambers. It was a day to see and be seen.

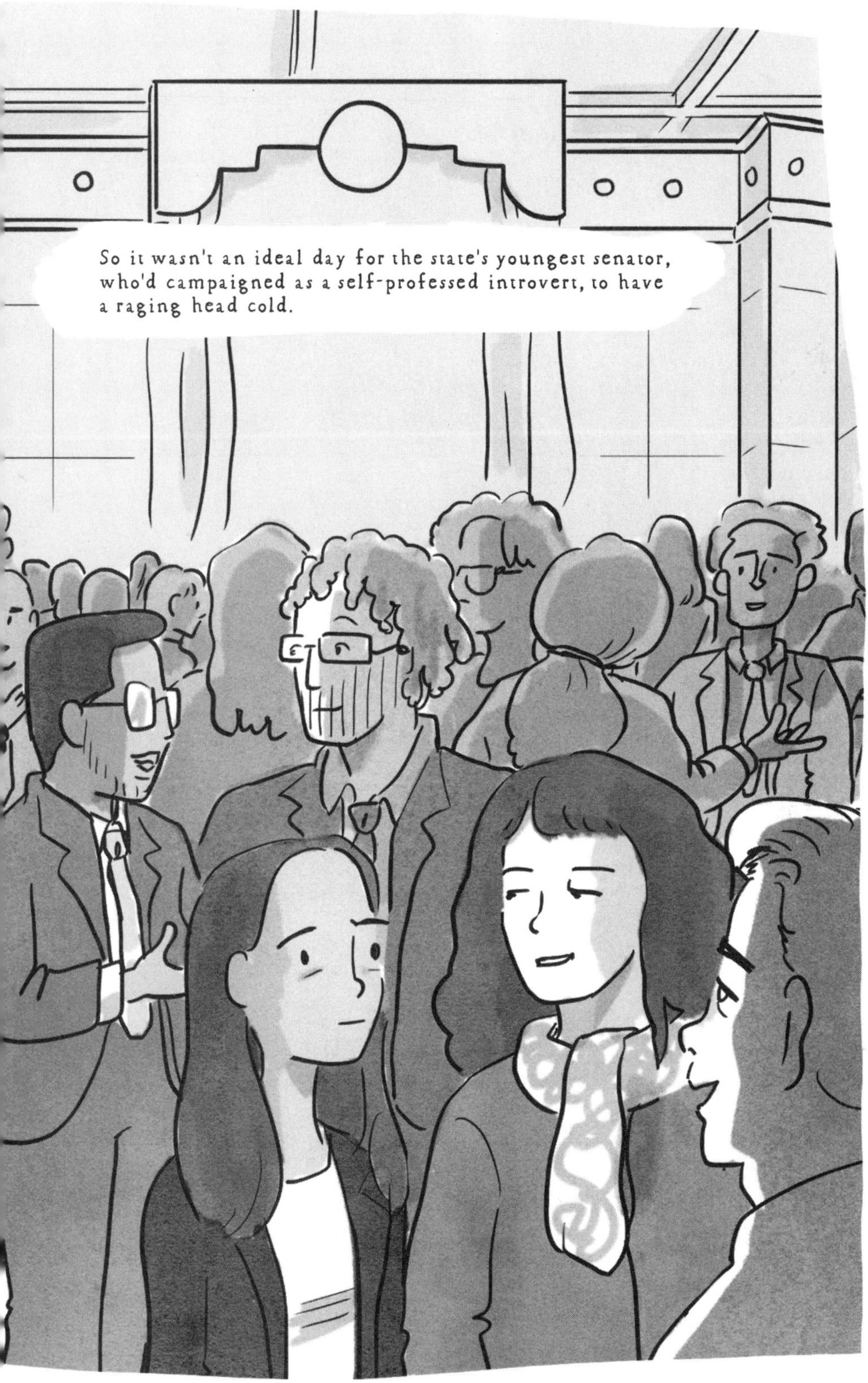
So it wasn't an ideal day for the state's youngest senator, who'd campaigned as a self-professed introvert, to have a raging head cold.

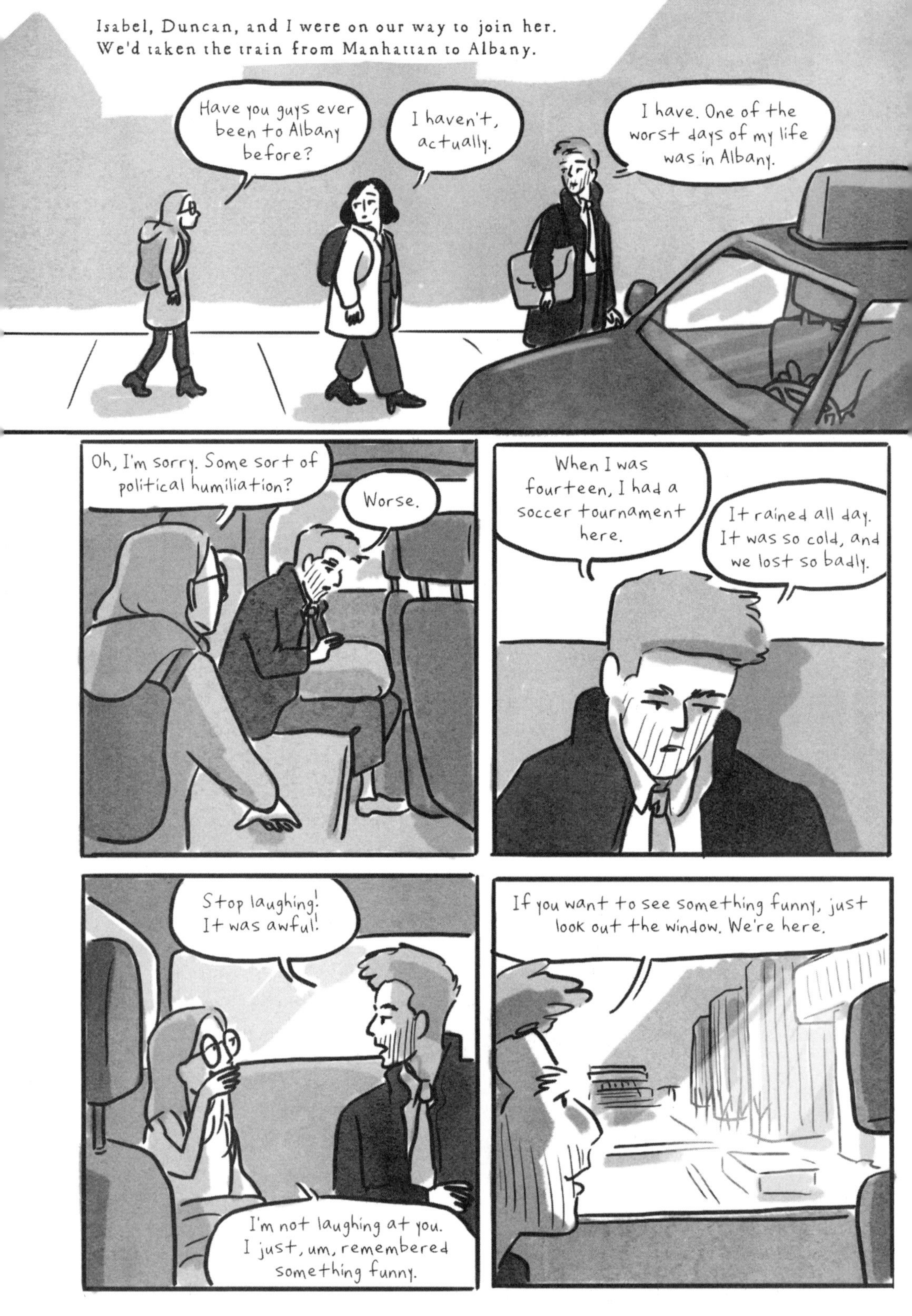
Isabel, Duncan, and I were on our way to join her. We'd taken the train from Manhattan to Albany.
Have you guys ever been to Albany before?
I haven't, actually.
I have. One of the worst days of my life was in Albany.
Oh, I'm sorry. Some sort of political humiliation?
Worse.
When I was fourteen, I had a soccer tournament here.
It rained all day. It was so cold, and we lost so badly.
Stop laughing! It was awful!
I'm not laughing at you. I just, um, remembered something funny.
If you want to see something funny, just look out the window. We're here.

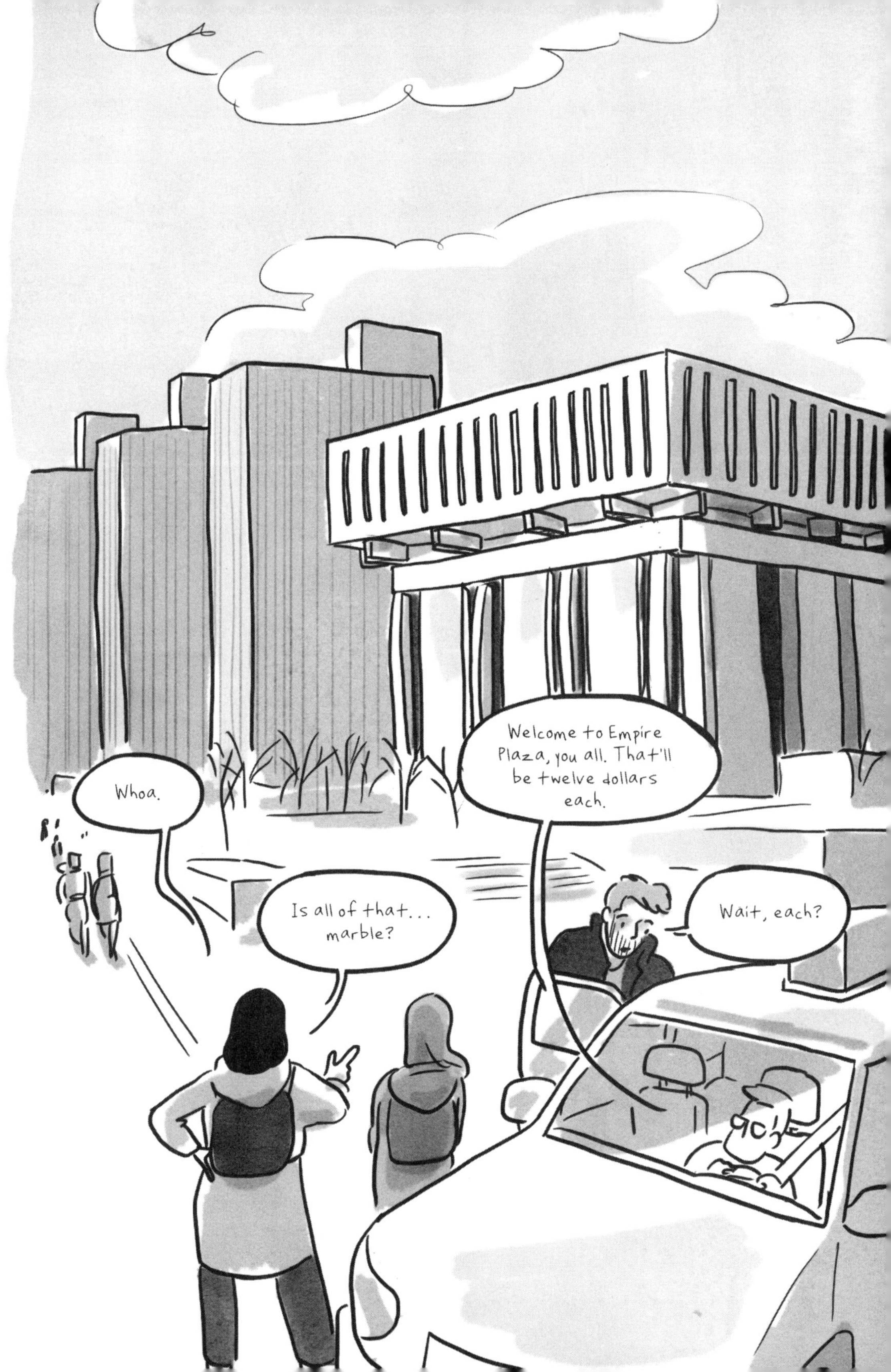
Whoa.
Is all of that... marble?
Welcome to Empire Plaza, you all. That'll be twelve dollars each.
Wait, each?

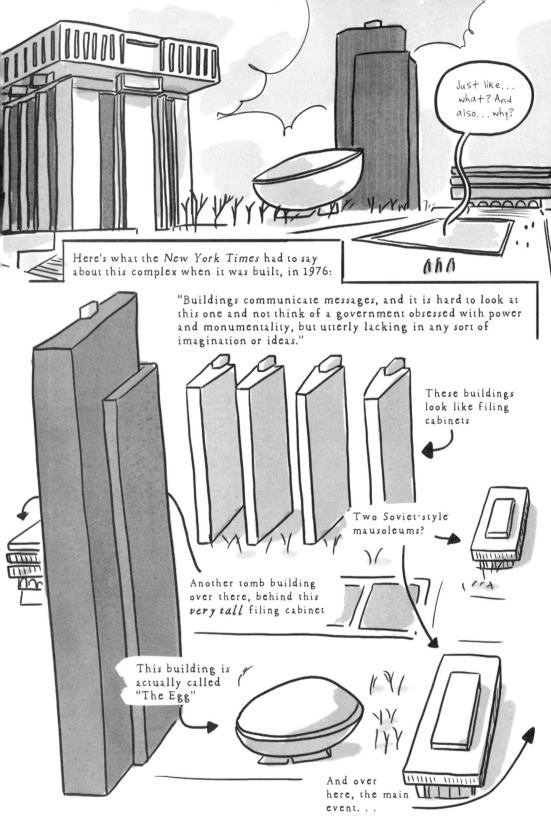

Just like... what? And also... why?

Here's what the *New York Times* had to say about this complex when it was built, in 1976:

"Buildings communicate messages, and it is hard to look at this one and not think of a government obsessed with power and monumentality, but utterly lacking in any sort of imagination or ideas."

These buildings look like filing cabinets

Two Soviet-style mausoleums?

Another tomb building over there, behind this *very tall* filing cabinet

This building is actually called "The Egg"

And over here, the main event...

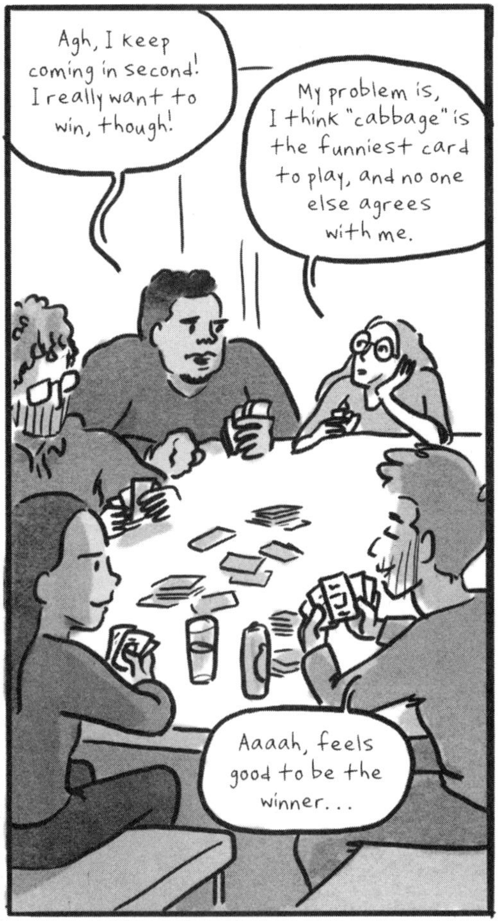
Agh, I keep coming in second! I really want to win, though!
My problem is, I think "cabbage" is the funniest card to play, and no one else agrees with me.
Aaaah, feels good to be the winner...

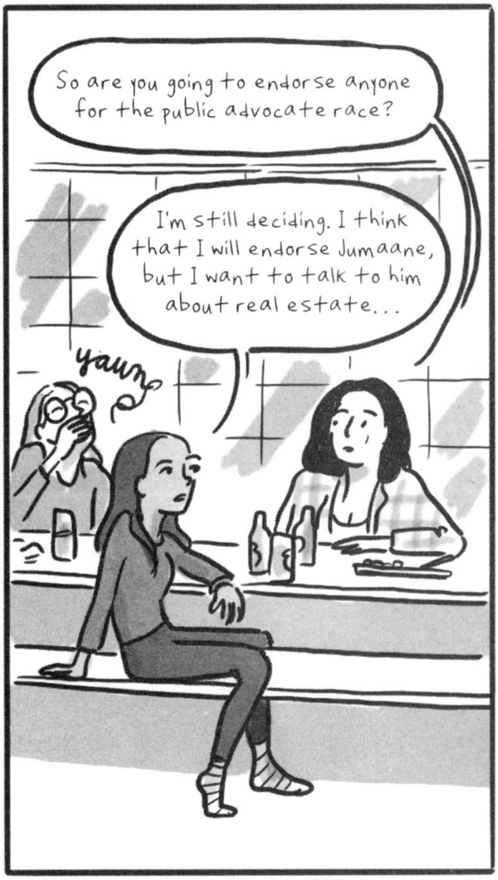
So are you going to endorse anyone for the public advocate race?
I'm still deciding. I think that I will endorse Jumaane, but I want to talk to him about real estate...
yawn

At 2AM, a discussion of the state constitution was still going strong, but I could barely keep my eyes open.

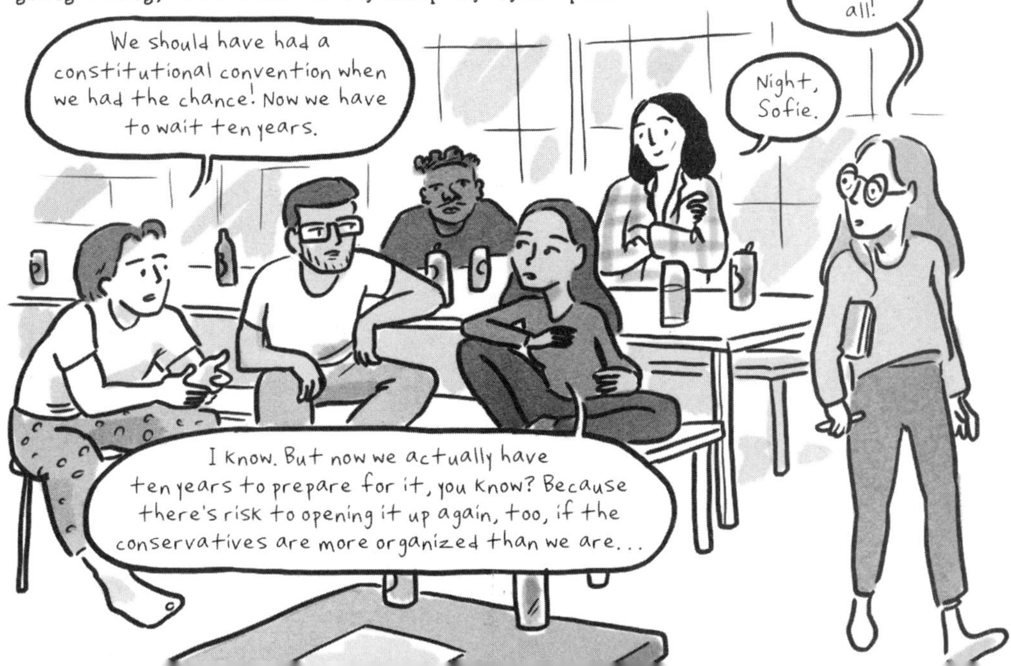
Goodnight, all!
We should have had a constitutional convention when we had the chance! Now we have to wait ten years.
Night, Sofie.
I know. But now we actually have ten years to prepare for it, you know? Because there's risk to opening it up again, too, if the conservatives are more organized than we are...

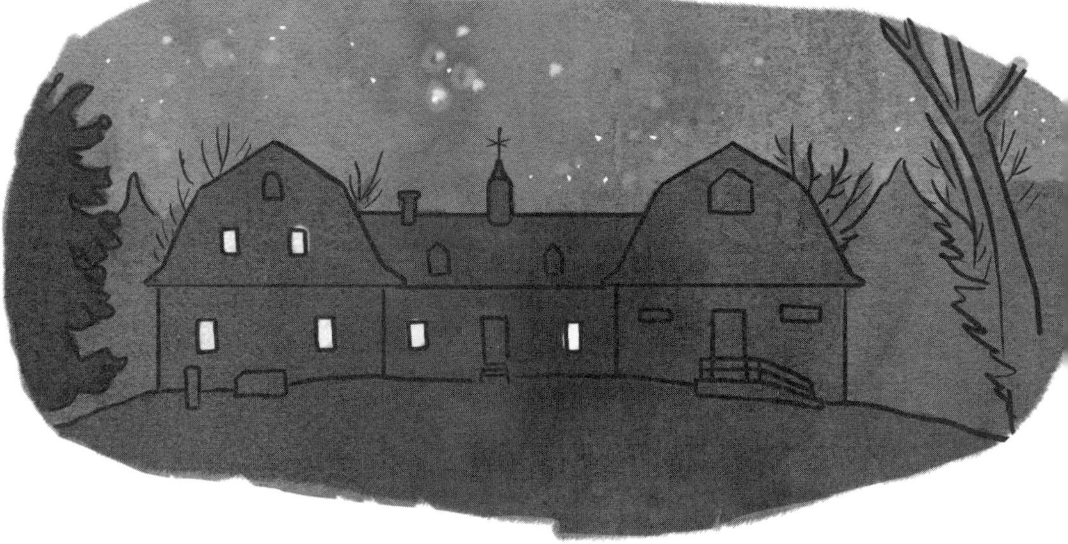

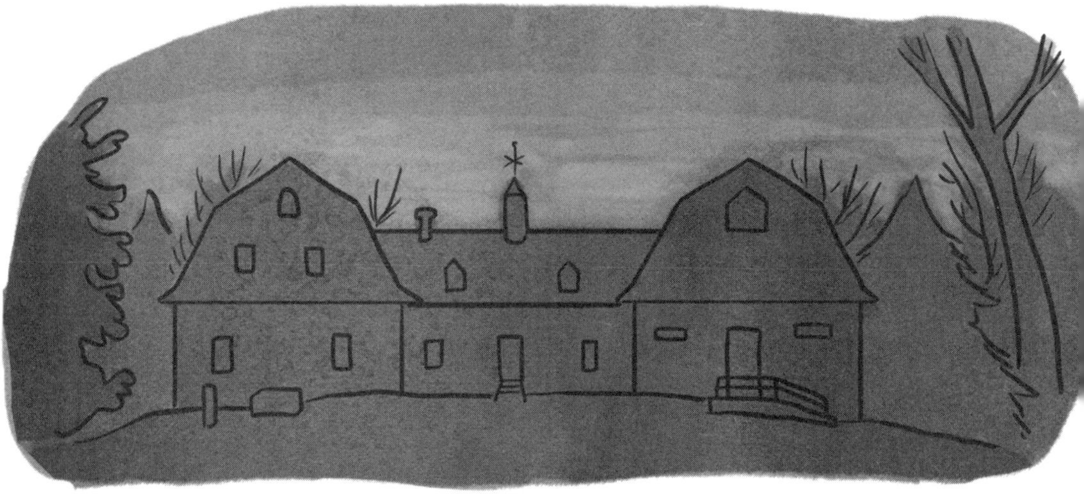

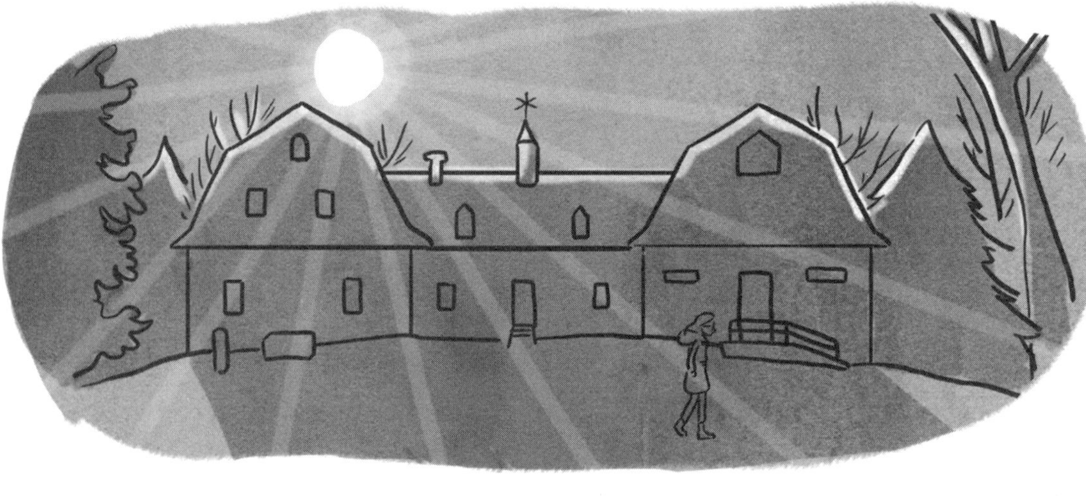

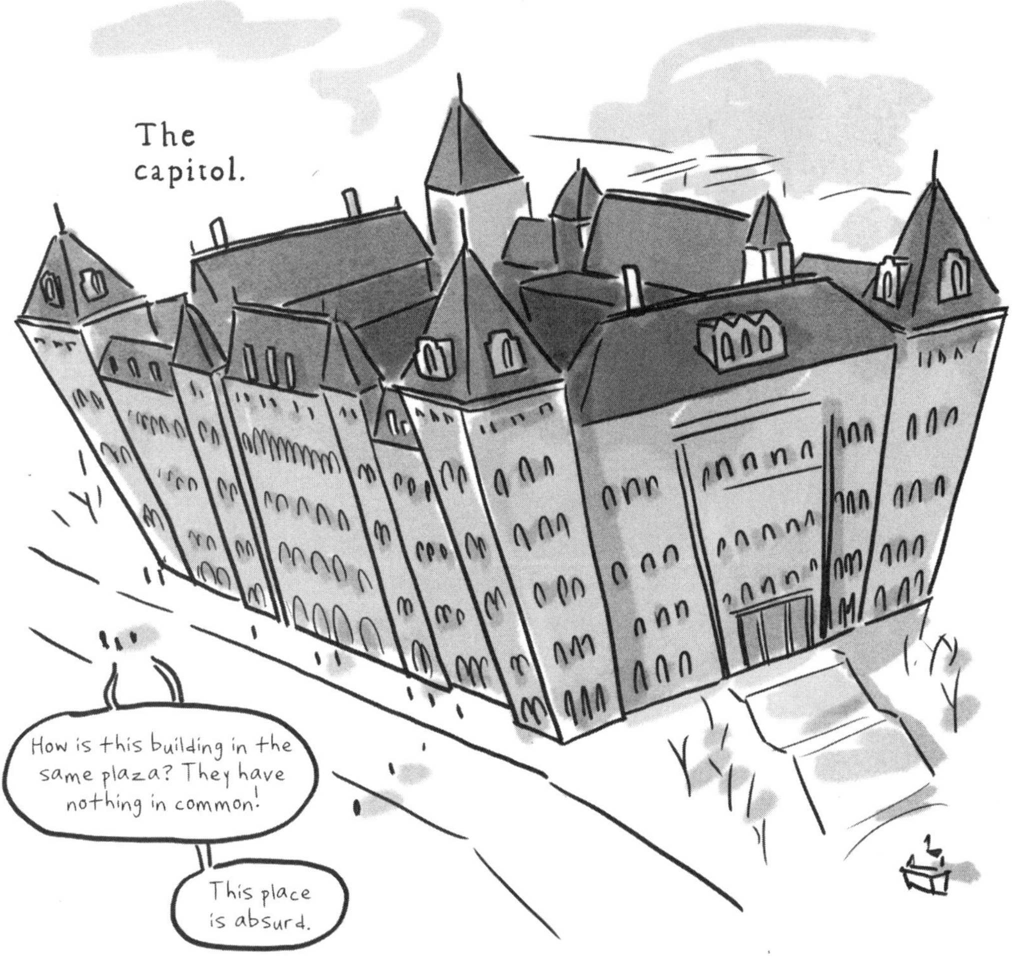
The capitol.
How is this building in the same plaza? They have nothing in common!
This place is absurd.

(Later, I looked up more about the building: how it was built by three different architects, and was the most expensive government building in its time. . .)

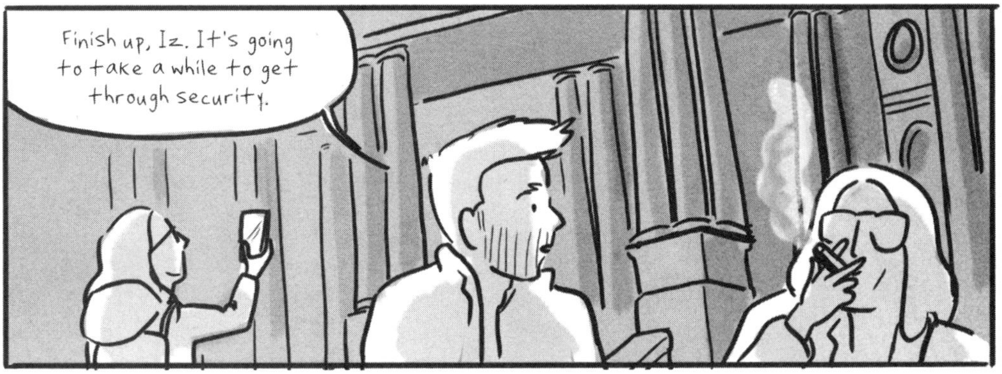
Finish up, Iz. It's going to take a while to get through security.

(. . . But that was later. For now, a few blurry pictures would have to do.)

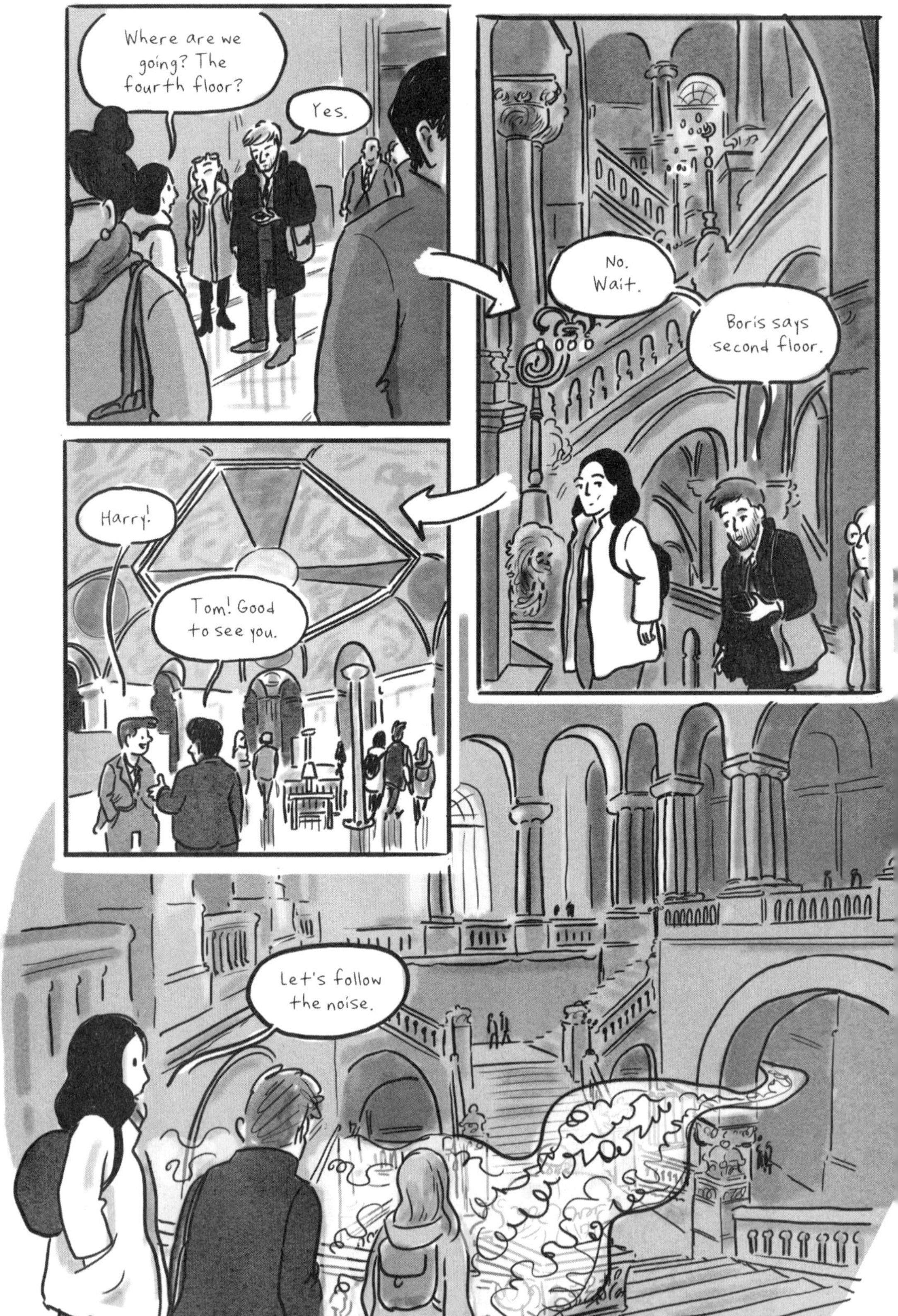
Where are we going? The fourth floor?
Yes.
No. Wait.
Boris says second floor.
Harry!
Tom! Good to see you.
Let's follow the noise.

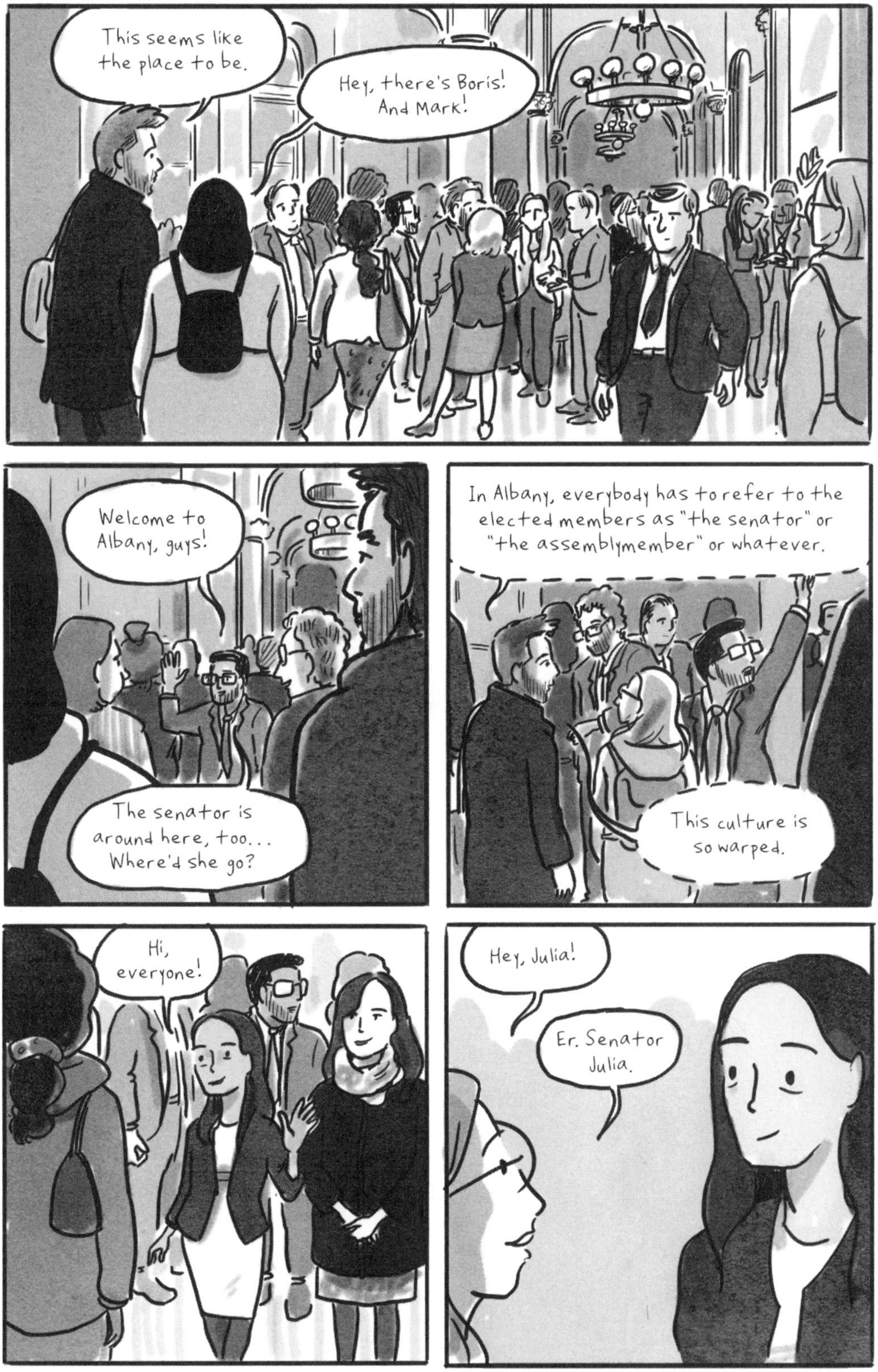
This seems like the place to be.
Hey, there's Boris! And Mark!
Welcome to Albany, guys!
The senator is around here, too... Where'd she go?
In Albany, everybody has to refer to the elected members as "the senator" or "the assemblymember" or whatever.
This culture is so warped.
Hi, everyone!
Hey, Julia!
Er. Senator Julia.

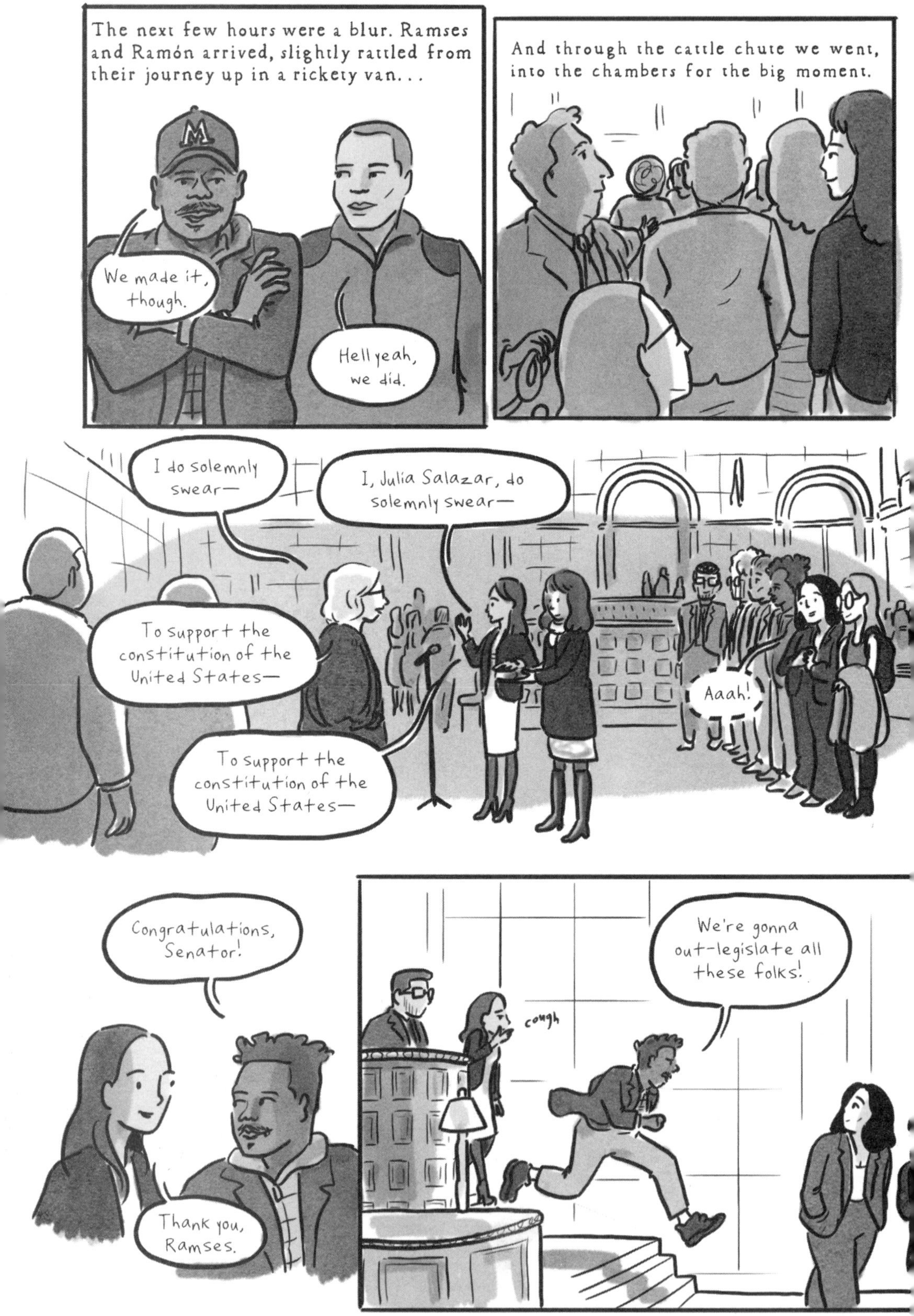
The next few hours were a blur. Ramses and Ramón arrived, slightly rattled from their journey up in a rickety van...
We made it, though.
Hell yeah, we did.
And through the cattle chute we went, into the chambers for the big moment.
I do solemnly swear—
I, Julia Salazar, do solemnly swear—
To support the constitution of the United States—
To support the constitution of the United States—
Aaah!
Congratulations, Senator!
Thank you, Ramses.
We're gonna out-legislate all these folks!
cough

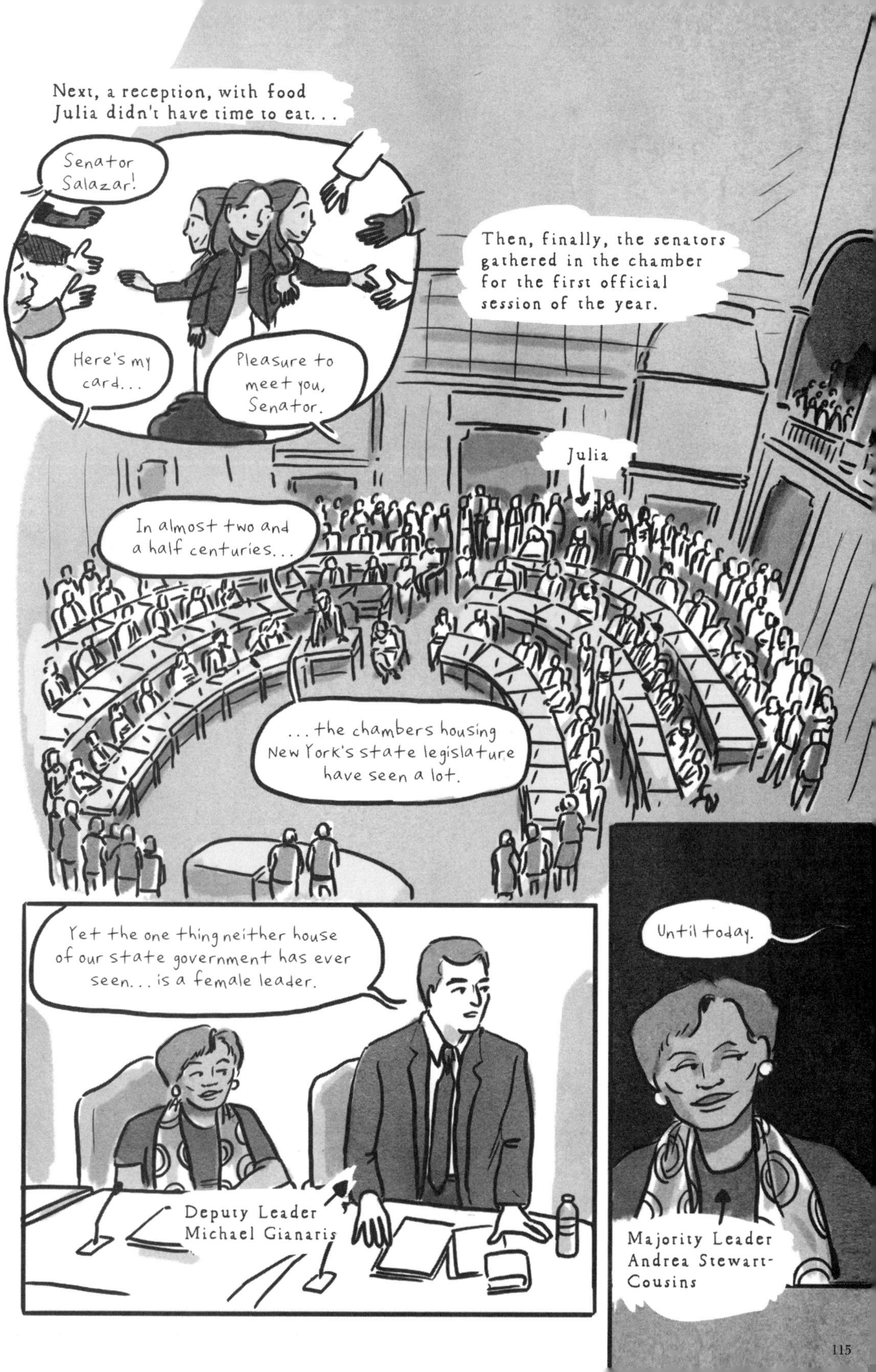

Next, a reception, with food Julia didn't have time to eat...
Senator Salazar!
Here's my card...
Pleasure to meet you, Senator.
Then, finally, the senators gathered in the chamber for the first official session of the year.
Julia
In almost two and a half centuries...
...the chambers housing New York's state legislature have seen a lot.
Yet the one thing neither house of our state government has ever seen... is a female leader.
Deputy Leader Michael Gianaris
Until today.
Majority Leader Andrea Stewart-Cousins

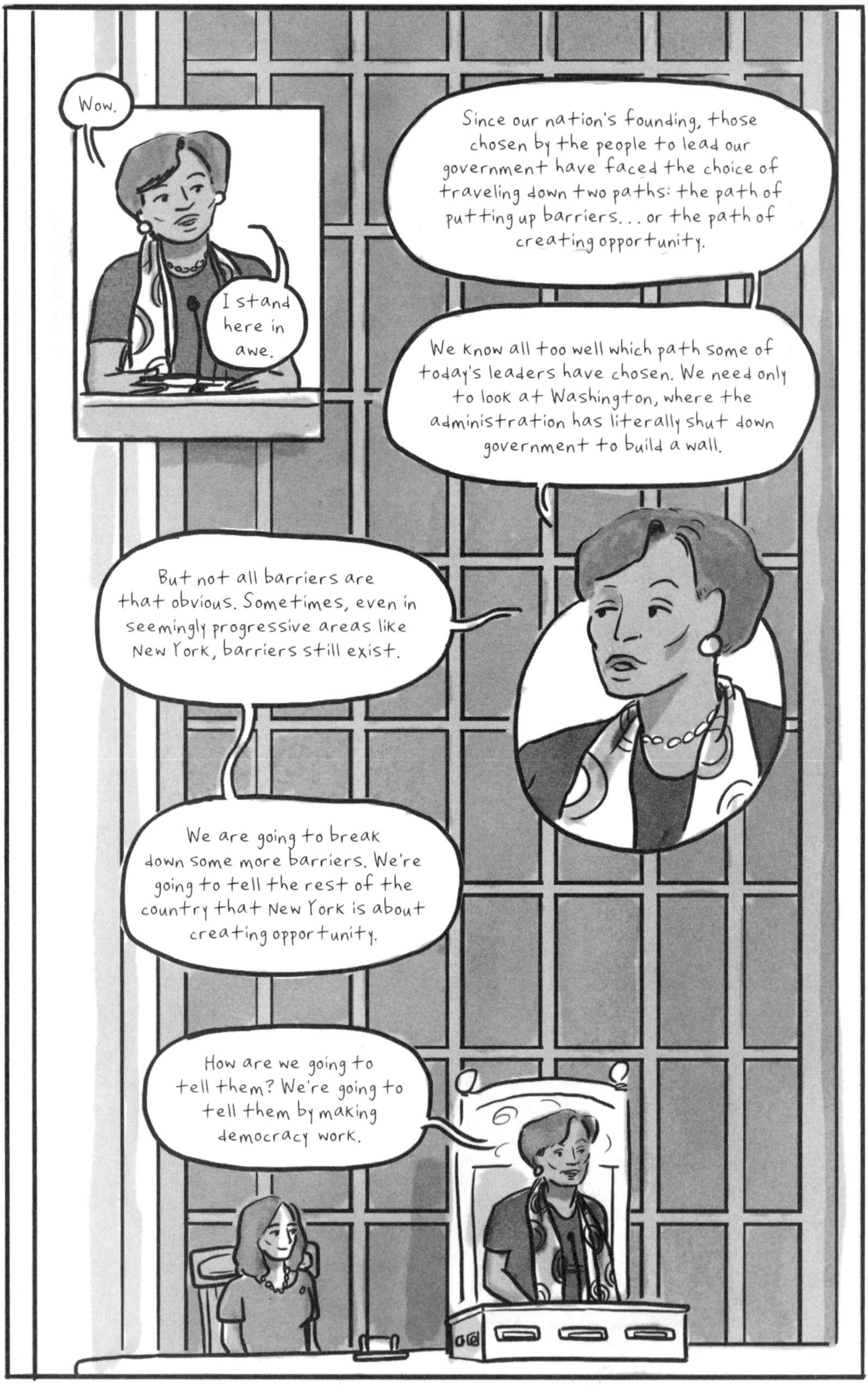
Wow.
I stand here in awe.
Since our nation's founding, those chosen by the people to lead our government have faced the choice of traveling down two paths: the path of putting up barriers... or the path of creating opportunity.
We know all too well which path some of today's leaders have chosen. We need only to look at Washington, where the administration has literally shut down government to build a wall.
But not all barriers are that obvious. Sometimes, even in seemingly progressive areas like New York, barriers still exist.
We are going to break down some more barriers. We're going to tell the rest of the country that New York is about creating opportunity.
How are we going to tell them? We're going to tell them by making democracy work.

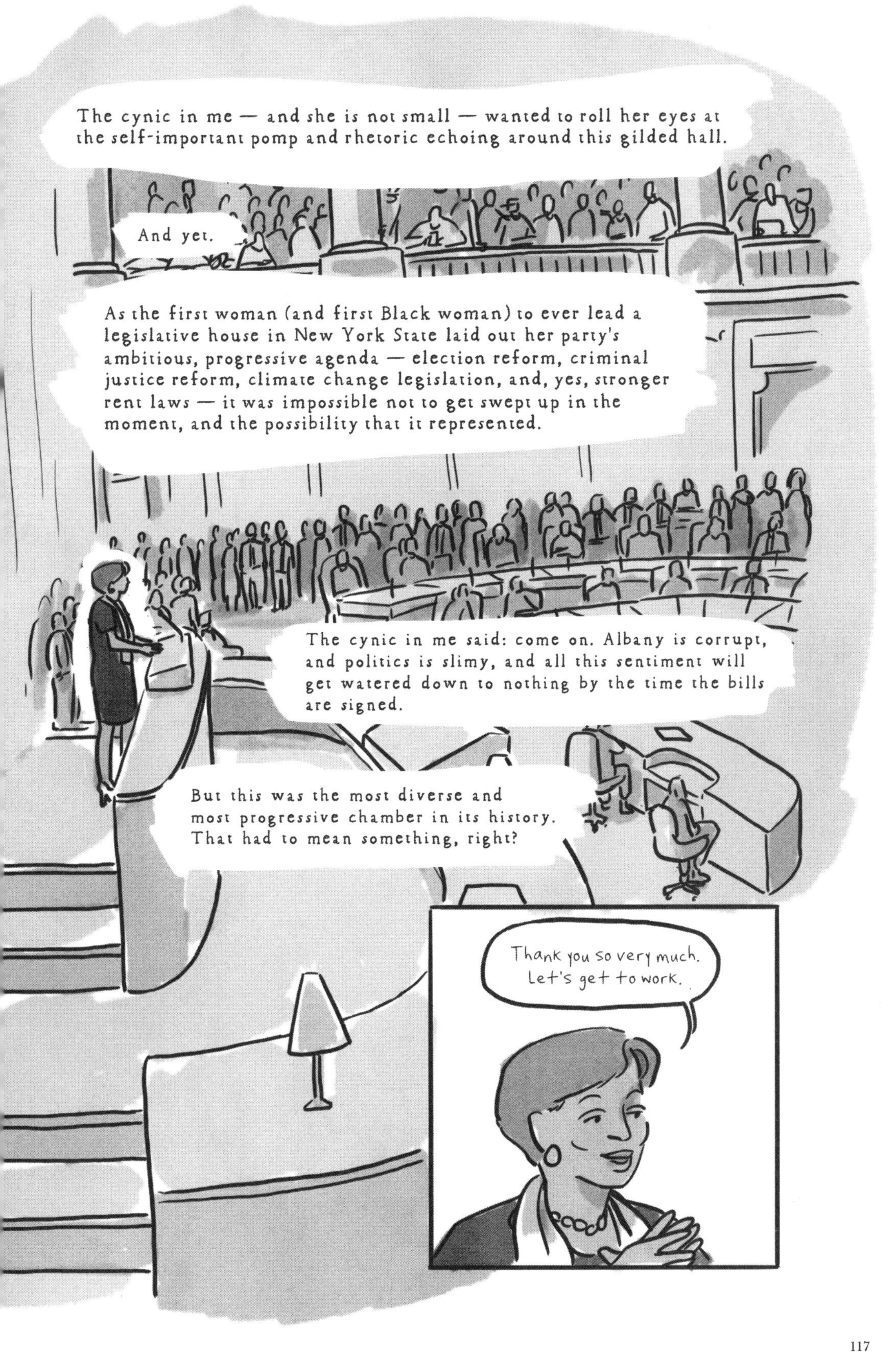
The cynic in me — and she is not small — wanted to roll her eyes at the self-important pomp and rhetoric echoing around this gilded hall.
And yet.
As the first woman (and first Black woman) to ever lead a legislative house in New York State laid out her party's ambitious, progressive agenda — election reform, criminal justice reform, climate change legislation, and, yes, stronger rent laws — it was impossible not to get swept up in the moment, and the possibility that it represented.
The cynic in me said: come on. Albany is corrupt, and politics is slimy, and all this sentiment will get watered down to nothing by the time the bills are signed.
But this was the most diverse and most progressive chamber in its history. That had to mean something, right?
Thank you so very much. Let's get to work.

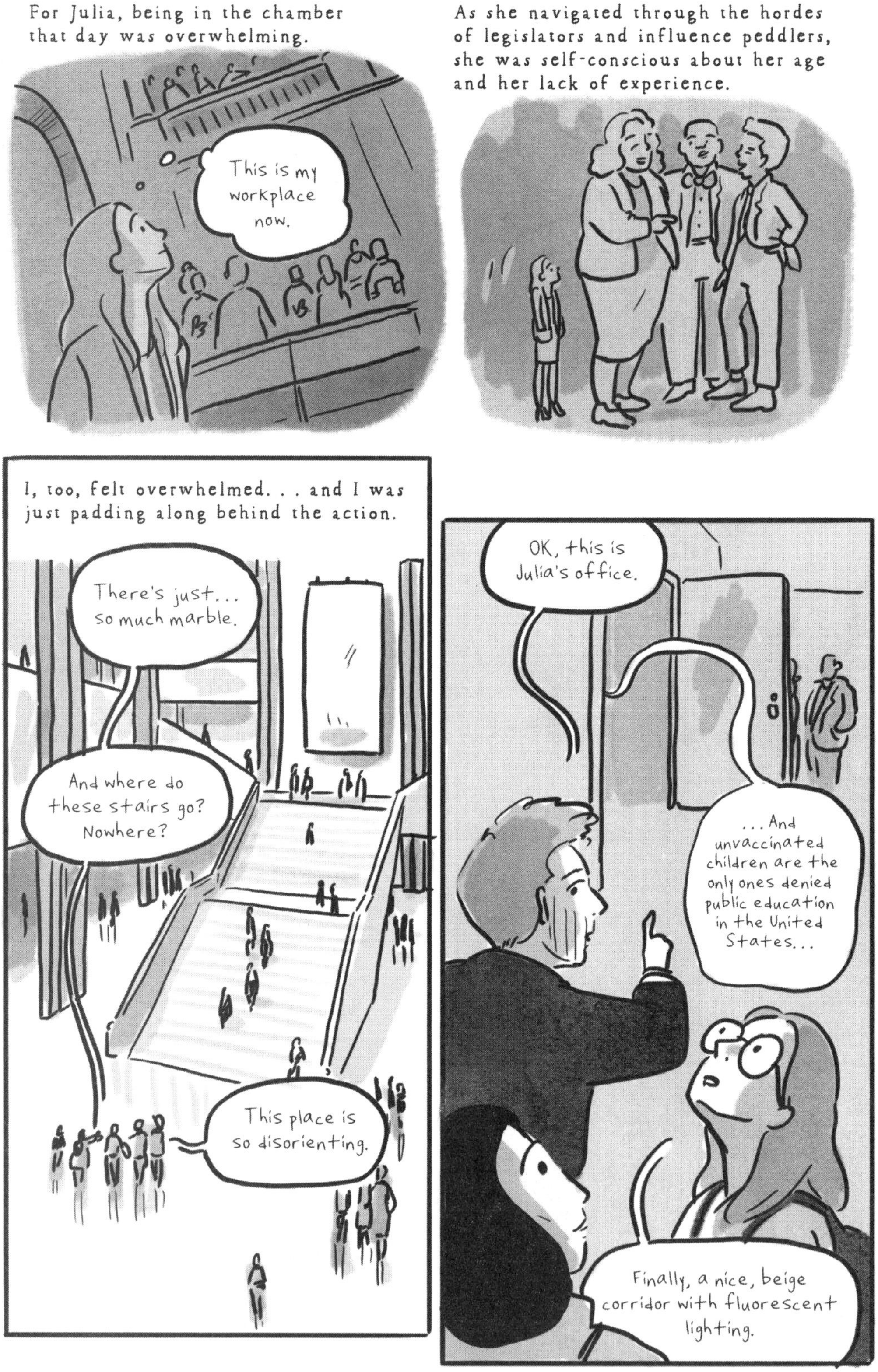
For Julia, being in the chamber that day was overwhelming.
This is my workplace now.
As she navigated through the hordes of legislators and influence peddlers, she was self-conscious about her age and her lack of experience.
I, too, felt overwhelmed. . . and I was just padding along behind the action.
There's just... so much marble.
And where do these stairs go? Nowhere?
This place is so disorienting.
OK, this is Julia's office.
...And unvaccinated children are the only ones denied public education in the United States...
Finally, a nice, beige corridor with fluorescent lighting.

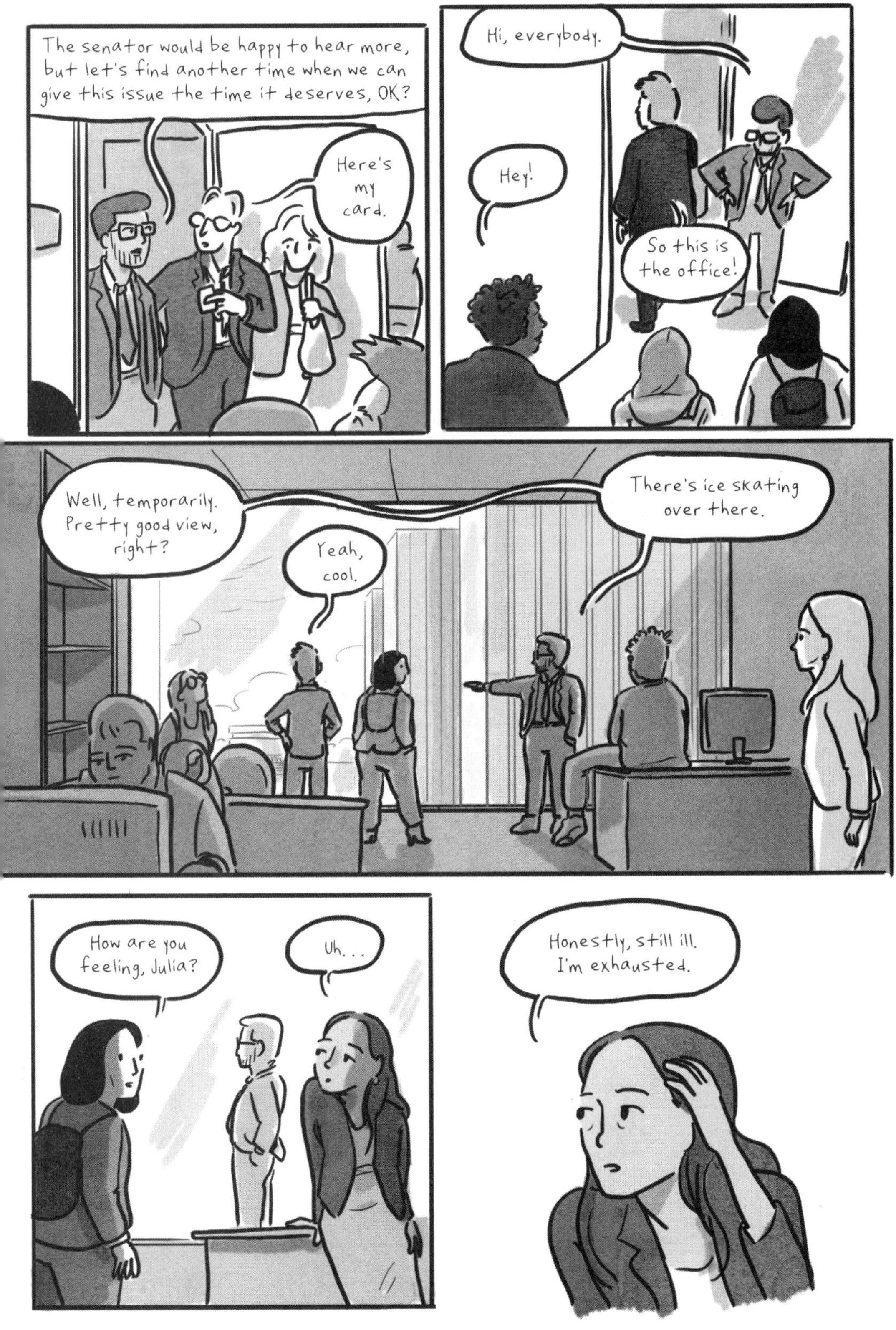
The senator would be happy to hear more, but let's find another time when we can give this issue the time it deserves, OK?
Here's my card.
Hi, everybody.
Hey!
So this is the office!
Well, temporarily. Pretty good view, right?
Yeah, cool.
There's ice skating over there.
How are you feeling, Julia?
Uh...
Honestly, still ill. I'm exhausted.

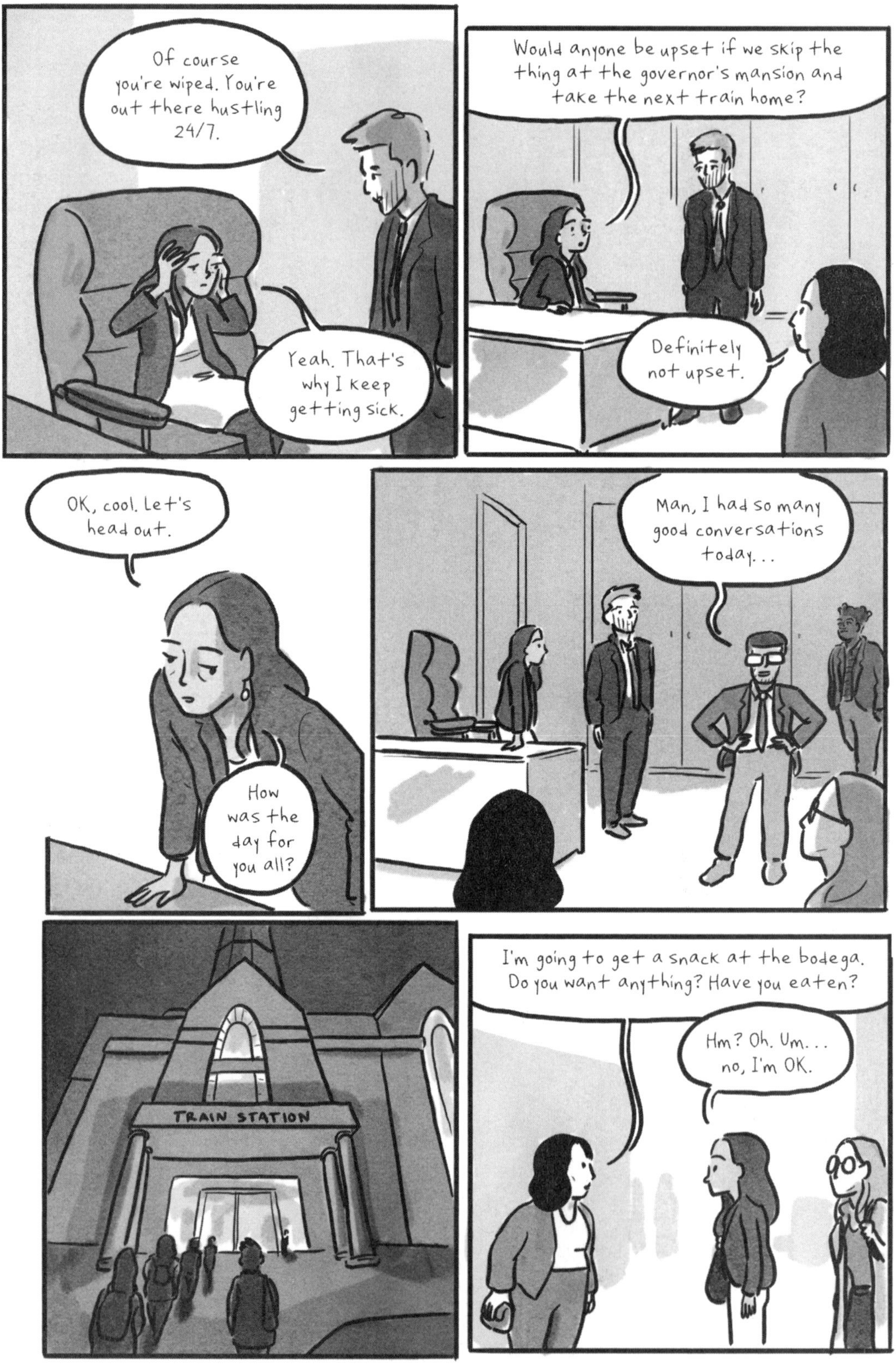
Of course you're wiped. You're out there hustling 24/7.
Yeah. That's why I keep getting sick.
Would anyone be upset if we skip the thing at the governor's mansion and take the next train home?
Definitely not upset.
OK, cool. Let's head out.
How was the day for you all?
Man, I had so many good conversations today...
TRAIN STATION
I'm going to get a snack at the bodega. Do you want anything? Have you eaten?
Hm? Oh. Um... no, I'm OK.

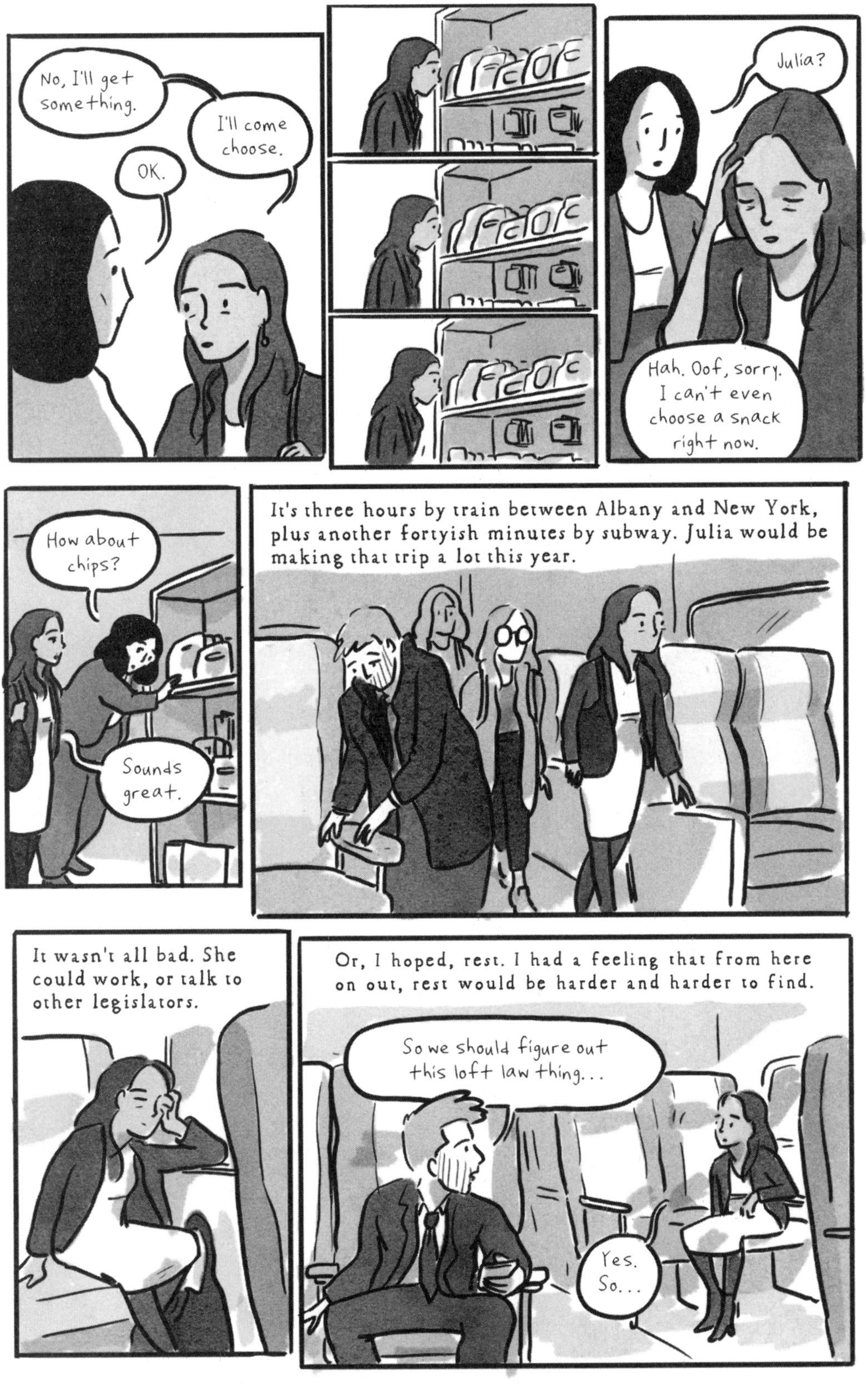

No, I'll get something.
I'll come choose.
OK.
Julia?
Hah. Oof, sorry. I can't even choose a snack right now.
How about chips?
Sounds great.
It's three hours by train between Albany and New York, plus another fortyish minutes by subway. Julia would be making that trip a lot this year.
It wasn't all bad. She could work, or talk to other legislators.
Or, I hoped, rest. I had a feeling that from here on out, rest would be harder and harder to find.
So we should figure out this loft law thing...
Yes. So...

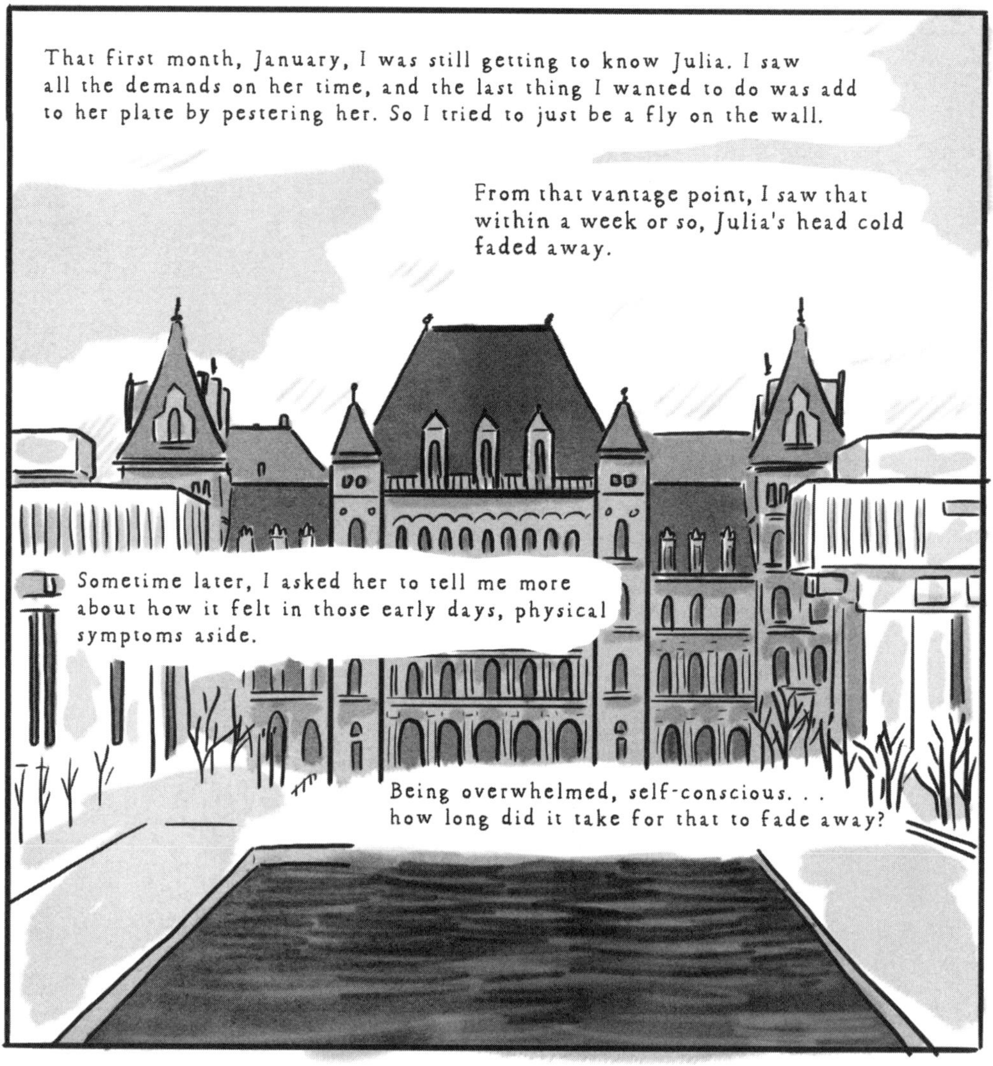
That first month, January, I was still getting to know Julia. I saw all the demands on her time, and the last thing I wanted to do was add to her plate by pestering her. So I tried to just be a fly on the wall.
From that vantage point, I saw that within a week or so, Julia's head cold faded away.
Sometime later, I asked her to tell me more about how it felt in those early days, physical symptoms aside.
Being overwhelmed, self-conscious. . . how long did it take for that to fade away?

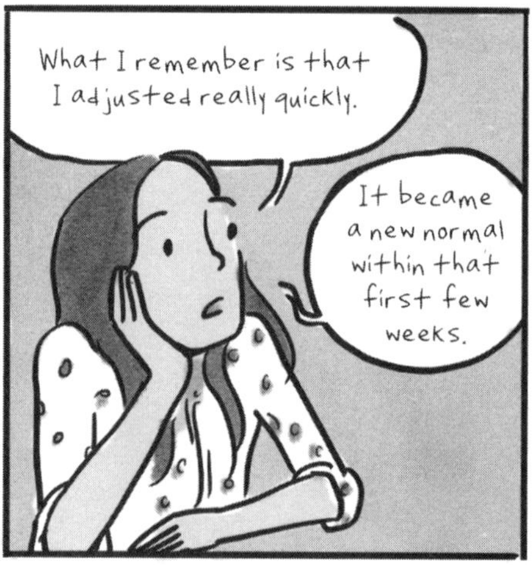
What I remember is that I adjusted really quickly.
It became a new normal within that first few weeks.

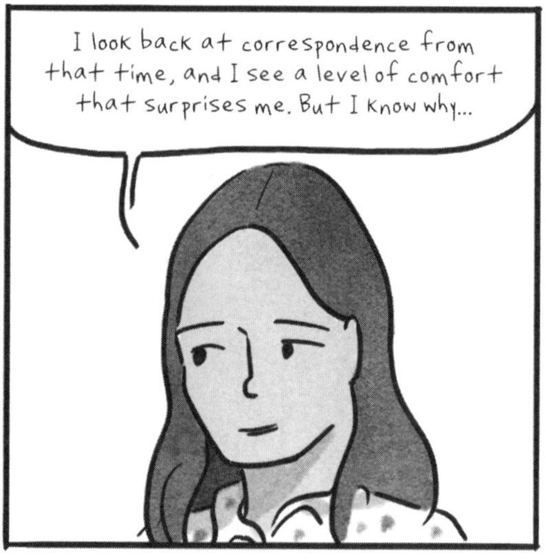
I look back at correspondence from that time, and I see a level of comfort that surprises me. But I know why...

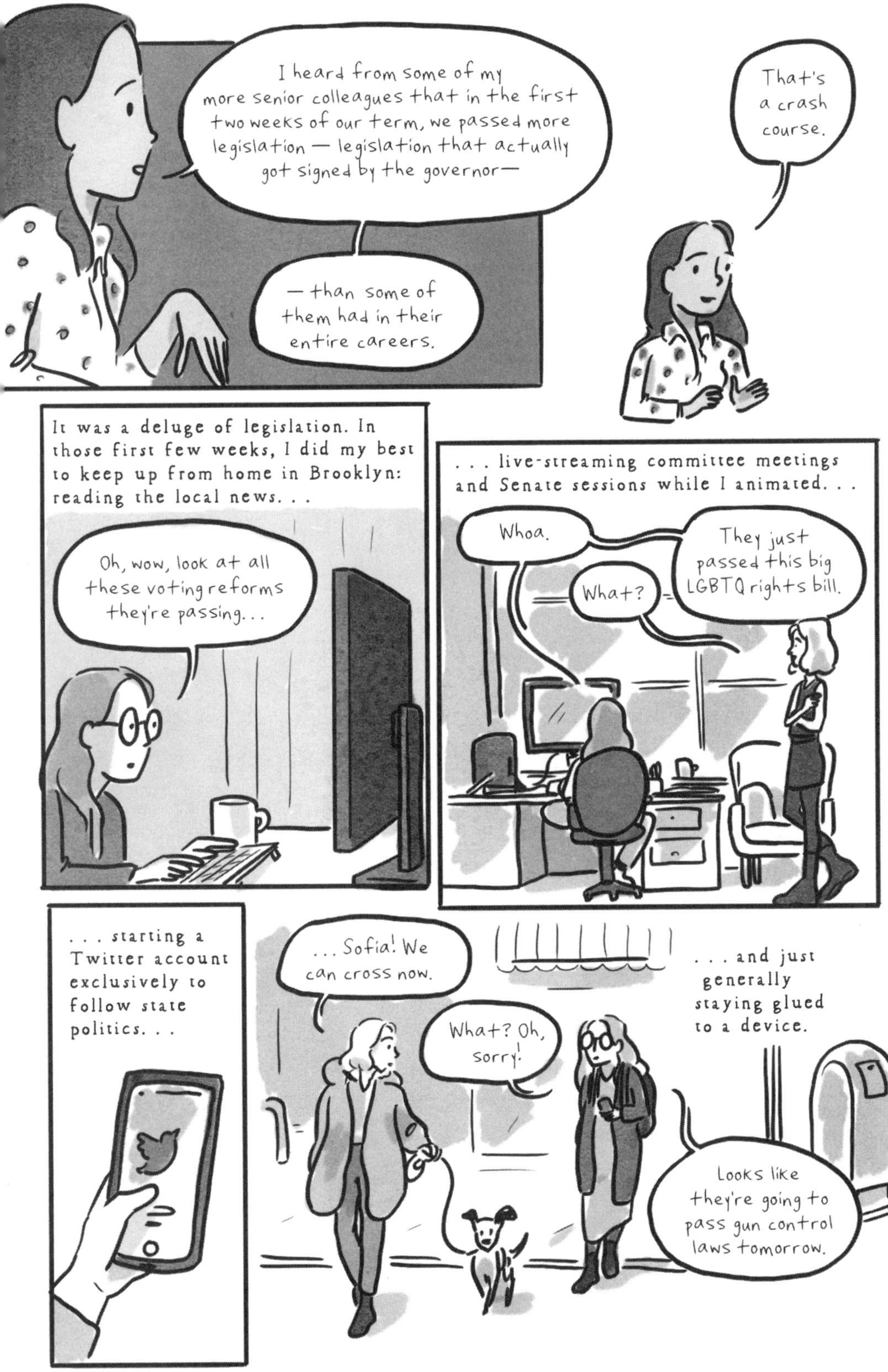
I heard from some of my more senior colleagues that in the first two weeks of our term, we passed more legislation — legislation that actually got signed by the governor—
— than some of them had in their entire careers.
That's a crash course.
It was a deluge of legislation. In those first few weeks, I did my best to keep up from home in Brooklyn: reading the local news. . .
Oh, wow, look at all these voting reforms they're passing. . .
. . . live-streaming committee meetings and Senate sessions while I animated. . .
Whoa.
What?
They just passed this big LGBTQ rights bill.
. . . starting a Twitter account exclusively to follow state politics. . .
. . . Sofia! We can cross now.
What? Oh, sorry!
. . . and just generally staying glued to a device.
Looks like they're going to pass gun control laws tomorrow.

You're getting pretty deep into this, huh?

Well, it's just that a lot is happening really fast and it's hard to keep up.

Yes, hello, Birdie.

My friend Hanna

My friend Birdie

It's like there's been this logjam of progressive bills for the past decade or more...

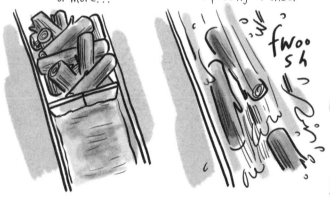

...And now they've just opened the dam. Everything is passing at once.

fwoosh

Doesn't it usually take forever to get through committee and all that? That's what I remember from Schoolhouse Rock.

♪ "I'm just a bill, yeah, I'm only a bill..."

What a banger.

I guess because these bills have been kicking around Albany for years, all the debates have already been had. And the Assembly has already passed them all so many times.

So even though these are big, consequential bills — like, for example, campaign finance reform — there's actually not a lot of conflict getting them passed.

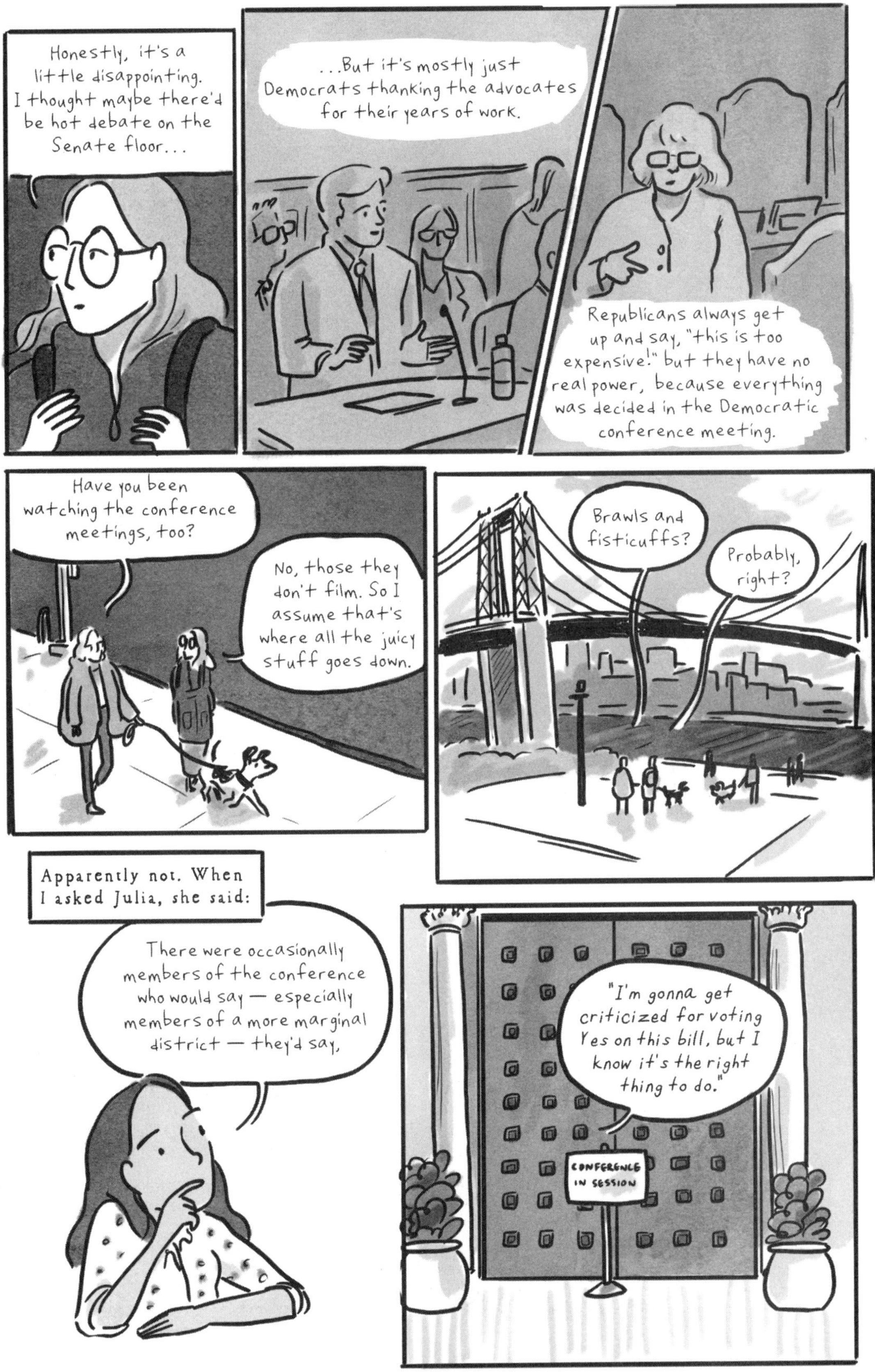

Honestly, it's a little disappointing. I thought maybe there'd be hot debate on the Senate floor...
...But it's mostly just Democrats thanking the advocates for their years of work.
Republicans always get up and say, "this is too expensive!" but they have no real power, because everything was decided in the Democratic conference meeting.
Have you been watching the conference meetings, too?
No, those they don't film. So I assume that's where all the juicy stuff goes down.
Brawls and fisticuffs?
Probably, right?
Apparently not. When I asked Julia, she said:
There were occasionally members of the conference who would say — especially members of a more marginal district — they'd say,
"I'm gonna get criticized for voting Yes on this bill, but I know it's the right thing to do."
CONFERENCE IN SESSION

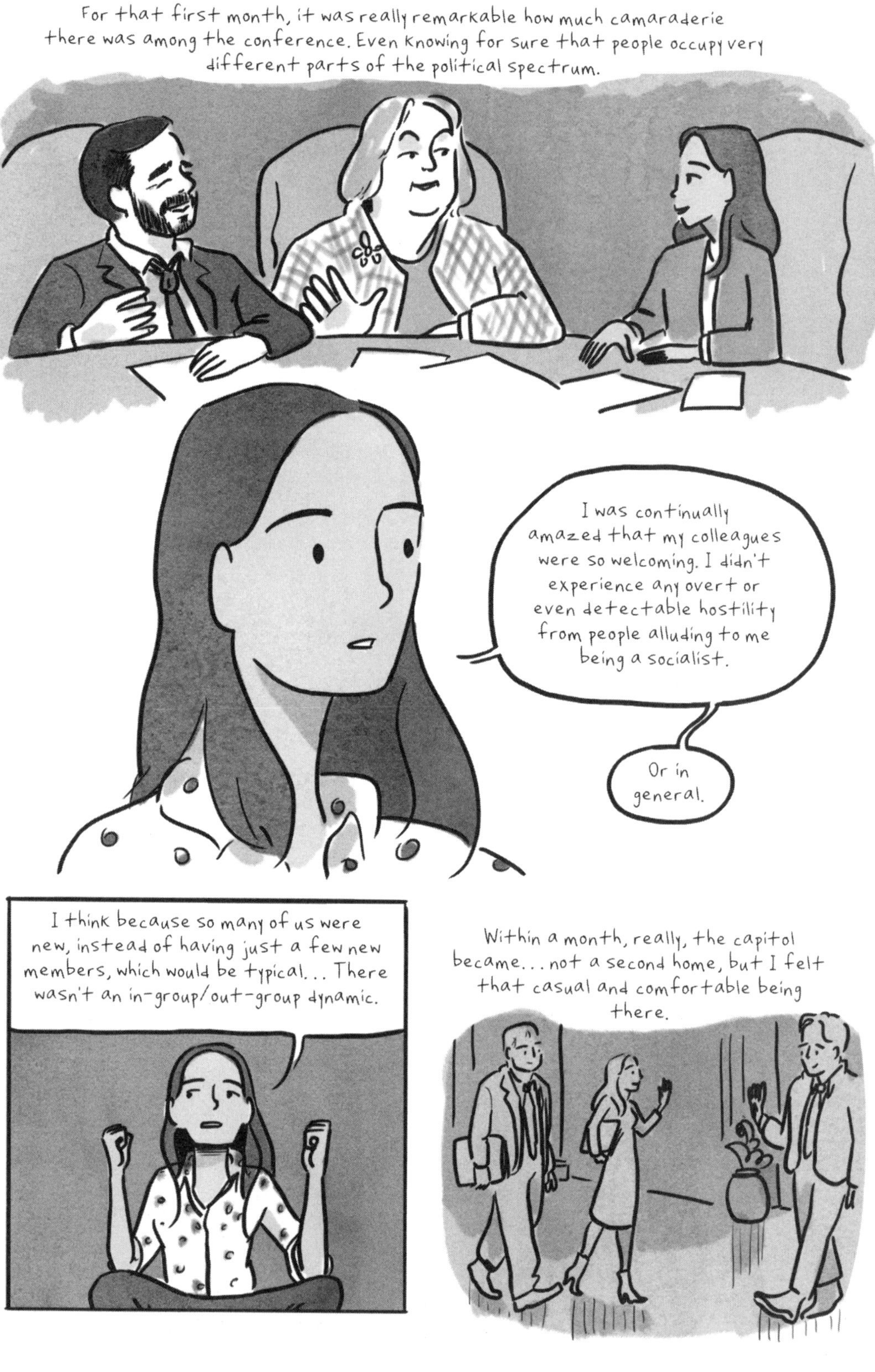
For that first month, it was really remarkable how much camaraderie there was among the conference. Even knowing for sure that people occupy very different parts of the political spectrum.
I was continually amazed that my colleagues were so welcoming. I didn't experience any overt or even detectable hostility from people alluding to me being a socialist.
Or in general.
I think because so many of us were new, instead of having just a few new members, which would be typical... There wasn't an in-group/out-group dynamic.
Within a month, really, the capitol became... not a second home, but I felt that casual and comfortable being there.

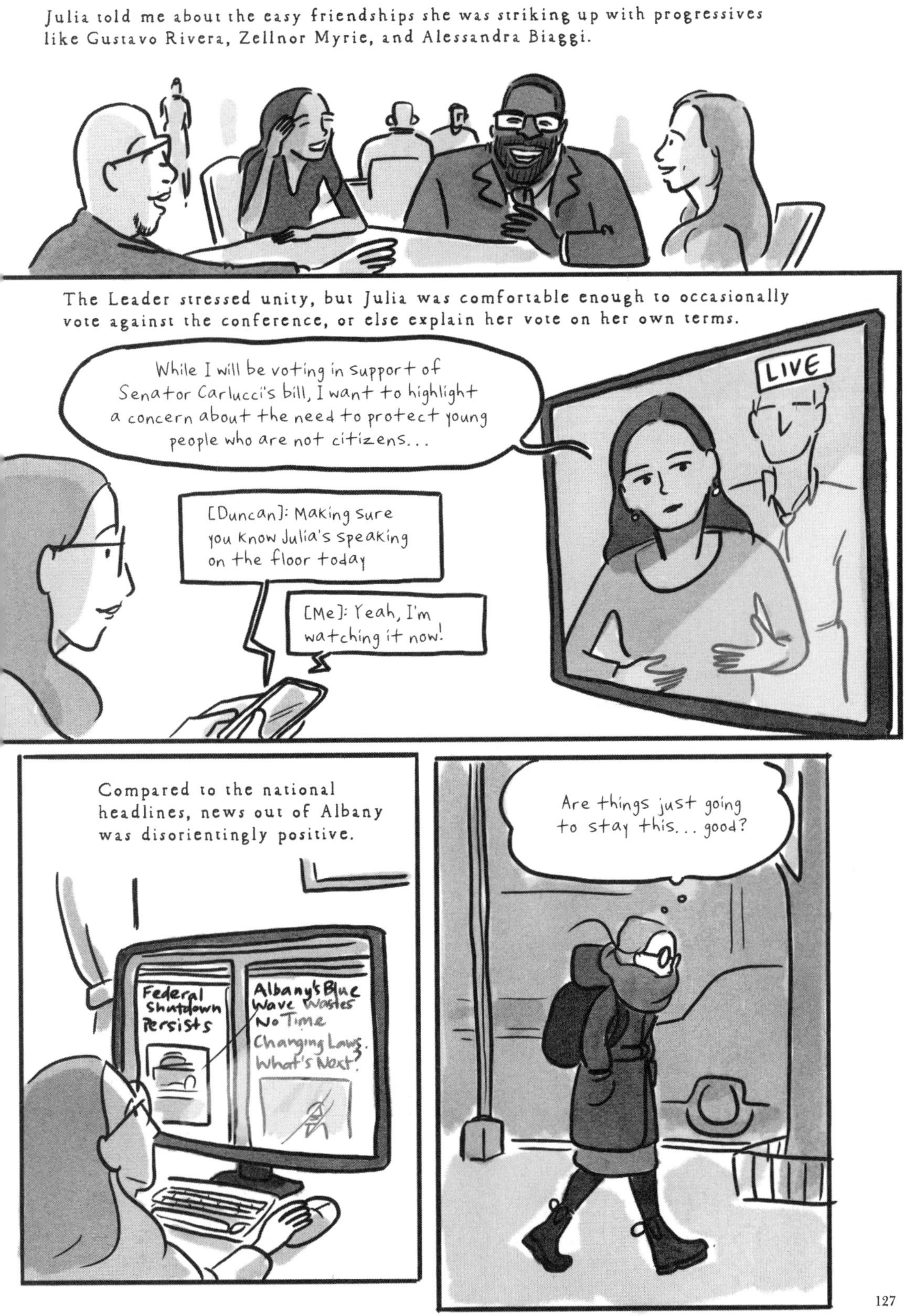
Julia told me about the easy friendships she was striking up with progressives like Gustavo Rivera, Zellnor Myrie, and Alessandra Biaggi.
The Leader stressed unity, but Julia was comfortable enough to occasionally vote against the conference, or else explain her vote on her own terms.
While I will be voting in support of Senator Carlucci's bill, I want to highlight a concern about the need to protect young people who are not citizens...
LIVE
[Duncan]: Making sure you know Julia's speaking on the floor today
[Me]: Yeah, I'm watching it now!
Compared to the national headlines, news out of Albany was disorientingly positive.
Federal Shutdown Persists
Albany's Blue Wave Wastes No Time Changing Laws. What's Next?
Are things just going to stay this... good?

Chapter Five

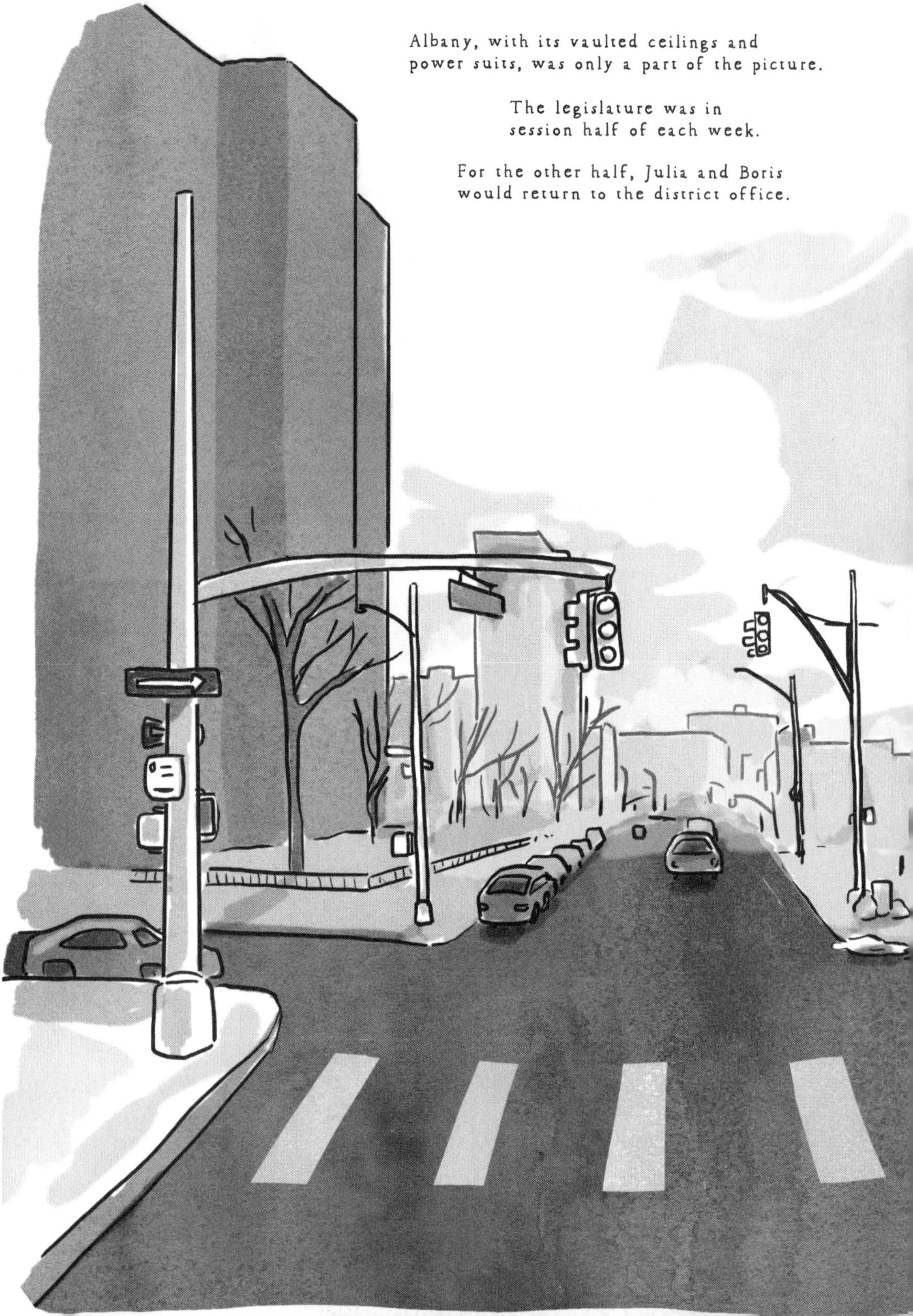

Albany, with its vaulted ceilings and power suits, was only a part of the picture.
The legislature was in session half of each week.
For the other half, Julia and Boris would return to the district office.

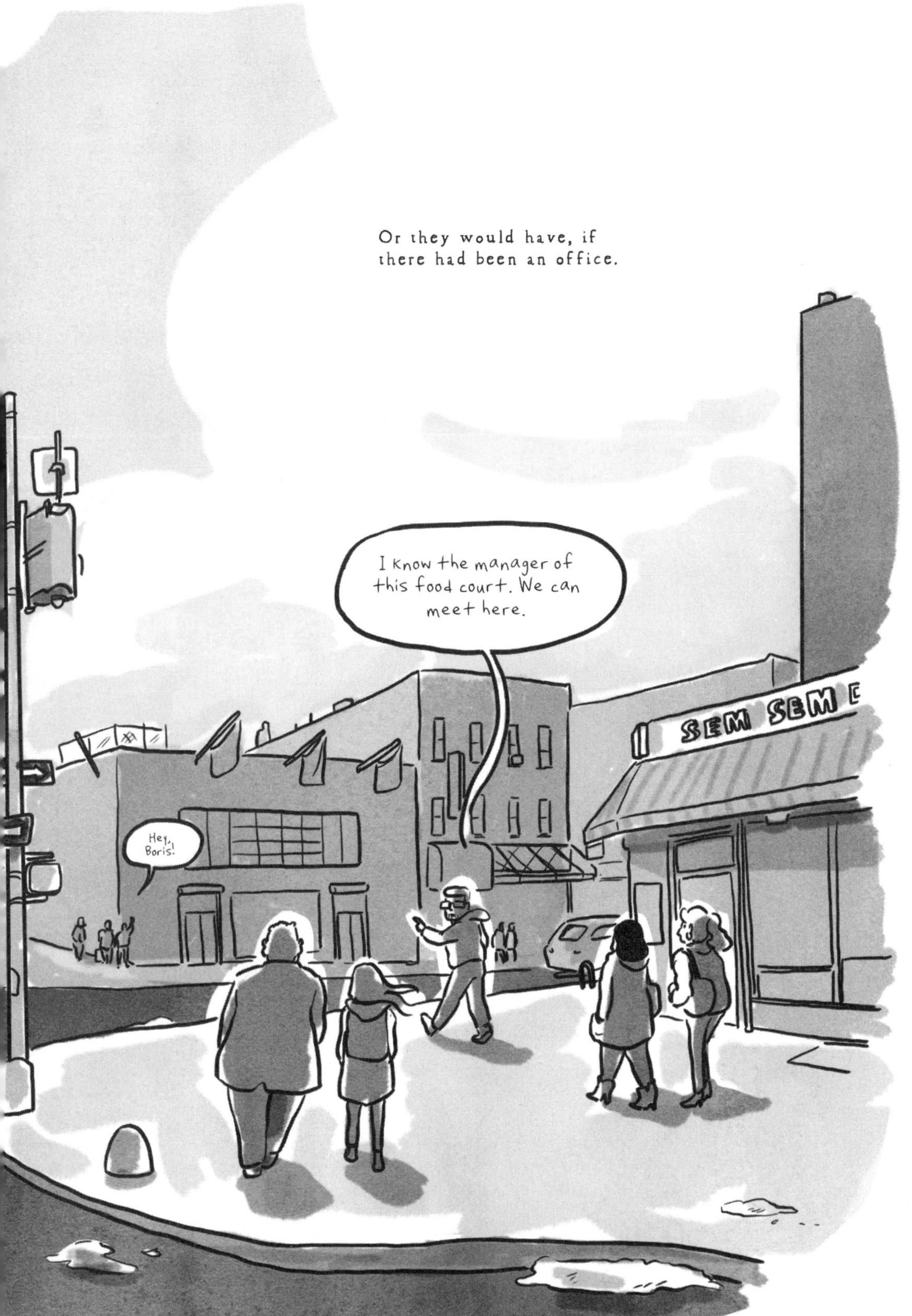
Or they would have, if
there had been an office.
I know the manager of
this food court. We can
meet here.
Hey,
Boris!
SEM SEM

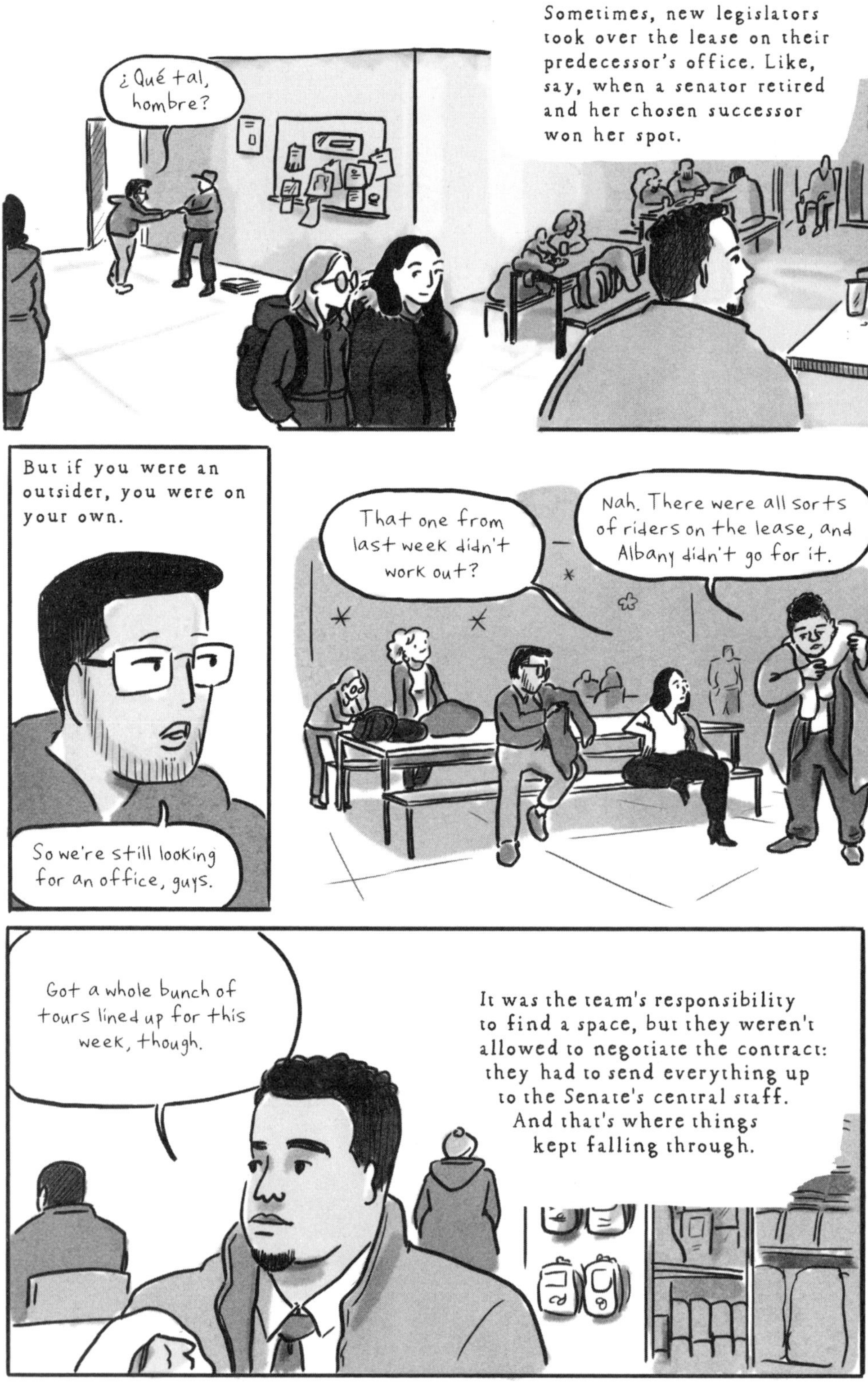
¿Qué tal, hombre?
Sometimes, new legislators took over the lease on their predecessor's office. Like, say, when a senator retired and her chosen successor won her spot.
But if you were an outsider, you were on your own.
So we're still looking for an office, guys.
That one from last week didn't work out?
Nah. There were all sorts of riders on the lease, and Albany didn't go for it.
Got a whole bunch of tours lined up for this week, though.
It was the team's responsibility to find a space, but they weren't allowed to negotiate the contract: they had to send everything up to the Senate's central staff. And that's where things kept falling through.

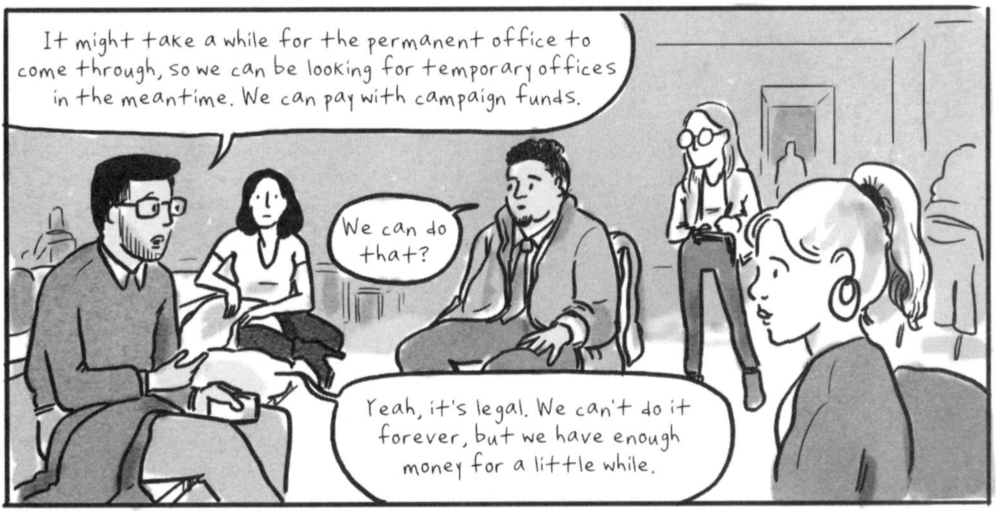
It might take a while for the permanent office to come through, so we can be looking for temporary offices in the meantime. We can pay with campaign funds.
We can do that?
Yeah, it's legal. We can't do it forever, but we have enough money for a little while.

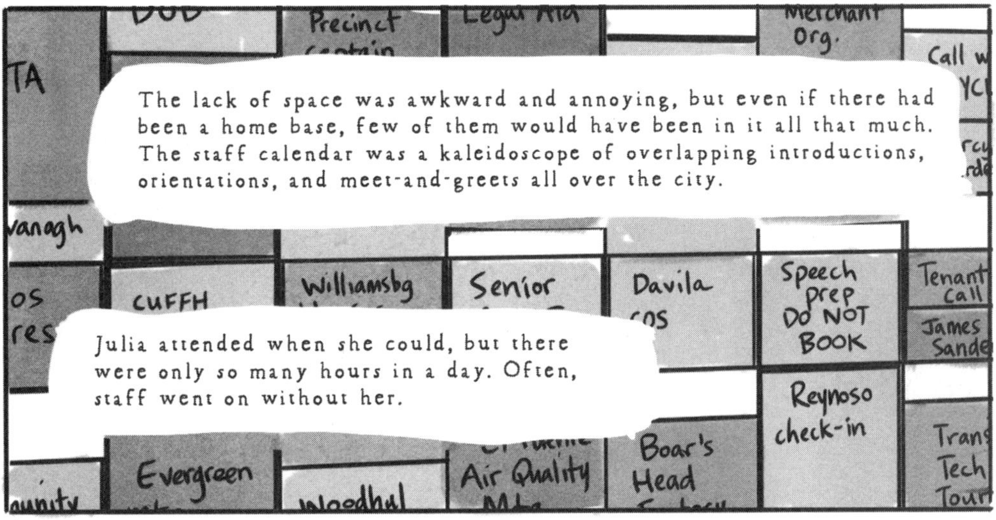
Precinct
Org.
The lack of space was awkward and annoying, but even if there had been a home base, few of them would have been in it all that much. The staff calendar was a kaleidoscope of overlapping introductions, orientations, and meet-and-greets all over the city.
CUFFH
Williamsbg
Senior
Davila
Speech prep DO NOT BOOK
Tenant call
Julia attended when she could, but there were only so many hours in a day. Often, staff went on without her.
Reynoso check-in
Evergreen
Air Quality
Boar's Head

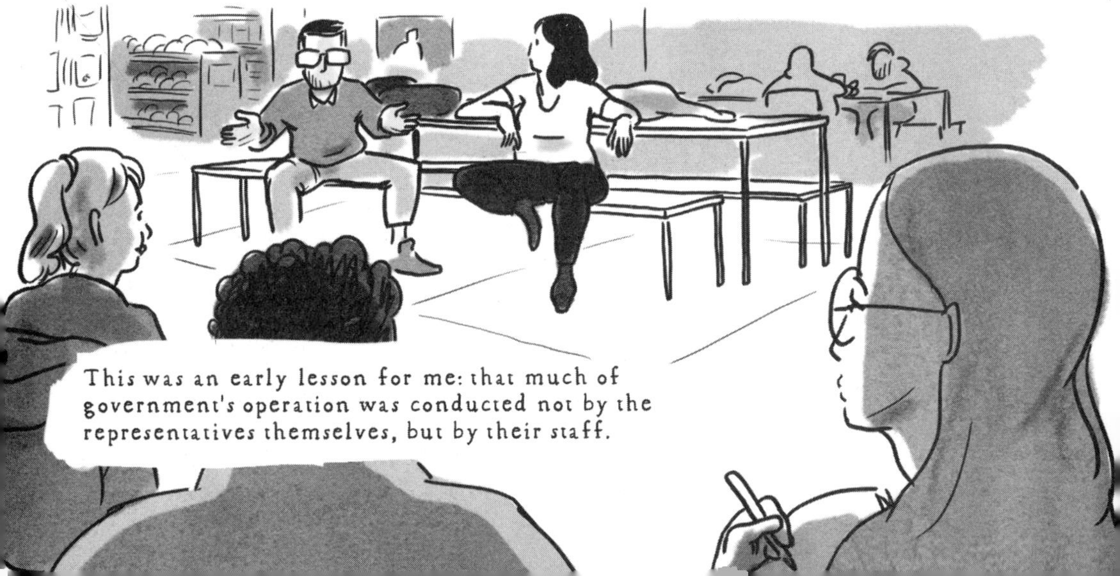
This was an early lesson for me: that much of government's operation was conducted not by the representatives themselves, but by their staff.

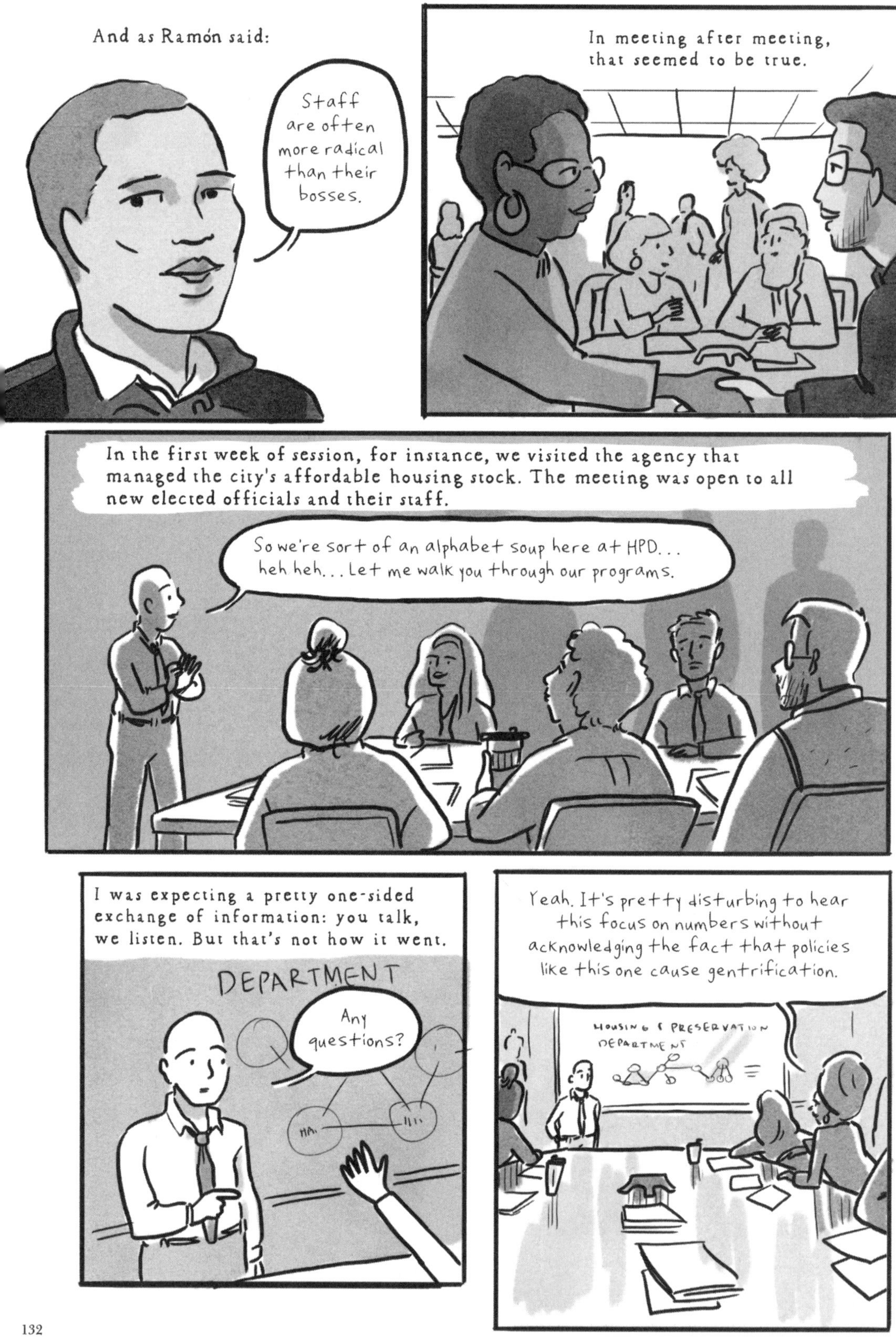
And as Ramón said:
Staff are often more radical than their bosses.
In meeting after meeting, that seemed to be true.
In the first week of session, for instance, we visited the agency that managed the city's affordable housing stock. The meeting was open to all new elected officials and their staff.
So we're sort of an alphabet soup here at HPD... heh heh... Let me walk you through our programs.
I was expecting a pretty one-sided exchange of information: you talk, we listen. But that's not how it went.
DEPARTMENT
Any questions?
Yeah. It's pretty disturbing to hear this focus on numbers without acknowledging the fact that policies like this one cause gentrification.
HOUSING & PRESERVATION DEPARTMENT

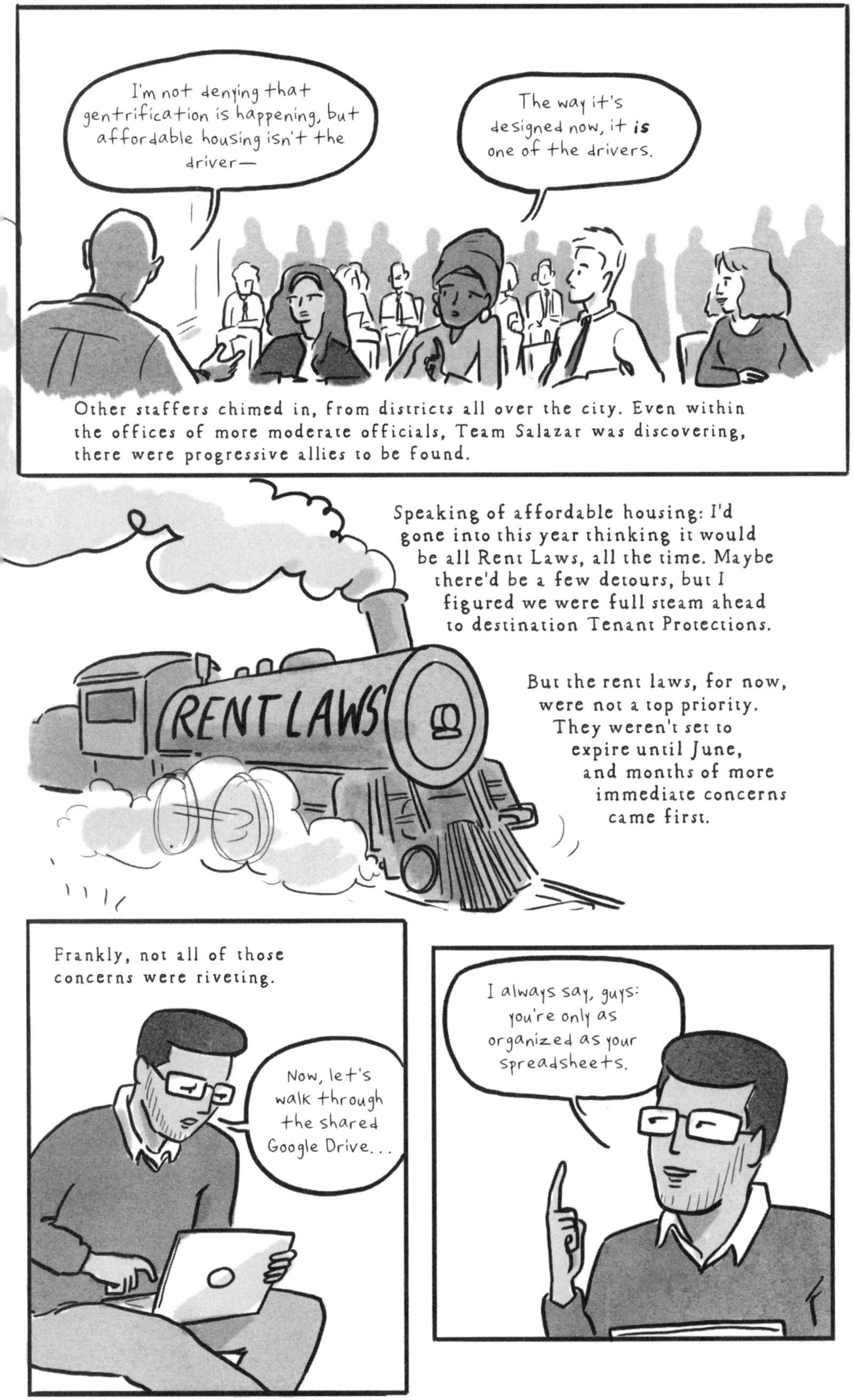
I'm not denying that gentrification is happening, but affordable housing isn't the driver—
The way it's designed now, it **is** one of the drivers.
Other staffers chimed in, from districts all over the city. Even within the offices of more moderate officials, Team Salazar was discovering, there were progressive allies to be found.
Speaking of affordable housing: I'd gone into this year thinking it would be all Rent Laws, all the time. Maybe there'd be a few detours, but I figured we were full steam ahead to destination Tenant Protections.
RENT LAWS
But the rent laws, for now, were not a top priority. They weren't set to expire until June, and months of more immediate concerns came first.
Frankly, not all of those concerns were riveting.
Now, let's walk through the shared Google Drive...
I always say, guys: you're only as organized as your spreadsheets.

And some concerns were just disparate. On any given day, the district staff were literally all over the place:

Connecting a constituent with legal representation for a worker's comp case

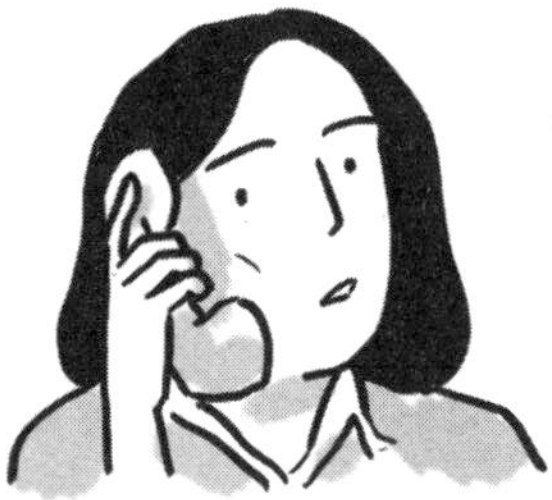

Touring potential office spaces

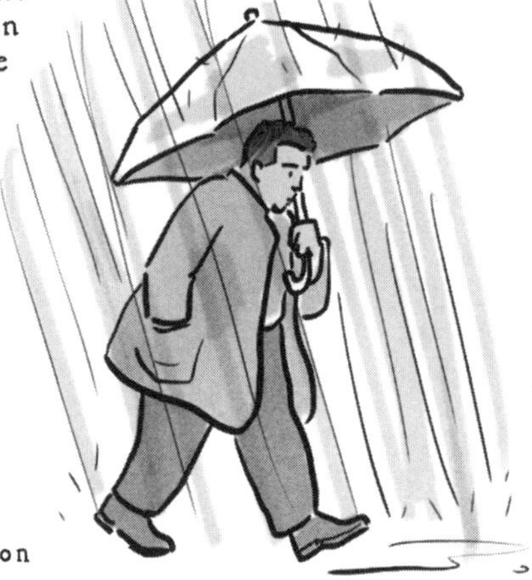

Researching recycling legislation

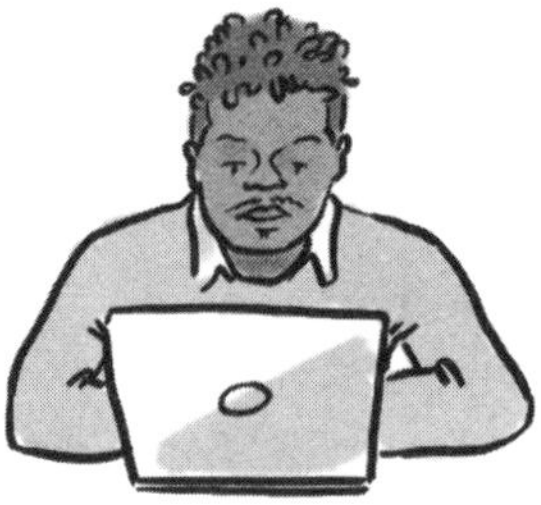

Talking to the taxi union

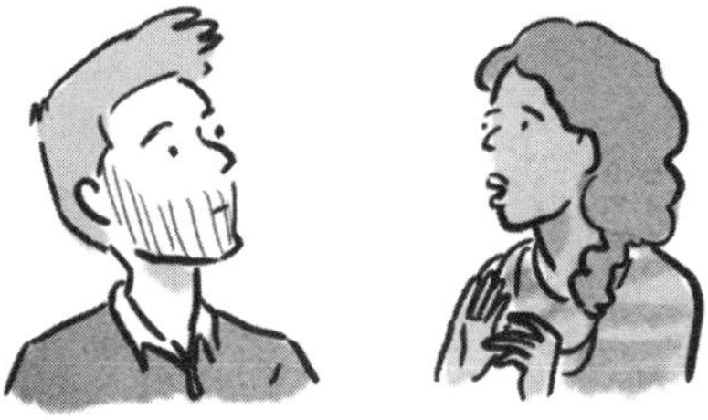

Meeting with the head of a local merchants' organization

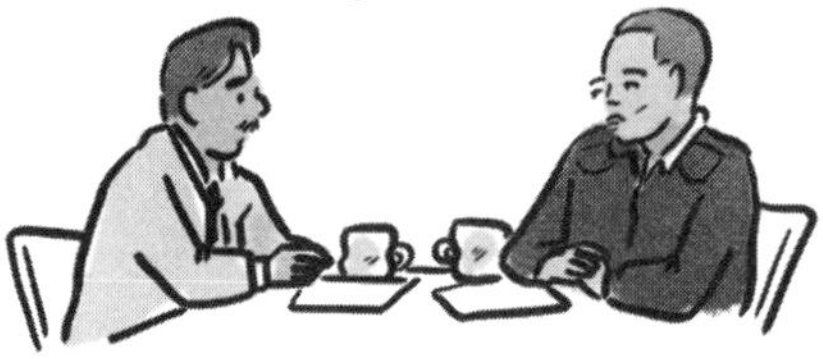

Discussing resource needs with the principal of a local high school

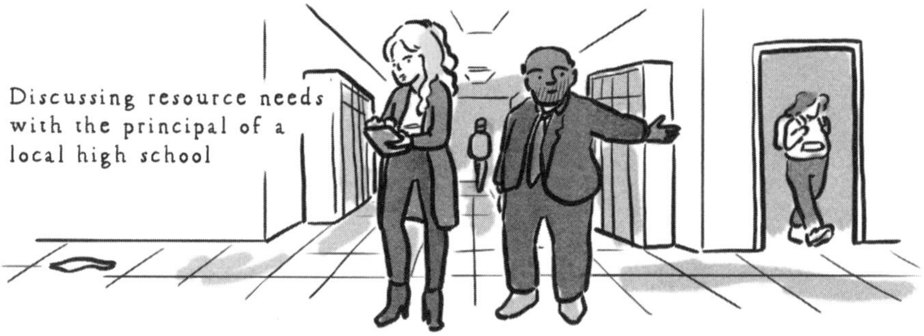

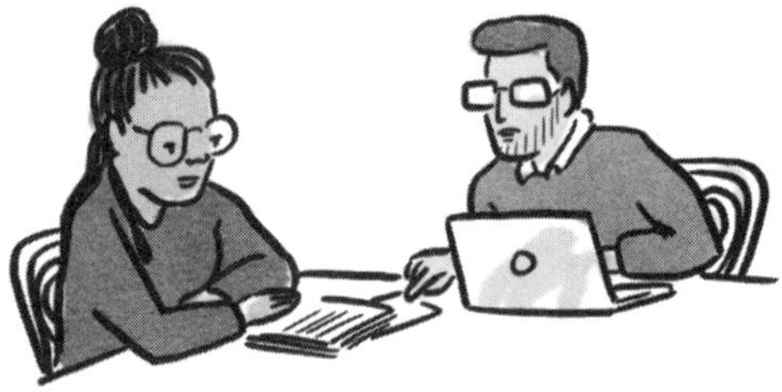

Sitting down with local non-profits about upcoming budgetary needs

Putting together a digital organizing strategy

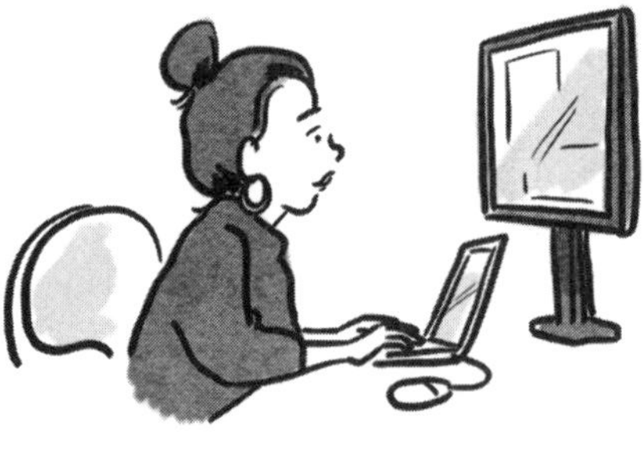

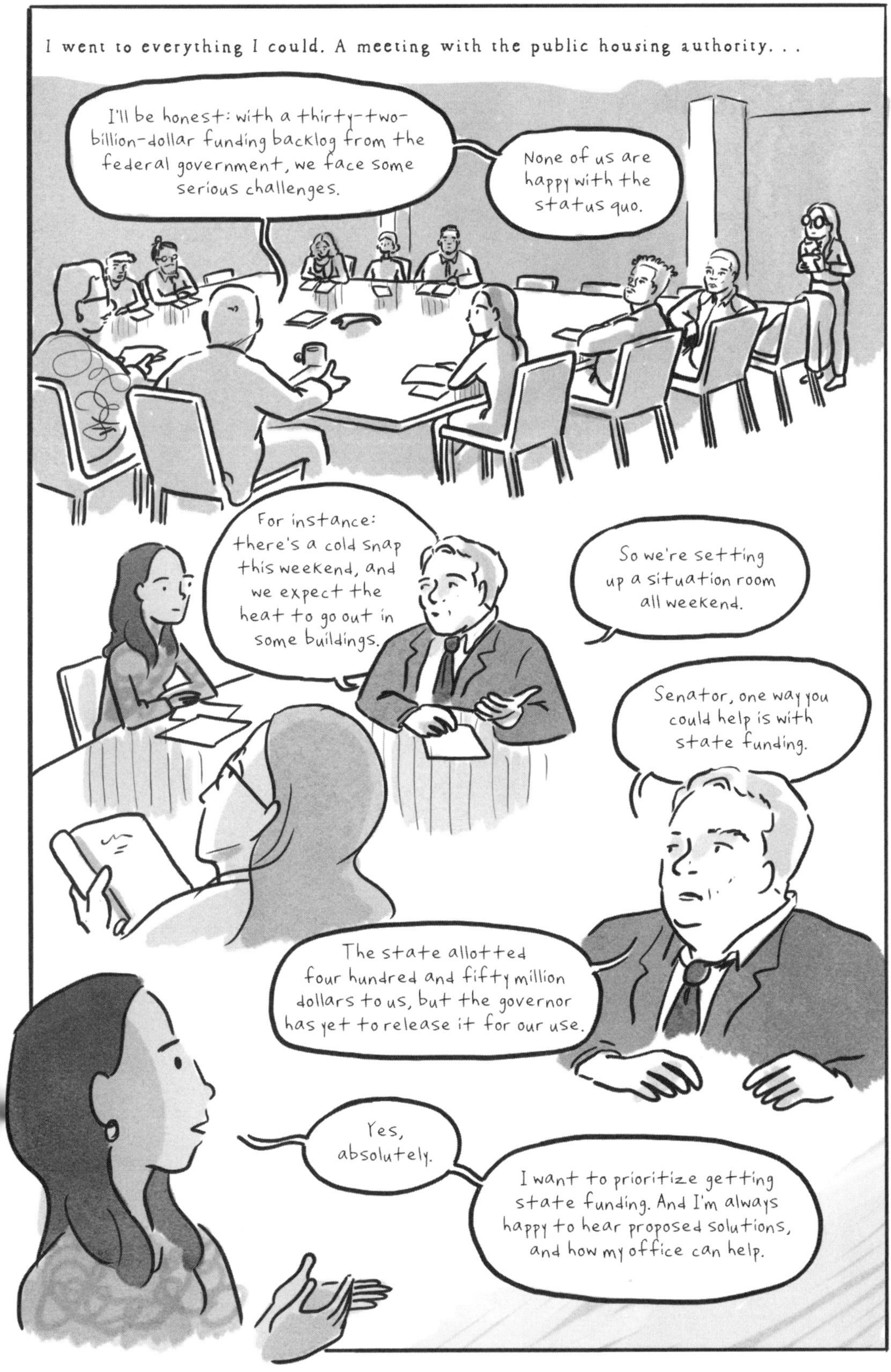
I went to everything I could. A meeting with the public housing authority. . .
I'll be honest: with a thirty-two-billion-dollar funding backlog from the federal government, we face some serious challenges.
None of us are happy with the status quo.
For instance: there's a cold snap this weekend, and we expect the heat to go out in some buildings.
So we're setting up a situation room all weekend.
Senator, one way you could help is with state funding.
The state allotted four hundred and fifty million dollars to us, but the governor has yet to release it for our use.
Yes, absolutely.
I want to prioritize getting state funding. And I'm always happy to hear proposed solutions, and how my office can help.

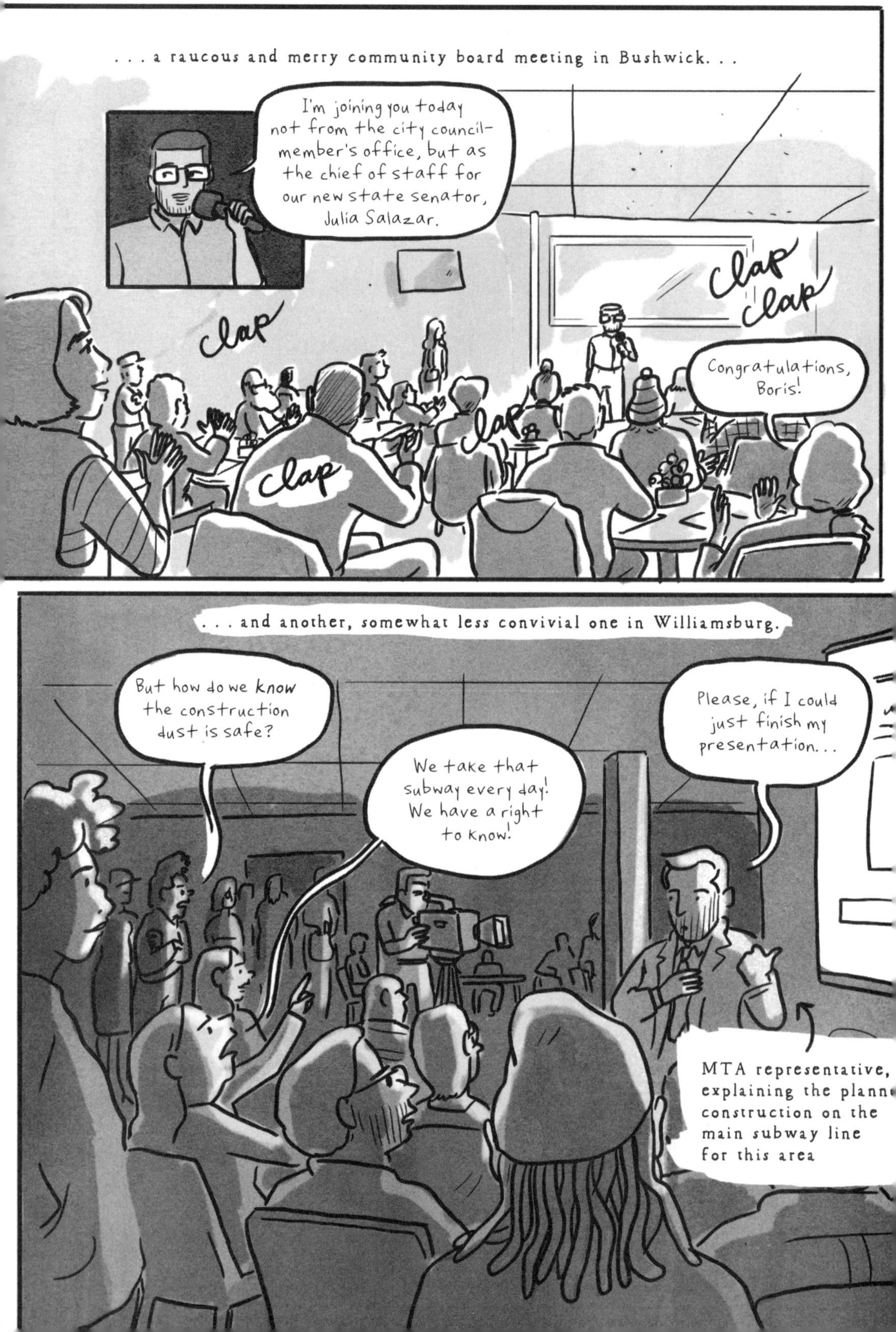
. . . a raucous and merry community board meeting in Bushwick. . .
I'm joining you today not from the city council-member's office, but as the chief of staff for our new state senator, Julia Salazar.
clap
clap
clap
clap clap
Congratulations, Boris!
. . . and another, somewhat less convivial one in Williamsburg.
But how do we know the construction dust is safe?
We take that subway every day! We have a right to know!
Please, if I could just finish my presentation...
MTA representative, explaining the planne construction on the main subway line for this area

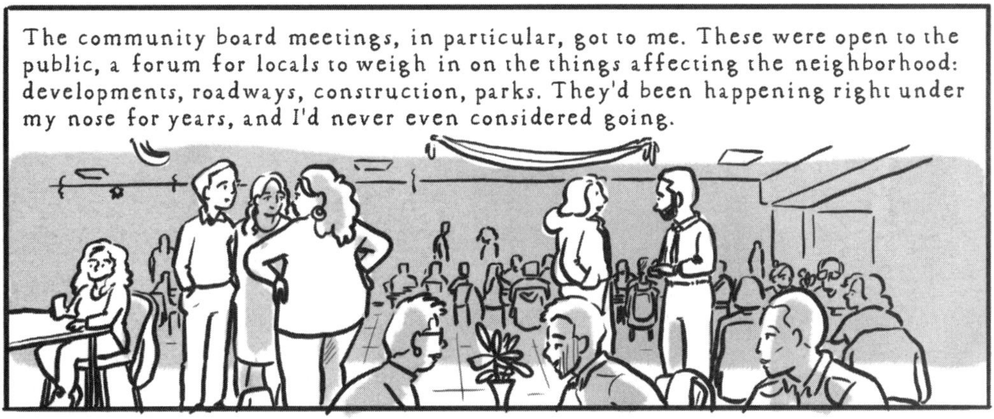
The community board meetings, in particular, got to me. These were open to the public, a forum for locals to weigh in on the things affecting the neighborhood: developments, roadways, construction, parks. They'd been happening right under my nose for years, and I'd never even considered going.

In part, that was because I felt guilty for being a gentrifier, and avoided situations where I was confronted with that awkwardness.

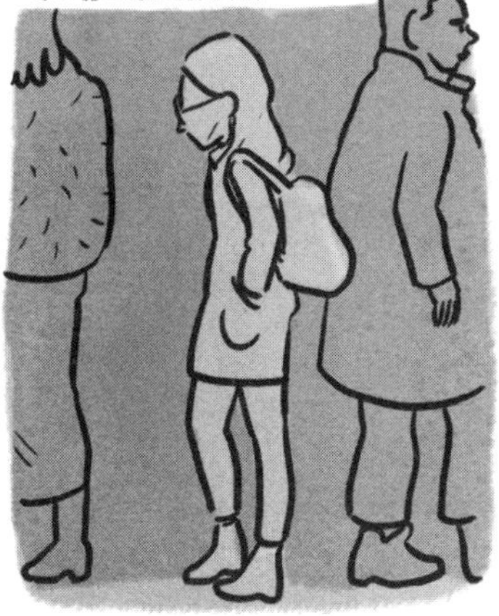

But also, I didn't consider this neighborhood to be my community... not really. New York was my community. My friends were my community.

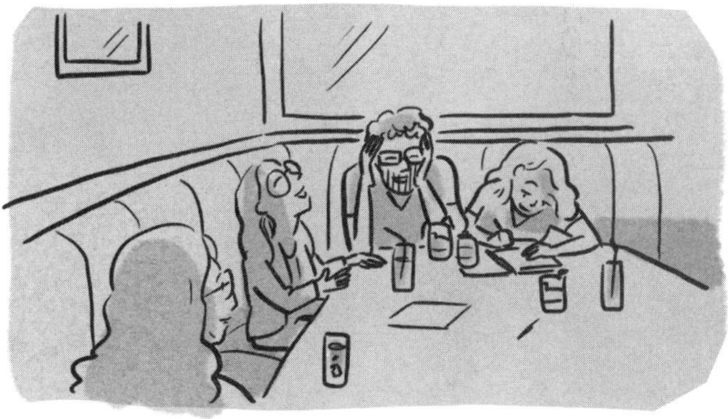

That was the narrative of the city I'd bought into: New York has everything, so you can cherry-pick what to have in your life. I had my own New York, filled with my people, my places.

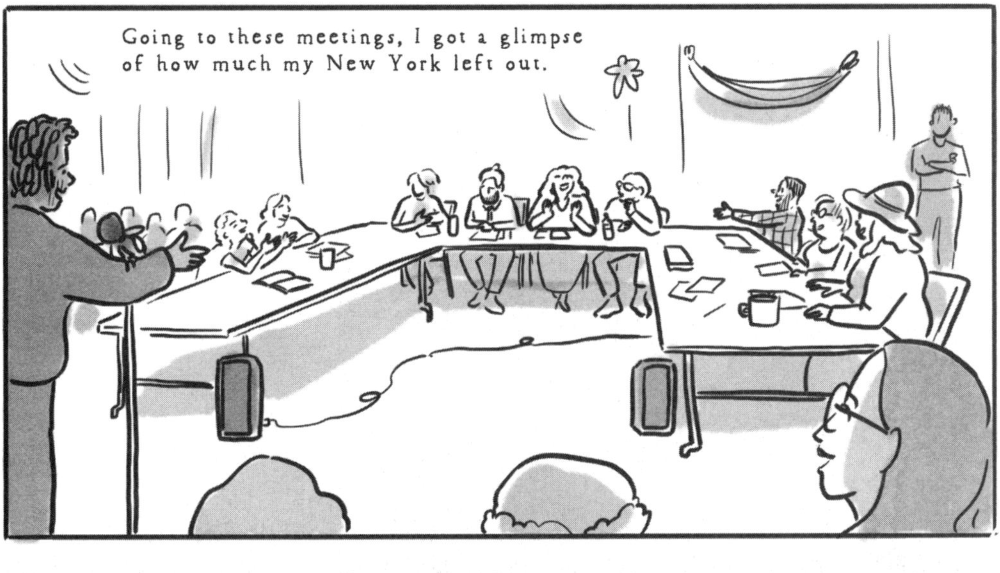
Going to these meetings, I got a glimpse of how much my New York left out.

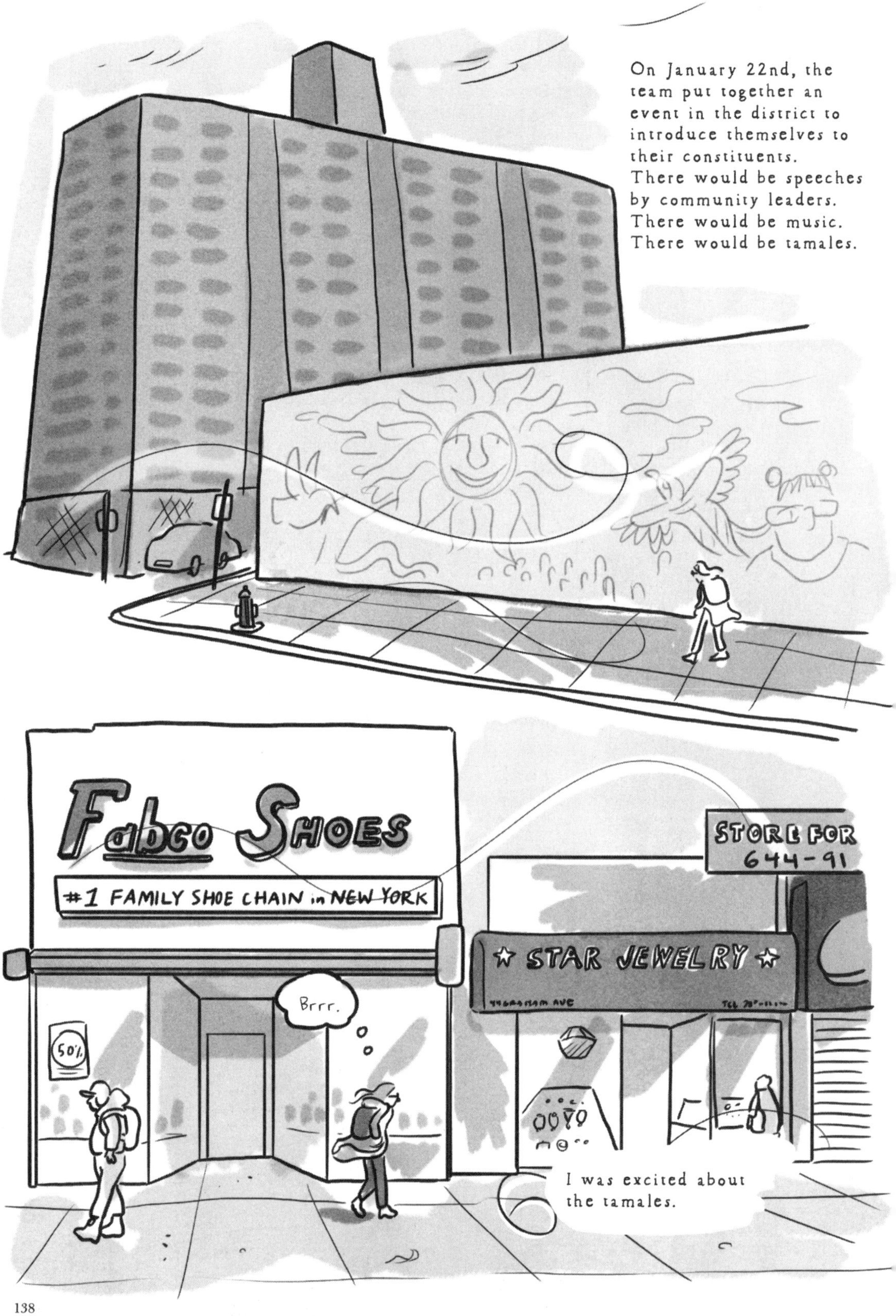
On January 22nd, the team put together an event in the district to introduce themselves to their constituents. There would be speeches by community leaders. There would be music. There would be tamales.
Fabco Shoes
#1 FAMILY SHOE CHAIN in NEW YORK
50%
STORE FOR
644-91
STAR JEWELRY
Brrr.
I was excited about the tamales.

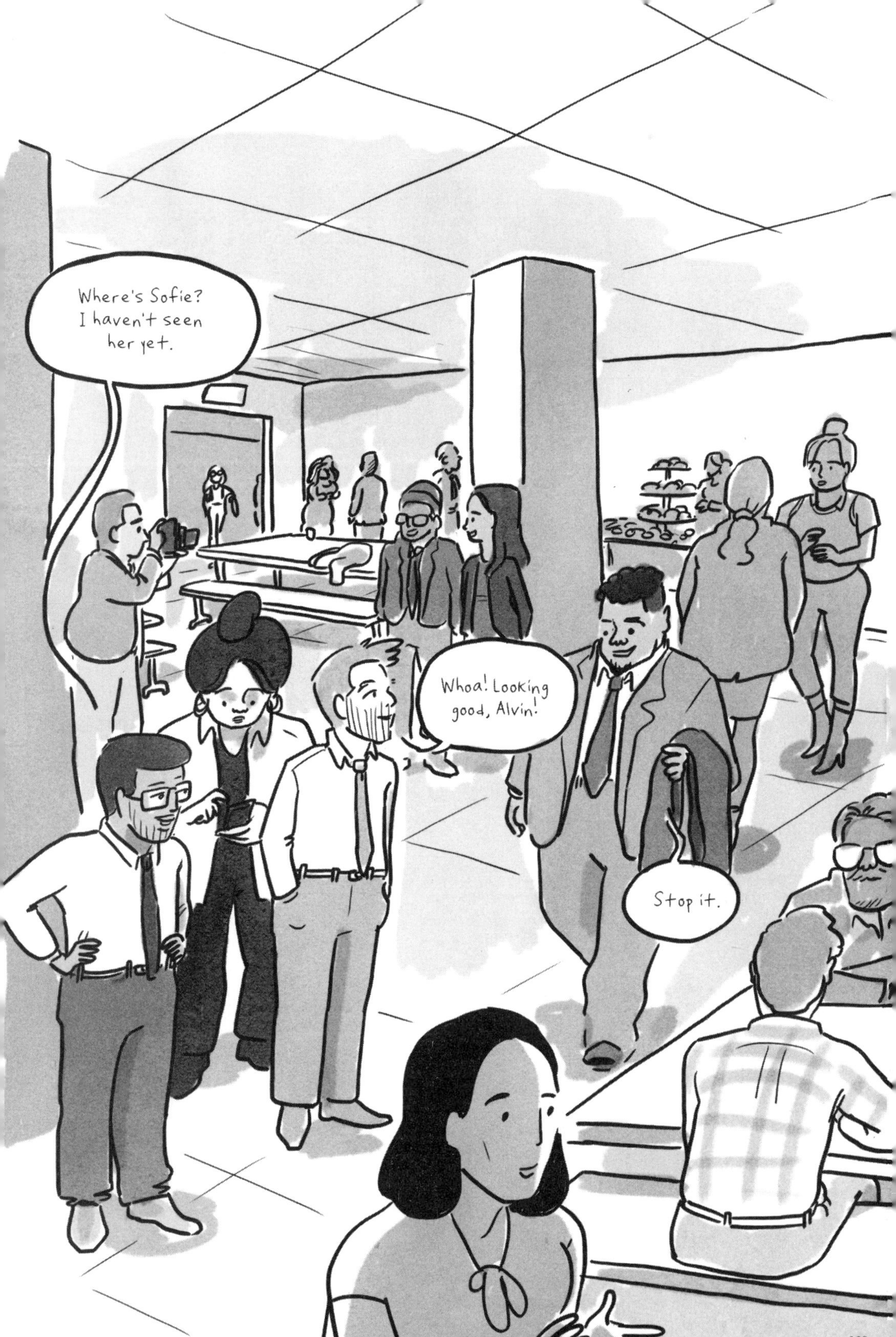
Where's Sofie? I haven't seen her yet.
Whoa! Looking good, Alvin!
Stop it.

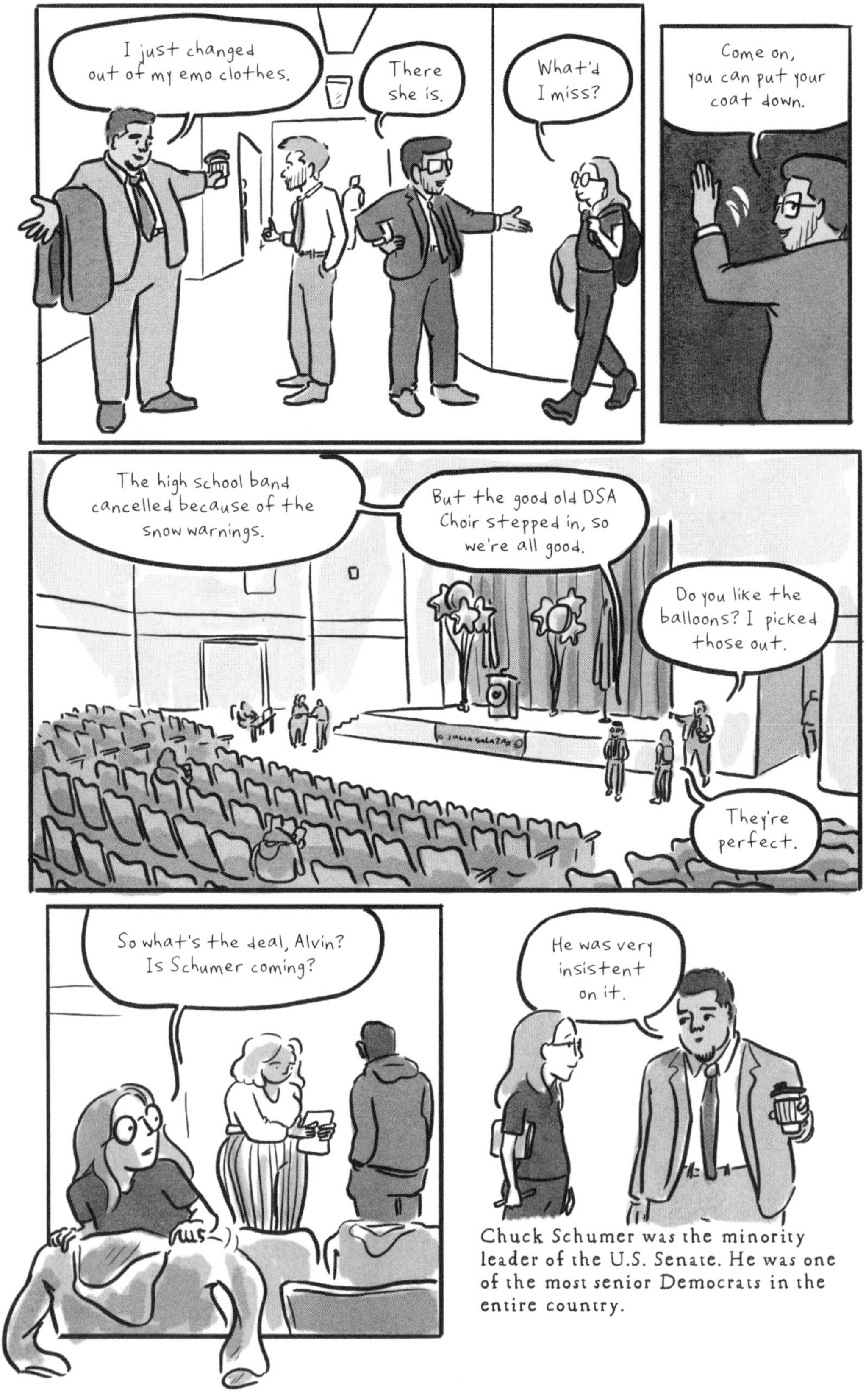
I just changed out of my emo clothes.
There she is.
What'd I miss?
Come on, you can put your coat down.
The high school band cancelled because of the snow warnings.
But the good old DSA Choir stepped in, so we're all good.
Do you like the balloons? I picked those out.
They're perfect.
So what's the deal, Alvin? Is Schumer coming?
He was very insistent on it.
Chuck Schumer was the minority leader of the U.S. Senate. He was one of the most senior Democrats in the entire country.

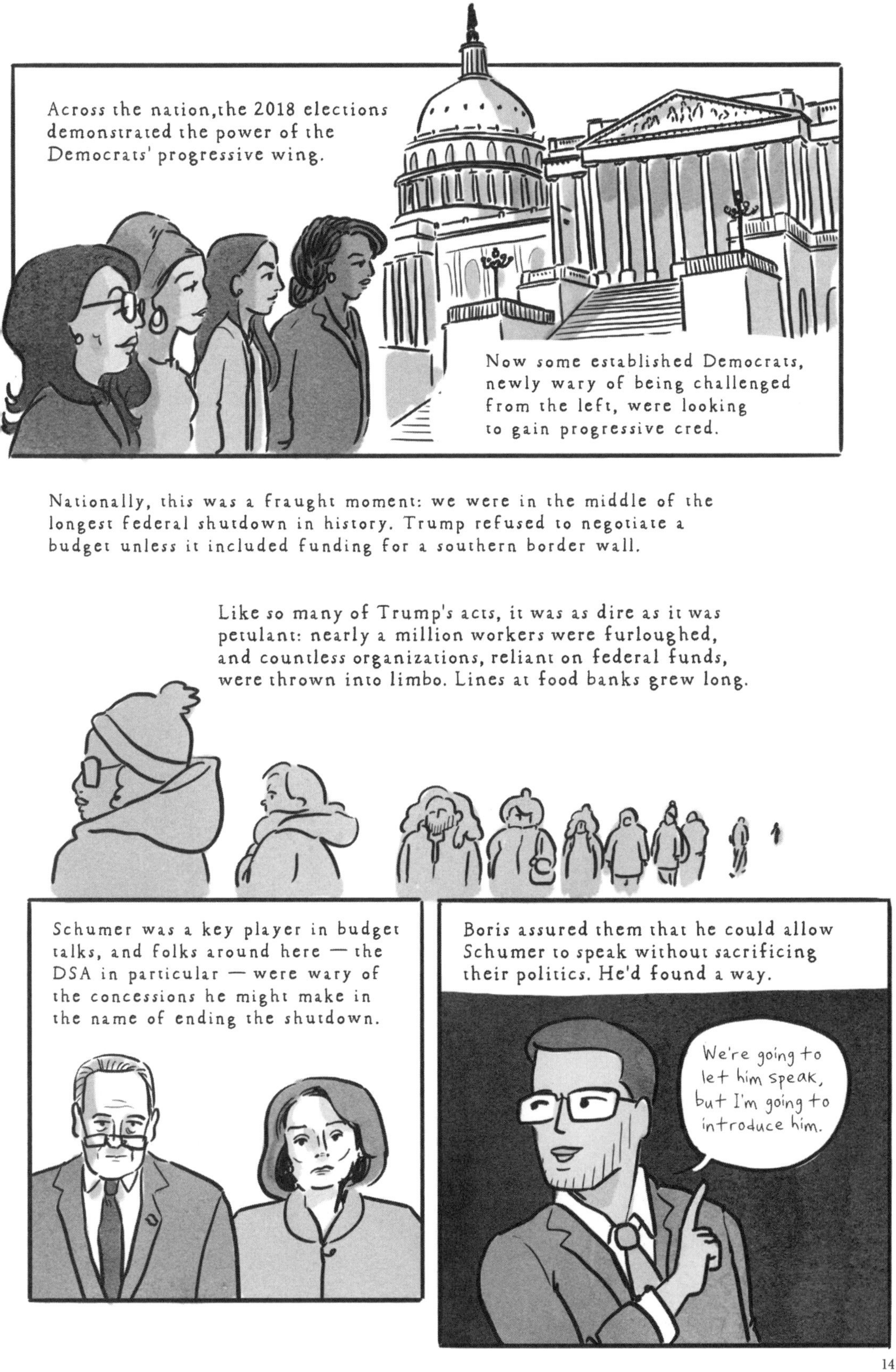
Across the nation, the 2018 elections demonstrated the power of the Democrats' progressive wing.
Now some established Democrats, newly wary of being challenged from the left, were looking to gain progressive cred.
Nationally, this was a fraught moment: we were in the middle of the longest federal shutdown in history. Trump refused to negotiate a budget unless it included funding for a southern border wall.
Like so many of Trump's acts, it was as dire as it was petulant: nearly a million workers were furloughed, and countless organizations, reliant on federal funds, were thrown into limbo. Lines at food banks grew long.
Schumer was a key player in budget talks, and folks around here — the DSA in particular — were wary of the concessions he might make in the name of ending the shutdown.
Boris assured them that he could allow Schumer to speak without sacrificing their politics. He'd found a way.
We're going to let him speak, but I'm going to introduce him.

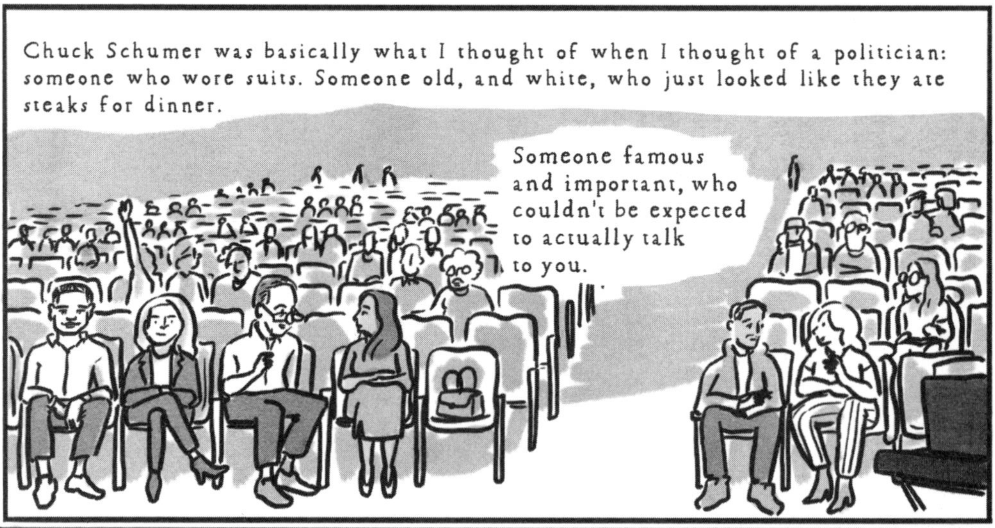
Chuck Schumer was basically what I thought of when I thought of a politician: someone who wore suits. Someone old, and white, who just looked like they ate steaks for dinner.
Someone famous and important, who couldn't be expected to actually talk to you.

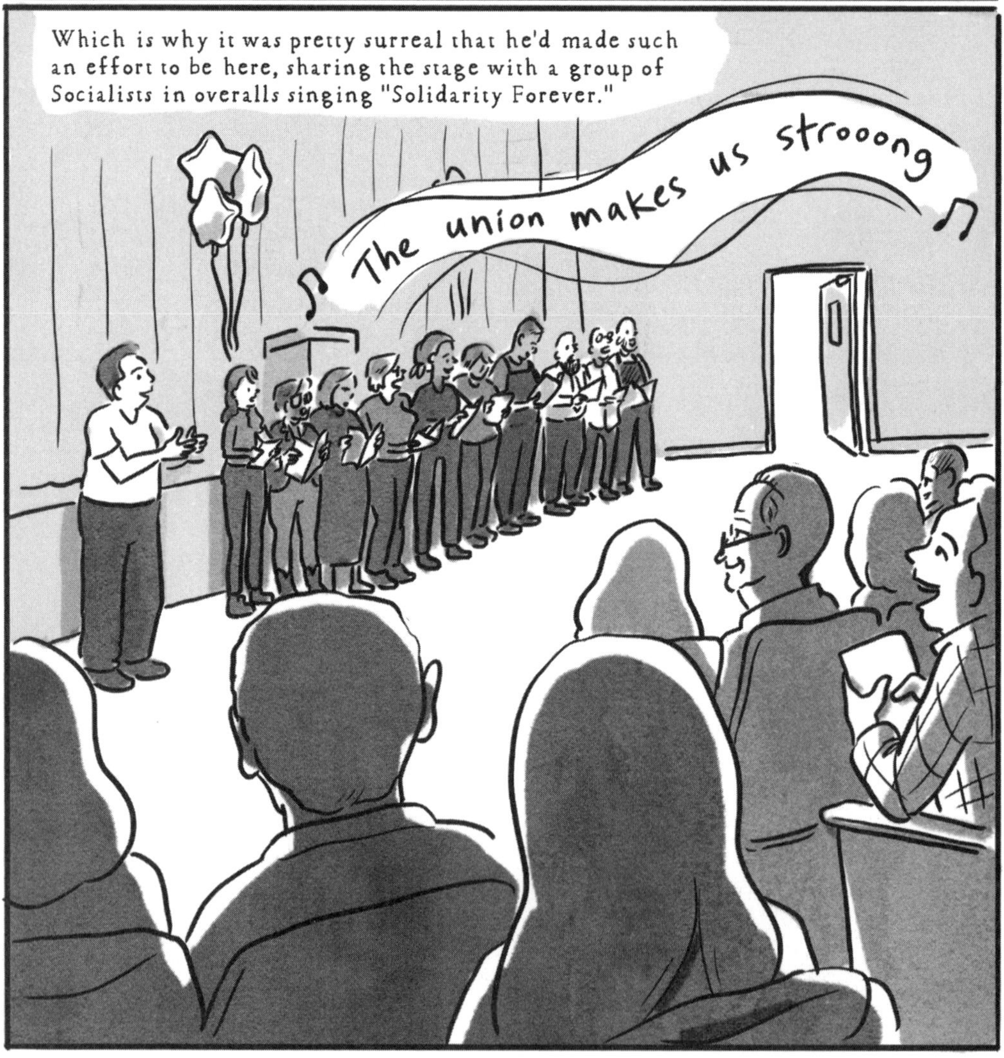
Which is why it was pretty surreal that he'd made such an effort to be here, sharing the stage with a group of Socialists in overalls singing "Solidarity Forever."
The union makes us strooong

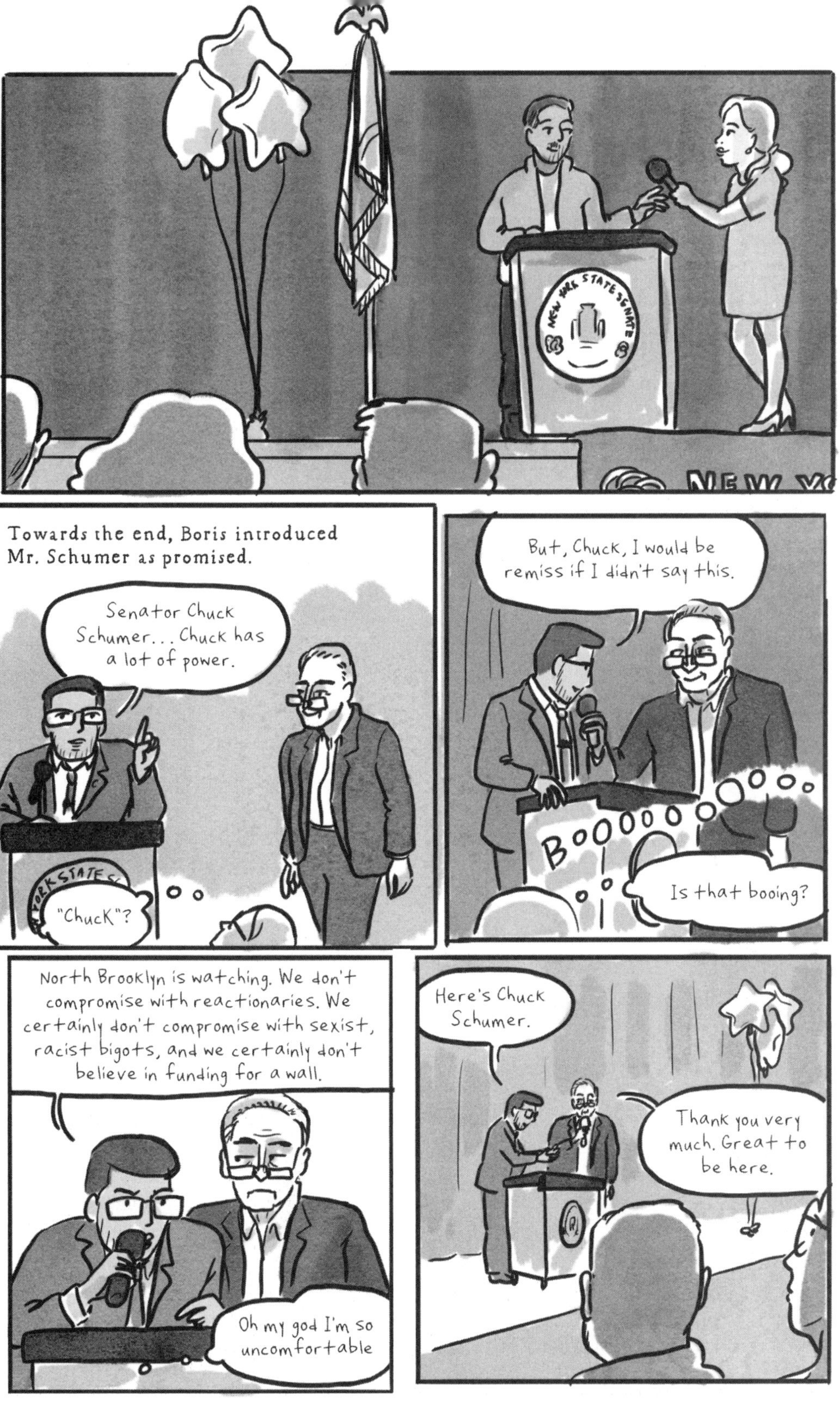
NEW YORK STATE SENATE
Towards the end, Boris introduced Mr. Schumer as promised.
Senator Chuck Schumer... Chuck has a lot of power.
"Chuck"?
But, Chuck, I would be remiss if I didn't say this.
BOOOOOOOOOOO
Is that booing?
North Brooklyn is watching. We don't compromise with reactionaries. We certainly don't compromise with sexist, racist bigots, and we certainly don't believe in funding for a wall.
Oh my god I'm so uncomfortable
Here's Chuck Schumer.
Thank you very much. Great to be here.

What Senator Schumer said — a familiar speech about his working-class roots — was less important than the fact of his speaking at all. It was a reminder that this little local office was part of a much bigger picture.

clap
clap
CLAP
clap clap clap clap clap
clap clap clap clap clap
clap clap CLAP clap
YEAH! clap
clap clap WOOOOO! clap clap clap
clap clap clap
clap clap CLAP clap clap
clap
clap
CLAP

It's my pleasure to introduce the state senator for District Eighteen: Julia Salazar.

Marty Needelman, community leader

Wow. This is incredible.

clap clap

As Marty said, I am a doer, not a talker. Emphasis on less of a talker... but I have some things to share with you.

After the Trump election, Julia said, she'd been demoralized and afraid. But she found hope and energy in the community of North Brooklyn.

Many of us had already been actively fighting for change long before this.

Fast-forward to this humble, insurgent State Senate campaign in 2018.

We were demanding change.

We raised voter turnout by nearly 300%, and we elected a woman of color.

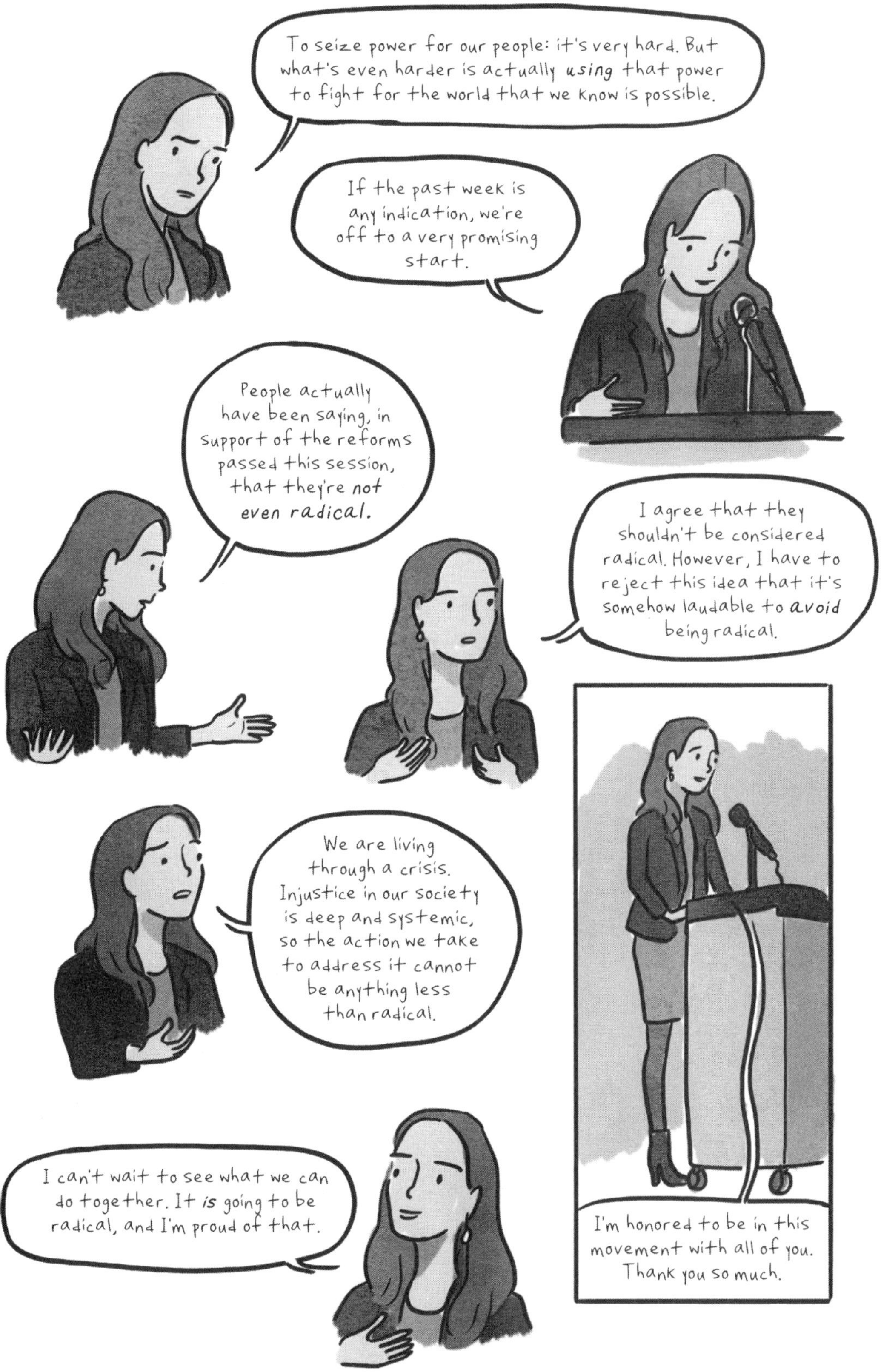
To seize power for our people: it's very hard. But what's even harder is actually *using* that power to fight for the world that we know is possible.
If the past week is any indication, we're off to a very promising start.
People actually have been saying, in support of the reforms passed this session, that they're *not even radical.*
I agree that they shouldn't be considered radical. However, I have to reject this idea that it's somehow laudable to *avoid* being radical.
We are living through a crisis. Injustice in our society is deep and systemic, so the action we take to address it cannot be anything less than radical.
I can't wait to see what we can do together. It *is* going to be radical, and I'm proud of that.
I'm honored to be in this movement with all of you. Thank you so much.

Throughout her speech, Julia spoke collectively.

"We were fighting for change."

"We elected a woman of color."

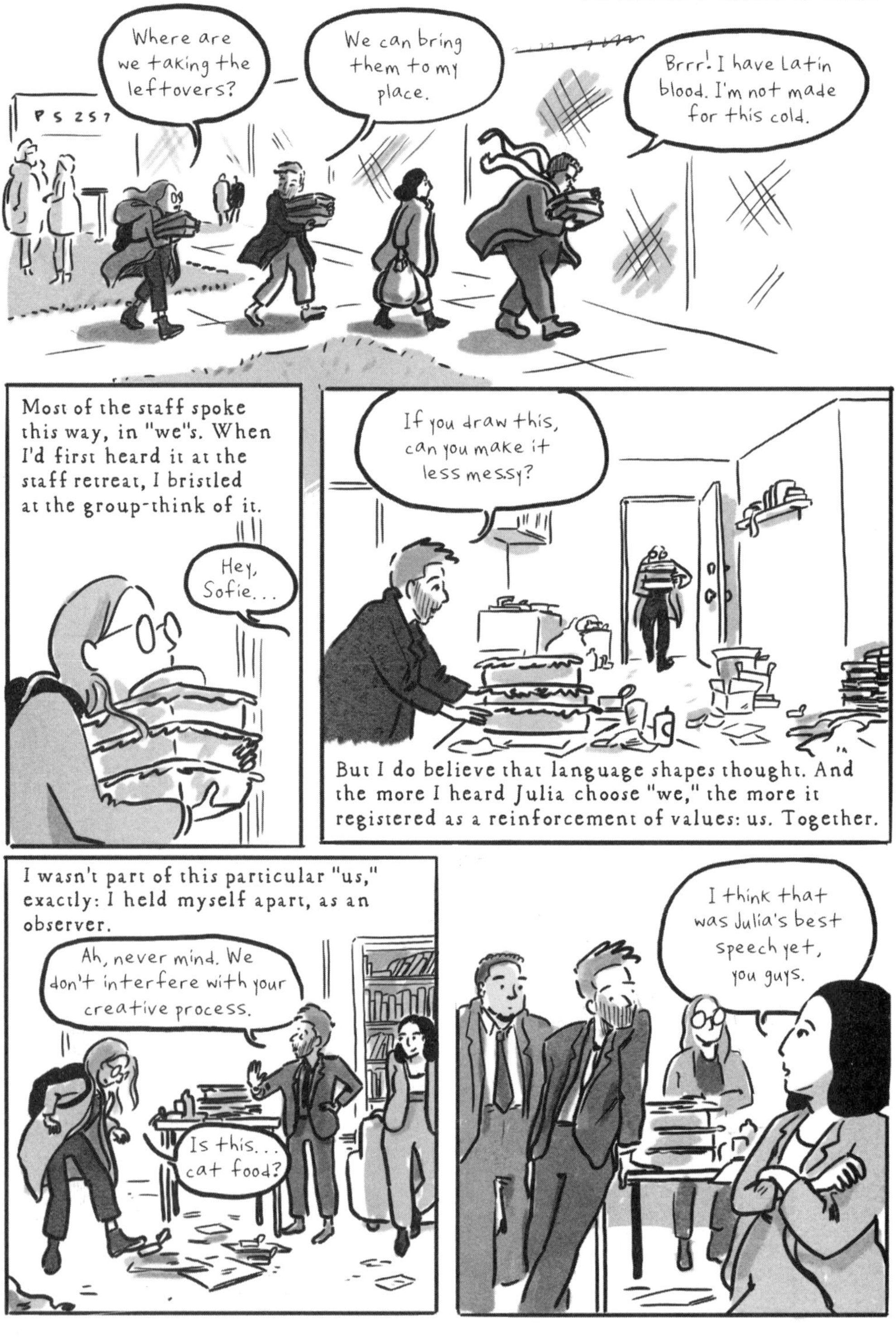
Where are we taking the leftovers?
We can bring them to my place.
Brrr! I have Latin blood. I'm not made for this cold.
PS 257
Most of the staff spoke this way, in "we"s. When I'd first heard it at the staff retreat, I bristled at the group-think of it.
Hey, Sofie...
If you draw this, can you make it less messy?
But I do believe that language shapes thought. And the more I heard Julia choose "we," the more it registered as a reinforcement of values: us. Together.
I wasn't part of this particular "us," exactly: I held myself apart, as an observer.
Ah, never mind. We don't interfere with your creative process.
Is this... cat food?
I think that was Julia's best speech yet, you guys.

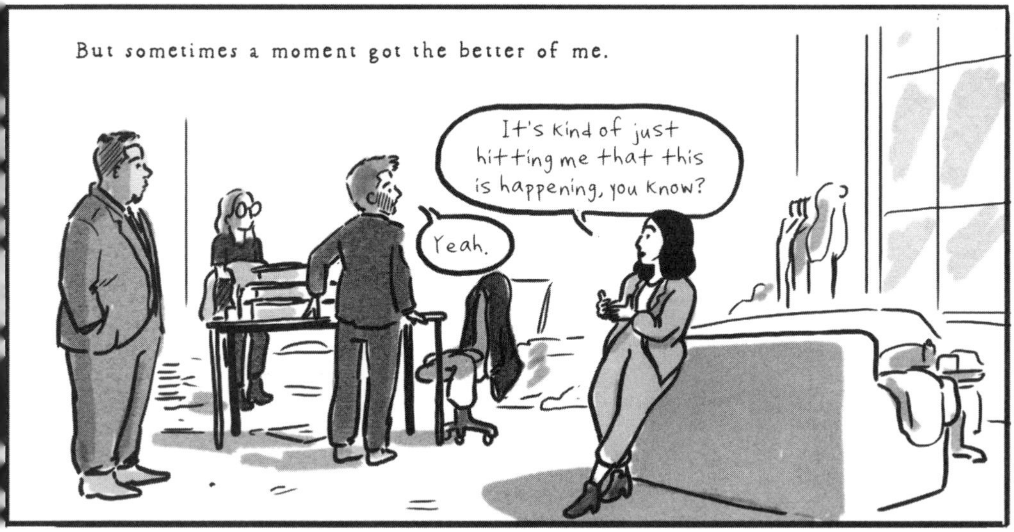
But sometimes a moment got the better of me.
It's kind of just hitting me that this is happening, you know?
Yeah.

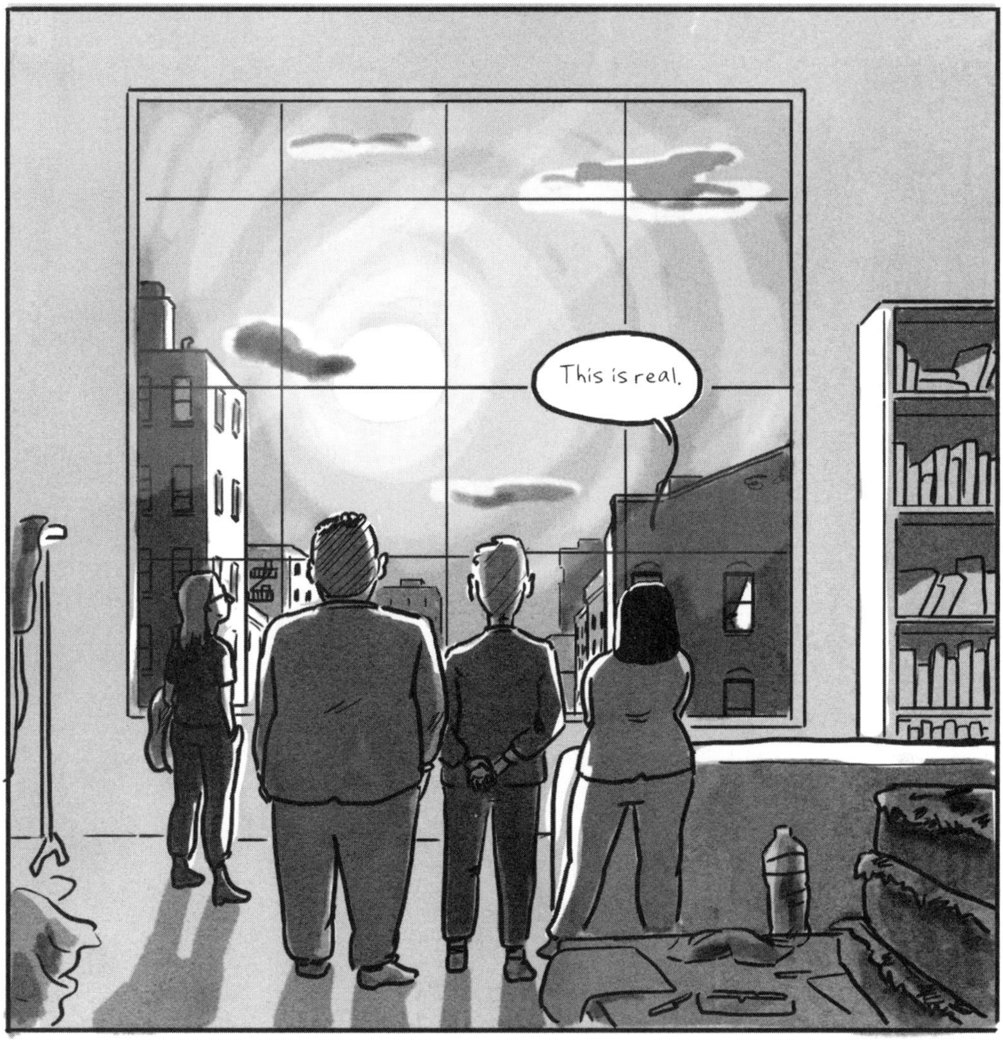
This is real.

Chapter Six

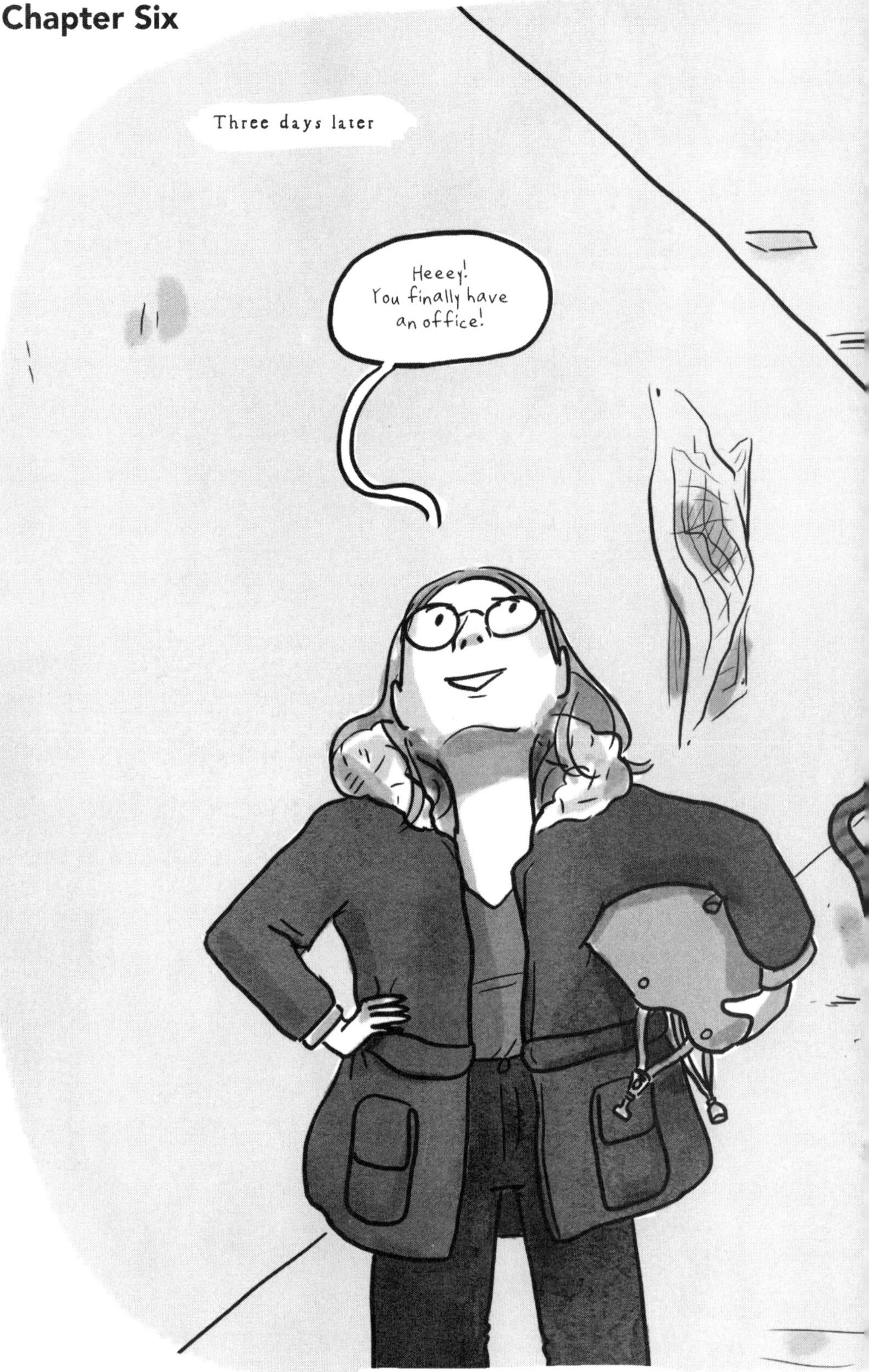
Three days later
Heeey! You finally have an office!

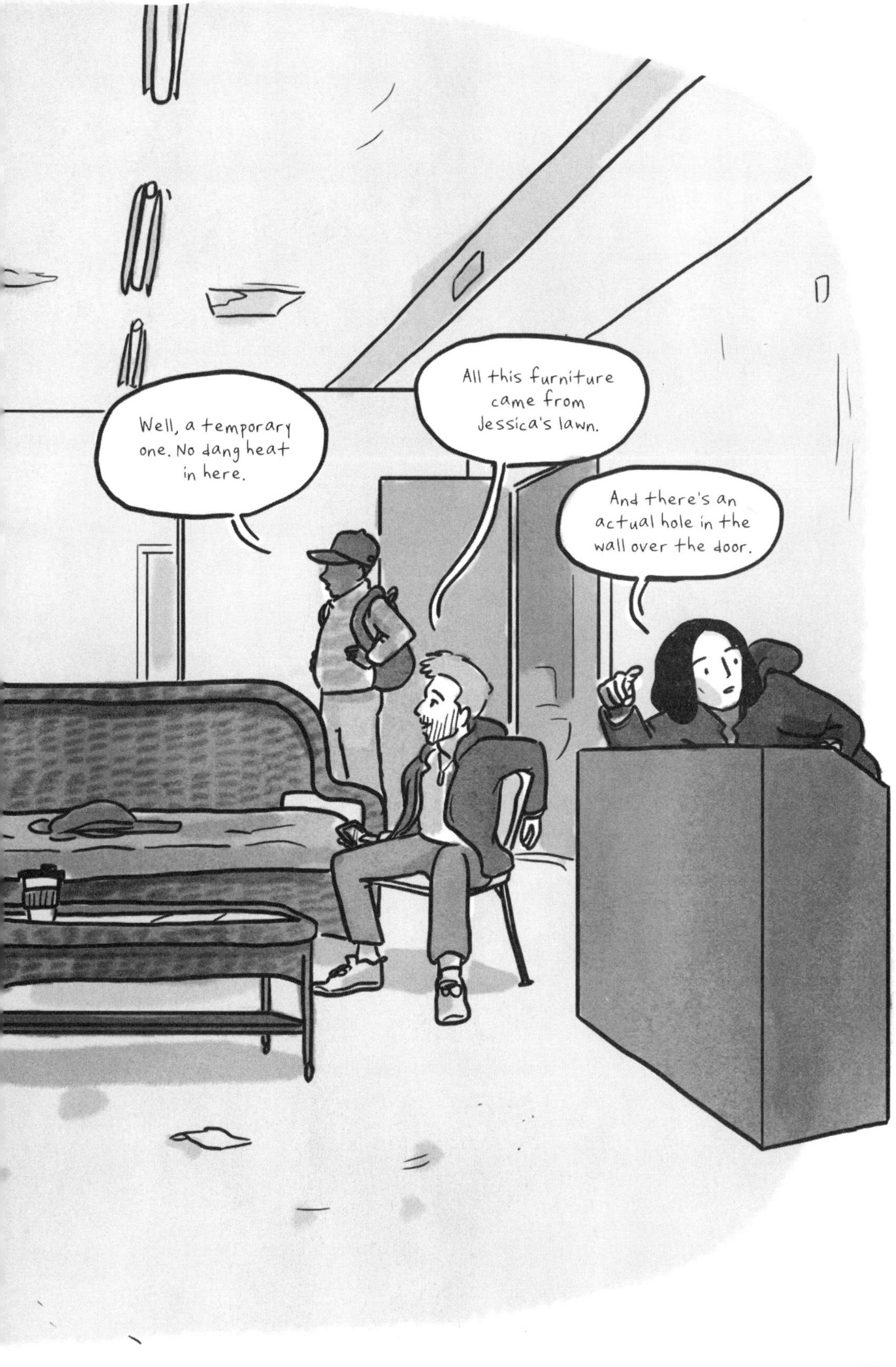
Well, a temporary one. No dang heat in here.
All this furniture came from Jessica's lawn.
And there's an actual hole in the wall over the door.

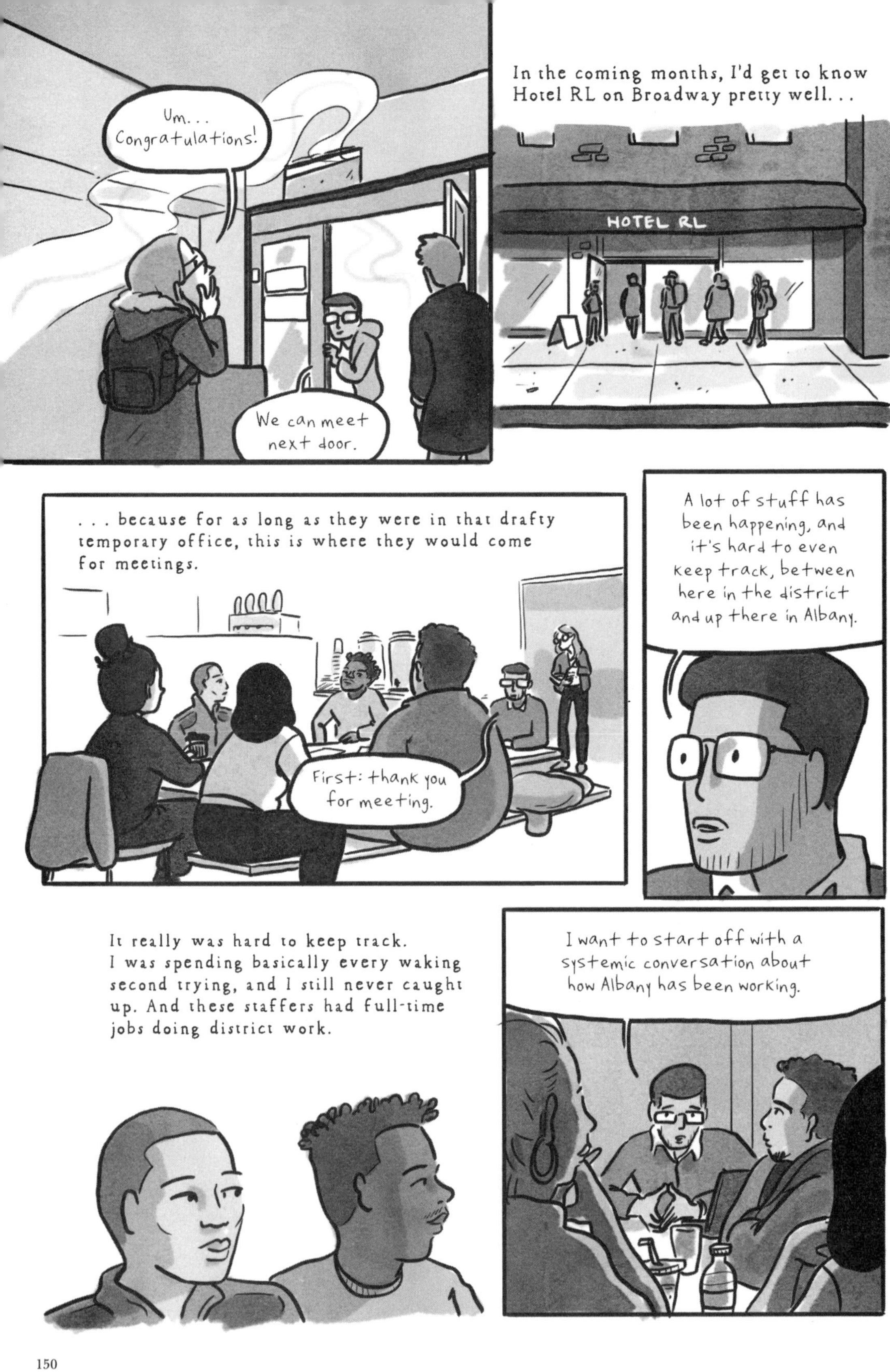
Um... Congratulations!
We can meet next door.
In the coming months, I'd get to know Hotel RL on Broadway pretty well. . .
HOTEL RL
. . . because for as long as they were in that drafty temporary office, this is where they would come for meetings.
First: thank you for meeting.
A lot of stuff has been happening, and it's hard to even keep track, between here in the district and up there in Albany.
It really was hard to keep track. I was spending basically every waking second trying, and I still never caught up. And these staffers had full-time jobs doing district work.
I want to start off with a systemic conversation about how Albany has been working.

Every week when legislature is in session, the Dems conference. Remember that room at the reception, with the food? That's the room.

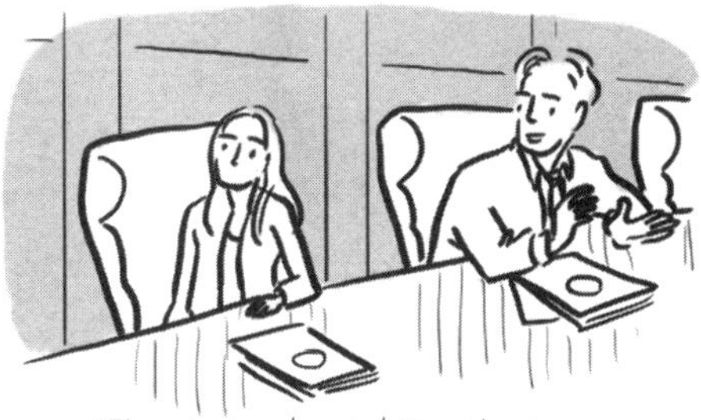

They talk about bills that are going to be voted on that same day and the next week.

But we don't get an idea of when session is going to take place, or conference, or committee meetings, until, like, two days before.

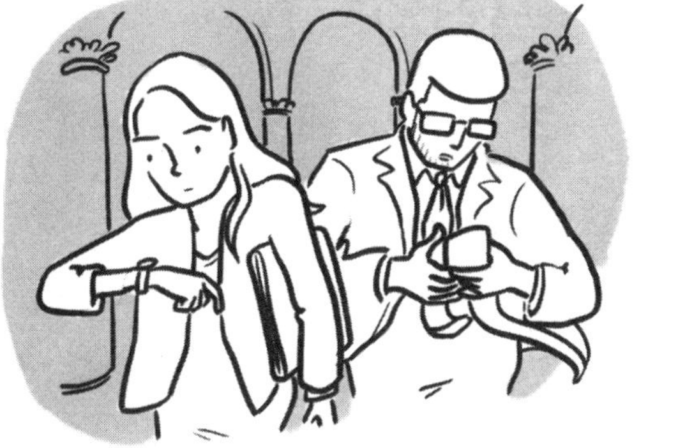

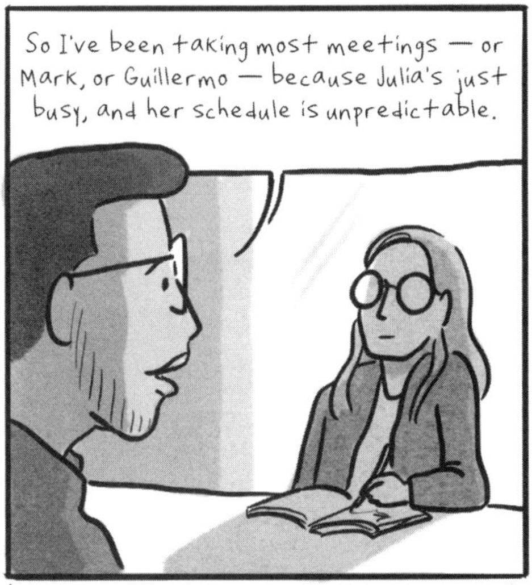
So I've been taking most meetings — or Mark, or Guillermo — because Julia's just busy, and her schedule is unpredictable.

A few days prior, I'd gone up to Albany to watch Julia pass her first bill. It would make contraception — eighteen different kinds — available to all New Yorkers without copay.

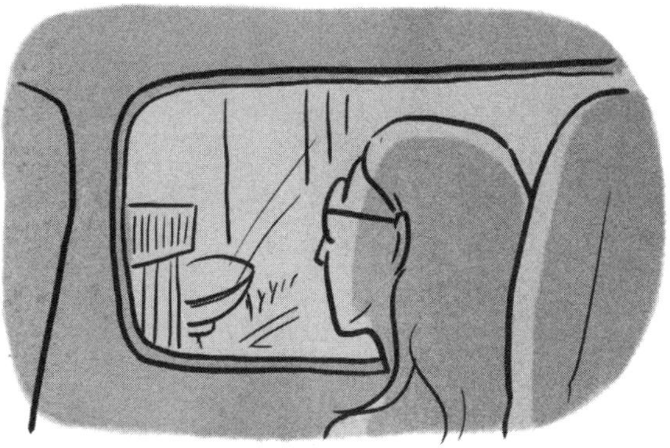

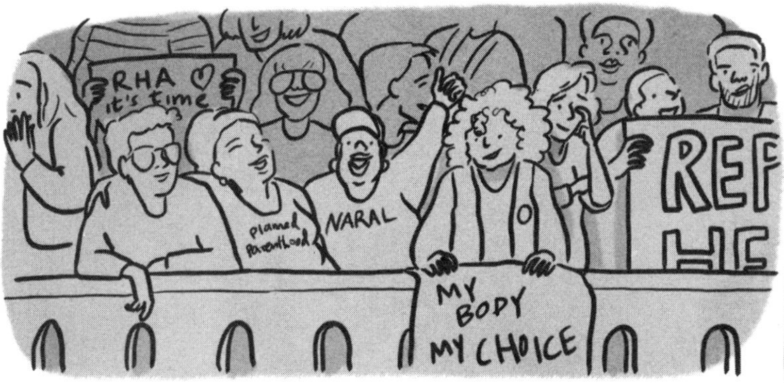
RHA ♡
it's time
Planned Parenthood
NARAL
MY BODY MY CHOICE

But another, higher-profile bill was passing that day: the Reproductive Health Act, which would protect abortion rights at the state level. The chamber galleries were so packed with advocates that I couldn't get in.

So I'd gone to hang out in Julia's Albany office instead. . .

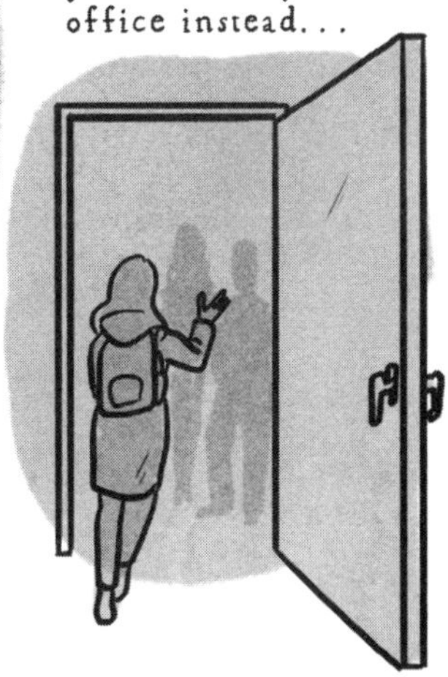

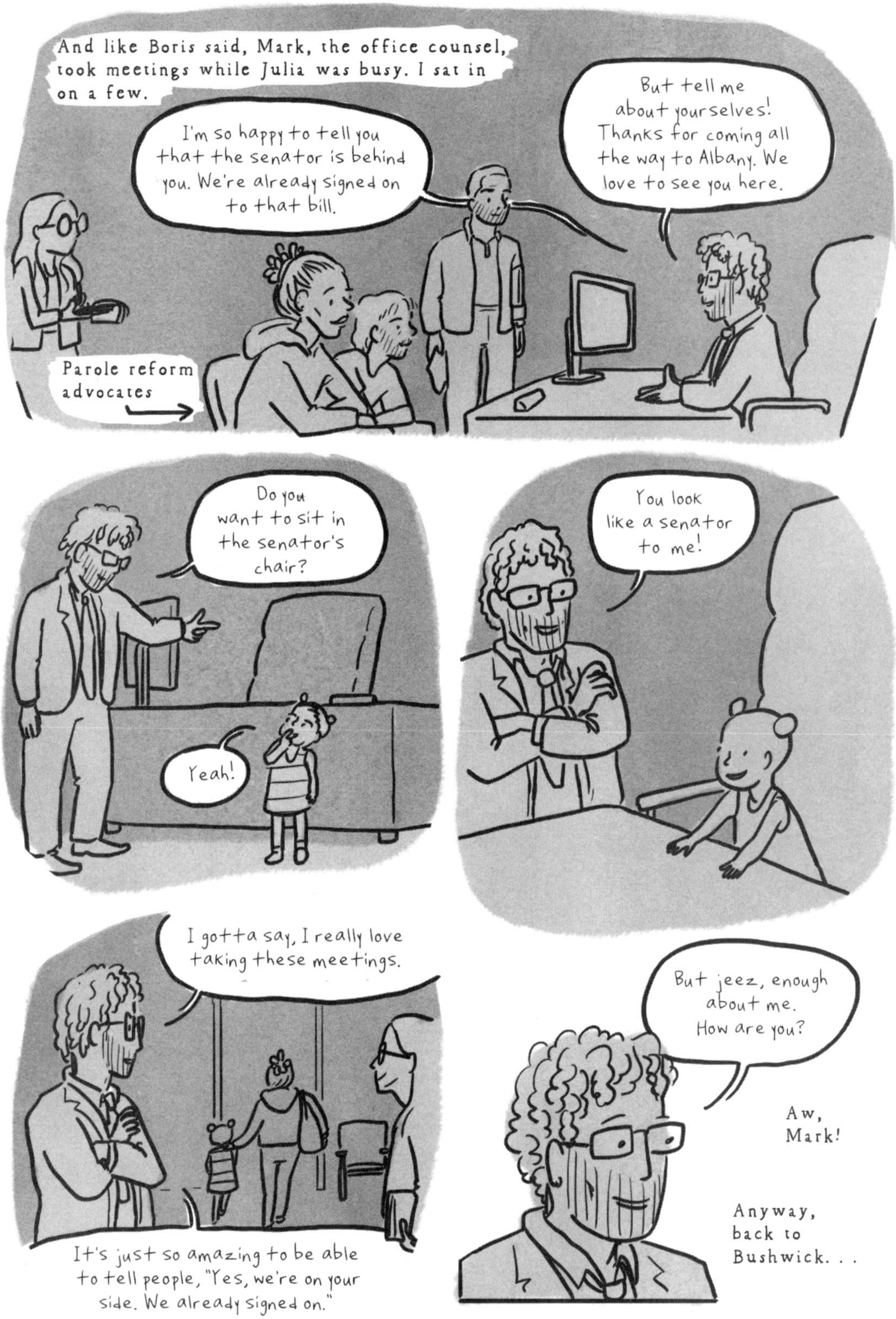

And like Boris said, Mark, the office counsel, took meetings while Julia was busy. I sat in on a few.
I'm so happy to tell you that the senator is behind you. We're already signed on to that bill.
But tell me about yourselves! Thanks for coming all the way to Albany. We love to see you here.
Parole reform advocates
Do you want to sit in the senator's chair?
Yeah!
You look like a senator to me!
I gotta say, I really love taking these meetings.
It's just so amazing to be able to tell people, "Yes, we're on your side. We already signed on."
But jeez, enough about me. How are you?
Aw, Mark!
Anyway, back to Bushwick. . .

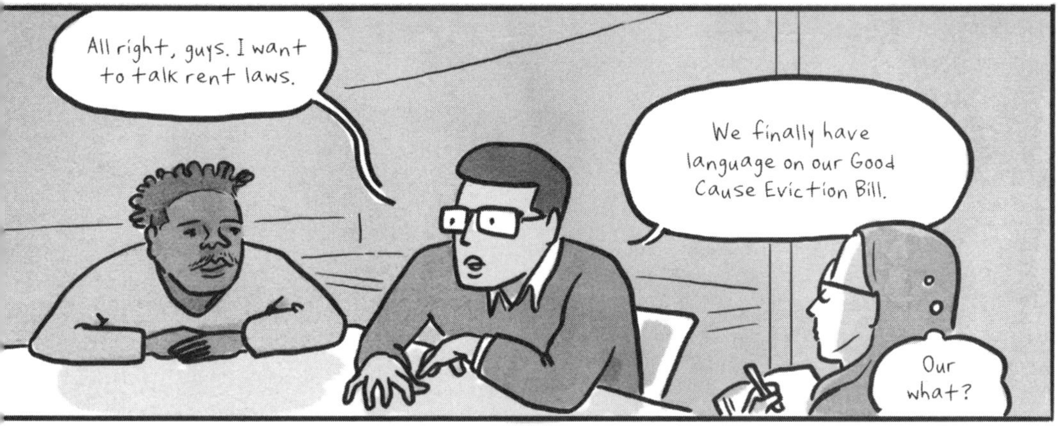
All right, guys. I want to talk rent laws.
We finally have language on our Good Cause Eviction Bill.
Our what?

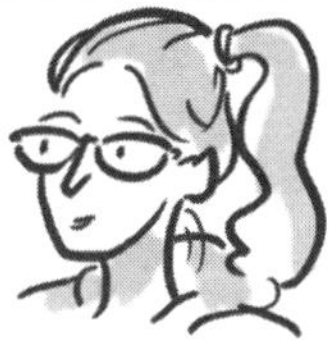

Remember when Cea told me that if legislators supported the Housing Justice for All platform from two years ago, that wasn't the same as supporting them now?

The new package of bills was called

UNIVERSAL RENT CONTROL

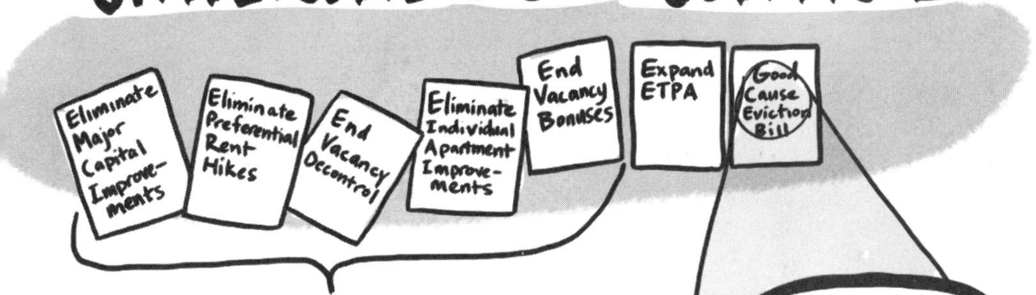
Eliminate Major Capital Improvements
Eliminate Preferential Rent Hikes
End Vacancy Decontrol
Eliminate Individual Apartment Improvements
End Vacancy Bonuses
Expand ETPA
Good Cause Eviction Bill

Most of the bills would close loopholes in the existing rent regulation system, and were very familiar to the legislators. These bills would be great for the roughly one million people in rent regulated units, but would do nothing for the millions of tenants outside of that system.

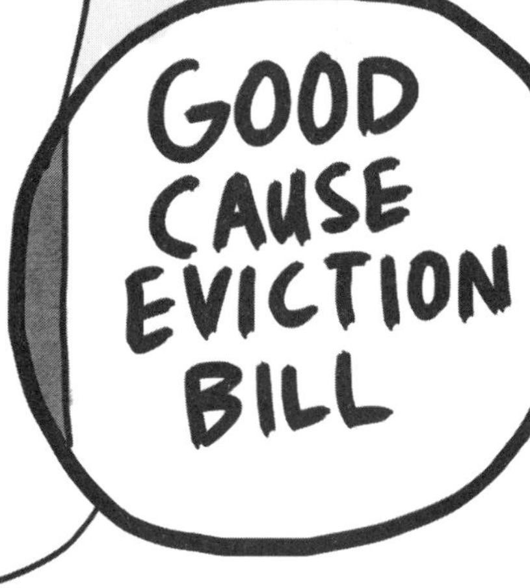
GOOD CAUSE EVICTION BILL

But this bill, on the other hand—

—would prevent eviction without good cause for the millions of tenants in ***unregulated*** units, all across the state. It was a brand new bill, and an ambitious one. Passing it would be a huge political lift.

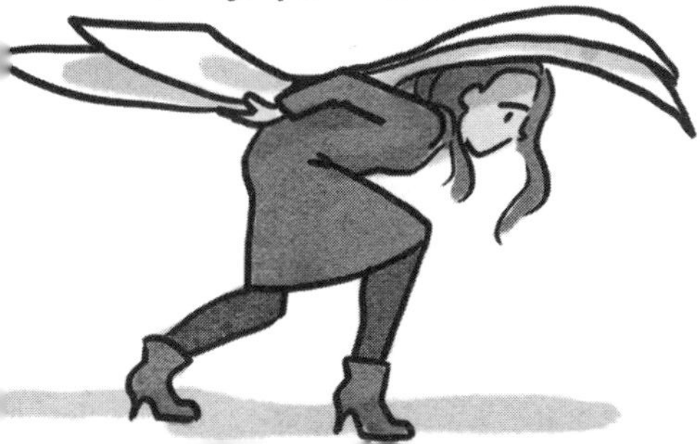

Julia was its lead Senate sponsor.

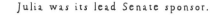

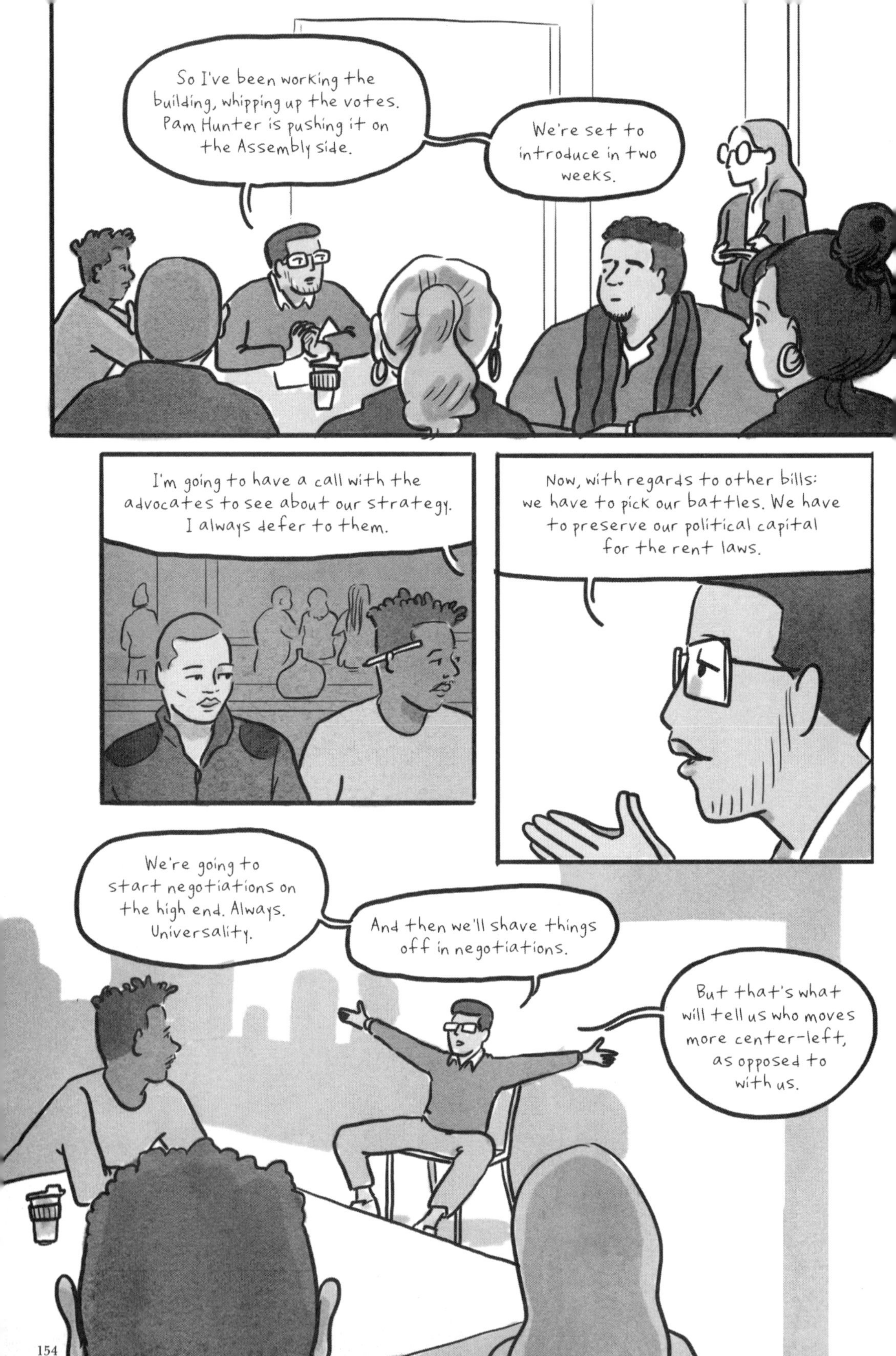
So I've been working the building, whipping up the votes. Pam Hunter is pushing it on the Assembly side.
We're set to introduce in two weeks.
I'm going to have a call with the advocates to see about our strategy. I always defer to them.
Now, with regards to other bills: we have to pick our battles. We have to preserve our political capital for the rent laws.
We're going to start negotiations on the high end. Always. Universality.
And then we'll shave things off in negotiations.
But that's what will tell us who moves more center-left, as opposed to with us.

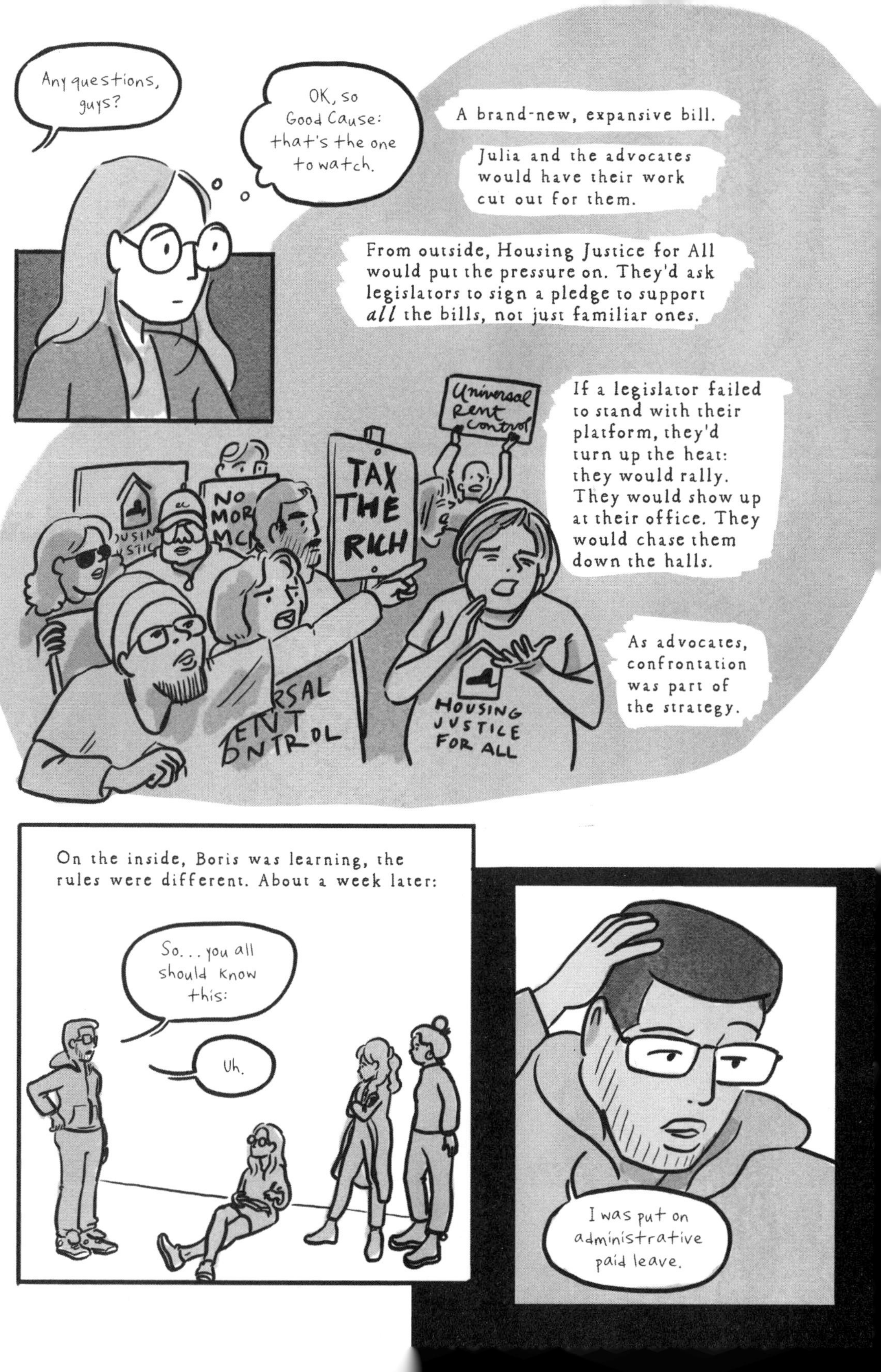

Any questions, guys?
OK, so Good Cause: that's the one to watch.
A brand-new, expansive bill.
Julia and the advocates would have their work cut out for them.
From outside, Housing Justice for All would put the pressure on. They'd ask legislators to sign a pledge to support *all* the bills, not just familiar ones.
Universal Rent control
TAX THE RICH
If a legislator failed to stand with their platform, they'd turn up the heat: they would rally. They would show up at their office. They would chase them down the halls.
HOUSING JUSTICE FOR ALL
As advocates, confrontation was part of the strategy.
On the inside, Boris was learning, the rules were different. About a week later:
So... you all should know this:
Uh.
I was put on administrative paid leave.

Boris told us what had happened: he'd run into an assemblymember (a Democrat) while waiting for the elevator.

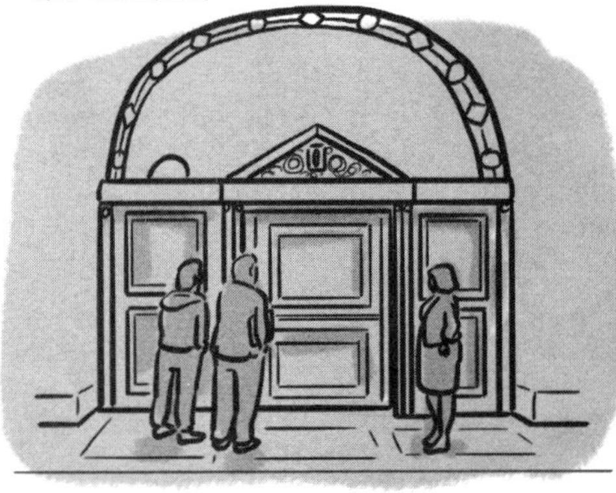

At first, she didn't recognize him, but once she did:

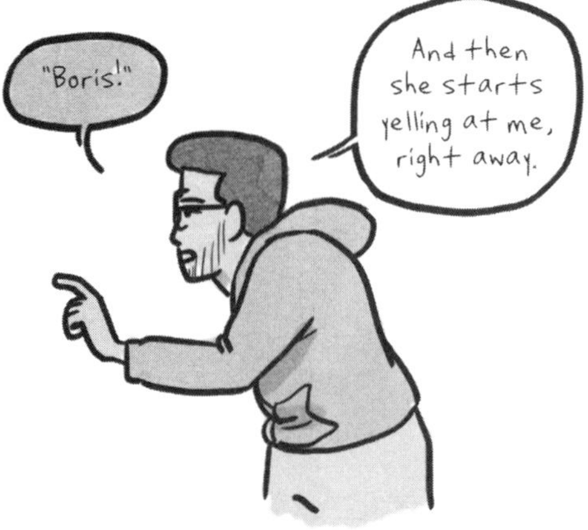
"Boris!"
And then she starts yelling at me, right away.

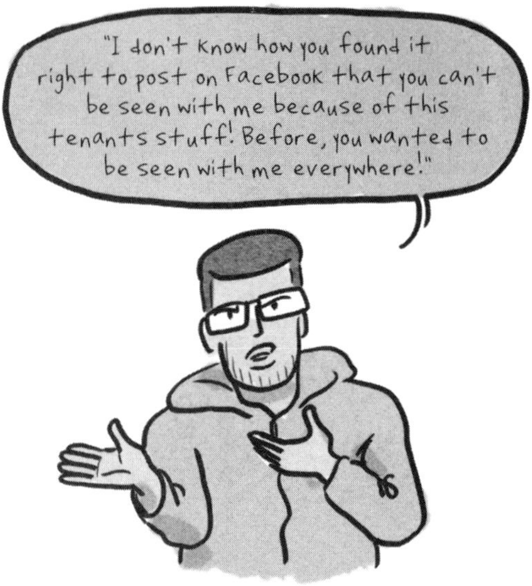
"I don't know how you found it right to post on Facebook that you can't be seen with me because of this tenants stuff! Before, you wanted to be seen with me everywhere!"

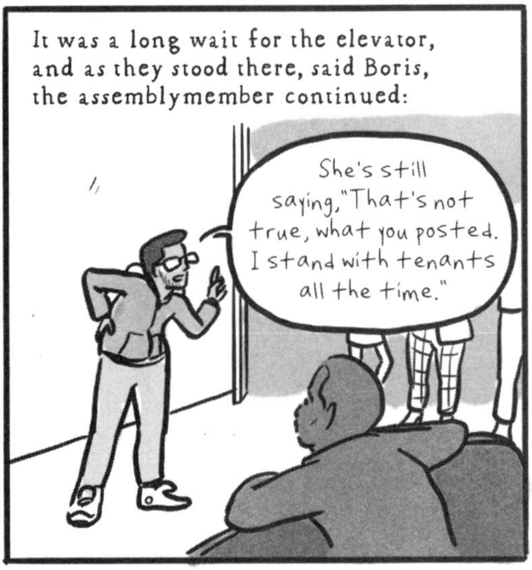
It was a long wait for the elevator, and as they stood there, said Boris, the assemblymember continued:
She's still saying, "That's not true, what you posted. I stand with tenants all the time."

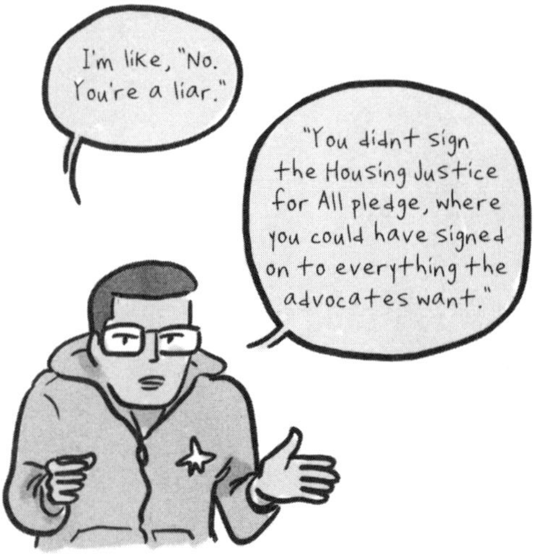
I'm like, "No. You're a liar."
"You didnt sign the Housing Justice for All pledge, where you could have signed on to everything the advocates want."

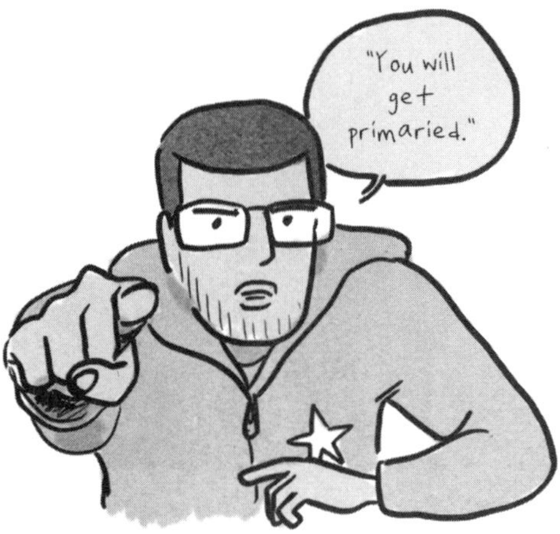
"You will get primaried."

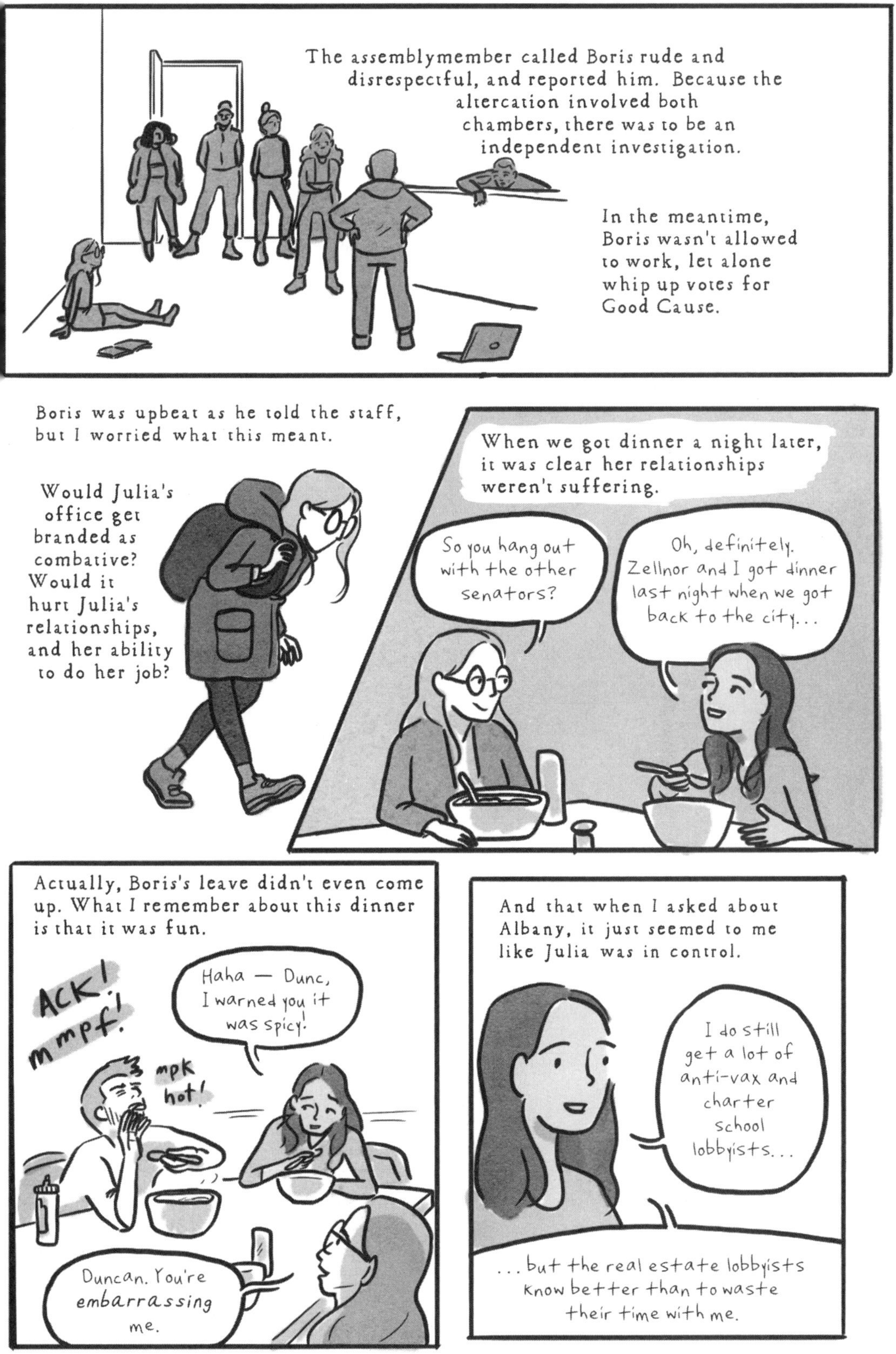
The assemblymember called Boris rude and disrespectful, and reported him. Because the altercation involved both chambers, there was to be an independent investigation.
In the meantime, Boris wasn't allowed to work, let alone whip up votes for Good Cause.
Boris was upbeat as he told the staff, but I worried what this meant.
Would Julia's office get branded as combative? Would it hurt Julia's relationships, and her ability to do her job?
When we got dinner a night later, it was clear her relationships weren't suffering.
So you hang out with the other senators?
Oh, definitely. Zellnor and I got dinner last night when we got back to the city...
Actually, Boris's leave didn't even come up. What I remember about this dinner is that it was fun.
ACK! mmpf!
Haha — Dunc, I warned you it was spicy!
mpk hot!
Duncan. You're embarrassing me.
And that when I asked about Albany, it just seemed to me like Julia was in control.
I do still get a lot of anti-vax and charter school lobbyists...
...but the real estate lobbyists know better than to waste their time with me.

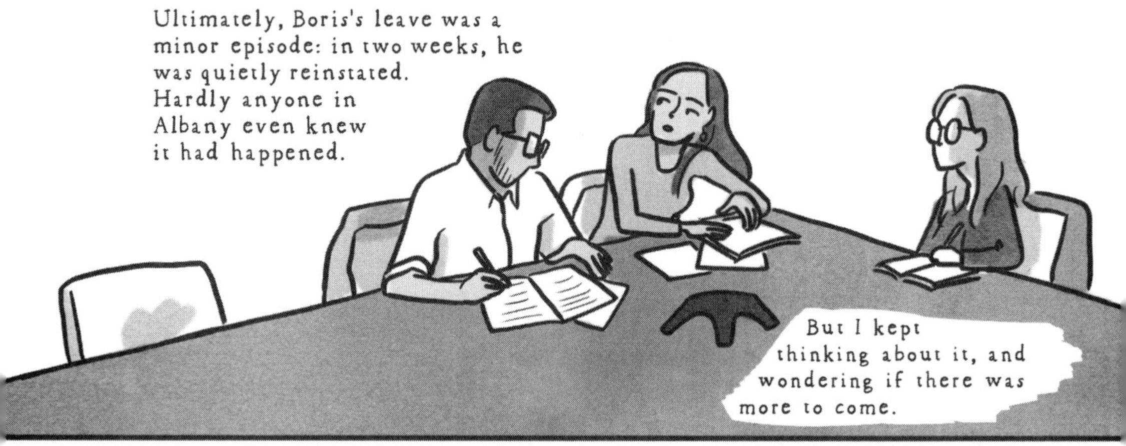
Ultimately, Boris's leave was a minor episode: in two weeks, he was quietly reinstated. Hardly anyone in Albany even knew it had happened.
But I kept thinking about it, and wondering if there was more to come.

Like every politician, Julia was in a tricky position:

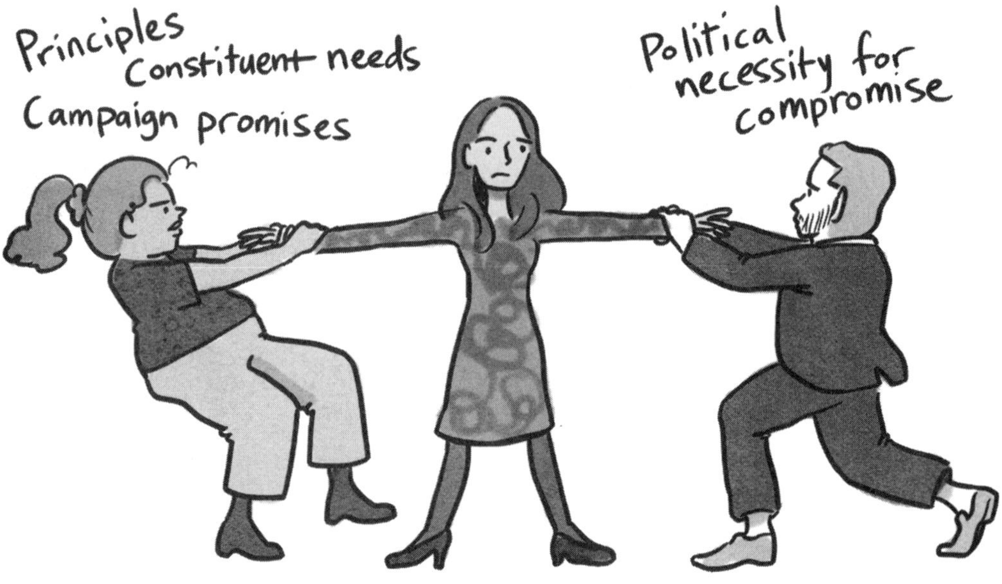
Principles
Constituent needs
Campaign promises
Political necessity for compromise

To lean too far this way risked political isolation. . .

. . . but too far this way, and what was the point of her being there at all?

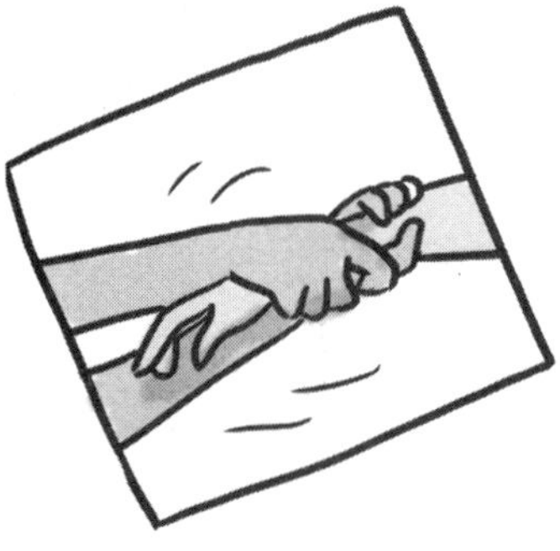

So far, Julia seemed to be handling those pressures pretty gracefully on a personal level. But she did represent a movement, and that movement would only get more confrontational to the legislature as time went on.

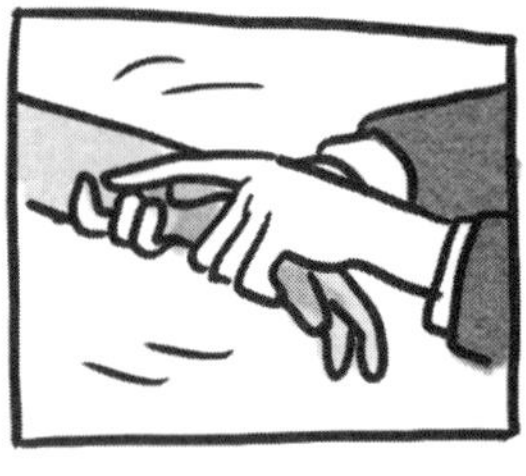

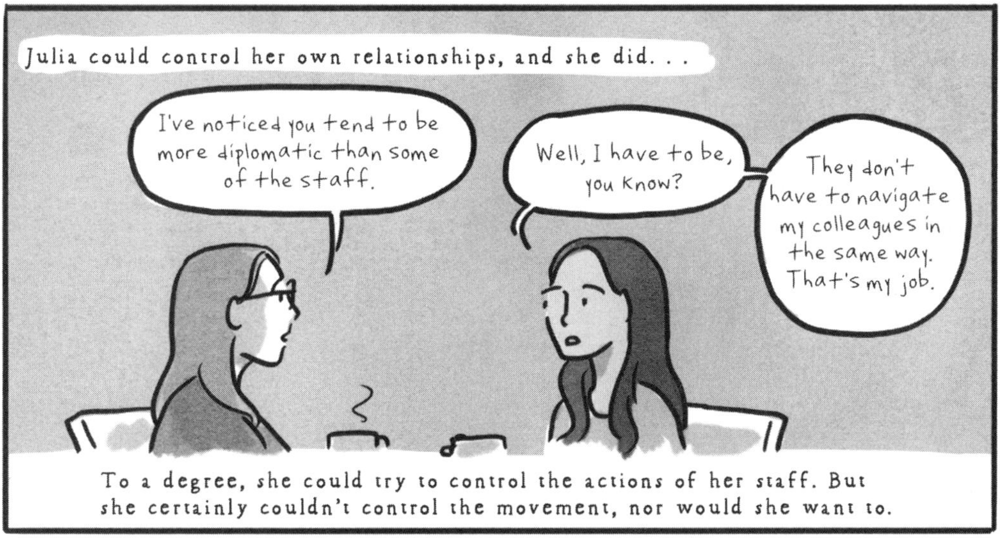
Julia could control her own relationships, and she did. . .
I've noticed you tend to be more diplomatic than some of the staff.
Well, I have to be, you know?
They don't have to navigate my colleagues in the same way. That's my job.
To a degree, she could try to control the actions of her staff. But she certainly couldn't control the movement, nor would she want to.

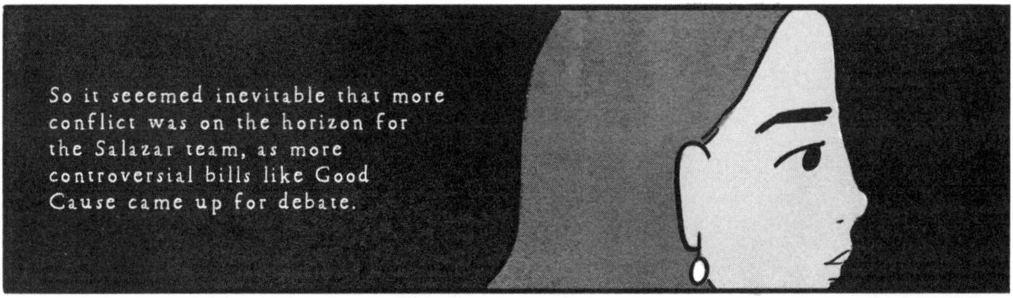
So it seeemed inevitable that more conflict was on the horizon for the Salazar team, as more controversial bills like Good Cause came up for debate.

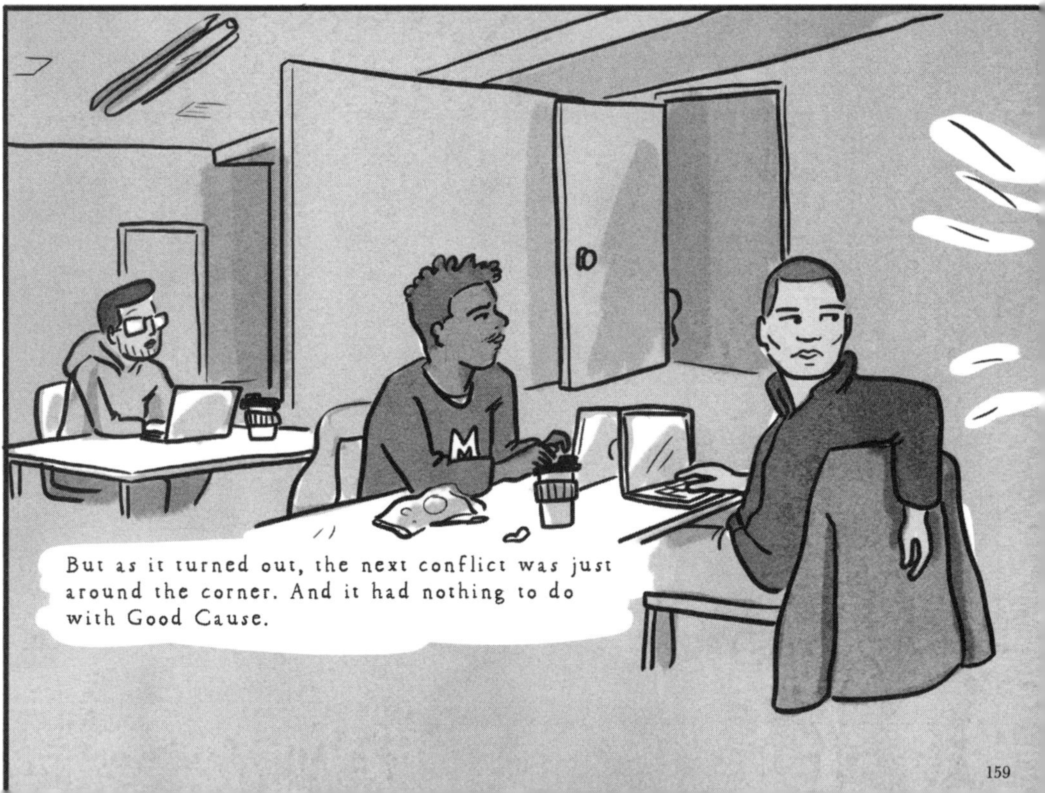
But as it turned out, the next conflict was just around the corner. And it had nothing to do with Good Cause.

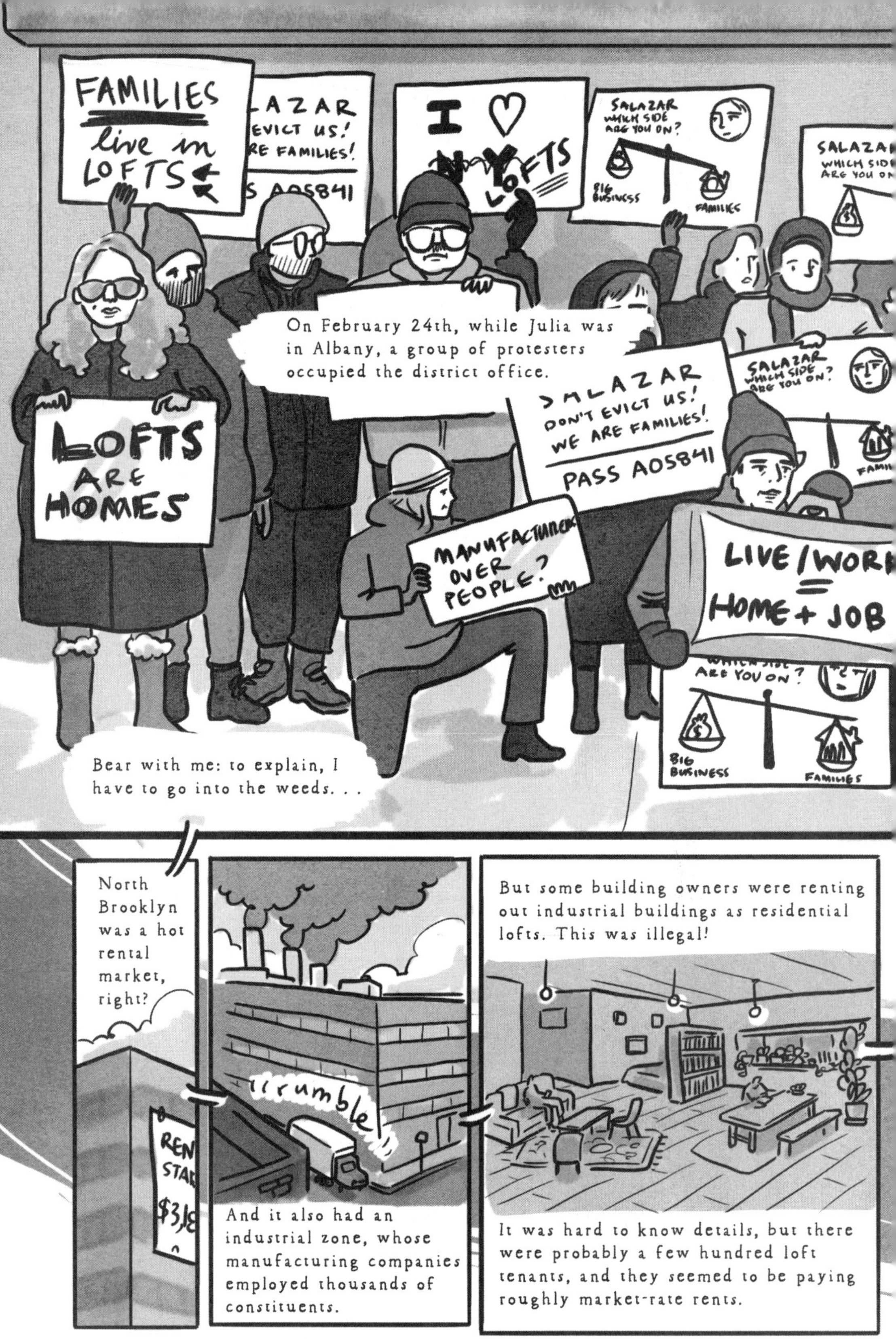

FAMILIES live in LOFTS
LAZAR EVICT US! RE FAMILIES! S A05841
I ♥ NY LOFTS
SALAZAR WHICH SIDE ARE YOU ON? BIG BUSINESS FAMILIES
On February 24th, while Julia was in Albany, a group of protesters occupied the district office.
LOFTS ARE HOMES
SALAZAR DON'T EVICT US! WE ARE FAMILIES! PASS A05841
MANUFACTURERS OVER PEOPLE?
LIVE/WORK = HOME + JOB
Bear with me: to explain, I have to go into the weeds. . .
North Brooklyn was a hot rental market, right?
rumble
And it also had an industrial zone, whose manufacturing companies employed thousands of constituents.
But some building owners were renting out industrial buildings as residential lofts. This was illegal!
It was hard to know details, but there were probably a few hundred loft tenants, and they seemed to be paying roughly market-rate rents.

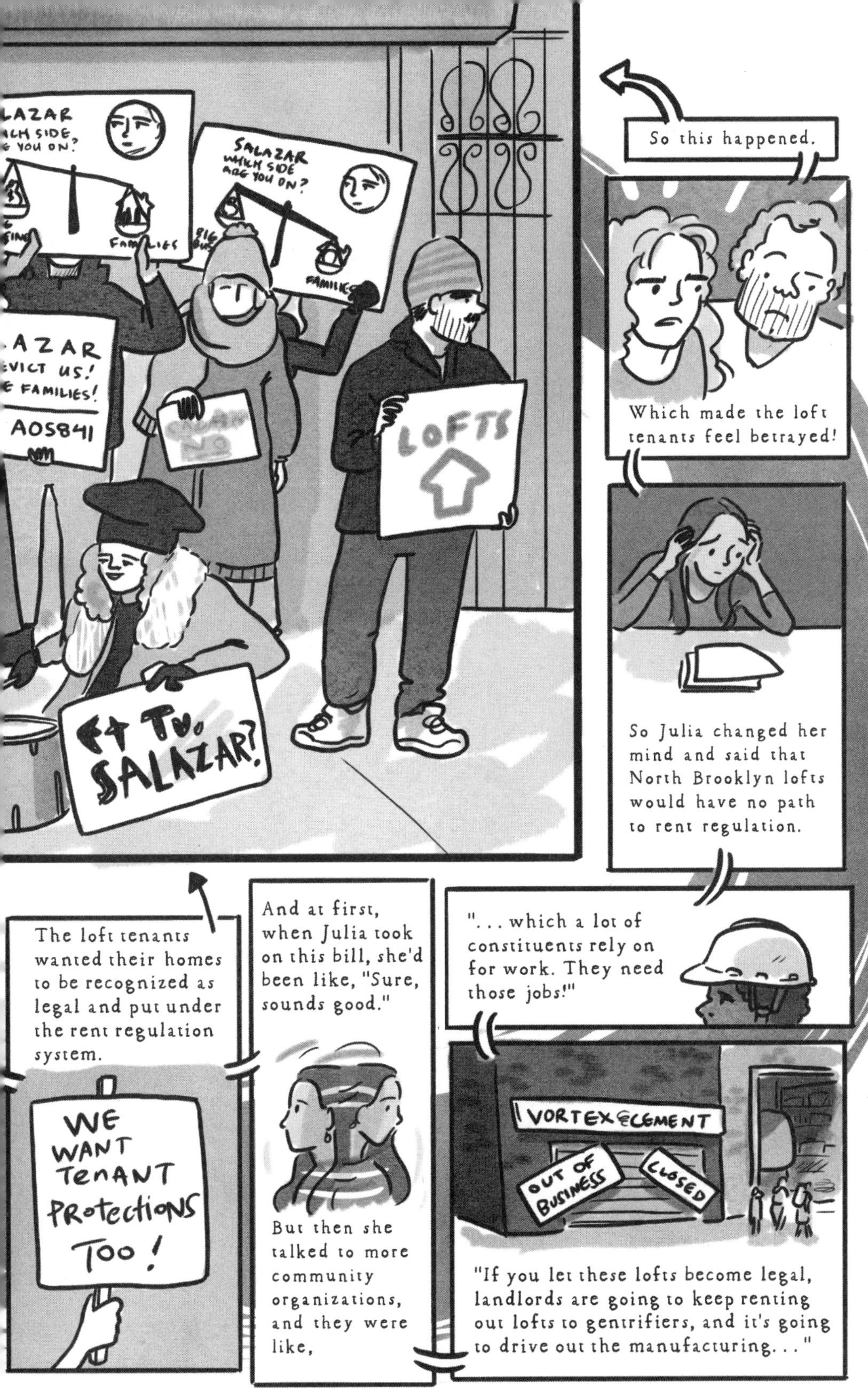

The loft tenants wanted their homes to be recognized as legal and put under the rent regulation system.
WE WANT TENANT PROTECTIONS TOO!
And at first, when Julia took on this bill, she'd been like, "Sure, sounds good."
But then she talked to more community organizations, and they were like,
VORTEX CEMENT
OUT OF BUSINESS
CLOSED
"If you let these lofts become legal, landlords are going to keep renting out lofts to gentrifiers, and it's going to drive out the manufacturing. . ."
". . . which a lot of constituents rely on for work. They need those jobs!"
So Julia changed her mind and said that North Brooklyn lofts would have no path to rent regulation.
Which made the loft tenants feel betrayed!
So this happened.
SALAZAR WHICH SIDE ARE YOU ON?
FAMILIES
A05841
LOFTS
ET TU, SALAZAR?

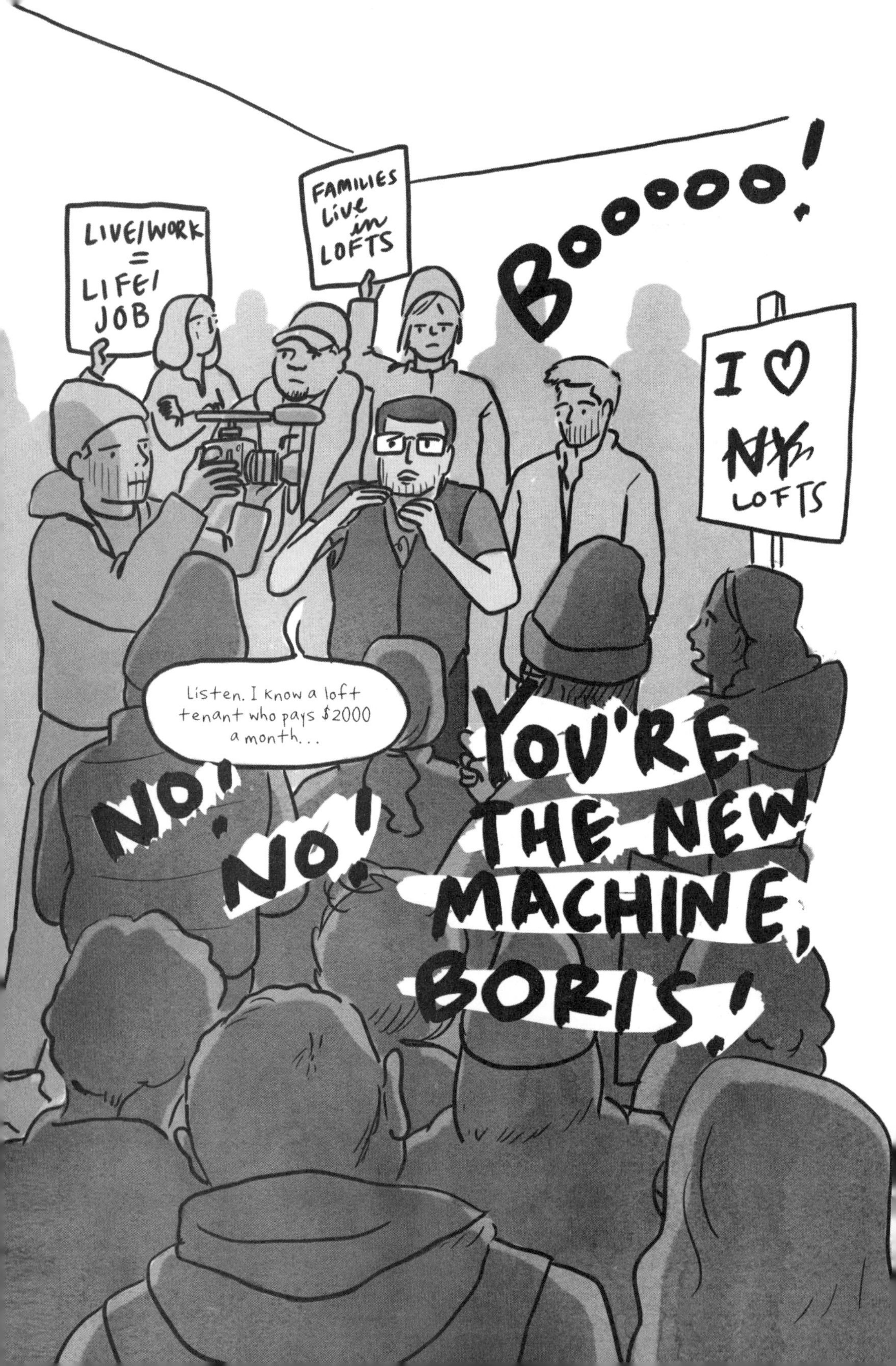
LIVE/WORK = LIFE/JOB
FAMILIES LIVE IN LOFTS
BOOOOOO!
I ♡ NY LOFTS
Listen. I know a loft tenant who pays $2000 a month...
NO!
NO!
YOU'RE THE NEW MACHINE, BORIS!

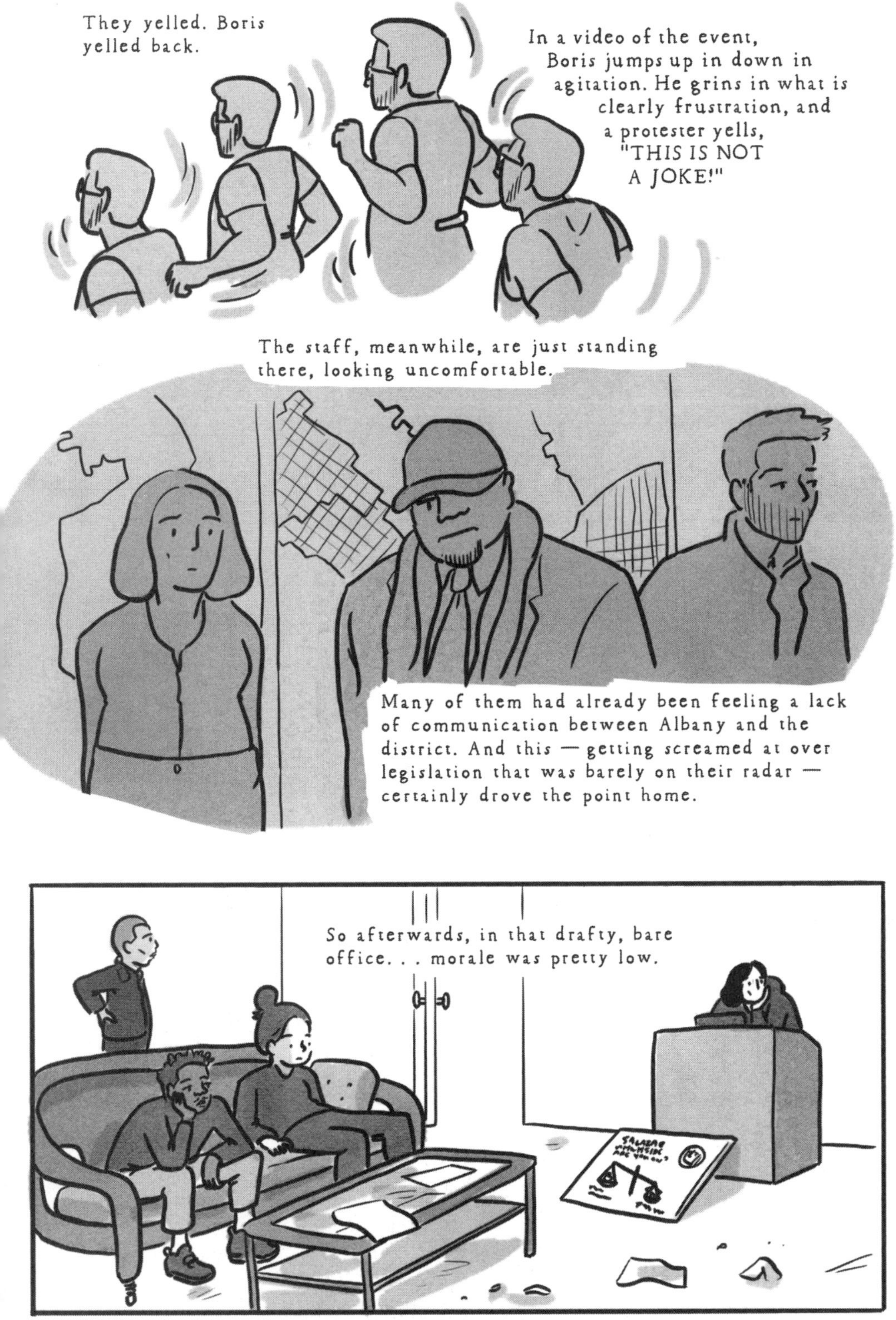
They yelled. Boris yelled back.
In a video of the event, Boris jumps up in down in agitation. He grins in what is clearly frustration, and a protester yells, "THIS IS NOT A JOKE!"
The staff, meanwhile, are just standing there, looking uncomfortable.
Many of them had already been feeling a lack of communication between Albany and the district. And this — getting screamed at over legislation that was barely on their radar — certainly drove the point home.
So afterwards, in that drafty, bare office. . . morale was pretty low.

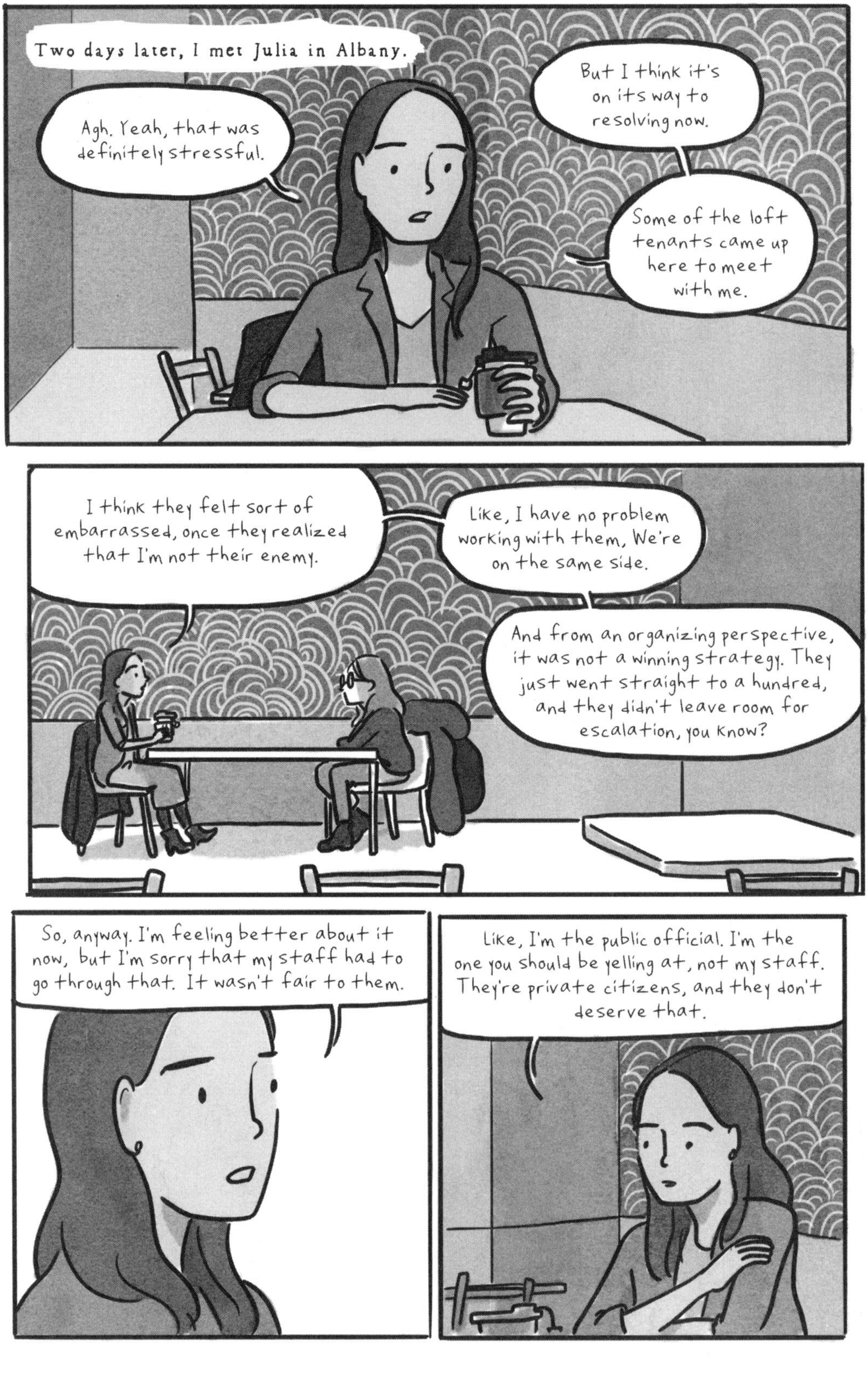
Two days later, I met Julia in Albany.
Agh. Yeah, that was definitely stressful.
But I think it's on its way to resolving now.
Some of the loft tenants came up here to meet with me.
I think they felt sort of embarrassed, once they realized that I'm not their enemy.
Like, I have no problem working with them, We're on the same side.
And from an organizing perspective, it was not a winning strategy. They just went straight to a hundred, and they didn't leave room for escalation, you know?
So, anyway. I'm feeling better about it now, but I'm sorry that my staff had to go through that. It wasn't fair to them.
Like, I'm the public official. I'm the one you should be yelling at, not my staff. They're private citizens, and they don't deserve that.

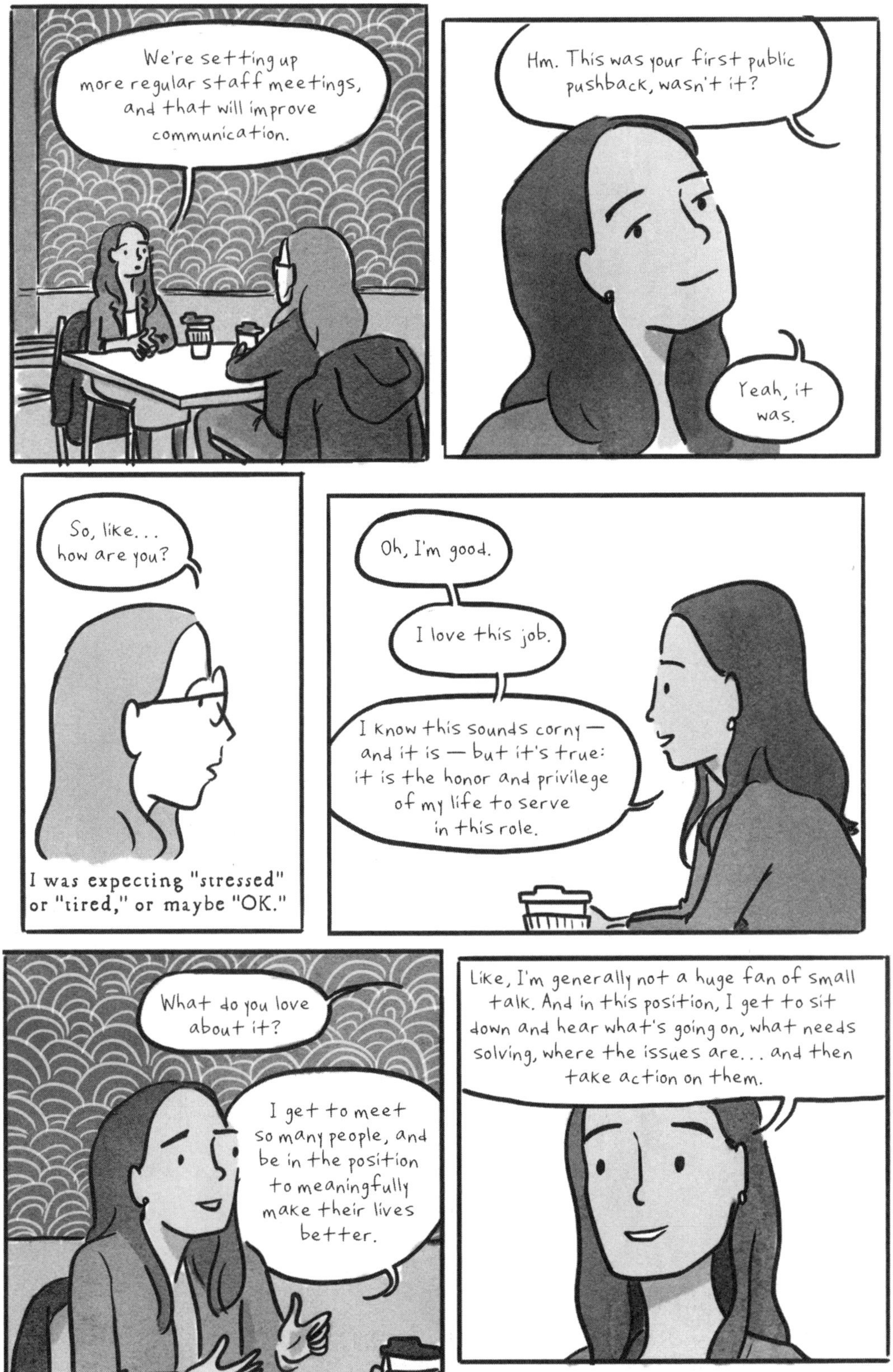

We're setting up more regular staff meetings, and that will improve communication.
Hm. This was your first public pushback, wasn't it?
Yeah, it was.
So, like... how are you?
I was expecting "stressed" or "tired," or maybe "OK."
Oh, I'm good.
I love this job.
I know this sounds corny — and it is — but it's true: it is the honor and privilege of my life to serve in this role.
What do you love about it?
I get to meet so many people, and be in the position to meaningfully make their lives better.
Like, I'm generally not a huge fan of small talk. And in this position, I get to sit down and hear what's going on, what needs solving, where the issues are... and then take action on them.

In a state of over nineteen million inhabitants, the loft law bill would affect only a few hundred.

But in spite of how small it was in the grand scheme of state legislation, it would become an ongoing headache for Julia.

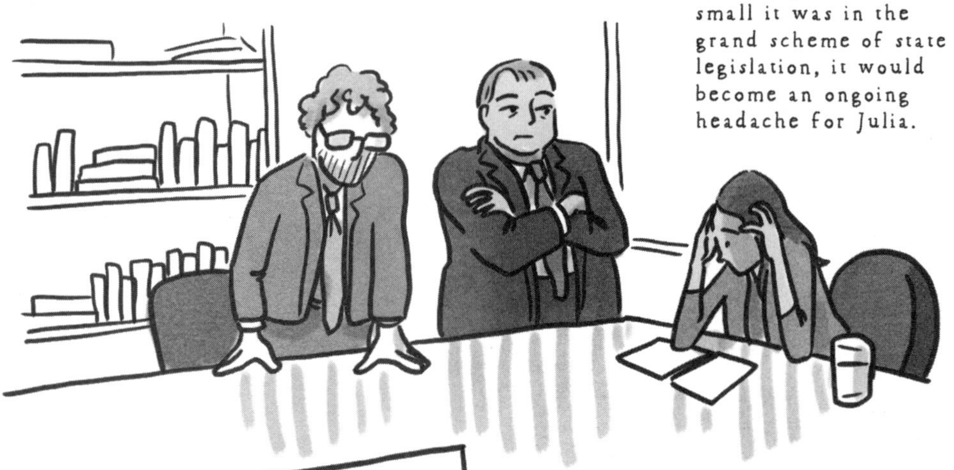

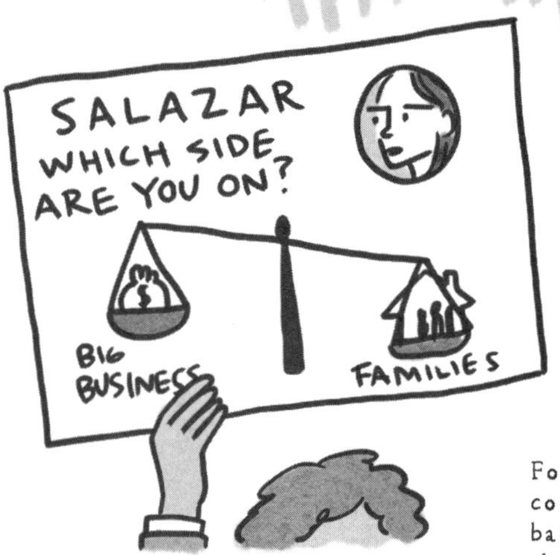
SALAZAR
WHICH SIDE ARE YOU ON?
BIG BUSINESS
FAMILIES

In the months to come, Julia would face rancor from all sides: the loft law tenants would call her a hypocrite. Community groups would tell her not to cow to gentrifiers. Her Assembly co-sponsor would grow impatient, and there would be talk of removing Julia from the bill entirely.

For the rest of session, loft law continued to percolate moodily on the backburner, as Julia agonized over the best solution for all involved.

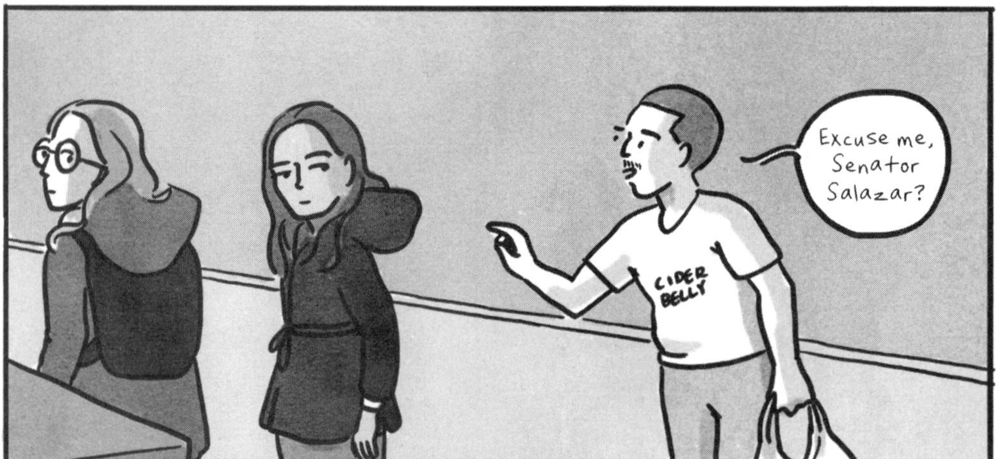
Excuse me, Senator Salazar?
CIDER BELLY

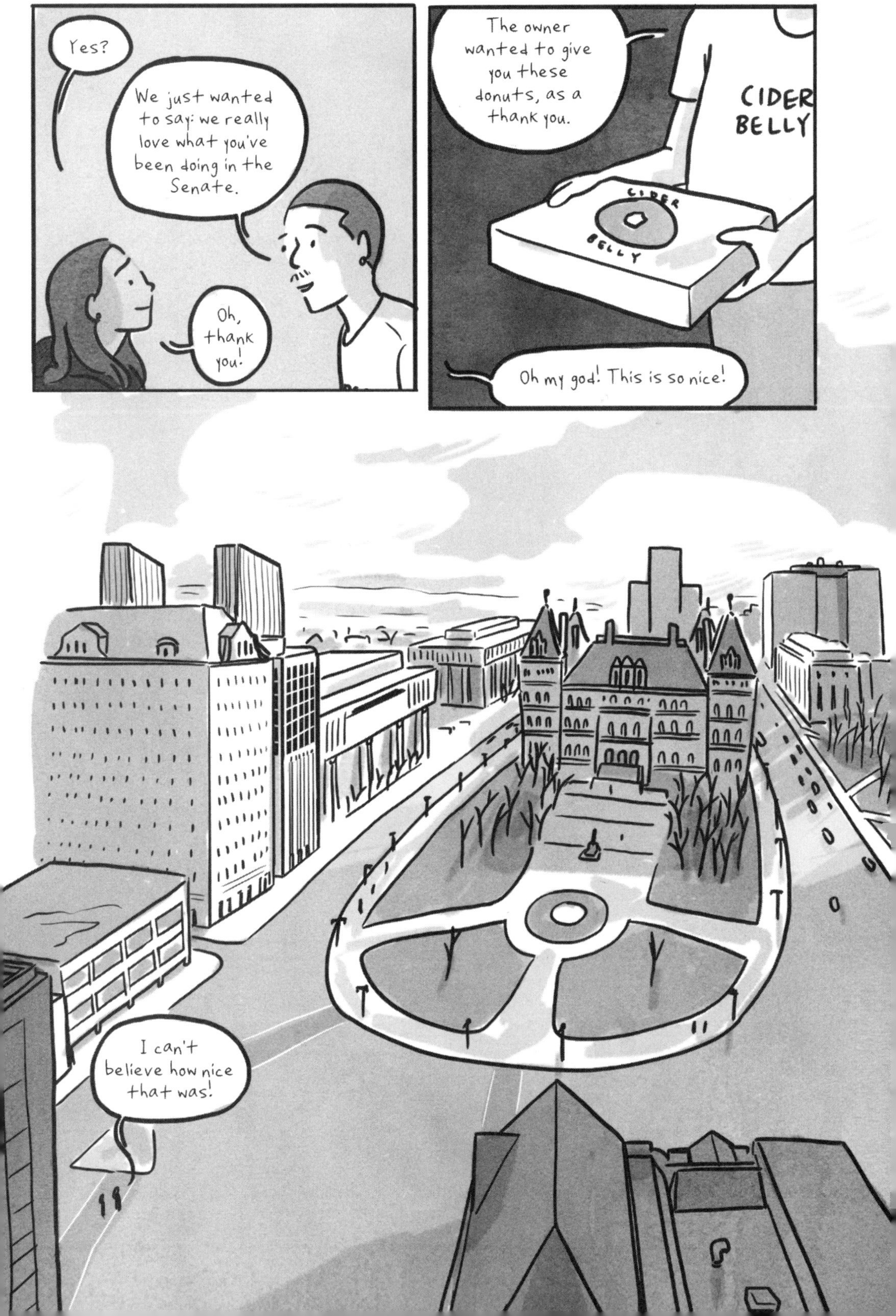
Yes?
We just wanted to say: we really love what you've been doing in the Senate.
Oh, thank you!
The owner wanted to give you these donuts, as a thank you.
CIDER BELLY
CIDER BELLY
Oh my god! This is so nice!
I can't believe how nice that was!

Chapter Seven

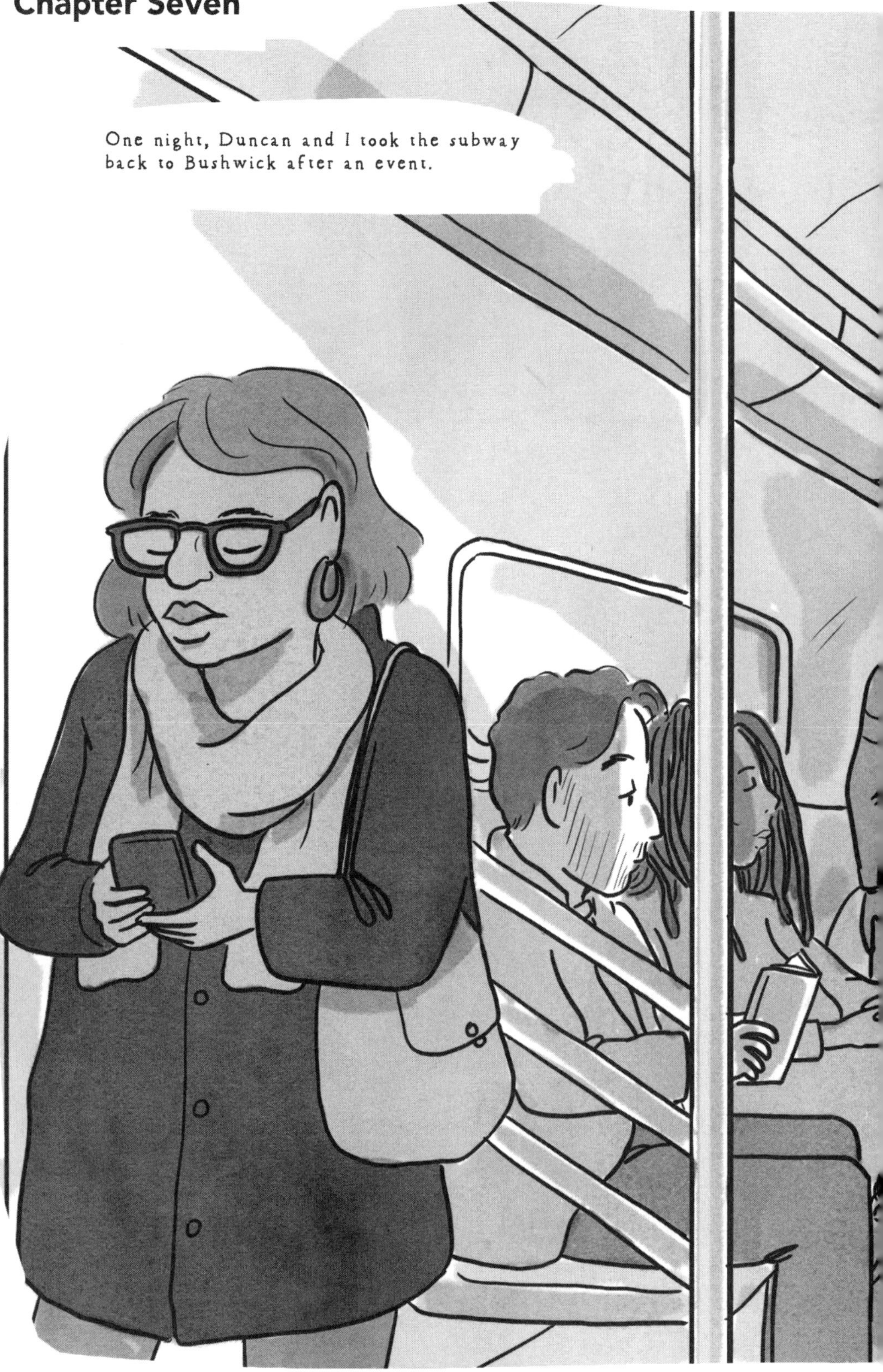
One night, Duncan and I took the subway back to Bushwick after an event.

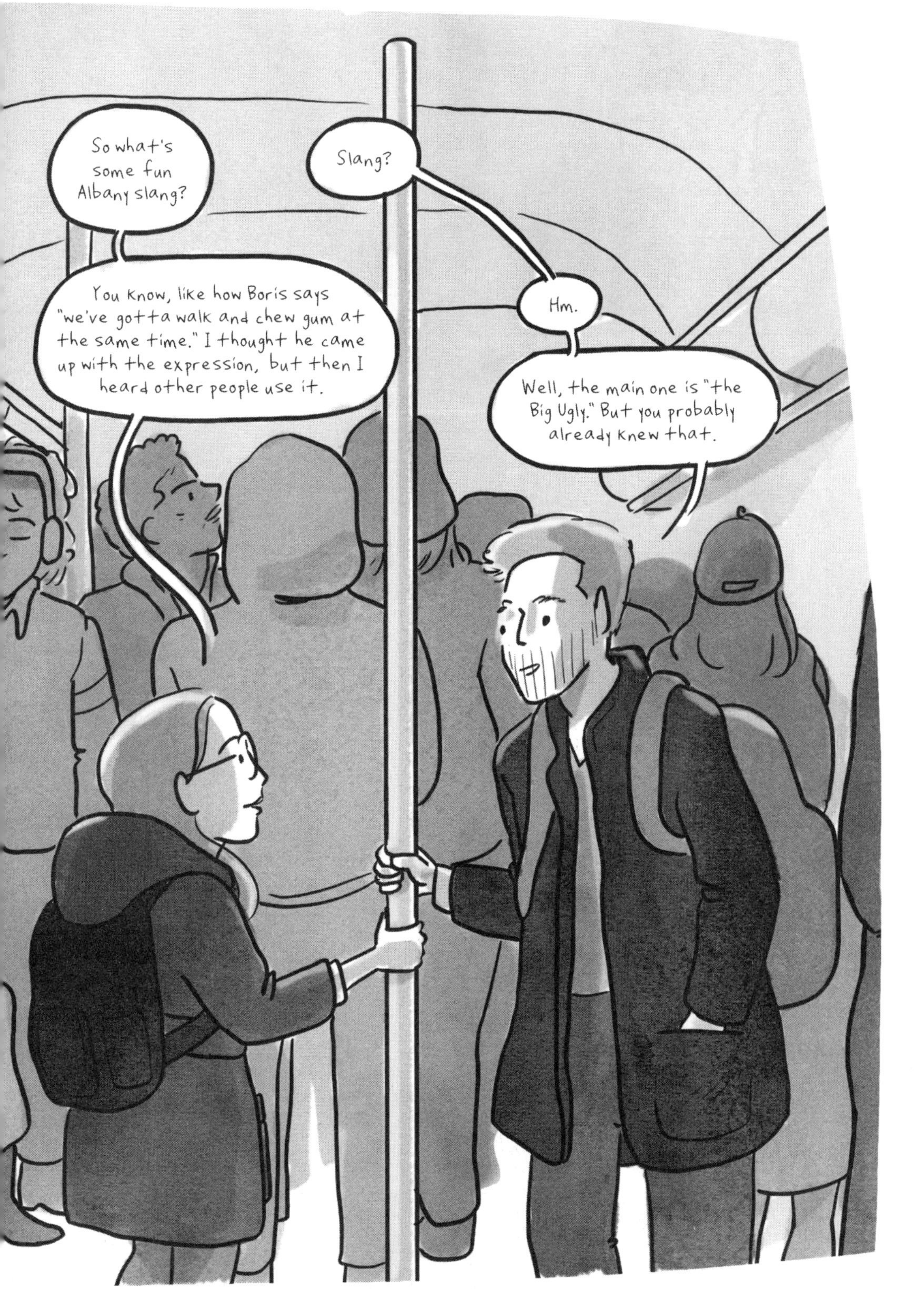
So what's some fun Albany slang?
Slang?
You know, like how Boris says "we've gotta walk and chew gum at the same time." I thought he came up with the expression, but then I heard other people use it.
Hm.
Well, the main one is "the Big Ugly." But you probably already knew that.

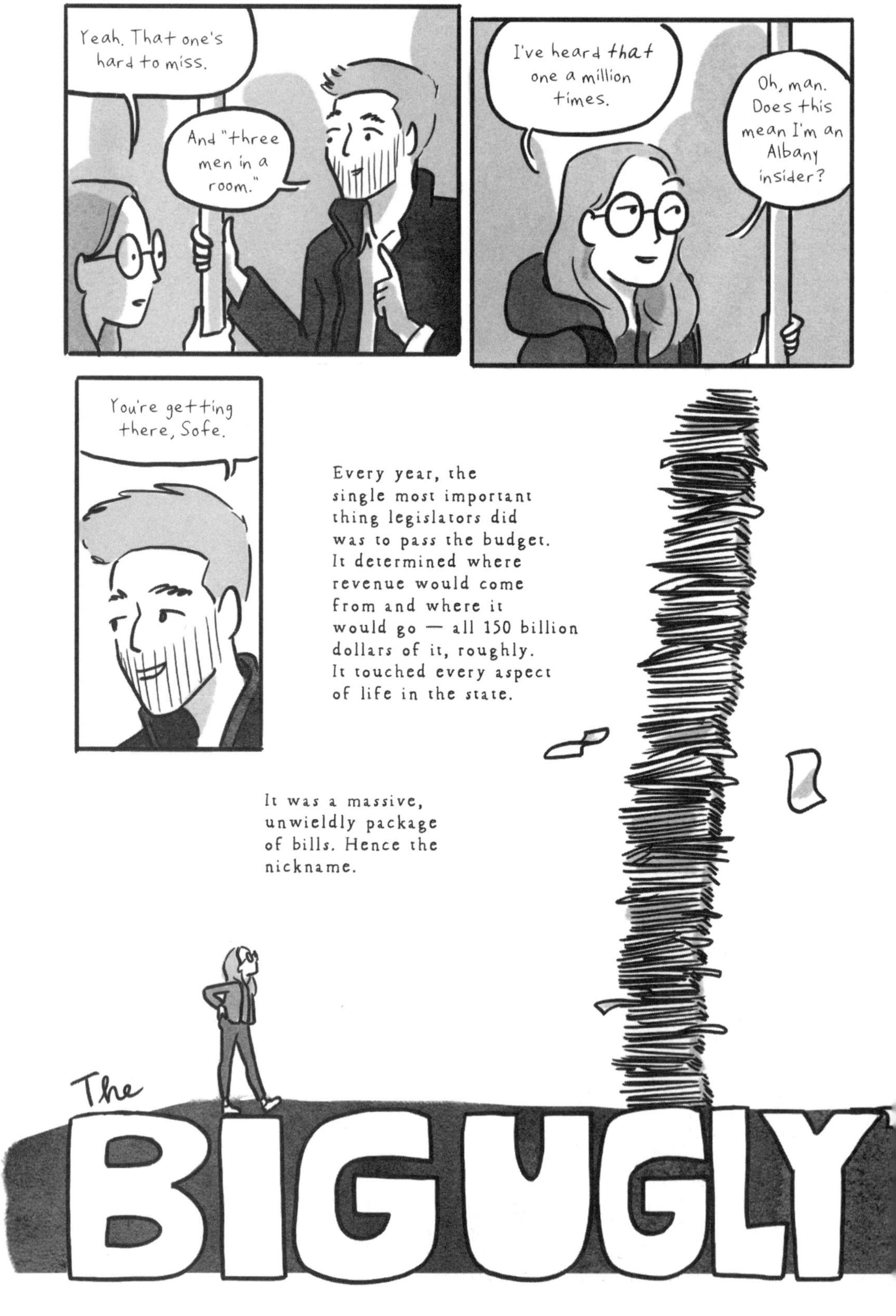
Yeah. That one's hard to miss.
And "three men in a room."
I've heard *that* one a million times.
Oh, man. Does this mean I'm an Albany insider?
You're getting there, Sofe.
Every year, the single most important thing legislators did was to pass the budget. It determined where revenue would come from and where it would go — all 150 billion dollars of it, roughly. It touched every aspect of life in the state.
It was a massive, unwieldly package of bills. Hence the nickname.
The BIG UGLY

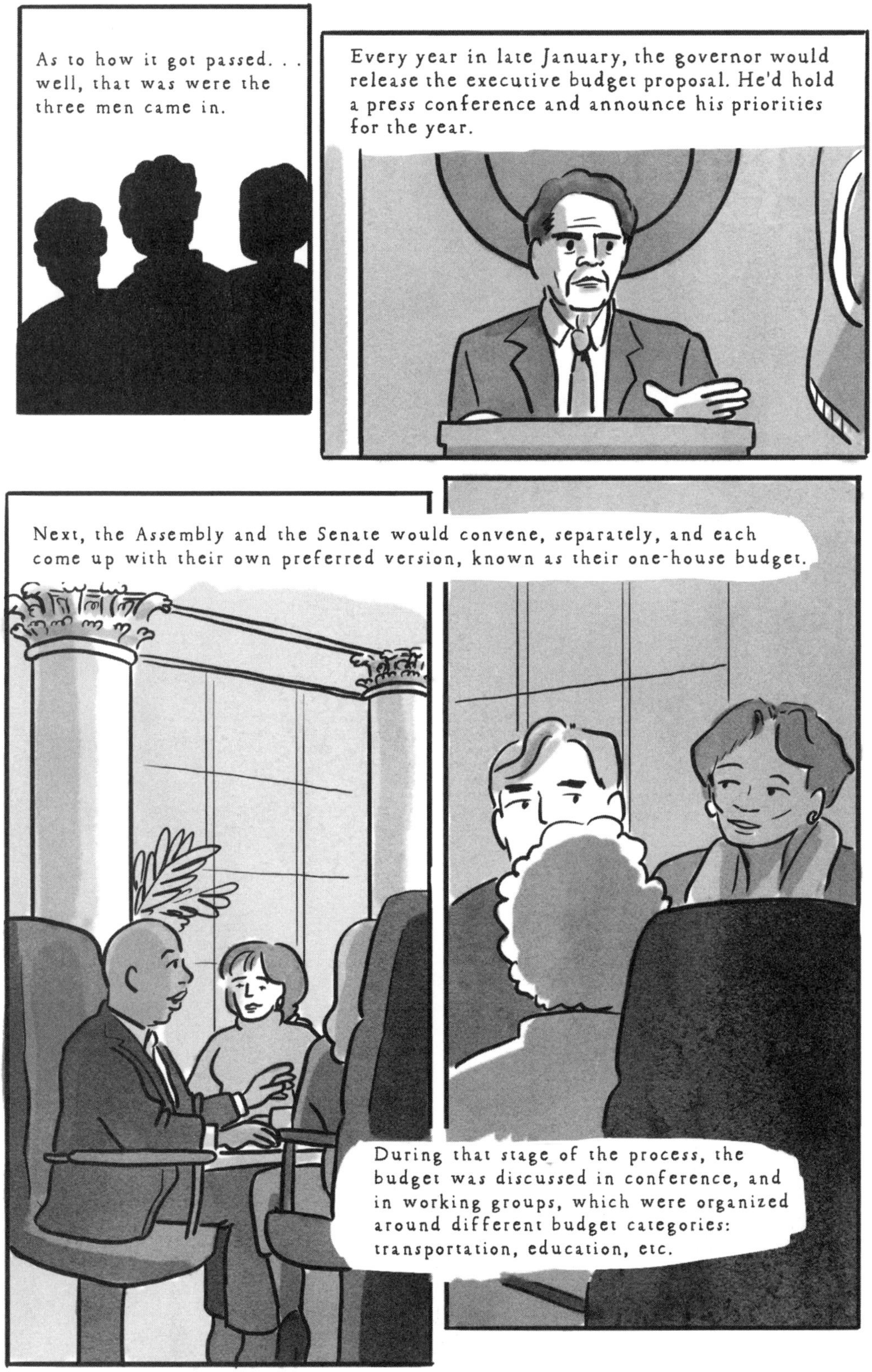
As to how it got passed. . . well, that was were the three men came in.
Every year in late January, the governor would release the executive budget proposal. He'd hold a press conference and announce his priorities for the year.
Next, the Assembly and the Senate would convene, separately, and each come up with their own preferred version, known as their one-house budget.
During that stage of the process, the budget was discussed in conference, and in working groups, which were organized around different budget categories: transportation, education, etc.

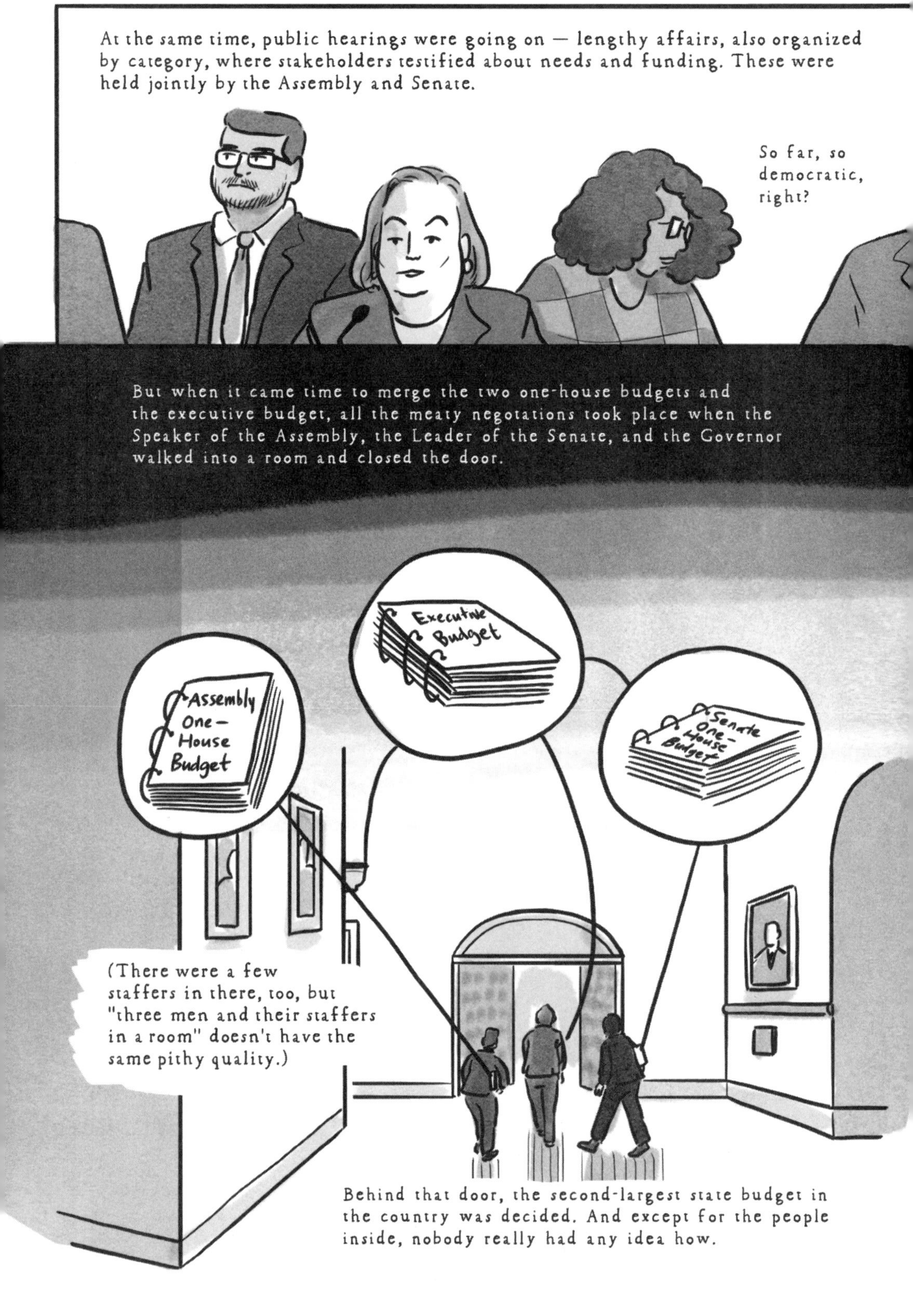
At the same time, public hearings were going on — lengthy affairs, also organized by category, where stakeholders testified about needs and funding. These were held jointly by the Assembly and Senate.
So far, so democratic, right?
But when it came time to merge the two one-house budgets and the executive budget, all the meaty negotations took place when the Speaker of the Assembly, the Leader of the Senate, and the Governor walked into a room and closed the door.
Executive Budget
Assembly One-House Budget
Senate One-House Budget
(There were a few staffers in there, too, but "three men and their staffers in a room" doesn't have the same pithy quality.)
Behind that door, the second-largest state budget in the country was decided. And except for the people inside, nobody really had any idea how.

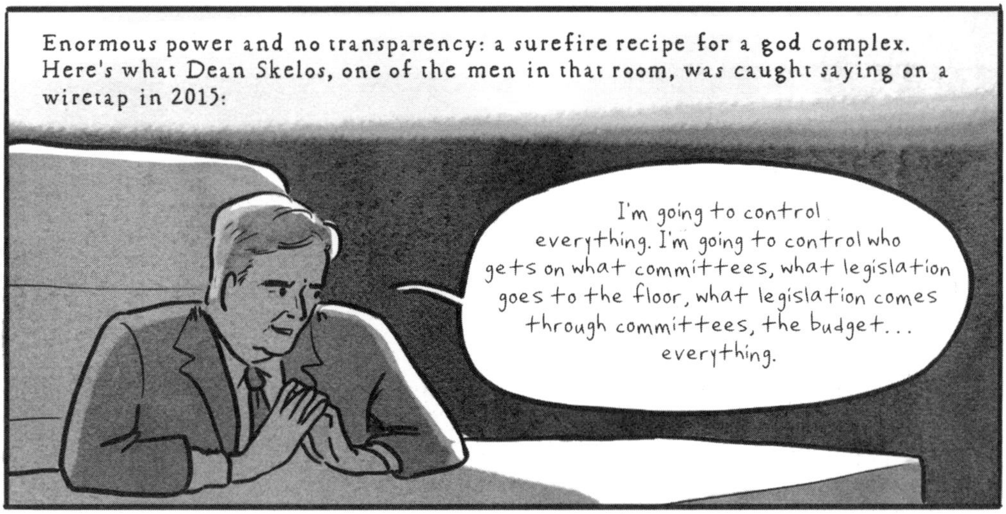
Enormous power and no transparency: a surefire recipe for a god complex. Here's what Dean Skelos, one of the men in that room, was caught saying on a wiretap in 2015:
I'm going to control everything. I'm going to control who gets on what committees, what legislation goes to the floor, what legislation comes through committees, the budget... everything.

Seymour Lachman, a Democratic state senator from 1996-2004, wrote a book* about the culture of corruption this power structure engendered.

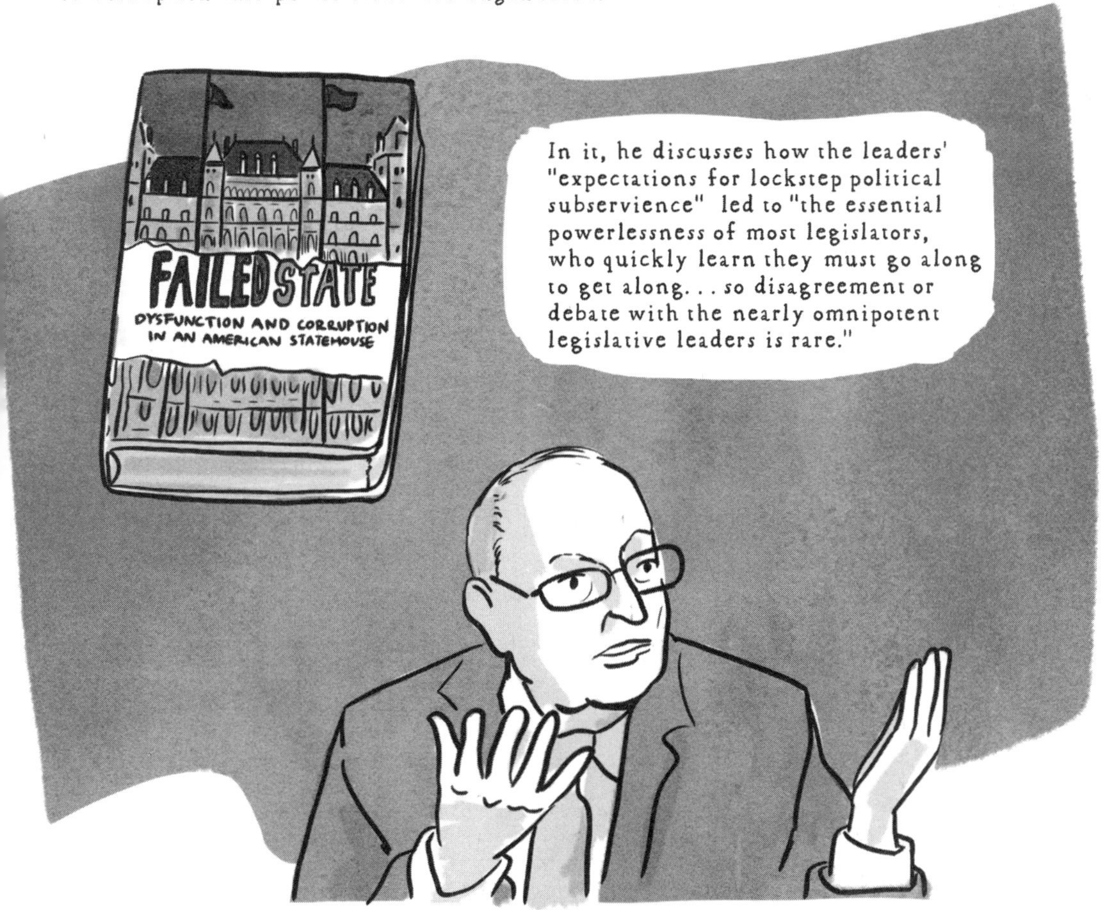
FAILED STATE
DYSFUNCTION AND CORRUPTION IN AN AMERICAN STATEHOUSE
In it, he discusses how the leaders' "expectations for lockstep political subservience" led to "the essential powerlessness of most legislators, who quickly learn they must go along to get along... so disagreement or debate with the nearly omnipotent legislative leaders is rare."

*Co-authored with Robert Polner, and originally published under the title *Three Men in a Room: The Inside Story of Power and Betrayal in an American Statehouse*

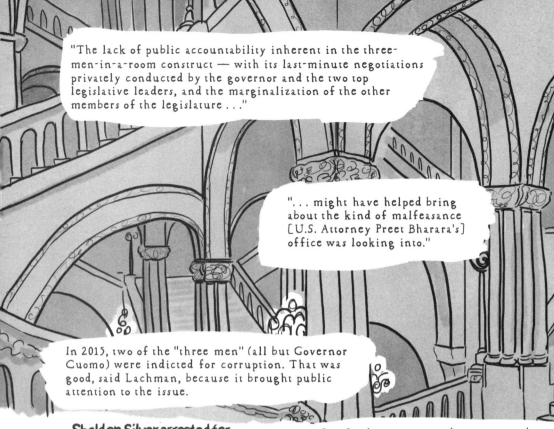

"The lack of public accountability inherent in the three-men-in-a-room construct — with its last-minute negotiations privately conducted by the governor and the two top legislative leaders, and the marginalization of the other members of the legislature . . ."

". . . might have helped bring about the kind of malfeasance [U.S. Attorney Preet Bharara's] office was looking into."

In 2015, two of the "three men" (all but Governor Cuomo) were indicted for corruption. That was good, said Lachman, because it brought public attention to the issue.

Sheldon Silver arrested for taking $4M in bribes, kickbacks

By Pam Belder, Chris Cuomo etc., Aaron Short and Bruce Golding   January 22, 2015 | 12:23pm

The New York Times

But Lachman remained unconvinced that much had changed. Maybe the players were different, but the structure was still in place. And the structure was rotten.

POLITICO MAGAZINE

POLITICO

Congratulations, New York, You're #1 in Corruption

How the Empire State created such a toxic (and criminal) political culture.

By LAWRENCE LANATT | May 4, 2015

Dean Skelos, Ex-New York Senate Leader, and His Son Are Convicted of Corruption

State Senator Dean G. Skelos and his son, Adam, left the federal courthouse in Manhattan after the verdict on Friday. Andrew Lenscher for The New York Times

"New York . . . has learned that it takes just three men in a room to cause devastating harm to a democratic system of governance."

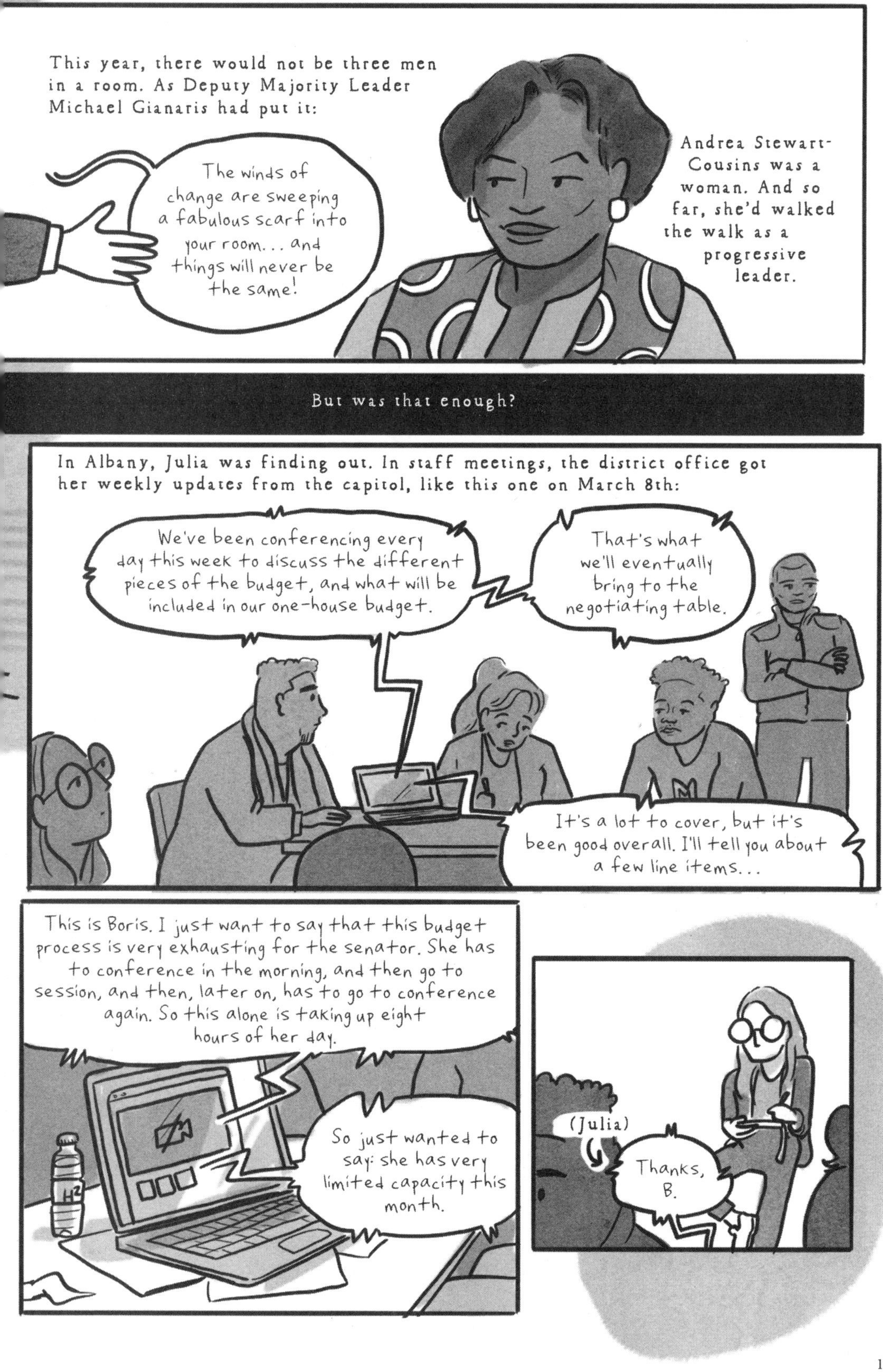
This year, there would not be three men in a room. As Deputy Majority Leader Michael Gianaris had put it:
The winds of change are sweeping a fabulous scarf into your room... and things will never be the same!
Andrea Stewart-Cousins was a woman. And so far, she'd walked the walk as a progressive leader.
But was that enough?
In Albany, Julia was finding out. In staff meetings, the district office got her weekly updates from the capitol, like this one on March 8th:
We've been conferencing every day this week to discuss the different pieces of the budget, and what will be included in our one-house budget.
That's what we'll eventually bring to the negotiating table.
It's a lot to cover, but it's been good overall. I'll tell you about a few line items...
This is Boris. I just want to say that this budget process is very exhausting for the senator. She has to conference in the morning, and then go to session, and then, later on, has to go to conference again. So this alone is taking up eight hours of her day.
So just wanted to say: she has very limited capacity this month.
(Julia)
Thanks, B.

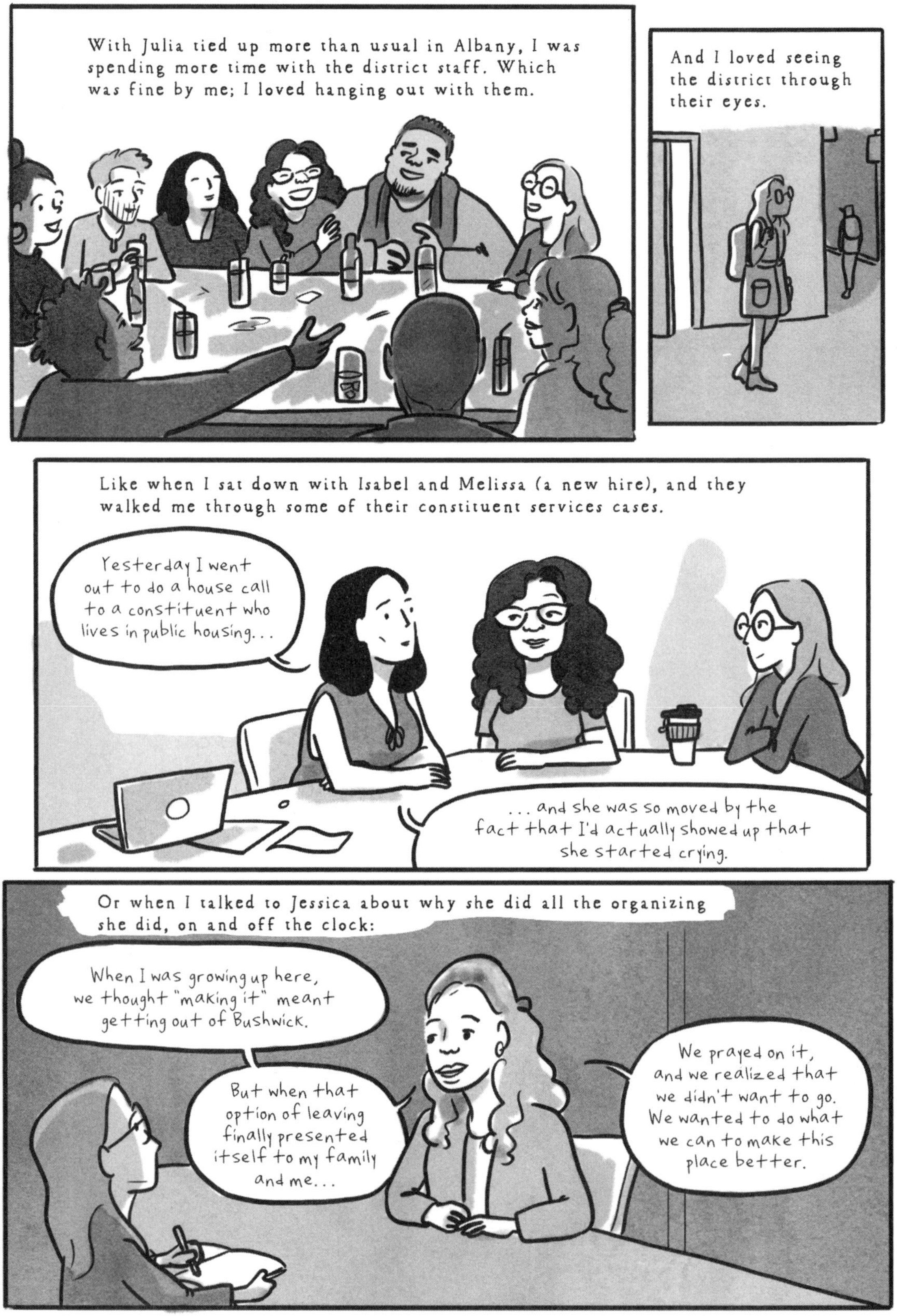
With Julia tied up more than usual in Albany, I was spending more time with the district staff. Which was fine by me; I loved hanging out with them.
And I loved seeing the district through their eyes.
Like when I sat down with Isabel and Melissa (a new hire), and they walked me through some of their constituent services cases.
Yesterday I went out to do a house call to a constituent who lives in public housing...
...and she was so moved by the fact that I'd actually showed up that she started crying.
Or when I talked to Jessica about why she did all the organizing she did, on and off the clock:
When I was growing up here, we thought "making it" meant getting out of Bushwick.
But when that option of leaving finally presented itself to my family and me...
We prayed on it, and we realized that we didn't want to go. We wanted to do what we can to make this place better.

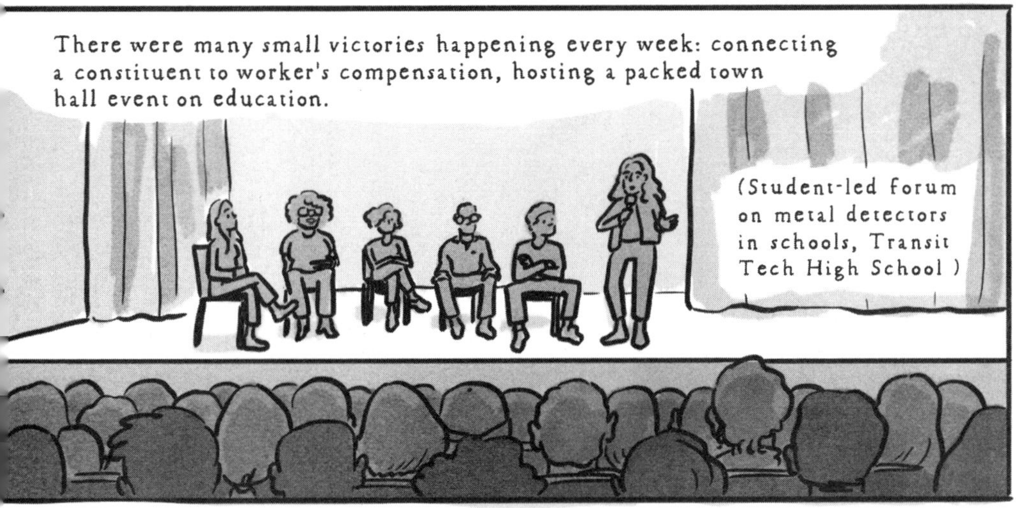
There were many small victories happening every week: connecting a constituent to worker's compensation, hosting a packed town hall event on education.
(Student-led forum on metal detectors in schools, Transit Tech High School)

But for every success story, there were also so many problems without easy fixes:

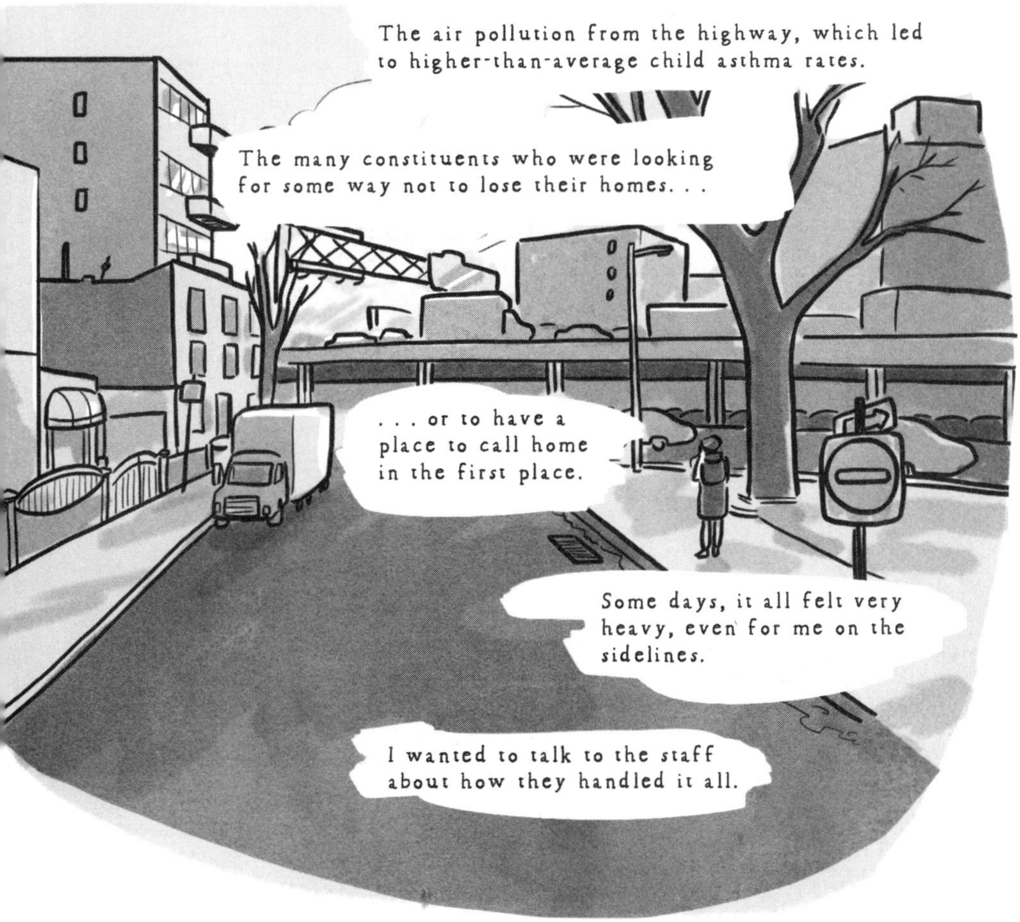
The air pollution from the highway, which led to higher-than-average child asthma rates.
The many constituents who were looking for some way not to lose their homes. . .
. . . or to have a place to call home in the first place.
Some days, it all felt very heavy, even for me on the sidelines.
I wanted to talk to the staff about how they handled it all.

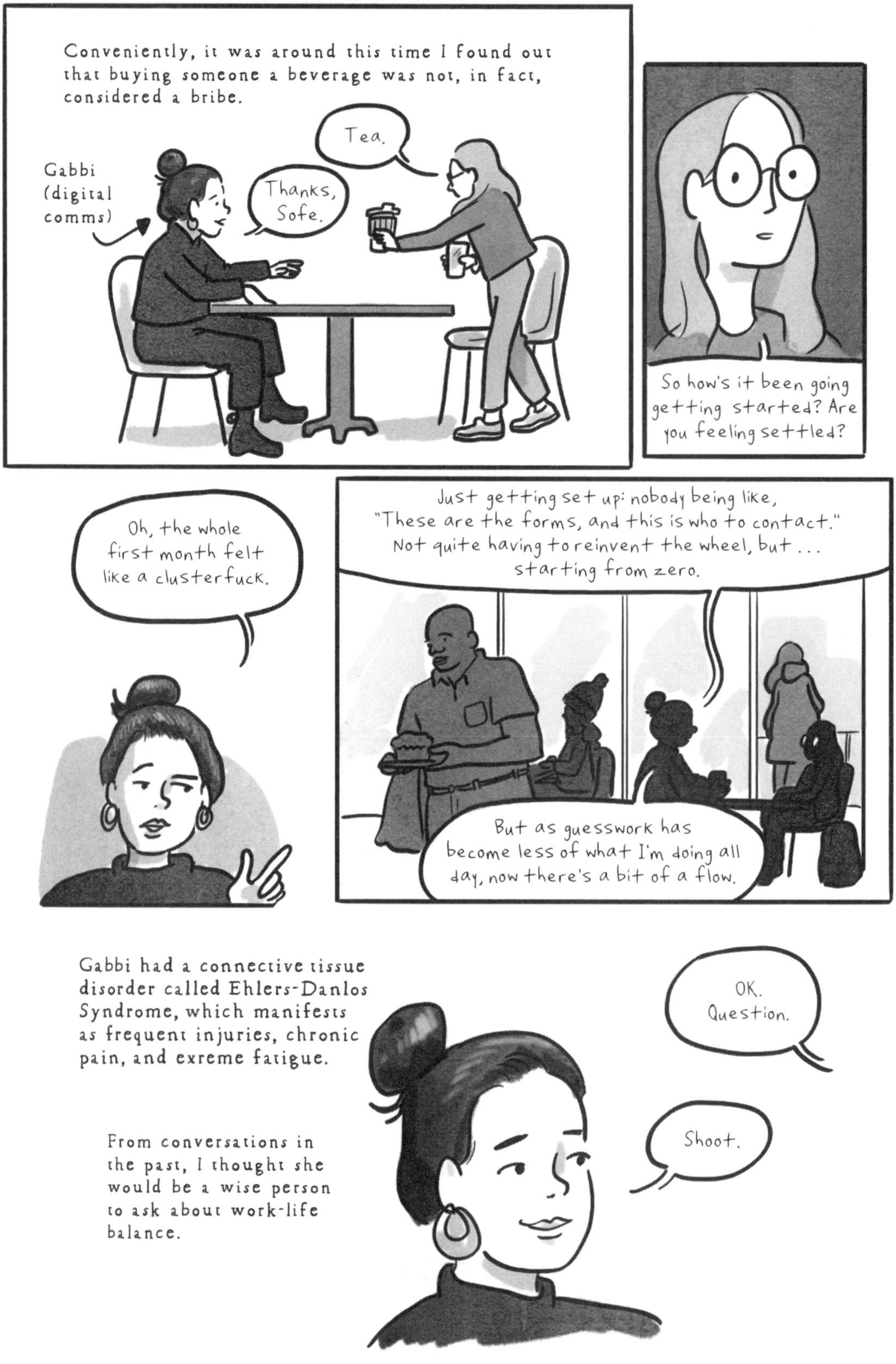
Conveniently, it was around this time I found out that buying someone a beverage was not, in fact, considered a bribe.
Gabbi (digital comms)
Tea.
Thanks, Sofe.
So how's it been going getting started? Are you feeling settled?
Oh, the whole first month felt like a clusterfuck.
Just getting set up: nobody being like, "These are the forms, and this is who to contact." Not quite having to reinvent the wheel, but . . . starting from zero.
But as guesswork has become less of what I'm doing all day, now there's a bit of a flow.
Gabbi had a connective tissue disorder called Ehlers-Danlos Syndrome, which manifests as frequent injuries, chronic pain, and exreme fatigue.
OK. Question.
From conversations in the past, I thought she would be a wise person to ask about work-life balance.
Shoot.

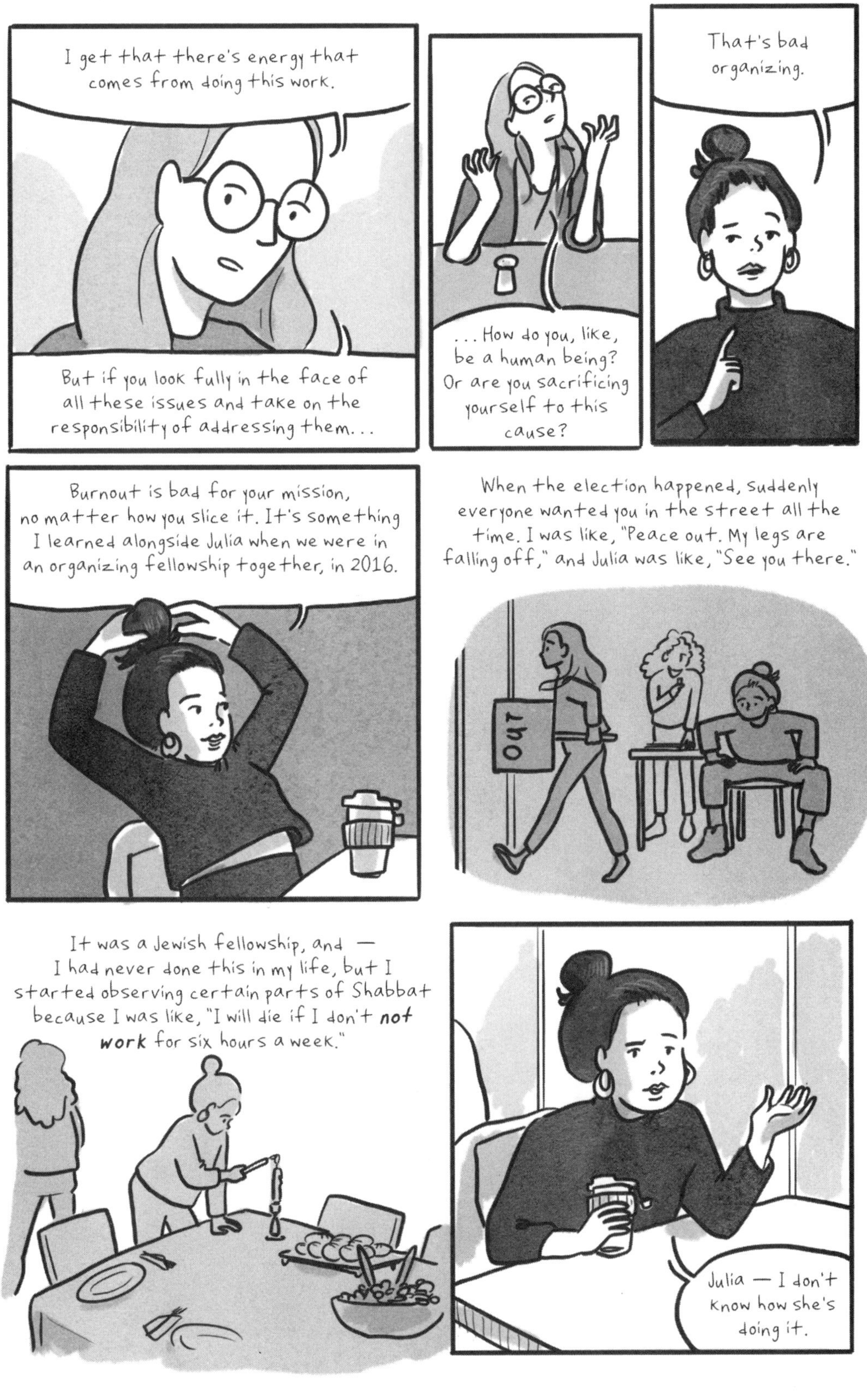
I get that there's energy that comes from doing this work.
But if you look fully in the face of all these issues and take on the responsibility of addressing them. . .
. . . How do you, like, be a human being? Or are you sacrificing yourself to this cause?
That's bad organizing.
Burnout is bad for your mission, no matter how you slice it. It's something I learned alongside Julia when we were in an organizing fellowship together, in 2016.
When the election happened, suddenly everyone wanted you in the street all the time. I was like, "Peace out. My legs are falling off," and Julia was like, "See you there."
OUT
It was a Jewish fellowship, and — I had never done this in my life, but I started observing certain parts of Shabbat because I was like, "I will die if I don't **not work** for six hours a week."
Julia — I don't know how she's doing it.

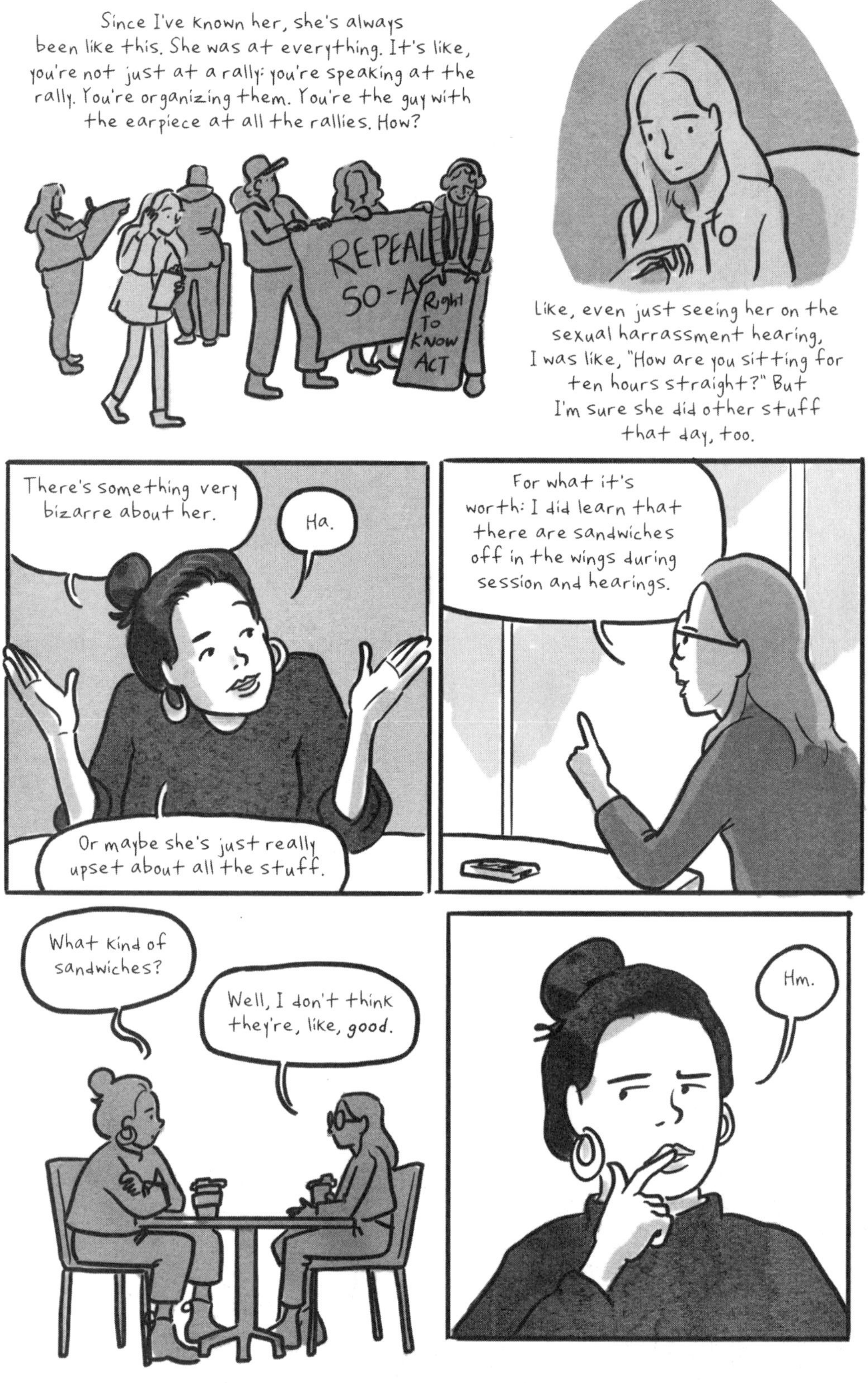
Since I've known her, she's always been like this. She was at everything. It's like, you're not just at a rally: you're speaking at the rally. You're organizing them. You're the guy with the earpiece at all the rallies. How?
REPEAL SO-A
Right To Know ACT
Like, even just seeing her on the sexual harrassment hearing, I was like, "How are you sitting for ten hours straight?" But I'm sure she did other stuff that day, too.
There's something very bizarre about her.
Ha.
Or maybe she's just really upset about all the stuff.
For what it's worth: I did learn that there are sandwiches off in the wings during session and hearings.
What kind of sandwiches?
Well, I don't think they're, like, good.
Hm.

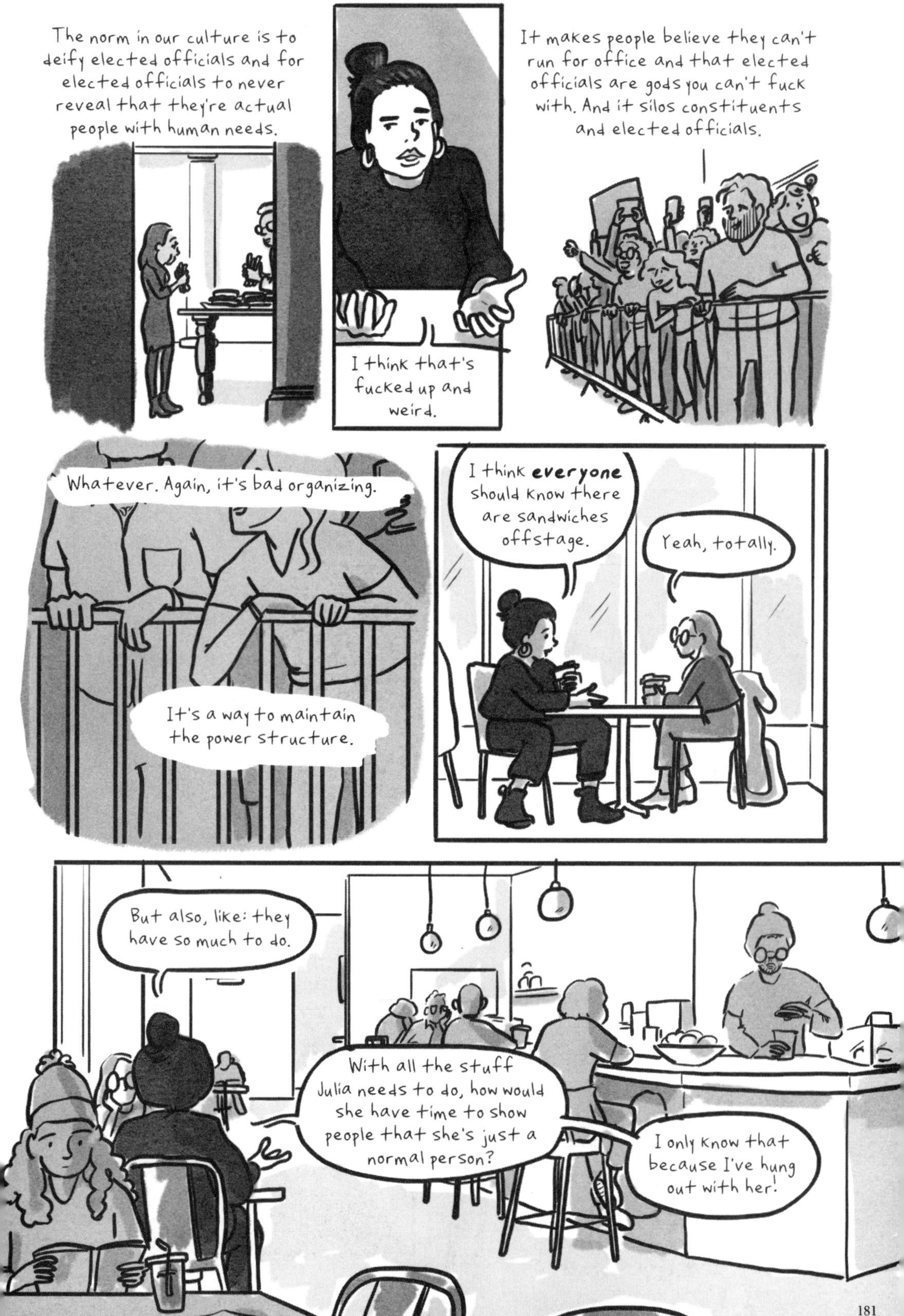
The norm in our culture is to deify elected officials and for elected officials to never reveal that they're actual people with human needs.
I think that's fucked up and weird.
It makes people believe they can't run for office and that elected officials are gods you can't fuck with. And it silos constituents and elected officials.
Whatever. Again, it's bad organizing.
It's a way to maintain the power structure.
I think **everyone** should know there are sandwiches offstage.
Yeah, totally.
But also, like: they have so much to do.
With all the stuff Julia needs to do, how would she have time to show people that she's just a normal person?
I only know that because I've hung out with her!

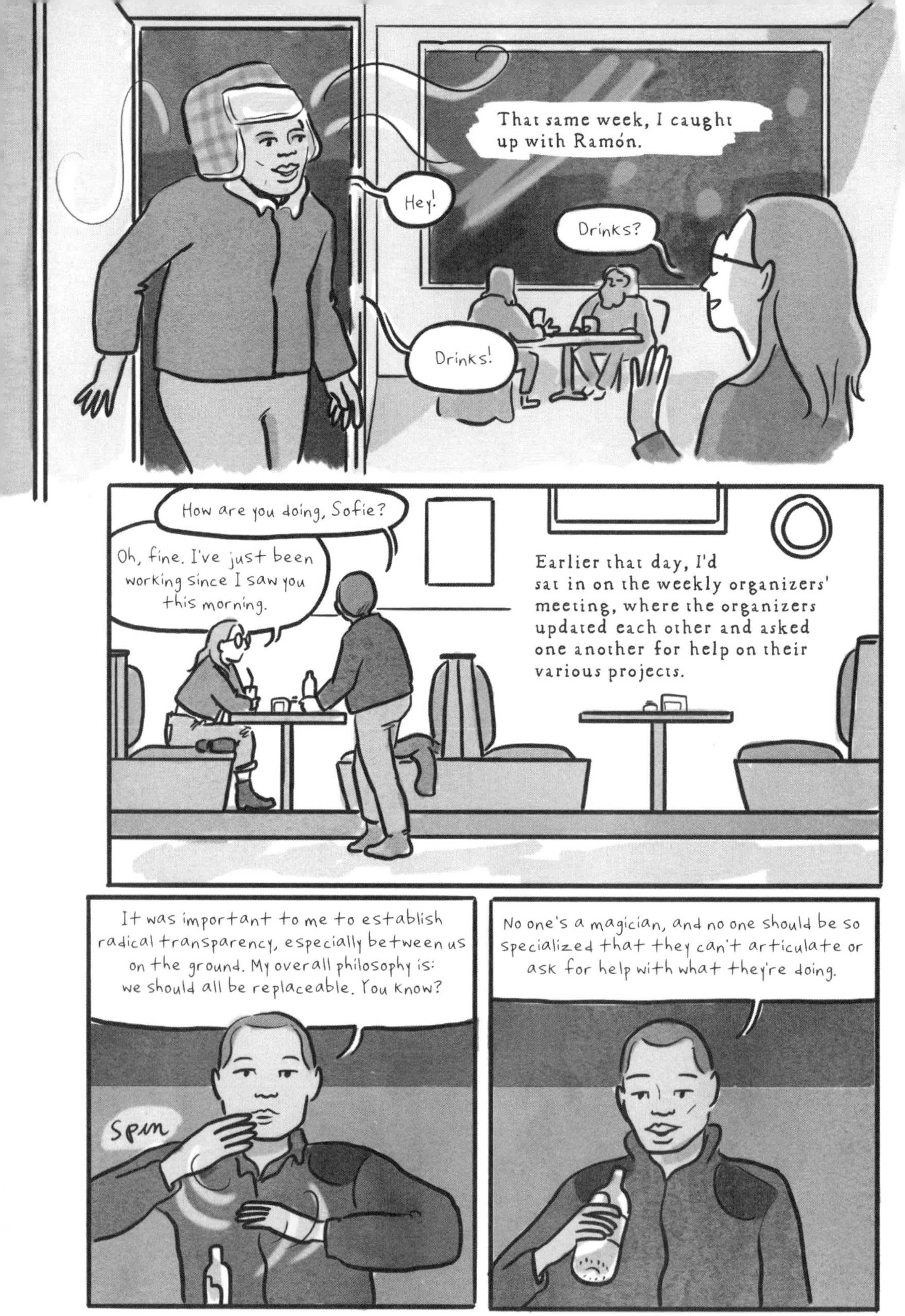

That same week, I caught up with Ramón.
Hey!
Drinks?
Drinks!
How are you doing, Sofie?
Oh, fine. I've just been working since I saw you this morning.
Earlier that day, I'd sat in on the weekly organizers' meeting, where the organizers updated each other and asked one another for help on their various projects.
It was important to me to establish radical transparency, especially between us on the ground. My overall philosophy is: we should all be replaceable. You know?
Spin
No one's a magician, and no one should be so specialized that they can't articulate or ask for help with what they're doing.

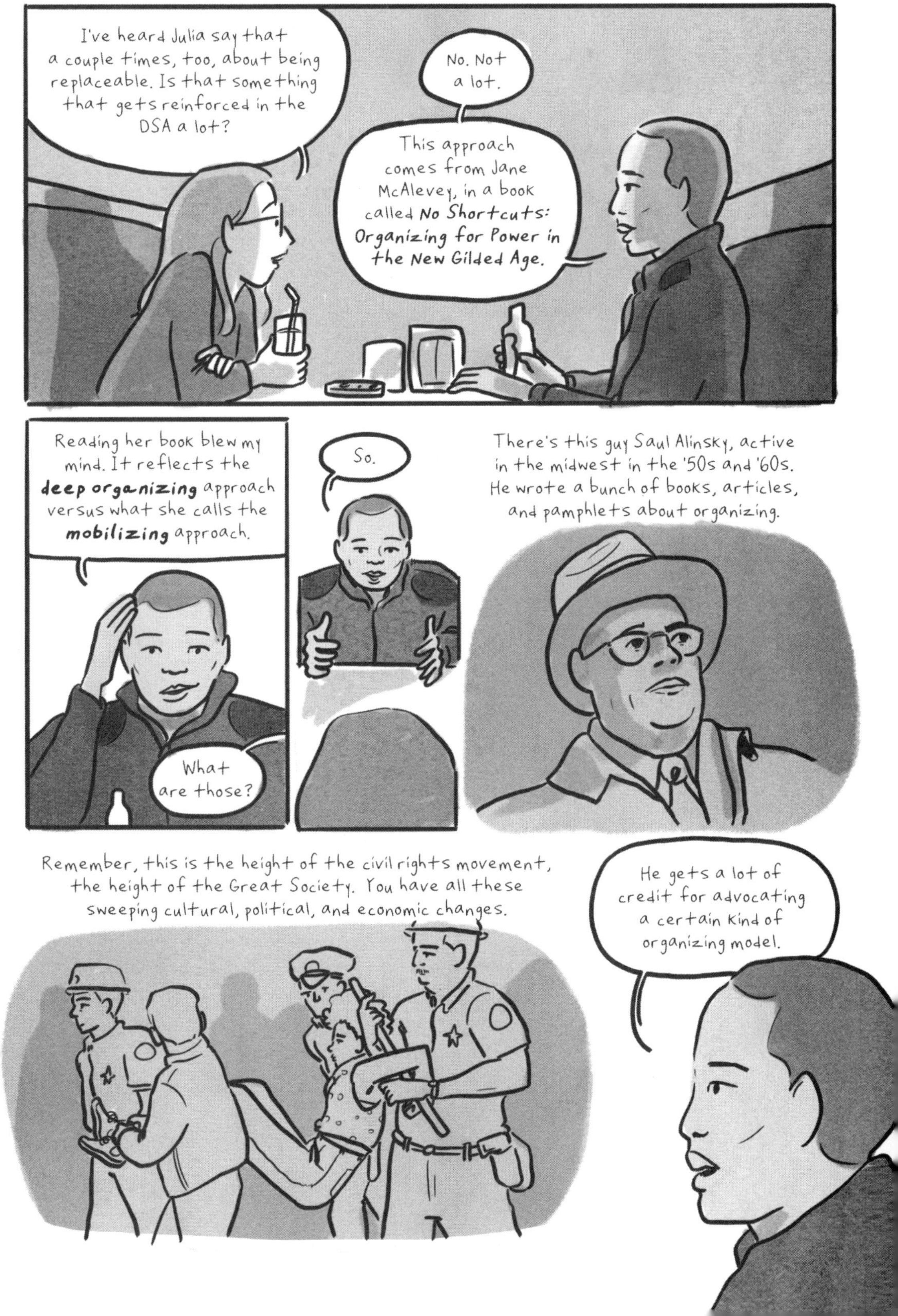
I've heard Julia say that a couple times, too, about being replaceable. Is that something that gets reinforced in the DSA a lot?
No. Not a lot.
This approach comes from Jane McAlevey, in a book called **No Shortcuts: Organizing for Power in the New Gilded Age.**
Reading her book blew my mind. It reflects the **deep organizing** approach versus what she calls the **mobilizing** approach.
What are those?
So.
There's this guy Saul Alinsky, active in the midwest in the '50s and '60s. He wrote a bunch of books, articles, and pamphlets about organizing.
Remember, this is the height of the civil rights movement, the height of the Great Society. You have all these sweeping cultural, political, and economic changes.
He gets a lot of credit for advocating a certain kind of organizing model.

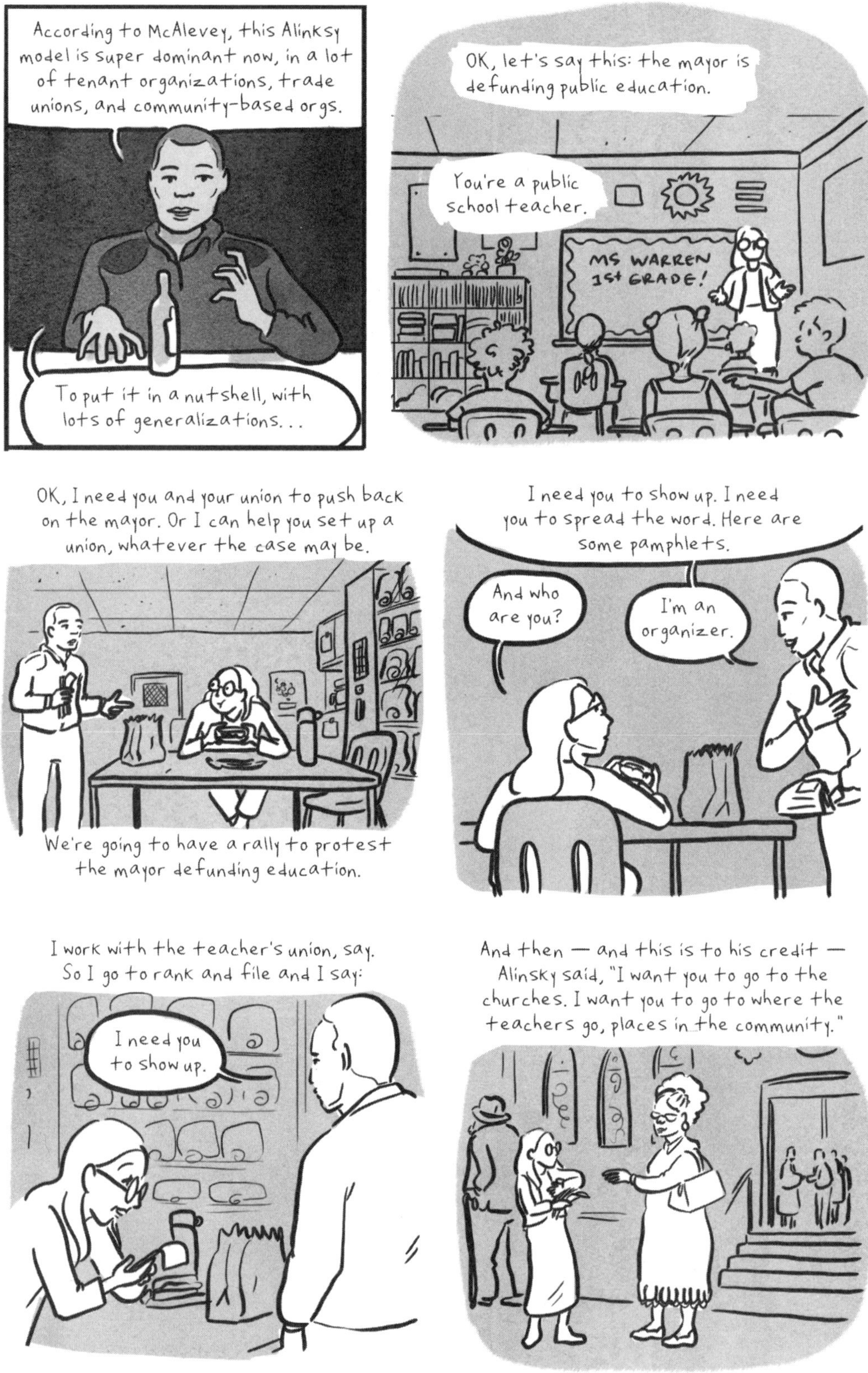

According to McAlevey, this Alinksy model is super dominant now, in a lot of tenant organizations, trade unions, and community-based orgs.
To put it in a nutshell, with lots of generalizations...
OK, let's say this: the mayor is defunding public education.
You're a public school teacher.
MS WARREN 1st GRADE!
OK, I need you and your union to push back on the mayor. Or I can help you set up a union, whatever the case may be.
We're going to have a rally to protest the mayor defunding education.
I need you to show up. I need you to spread the word. Here are some pamphlets.
And who are you?
I'm an organizer.
I work with the teacher's union, say. So I go to rank and file and I say:
I need you to show up.
And then — and this is to his credit — Alinsky said, "I want you to go to the churches. I want you to go to where the teachers go, places in the community."

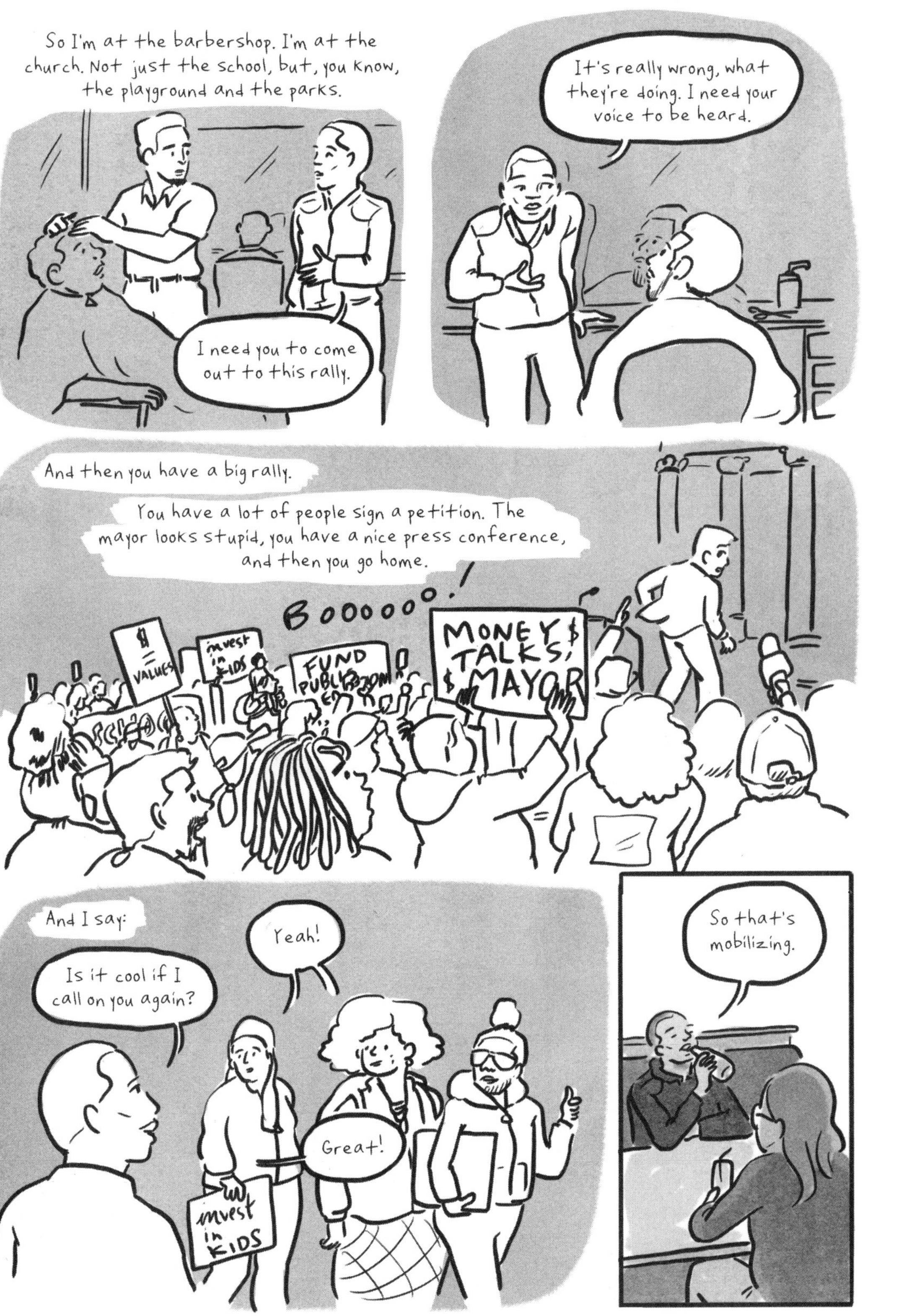
So I'm at the barbershop. I'm at the church. Not just the school, but, you know, the playground and the parks.
I need you to come out to this rally.
It's really wrong, what they're doing. I need your voice to be heard.
And then you have a big rally.
You have a lot of people sign a petition. The mayor looks stupid, you have a nice press conference, and then you go home.
Boooooo..!
$ = VALUES
invest in KIDS
MONEY$ TALKS, $MAYOR
And I say:
Is it cool if I call on you again?
Yeah!
Great!
invest in KIDS
So that's mobilizing.

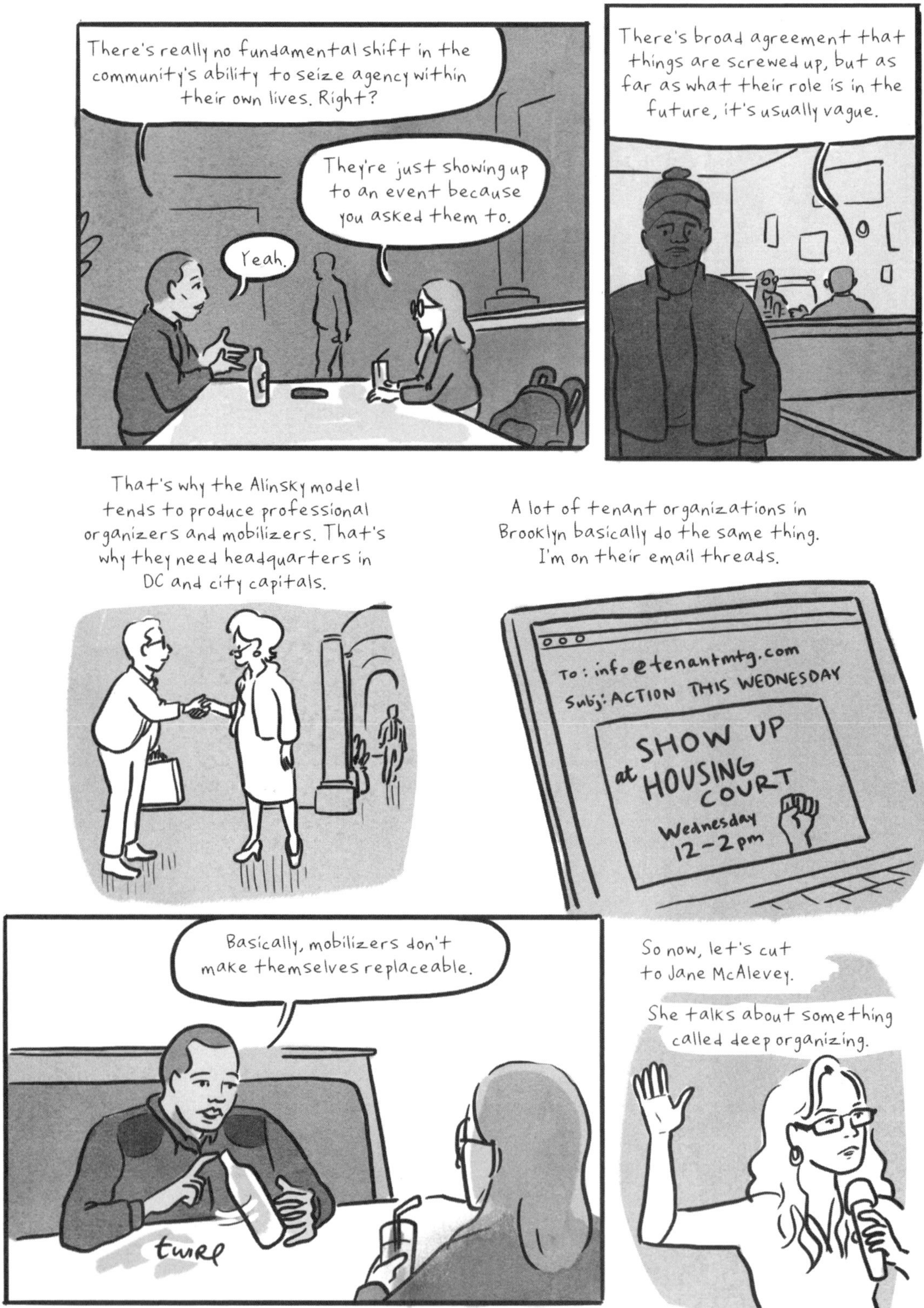
There's really no fundamental shift in the community's ability to seize agency within their own lives. Right?
They're just showing up to an event because you asked them to.
Yeah.
There's broad agreement that things are screwed up, but as far as what their role is in the future, it's usually vague.
That's why the Alinsky model tends to produce professional organizers and mobilizers. That's why they need headquarters in DC and city capitals.
A lot of tenant organizations in Brooklyn basically do the same thing. I'm on their email threads.
To: info@tenantmtg.com
Subj: ACTION THIS WEDNESDAY
SHOW UP at HOUSING COURT
Wednesday 12-2pm
Basically, mobilizers don't make themselves replaceable.
twirl
So now, let's cut to Jane McAlevey.
She talks about something called deep organizing.

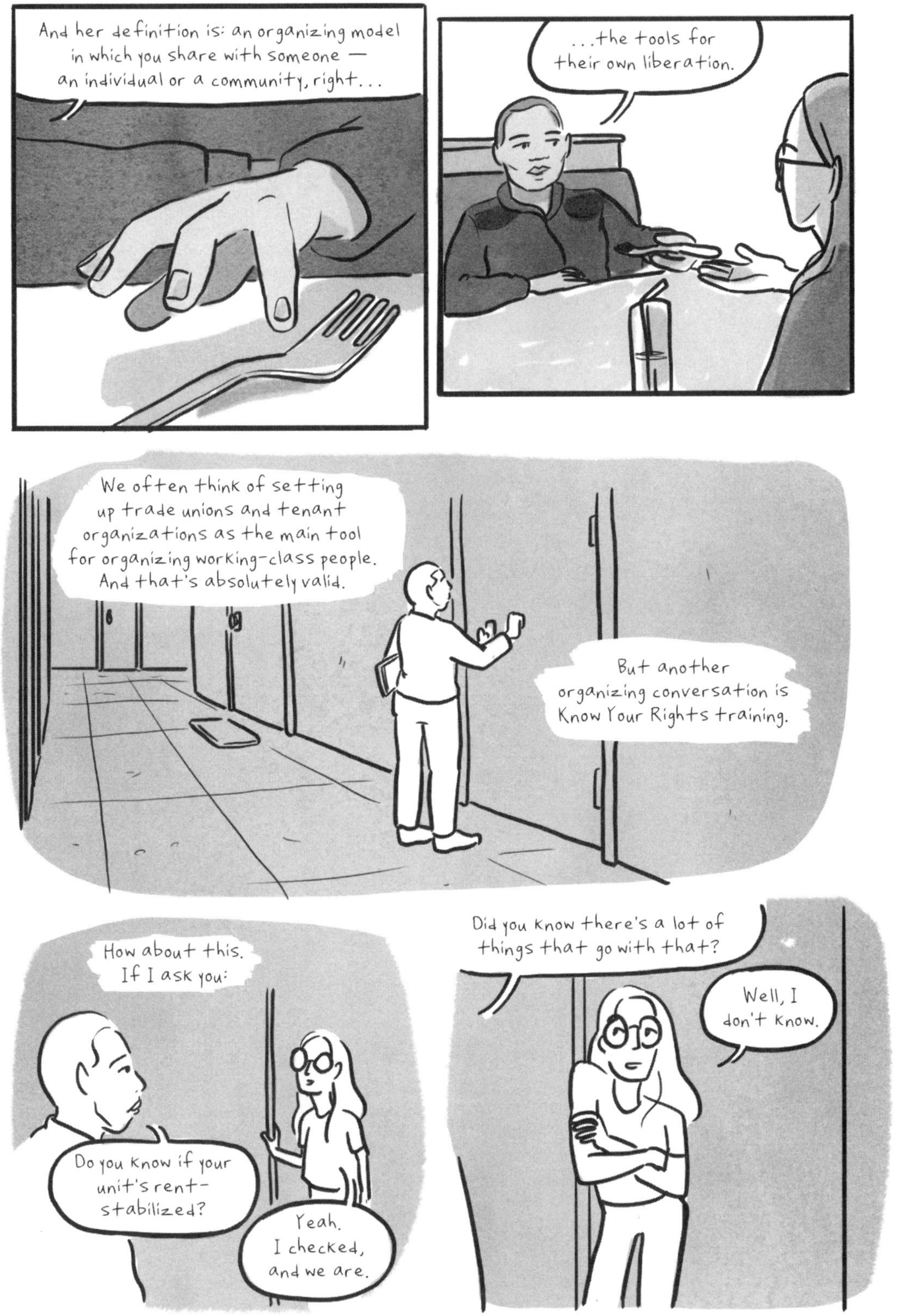
And her definition is: an organizing model in which you share with someone — an individual or a community, right...
...the tools for their own liberation.
We often think of setting up trade unions and tenant organizations as the main tool for organizing working-class people. And that's absolutely valid.
But another organizing conversation is Know Your Rights training.
How about this. If I ask you:
Do you know if your unit's rent-stabilized?
Yeah. I checked, and we are.
Did you know there's a lot of things that go with that?
Well, I don't know.

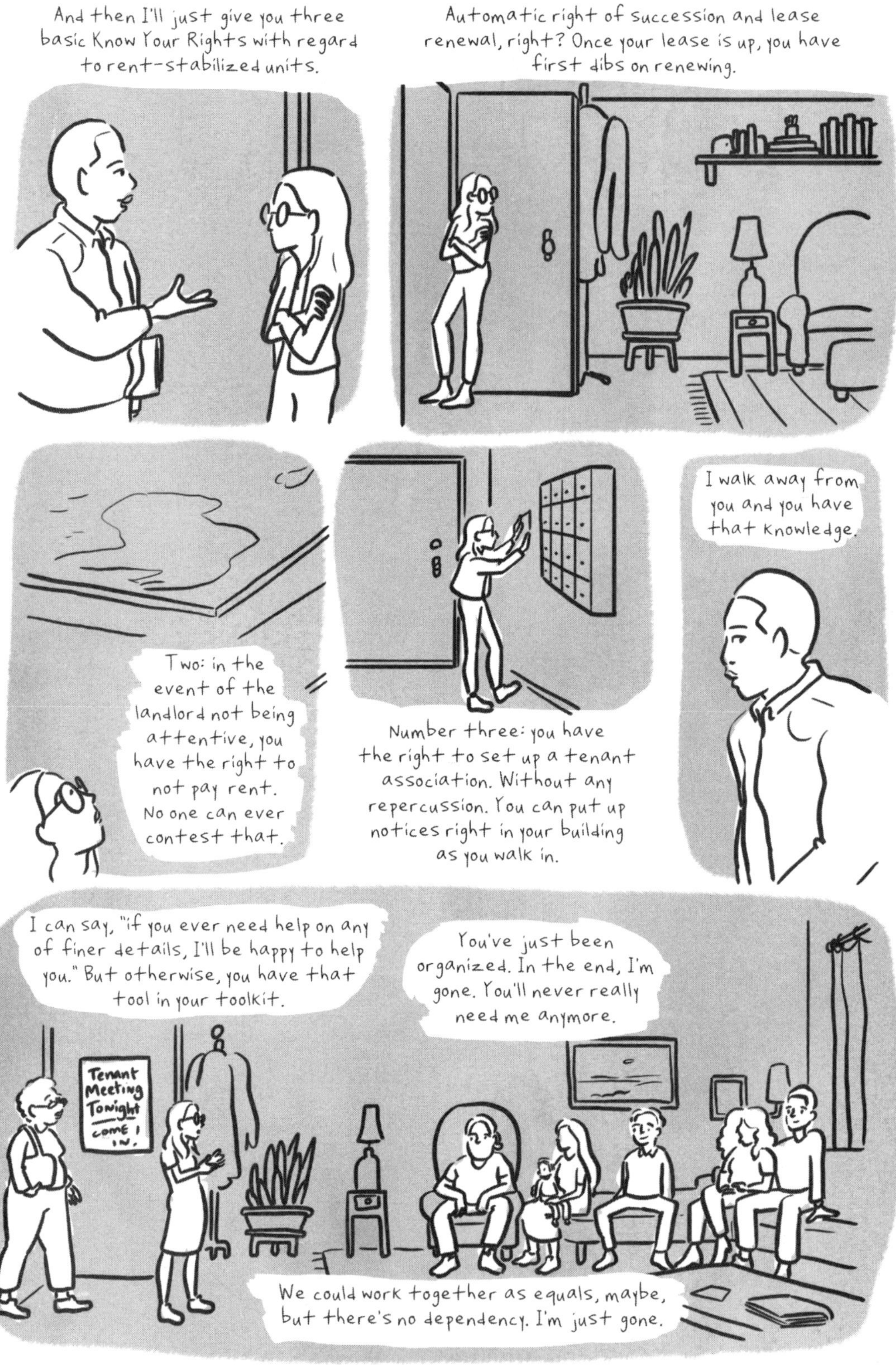
And then I'll just give you three basic Know Your Rights with regard to rent-stabilized units.
Automatic right of succession and lease renewal, right? Once your lease is up, you have first dibs on renewing.
Two: in the event of the landlord not being attentive, you have the right to not pay rent. No one can ever contest that.
Number three: you have the right to set up a tenant association. Without any repercussion. You can put up notices right in your building as you walk in.
I walk away from you and you have that knowledge.
I can say, "if you ever need help on any of finer details, I'll be happy to help you." But otherwise, you have that tool in your toolkit.
You've just been organized. In the end, I'm gone. You'll never really need me anymore.
Tenant Meeting Tonight COME IN.
We could work together as equals, maybe, but there's no dependency. I'm just gone.

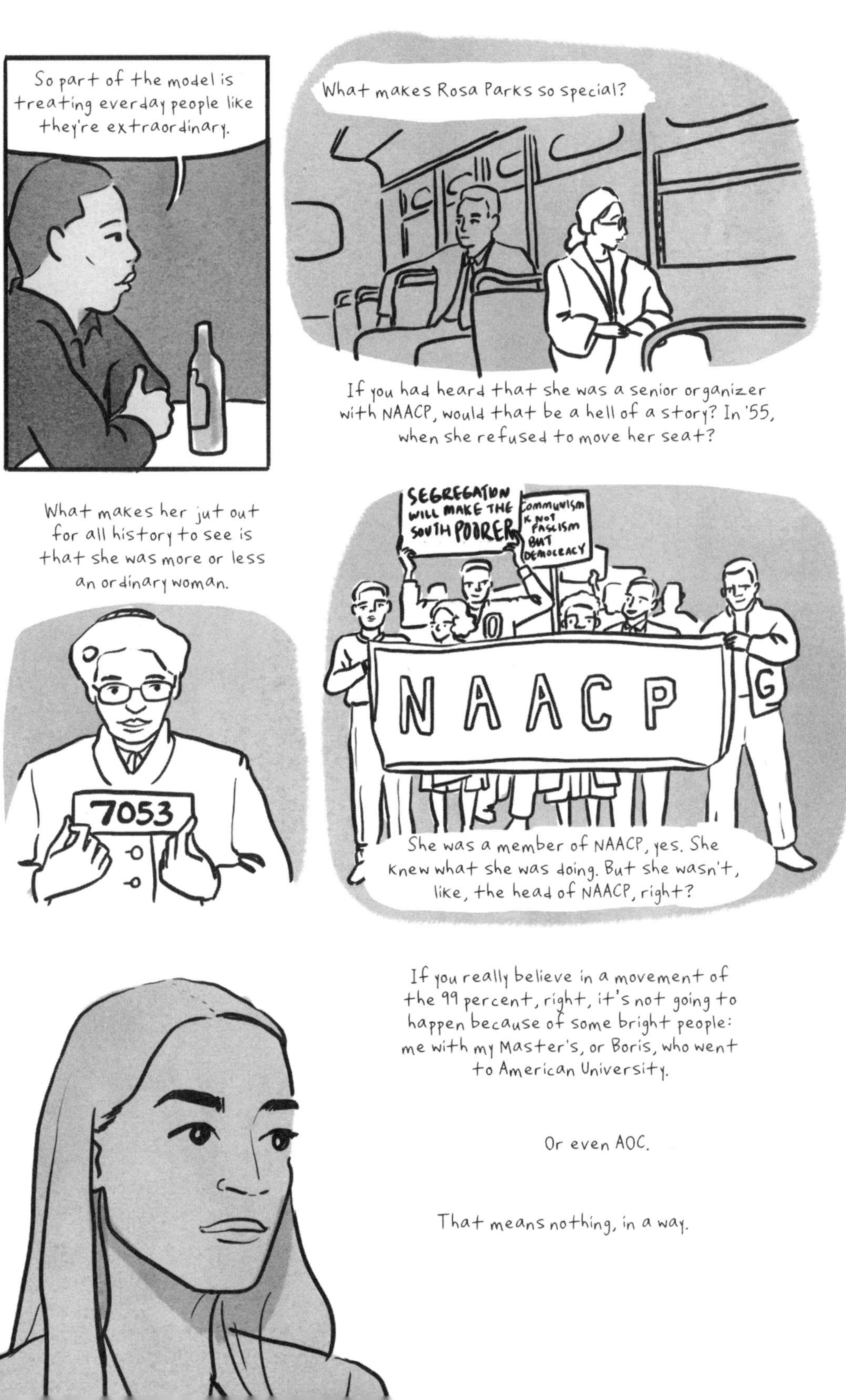
So part of the model is treating everday people like they're extraordinary.
What makes Rosa Parks so special?
If you had heard that she was a senior organizer with NAACP, would that be a hell of a story? In '55, when she refused to move her seat?
What makes her jut out for all history to see is that she was more or less an ordinary woman.
7053
SEGREGATION WILL MAKE THE SOUTH POORER
COMMUNISM IS NOT FASCISM BUT DEMOCRACY
NAACP
She was a member of NAACP, yes. She knew what she was doing. But she wasn't, like, the head of NAACP, right?
If you really believe in a movement of the 99 percent, right, it's not going to happen because of some bright people: me with my Master's, or Boris, who went to American University.
Or even AOC.
That means nothing, in a way.

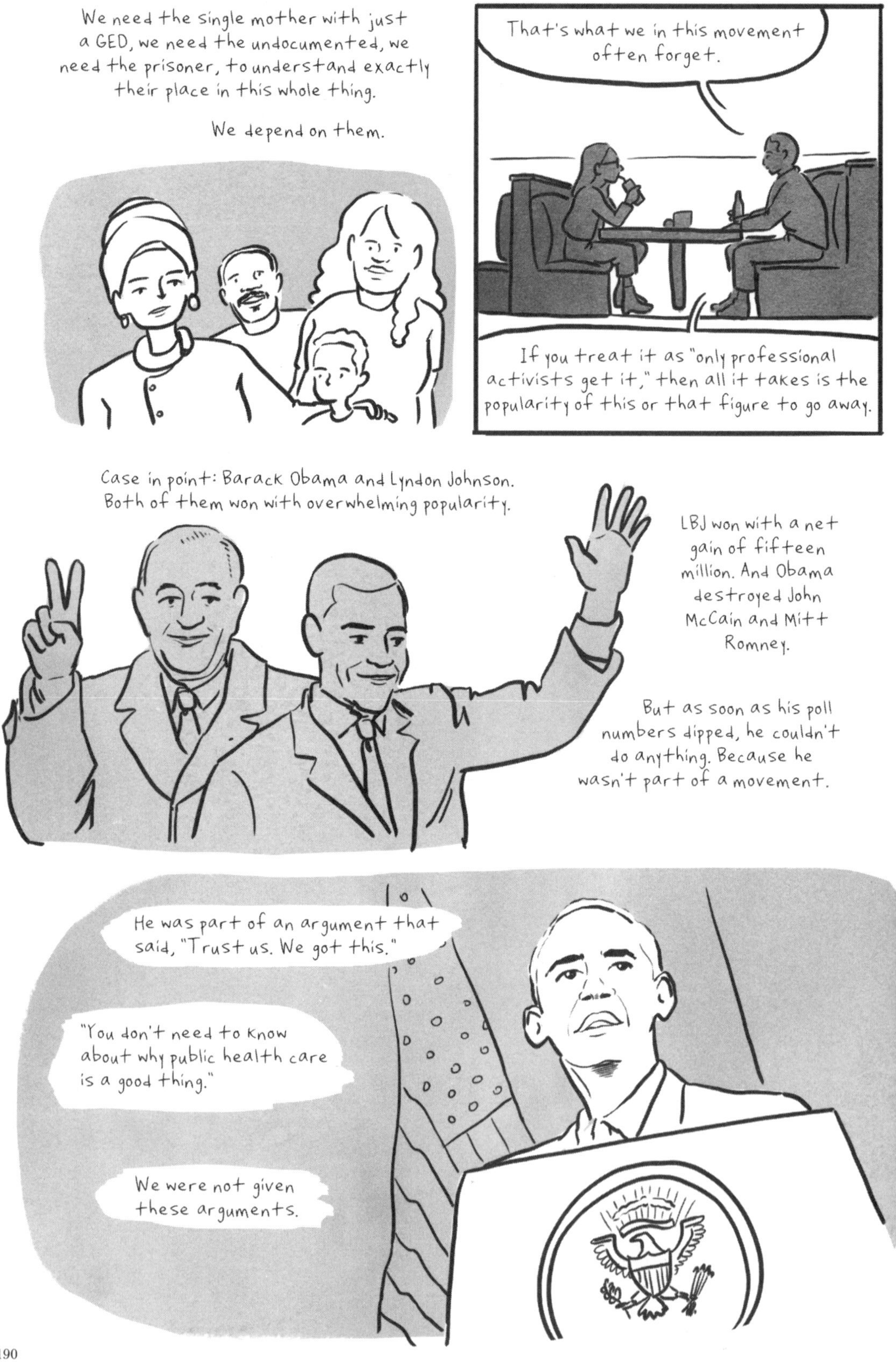
We need the single mother with just a GED, we need the undocumented, we need the prisoner, to understand exactly their place in this whole thing.
We depend on them.
That's what we in this movement often forget.
If you treat it as "only professional activists get it," then all it takes is the popularity of this or that figure to go away.
Case in point: Barack Obama and Lyndon Johnson. Both of them won with overwhelming popularity.
LBJ won with a net gain of fifteen million. And Obama destroyed John McCain and Mitt Romney.
But as soon as his poll numbers dipped, he couldn't do anything. Because he wasn't part of a movement.
He was part of an argument that said, "Trust us. We got this."
"You don't need to know about why public health care is a good thing."
We were not given these arguments.

Now fast-forward to 2016. Bernie Sanders, AOC, Elizabeth Warren. They don't have a monopoly on Medicare for All as an idea, right? Leftists have been arguing for national healthcare forever.

from *American Labor Legislation Review*, 1919

DESTITUTION
SICKNESS
HEALTH INSURANCE

Protected!

But what they did was simply let people know that there are other countries that do it for free.

"You need to know this."

"You need to know that the average life expectancy in Sweden, or Canada — very harsh climates, compared to ours..."

"...they live two or three years longer. They have lower rates of suicide. Higher general welfare. Lower infant mortality."

"Don't you want this?"

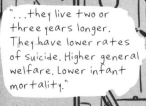

Average Life Span

Age

U.S.	Sweden	Canada
79	82	82

Those of us who are everday people: we don't have time to look up Sweden. We're inundated with a lot of propaganda.

That's an organizing question that Bernie posed to us. Liz Warren, AOC, Julia Salazar, other wonderful movers and shakers: they make it a point to let us know what we ought to know.

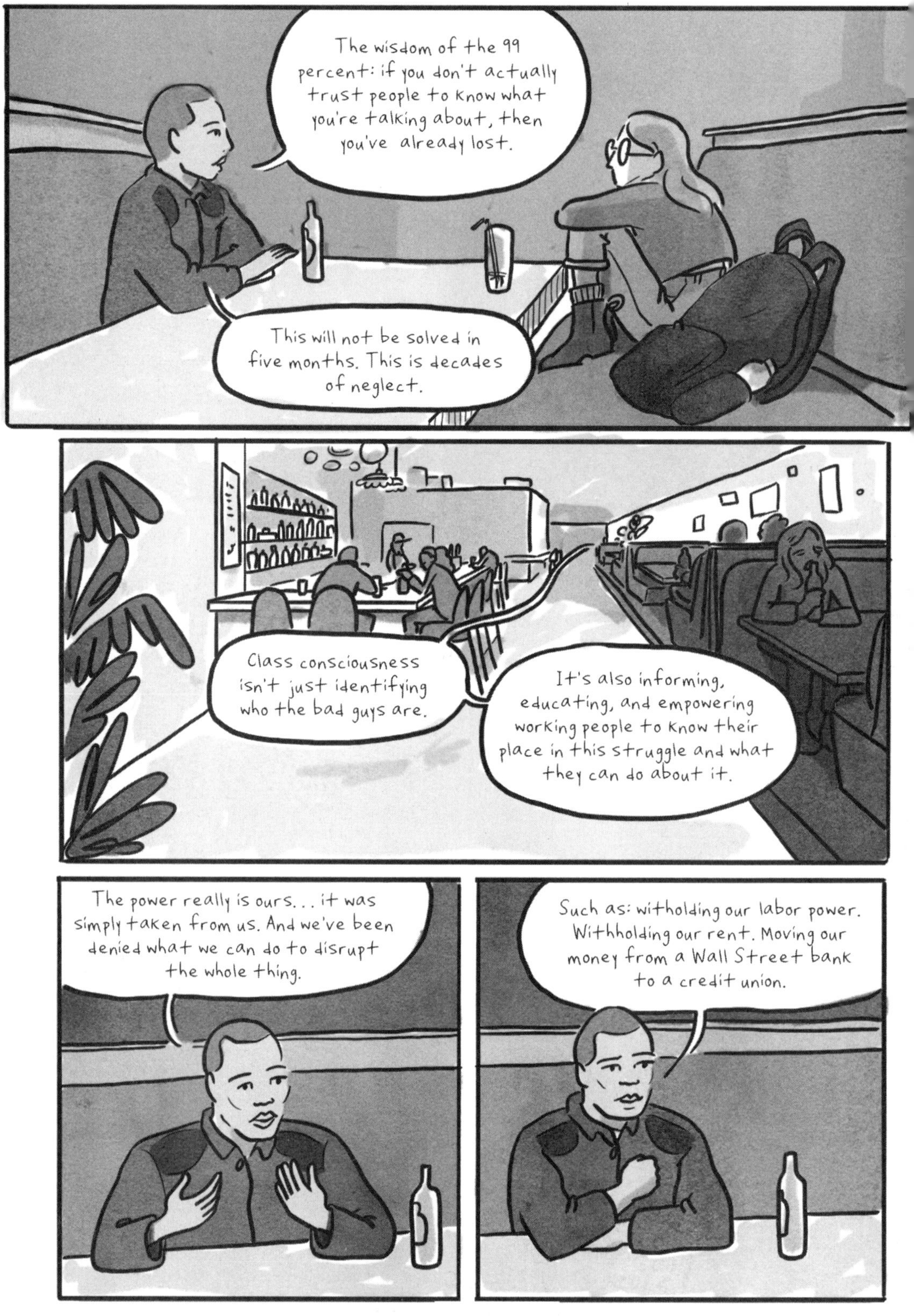
The wisdom of the 99 percent: if you don't actually trust people to know what you're talking about, then you've already lost.
This will not be solved in five months. This is decades of neglect.
Class consciousness isn't just identifying who the bad guys are.
It's also informing, educating, and empowering working people to know their place in this struggle and what they can do about it.
The power really is ours. . . it was simply taken from us. And we've been denied what we can do to disrupt the whole thing.
Such as: witholding our labor power. Withholding our rent. Moving our money from a Wall Street bank to a credit union.

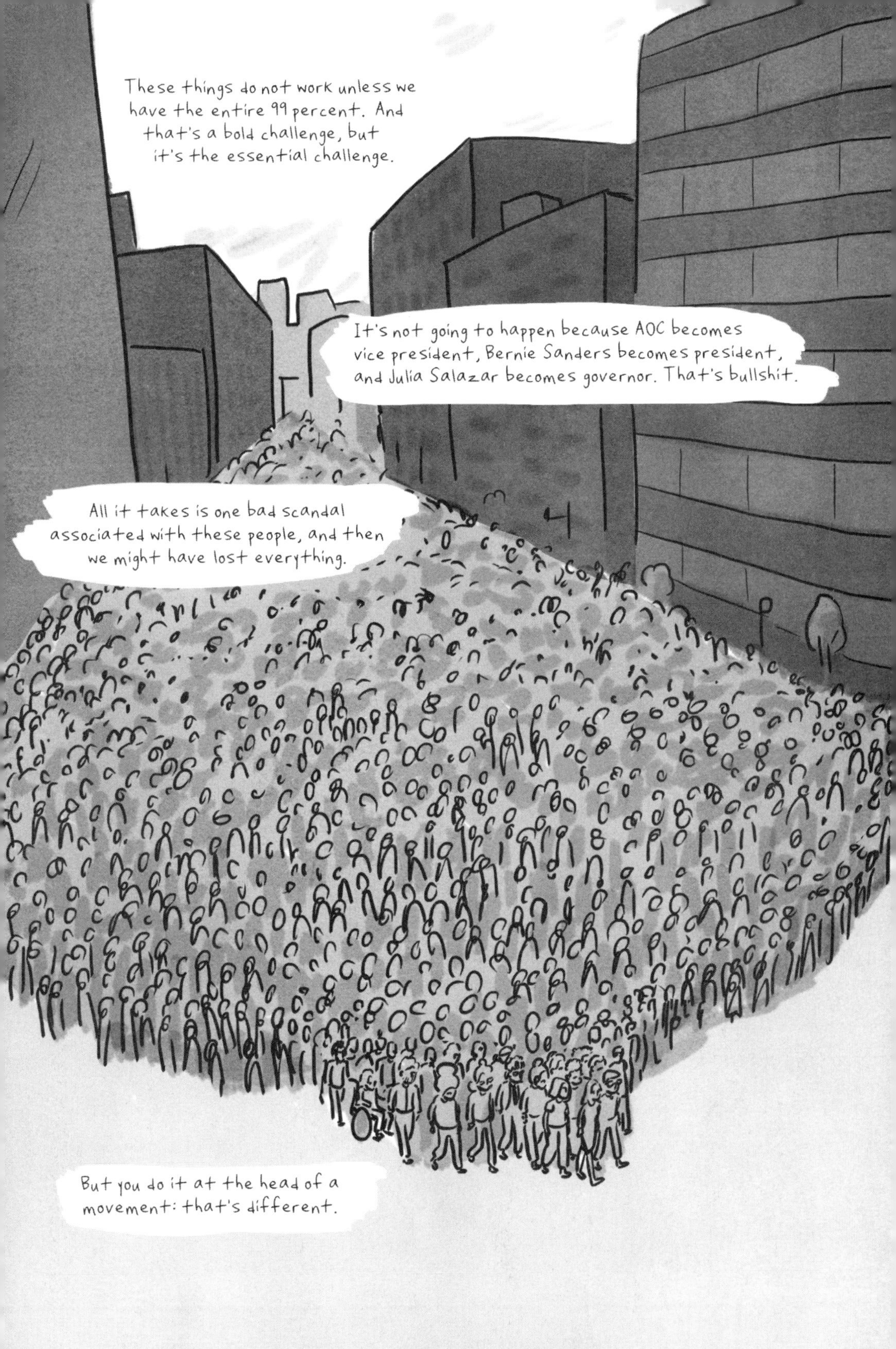
These things do not work unless we have the entire 99 percent. And that's a bold challenge, but it's the essential challenge.
It's not going to happen because AOC becomes vice president, Bernie Sanders becomes president, and Julia Salazar becomes governor. That's bullshit.
All it takes is one bad scandal associated with these people, and then we might have lost everything.
But you do it at the head of a movement: that's different.

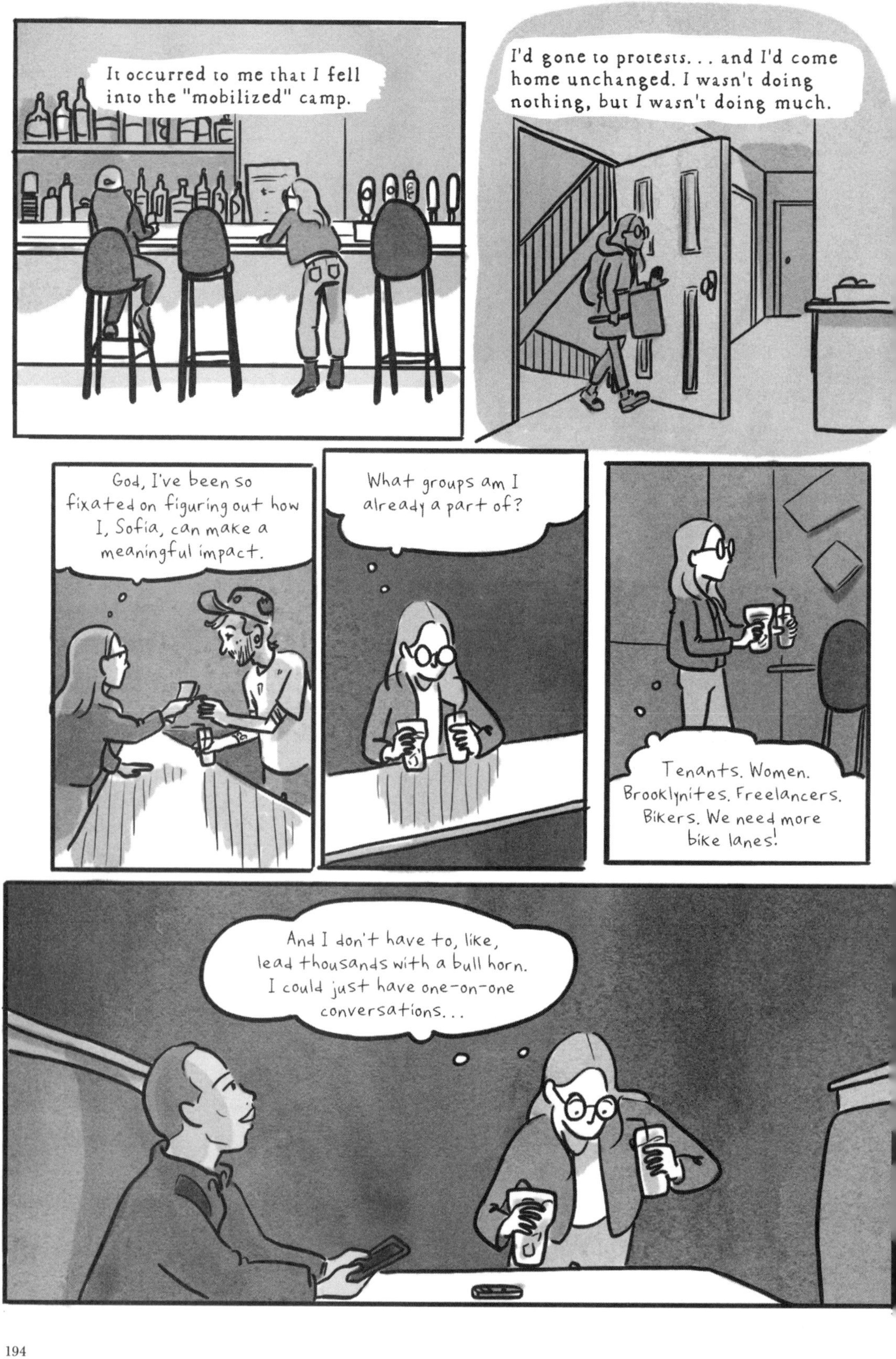

It occurred to me that I fell into the "mobilized" camp.
I'd gone to protests. . . and I'd come home unchanged. I wasn't doing nothing, but I wasn't doing much.
God, I've been so fixated on figuring out how I, Sofia, can make a meaningful impact.
What groups am I already a part of?
Tenants. Women. Brooklynites. Freelancers. Bikers. We need more bike lanes!
And I don't have to, like, lead thousands with a bull horn. I could just have one-on-one conversations. . .

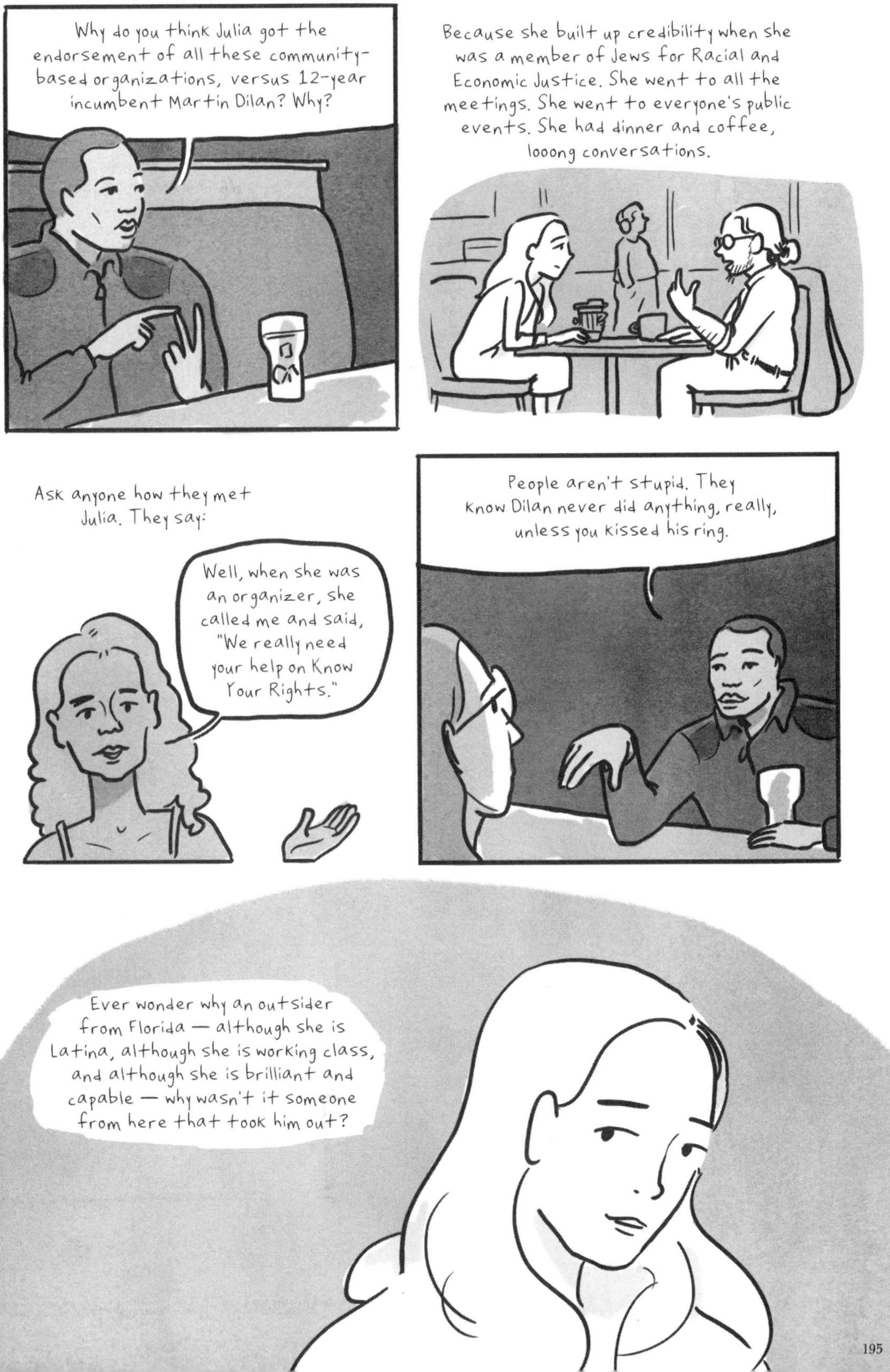

Why do you think Julia got the endorsement of all these community-based organizations, versus 12-year incumbent Martin Dilan? Why?
Because she built up credibility when she was a member of Jews for Racial and Economic Justice. She went to all the meetings. She went to everyone's public events. She had dinner and coffee, looong conversations.
Ask anyone how they met Julia. They say:
Well, when she was an organizer, she called me and said, "We really need your help on Know Your Rights."
People aren't stupid. They know Dilan never did anything, really, unless you kissed his ring.
Ever wonder why an outsider from Florida — although she is Latina, although she is working class, and although she is brilliant and capable — why wasn't it someone from here that took him out?

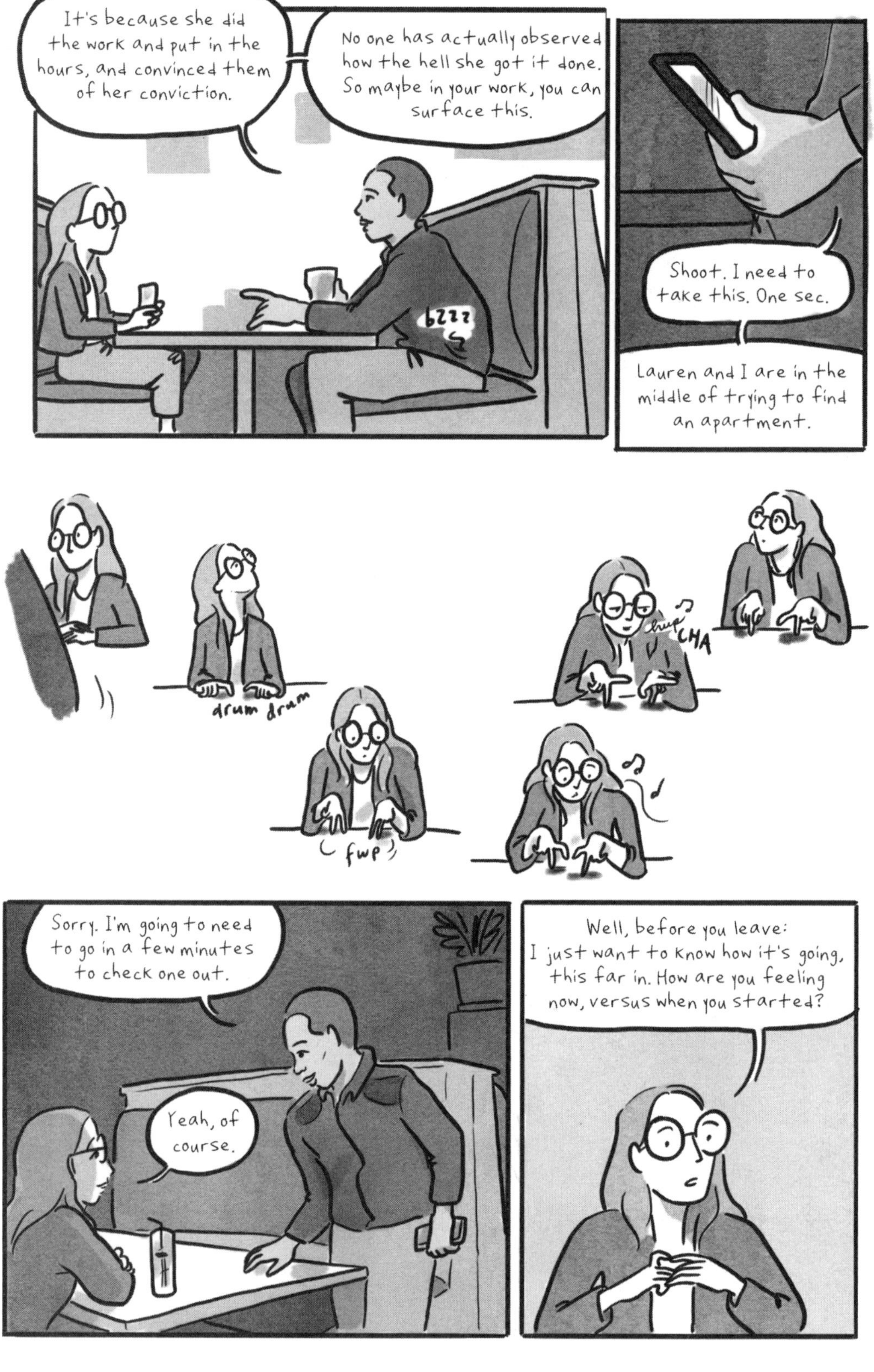
It's because she did the work and put in the hours, and convinced them of her conviction.
No one has actually observed how the hell she got it done. So maybe in your work, you can surface this.
bzzz
Shoot. I need to take this. One sec.
Lauren and I are in the middle of trying to find an apartment.
drum drum
fwp
CHA
Sorry. I'm going to need to go in a few minutes to check one out.
Yeah, of course.
Well, before you leave: I just want to know how it's going, this far in. How are you feeling now, versus when you started?

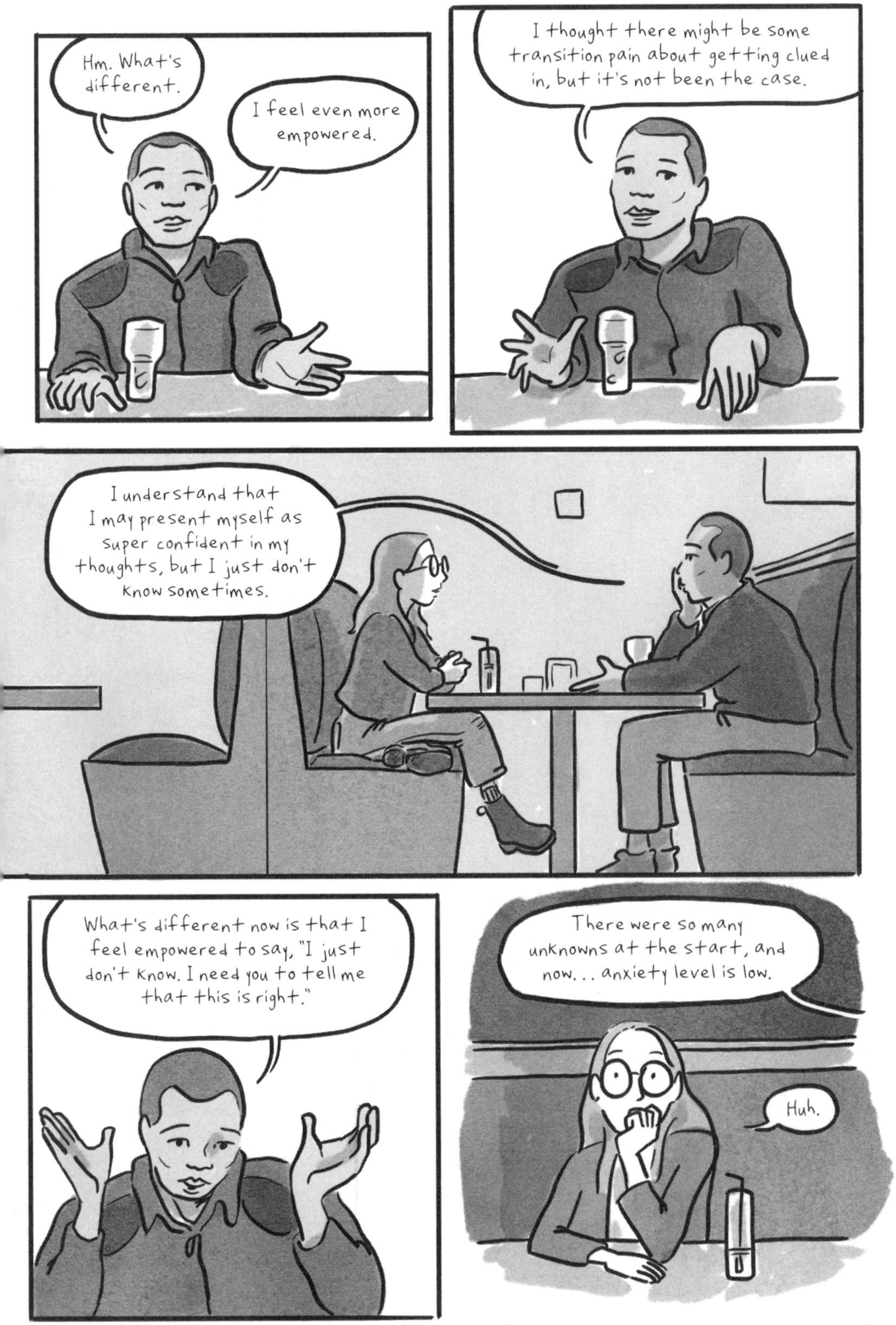
Hm. What's different.
I feel even more empowered.
I thought there might be some transition pain about getting clued in, but it's not been the case.
I understand that I may present myself as super confident in my thoughts, but I just don't know sometimes.
What's different now is that I feel empowered to say, "I just don't know. I need you to tell me that this is right."
There were so many unknowns at the start, and now... anxiety level is low.
Huh.

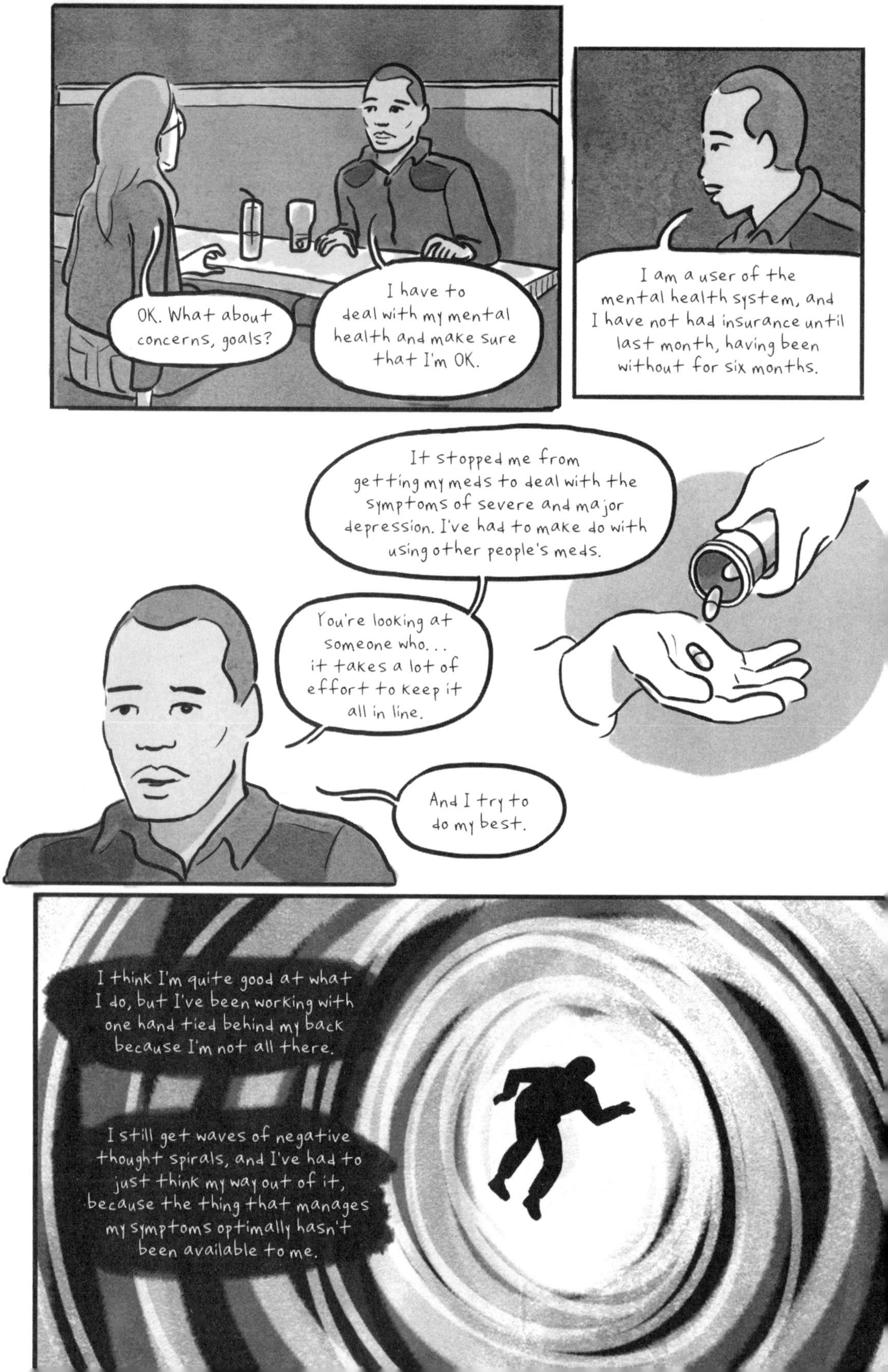
OK. What about concerns, goals?
I have to deal with my mental health and make sure that I'm OK.
I am a user of the mental health system, and I have not had insurance until last month, having been without for six months.
It stopped me from getting my meds to deal with the symptoms of severe and major depression. I've had to make do with using other people's meds.
You're looking at someone who... it takes a lot of effort to keep it all in line.
And I try to do my best.
I think I'm quite good at what I do, but I've been working with one hand tied behind my back because I'm not all there.
I still get waves of negative thought spirals, and I've had to just think my way out of it, because the thing that manages my symptoms optimally hasn't been available to me.

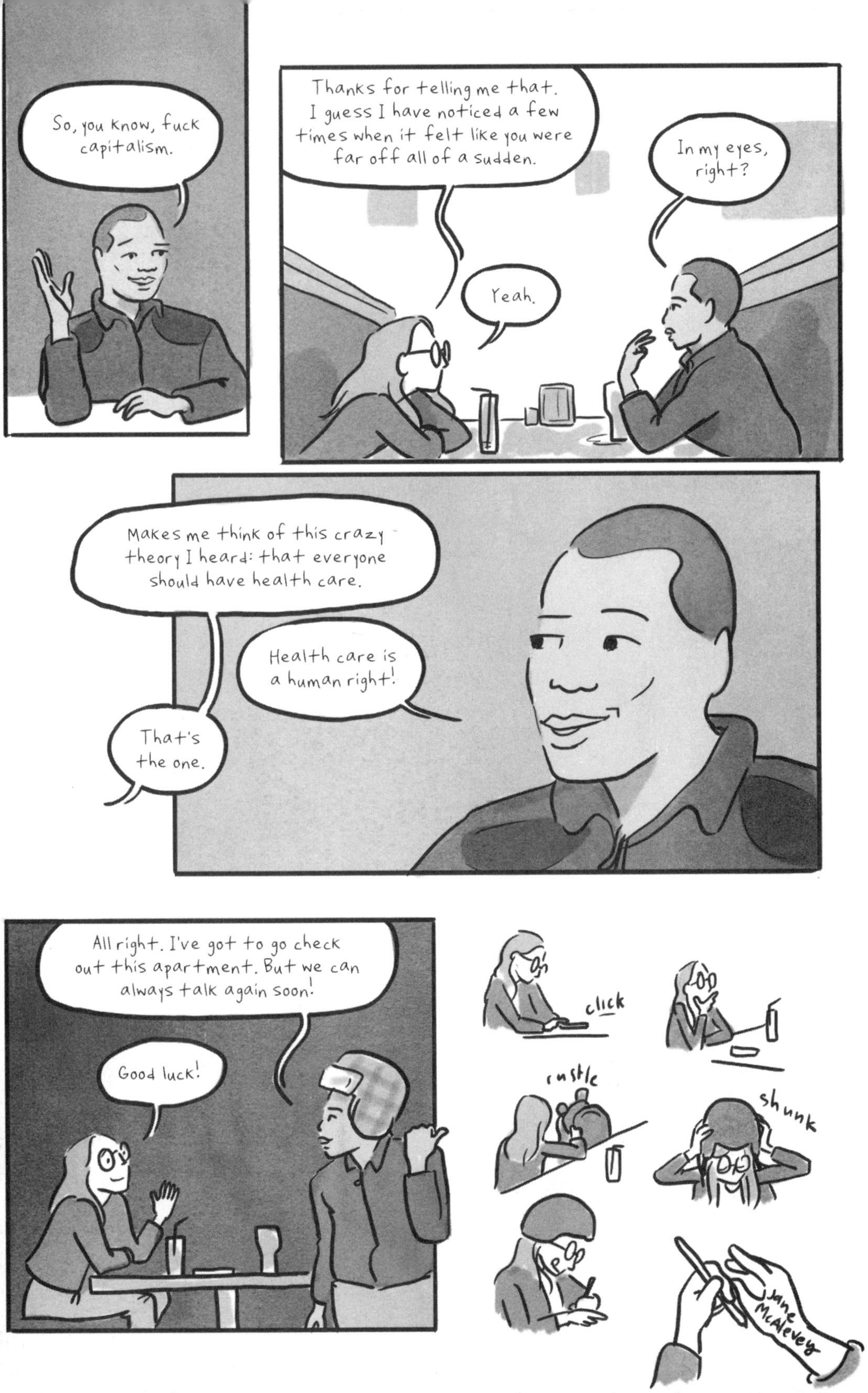
So, you know, fuck capitalism.
Thanks for telling me that. I guess I have noticed a few times when it felt like you were far off all of a sudden.
Yeah.
In my eyes, right?
Makes me think of this crazy theory I heard: that everyone should have health care.
Health care is a human right!
That's the one.
All right. I've got to go check out this apartment. But we can always talk again soon!
Good luck!
click
rustle
shunk
Jane McAlevey

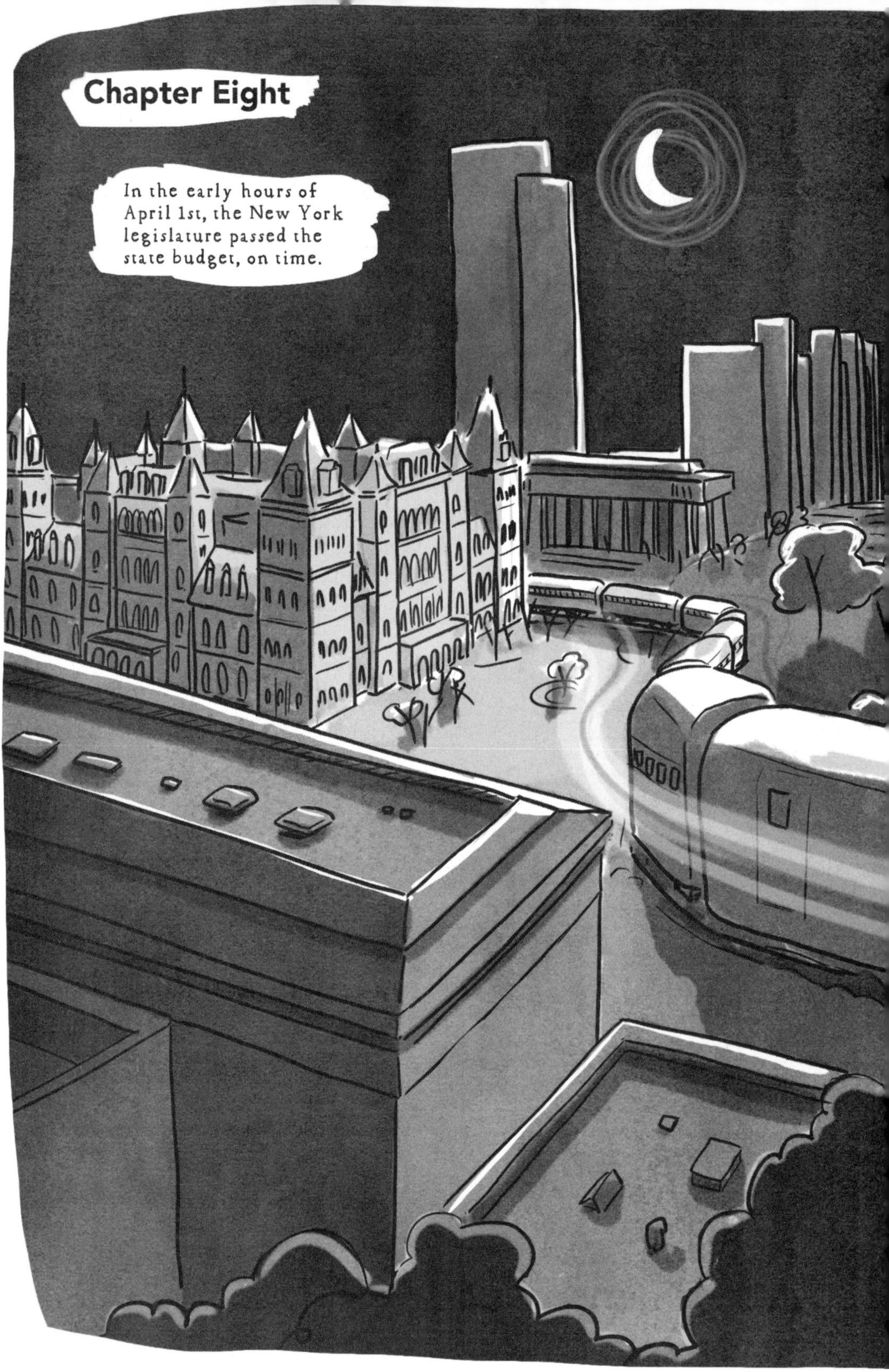
Chapter Eight
In the early hours of April 1st, the New York legislature passed the state budget, on time.

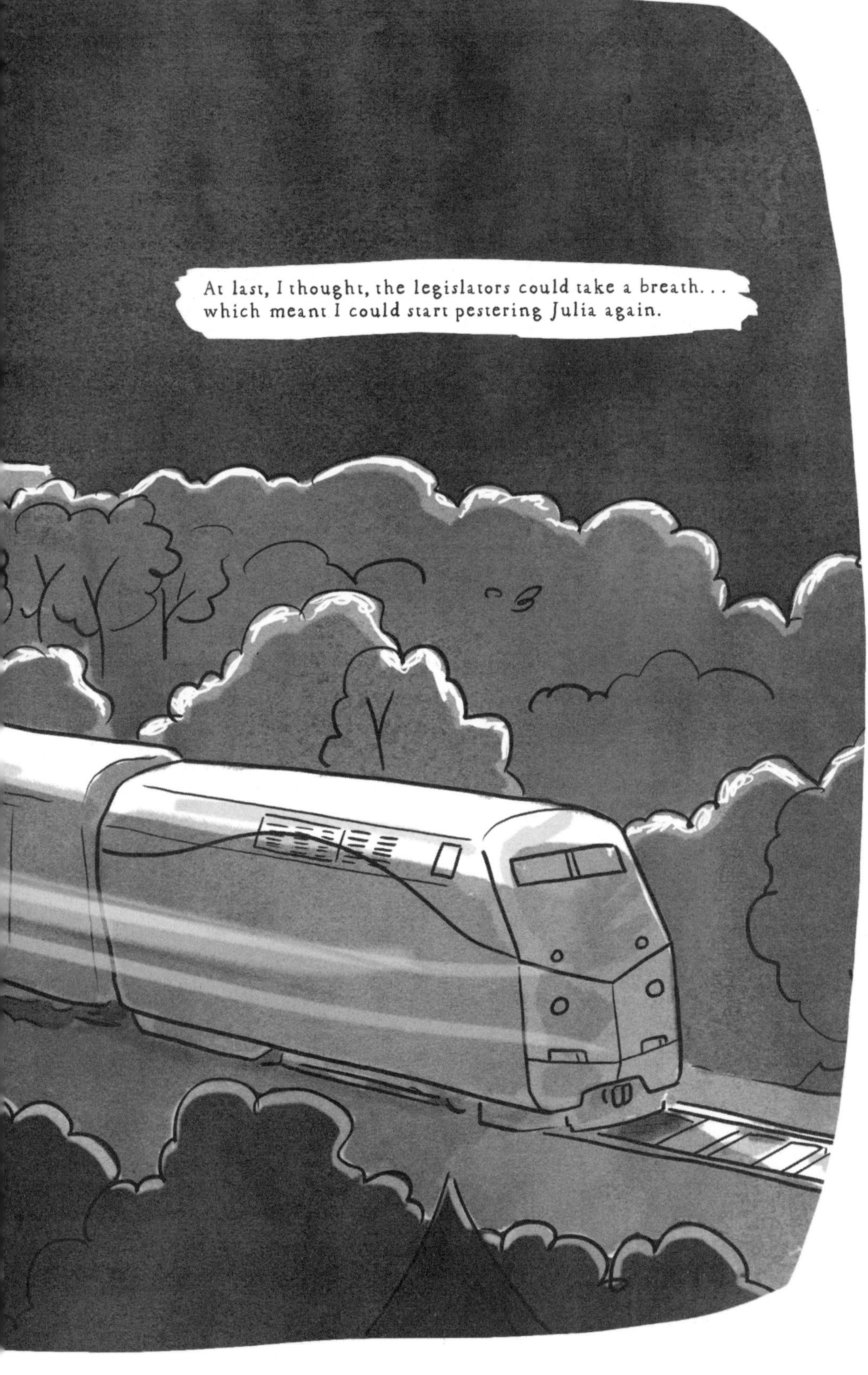
At last, I thought, the legislators could take a breath. . .
which meant I could start pestering Julia again.

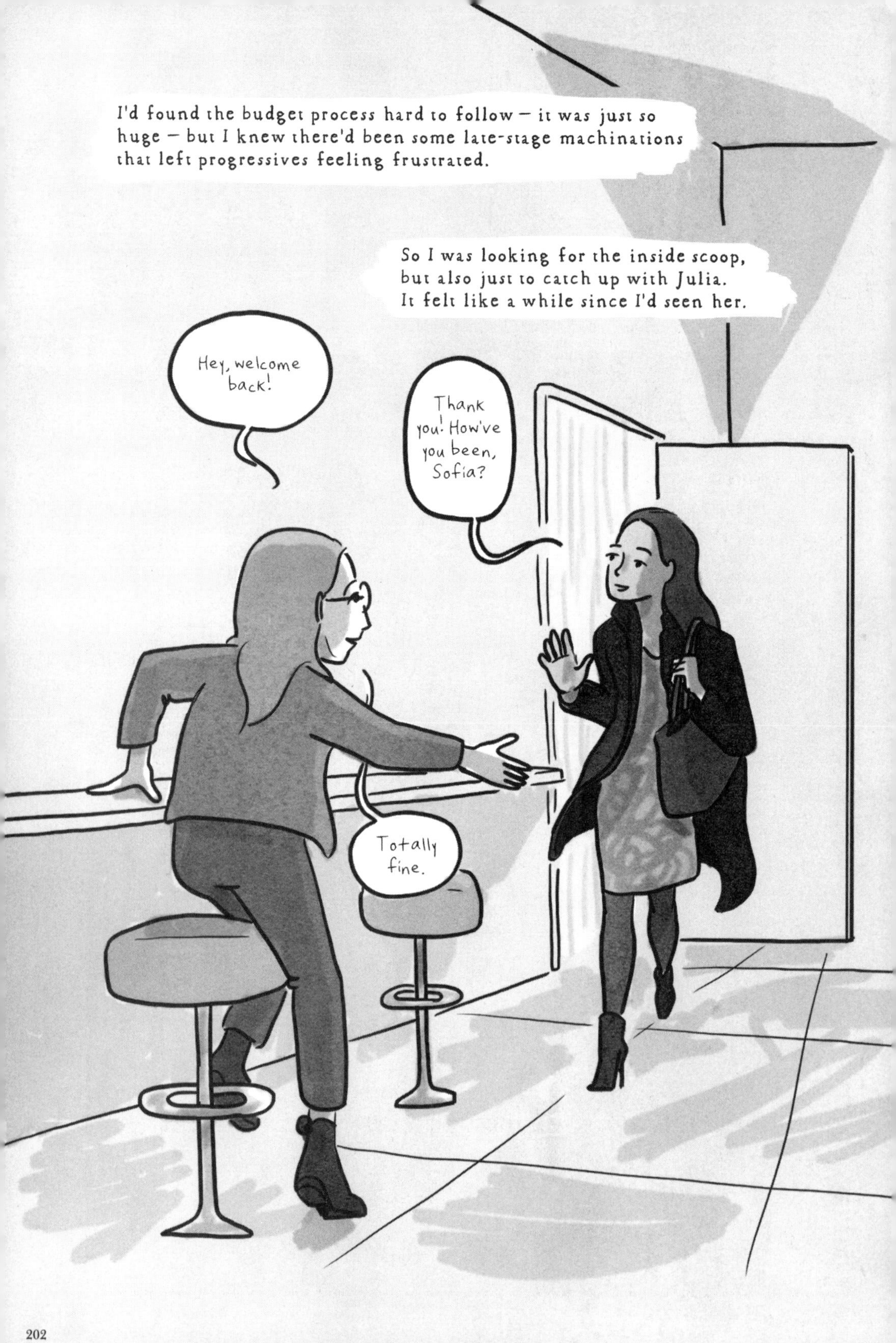
I'd found the budget process hard to follow — it was just so huge — but I knew there'd been some late-stage machinations that left progressives feeling frustrated.
So I was looking for the inside scoop, but also just to catch up with Julia. It felt like a while since I'd seen her.
Hey, welcome back!
Thank you! How've you been, Sofia?
Totally fine.

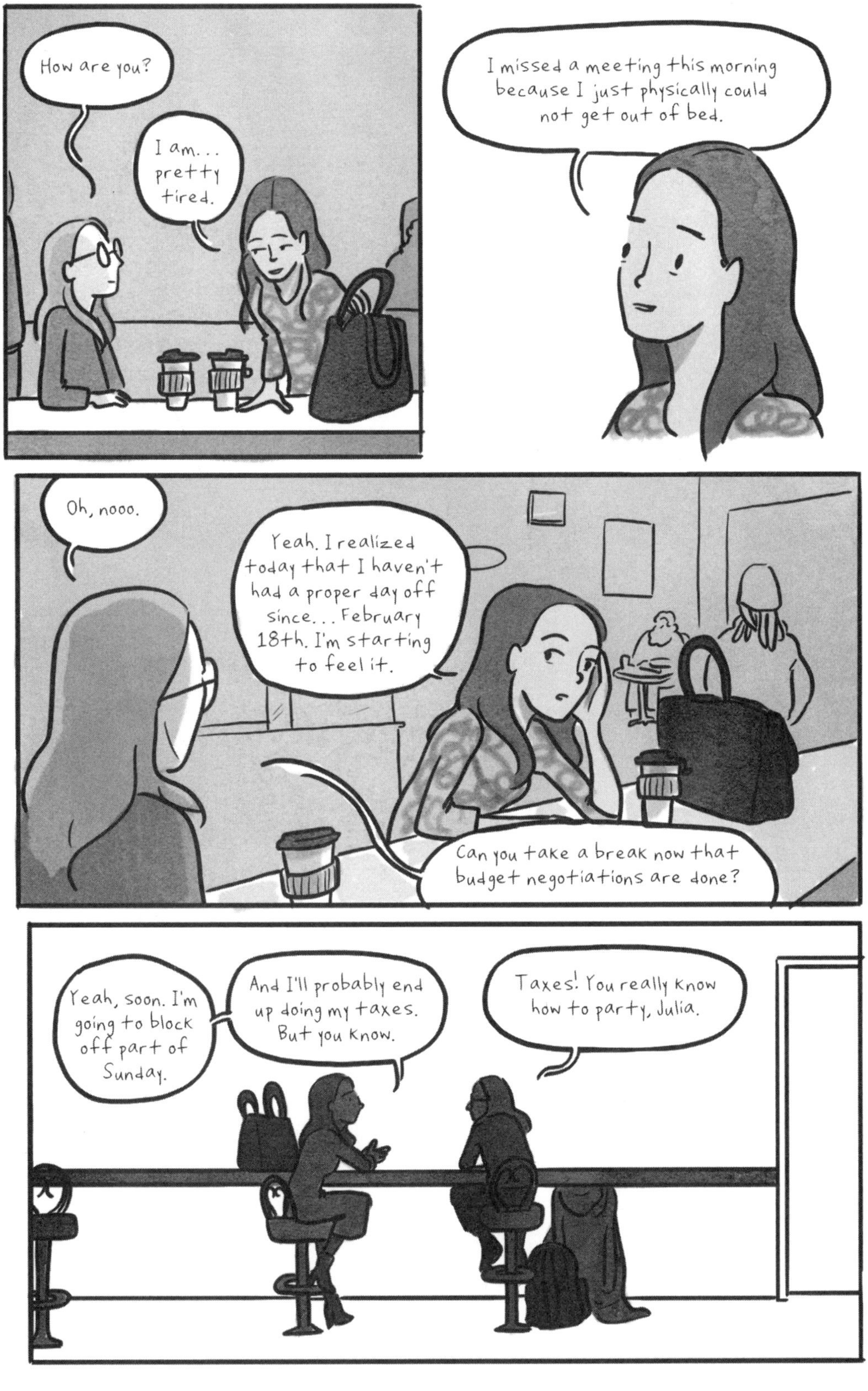
How are you?
I am... pretty tired.
I missed a meeting this morning because I just physically could not get out of bed.
Oh, nooo.
Yeah. I realized today that I haven't had a proper day off since... February 18th. I'm starting to feel it.
Can you take a break now that budget negotiations are done?
Yeah, soon. I'm going to block off part of Sunday.
And I'll probably end up doing my taxes. But you know.
Taxes! You really know how to party, Julia.

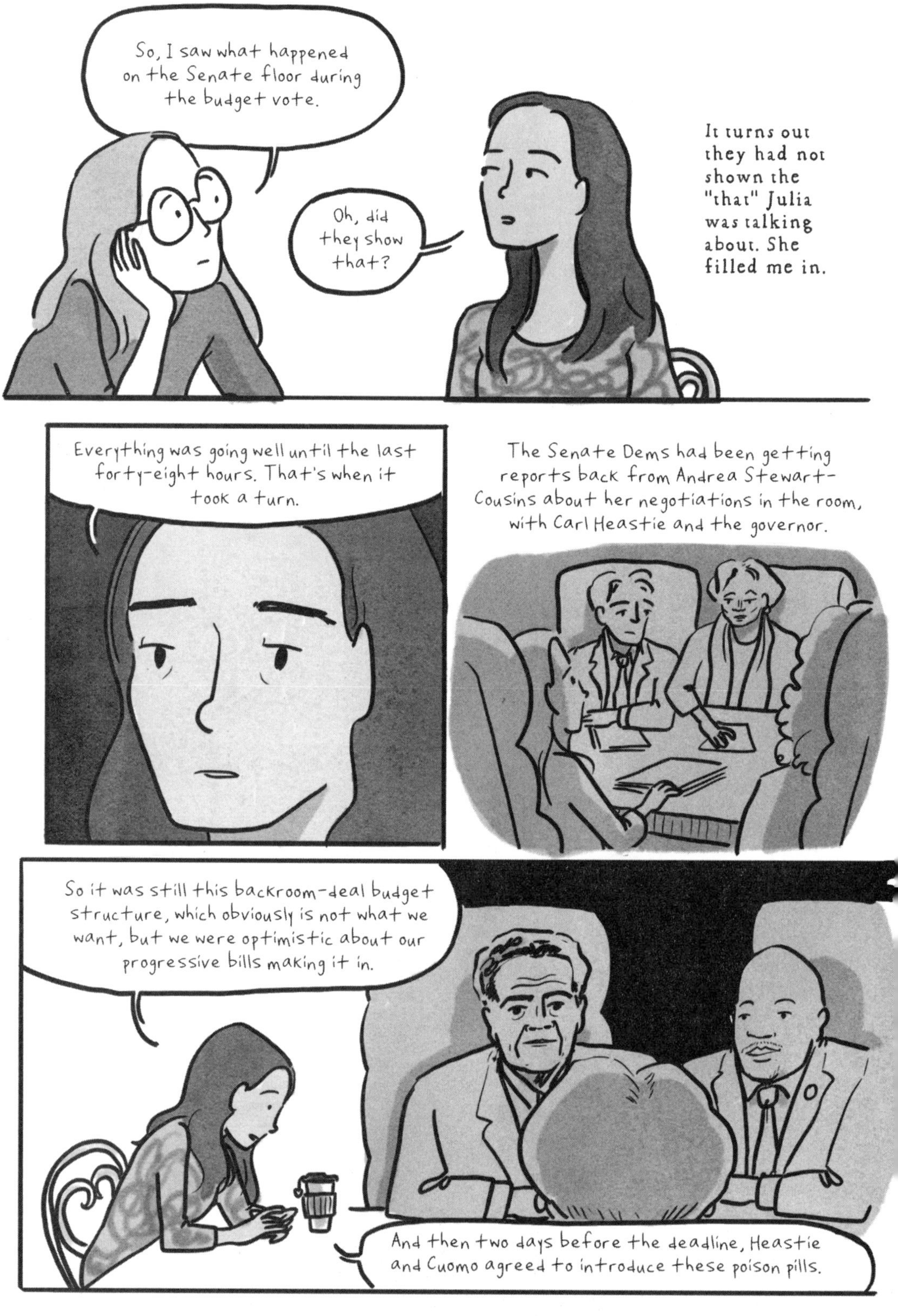
So, I saw what happened on the Senate floor during the budget vote.
Oh, did they show that?
It turns out they had not shown the "that" Julia was talking about. She filled me in.
Everything was going well until the last forty-eight hours. That's when it took a turn.
The Senate Dems had been getting reports back from Andrea Stewart-Cousins about her negotiations in the room, with Carl Heastie and the governor.
So it was still this backroom-deal budget structure, which obviously is not what we want, but we were optimistic about our progressive bills making it in.
And then two days before the deadline, Heastie and Cuomo agreed to introduce these poison pills.

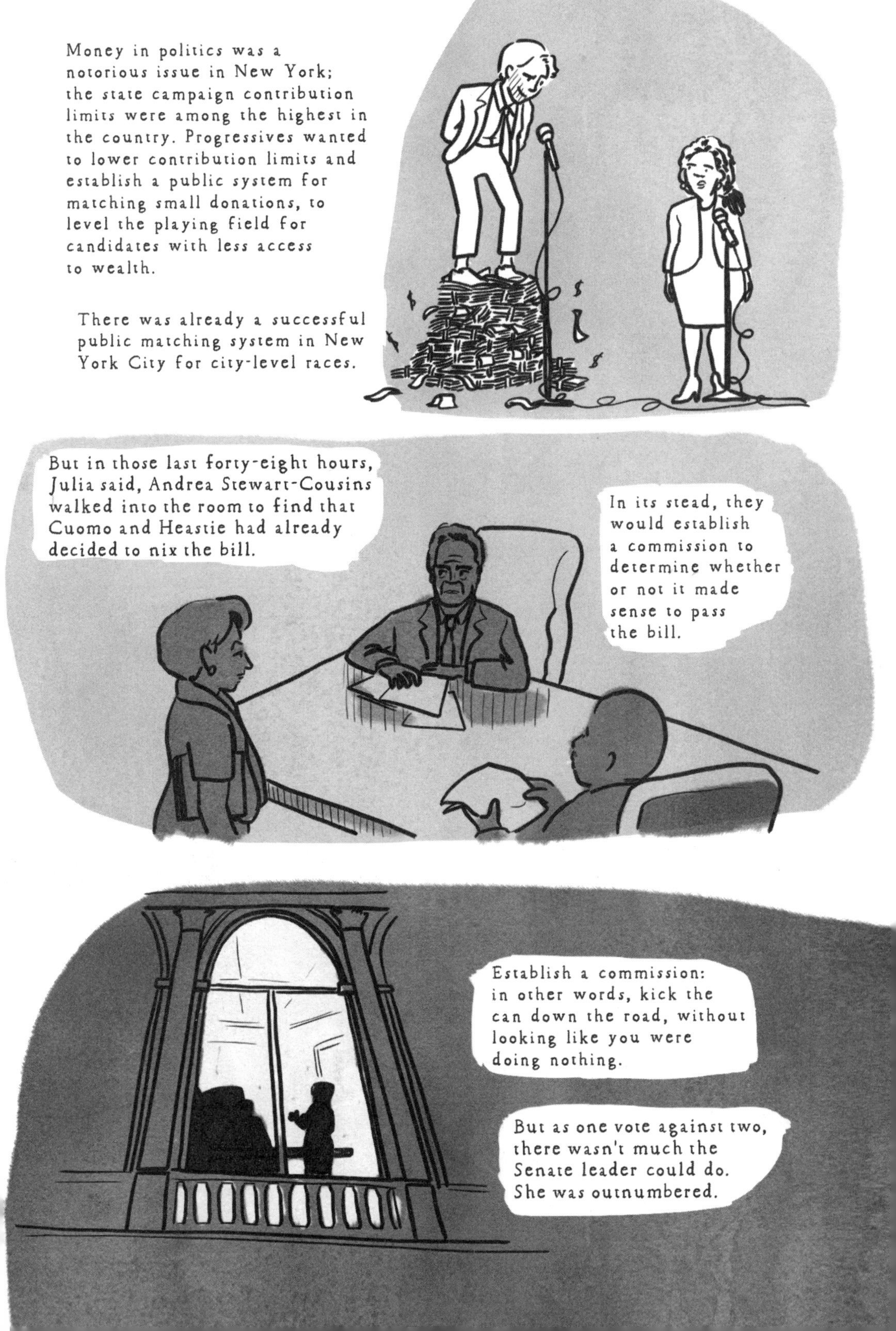
Money in politics was a notorious issue in New York; the state campaign contribution limits were among the highest in the country. Progressives wanted to lower contribution limits and establish a public system for matching small donations, to level the playing field for candidates with less access to wealth.
There was already a successful public matching system in New York City for city-level races.
But in those last forty-eight hours, Julia said, Andrea Stewart-Cousins walked into the room to find that Cuomo and Heastie had already decided to nix the bill.
In its stead, they would establish a commission to determine whether or not it made sense to pass the bill.
Establish a commission: in other words, kick the can down the road, without looking like you were doing nothing.
But as one vote against two, there wasn't much the Senate leader could do. She was outnumbered.

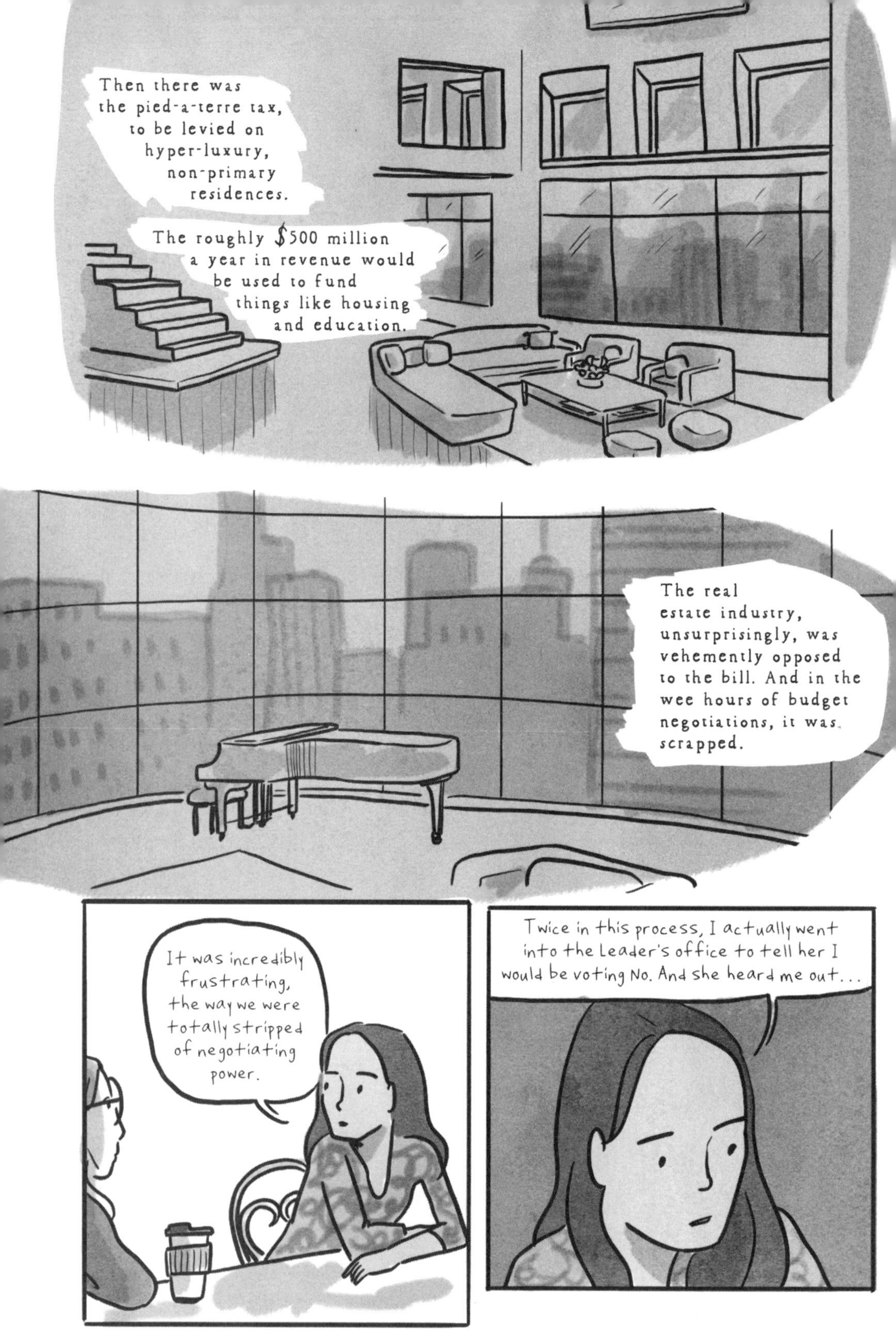
Then there was the pied-a-terre tax, to be levied on hyper-luxury, non-primary residences.
The roughly $500 million a year in revenue would be used to fund things like housing and education.
The real estate industry, unsurprisingly, was vehemently opposed to the bill. And in the wee hours of budget negotiations, it was scrapped.
It was incredibly frustrating, the way we were totally stripped of negotiating power.
Twice in this process, I actually went into the Leader's office to tell her I would be voting No. And she heard me out...

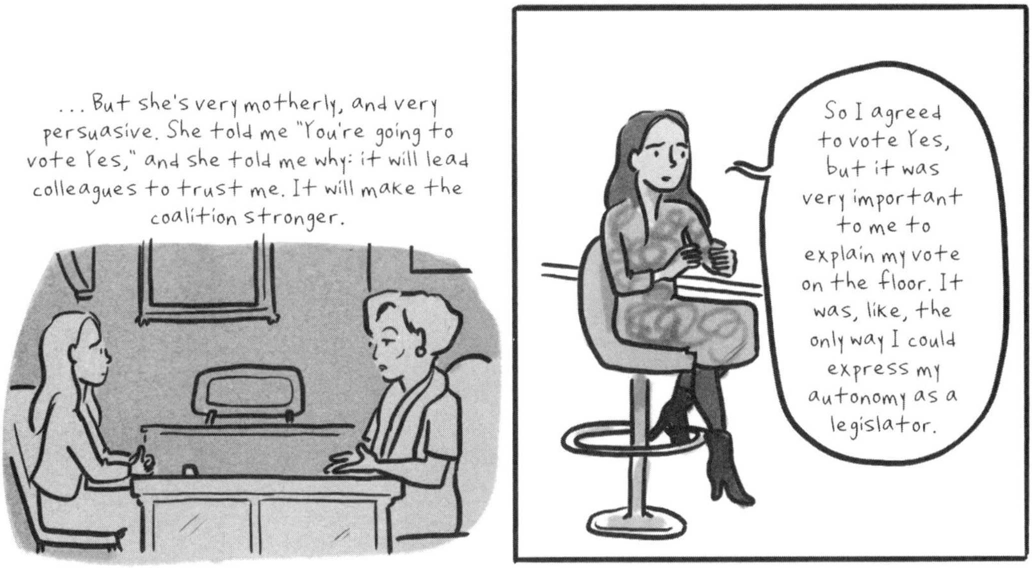
. . . But she's very motherly, and very persuasive. She told me "You're going to vote Yes," and she told me why: it will lead colleagues to trust me. It will make the coalition stronger.
So I agreed to vote Yes, but it was very important to me to explain my vote on the floor. It was, like, the only way I could express my autonomy as a legislator.

Normally, senators have ample time to explain their vote. But by the time this article of the budget came up for a vote, they were running up against the midnight deadline, so they started limiting speeches to just two minutes.

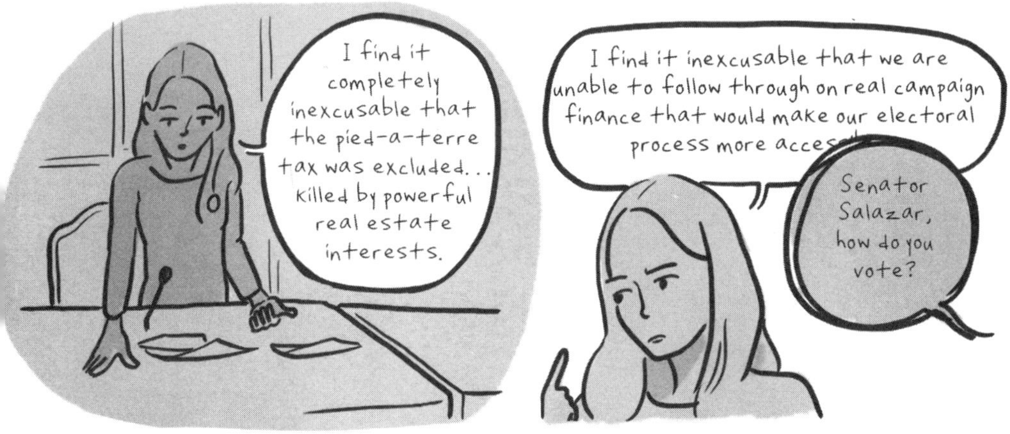
I find it completely inexcusable that the pied-a-terre tax was excluded. . . Killed by powerful real estate interests.
I find it inexcusable that we are unable to follow through on real campaign finance that would make our electoral process more acces
Senator Salazar, how do you vote?

In the video, you can feel Julia's frustration.

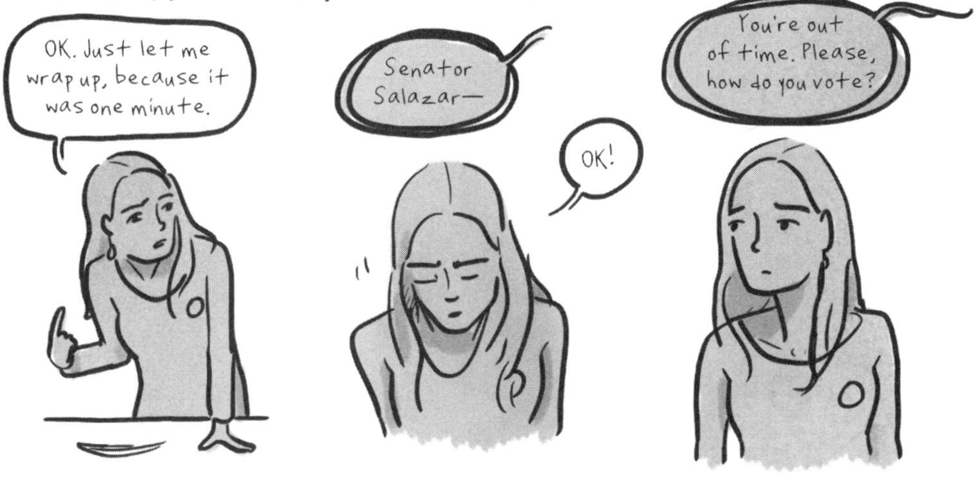
OK. Just let me wrap up, because it was one minute.
Senator Salazar—
OK!
You're out of time. Please, how do you vote?

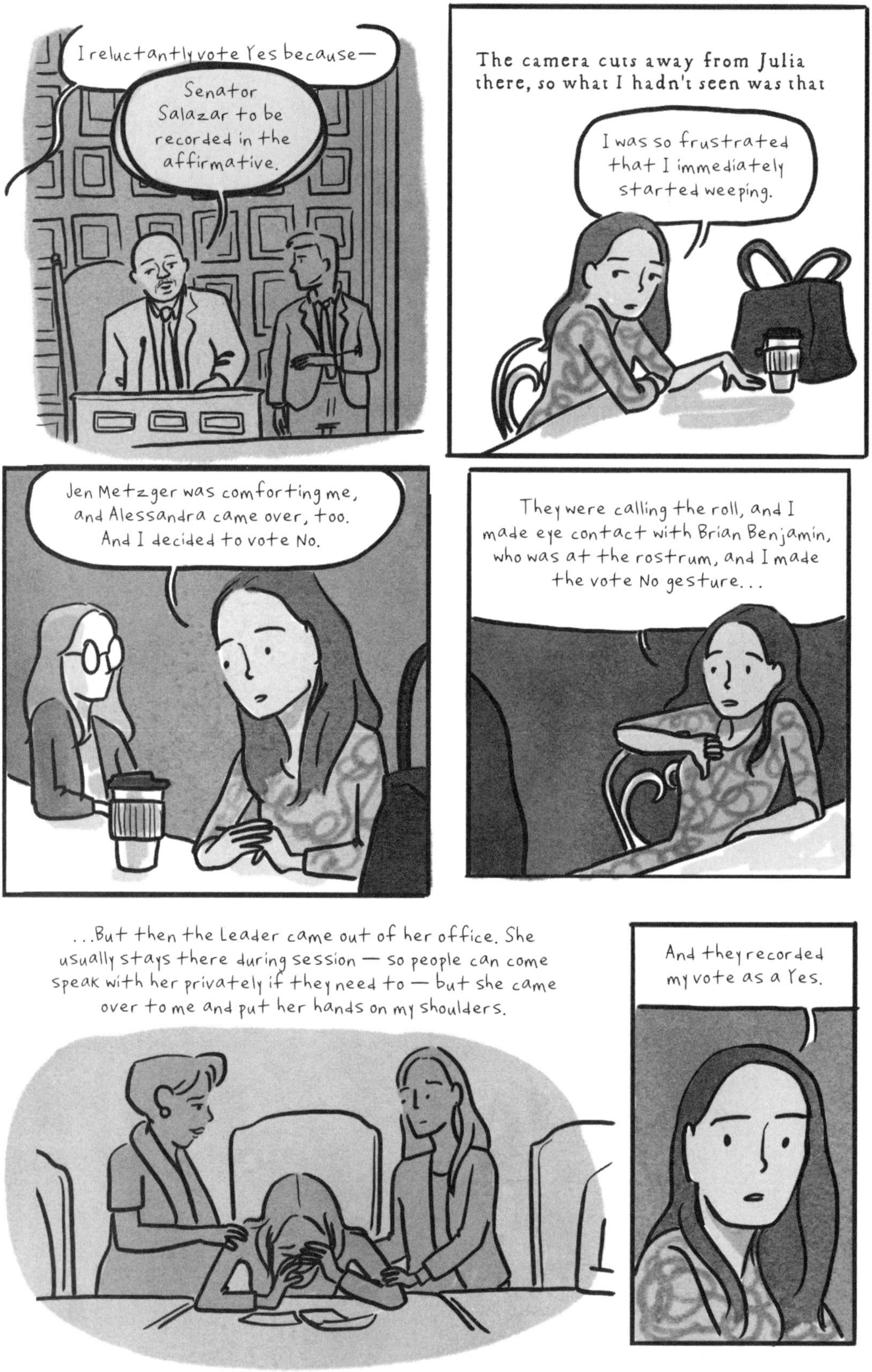
I reluctantly vote Yes because—
Senator Salazar to be recorded in the affirmative.
The camera cuts away from Julia there, so what I hadn't seen was that
I was so frustrated that I immediately started weeping.
Jen Metzger was comforting me, and Alessandra came over, too. And I decided to vote No.
They were calling the roll, and I made eye contact with Brian Benjamin, who was at the rostrum, and I made the vote No gesture...
...But then the Leader came out of her office. She usually stays there during session — so people can come speak with her privately if they need to — but she came over to me and put her hands on my shoulders.
And they recorded my vote as a Yes.

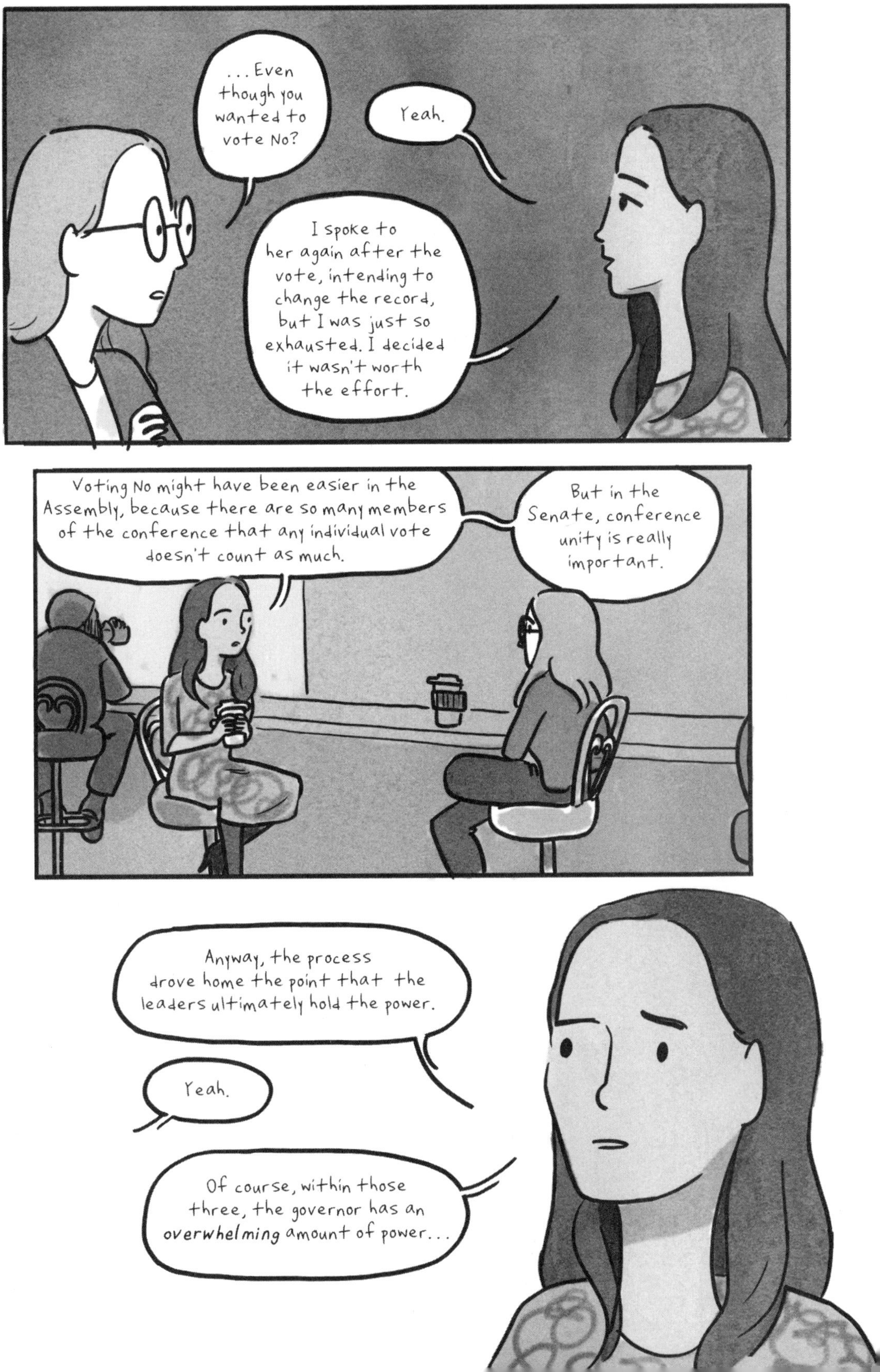
...Even though you wanted to vote No?
Yeah.
I spoke to her again after the vote, intending to change the record, but I was just so exhausted. I decided it wasn't worth the effort.
Voting No might have been easier in the Assembly, because there are so many members of the conference that any individual vote doesn't count as much.
But in the Senate, conference unity is really important.
Anyway, the process drove home the point that the leaders ultimately hold the power.
Yeah.
Of course, within those three, the governor has an *overwhelming* amount of power...

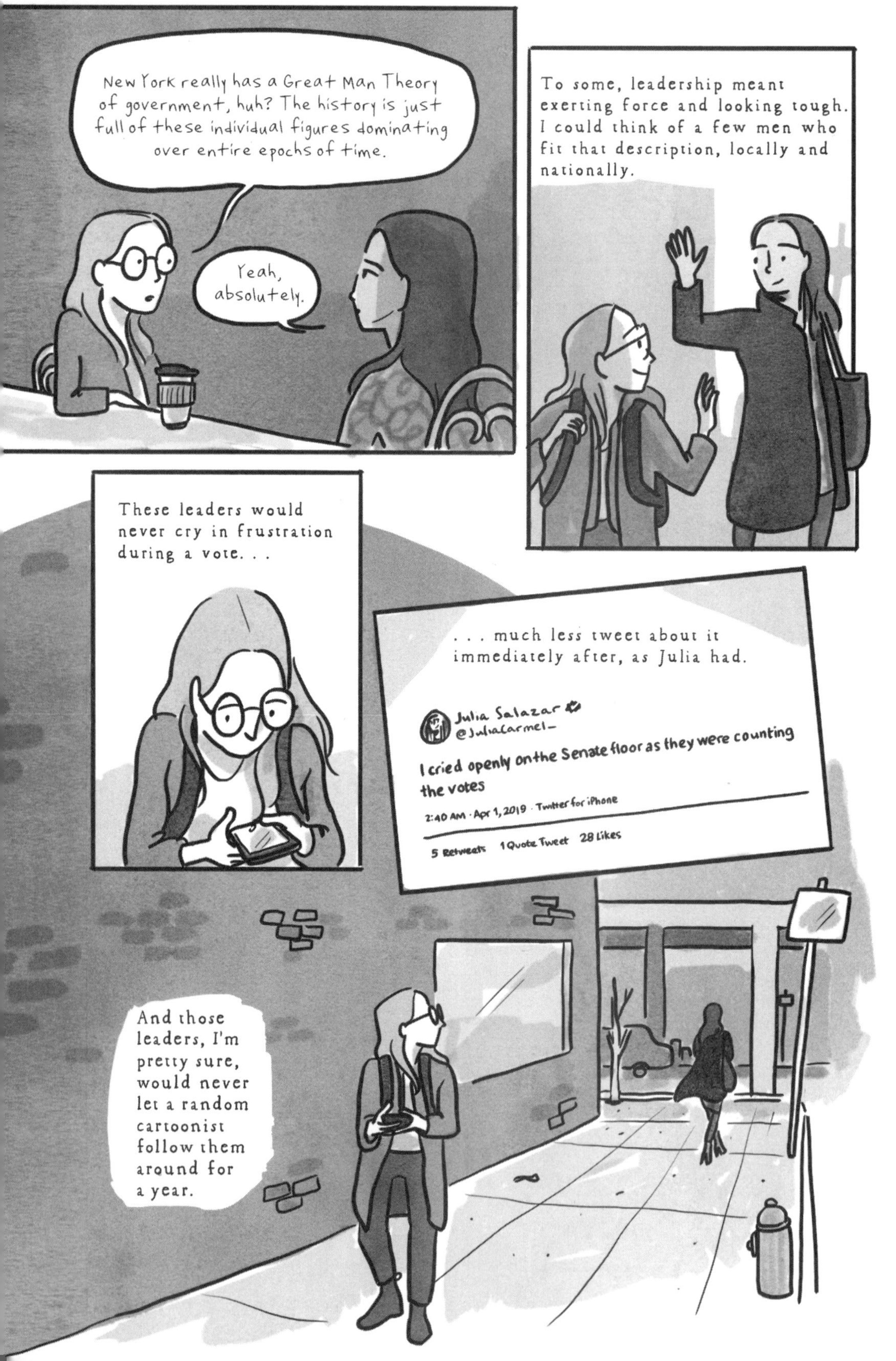
New York really has a Great Man Theory of government, huh? The history is just full of these individual figures dominating over entire epochs of time.
Yeah, absolutely.
To some, leadership meant exerting force and looking tough. I could think of a few men who fit that description, locally and nationally.
These leaders would never cry in frustration during a vote. . .
. . . much less tweet about it immediately after, as Julia had.
Julia Salazar
@JuliaCarmel_
I cried openly on the Senate floor as they were counting the votes
2:40 AM · Apr 1, 2019 · Twitter for iPhone
5 Retweets 1 Quote Tweet 28 Likes
And those leaders, I'm pretty sure, would never let a random cartoonist follow them around for a year.

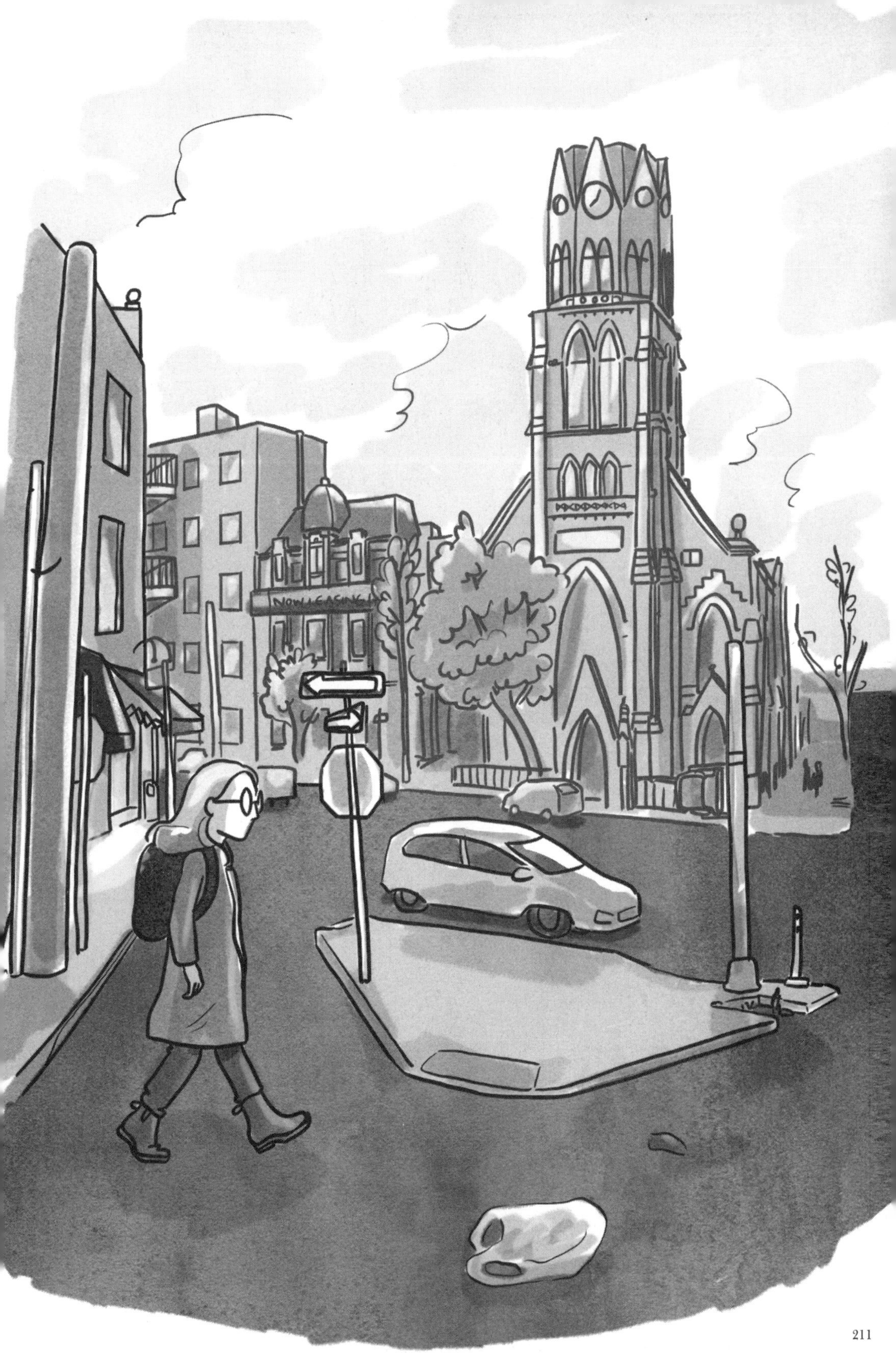
NOW LEASING

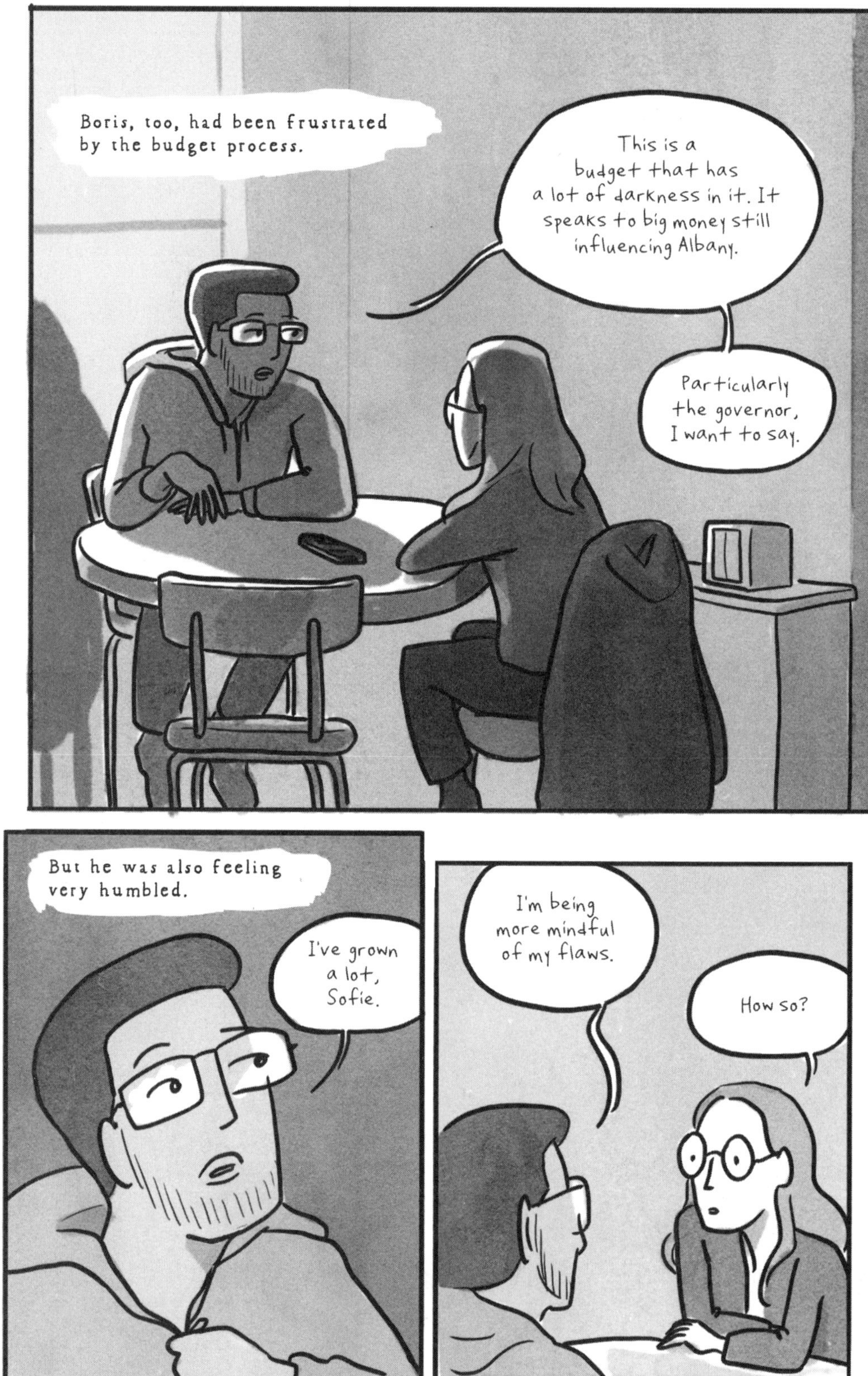

Boris, too, had been frustrated by the budget process.
This is a budget that has a lot of darkness in it. It speaks to big money still influencing Albany.
Particularly the governor, I want to say.
But he was also feeling very humbled.
I've grown a lot, Sofie.
I'm being more mindful of my flaws.
How so?

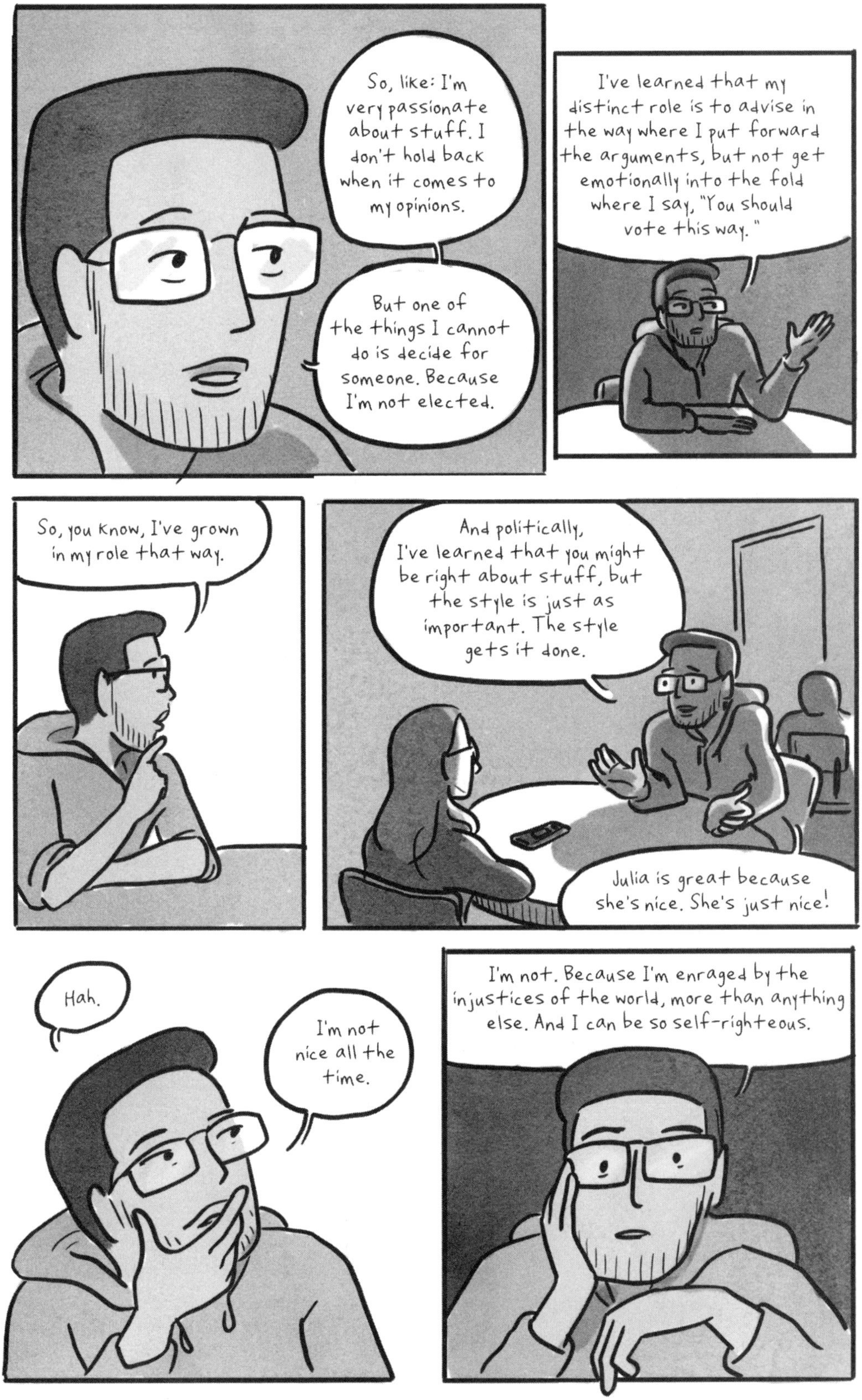
So, like: I'm very passionate about stuff. I don't hold back when it comes to my opinions.
But one of the things I cannot do is decide for someone. Because I'm not elected.
I've learned that my distinct role is to advise in the way where I put forward the arguments, but not get emotionally into the fold where I say, "You should vote this way."
So, you know, I've grown in my role that way.
And politically, I've learned that you might be right about stuff, but the style is just as important. The style gets it done.
Julia is great because she's nice. She's just nice!
Hah.
I'm not nice all the time.
I'm not. Because I'm enraged by the injustices of the world, more than anything else. And I can be so self-righteous.

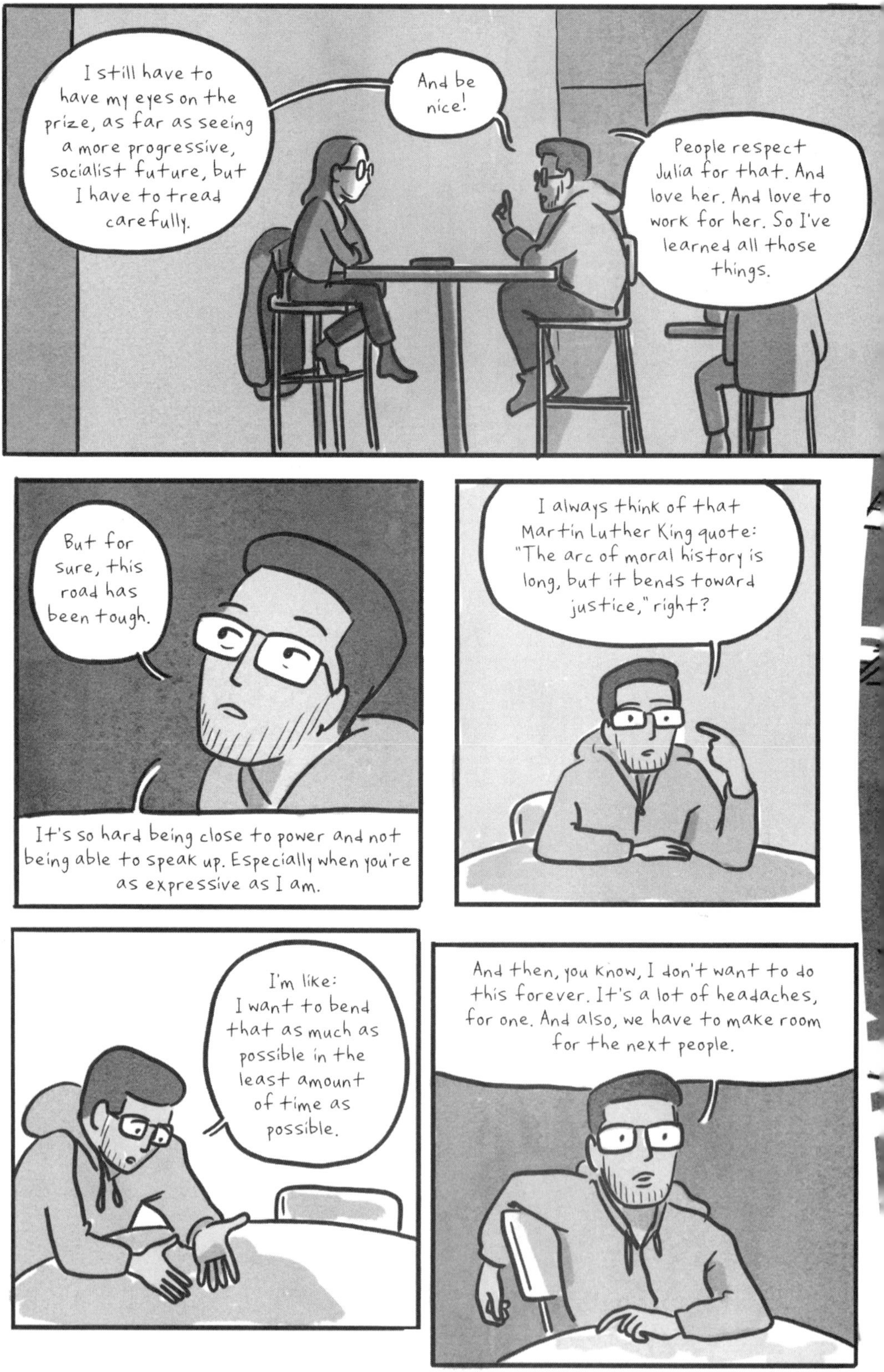
I still have to have my eyes on the prize, as far as seeing a more progressive, socialist future, but I have to tread carefully.
And be nice!
People respect Julia for that. And love her. And love to work for her. So I've learned all those things.
But for sure, this road has been tough.
It's so hard being close to power and not being able to speak up. Especially when you're as expressive as I am.
I always think of that Martin Luther King quote: "The arc of moral history is long, but it bends toward justice," right?
I'm like: I want to bend that as much as possible in the least amount of time as possible.
And then, you know, I don't want to do this forever. It's a lot of headaches, for one. And also, we have to make room for the next people.

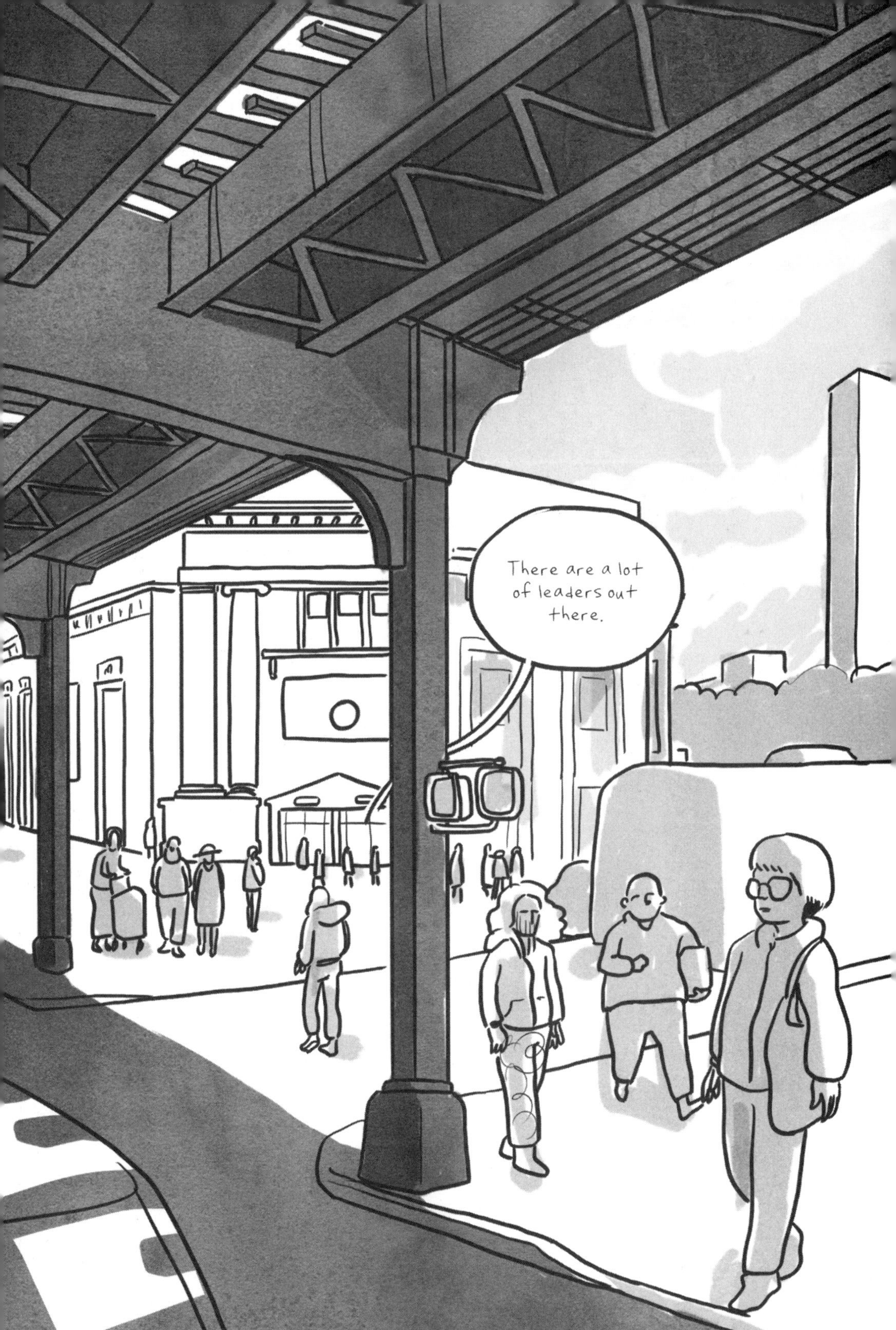
There are a lot of leaders out there.

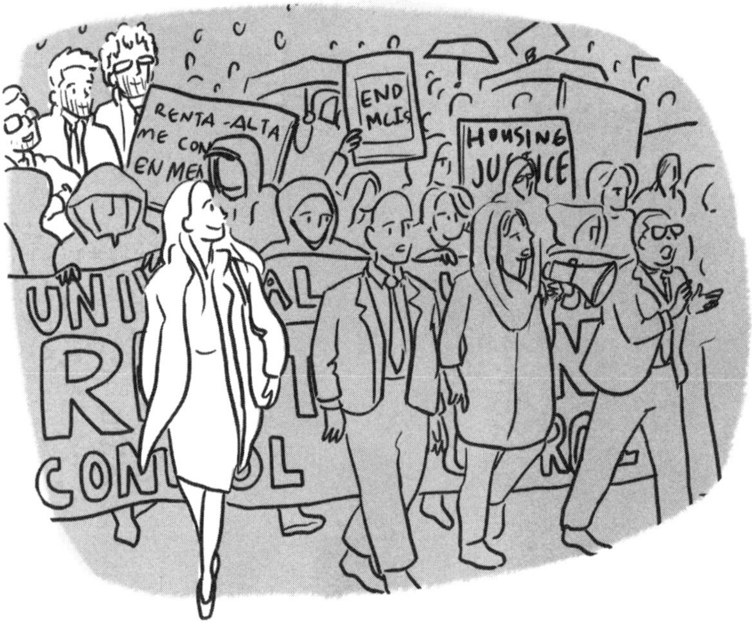
RENTA -ALTA
END MCIs
HOUSING

Part III

Chapter Nine

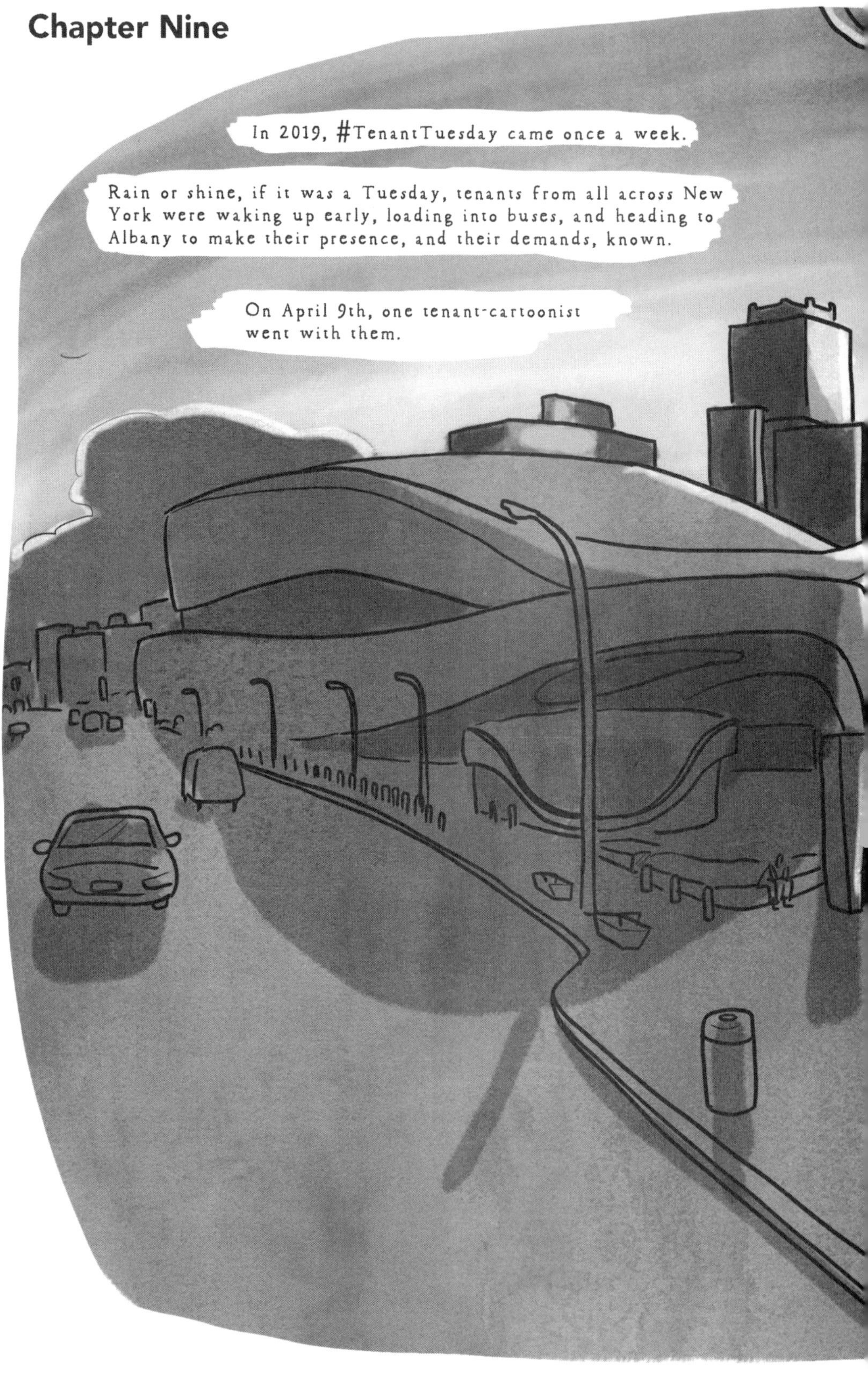
In 2019, #TenantTuesday came once a week.
Rain or shine, if it was a Tuesday, tenants from all across New York were waking up early, loading into buses, and heading to Albany to make their presence, and their demands, known.
On April 9th, one tenant-cartoonist went with them.

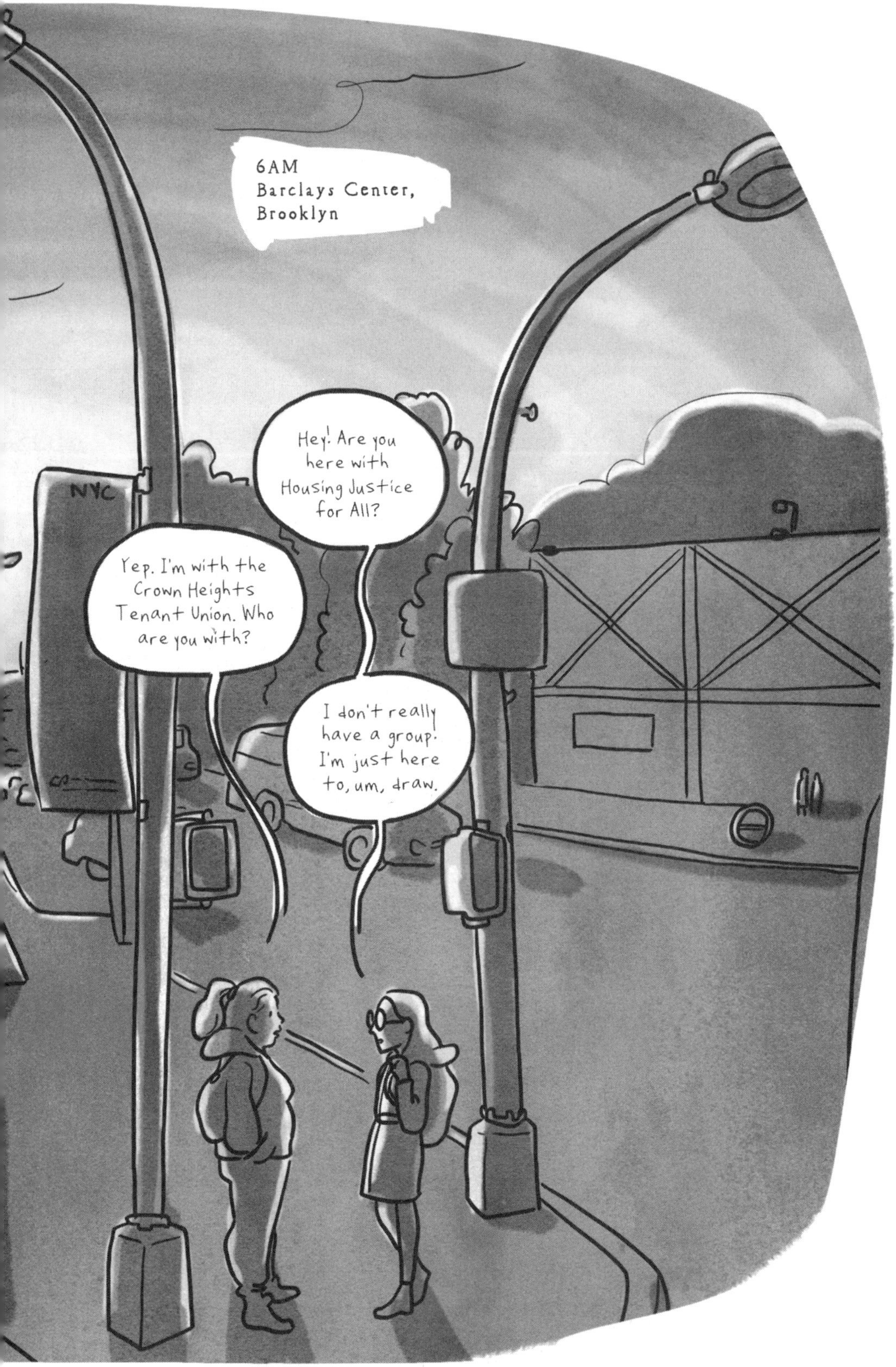
6AM
Barclays Center,
Brooklyn
Hey! Are you here with Housing Justice for All?
Yep. I'm with the Crown Heights Tenant Union. Who are you with?
I don't really have a group! I'm just here to, um, draw.
NYC

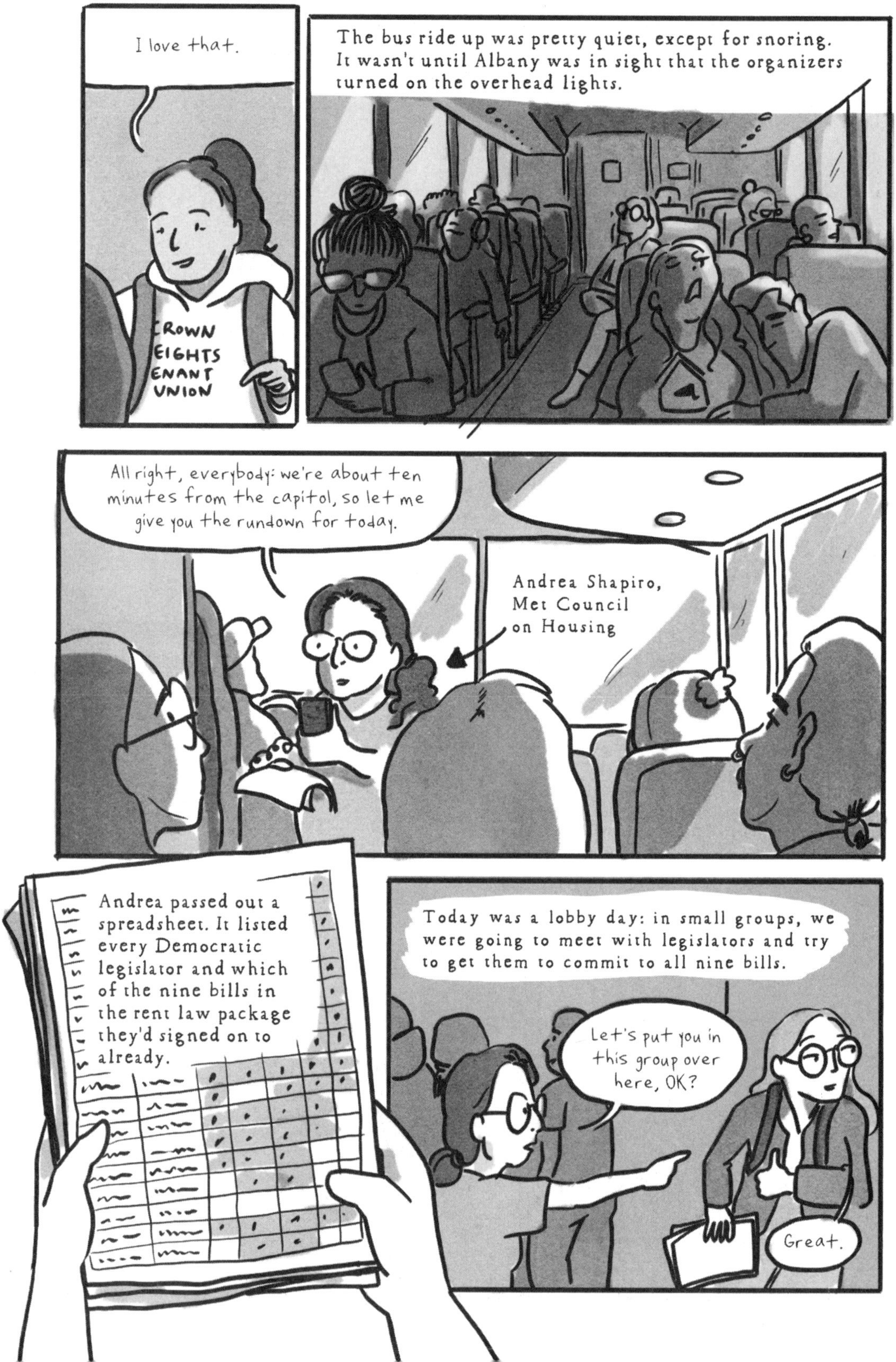
I love that.
CROWN EIGHTS ENANT UNION
The bus ride up was pretty quiet, except for snoring. It wasn't until Albany was in sight that the organizers turned on the overhead lights.
All right, everybody: we're about ten minutes from the capitol, so let me give you the rundown for today.
Andrea Shapiro, Met Council on Housing
Andrea passed out a spreadsheet. It listed every Democratic legislator and which of the nine bills in the rent law package they'd signed on to already.
Today was a lobby day: in small groups, we were going to meet with legislators and try to get them to commit to all nine bills.
Let's put you in this group over here, OK?
Great.

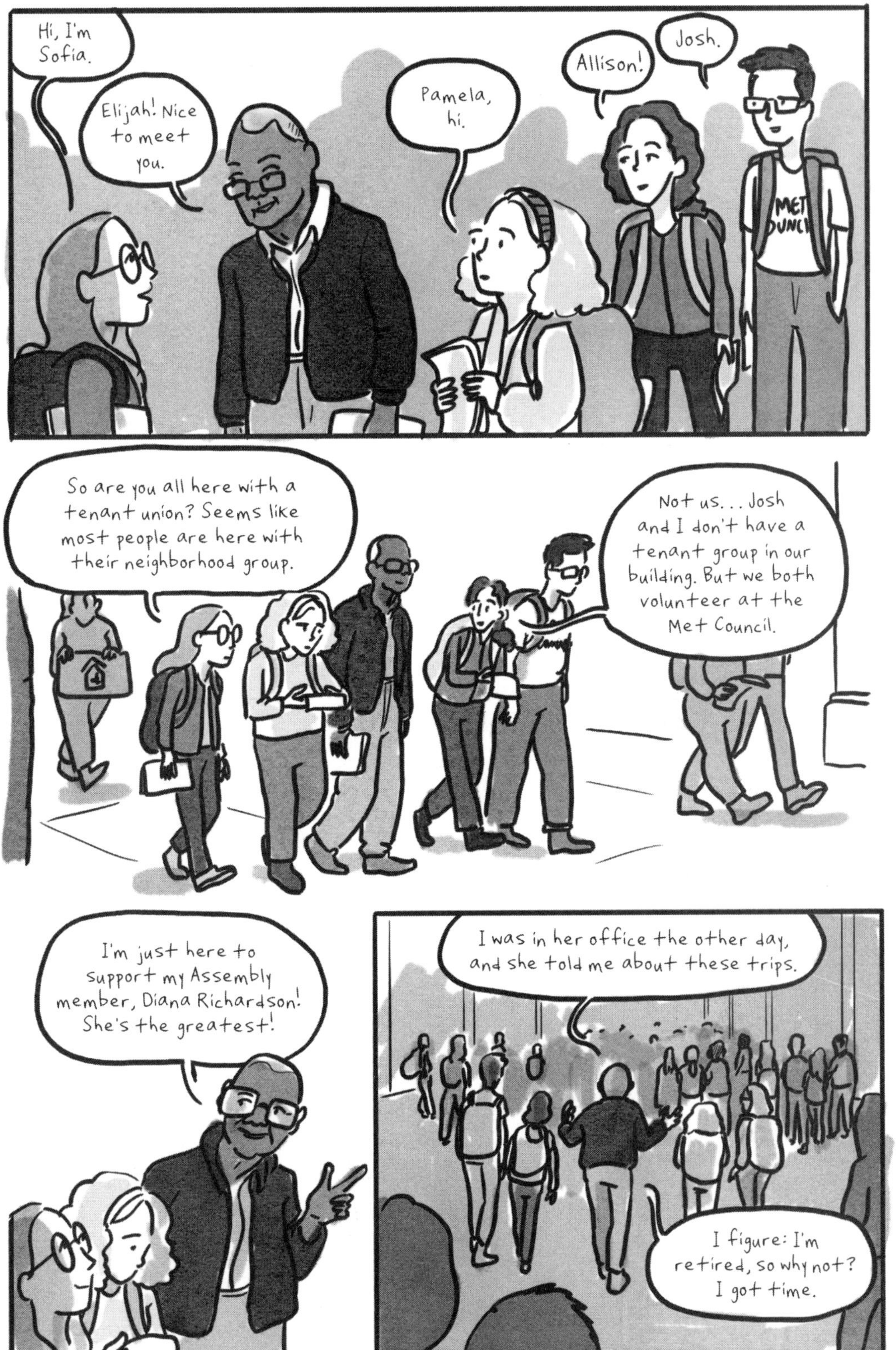
Hi, I'm Sofia.
Elijah! Nice to meet you.
Pamela, hi.
Allison!
Josh.
So are you all here with a tenant union? Seems like most people are here with their neighborhood group.
Not us... Josh and I don't have a tenant group in our building. But we both volunteer at the Met Council.
I'm just here to support my Assembly member, Diana Richardson! She's the greatest!
I was in her office the other day, and she told me about these trips.
I figure: I'm retired, so why not? I got time.

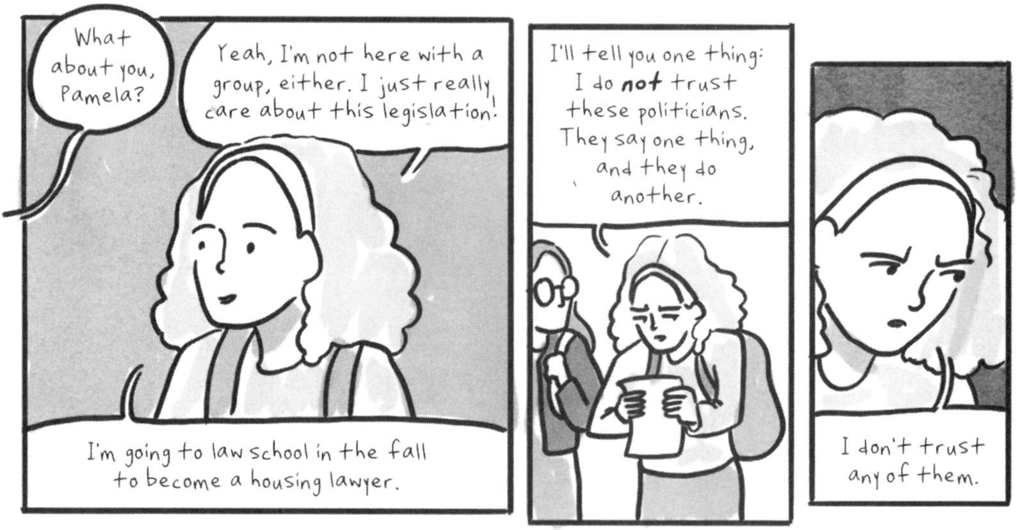
What about you, Pamela?
Yeah, I'm not here with a group, either. I just really care about this legislation!
I'm going to law school in the fall to become a housing lawyer.
I'll tell you one thing: I do **not** trust these politicians. They say one thing, and they do another.
I don't trust any of them.

The spreadsheet sent us to Helene Weinstein, a longtime assemblymember from Brooklyn. She'd signed on to some, but not all, of the nine bills.

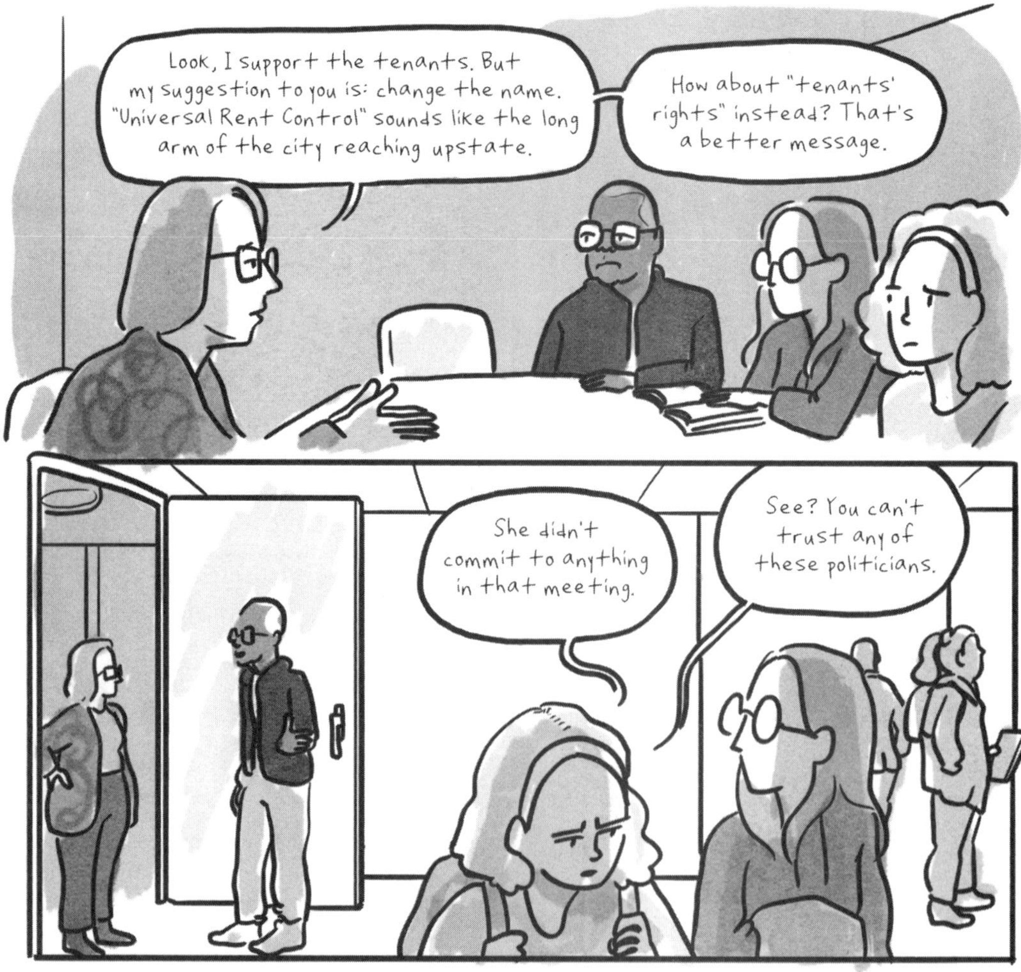
Look, I support the tenants. But my suggestion to you is: change the name. "Universal Rent Control" sounds like the long arm of the city reaching upstate.
How about "tenants' rights" instead? That's a better message.
She didn't commit to anything in that meeting.
See? You can't trust any of these politicians.

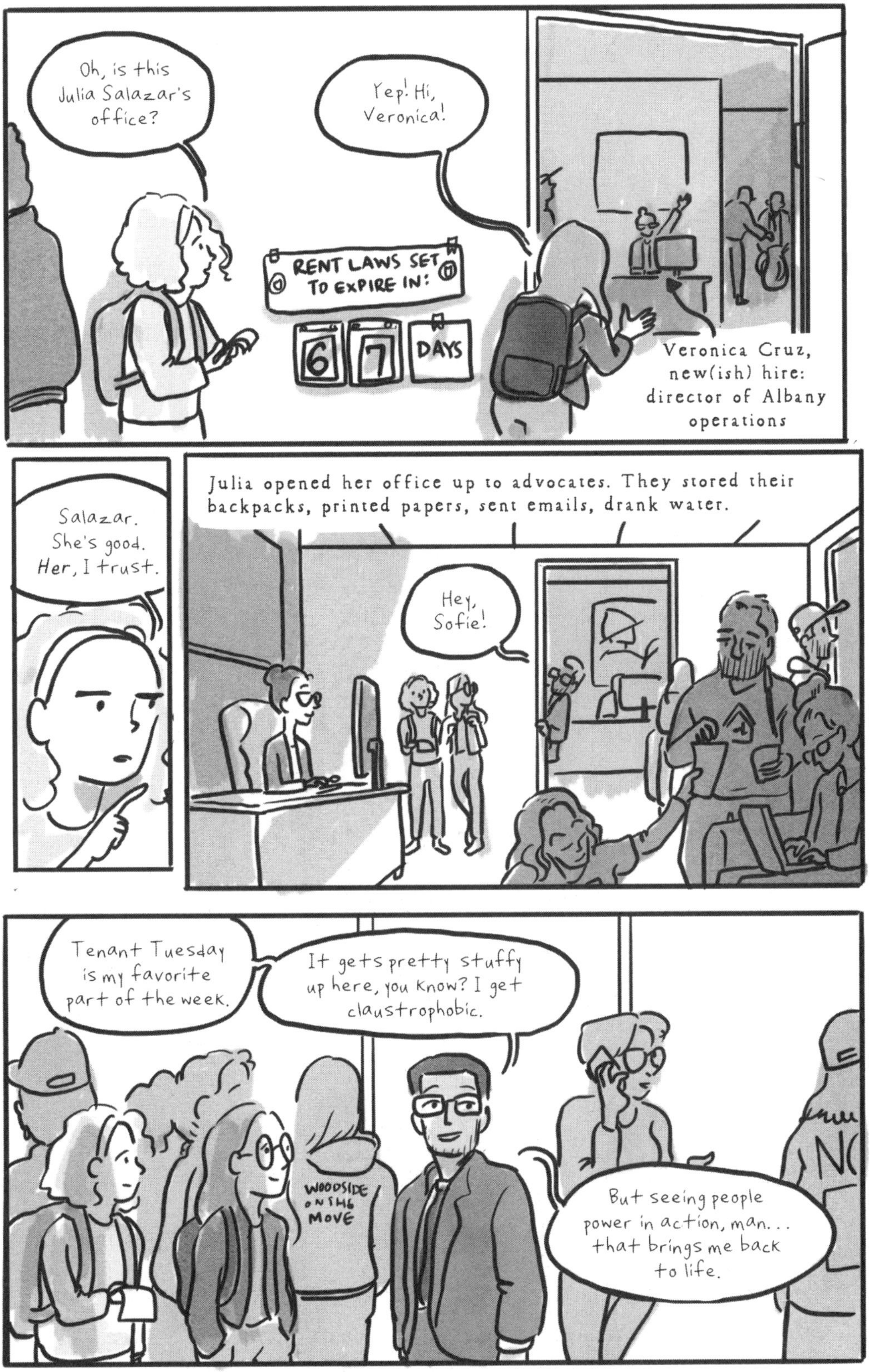
Oh, is this Julia Salazar's office?
RENT LAWS SET TO EXPIRE IN:
67 DAYS
Yep! Hi, Veronica!
Veronica Cruz, new(ish) hire: director of Albany operations
Salazar. She's good. Her, I trust.
Julia opened her office up to advocates. They stored their backpacks, printed papers, sent emails, drank water.
Hey, Sofie!
Tenant Tuesday is my favorite part of the week.
It gets pretty stuffy up here, you know? I get claustrophobic.
WOODSIDE ON THE MOVE
But seeing people power in action, man... that brings me back to life.

Meanwhile, as Pamela and I were heading into our next meeting. . .

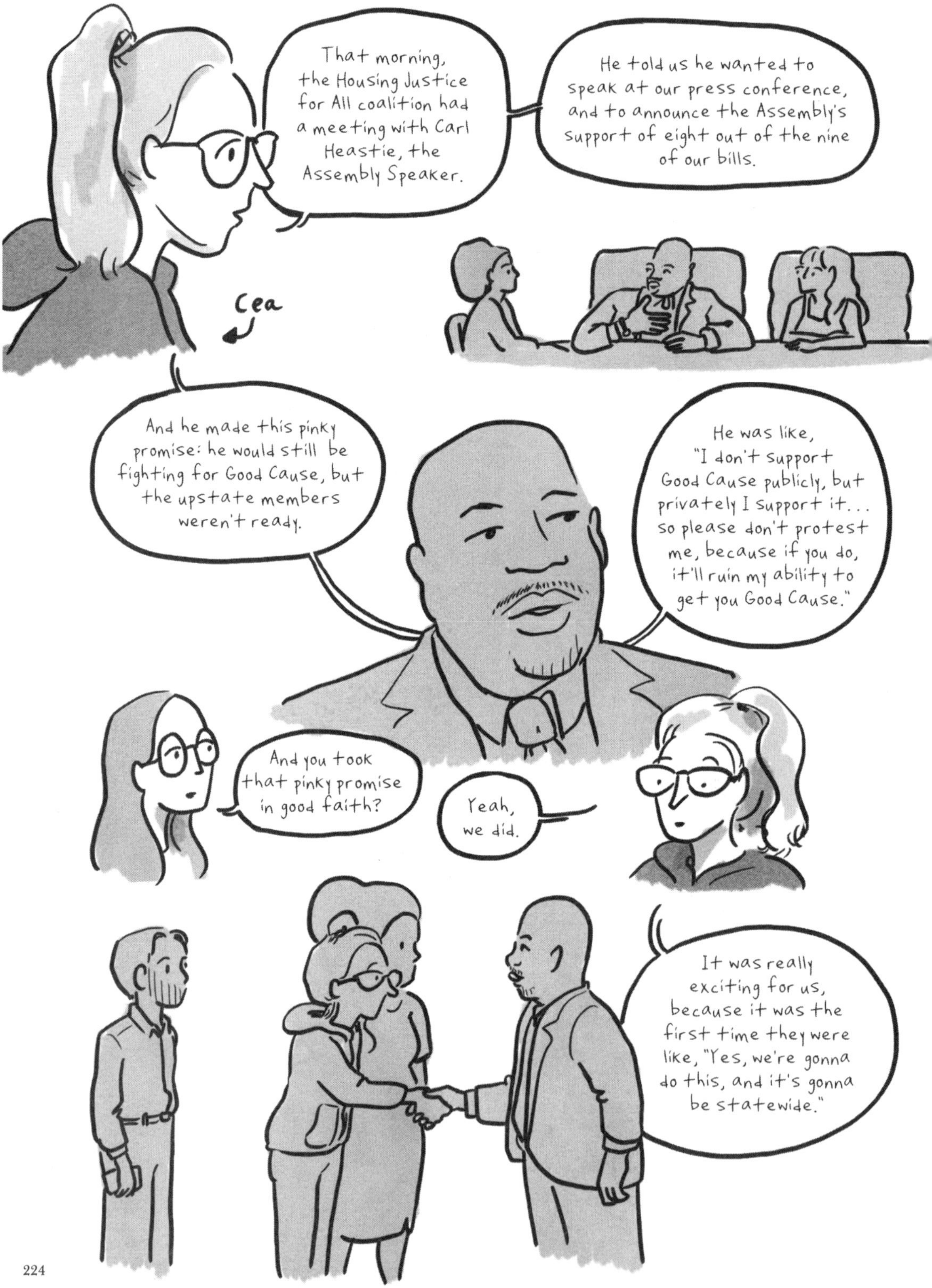
That morning, the Housing Justice for All coalition had a meeting with Carl Heastie, the Assembly Speaker.
He told us he wanted to speak at our press conference, and to announce the Assembly's support of eight out of the nine of our bills.
Cea
And he made this pinky promise: he would still be fighting for Good Cause, but the upstate members weren't ready.
He was like, "I don't support Good Cause publicly, but privately I support it. . . so please don't protest me, because if you do, it'll ruin my ability to get you Good Cause."
And you took that pinky promise in good faith?
Yeah, we did.
It was really exciting for us, because it was the first time they were like, "Yes, we're gonna do this, and it's gonna be statewide."

So, later that day, when tenants convened for a press conference, Carl Heastie took center stage. He said the Assembly had conferenced, and they had sorted out where they would stand on each of the nine Housing Justice for All bills.

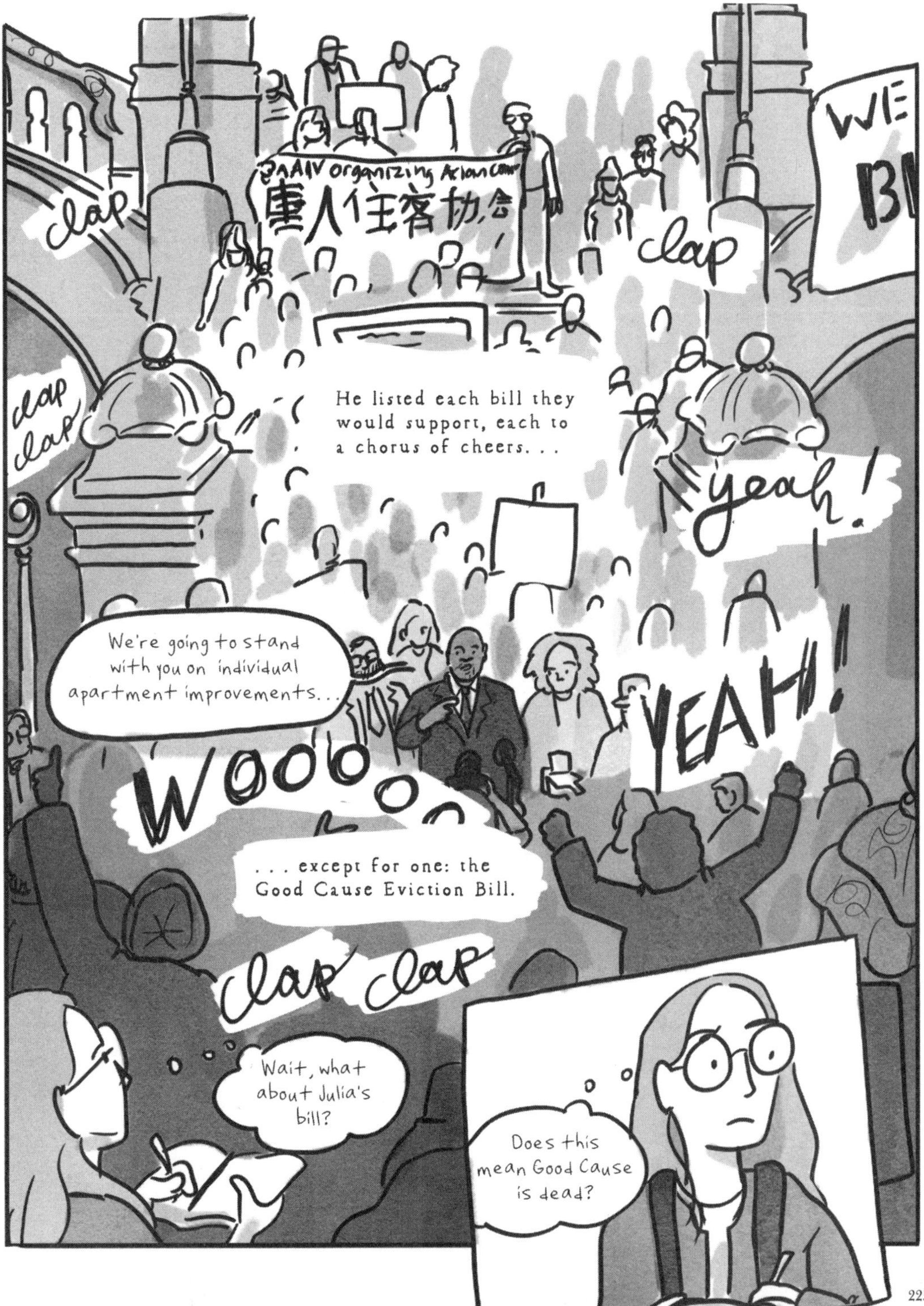

clap
clap
clap
clap
He listed each bill they would support, each to a chorus of cheers. . .
yeah!
We're going to stand with you on individual apartment improvements...
YEAH!
Wooooo
. . . except for one: the Good Cause Eviction Bill.
clap clap
Wait, what about Julia's bill?
Does this mean Good Cause is dead?

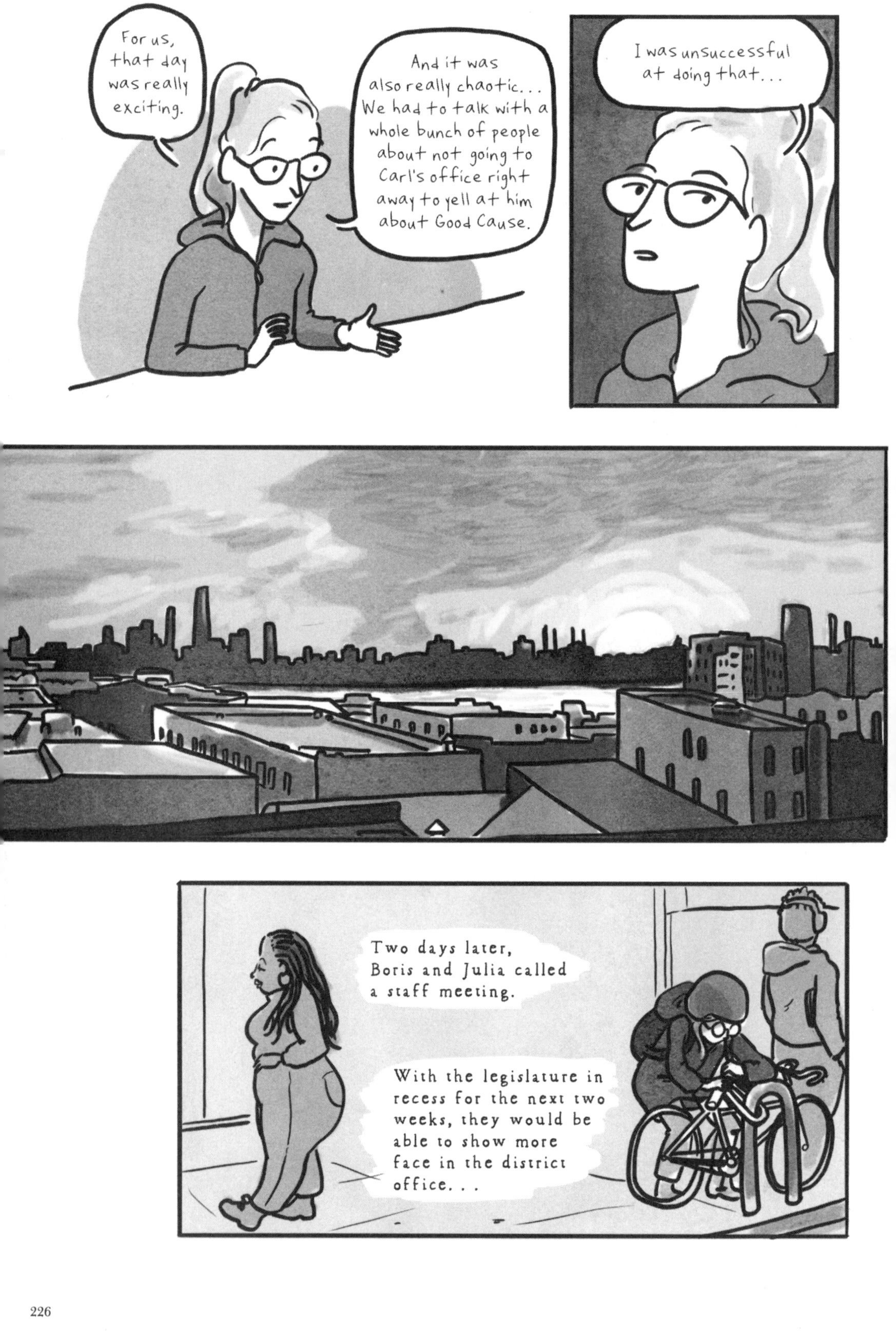
For us, that day was really exciting.
And it was also really chaotic... We had to talk with a whole bunch of people about not going to Carl's office right away to yell at him about Good Cause.
I was unsuccessful at doing that...
Two days later, Boris and Julia called a staff meeting.
With the legislature in recess for the next two weeks, they would be able to show more face in the district office...

. . . except that, once again, there was no district office. Their temporary lease had ended, and the permanent lease seemed no closer than it had months ago.

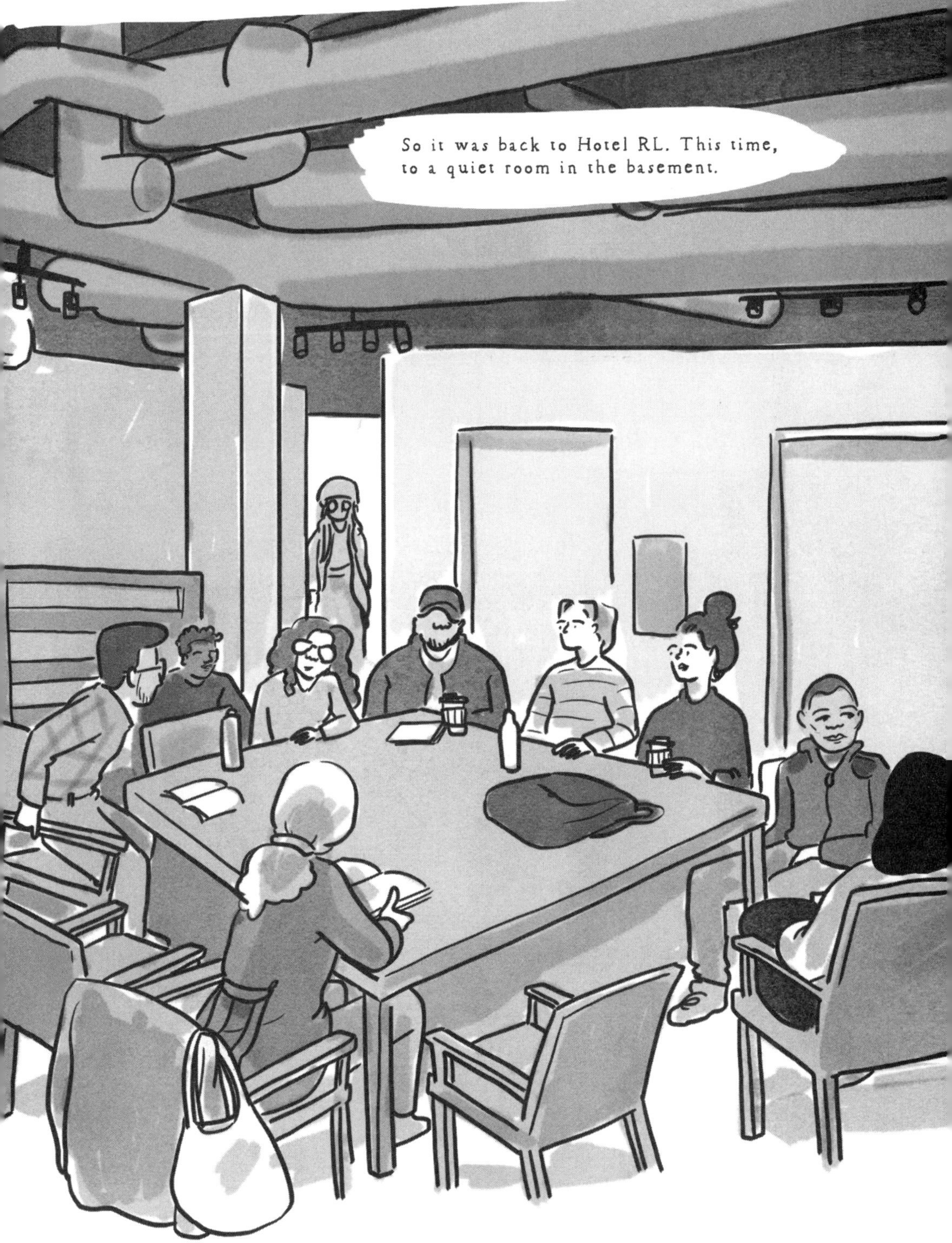
So it was back to Hotel RL. This time, to a quiet room in the basement.

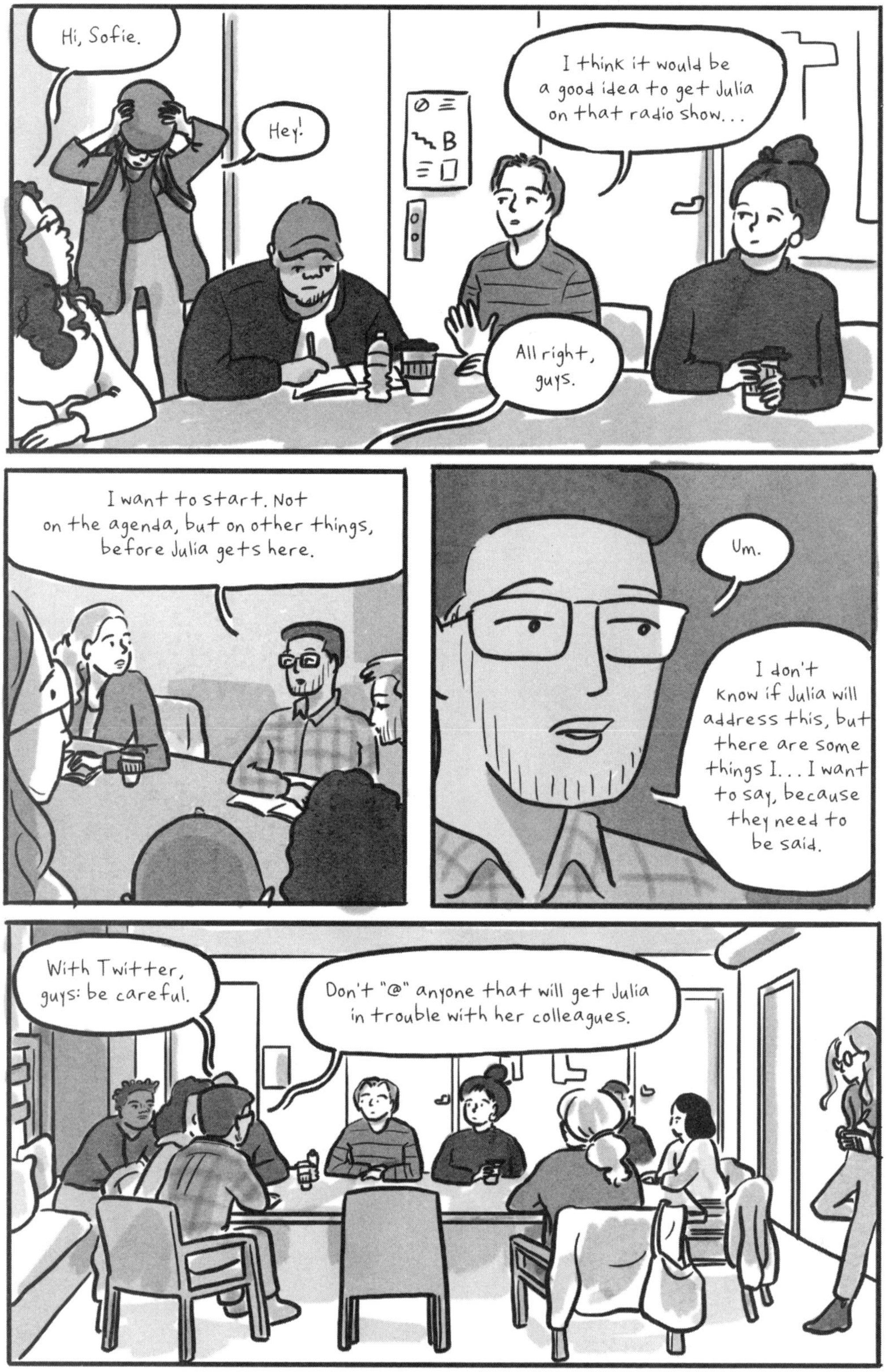
Hi, Sofie.
Hey!
I think it would be a good idea to get Julia on that radio show...
All right, guys.
I want to start. Not on the agenda, but on other things, before Julia gets here.
Um.
I don't know if Julia will address this, but there are some things I... I want to say, because they need to be said.
With Twitter, guys: be careful.
Don't "@" anyone that will get Julia in trouble with her colleagues.

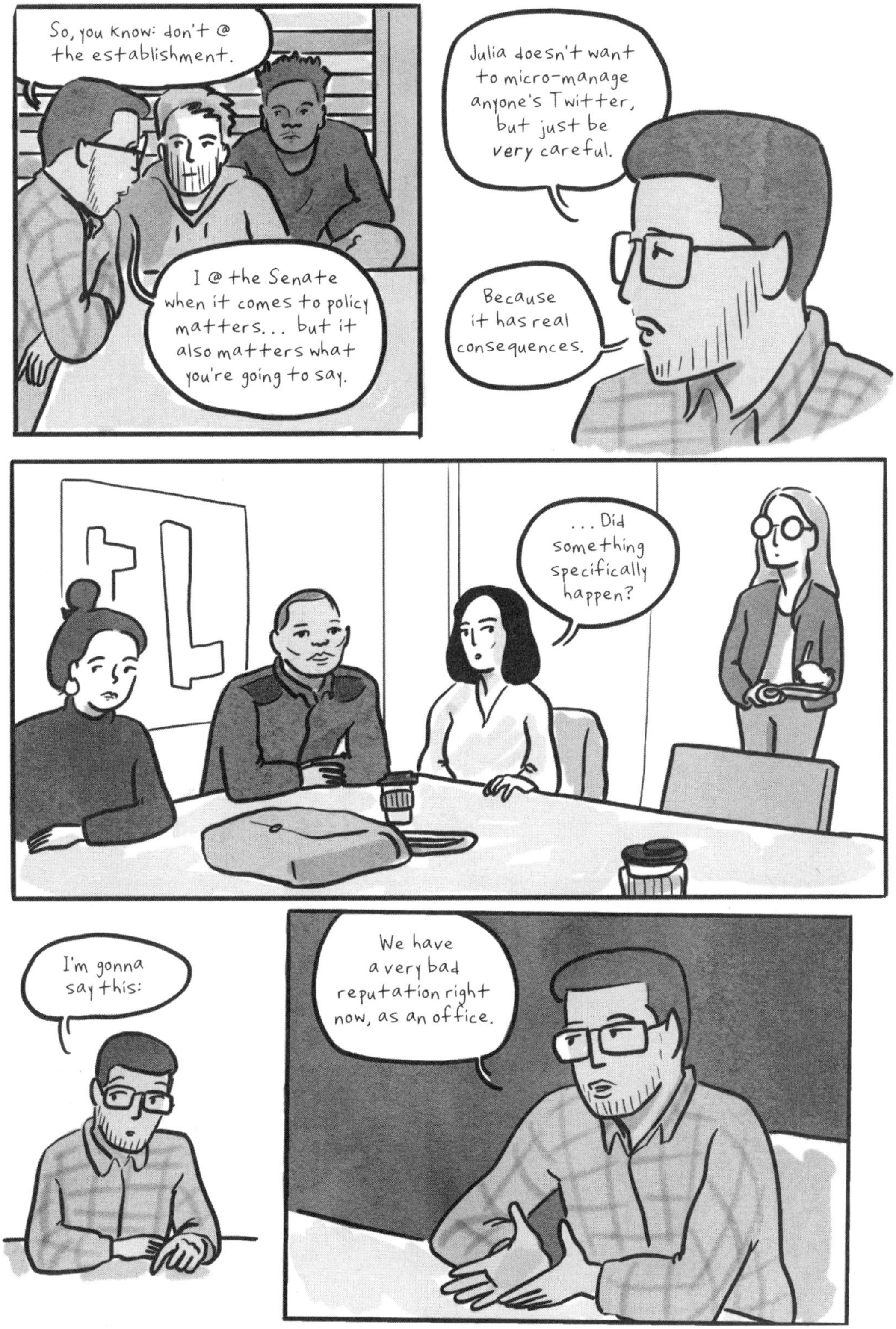
So, you know: don't @ the establishment.
I @ the Senate when it comes to policy matters... but it also matters what you're going to say.
Julia doesn't want to micro-manage anyone's Twitter, but just be very careful.
Because it has real consequences.
...Did something specifically happen?
I'm gonna say this:
We have a very bad reputation right now, as an office.

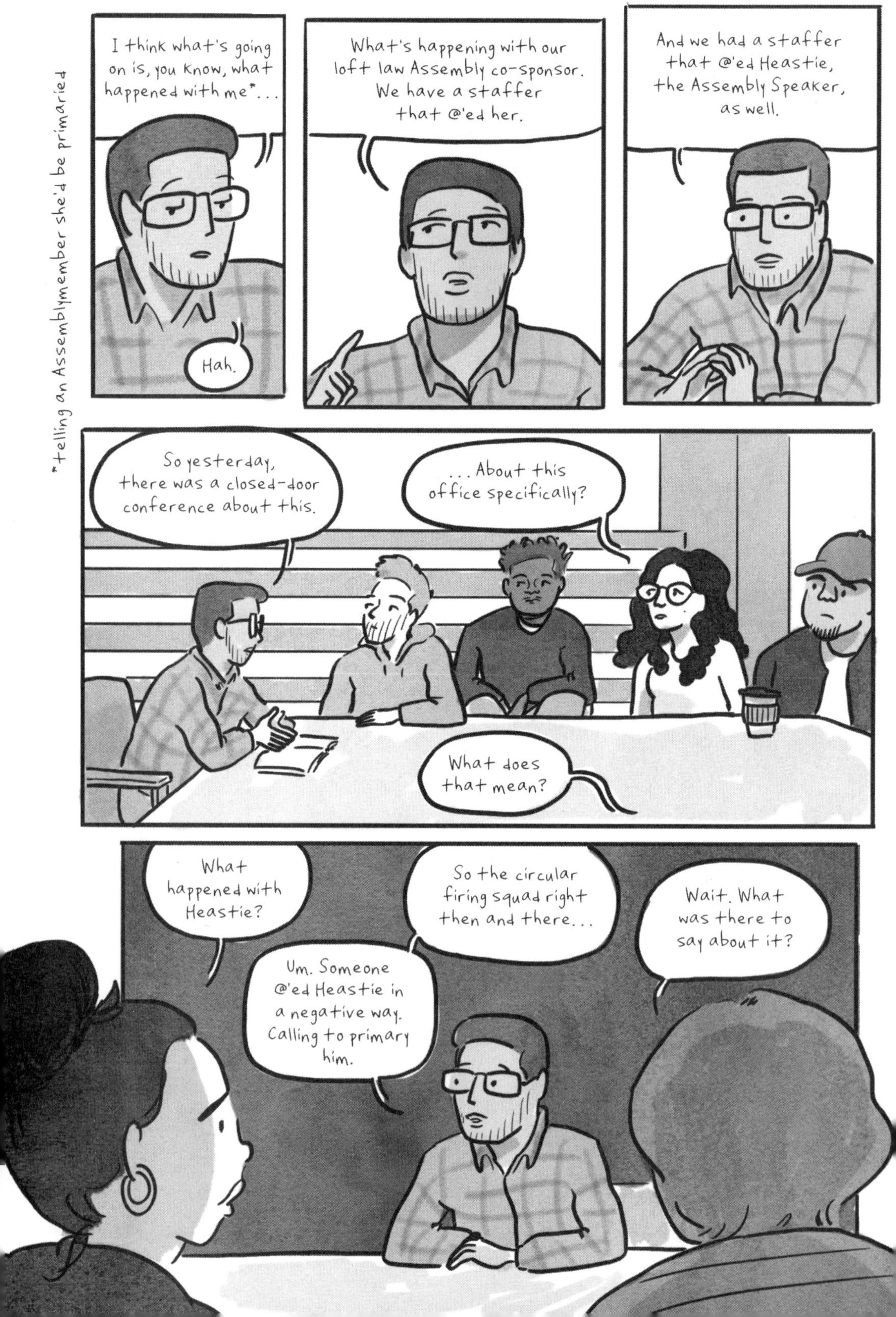
I think what's going on is, you know, what happened with me*...
Hah.
What's happening with our loft law Assembly co-sponsor. We have a staffer that @'ed her.
And we had a staffer that @'ed Heastie, the Assembly Speaker, as well.
So yesterday, there was a closed-door conference about this.
... About this office specifically?
What does that mean?
What happened with Heastie?
Um. Someone @'ed Heastie in a negative way. Calling to primary him.
So the circular firing squad right then and there...
Wait. What was there to say about it?

*telling an Assemblymember she'd be primaried

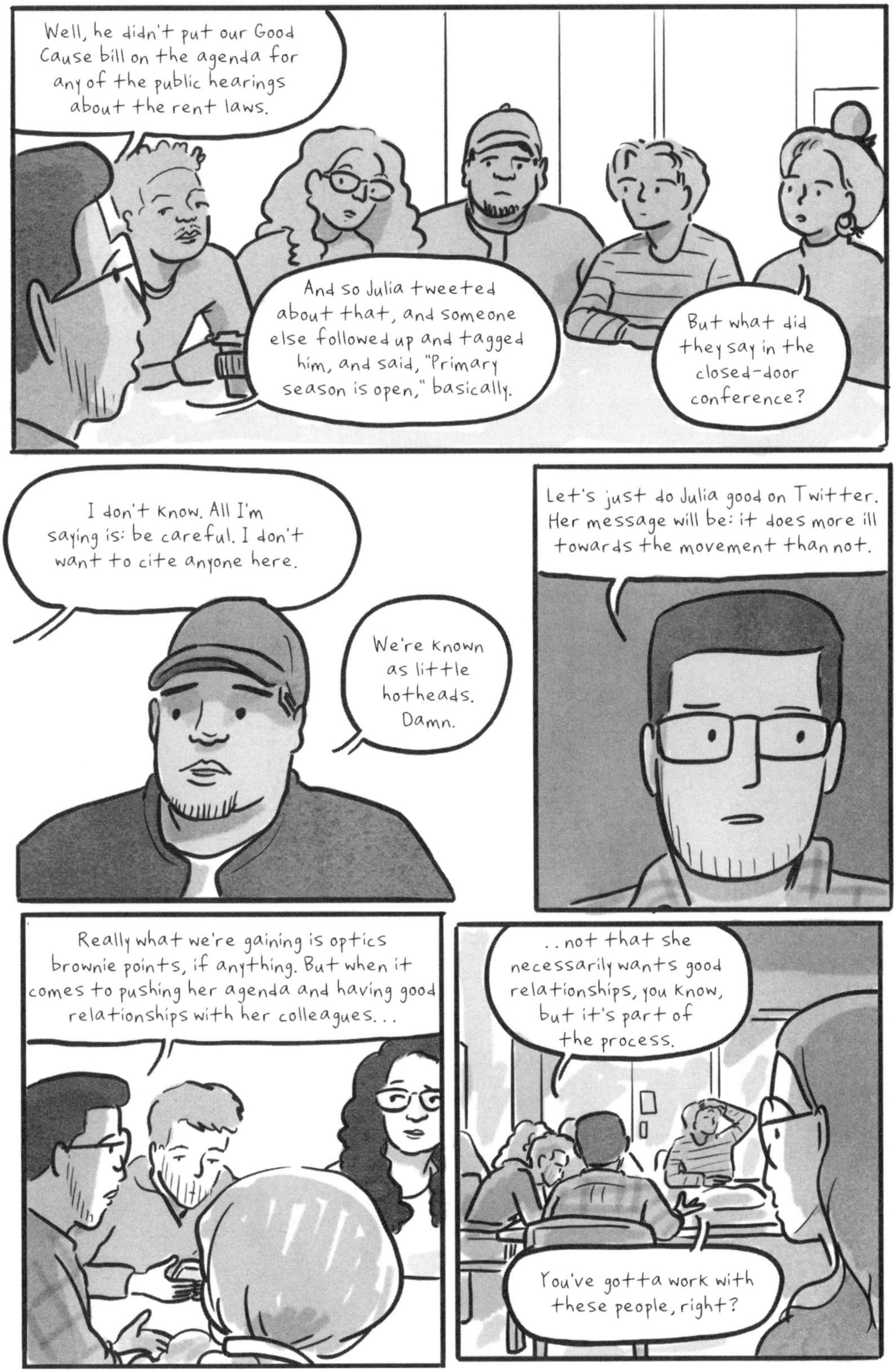
Well, he didn't put our Good Cause bill on the agenda for any of the public hearings about the rent laws.
And so Julia tweeted about that, and someone else followed up and tagged him, and said, "Primary season is open," basically.
But what did they say in the closed-door conference?
I don't know. All I'm saying is: be careful. I don't want to cite anyone here.
We're known as little hotheads. Damn.
Let's just do Julia good on Twitter. Her message will be: it does more ill towards the movement than not.
Really what we're gaining is optics brownie points, if anything. But when it comes to pushing her agenda and having good relationships with her colleagues...
..not that she necessarily wants good relationships, you know, but it's part of the process.
You've gotta work with these people, right?

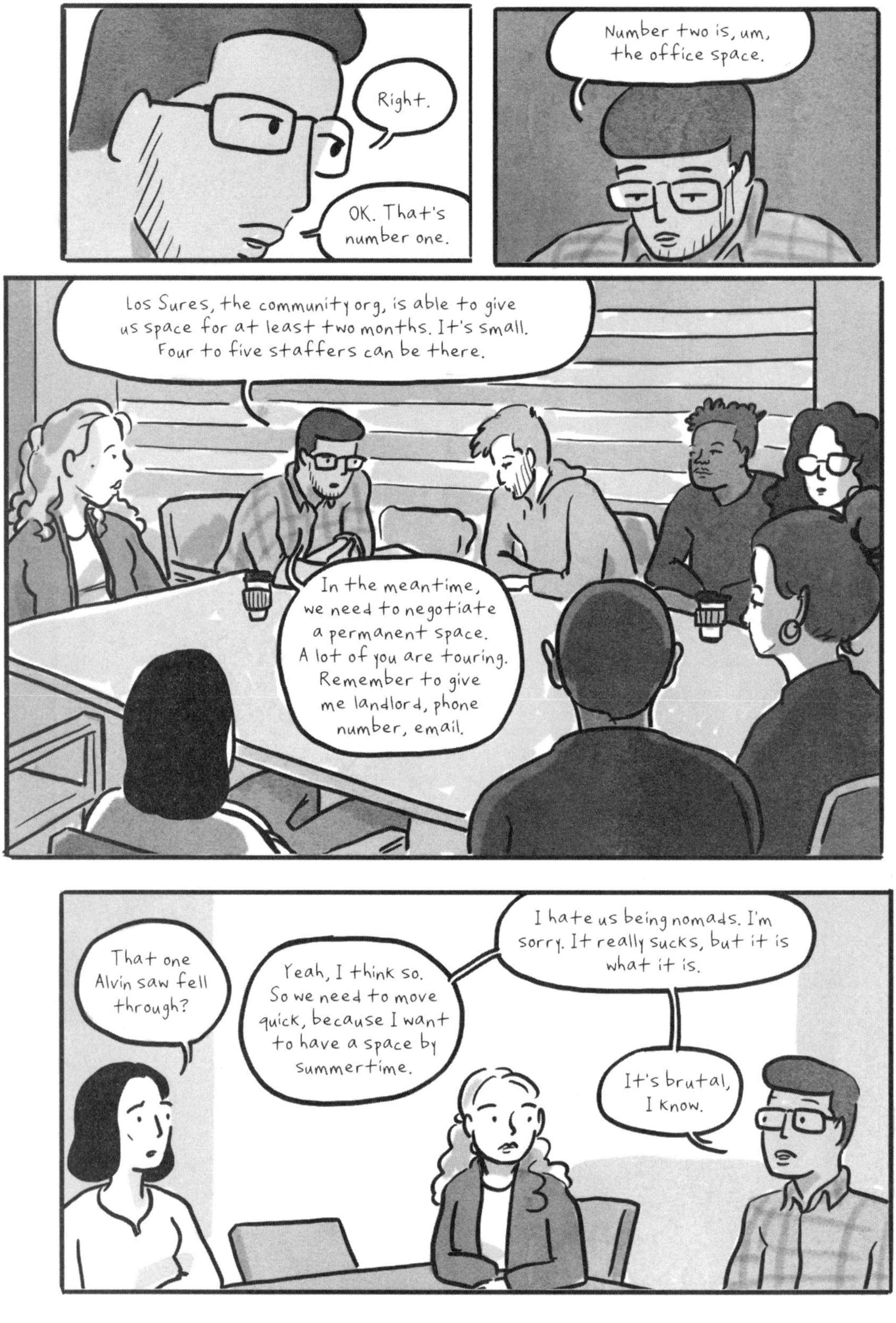
Right.
OK. That's number one.
Number two is, um, the office space.
Los Sures, the community org, is able to give us space for at least two months. It's small. Four to five staffers can be there.
In the meantime, we need to negotiate a permanent space. A lot of you are touring. Remember to give me landlord, phone number, email.
That one Alvin saw fell through?
Yeah, I think so. So we need to move quick, because I want to have a space by summertime.
I hate us being nomads. I'm sorry. It really sucks, but it is what it is.
It's brutal, I know.

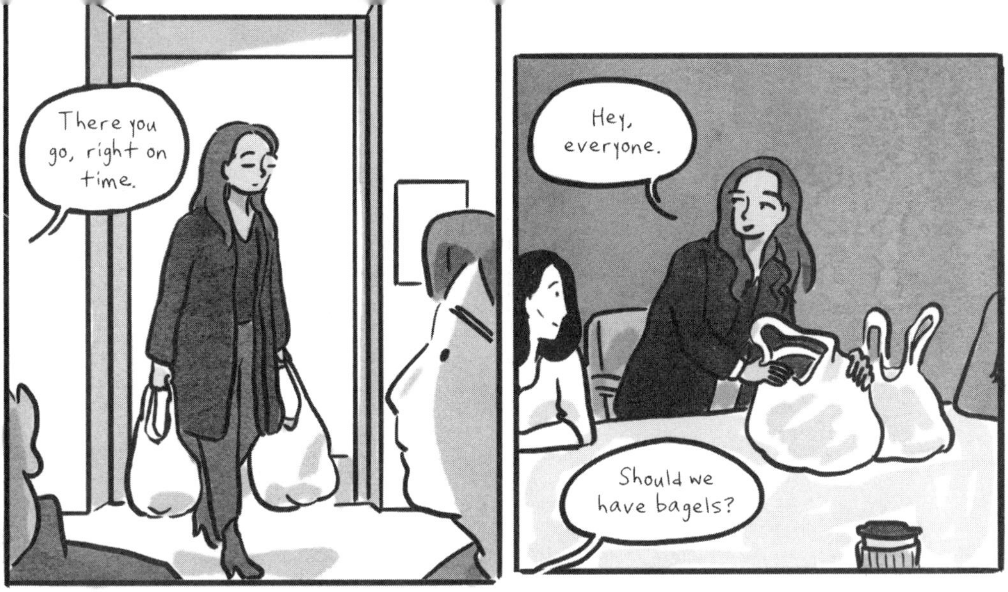
There you go, right on time.
Hey, everyone.
Should we have bagels?

We had bagels. For a while, the meeting ran smoothly. The team planned upcoming events in the district: a town hall on the budget, a forum on the student impact of metal detectors in schools, a roundtable on education.

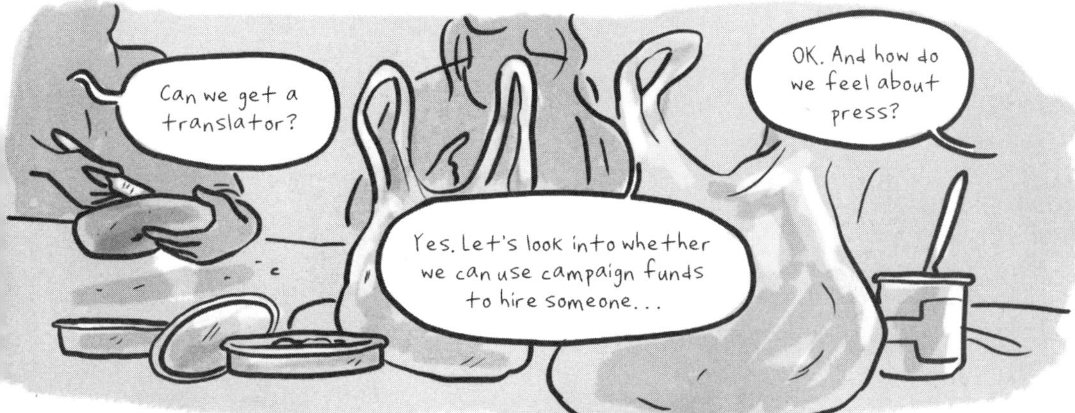
Can we get a translator?
Yes. Let's look into whether we can use campaign funds to hire someone...
OK. And how do we feel about press?

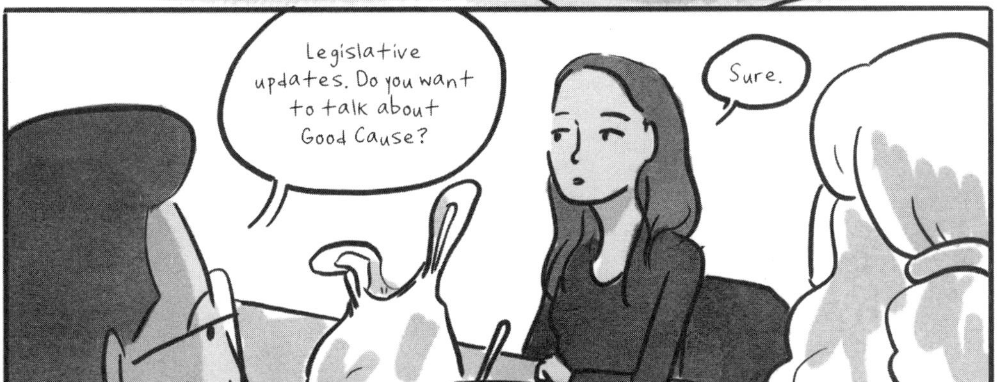
Legislative updates. Do you want to talk about Good Cause?
Sure.

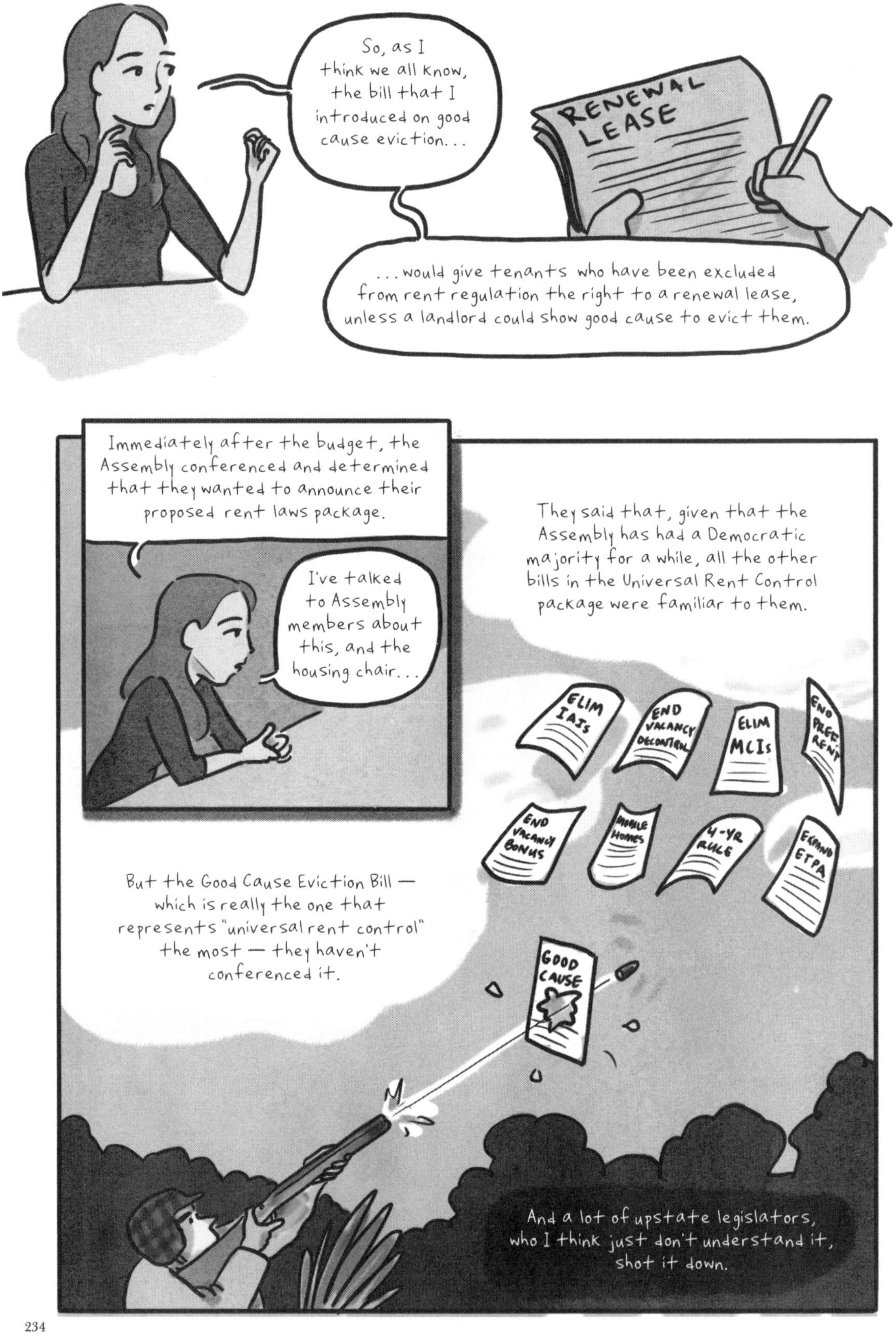
So, as I think we all know, the bill that I introduced on good cause eviction...
RENEWAL LEASE
...would give tenants who have been excluded from rent regulation the right to a renewal lease, unless a landlord could show good cause to evict them.
Immediately after the budget, the Assembly conferenced and determined that they wanted to announce their proposed rent laws package.
I've talked to Assembly members about this, and the housing chair...
They said that, given that the Assembly has had a Democratic majority for a while, all the other bills in the Universal Rent Control package were familiar to them.
ELIM IAIs
END VACANCY DECONTROL
ELIM MCIs
END PREF. RENT
END VACANCY BONUS
MOBILE HOMES
4-YR RULE
EXPAND ETPA
But the Good Cause Eviction Bill — which is really the one that represents "universal rent control" the most — they haven't conferenced it.
GOOD CAUSE
And a lot of upstate legislators, who I think just don't understand it, shot it down.

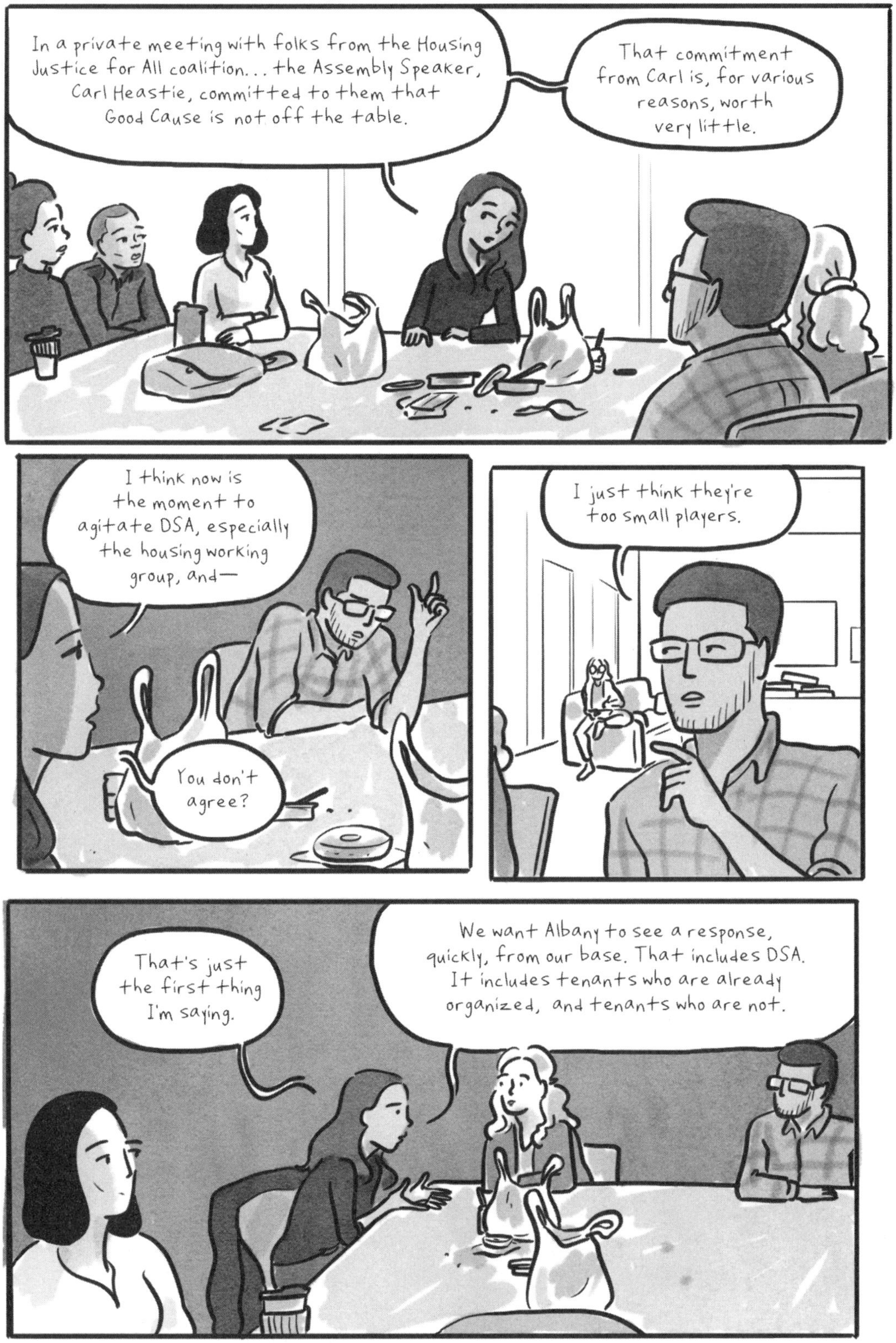
In a private meeting with folks from the Housing Justice for All coalition... the Assembly Speaker, Carl Heastie, committed to them that Good Cause is not off the table.
That commitment from Carl is, for various reasons, worth very little.
I think now is the moment to agitate DSA, especially the housing working group, and—
You don't agree?
I just think they're too small players.
That's just the first thing I'm saying.
We want Albany to see a response, quickly, from our base. That includes DSA. It includes tenants who are already organized, and tenants who are not.

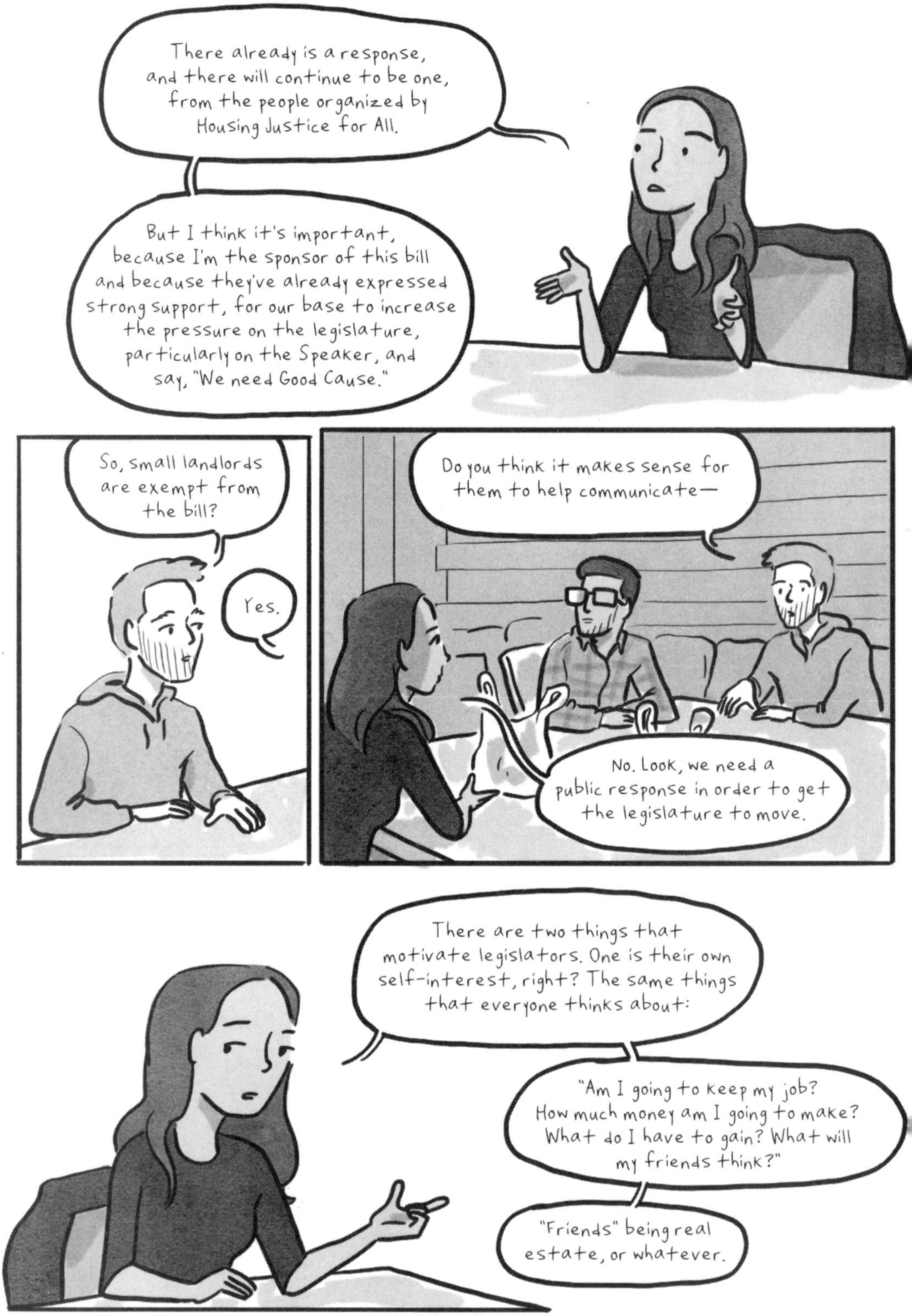

There already is a response, and there will continue to be one, from the people organized by Housing Justice for All.
But I think it's important, because I'm the sponsor of this bill and because they've already expressed strong support, for our base to increase the pressure on the legislature, particularly on the Speaker, and say, "We need Good Cause."
So, small landlords are exempt from the bill?
Yes.
Do you think it makes sense for them to help communicate—
No. Look, we need a public response in order to get the legislature to move.
There are two things that motivate legislators. One is their own self-interest, right? The same things that everyone thinks about:
"Am I going to keep my job? How much money am I going to make? What do I have to gain? What will my friends think?"
"Friends" being real estate, or whatever.

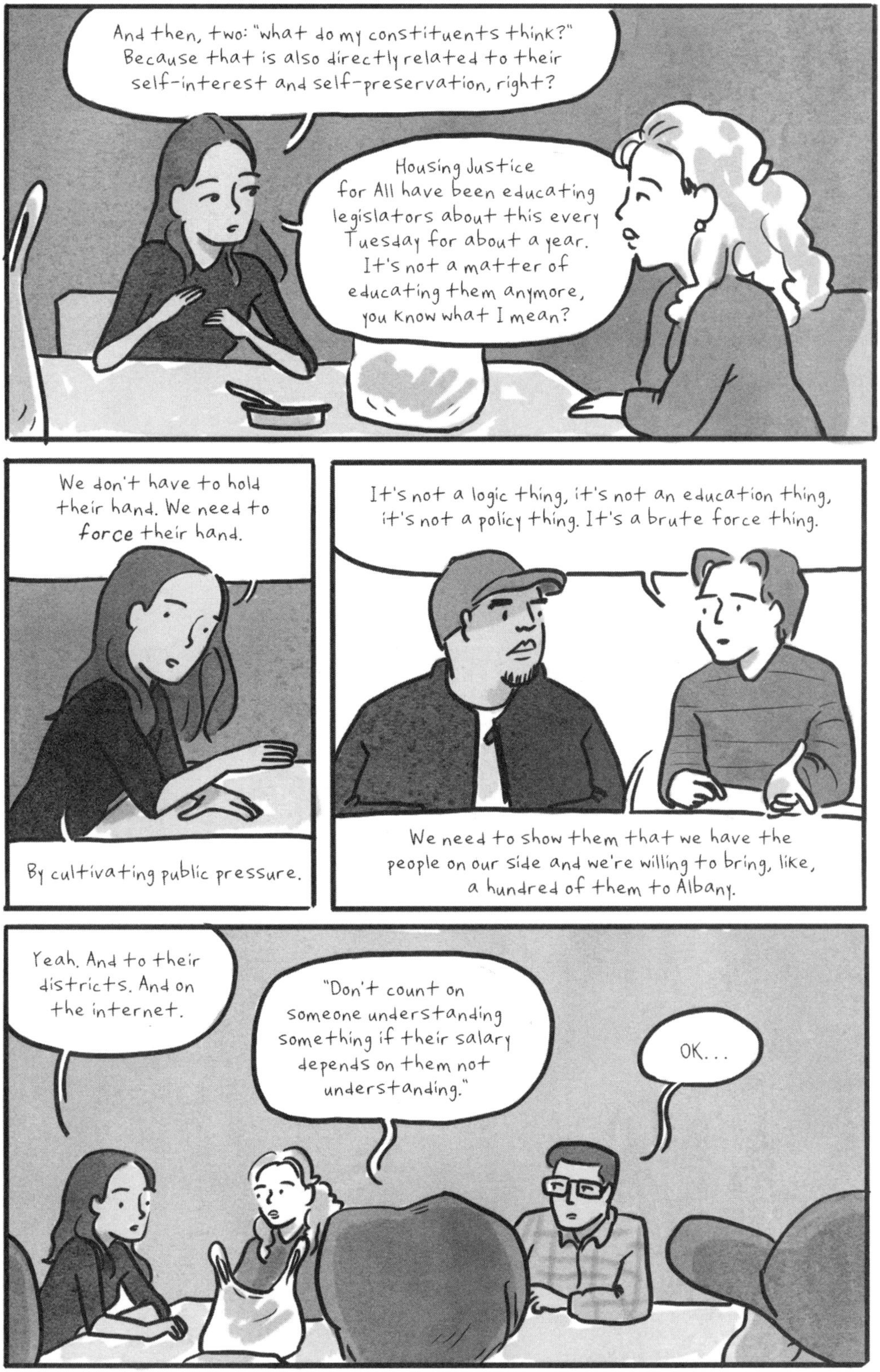

And then, two: "what do my constituents think?" Because that is also directly related to their self-interest and self-preservation, right?
Housing Justice for All have been educating legislators about this every Tuesday for about a year. It's not a matter of educating them anymore, you know what I mean?
We don't have to hold their hand. We need to force their hand.
By cultivating public pressure.
It's not a logic thing, it's not an education thing, it's not a policy thing. It's a brute force thing.
We need to show them that we have the people on our side and we're willing to bring, like, a hundred of them to Albany.
Yeah. And to their districts. And on the internet.
"Don't count on someone understanding something if their salary depends on them not understanding."
OK...

This is my biggest concern, is like: we have limited capacity. We're planning three events.

How do we talk to our base? What does it look like? How do we turn that into a strategy meeting to get them to do—

The whole reason we need to activate our base is because we don't have enough capacity to do this alone.

Right, but what I'm saying is, what does it look like and when—

Immediately.

But it needs to be structured, though. It's not like they just show up—

OK.

—to a meeting, and—

We're not just showing up! OK.

We build a structure so they'll come.

Right.

No, we don't have to build a structure. A structure exists.

Look.

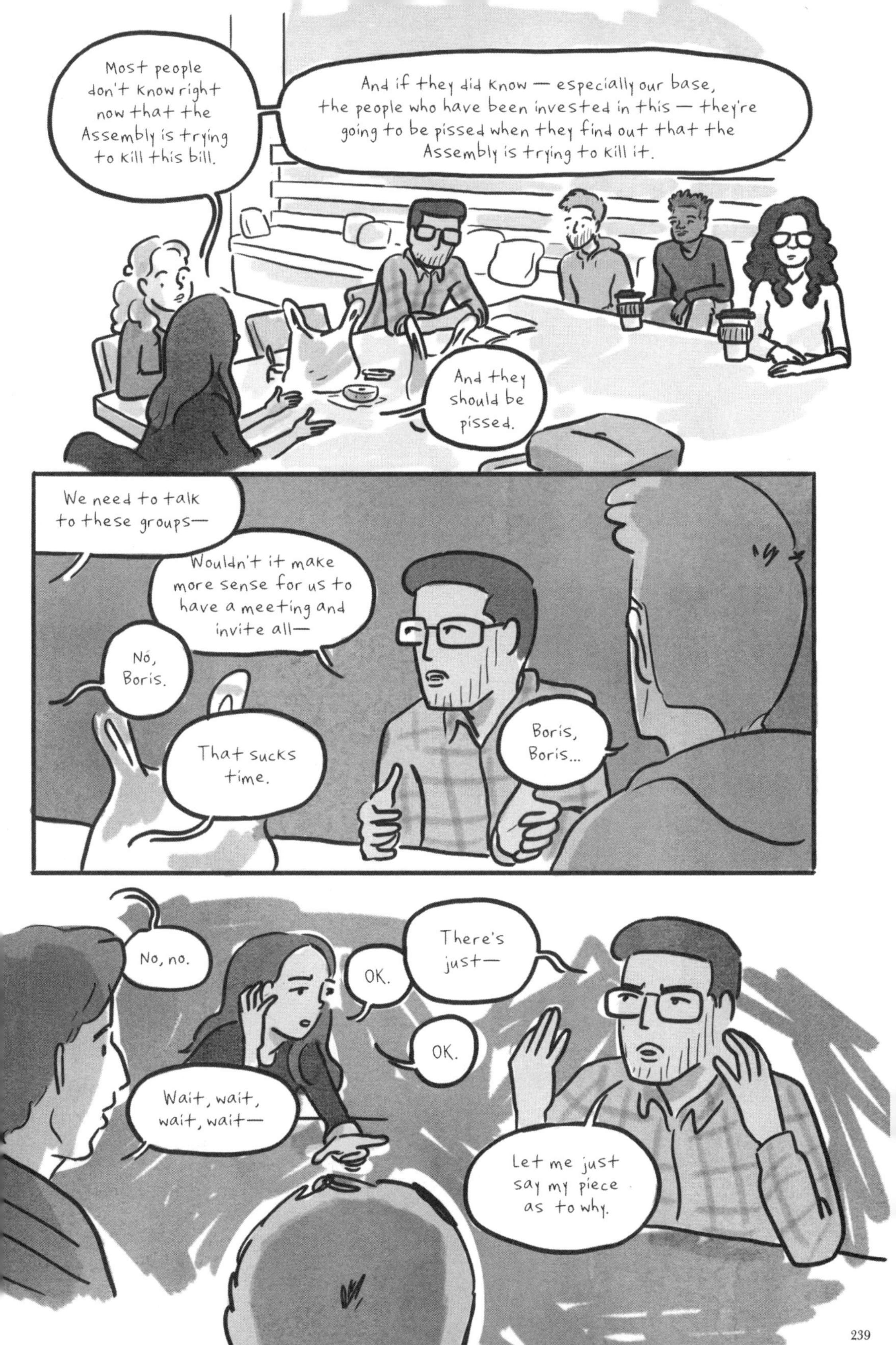
Most people don't know right now that the Assembly is trying to kill this bill.
And if they did know — especially our base, the people who have been invested in this — they're going to be pissed when they find out that the Assembly is trying to kill it.
And they should be pissed.
We need to talk to these groups—
Wouldn't it make more sense for us to have a meeting and invite all—
No, Boris.
That sucks time.
Boris, Boris...
No, no.
OK.
There's just—
OK.
Wait, wait, wait, wait—
Let me just say my piece as to why.

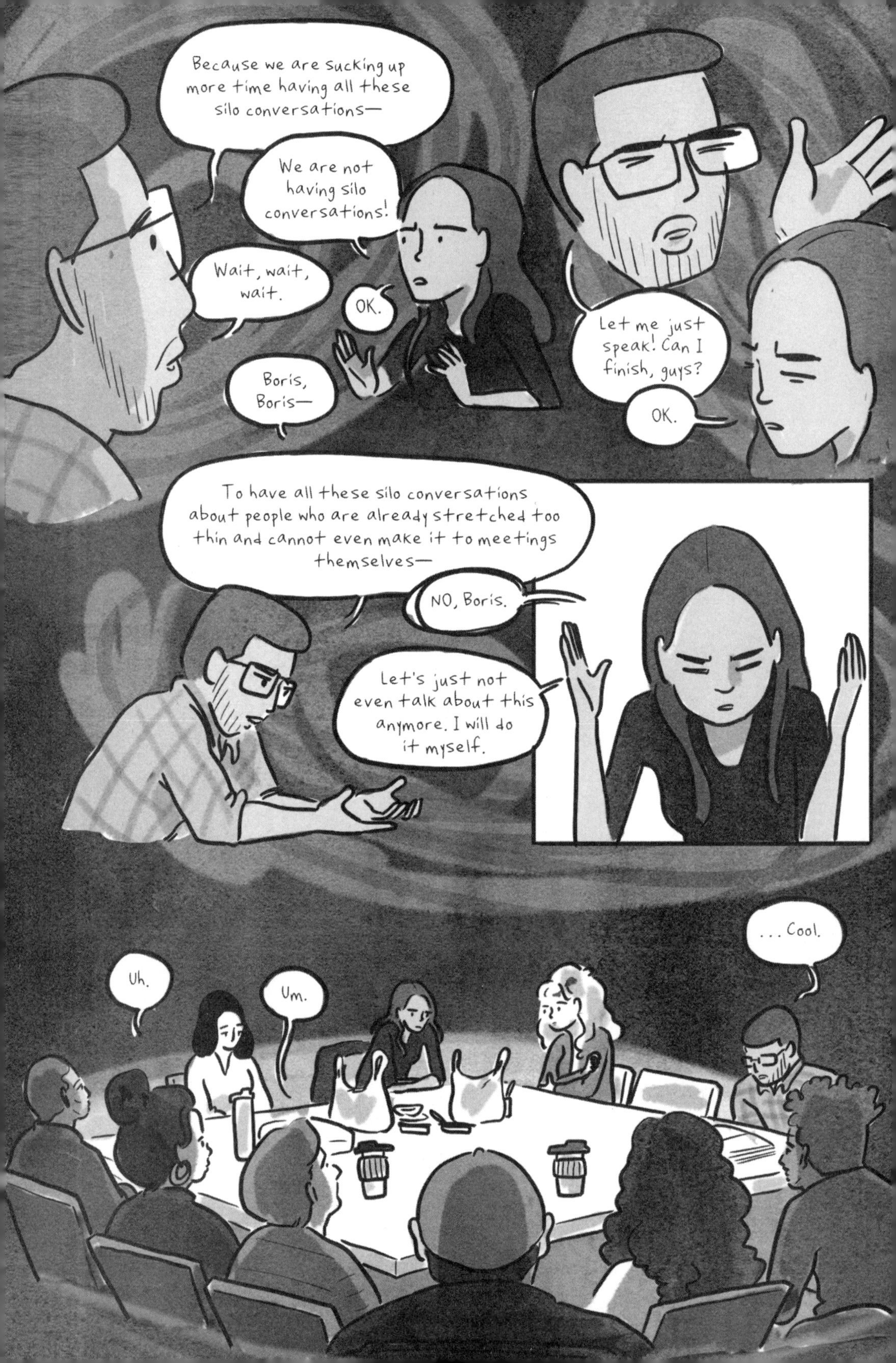
Because we are sucking up more time having all these silo conversations—
We are not having silo conversations!
Wait, wait, wait.
OK.
Boris, Boris—
Let me just speak! Can I finish, guys?
OK.
To have all these silo conversations about people who are already stretched too thin and cannot even make it to meetings themselves—
NO, Boris.
Let's just not even talk about this anymore. I will do it myself.
Uh.
Um.
...Cool.

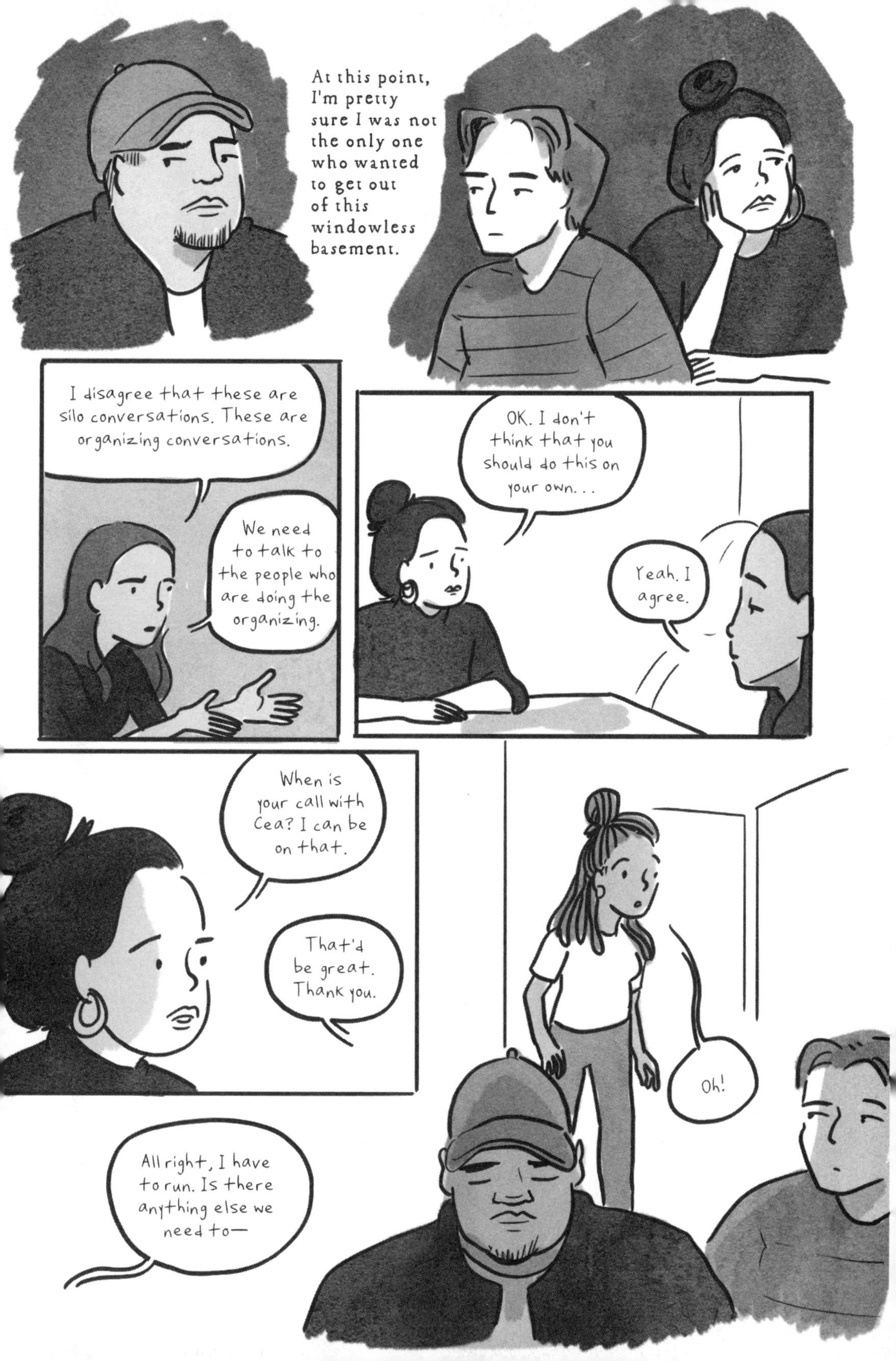
At this point, I'm pretty sure I was not the only one who wanted to get out of this windowless basement.
I disagree that these are silo conversations. These are organizing conversations.
We need to talk to the people who are doing the organizing.
OK. I don't think that you should do this on your own...
Yeah. I agree.
When is your call with Cea? I can be on that.
That'd be great. Thank you.
All right, I have to run. Is there anything else we need to—
Oh!

Sorry to interrupt.

No, it's OK.

Um... What do you guys do?

I'm the state senator, and this is my amazing staff.

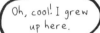

Oh, cool! I grew up here.

I'll just say... people are angry. I get angry.

I take the B52 bus to Downtown Brooklyn, and I can't tell the difference between Brooklyn and Manhattan.

Everything that was here is not here anymore.

Yeah. I hear you.

Anyway, kudos to you. I care in other ways, but I'm not politician material, myself.

Hey, you know what?

That's exactly what I thought a year ago!

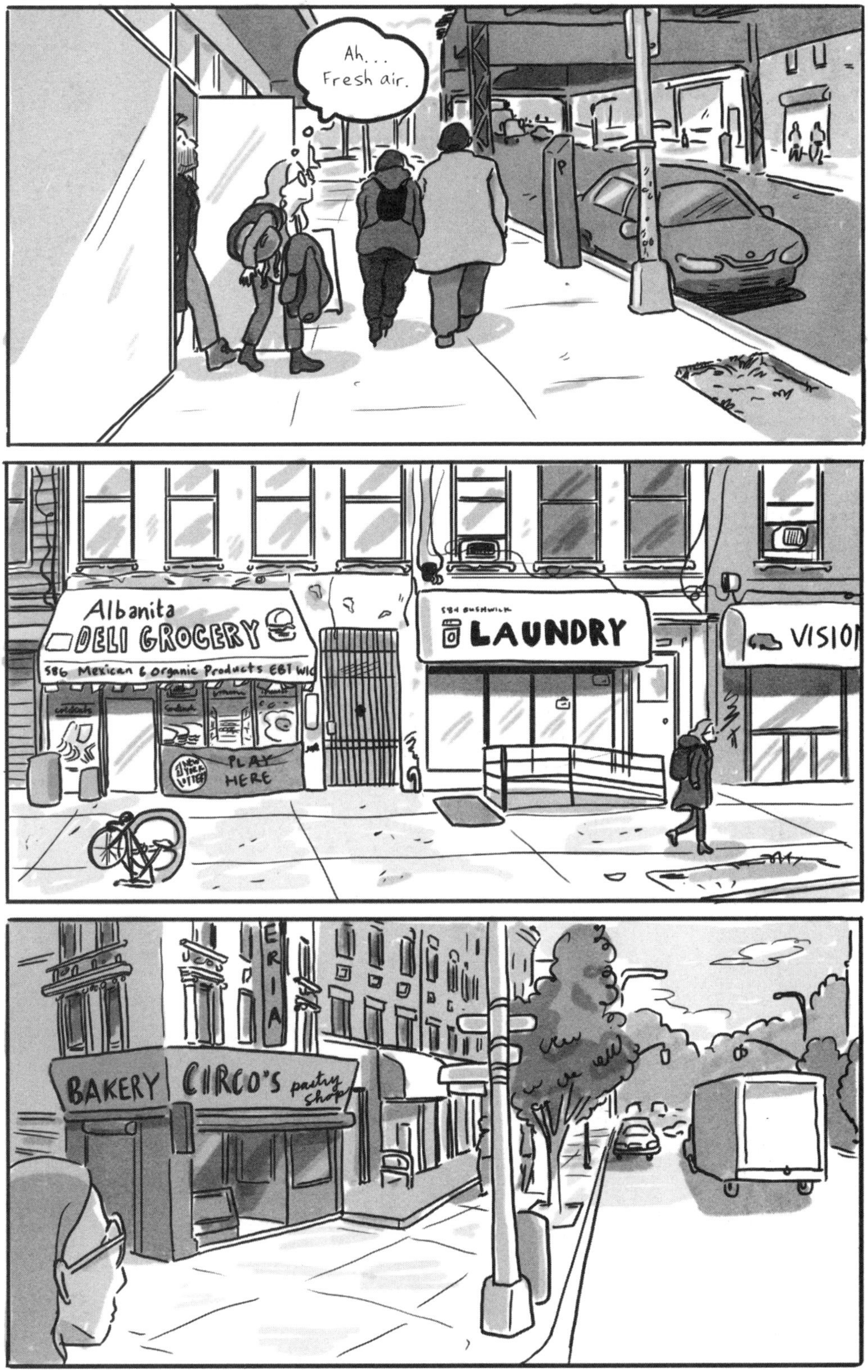
Ah...
Fresh air.
Albanita
DELI GROCERY
586 Mexican & Organic Products EBT WIC
PLAY
HERE
584 BUSHWICK
LAUNDRY
VISION
BAKERY
CIRCO's pastry shop

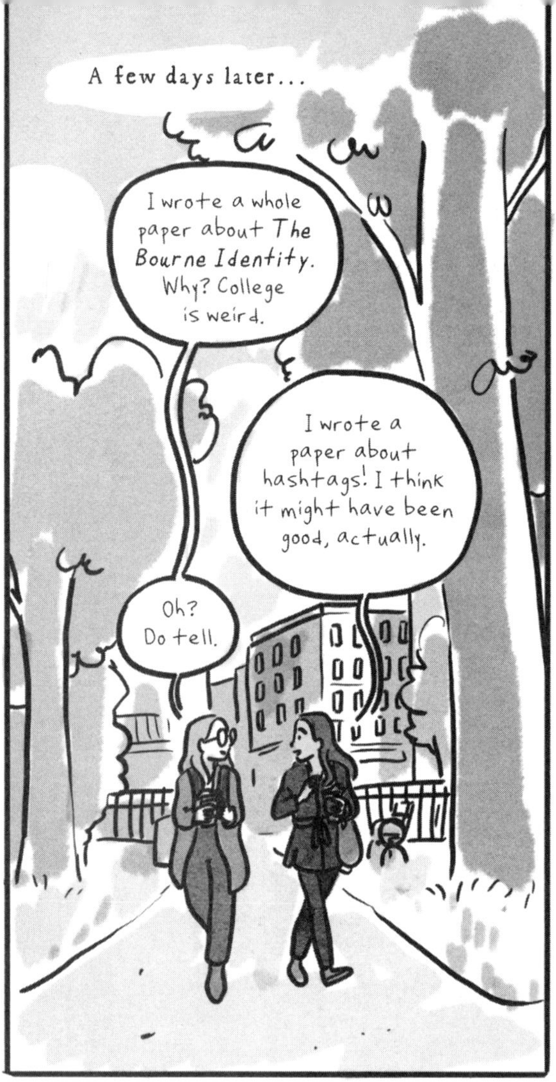
A few days later...
I wrote a whole paper about The Bourne Identity. Why? College is weird.
I wrote a paper about hashtags! I think it might have been good, actually.
Oh? Do tell.

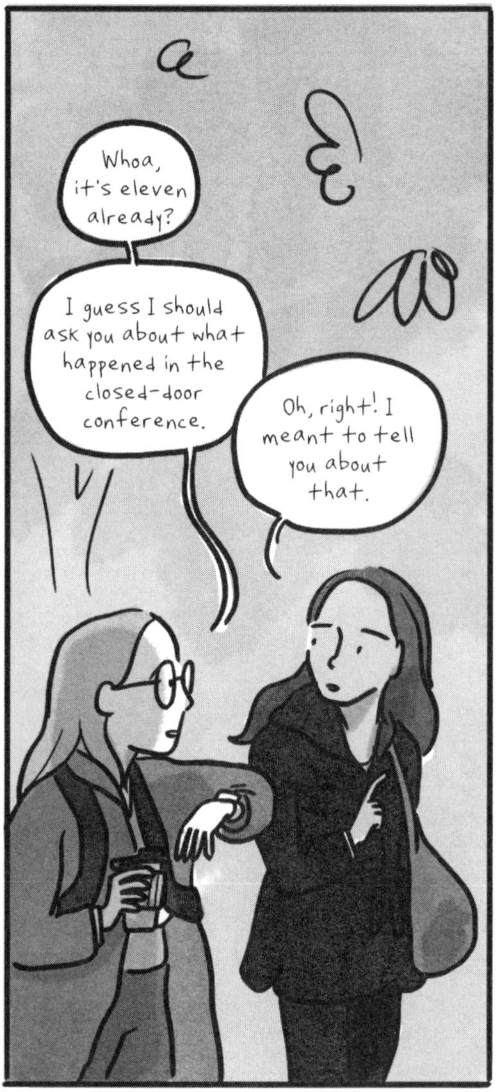
Whoa, it's eleven already?
I guess I should ask you about what happened in the closed-door conference.
Oh, right! I meant to tell you about that.

Julia said that Leadership had called the conference to caution new legislators about tweeting.

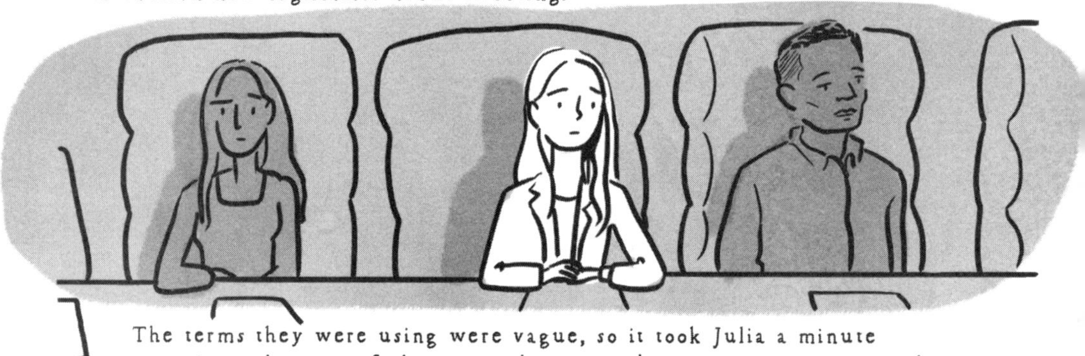

The terms they were using were vague, so it took Julia a minute to register that one of the tweets being cited — a tweet suggesting that Assembly Speaker Heastie would get primaried — came from her office.

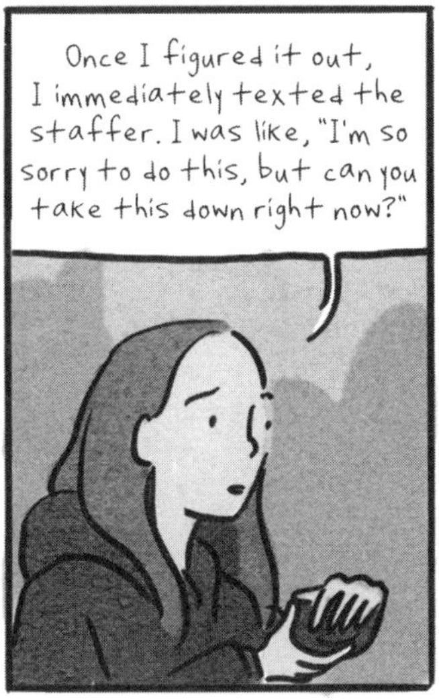
Once I figured it out, I immediately texted the staffer. I was like, "I'm so sorry to do this, but can you take this down right now?"

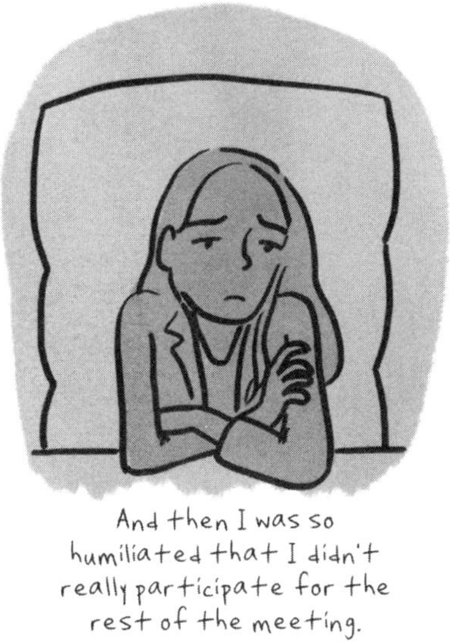
And then I was so humiliated that I didn't really participate for the rest of the meeting.

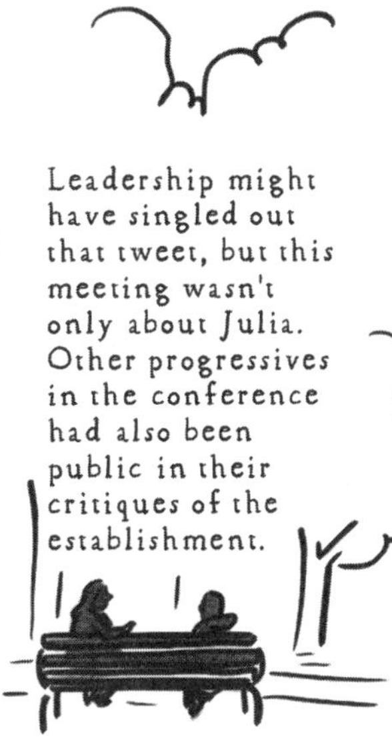
Leadership might have singled out that tweet, but this meeting wasn't only about Julia. Other progressives in the conference had also been public in their critiques of the establishment.

Jessica Ramos and Alessandra Biaggi, two other freshman senators (along with Assemblymember Yuh-Line Niou) had recently held an impromptu press conference to criticize the governor for holding a secret, $25,000-a-head fundraiser in the middle of budget season.

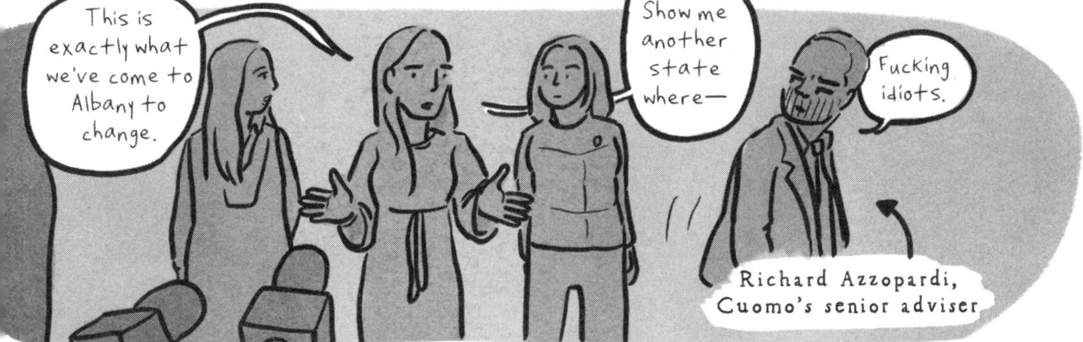
This is exactly what we've come to Albany to change.
Show me another state where—
Fucking idiots.
Richard Azzopardi, Cuomo's senior adviser

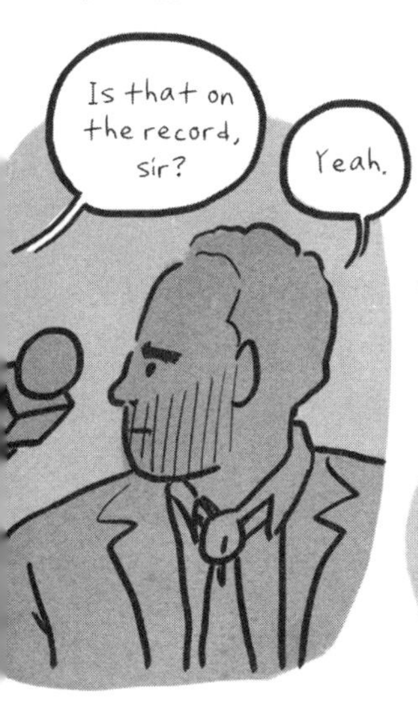
Is that on the record, sir?
Yeah.

So that spat, too, had been playing out on Twitter. Cuomo's top aides accused the senators of hypocrisy, because they, too, held fundraisers in Albany.

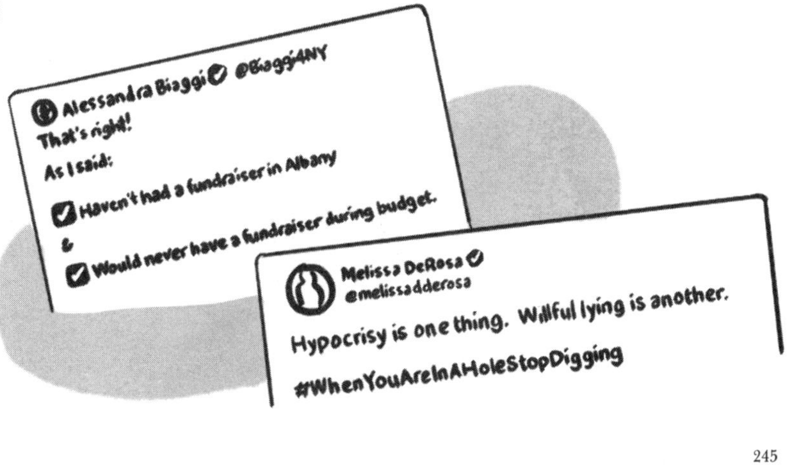
Alessandra Biaggi @Biaggi4NY
That's right!
As I said:
Haven't had a fundraiser in Albany
&
Would never have a fundraiser during budget.
Melissa DeRosa @melissadderosa
Hypocrisy is one thing. Willful lying is another.
#WhenYouAreInAHoleStopDigging

The rest of the conference was summarized in a *New York Times* article, which Julia confirmed to me.

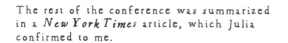

Kevin Parker, a nine-term senator, spoke up to chastise the new progressives. He said that while they might be used to being grassroots activists loudly pushing for change, legislating was different.

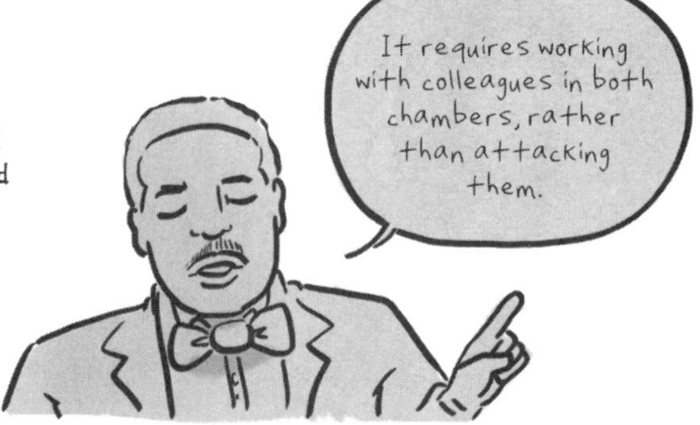
It requires working with colleagues in both chambers, rather than attacking them.

That was interesting to hear from Senator Parker, who less than a year prior had caused a scandal by tweeting "kill yourself" to a Republican staffer.

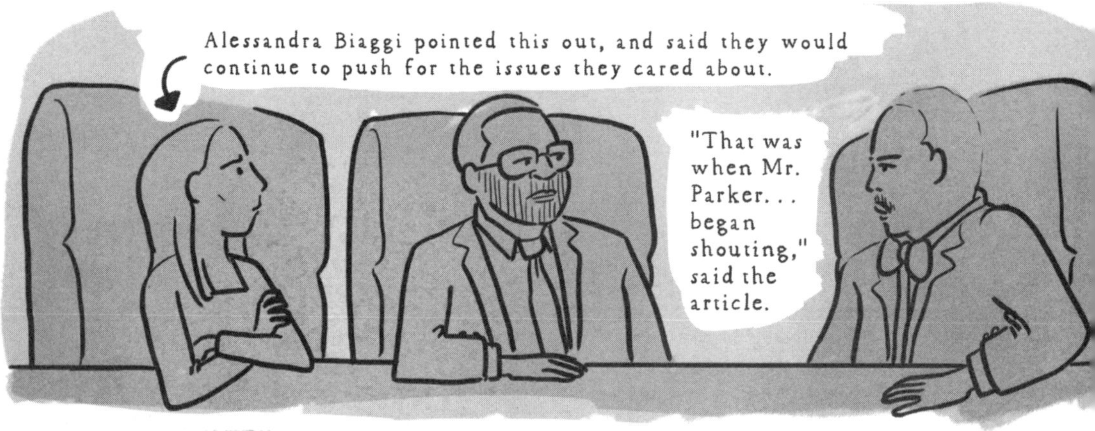
Alessandra Biaggi pointed this out, and said they would continue to push for the issues they cared about.
"That was when Mr. Parker. . . began shouting," said the article.

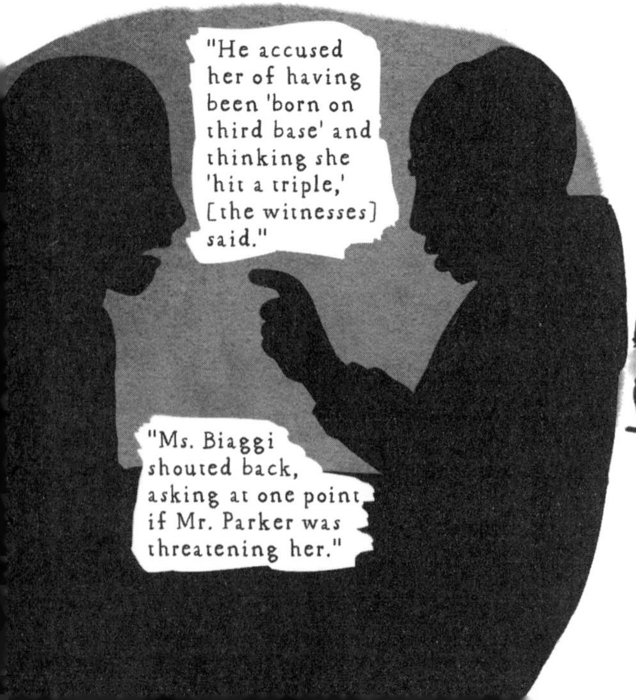
"He accused her of having been 'born on third base' and thinking she 'hit a triple,' [the witnesses] said."
"Ms. Biaggi shouted back, asking at one point if Mr. Parker was threatening her."

"At another point, Mr. Parker took off his tie and threw it down. 'I am unbeatable,' he said, in an apparent reference to any attempts to challenge him in a primary."

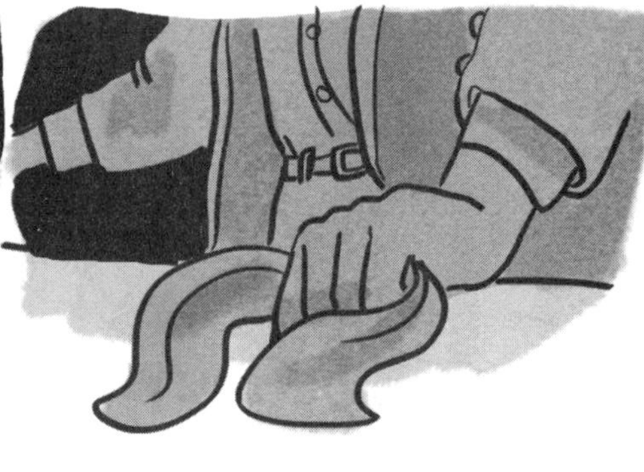

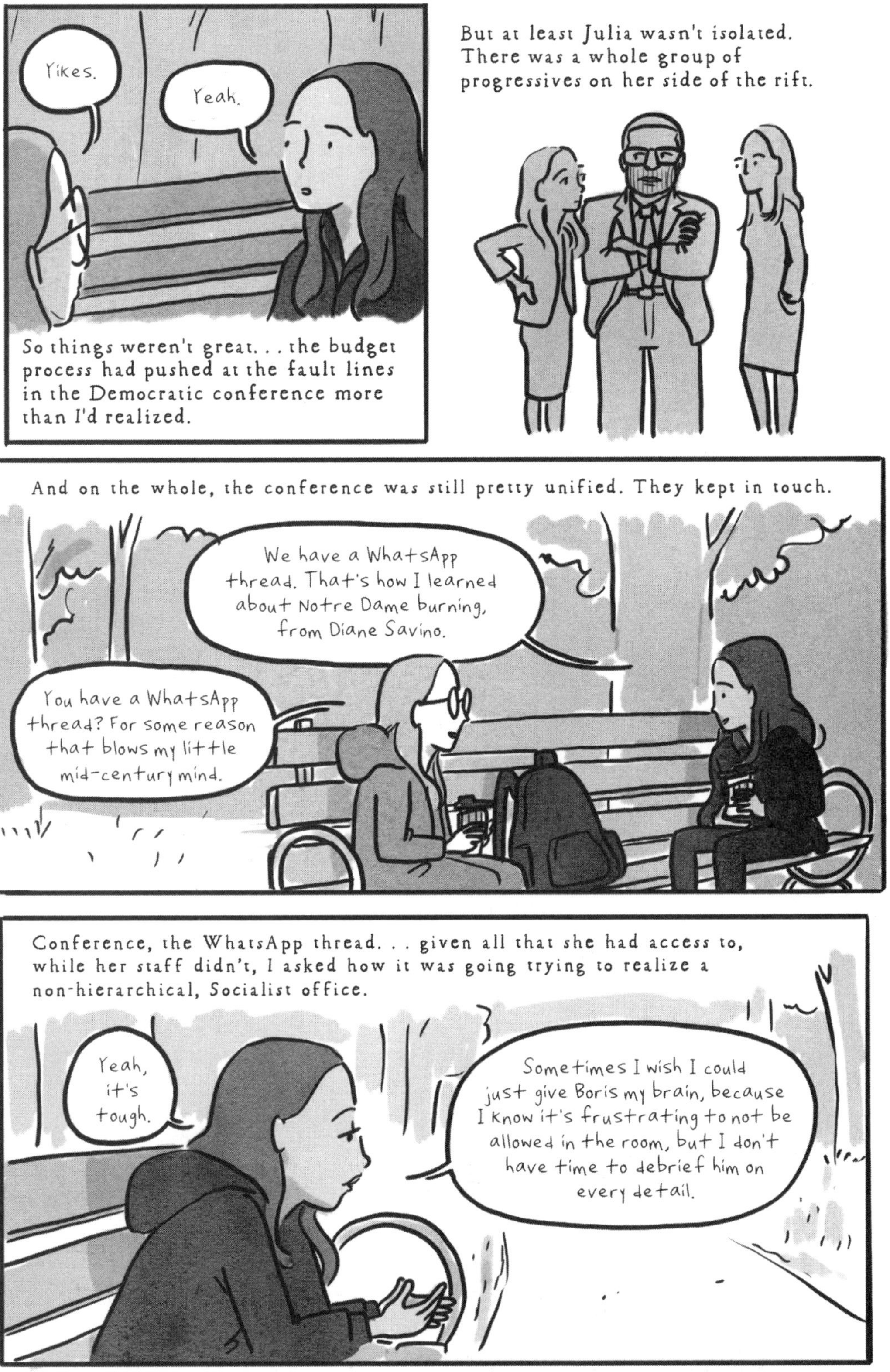
Yikes.
Yeah.
So things weren't great. . . the budget process had pushed at the fault lines in the Democratic conference more than I'd realized.
But at least Julia wasn't isolated. There was a whole group of progressives on her side of the rift.
And on the whole, the conference was still pretty unified. They kept in touch.
We have a WhatsApp thread. That's how I learned about Notre Dame burning, from Diane Savino.
You have a WhatsApp thread? For some reason that blows my little mid-century mind.
Conference, the WhatsApp thread. . . given all that she had access to, while her staff didn't, I asked how it was going trying to realize a non-hierarchical, Socialist office.
Yeah, it's tough.
Sometimes I wish I could just give Boris my brain, because I know it's frustrating to not be allowed in the room, but I don't have time to debrief him on every detail.

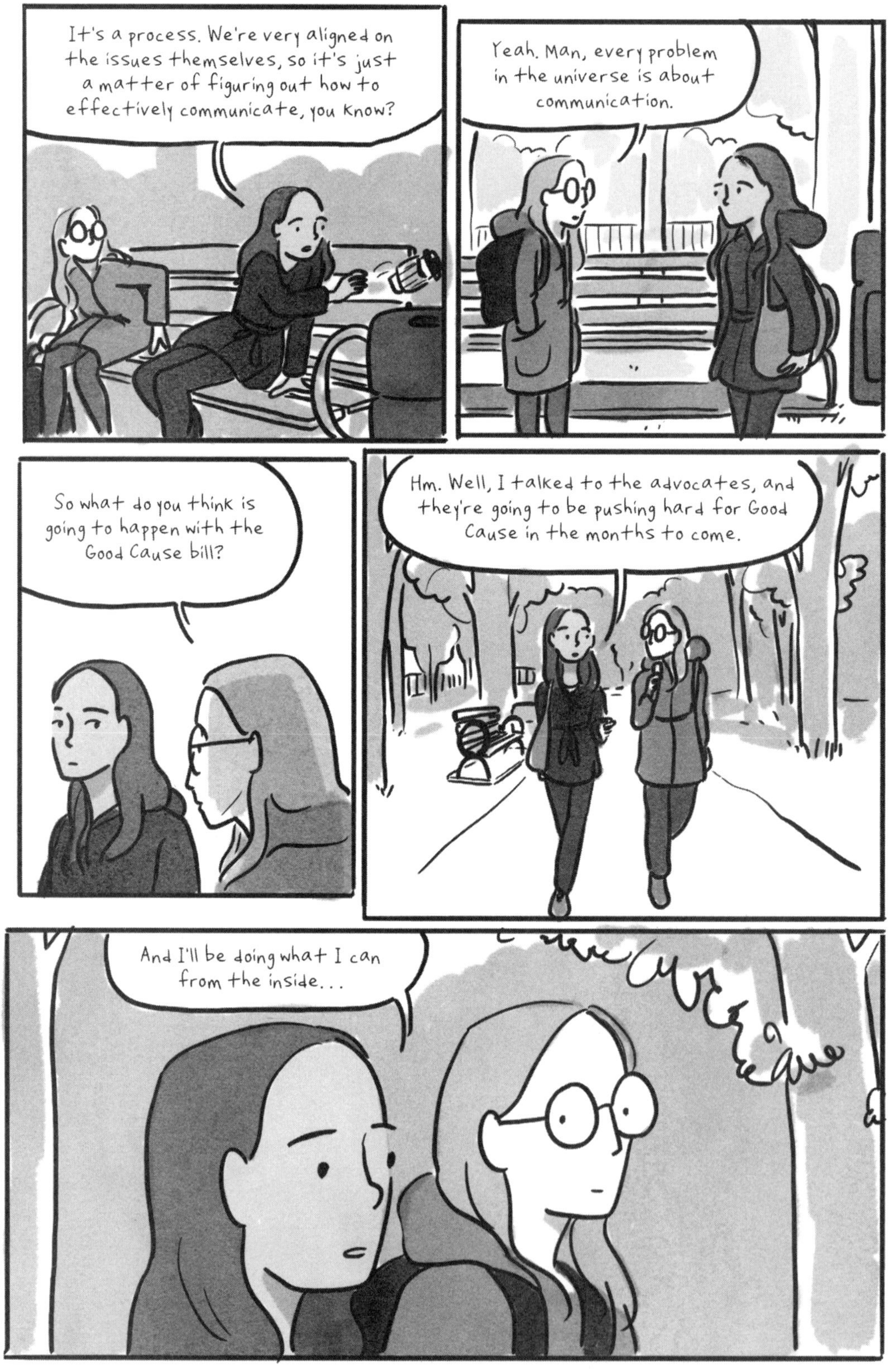
It's a process. We're very aligned on the issues themselves, so it's just a matter of figuring out how to effectively communicate, you know?
Yeah. Man, every problem in the universe is about communication.
So what do you think is going to happen with the Good Cause bill?
Hm. Well, I talked to the advocates, and they're going to be pushing hard for Good Cause in the months to come.
And I'll be doing what I can from the inside...

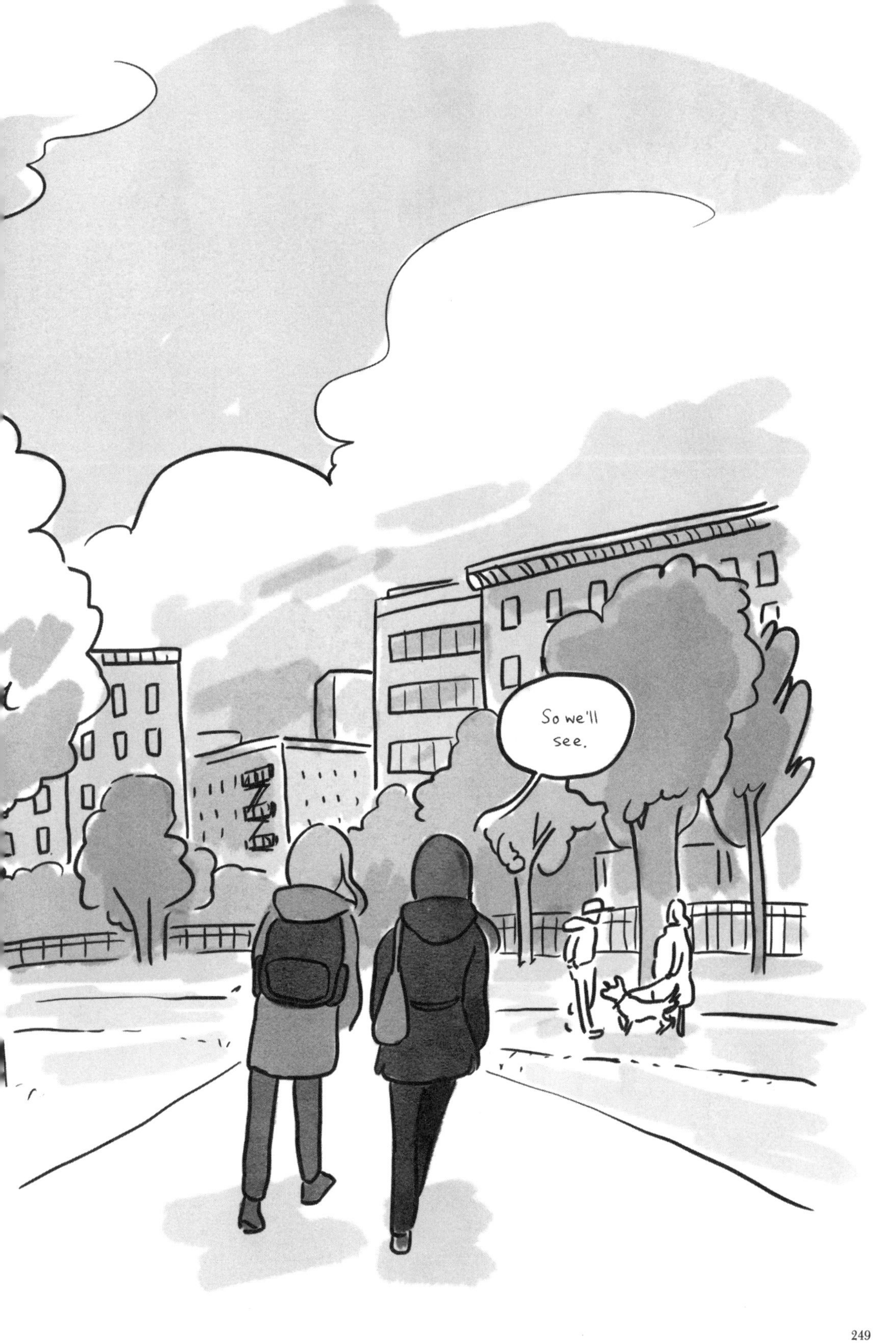
So we'll
see.

Chapter Ten

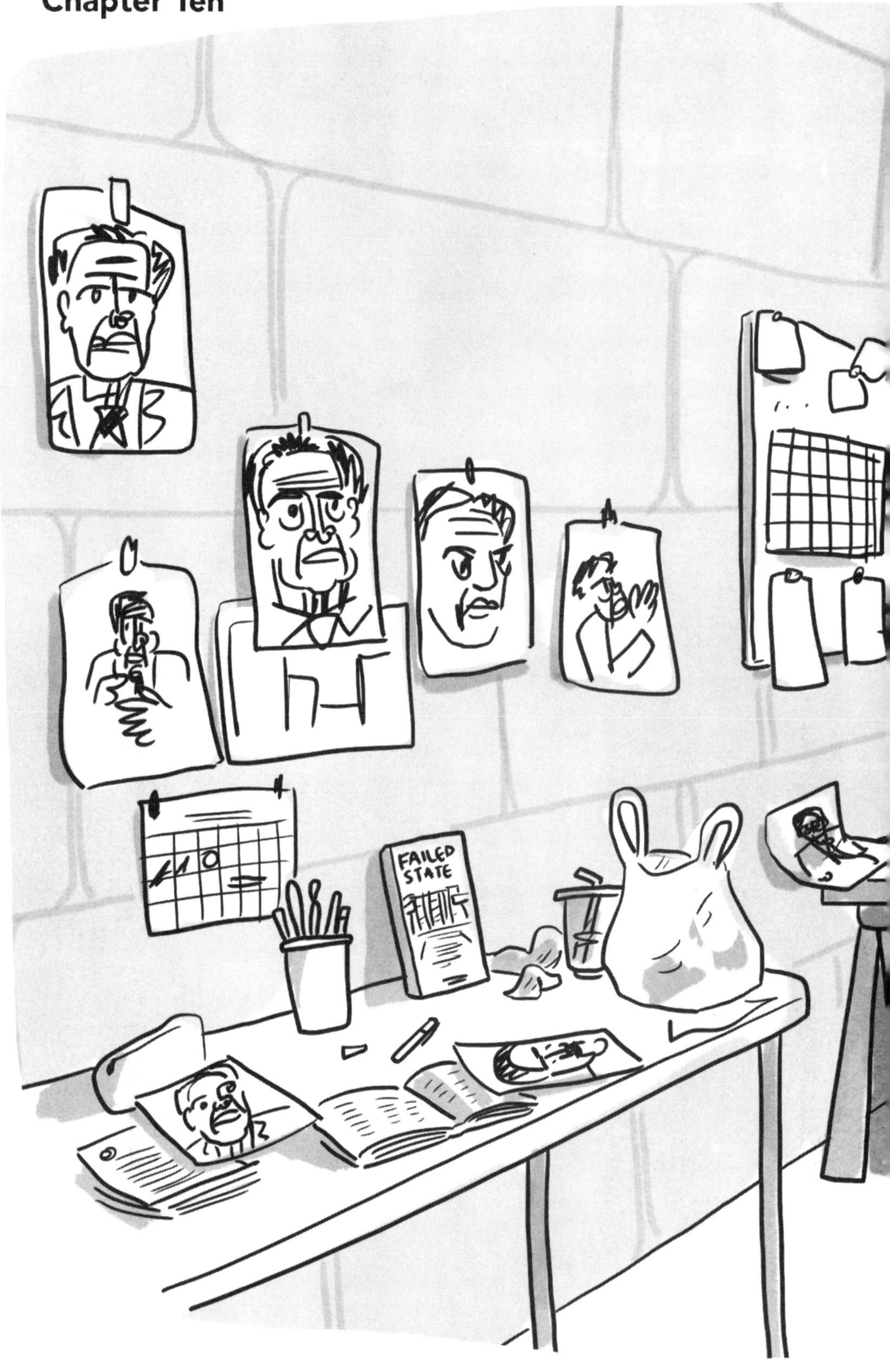
FAILED STATE

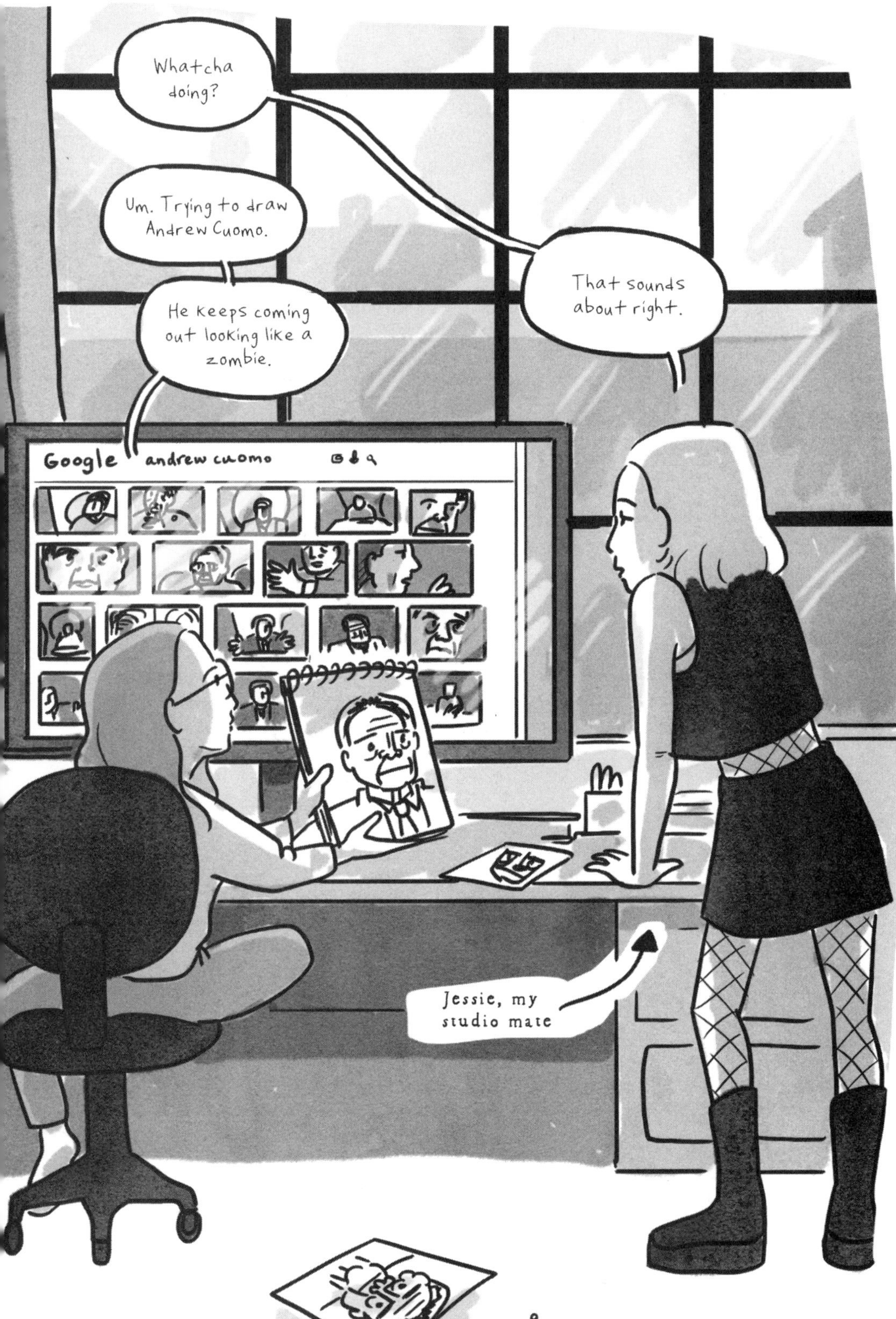
Whatcha doing?
Um. Trying to draw Andrew Cuomo.
He keeps coming out looking like a zombie.
That sounds about right.
Google andrew cuomo
Jessie, my studio mate

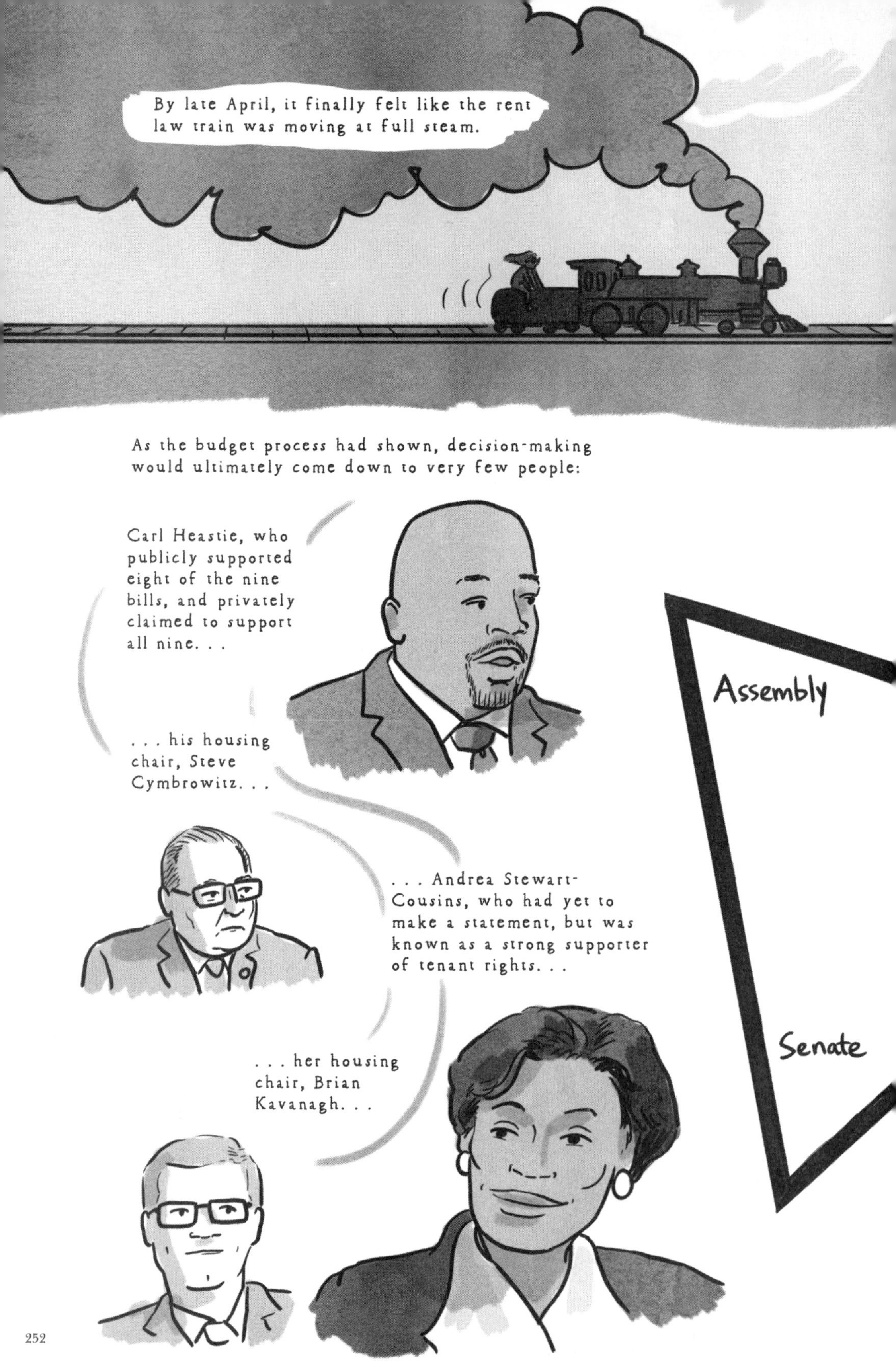
By late April, it finally felt like the rent law train was moving at full steam.
As the budget process had shown, decision-making would ultimately come down to very few people:
Carl Heastie, who publicly supported eight of the nine bills, and privately claimed to support all nine. . .
. . . his housing chair, Steve Cymbrowitz. . .
. . . Andrea Stewart-Cousins, who had yet to make a statement, but was known as a strong supporter of tenant rights. . .
. . . her housing chair, Brian Kavanagh. . .
Assembly
Senate

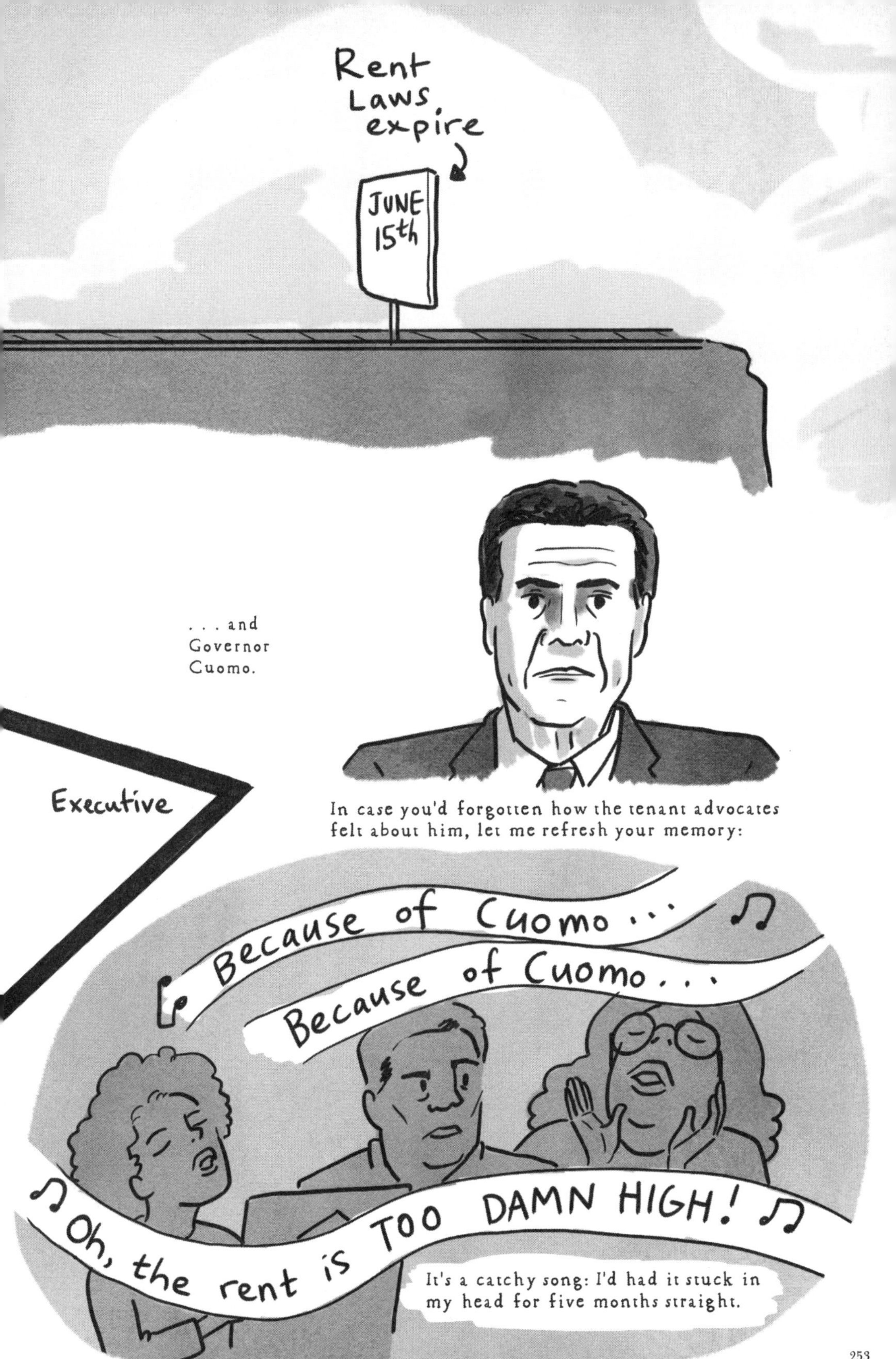
Rent Laws expire
JUNE 15th
. . . and Governor Cuomo.
Executive
In case you'd forgotten how the tenant advocates felt about him, let me refresh your memory:
Because of Cuomo . . .
Because of Cuomo . . .
Oh, the rent is TOO DAMN HIGH!
It's a catchy song: I'd had it stuck in my head for five months straight.

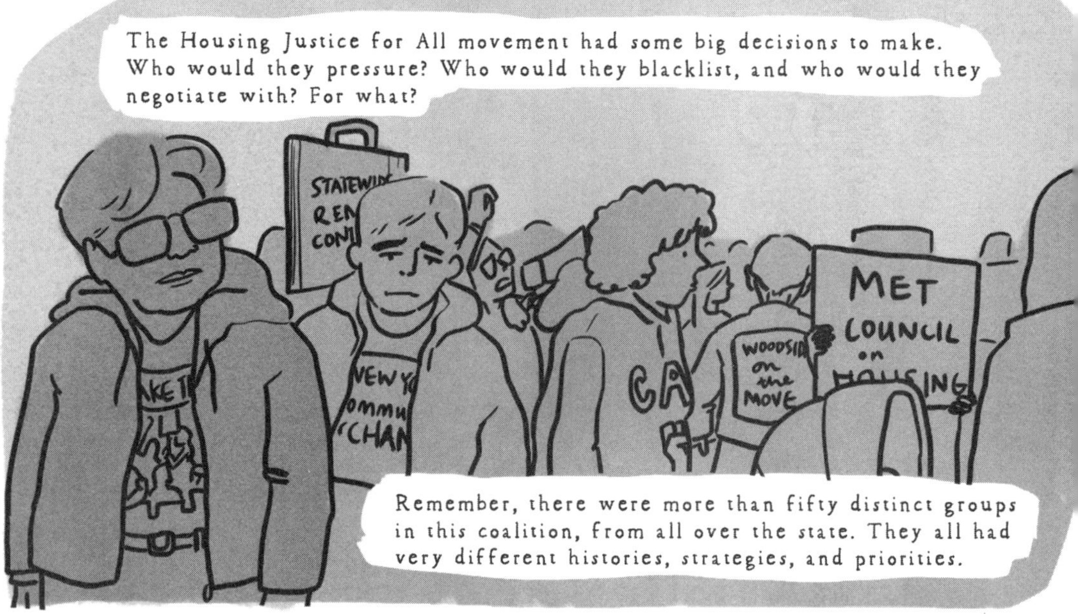
The Housing Justice for All movement had some big decisions to make. Who would they pressure? Who would they blacklist, and who would they negotiate with? For what?
MET COUNCIL on
WOODSIDE on the MOVE
Remember, there were more than fifty distinct groups in this coalition, from all over the state. They all had very different histories, strategies, and priorities.

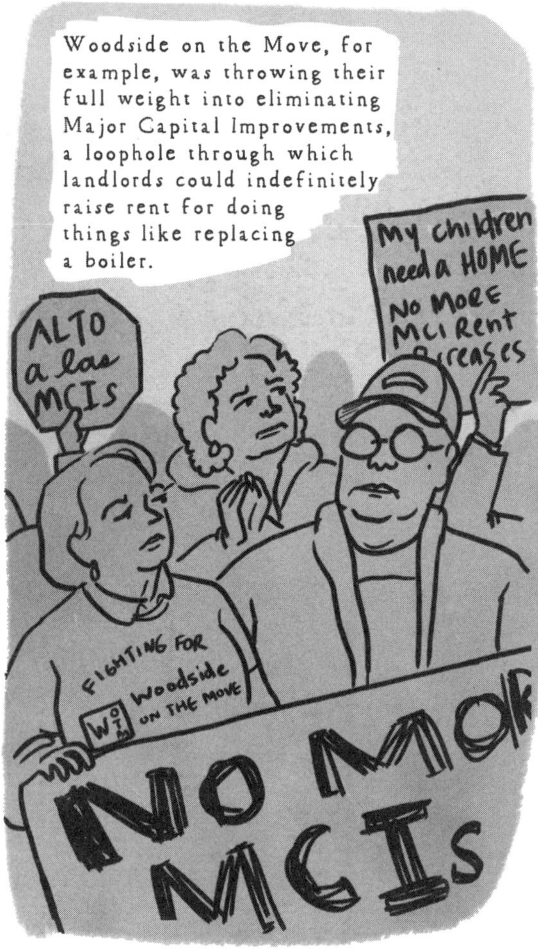
Woodside on the Move, for example, was throwing their full weight into eliminating Major Capital Improvements, a loophole through which landlords could indefinitely raise rent for doing things like replacing a boiler.
My children need a HOME
NO MORE MCI Rent
ALTO a las MCIs
FIGHTING FOR Woodside ON THE MOVE
NO MCIs

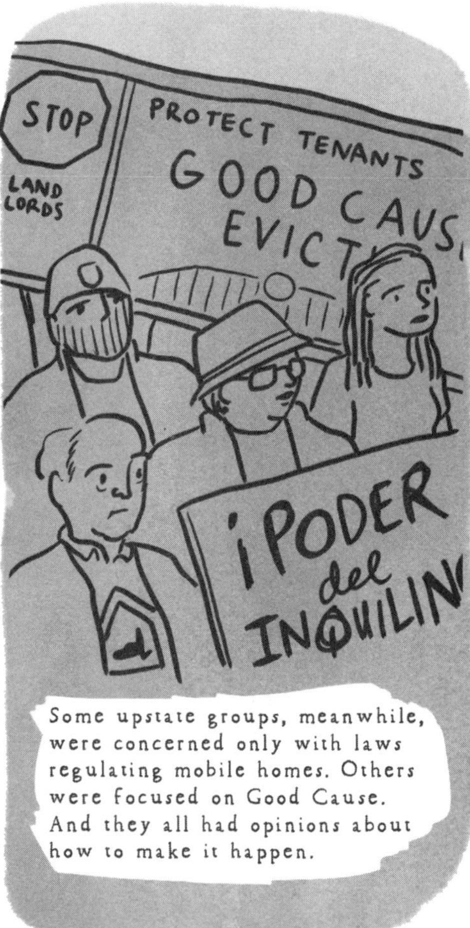
STOP LANDLORDS
PROTECT TENANTS
GOOD CAUS
EVICT
¡PODER del INQUILIN
Some upstate groups, meanwhile, were concerned only with laws regulating mobile homes. Others were focused on Good Cause. And they all had opinions about how to make it happen.

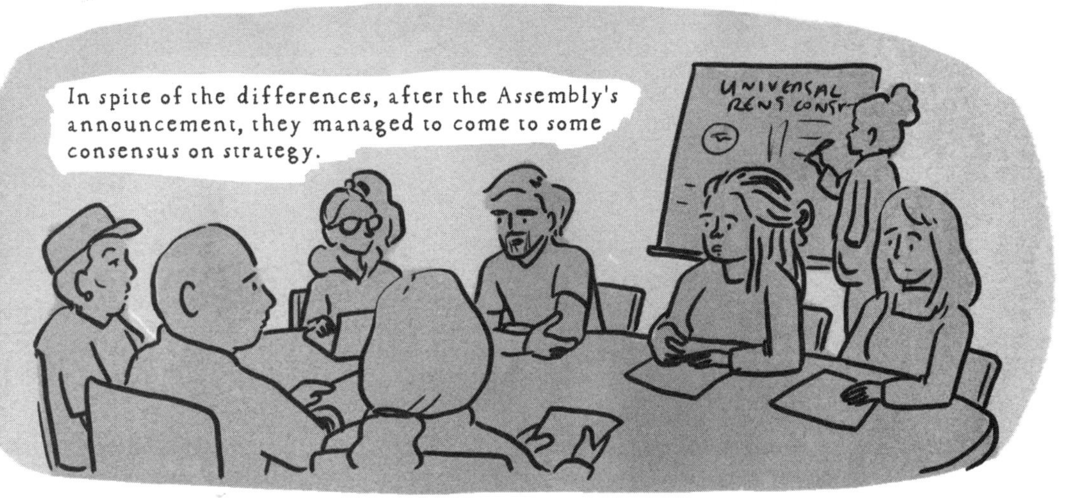

In spite of the differences, after the Assembly's announcement, they managed to come to some consensus on strategy.

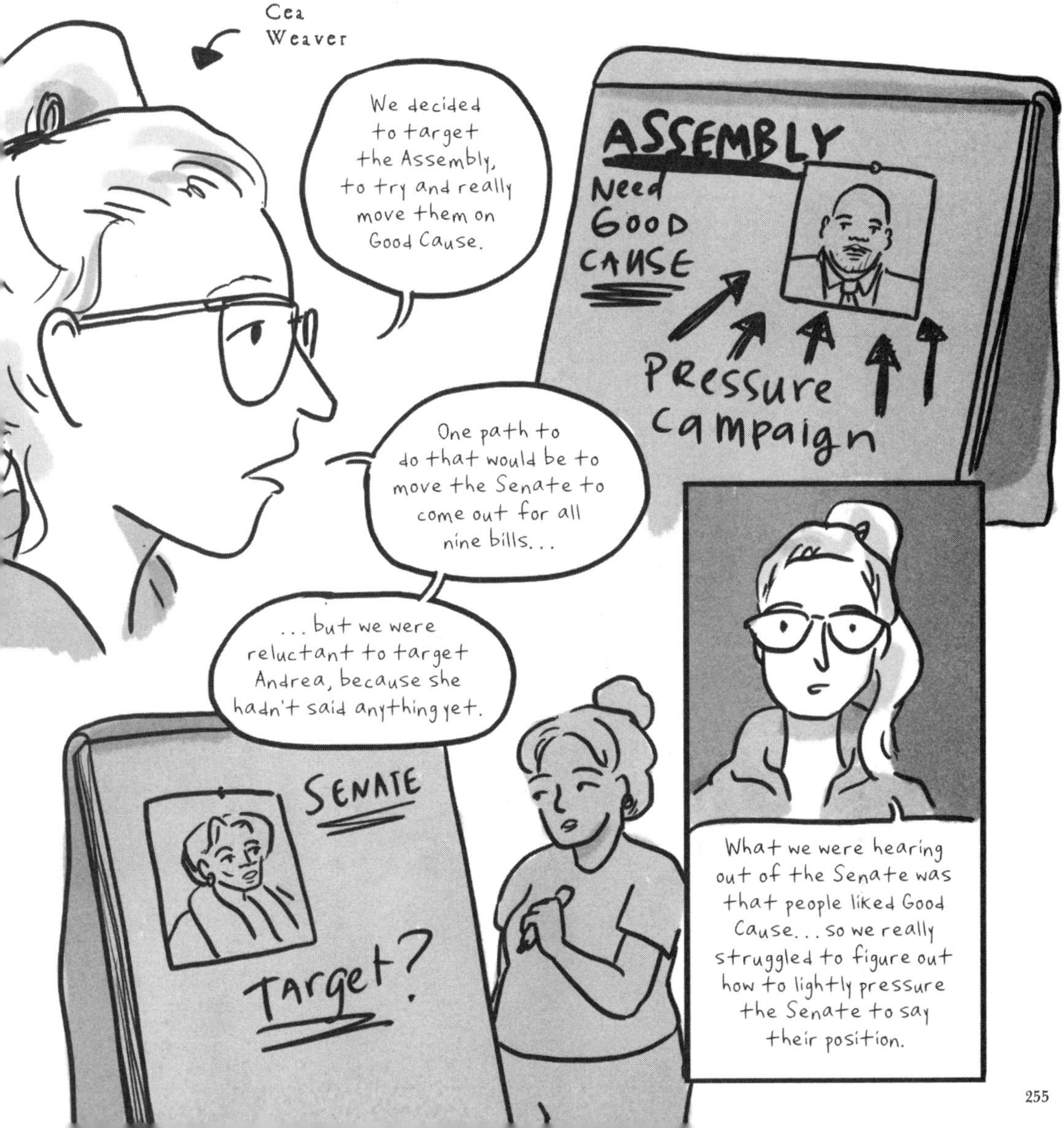

Cea Weaver
We decided to target the Assembly, to try and really move them on Good Cause.
ASSEMBLY
Need GOOD CAUSE
Pressure campaign
One path to do that would be to move the Senate to come out for all nine bills...
...but we were reluctant to target Andrea, because she hadn't said anything yet.
SENATE
Target?
What we were hearing out of the Senate was that people liked Good Cause... so we really struggled to figure out how to lightly pressure the Senate to say their position.

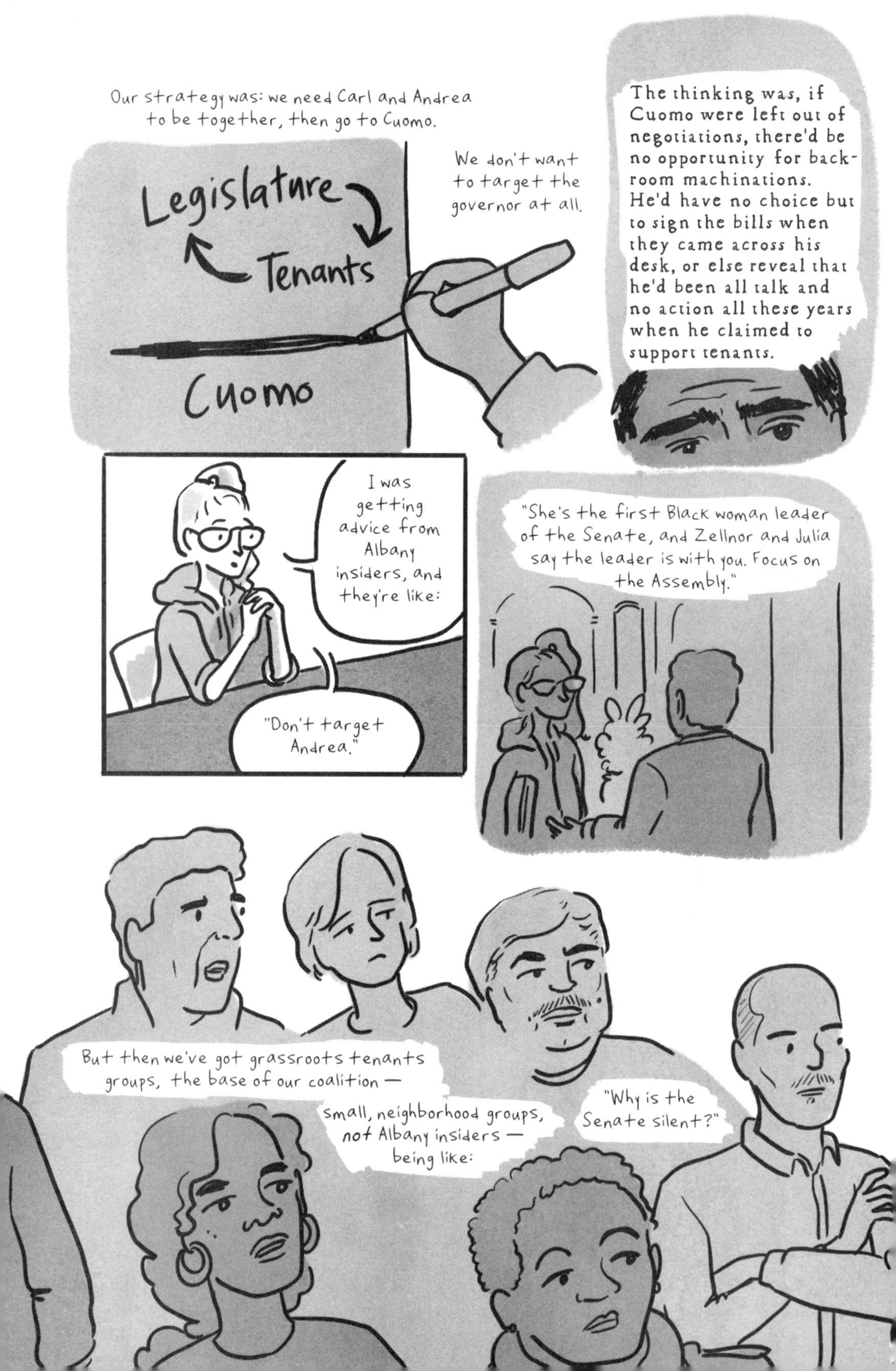

Our strategy was: we need Carl and Andrea to be together, then go to Cuomo.
Legislature
Tenants
Cuomo
We don't want to target the governor at all.
The thinking was, if Cuomo were left out of negotiations, there'd be no opportunity for back-room machinations. He'd have no choice but to sign the bills when they came across his desk, or else reveal that he'd been all talk and no action all these years when he claimed to support tenants.
I was getting advice from Albany insiders, and they're like:
"Don't target Andrea."
"She's the first Black woman leader of the Senate, and Zellnor and Julia say the leader is with you. Focus on the Assembly."
But then we've got grassroots tenants groups, the base of our coalition —
small, neighborhood groups, *not* Albany insiders — being like:
"Why is the Senate silent?"

They might have been silent, but they were not static. . . Behind closed doors, the Senate had assembled a self-selecting working group to hammer out the details of the rent package. Julia was heavily involved.

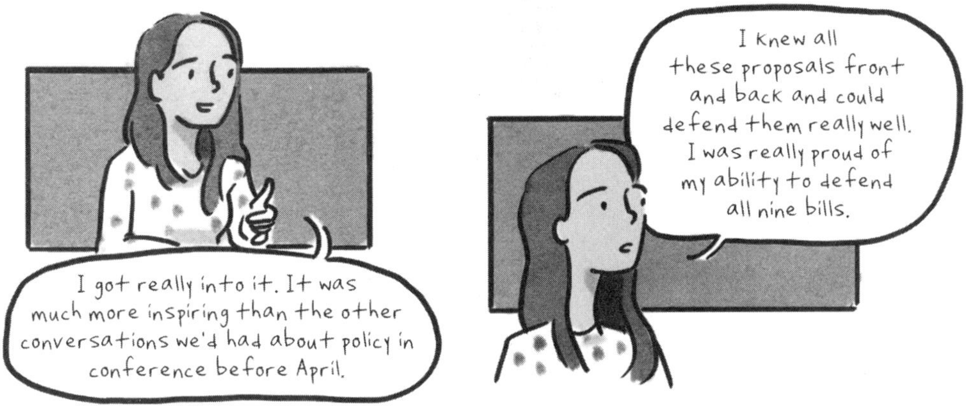
I got really into it. It was much more inspiring than the other conversations we'd had about policy in conference before April.
I knew all these proposals front and back and could defend them really well. I was really proud of my ability to defend all nine bills.

But as the days passed with no official statement, the advocates got more restless, and Cea's report-backs from Albany did little to calm them.

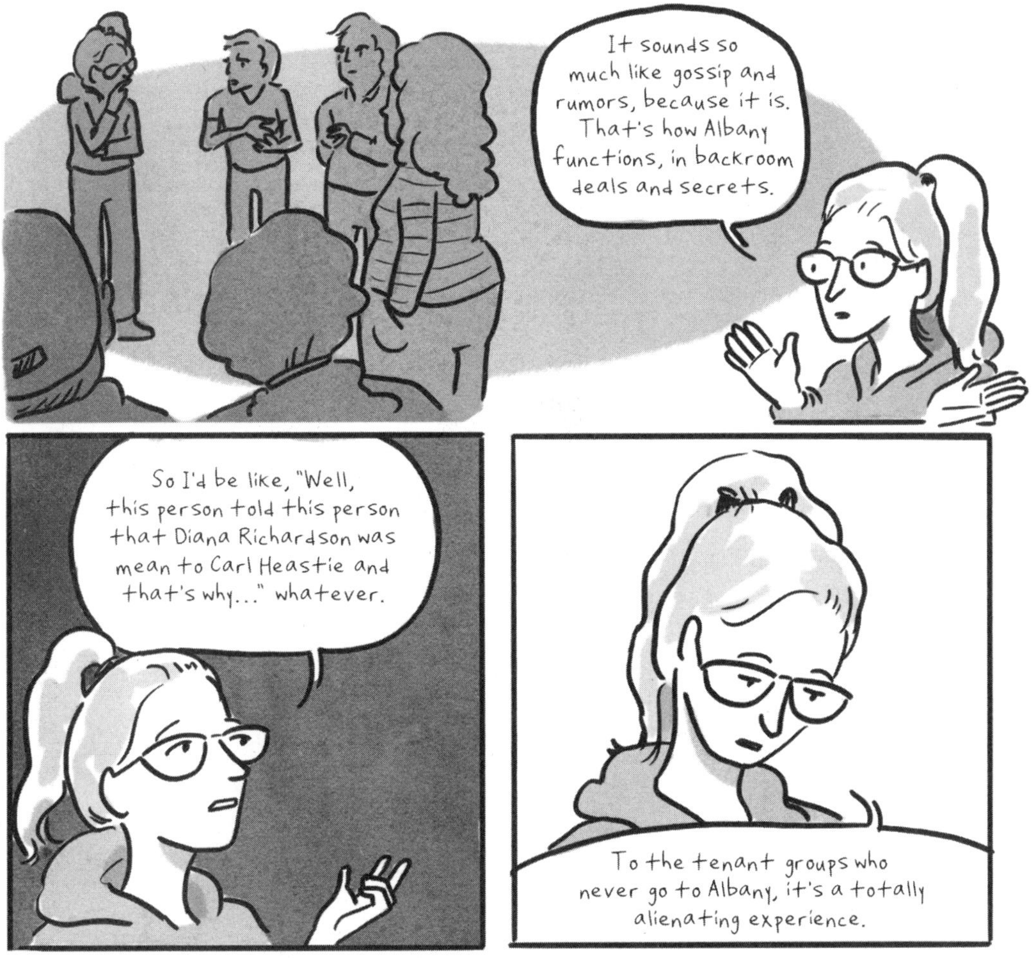
It sounds so much like gossip and rumors, because it is. That's how Albany functions, in backroom deals and secrets.
So I'd be like, "Well, this person told this person that Diana Richardson was mean to Carl Heastie and that's why..." whatever.
To the tenant groups who never go to Albany, it's a totally alienating experience.

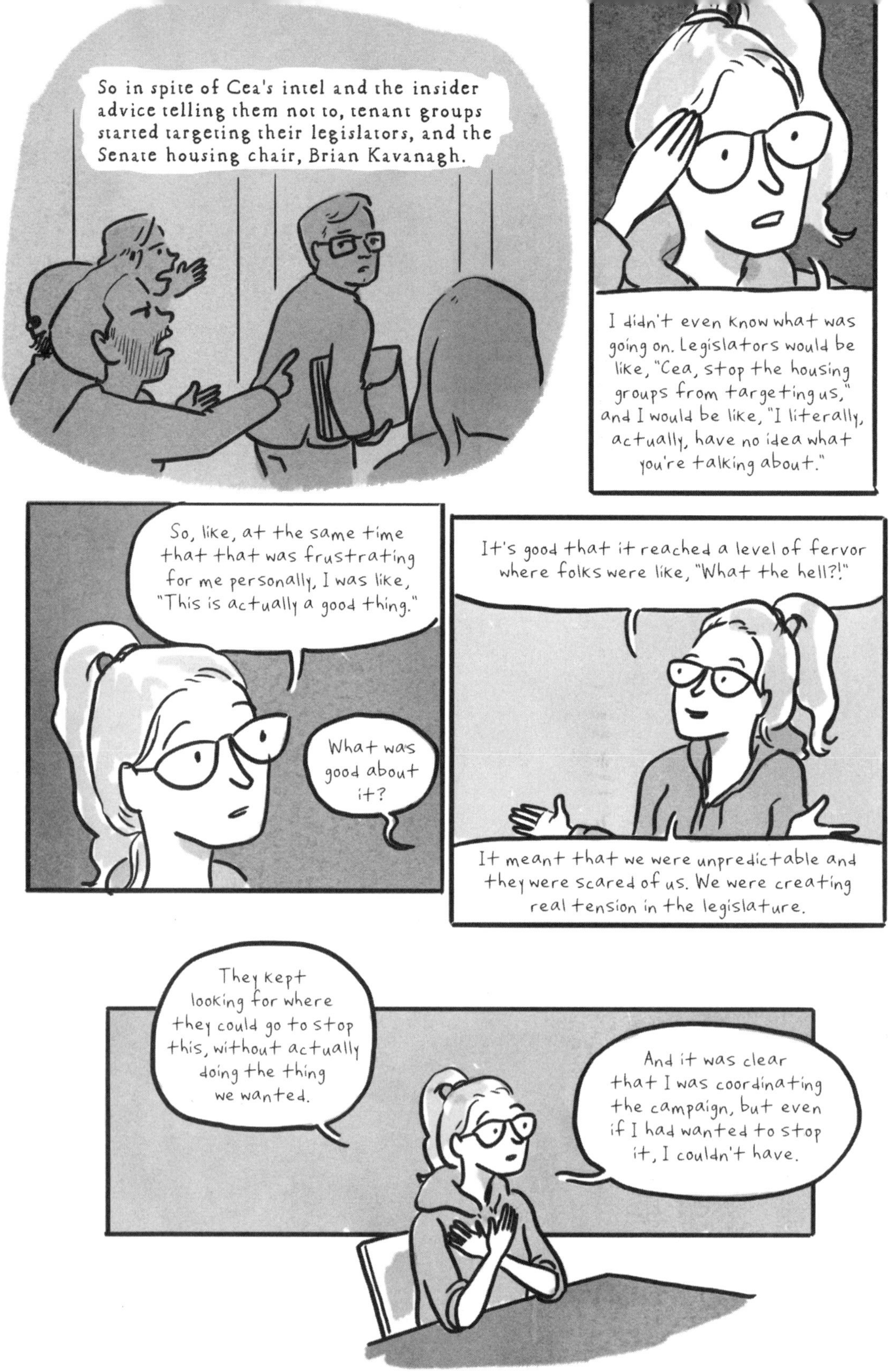
So in spite of Cea's intel and the insider advice telling them not to, tenant groups started targeting their legislators, and the Senate housing chair, Brian Kavanagh.
I didn't even know what was going on. Legislators would be like, "Cea, stop the housing groups from targeting us," and I would be like, "I literally, actually, have no idea what you're talking about."
So, like, at the same time that that was frustrating for me personally, I was like, "This is actually a good thing."
What was good about it?
It's good that it reached a level of fervor where folks were like, "What the hell?!"
It meant that we were unpredictable and they were scared of us. We were creating real tension in the legislature.
They kept looking for where they could go to stop this, without actually doing the thing we wanted.
And it was clear that I was coordinating the campaign, but even if I had wanted to stop it, I couldn't have.

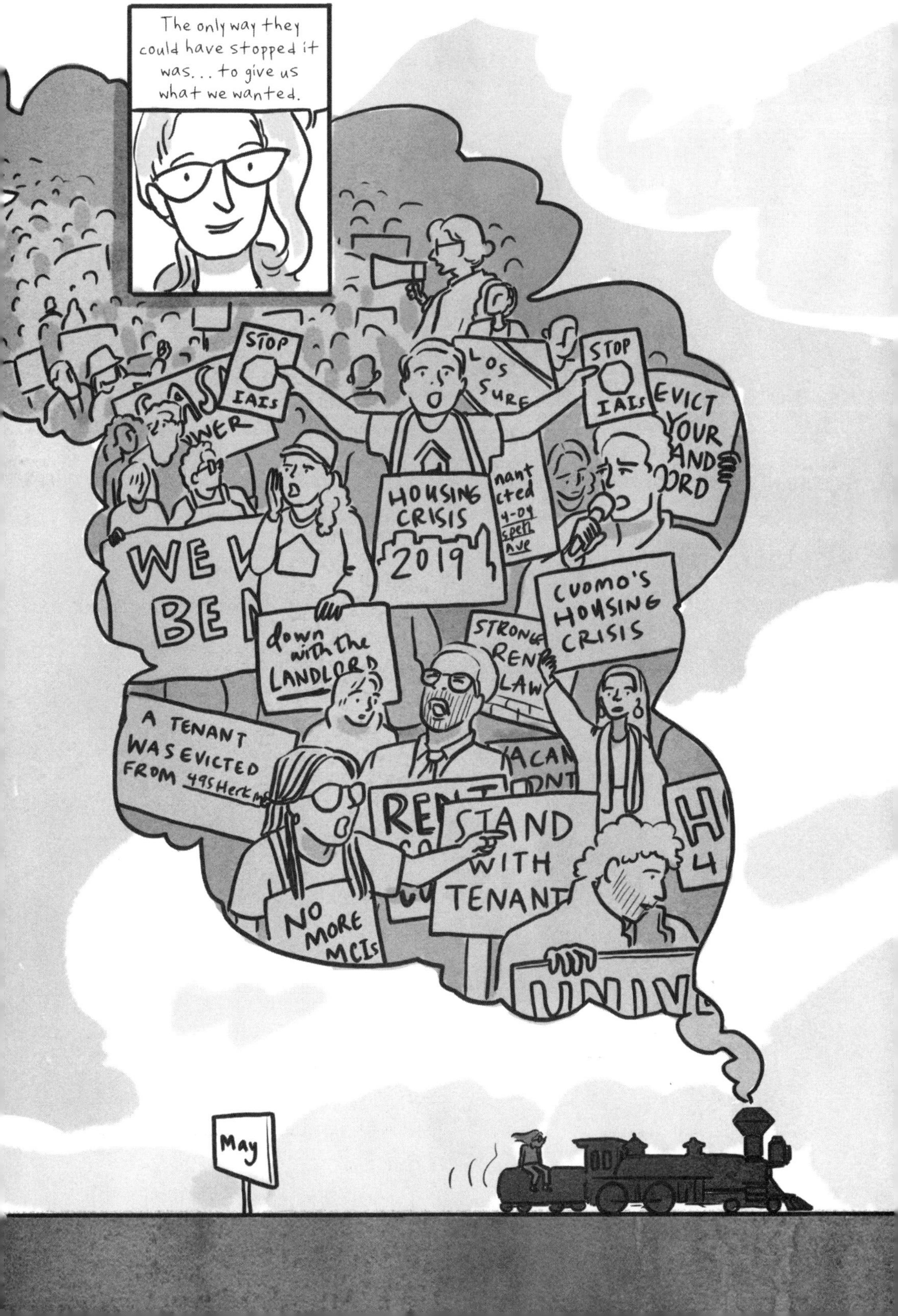

The only way they could have stopped it was... to give us what we wanted.
STOP IAIS
LOS SURE
STOP IAIS
EVICT YOUR
HOUSING CRISIS 2019
CUOMO'S HOUSING CRISIS
down with the LANDLORD
A TENANT WAS EVICTED FROM 495 Herk
STAND WITH TENANT
NO MORE MCIs
May

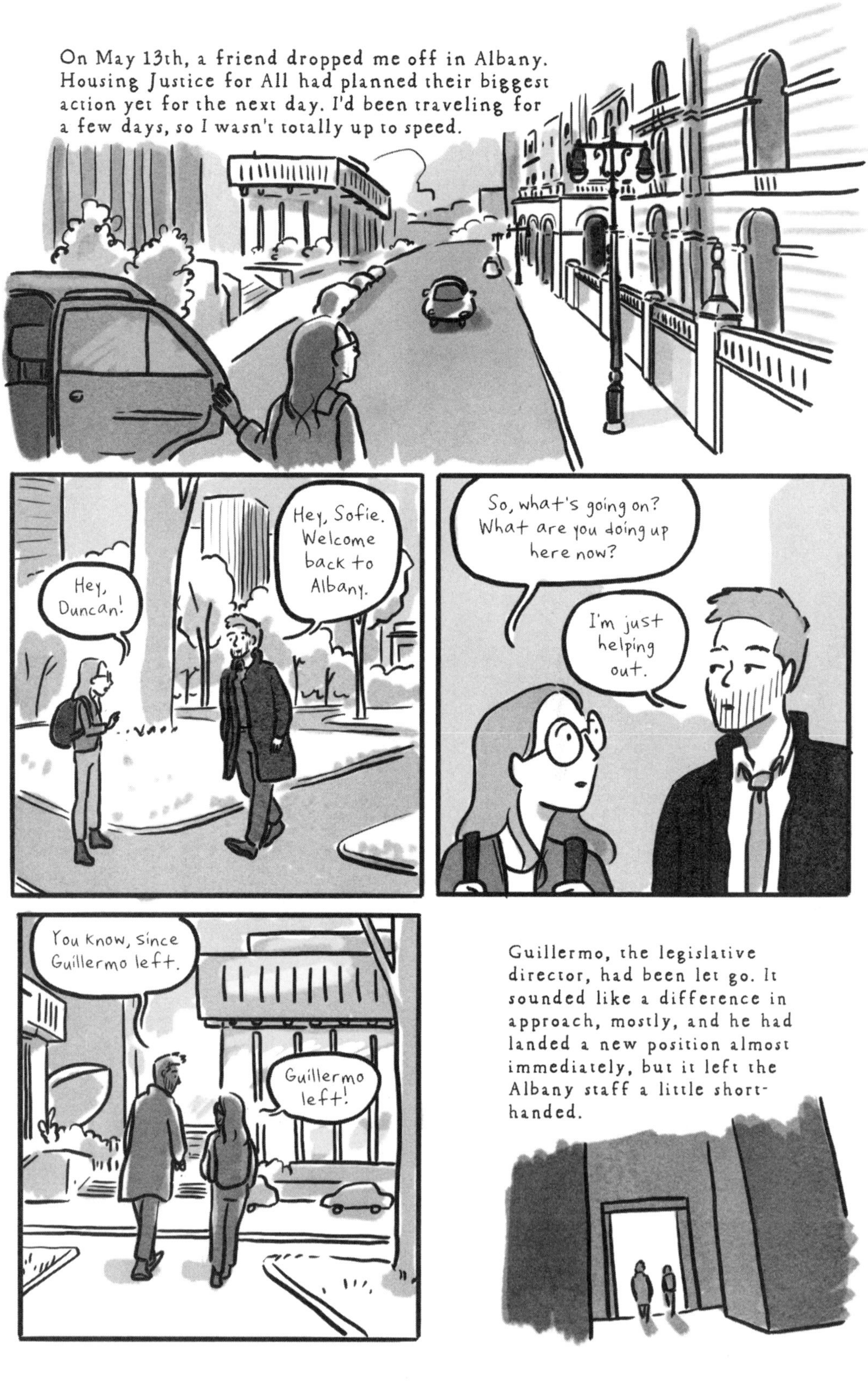
On May 13th, a friend dropped me off in Albany. Housing Justice for All had planned their biggest action yet for the next day. I'd been traveling for a few days, so I wasn't totally up to speed.
Hey, Duncan!
Hey, Sofie. Welcome back to Albany.
So, what's going on? What are you doing up here now?
I'm just helping out.
You know, since Guillermo left.
Guillermo left!
Guillermo, the legislative director, had been let go. It sounded like a difference in approach, mostly, and he had landed a new position almost immediately, but it left the Albany staff a little short-handed.

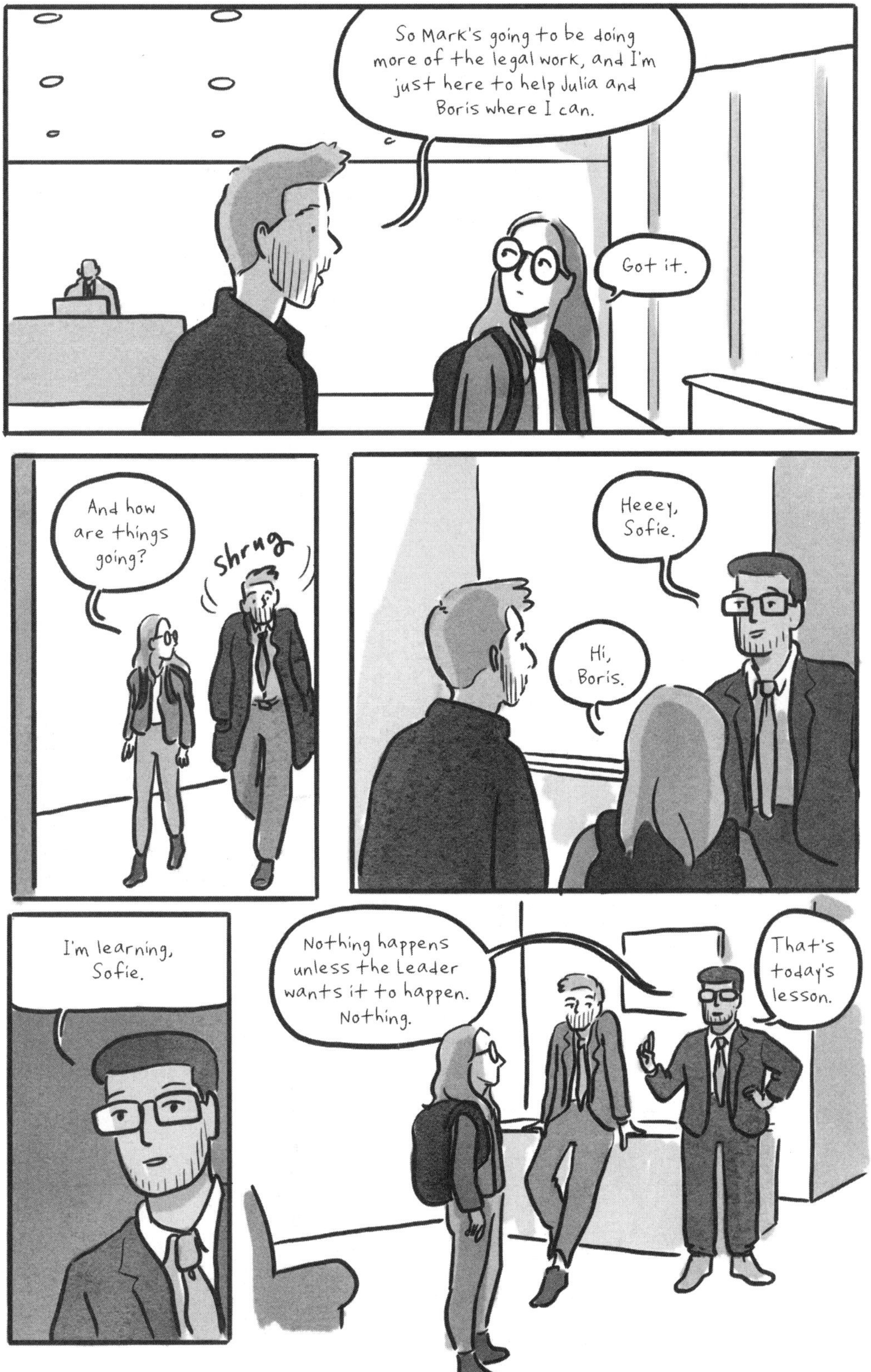
So Mark's going to be doing more of the legal work, and I'm just here to help Julia and Boris where I can.
Got it.
And how are things going?
Shrug
Heeey, Sofie.
Hi, Boris.
I'm learning, Sofie.
Nothing happens unless the leader wants it to happen. Nothing.
That's today's lesson.

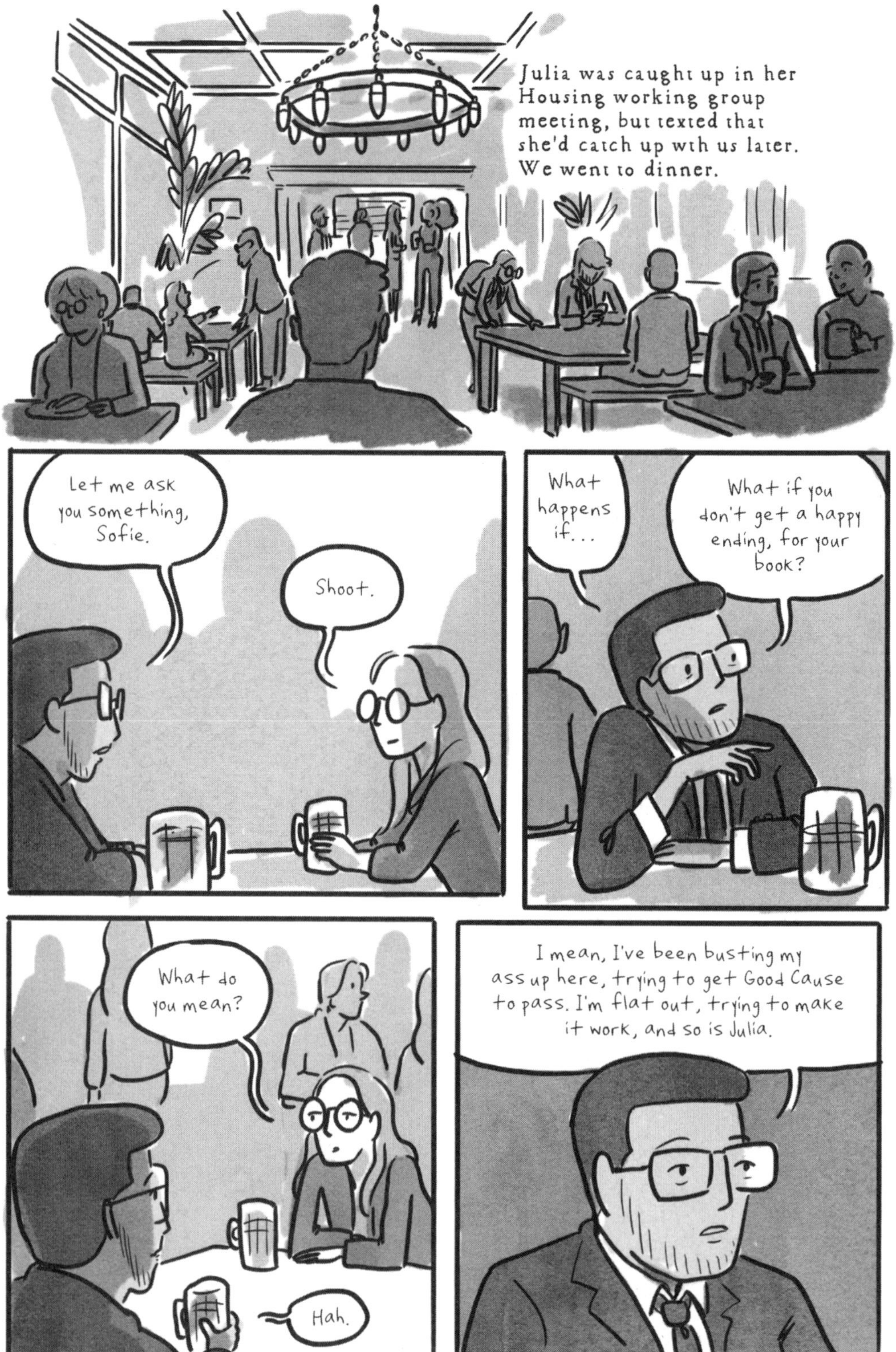
Julia was caught up in her Housing working group meeting, but texted that she'd catch up wth us later. We went to dinner.
Let me ask you something, Sofie.
Shoot.
What happens if...
What if you don't get a happy ending, for your book?
What do you mean?
Hah.
I mean, I've been busting my ass up here, trying to get Good Cause to pass. I'm flat out, trying to make it work, and so is Julia.

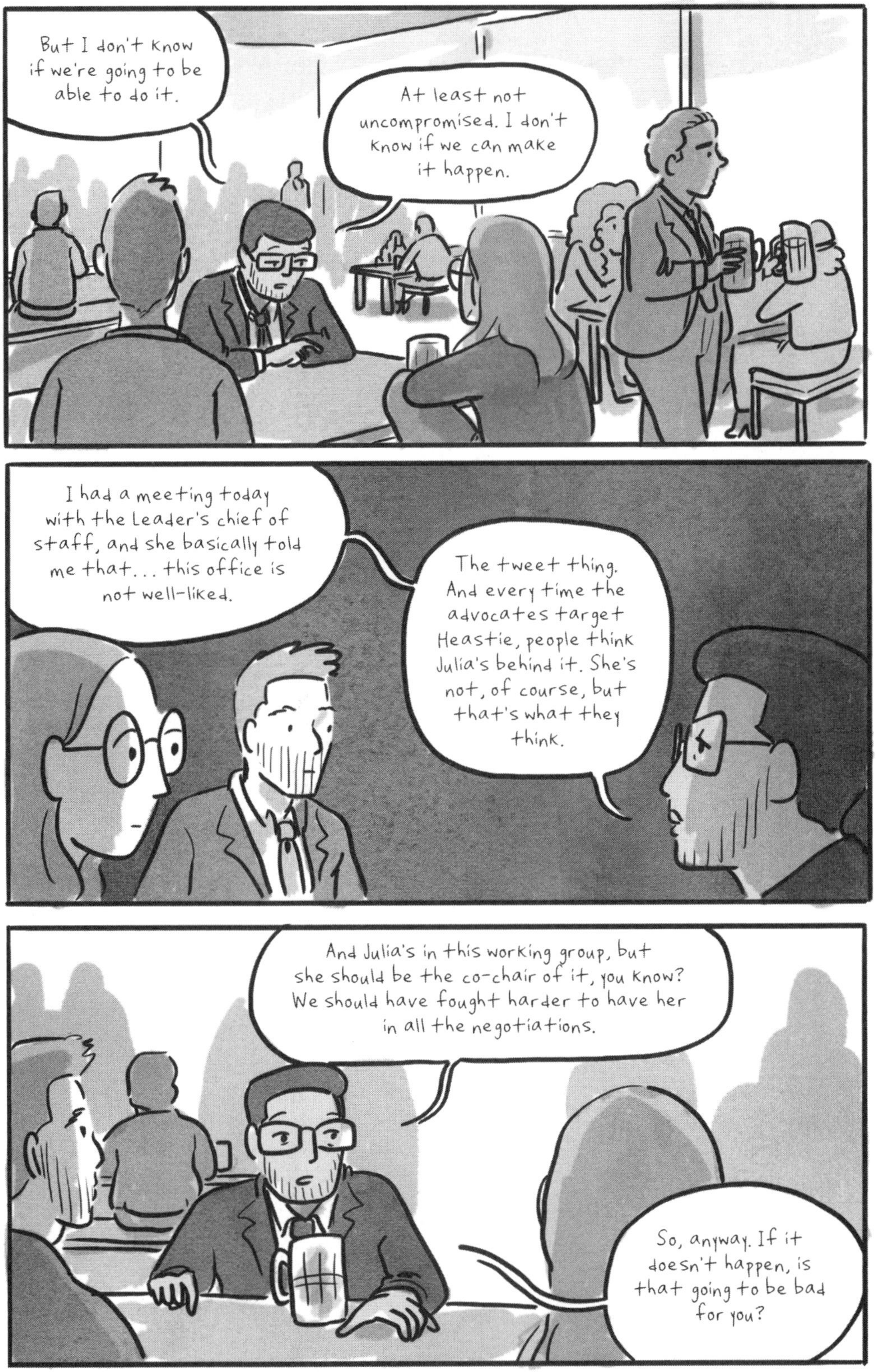
But I don't know if we're going to be able to do it.
At least not uncompromised. I don't know if we can make it happen.
I had a meeting today with the Leader's chief of staff, and she basically told me that... this office is not well-liked.
The tweet thing. And every time the advocates target Heastie, people think Julia's behind it. She's not, of course, but that's what they think.
And Julia's in this working group, but she should be the co-chair of it, you know? We should have fought harder to have her in all the negotiations.
So, anyway. If it doesn't happen, is that going to be bad for you?

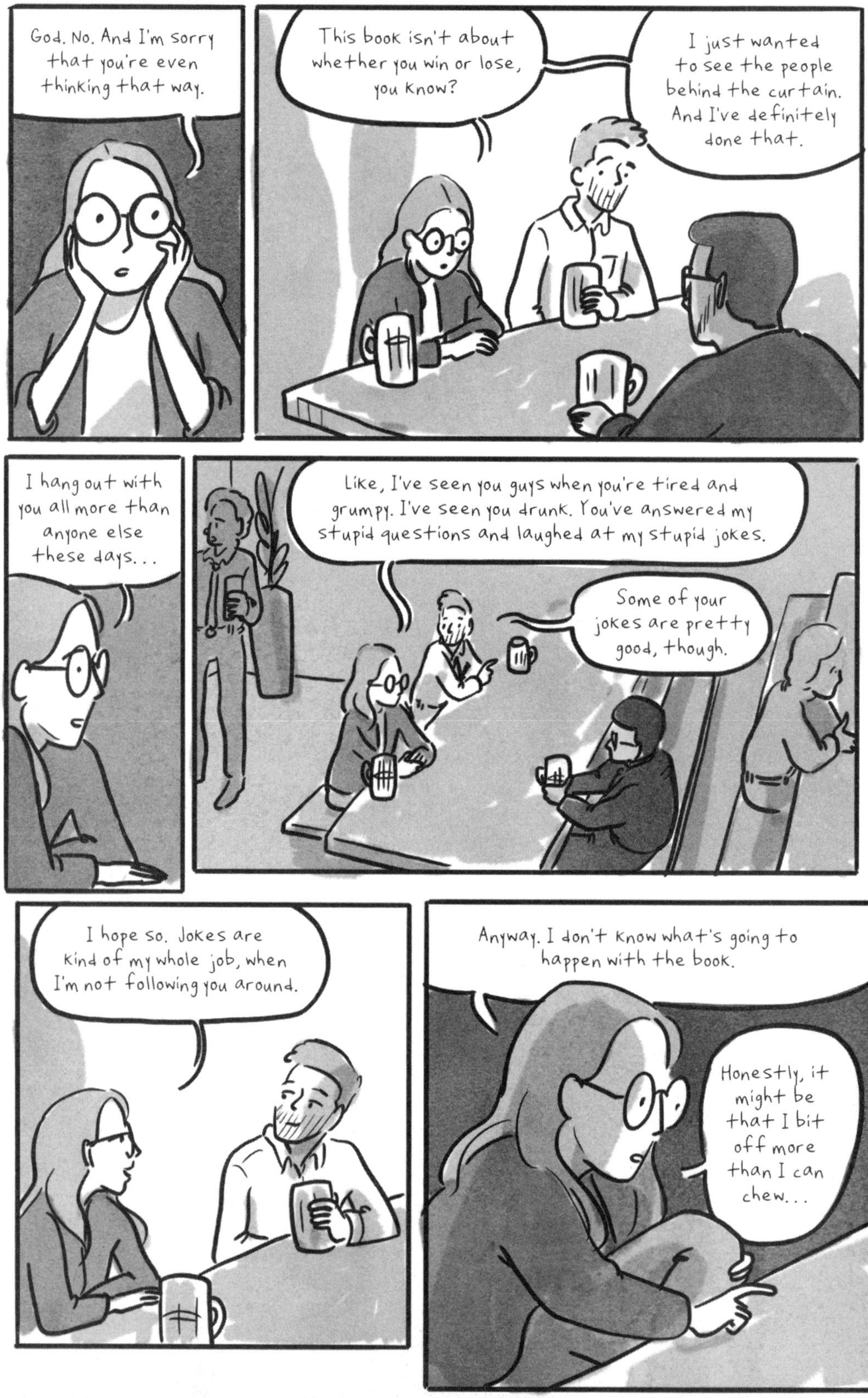
God. No. And I'm sorry that you're even thinking that way.
This book isn't about whether you win or lose, you know?
I just wanted to see the people behind the curtain. And I've definitely done that.
I hang out with you all more than anyone else these days...
Like, I've seen you guys when you're tired and grumpy. I've seen you drunk. You've answered my stupid questions and laughed at my stupid jokes.
Some of your jokes are pretty good, though.
I hope so. Jokes are kind of my whole job, when I'm not following you around.
Anyway. I don't know what's going to happen with the book.
Honestly, it might be that I bit off more than I can chew...

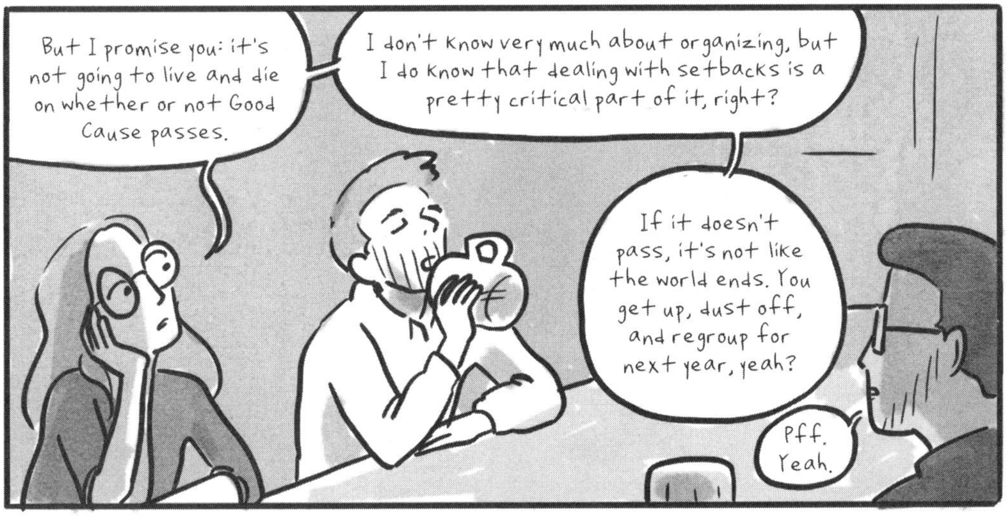
But I promise you: it's not going to live and die on whether or not Good Cause passes.
I don't know very much about organizing, but I do know that dealing with setbacks is a pretty critical part of it, right?
If it doesn't pass, it's not like the world ends. You get up, dust off, and regroup for next year, yeah?
Pff. Yeah.

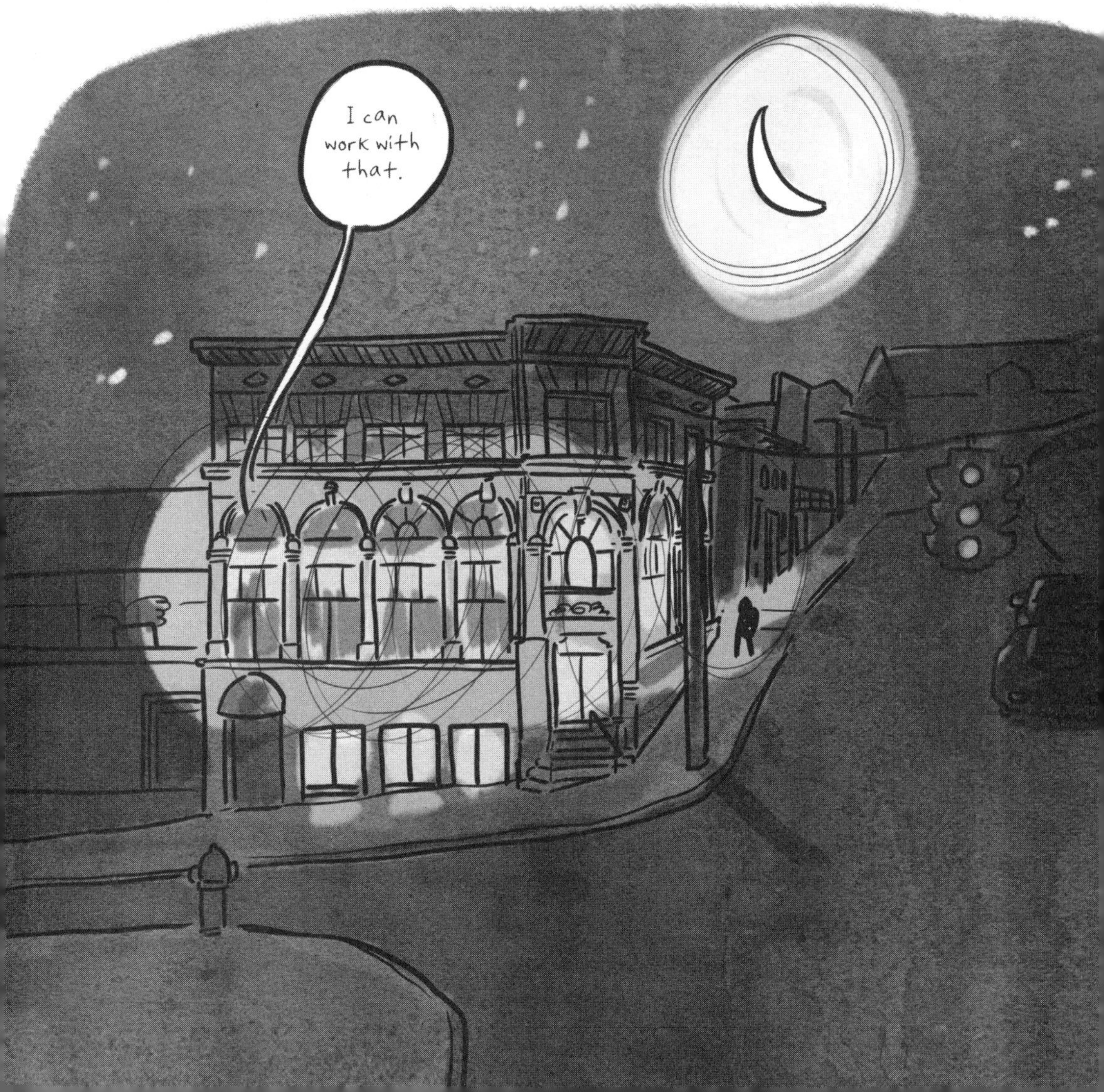
I can work with that.

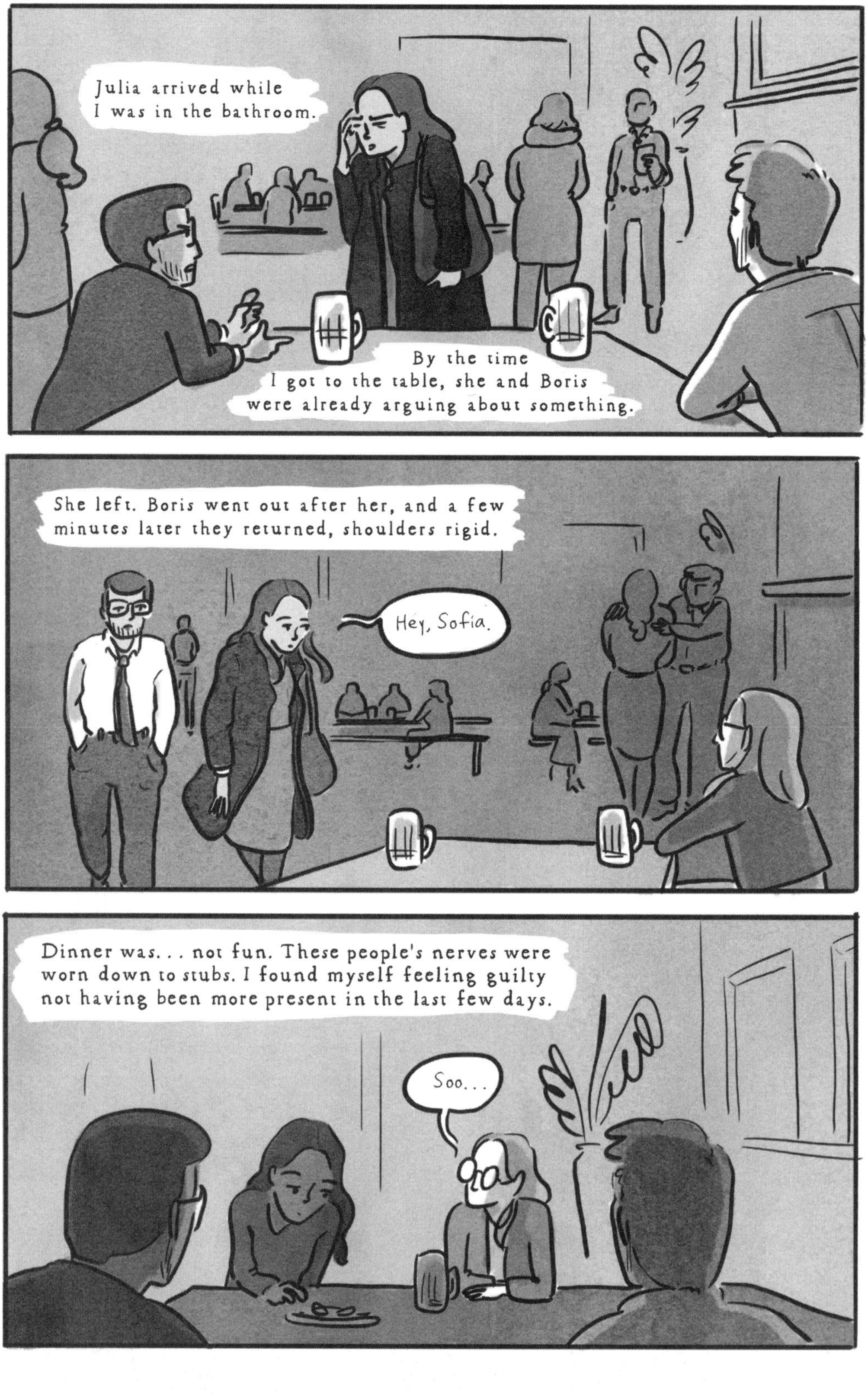
Julia arrived while I was in the bathroom.
By the time I got to the table, she and Boris were already arguing about something.
She left. Boris went out after her, and a few minutes later they returned, shoulders rigid.
Hey, Sofia.
Dinner was. . . not fun. These people's nerves were worn down to stubs. I found myself feeling guilty not having been more present in the last few days.
Soo. . .

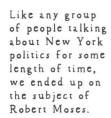

Like any group of people talking about New York politics for some length of time, we ended up on the subject of Robert Moses.

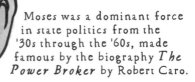

Moses was a dominant force in state politics from the '30s through the '60s, made famous by the biography *The Power Broker* by Robert Caro.

He was known for relentlessly accruing power and forcing his vision of the city into reality. He was bullying and despotic, but undeniably brilliant and effective.

Every politician just wants to be Robert Moses. Everyone wants to see their vision executed.

Well, I never wanted to be a politician.

But maybe you should be. You should run, Boris.

Otherwise, it's just going to be another year of you trying to be the senator.

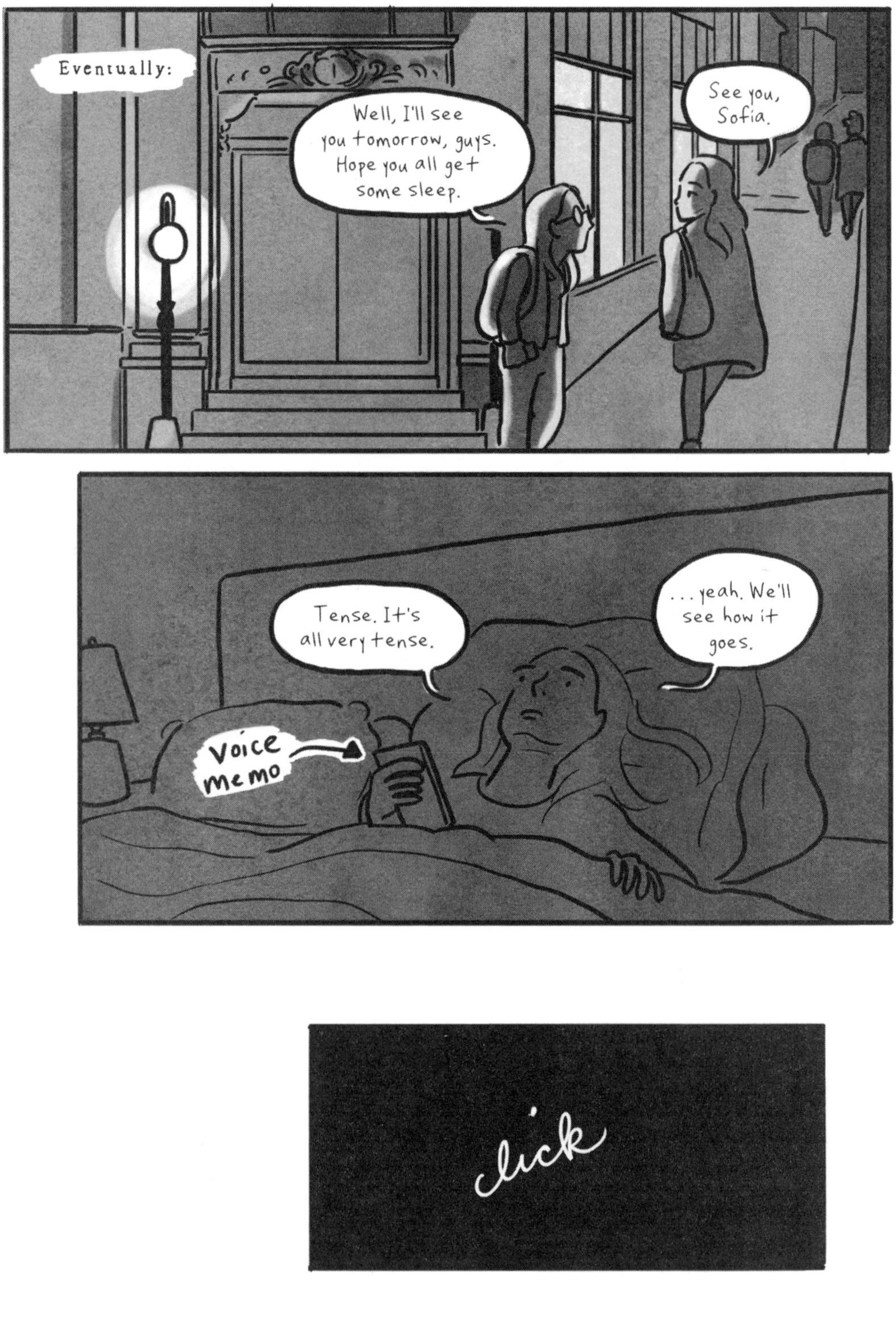
Eventually:
Well, I'll see you tomorrow, guys. Hope you all get some sleep.
See you, Sofia.
Tense. It's all very tense.
...yeah. We'll see how it goes.
Voice memo
click

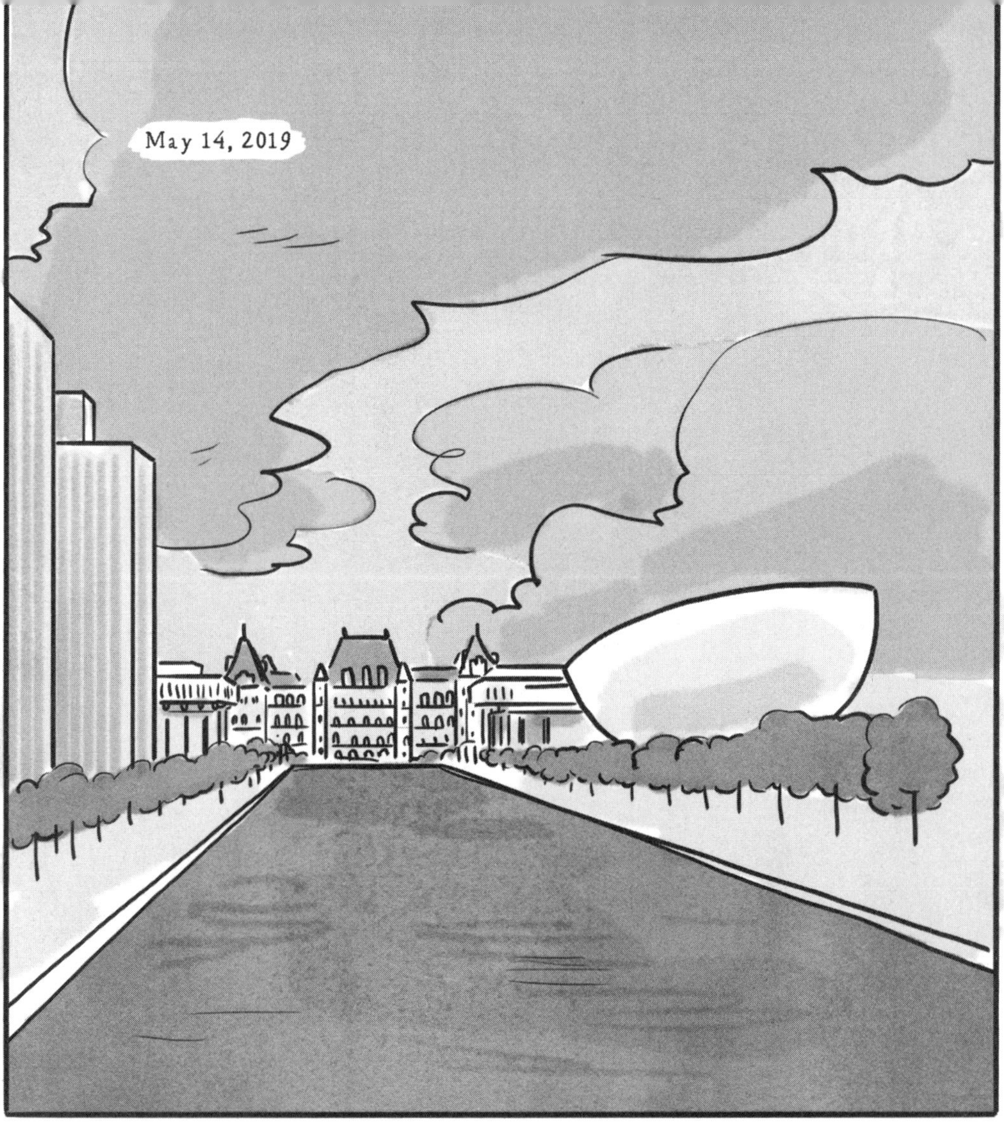
May 14, 2019

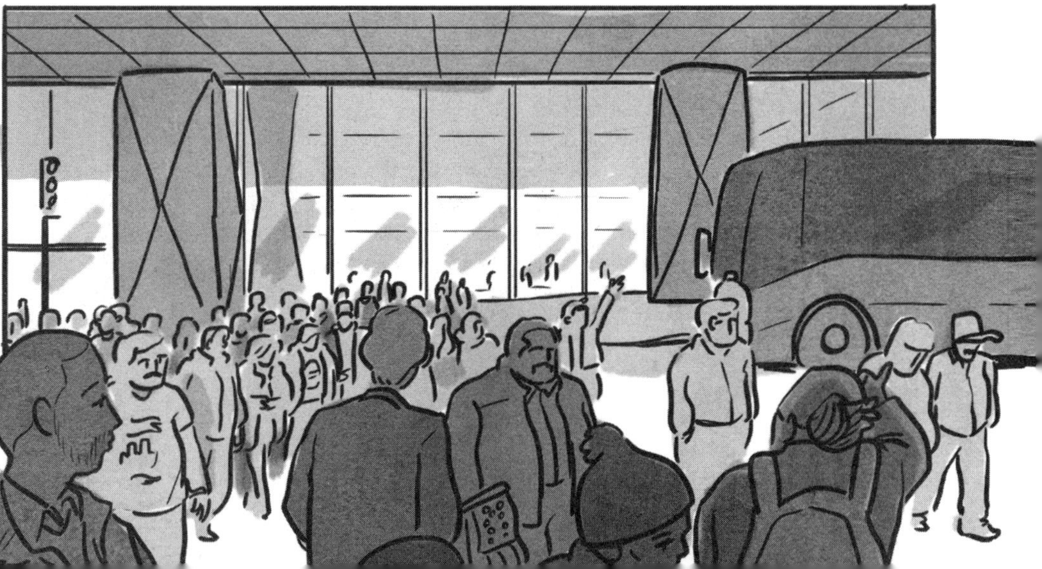

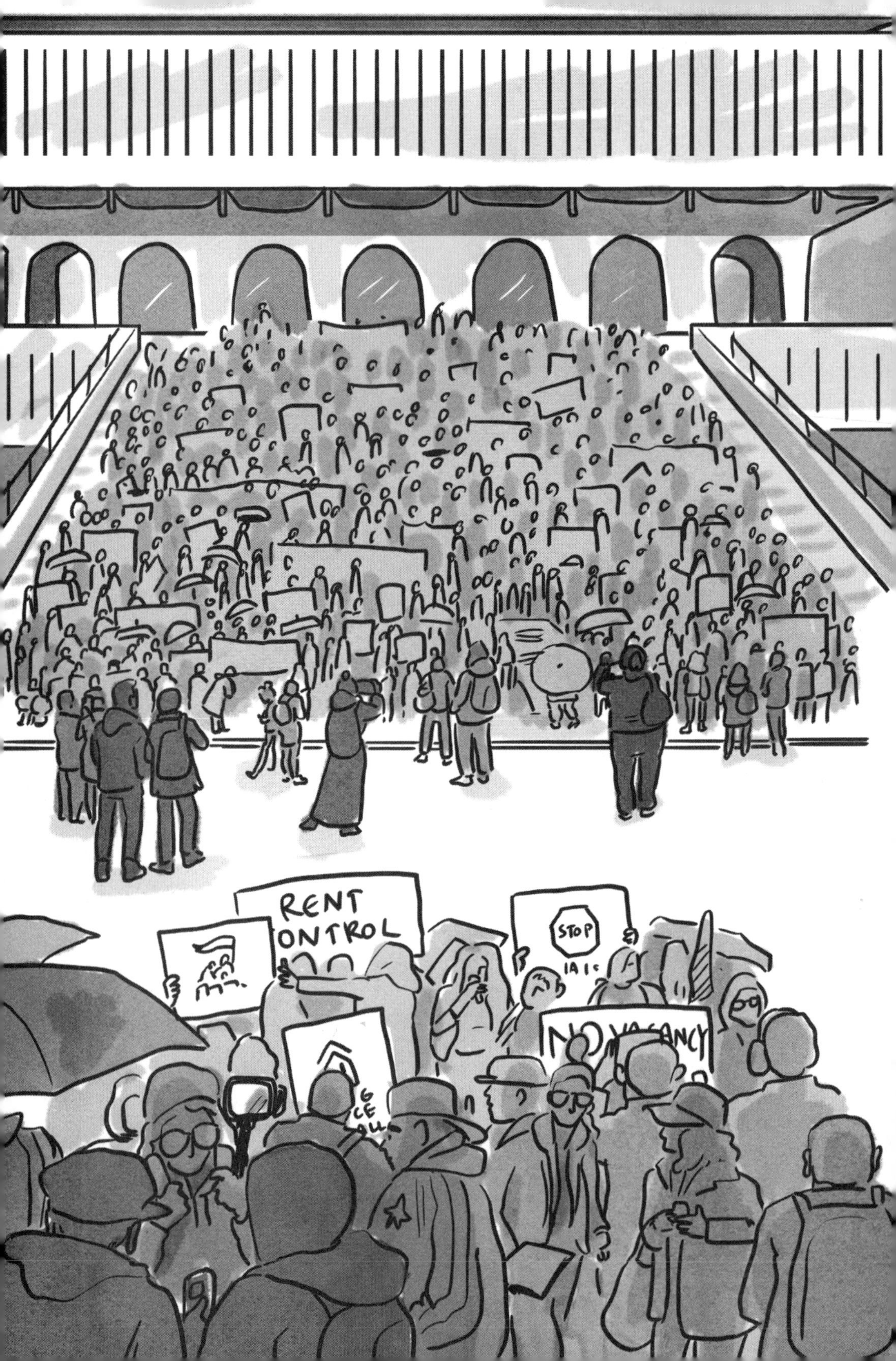
RENT
ONTROL
STOP
NO VA ANCY

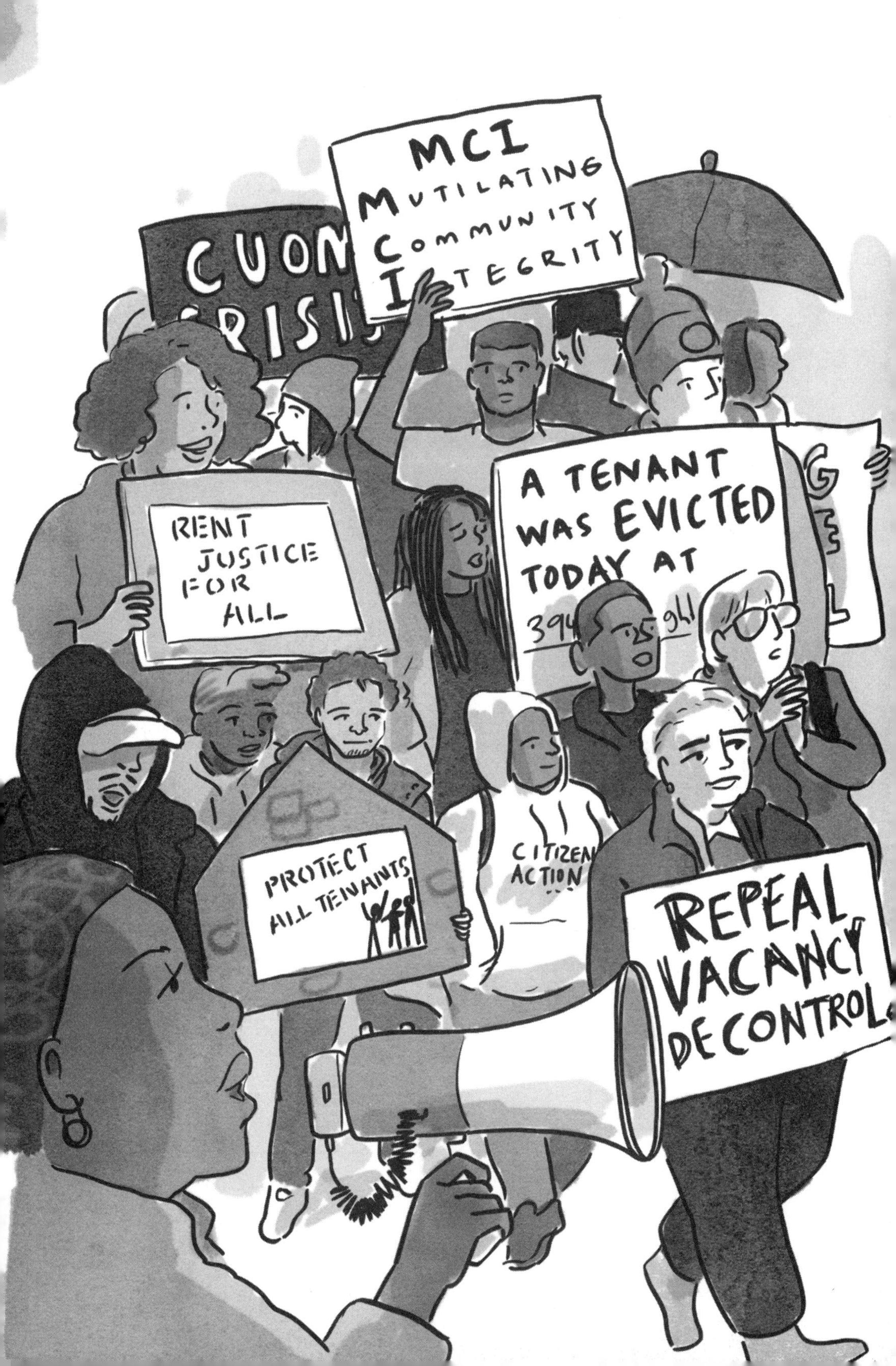
MCI
MUTILATING
COMMUNITY
INTEGRITY
A TENANT WAS EVICTED TODAY AT
RENT JUSTICE FOR ALL
PROTECT ALL TENANTS
CITIZEN ACTION
REPEAL VACANCY DECONTROL

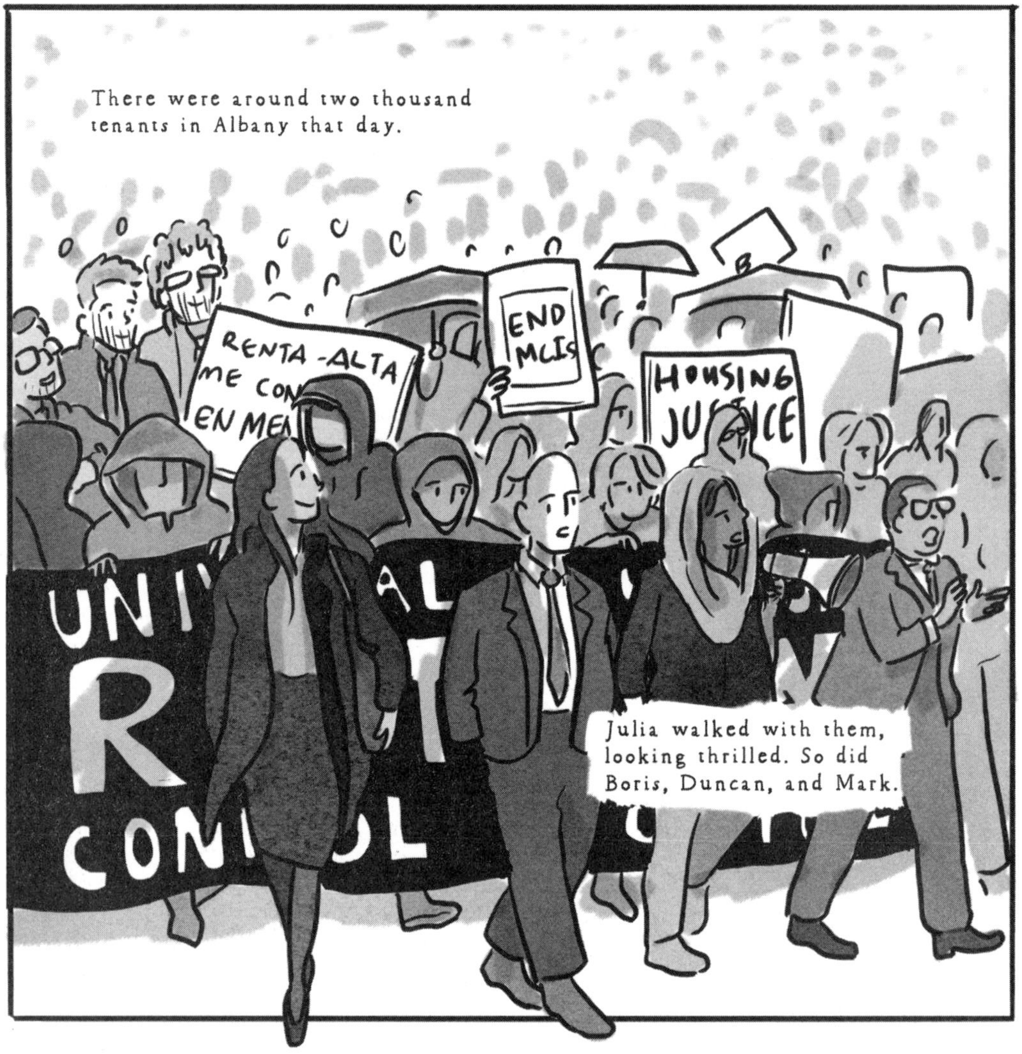
There were around two thousand tenants in Albany that day.
END MCIs
Julia walked with them, looking thrilled. So did Boris, Duncan, and Mark.

Tenants swarmed the legislature. They packed the iconic Million Dollar Staircase. They blocked the Assembly chambers. They found the Senate housing chair and chased him through the halls, demanding that he come out for all nine bills.

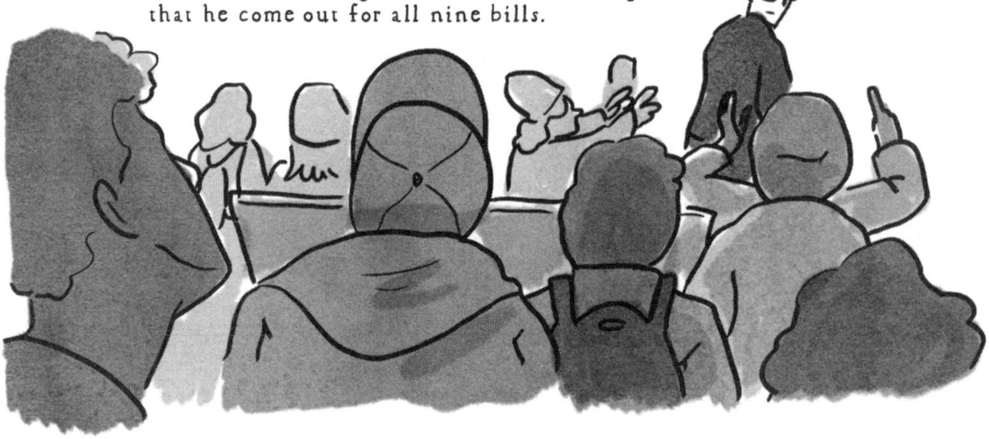

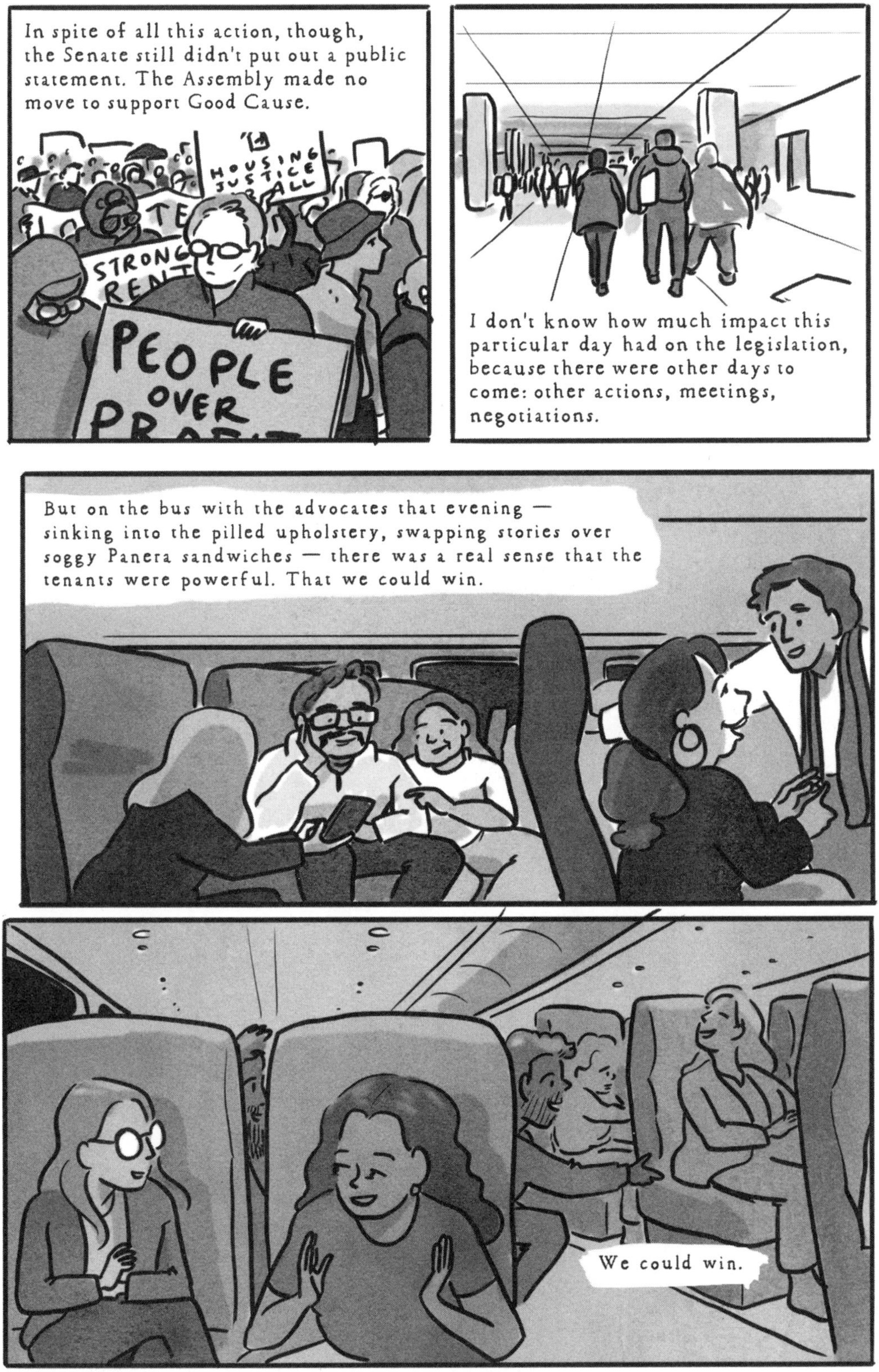
In spite of all this action, though, the Senate still didn't put out a public statement. The Assembly made no move to support Good Cause.
HOUSING
JUSTICE
STRONG
RENT
PEOPLE
OVER
I don't know how much impact this particular day had on the legislation, because there were other days to come: other actions, meetings, negotiations.
But on the bus with the advocates that evening — sinking into the pilled upholstery, swapping stories over soggy Panera sandwiches — there was a real sense that the tenants were powerful. That we could win.
We could win.

Chapter Eleven

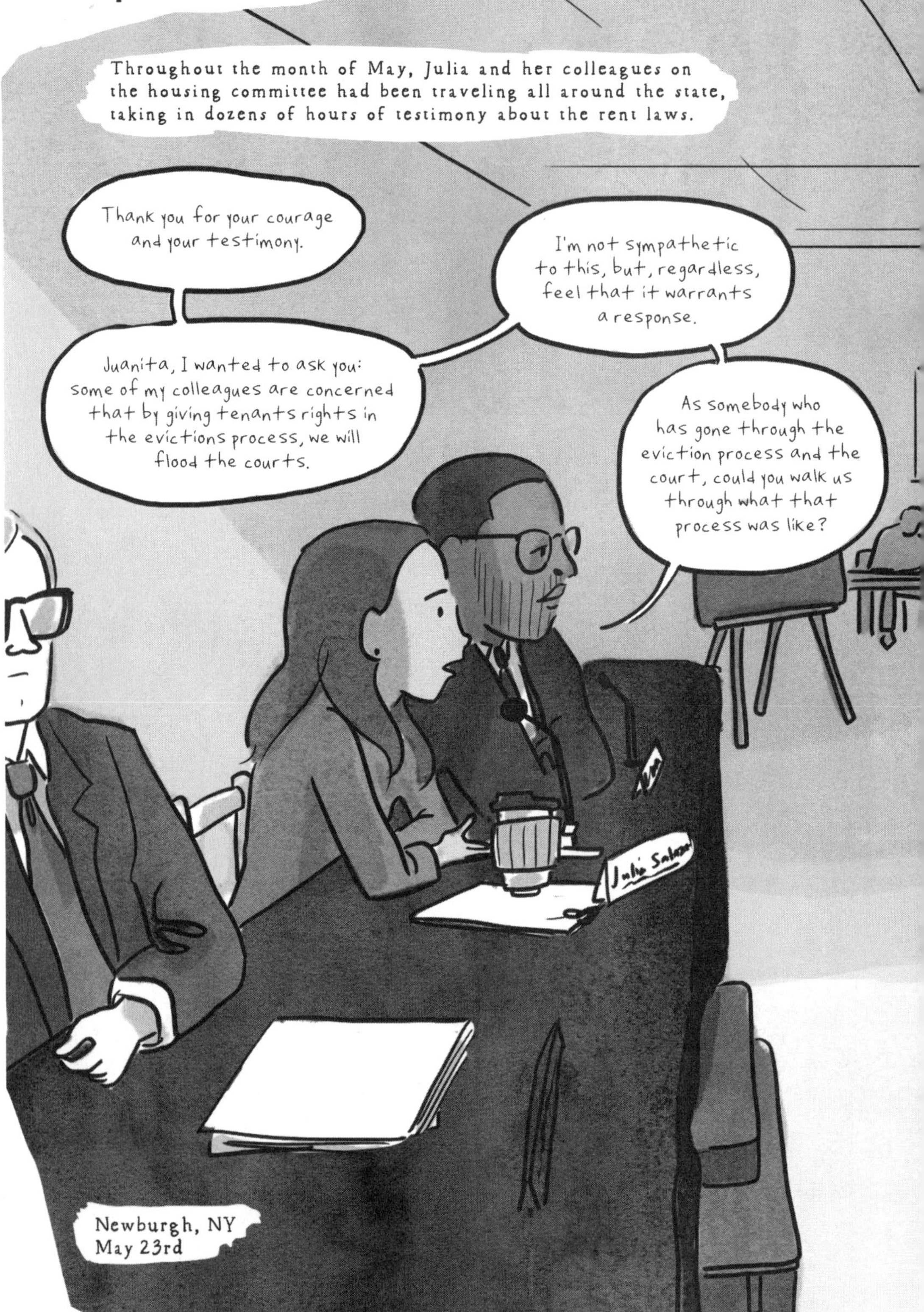
Throughout the month of May, Julia and her colleagues on the housing committee had been traveling all around the state, taking in dozens of hours of testimony about the rent laws.
Thank you for your courage and your testimony.
Juanita, I wanted to ask you: some of my colleagues are concerned that by giving tenants rights in the evictions process, we will flood the courts.
I'm not sympathetic to this, but, regardless, feel that it warrants a response.
As somebody who has gone through the eviction process and the court, could you walk us through what that process was like?
Newburgh, NY
May 23rd

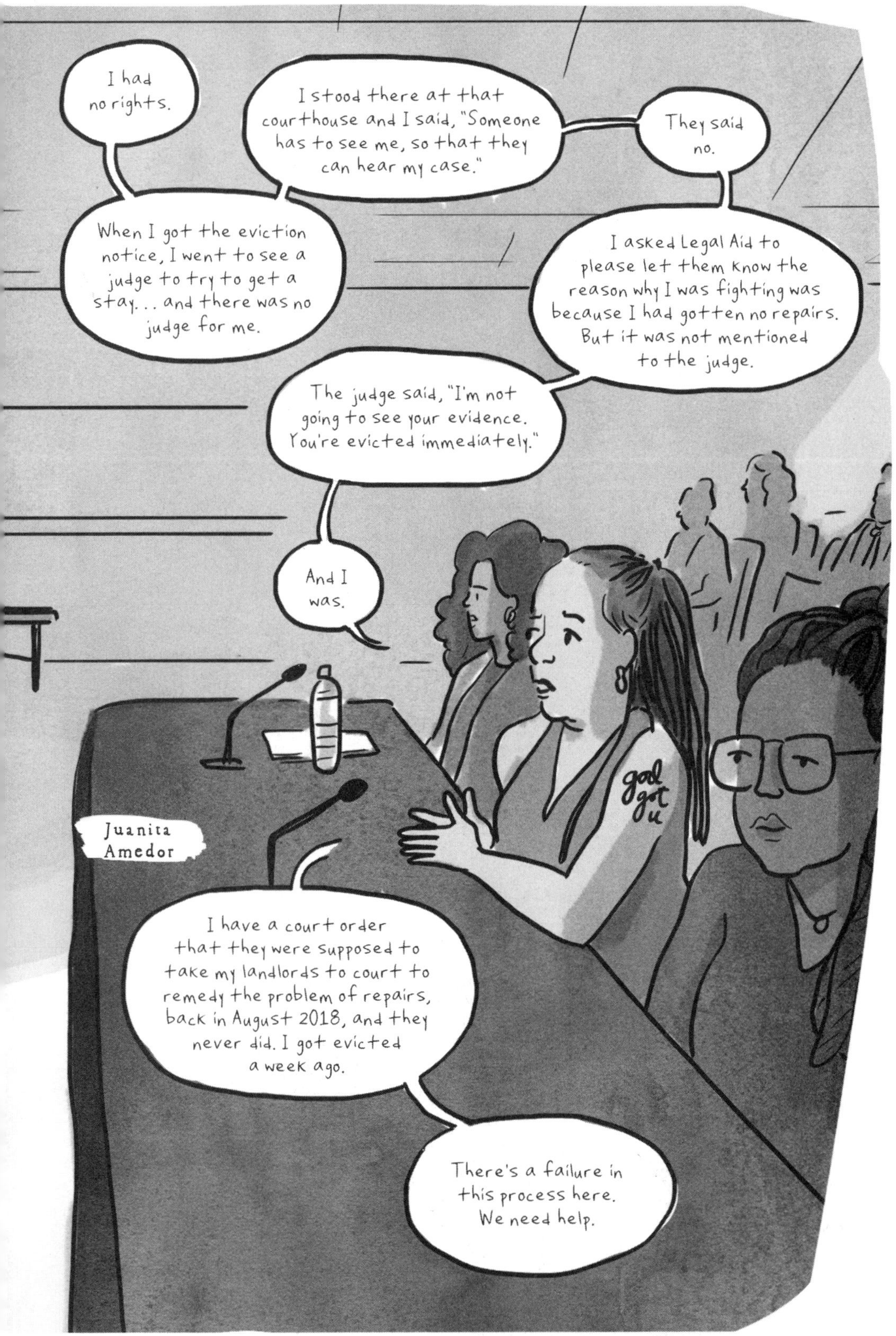
I had no rights.
When I got the eviction notice, I went to see a judge to try to get a stay... and there was no judge for me.
I stood there at that courthouse and I said, "Someone has to see me, so that they can hear my case."
They said no.
I asked Legal Aid to please let them know the reason why I was fighting was because I had gotten no repairs. But it was not mentioned to the judge.
The judge said, "I'm not going to see your evidence. You're evicted immediately."
And I was.
god got u
Juanita Amedor
I have a court order that they were supposed to take my landlords to court to remedy the problem of repairs, back in August 2018, and they never did. I got evicted a week ago.
There's a failure in this process here. We need help.

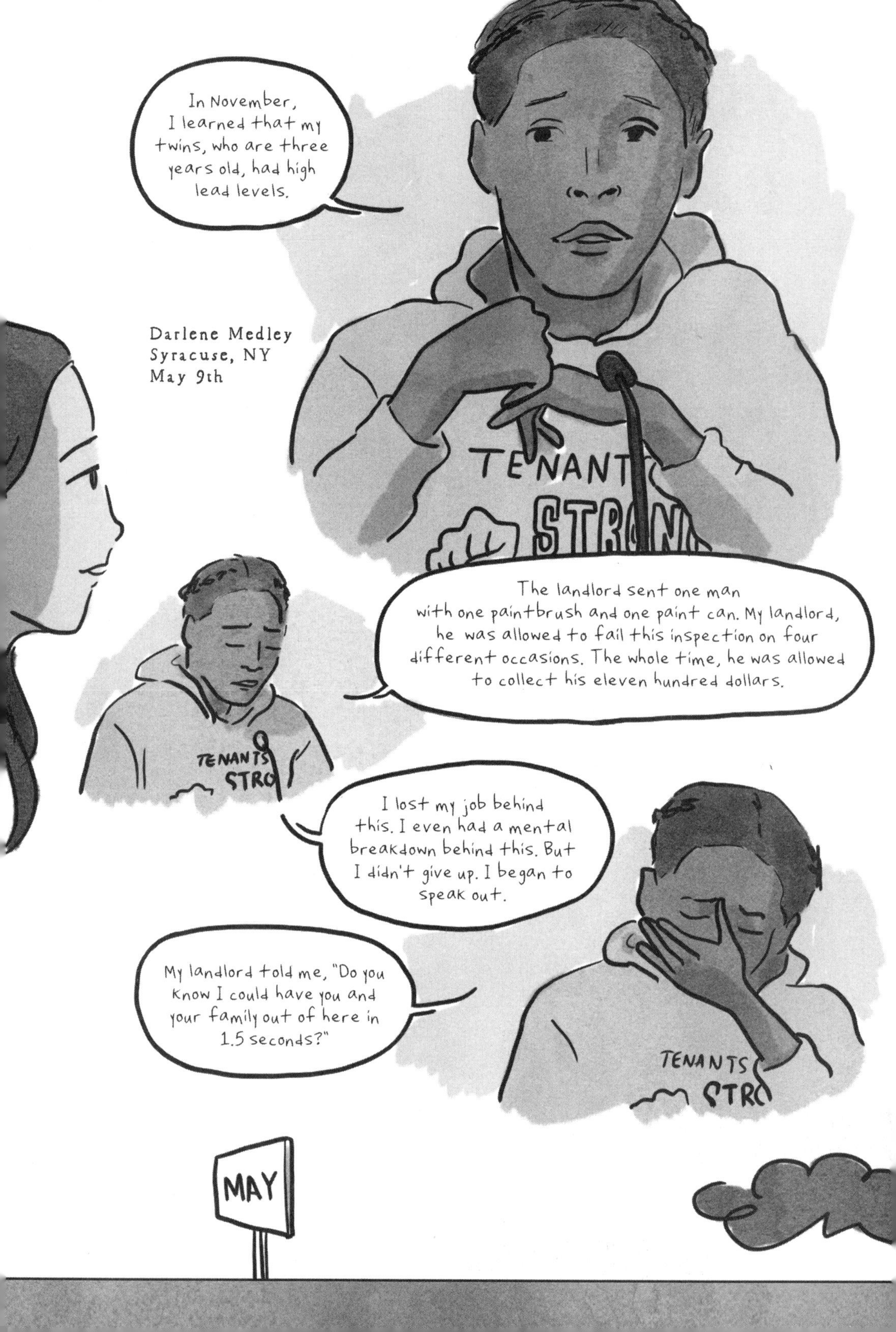
In November, I learned that my twins, who are three years old, had high lead levels.
Darlene Medley
Syracuse, NY
May 9th
TENANTS STRO
The landlord sent one man with one paintbrush and one paint can. My landlord, he was allowed to fail this inspection on four different occasions. The whole time, he was allowed to collect his eleven hundred dollars.
TENANTS STRO
I lost my job behind this. I even had a mental breakdown behind this. But I didn't give up. I began to speak out.
My landlord told me, "Do you know I could have you and your family out of here in 1.5 seconds?"
TENANTS STRO
MAY

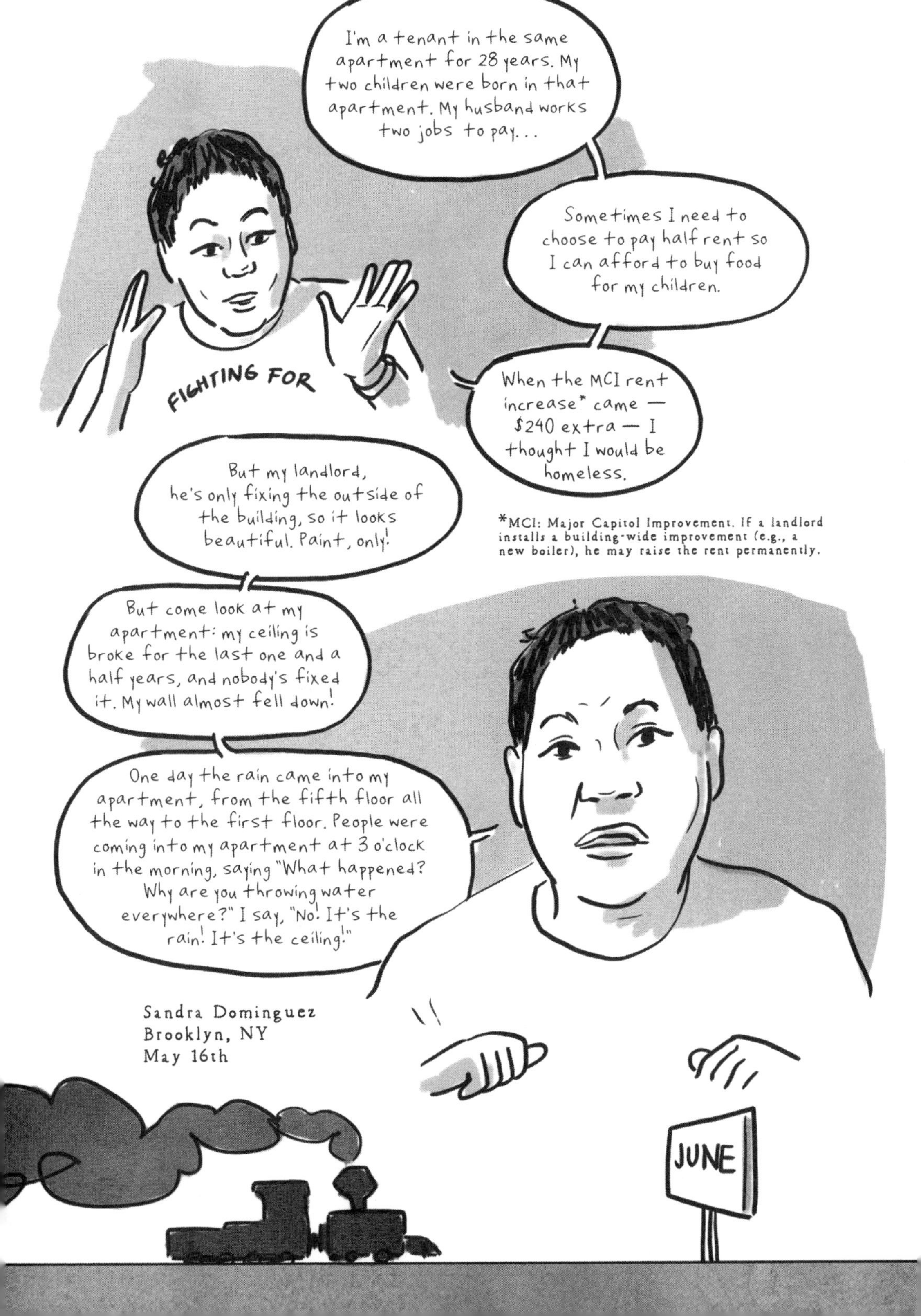
I'm a tenant in the same apartment for 28 years. My two children were born in that apartment. My husband works two jobs to pay...
Sometimes I need to choose to pay half rent so I can afford to buy food for my children.
FIGHTING FOR
When the MCI rent increase* came — $240 extra — I thought I would be homeless.
But my landlord, he's only fixing the outside of the building, so it looks beautiful. Paint, only!
*MCI: Major Capitol Improvement. If a landlord installs a building-wide improvement (e.g., a new boiler), he may raise the rent permanently.
But come look at my apartment: my ceiling is broke for the last one and a half years, and nobody's fixed it. My wall almost fell down!
One day the rain came into my apartment, from the fifth floor all the way to the first floor. People were coming into my apartment at 3 o'clock in the morning, saying "What happened? Why are you throwing water everywhere?" I say, "No! It's the rain! It's the ceiling!"
Sandra Dominguez
Brooklyn, NY
May 16th
JUNE

In the hearings, a few real estate representatives showed up, but tenant advocates far outweighed them. This was not surprising.

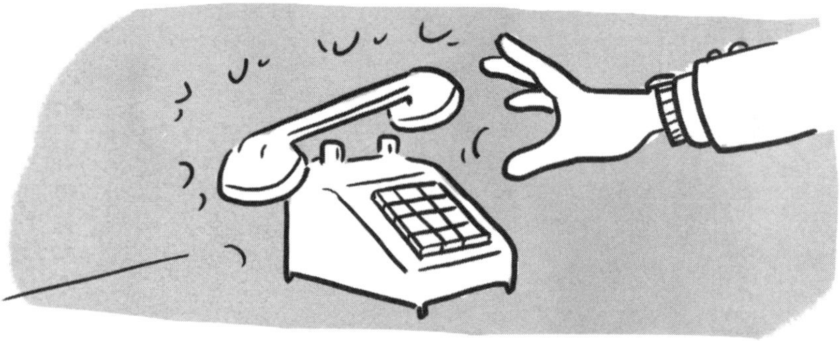

If I had a direct line to the powers that be, I probably wouldn't have waited for hours to speak my piece at a public forum, either.

That said, the real estate lobby did give some thought to public opinion. For instance, there was this counter-protest, which took place outside the public hearing in Brooklyn on May 16th. . .

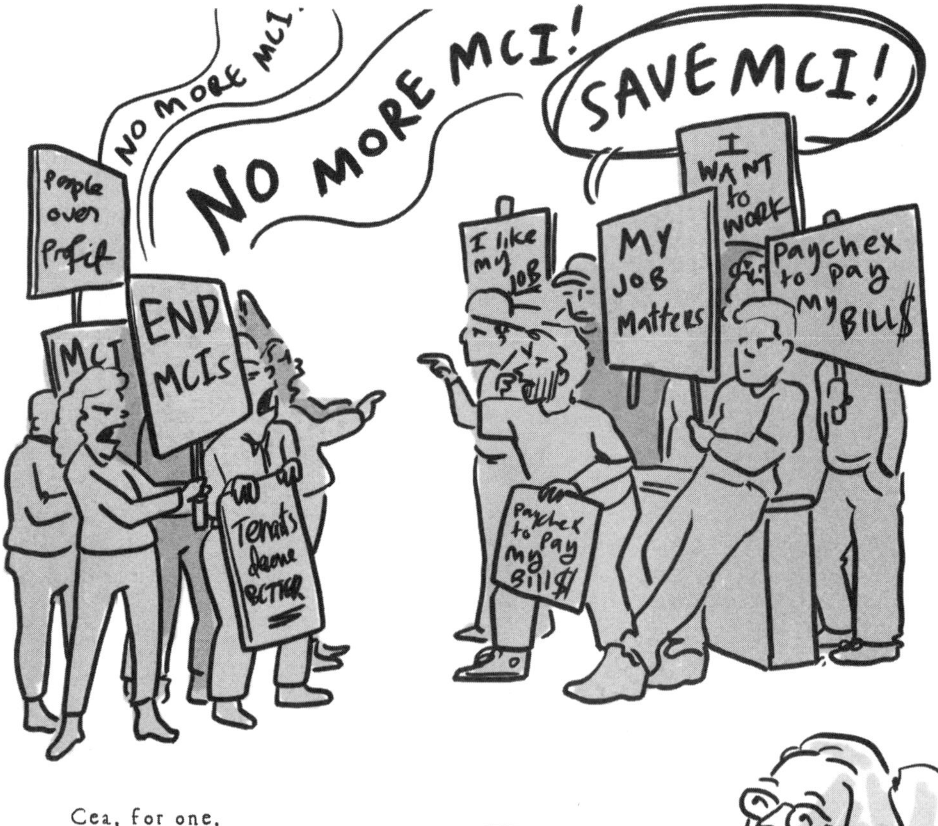
NO MORE MCI!
NO MORE MCI!
SAVE MCI!
people over profit
MCI
END MCIs
I WANT to WORK
I like my JOB
My JOB Matters
Paychex to pay my BILL$
Paychex to Pay my BILL$

Cea, for one, was unimpressed with the organizing.

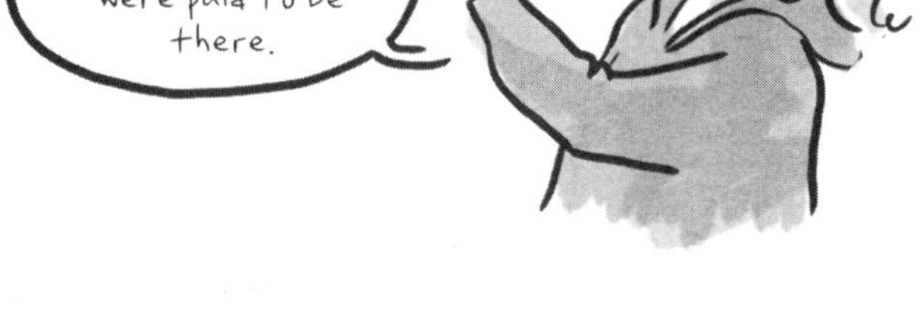
Those beefy guys from Queens? They were paid to be there.

Mostly, though, grassroots campaigns were not the way the real estate lobby did business.

While HJ4A ramped up their organizing – more protests, more bus trips, more targeting legislators – real estate interests poured money into lobbying. . .

. . . and ad campaigns.

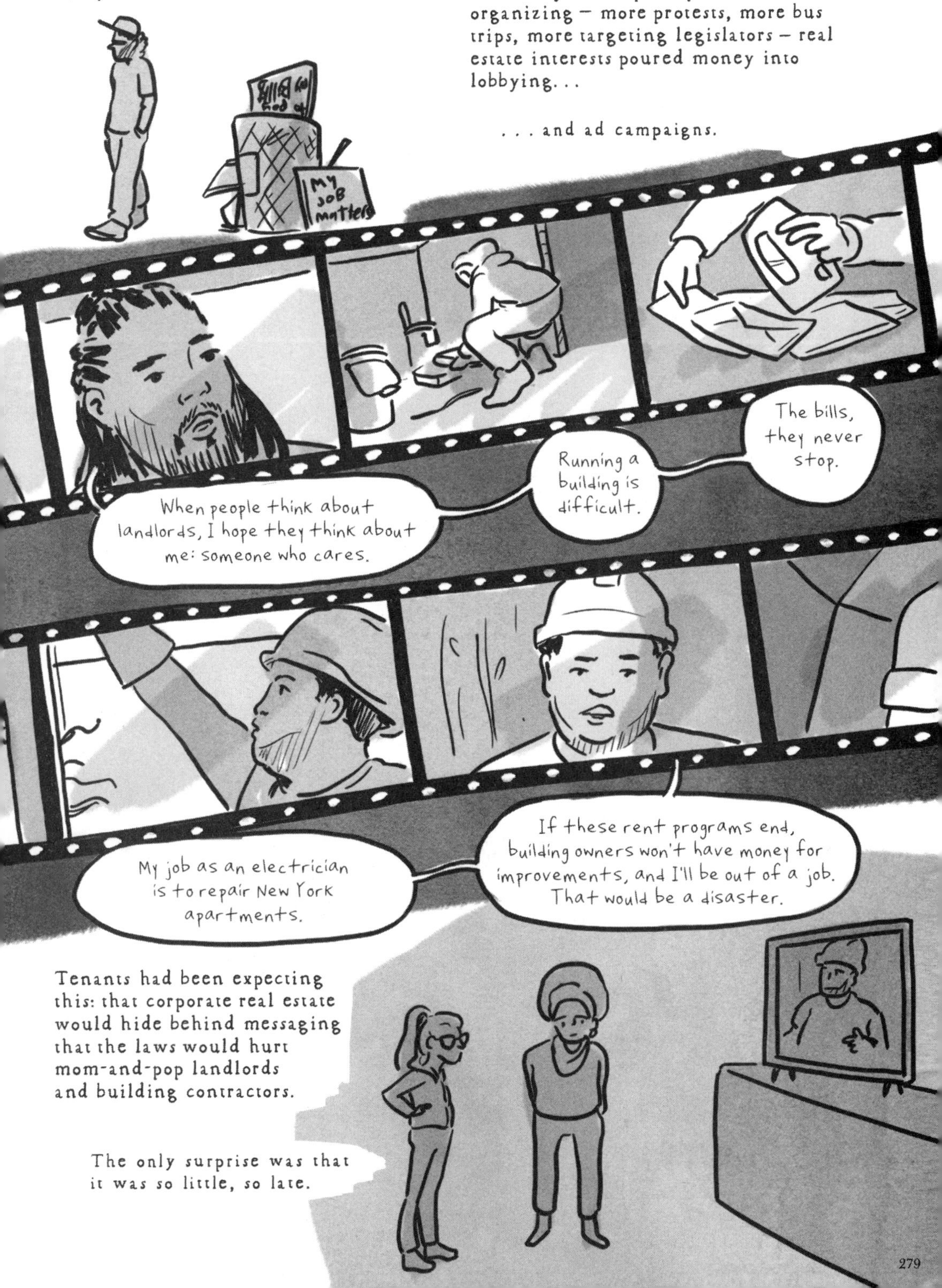
MY JOB MATTERS
When people think about landlords, I hope they think about me: someone who cares.
Running a building is difficult.
The bills, they never stop.
My job as an electrician is to repair New York apartments.
If these rent programs end, building owners won't have money for improvements, and I'll be out of a job. That would be a disaster.

Tenants had been expecting this: that corporate real estate would hide behind messaging that the laws would hurt mom-and-pop landlords and building contractors.

The only surprise was that it was so little, so late.

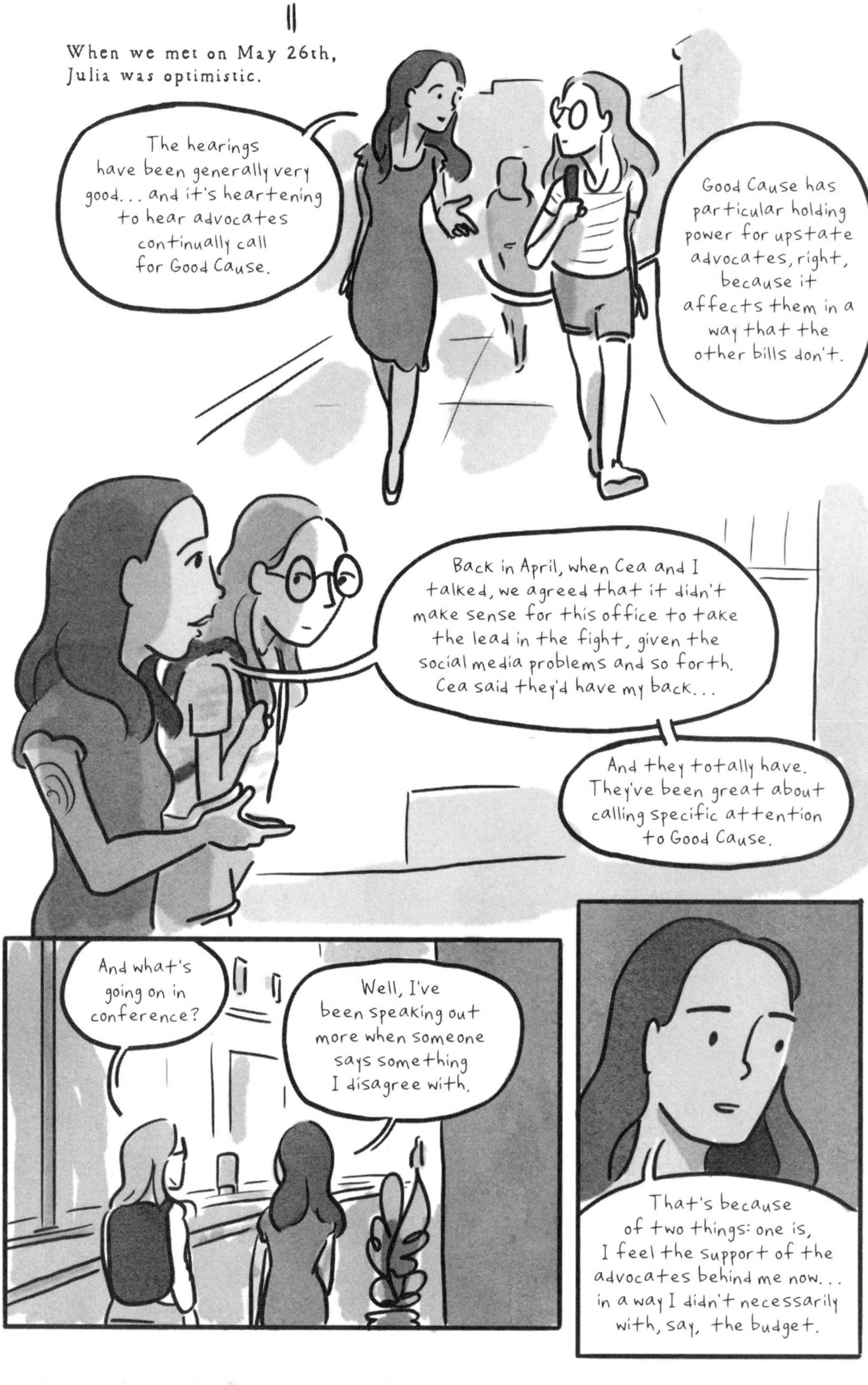
||
When we met on May 26th, Julia was optimistic.
The hearings have been generally very good... and it's heartening to hear advocates continually call for Good Cause.
Good Cause has particular holding power for upstate advocates, right, because it affects them in a way that the other bills don't.
Back in April, when Cea and I talked, we agreed that it didn't make sense for this office to take the lead in the fight, given the social media problems and so forth. Cea said they'd have my back...
And they totally have. They've been great about calling specific attention to Good Cause.
And what's going on in conference?
Well, I've been speaking out more when someone says something I disagree with.
That's because of two things: one is, I feel the support of the advocates behind me now... in a way I didn't necessarily with, say, the budget.

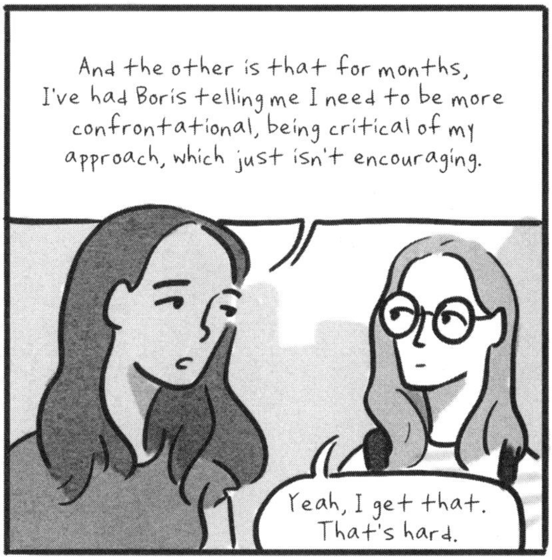
And the other is that for months, I've had Boris telling me I need to be more confrontational, being critical of my approach, which just isn't encouraging.
Yeah, I get that. That's hard.

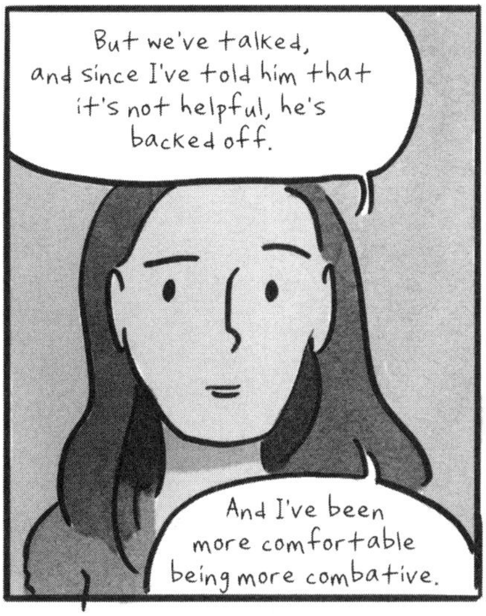
But we've talked, and since I've told him that it's not helpful, he's backed off.
And I've been more comfortable being more combative.

Speaking of combative: as the days wore on and the Senate still had yet to put out a public statement, the tenants were growing restless. They were still reluctant to target Andrea Stewart-Cousins specifically, but they were ramping up their actions on legislators.

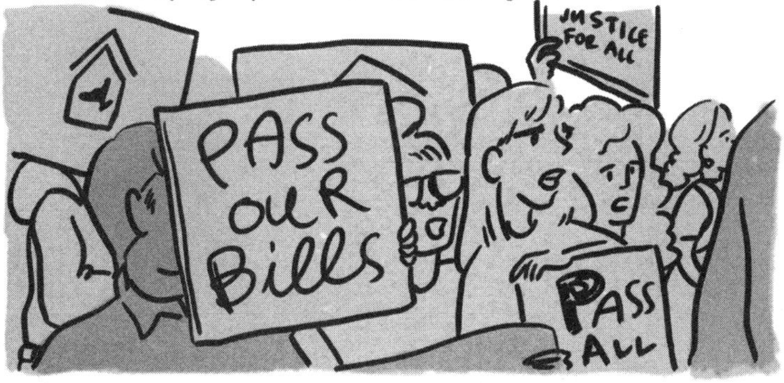
JUSTICE FOR ALL
PASS OUR BILLS
PASS ALL

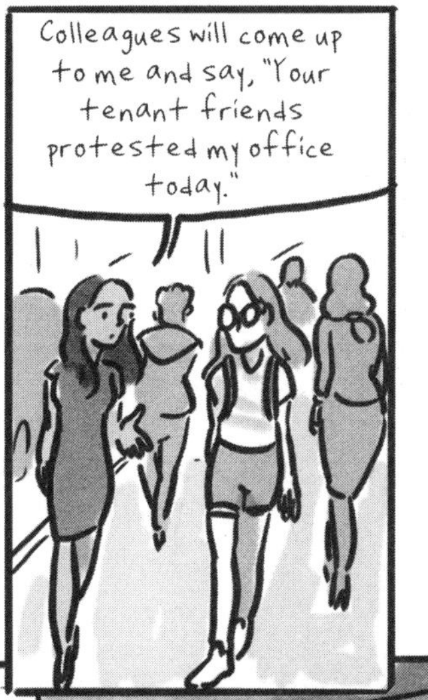
Colleagues will come up to me and say, "Your tenant friends protested my office today."

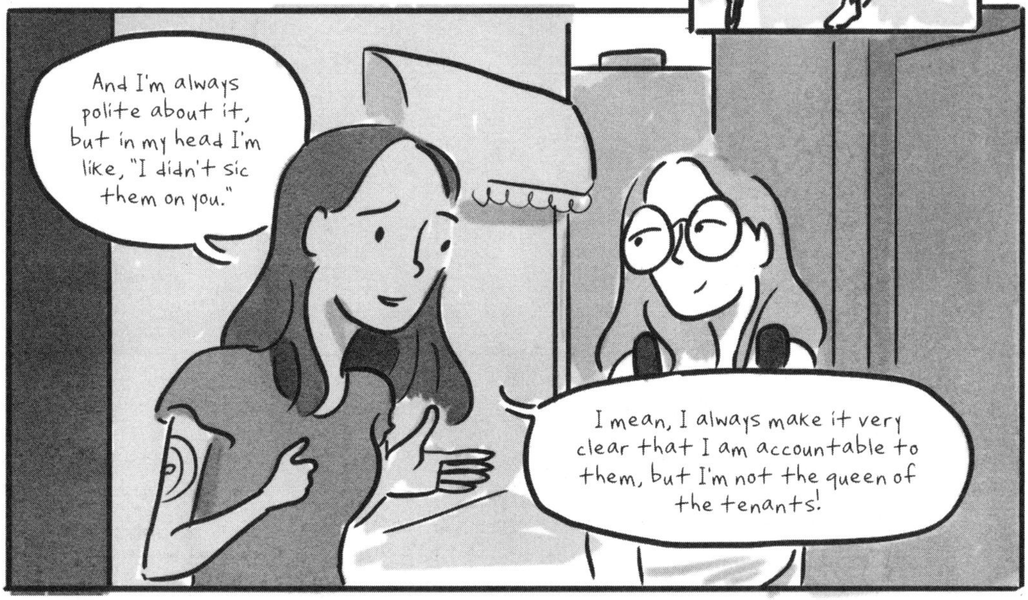
And I'm always polite about it, but in my head I'm like, "I didn't sic them on you."
I mean, I always make it very clear that I am accountable to them, but I'm not the queen of the tenants!

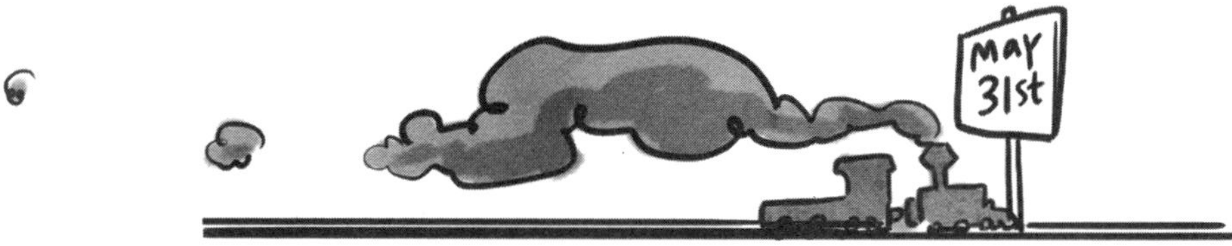
May 31st

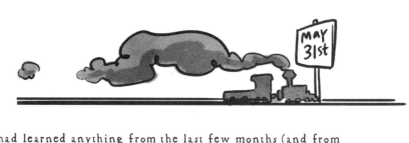

If I had learned anything from the last few months (and from growing up with hens, but that's another story), it was to not count chickens before they hatched. Sure enough, a few days later, in the new temporary office:

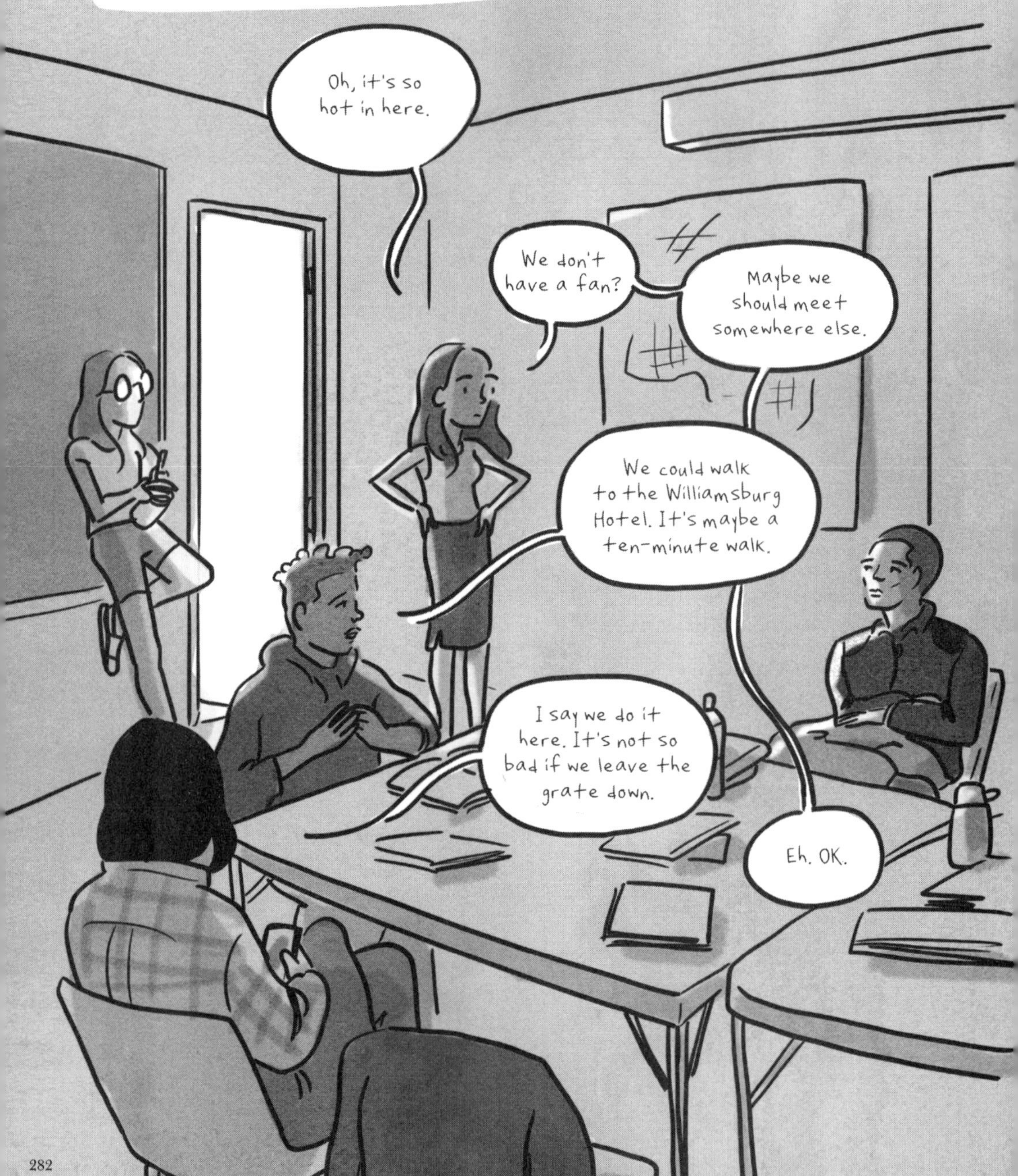
Oh, it's so hot in here.
We don't have a fan?
Maybe we should meet somewhere else.
We could walk to the Williamsburg Hotel. It's maybe a ten-minute walk.
I say we do it here. It's not so bad if we leave the grate down.
Eh. OK.

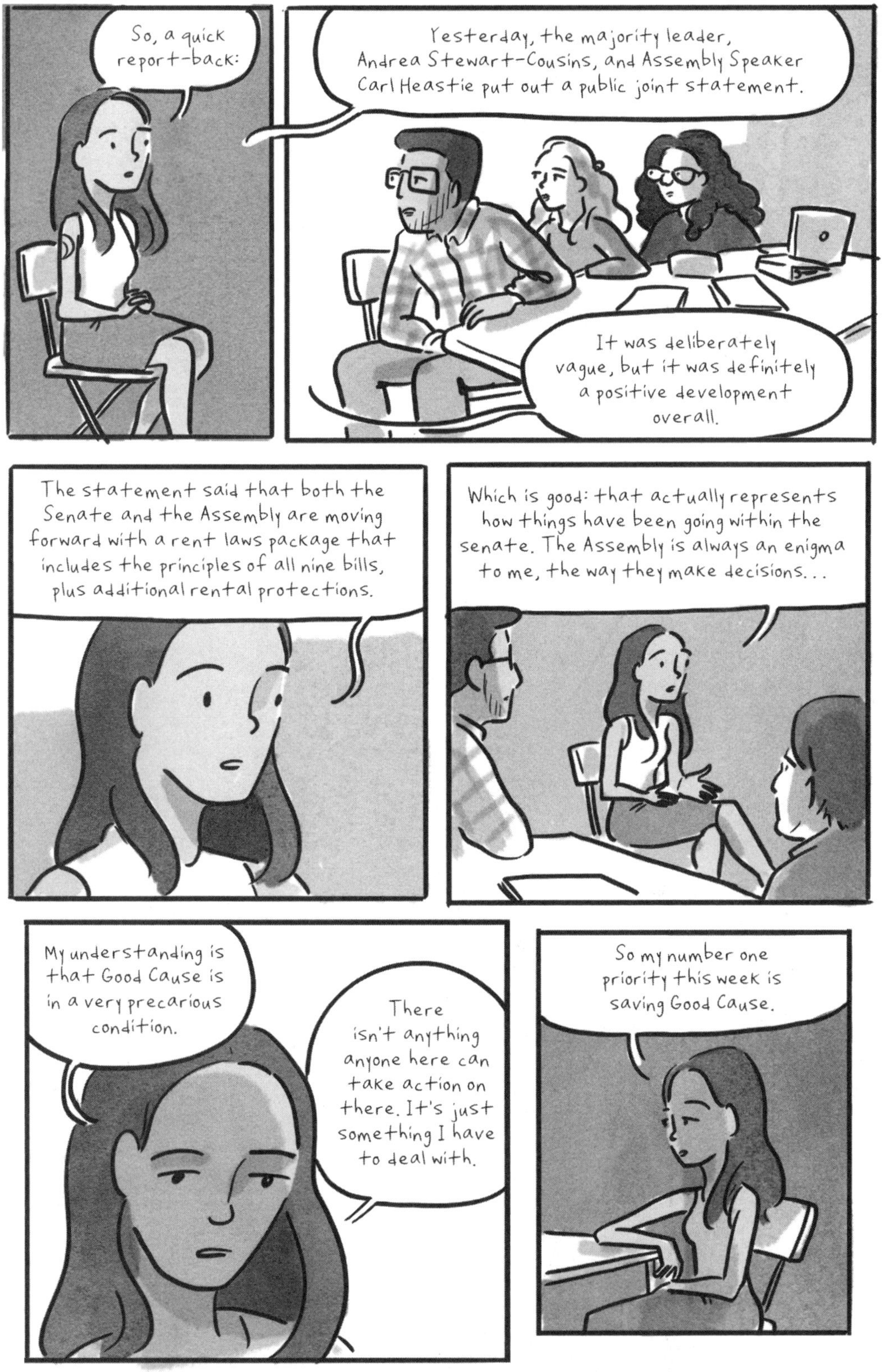
So, a quick report-back:
Yesterday, the majority leader, Andrea Stewart-Cousins, and Assembly Speaker Carl Heastie put out a public joint statement.
It was deliberately vague, but it was definitely a positive development overall.
The statement said that both the Senate and the Assembly are moving forward with a rent laws package that includes the principles of all nine bills, plus additional rental protections.
Which is good: that actually represents how things have been going within the senate. The Assembly is always an enigma to me, the way they make decisions...
My understanding is that Good Cause is in a very precarious condition.
There isn't anything anyone here can take action on there. It's just something I have to deal with.
So my number one priority this week is saving Good Cause.

So this was it: this was the end-game.

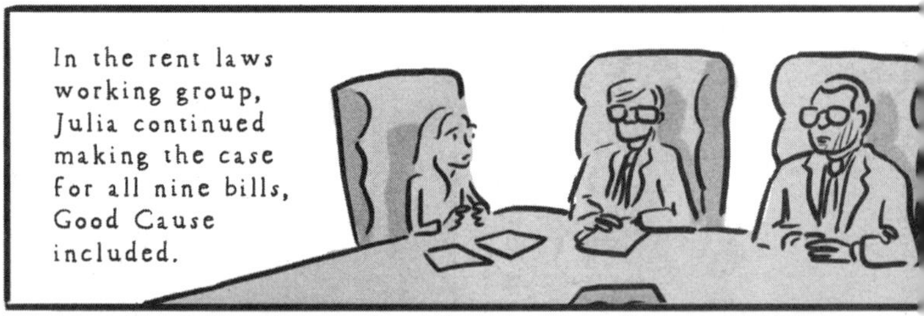
In the rent laws working group, Julia continued making the case for all nine bills, Good Cause included.

And on the outside:

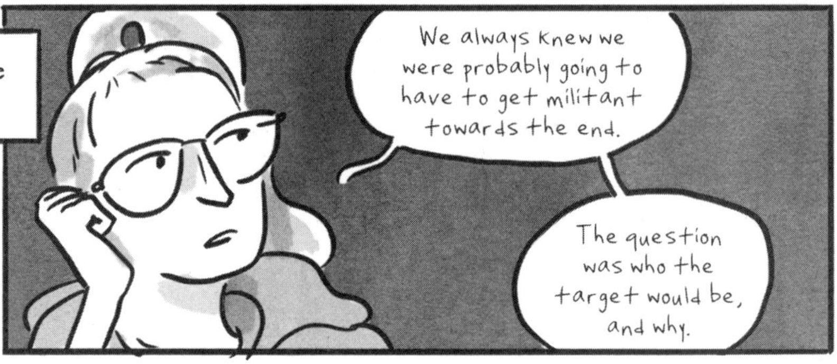
We always knew we were probably going to have to get militant towards the end.
The question was who the target would be, and why.

Why? The Good Cause bill.

Who? That was a bit trickier.

The most efficient thing to do would be to put pressure on the Senate to come out publicly for all nine bills already.

Because that would put pressure on the Assembly to add Good Cause to their platform. . .

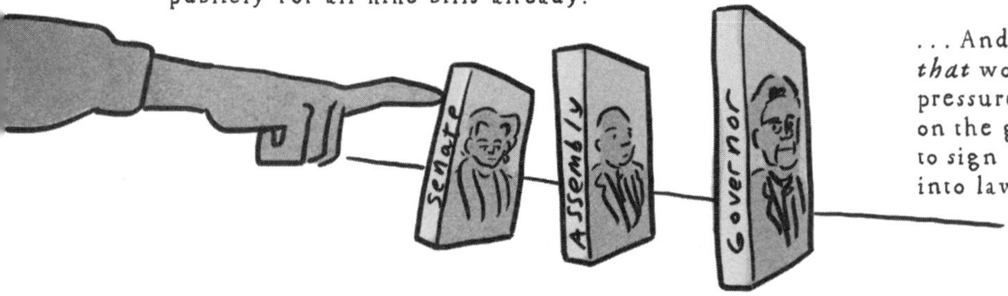
Senate
Assembly
Governor

. . . And *that* would put pressure on the governor to sign it all into law.

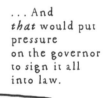

But they were still hearing that targeting Andrea Stewart-Cousins in the Senate would be counter-productive, because she was on their side.

So Housing Justice for All came up with a compromise. They would target Andrea Stewart-Cousins. . .

. . . But they would *also* target the Assembly and the governor.

An escalation, but spread out.

So on June 4th. . .

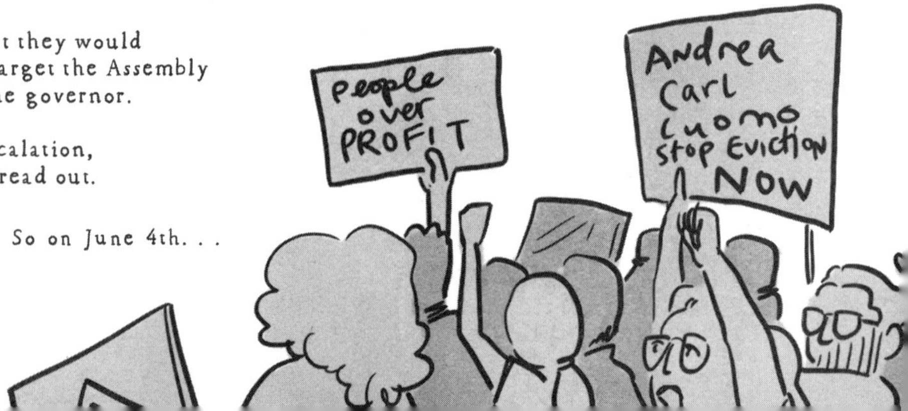
people over PROFIT
Andrea Carl Cuomo stop Eviction NOW

WHICH SIDE ARE YOU ON?
Landlords
Tenants
HOUSING JUSTICE
Assembly
Senate
HOUSING JUSTICE FOR ALL
HOUSING JUSTICE FOR ALL
Governor's Office

Tenants blocked the entry to both chambers and the executive office. It was chaotic: lobbyists were stepping over them, and sometimes on them. Things got physical. People got arrested.

It worked. Immediately after:

Statement From Senate Majority Leader Andrea Stewart-Cousins On Housing Legislation

ANDREA STEWART-COUSINS June 04, 2019 | ISSUE: HOUSING REGULATION

"Following a long discussion within the Senate Majority Conference, it is clear that we have support for all nine priority housing bills. We have 11 days remaining before current rent regulations expire, and we will use that time to advance this legislation. We have committed to providing New Yorkers with the strongest housing protections in state history."

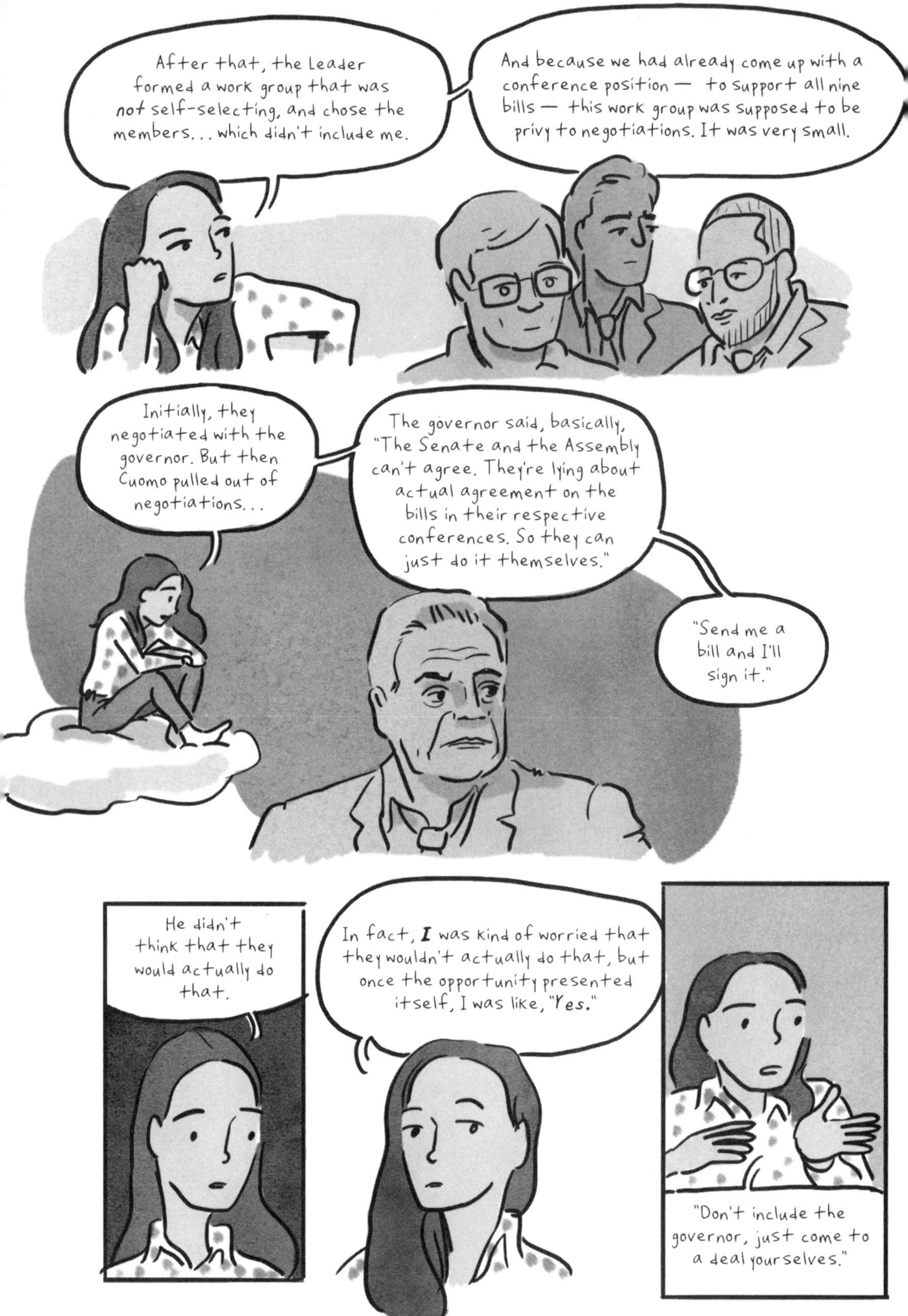
After that, the leader formed a work group that was not self-selecting, and chose the members... which didn't include me.
And because we had already come up with a conference position — to support all nine bills — this work group was supposed to be privy to negotiations. It was very small.
Initially, they negotiated with the governor. But then Cuomo pulled out of negotiations...
The governor said, basically, "The Senate and the Assembly can't agree. They're lying about actual agreement on the bills in their respective conferences. So they can just do it themselves."
"Send me a bill and I'll sign it."
He didn't think that they would actually do that.
In fact, *I* was kind of worried that they wouldn't actually do that, but once the opportunity presented itself, I was like, "*Yes.*"
"Don't include the governor, just come to a deal yourselves."

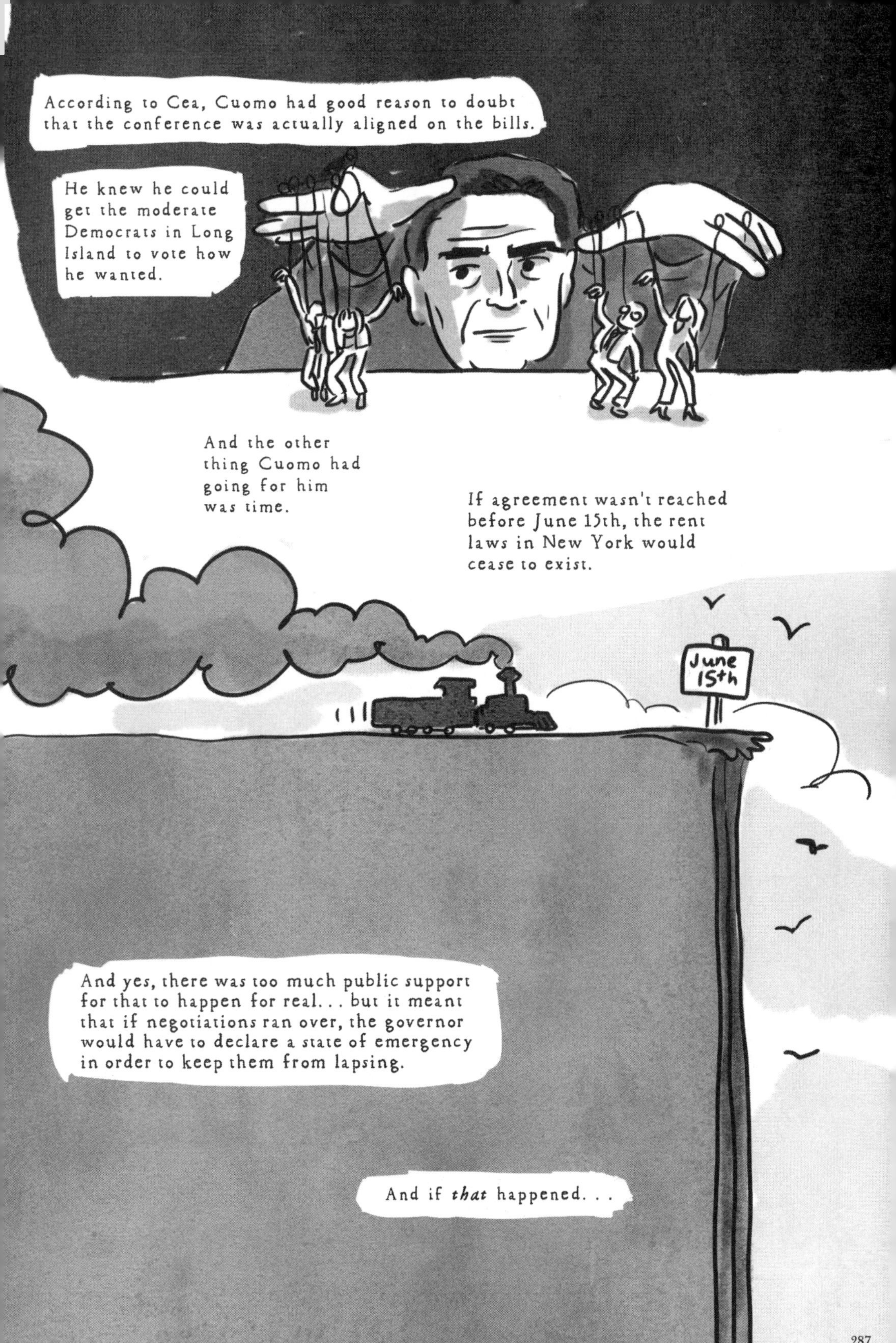
According to Cea, Cuomo had good reason to doubt that the conference was actually aligned on the bills.
He knew he could get the moderate Democrats in Long Island to vote how he wanted.
And the other thing Cuomo had going for him was time.
If agreement wasn't reached before June 15th, the rent laws in New York would cease to exist.
June 15th
And yes, there was too much public support for that to happen for real. . . but it meant that if negotiations ran over, the governor would have to declare a state of emergency in order to keep them from lapsing.
And if *that* happened. . .

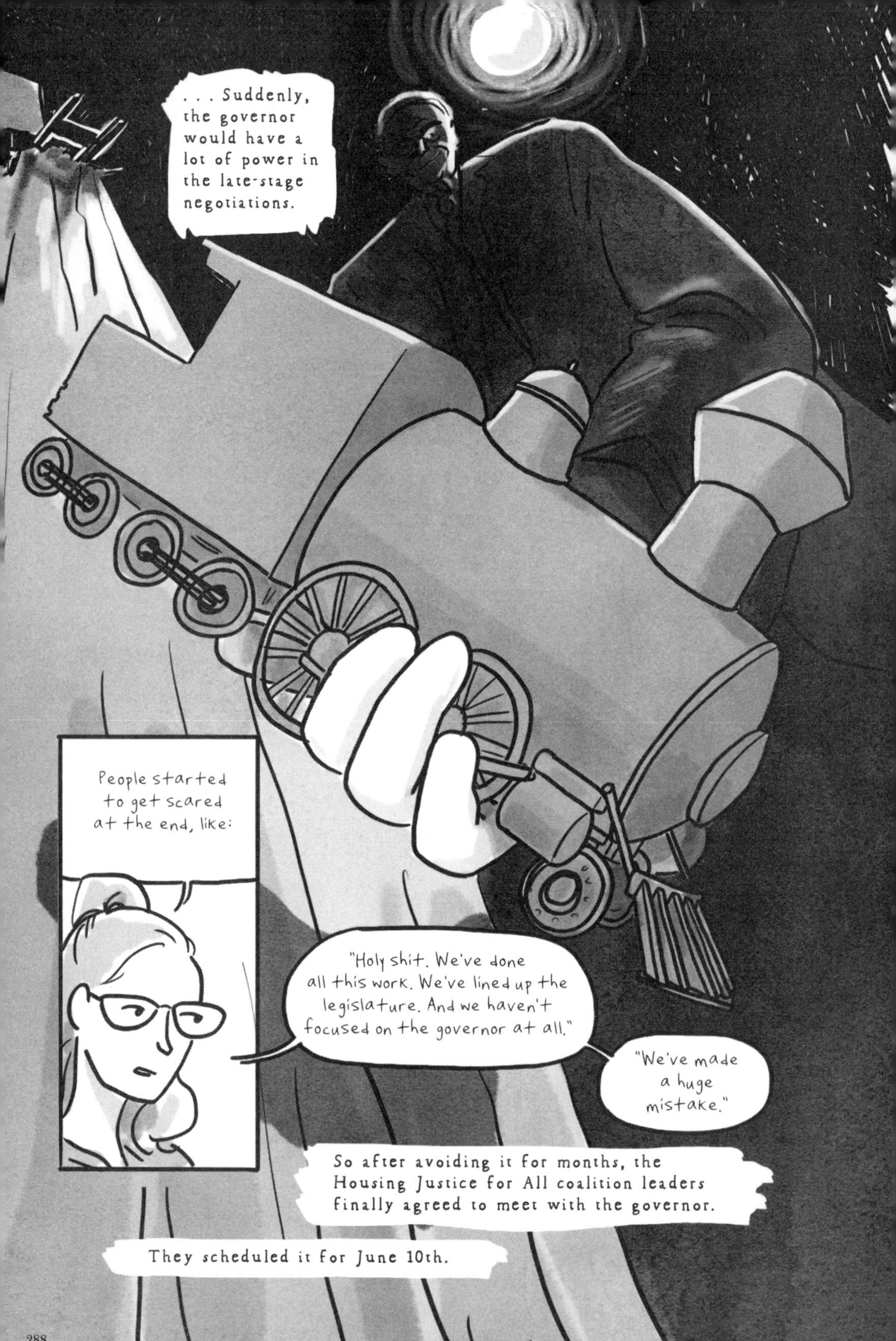
. . . Suddenly, the governor would have a lot of power in the late-stage negotiations.
People started to get scared at the end, like:
"Holy shit. We've done all this work. We've lined up the legislature. And we haven't focused on the governor at all."
"We've made a huge mistake."
So after avoiding it for months, the Housing Justice for All coalition leaders finally agreed to meet with the governor.
They scheduled it for June 10th.

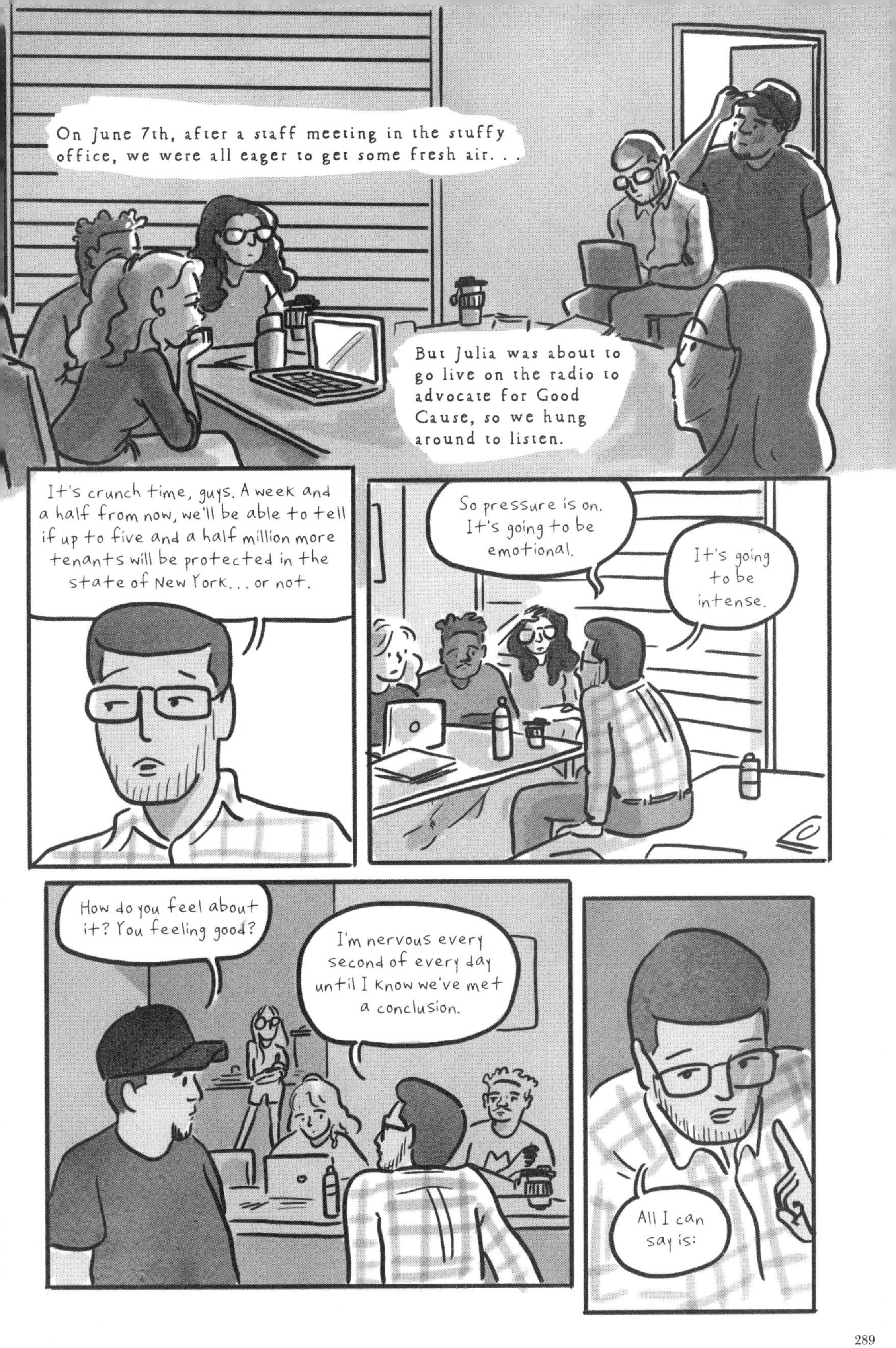
On June 7th, after a staff meeting in the stuffy office, we were all eager to get some fresh air. . .
But Julia was about to go live on the radio to advocate for Good Cause, so we hung around to listen.
It's crunch time, guys. A week and a half from now, we'll be able to tell if up to five and a half million more tenants will be protected in the state of New York. . . or not.
So pressure is on. It's going to be emotional.
It's going to be intense.
How do you feel about it? You feeling good?
I'm nervous every second of every day until I know we've met a conclusion.
All I can say is:

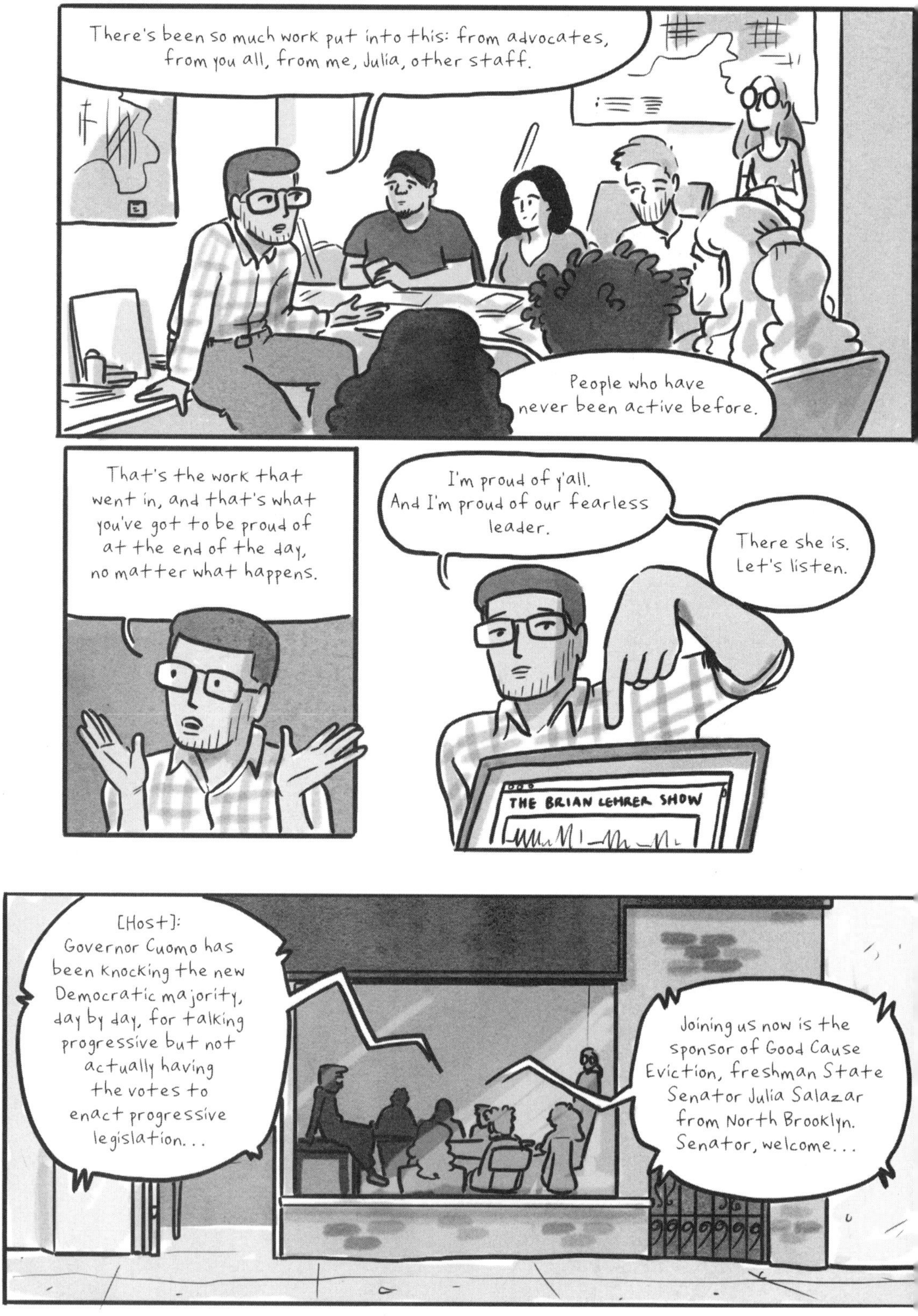
There's been so much work put into this: from advocates, from you all, from me, Julia, other staff.
People who have never been active before.
That's the work that went in, and that's what you've got to be proud of at the end of the day, no matter what happens.
I'm proud of y'all. And I'm proud of our fearless leader.
There she is. Let's listen.
THE BRIAN LEHRER SHOW
[Host]: Governor Cuomo has been knocking the new Democratic majority, day by day, for talking progressive but not actually having the votes to enact progressive legislation...
Joining us now is the sponsor of Good Cause Eviction, freshman State Senator Julia Salazar from North Brooklyn. Senator, welcome...

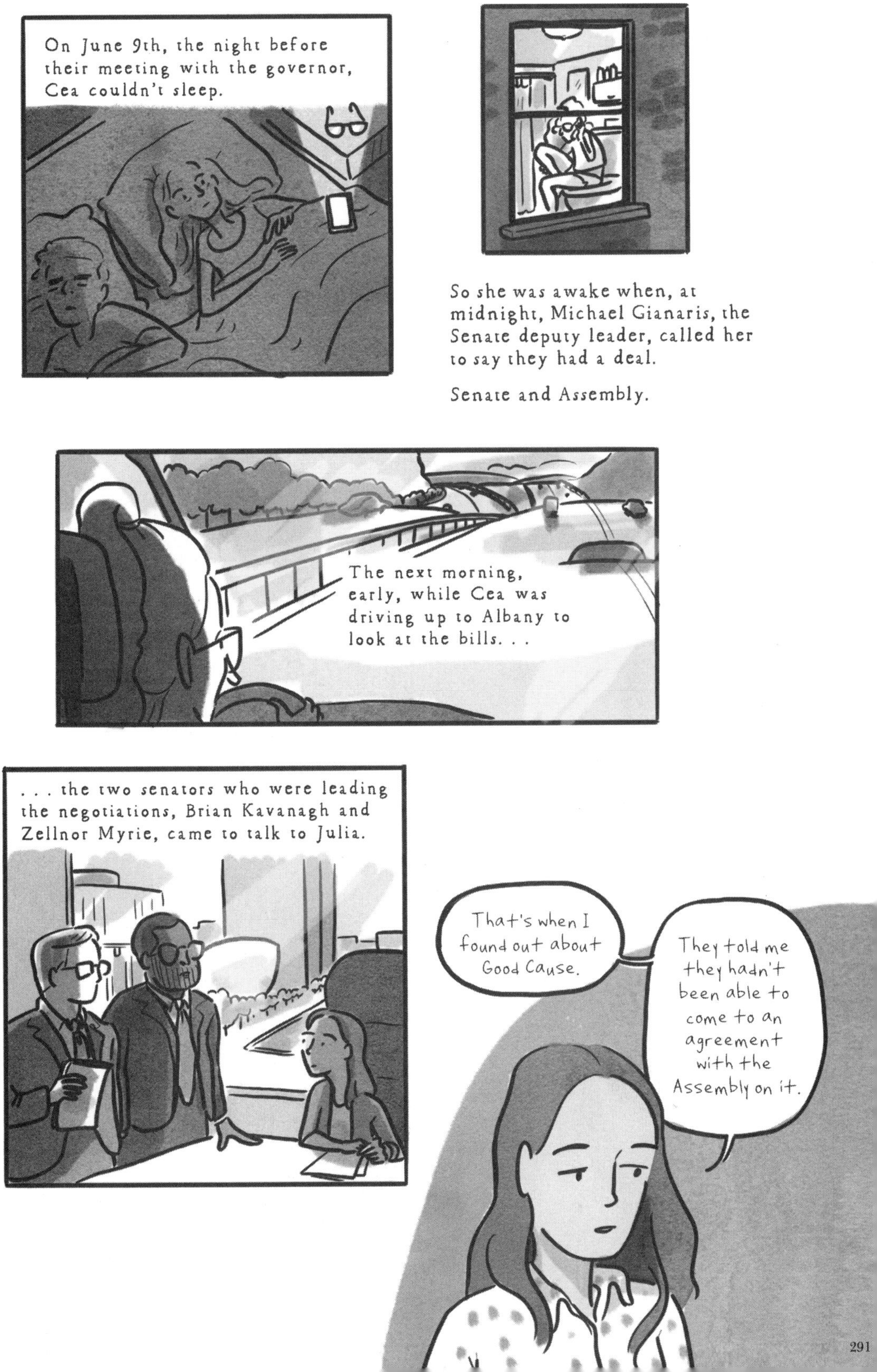
On June 9th, the night before their meeting with the governor, Cea couldn't sleep.
So she was awake when, at midnight, Michael Gianaris, the Senate deputy leader, called her to say they had a deal.
Senate and Assembly.
The next morning, early, while Cea was driving up to Albany to look at the bills. . .
. . . the two senators who were leading the negotiations, Brian Kavanagh and Zellnor Myrie, came to talk to Julia.
That's when I found out about Good Cause.
They told me they hadn't been able to come to an agreement with the Assembly on it.

No Good
Cause.

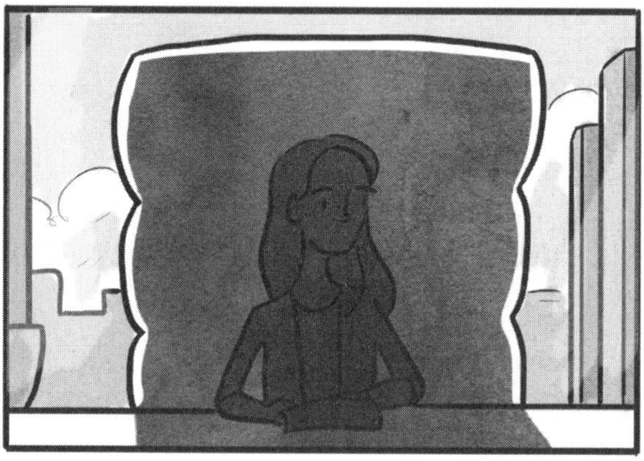

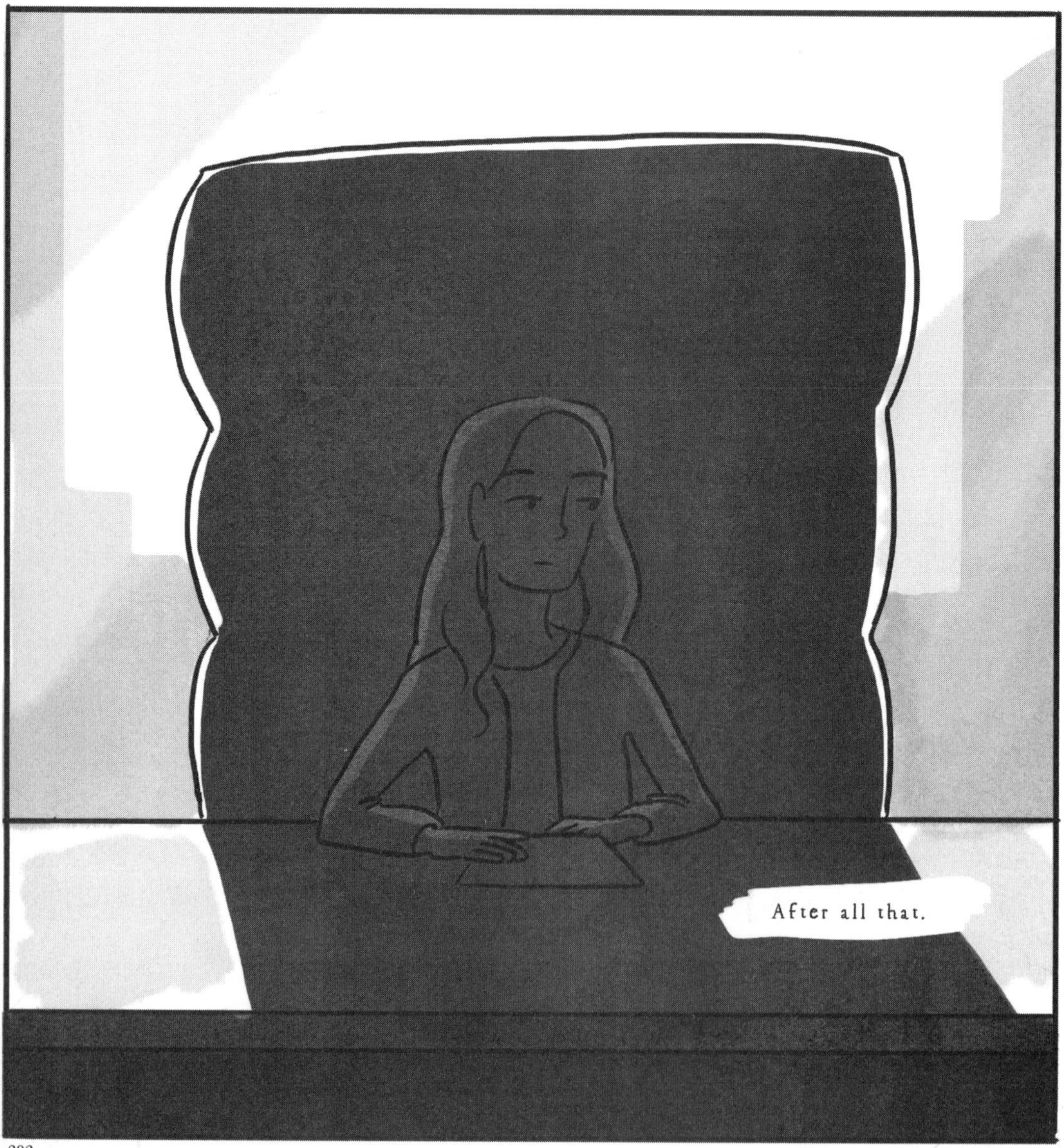
After all that.

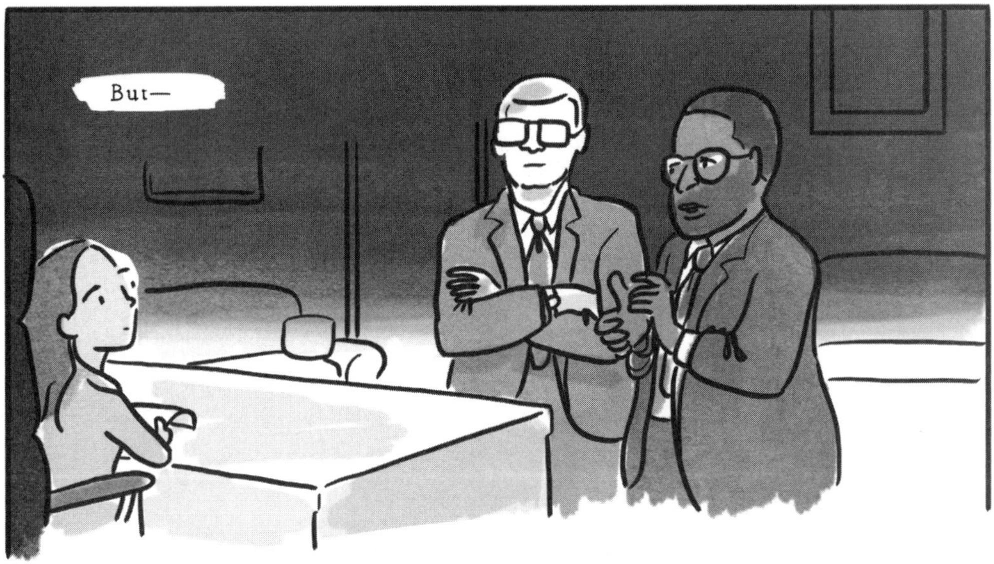
But—

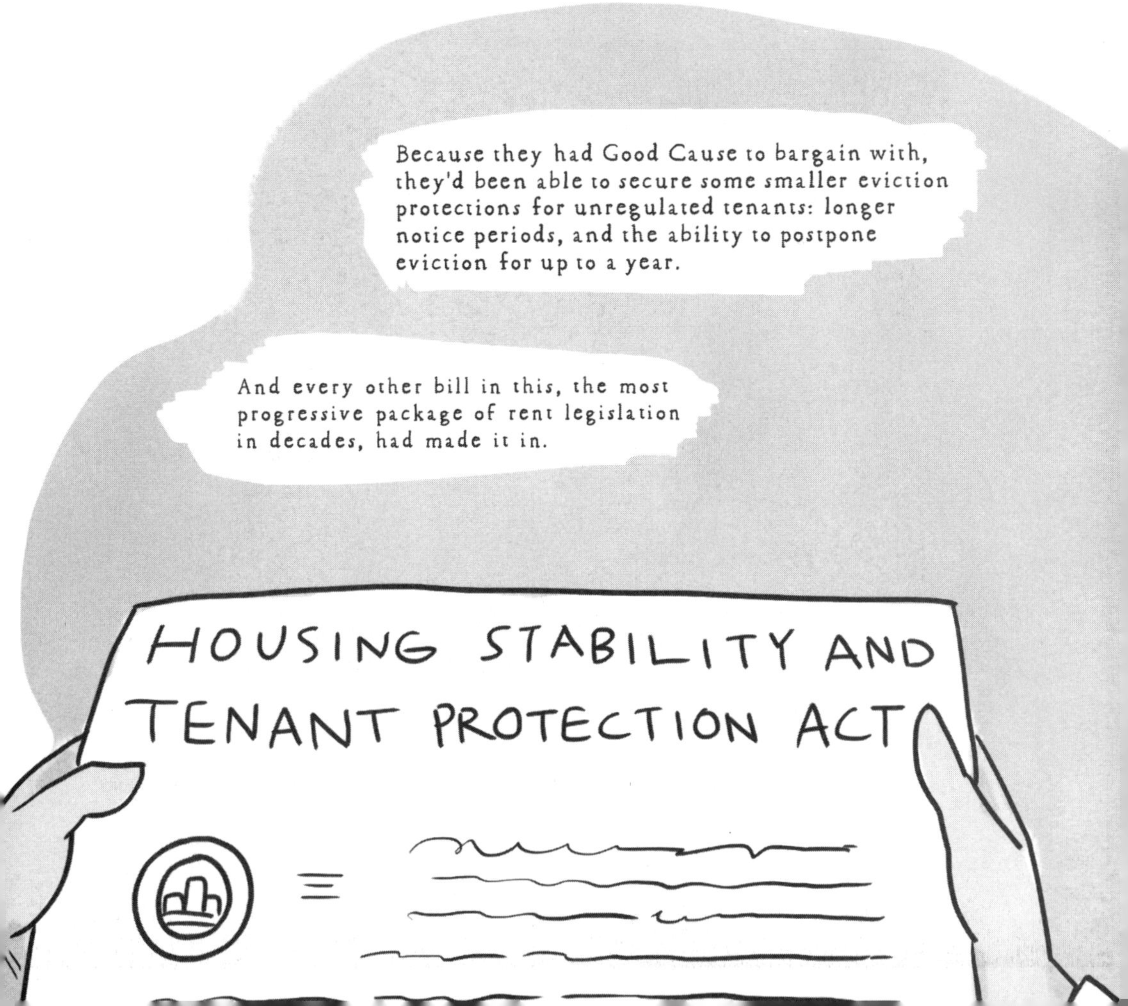
Because they had Good Cause to bargain with, they'd been able to secure some smaller eviction protections for unregulated tenants: longer notice periods, and the ability to postpone eviction for up to a year.
And every other bill in this, the most progressive package of rent legislation in decades, had made it in.
HOUSING STABILITY AND TENANT PROTECTION ACT

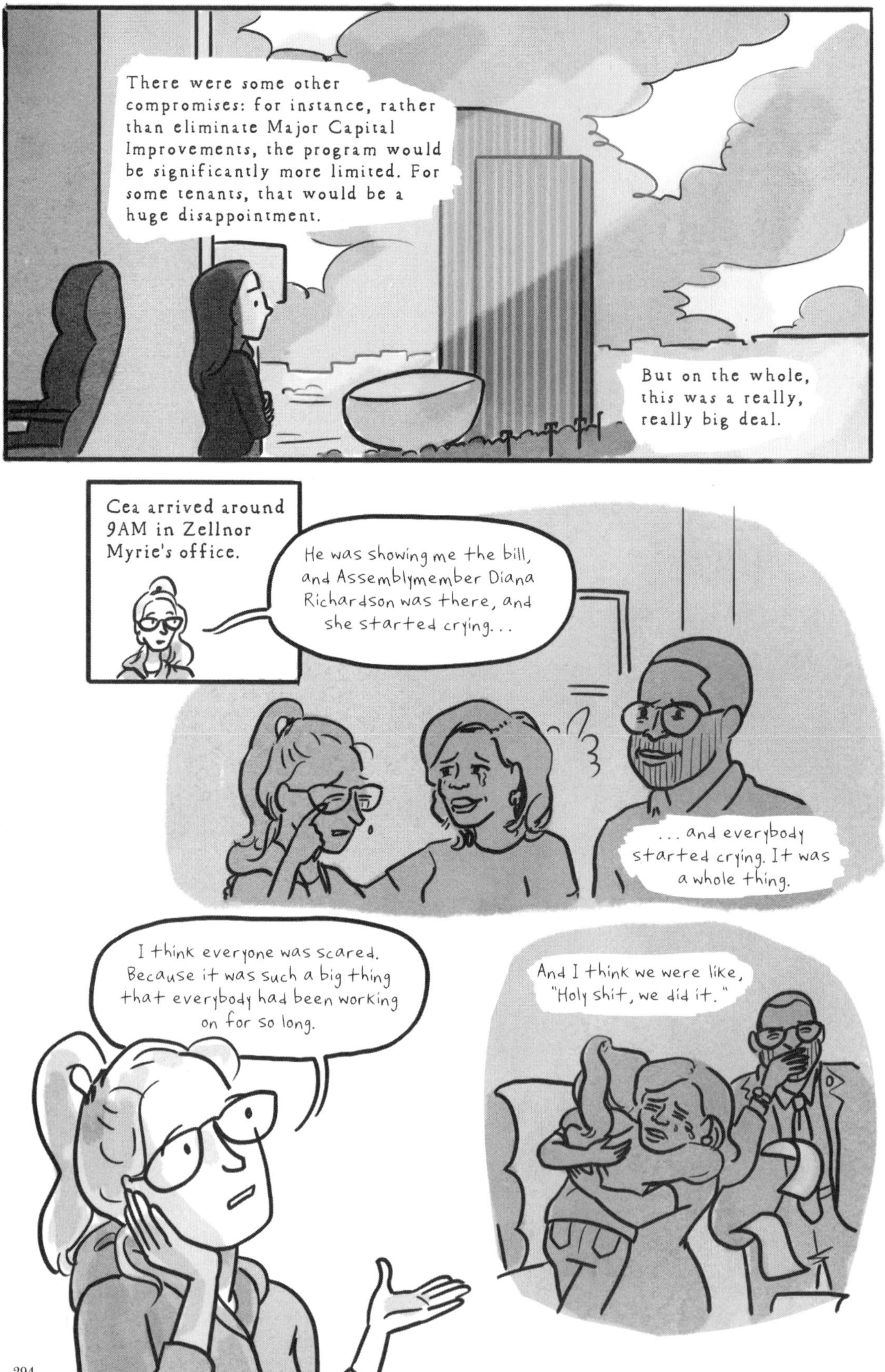
There were some other compromises: for instance, rather than eliminate Major Capital Improvements, the program would be significantly more limited. For some tenants, that would be a huge disappointment.
But on the whole, this was a really, really big deal.
Cea arrived around 9AM in Zellnor Myrie's office.
He was showing me the bill, and Assemblymember Diana Richardson was there, and she started crying...
...and everybody started crying. It was a whole thing.
I think everyone was scared. Because it was such a big thing that everybody had been working on for so long.
And I think we were like, "Holy shit, we did it."

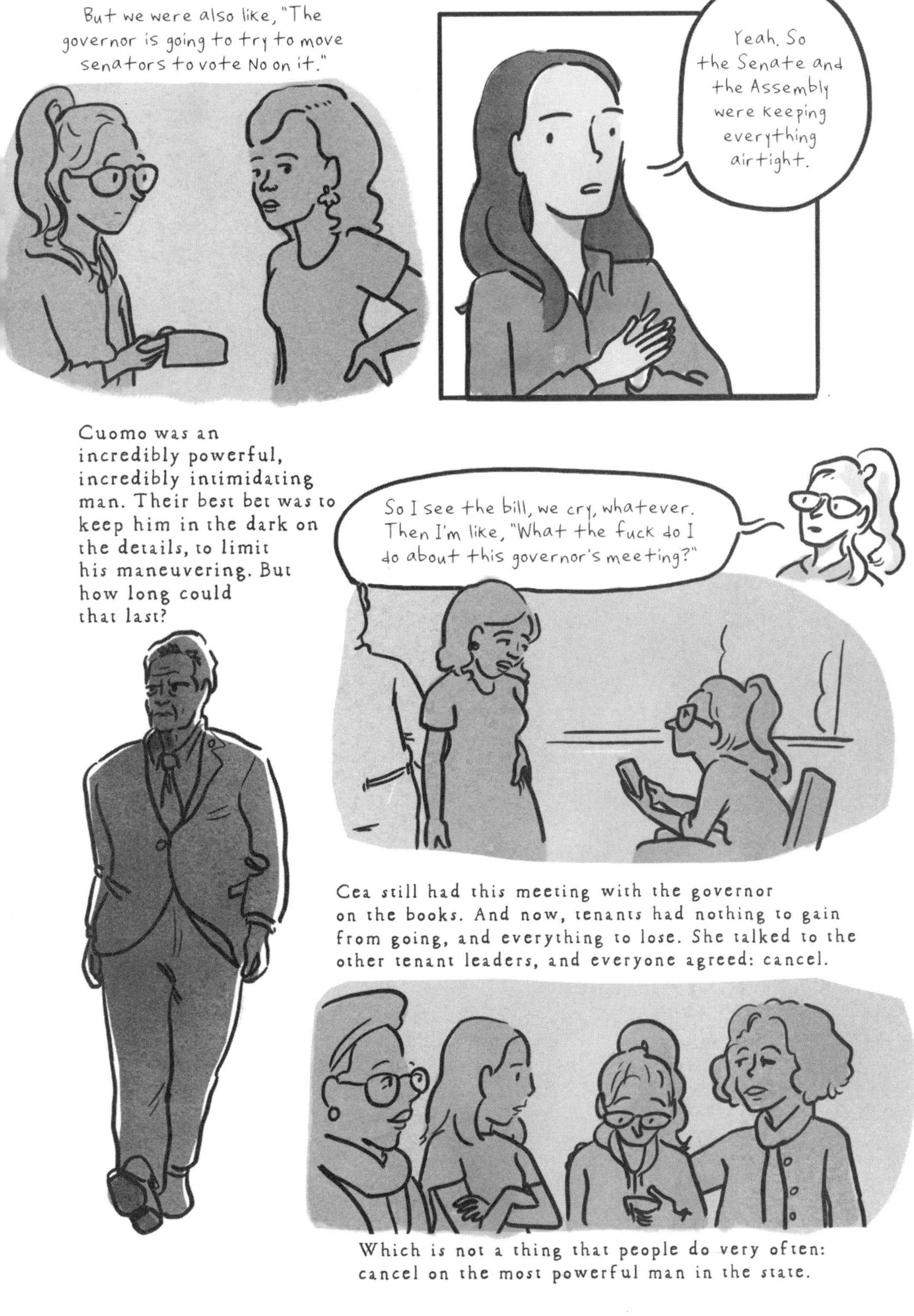
But we were also like, "The governor is going to try to move senators to vote No on it."
Yeah. So the Senate and the Assembly were keeping everything airtight.
Cuomo was an incredibly powerful, incredibly intimidating man. Their best bet was to keep him in the dark on the details, to limit his maneuvering. But how long could that last?
So I see the bill, we cry, whatever. Then I'm like, "What the fuck do I do about this governor's meeting?"
Cea still had this meeting with the governor on the books. And now, tenants had nothing to gain from going, and everything to lose. She talked to the other tenant leaders, and everyone agreed: cancel.
Which is not a thing that people do very often: cancel on the most powerful man in the state.

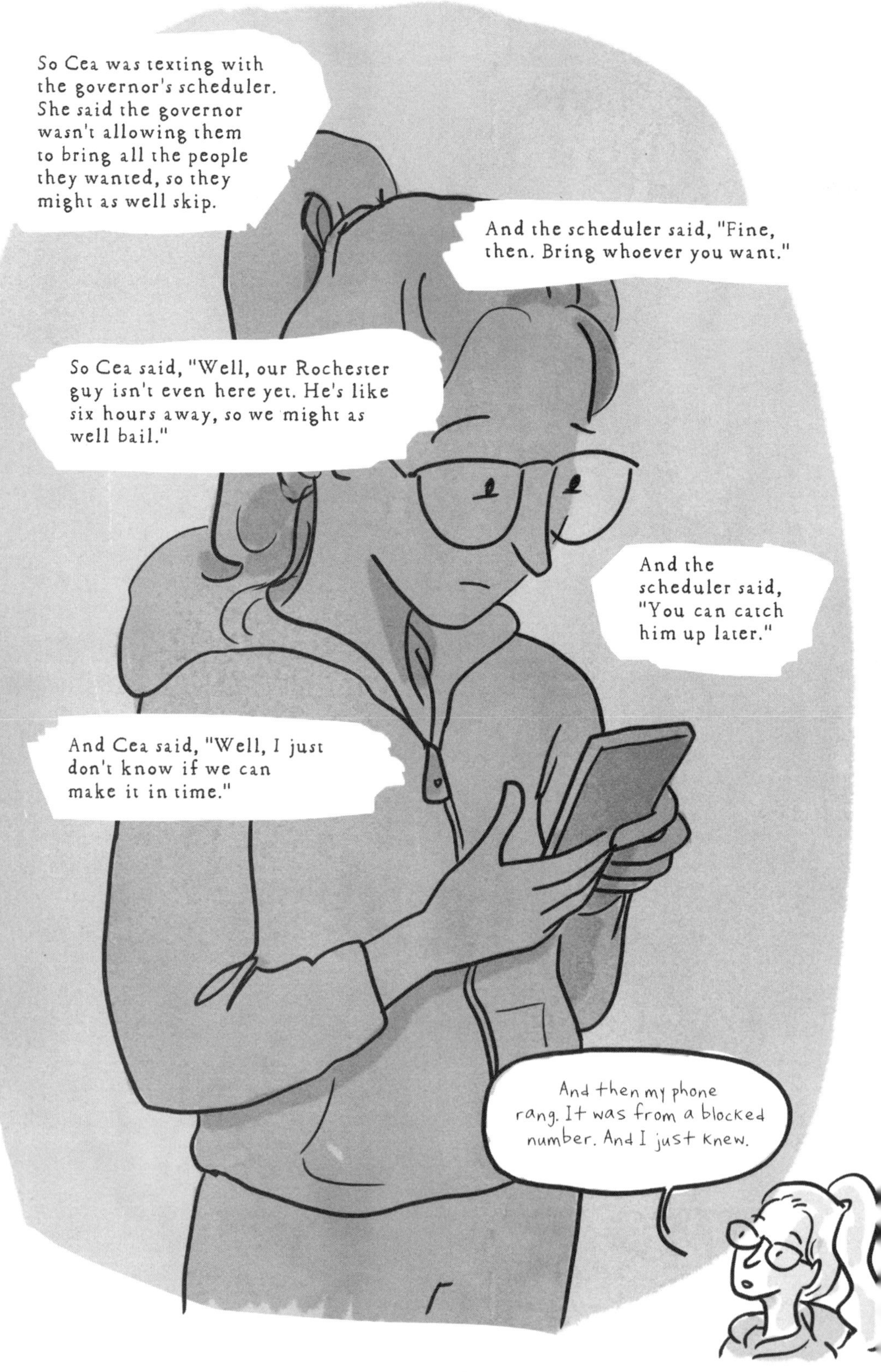
So Cea was texting with the governor's scheduler. She said the governor wasn't allowing them to bring all the people they wanted, so they might as well skip.
And the scheduler said, "Fine, then. Bring whoever you want."
So Cea said, "Well, our Rochester guy isn't even here yet. He's like six hours away, so we might as well bail."
And the scheduler said, "You can catch him up later."
And Cea said, "Well, I just don't know if we can make it in time."
And then my phone rang. It was from a blocked number. And I just knew.

Cea said the conversation went like this:

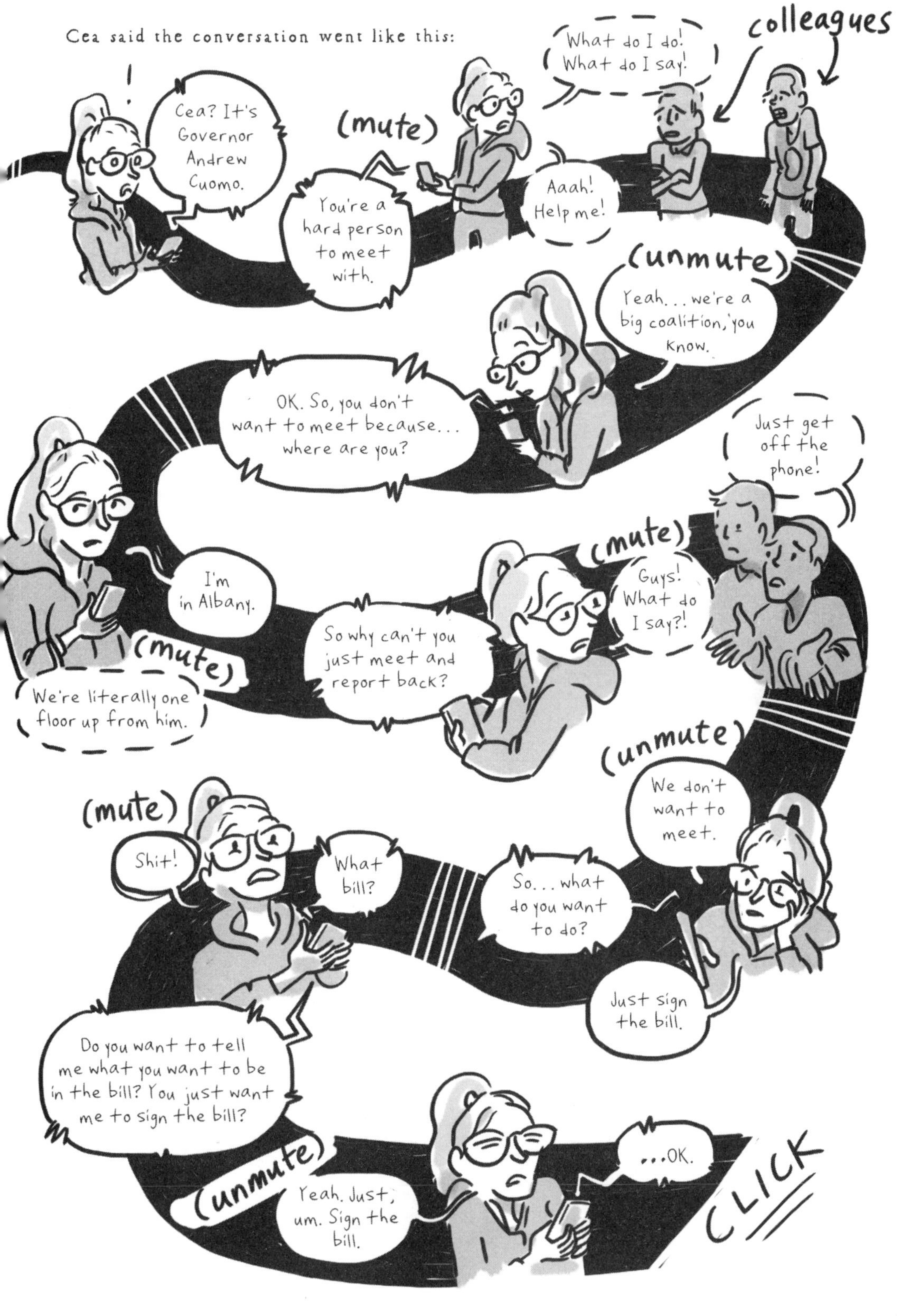

!
Cea? It's Governor Andrew Cuomo.
(mute)
You're a hard person to meet with.
What do I do! What do I say!
colleagues
Aaah! Help me!
(unmute)
Yeah... we're a big coalition, you know.
OK. So, you don't want to meet because... where are you?
I'm in Albany.
(mute)
We're literally one floor up from him.
So why can't you just meet and report back?
(mute)
Guys! What do I say?!
Just get off the phone!
(unmute)
We don't want to meet.
So... what do you want to do?
Just sign the bill.
What bill?
(mute)
Shit!
Do you want to tell me what you want to be in the bill? You just want me to sign the bill?
(unmute)
Yeah. Just, um. Sign the bill.
...OK.
CLICK

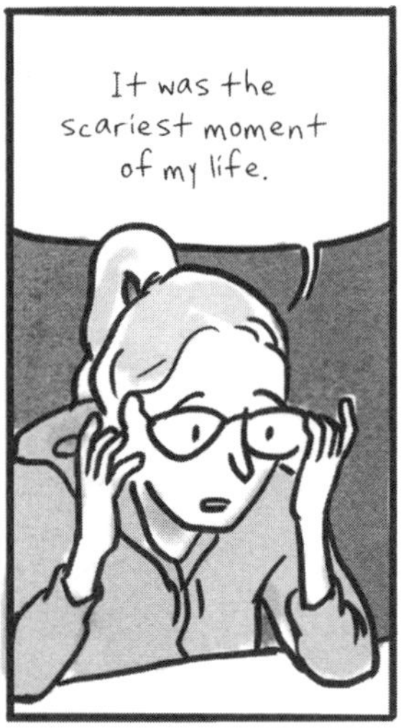
It was the scariest moment of my life.

Cea and the tenants holed up in Julia's conference room. They had to get on a call with tenants all over the state, communicate what was in the bill, and figure out how to respond. . . all without anything leaking out to the press or the governor.

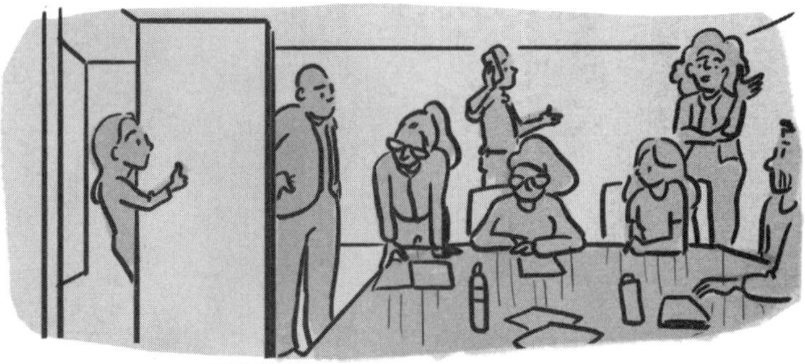

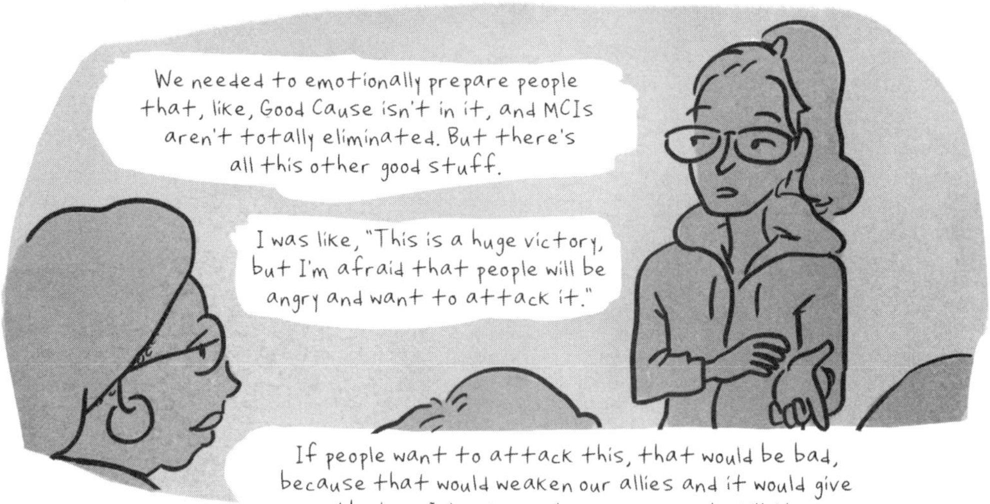
We needed to emotionally prepare people that, like, Good Cause isn't in it, and MCIs aren't totally eliminated. But there's all this other good stuff.
I was like, "This is a huge victory, but I'm afraid that people will be angry and want to attack it."
If people want to attack this, that would be bad, because that would weaken our allies and it would give the Long Island senators a reason to kill it.

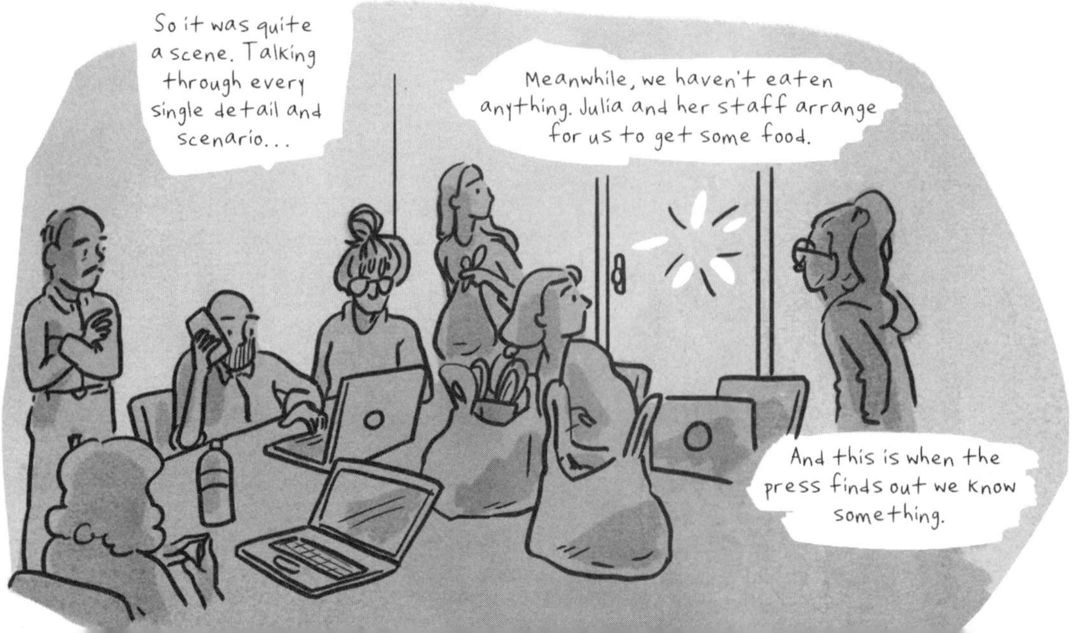
So it was quite a scene. Talking through every single detail and scenario. . .
Meanwhile, we haven't eaten anything. Julia and her staff arrange for us to get some food.
And this is when the press finds out we know something.

. . . All of a sudden, there are twenty reporters outside of Julia's conference room.

We were getting constant press calls. And the pressure to answer the press was pretty big.

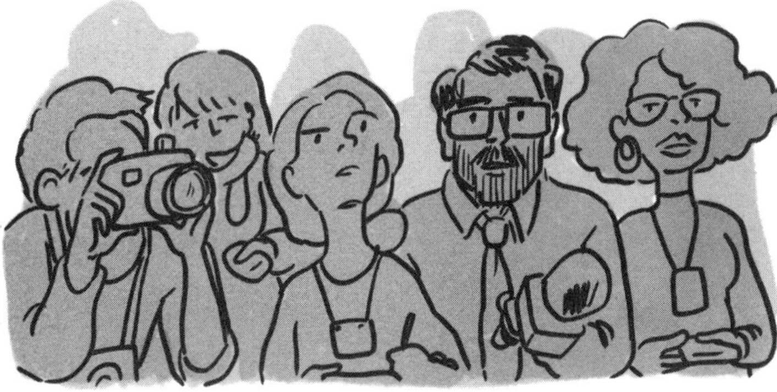

Like, the *New York Times* was like, "We heard there's a deal. What's in it?" They're trying to get the scoop and we just couldn't do it.

Within a couple of hours we finished explaining to our people what's in the bill, and everyone was really happy.

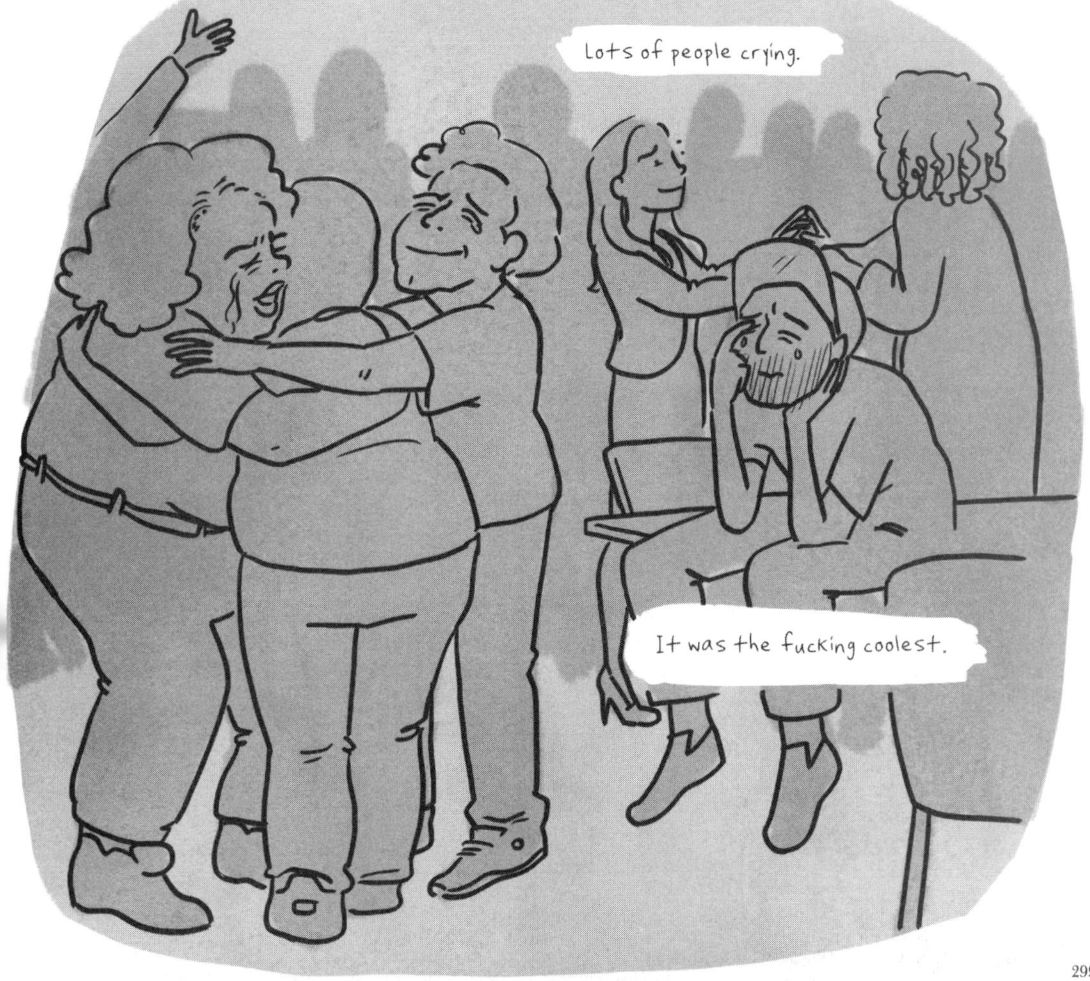
Lots of people crying.
It was the fucking coolest.

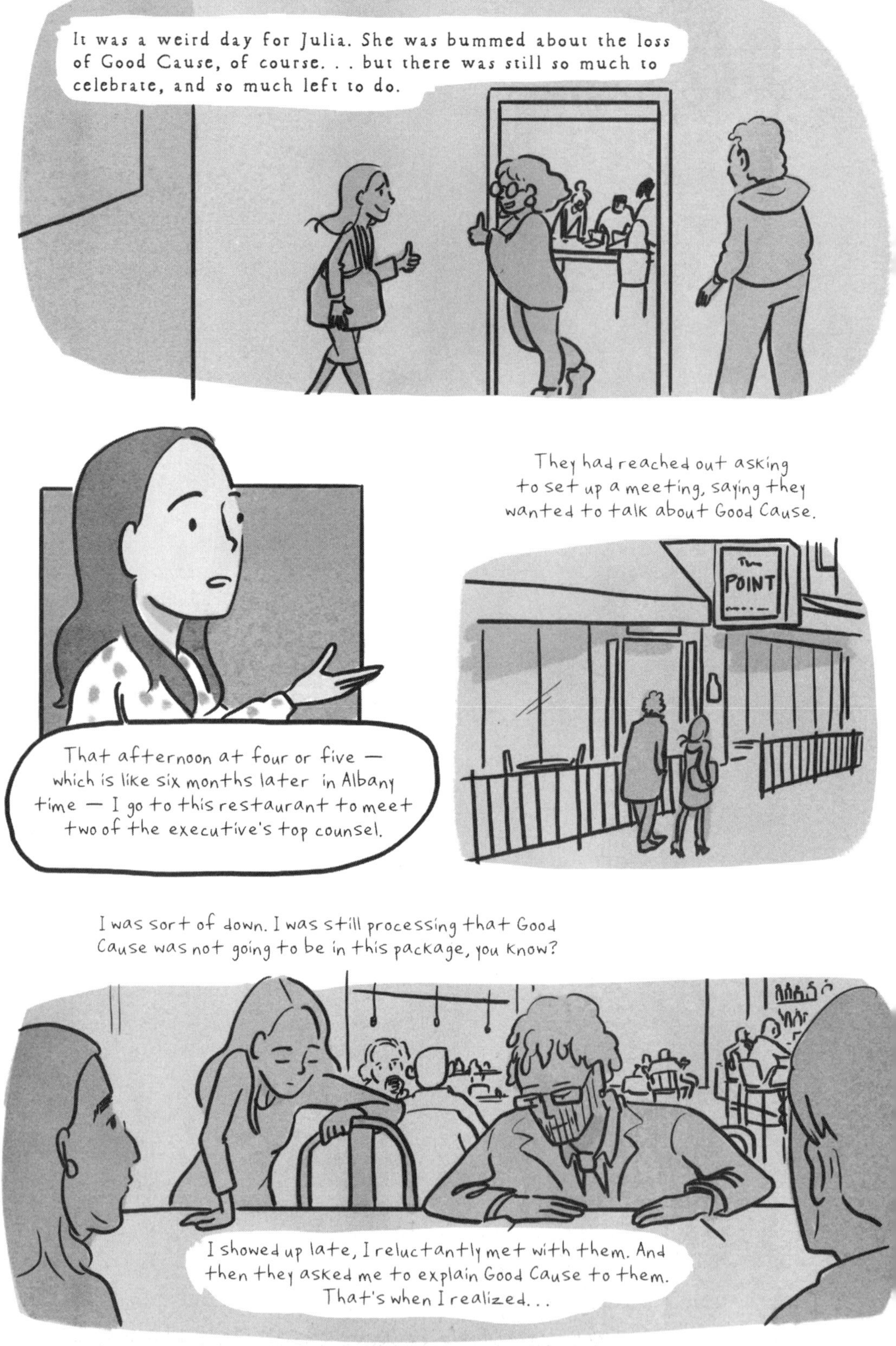
It was a weird day for Julia. She was bummed about the loss of Good Cause, of course. . . but there was still so much to celebrate, and so much left to do.
That afternoon at four or five — which is like six months later in Albany time — I go to this restaurant to meet two of the executive's top counsel.
They had reached out asking to set up a meeting, saying they wanted to talk about Good Cause.
POINT
I was sort of down. I was still processing that Good Cause was not going to be in this package, you know?
I showed up late, I reluctantly met with them. And then they asked me to explain Good Cause to them. That's when I realized. . .

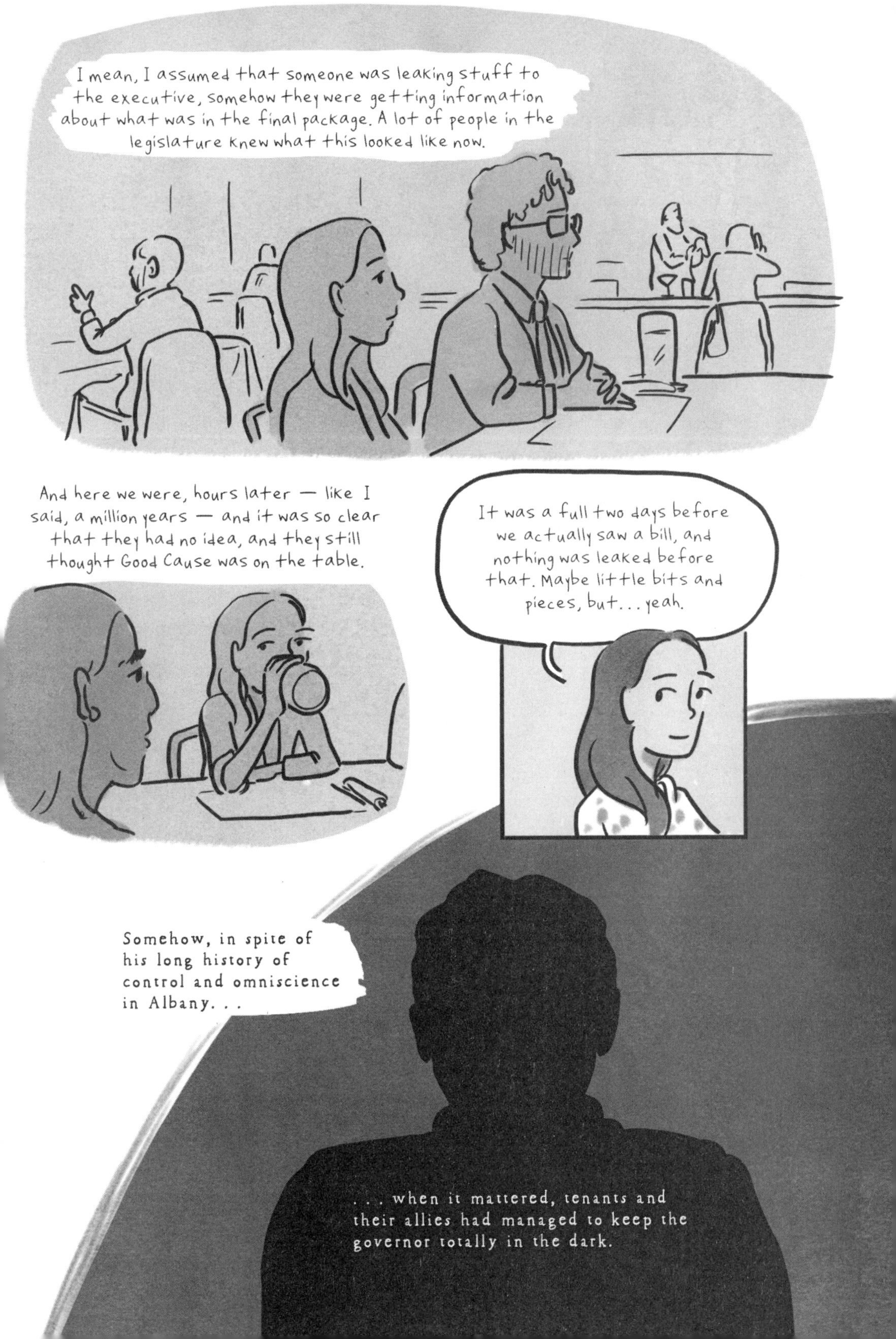
I mean, I assumed that someone was leaking stuff to the executive, somehow they were getting information about what was in the final package. A lot of people in the legislature knew what this looked like now.
And here we were, hours later — like I said, a million years — and it was so clear that they had no idea, and they still thought Good Cause was on the table.
It was a full two days before we actually saw a bill, and nothing was leaked before that. Maybe little bits and pieces, but... yeah.
Somehow, in spite of his long history of control and omniscience in Albany...
... when it mattered, tenants and their allies had managed to keep the governor totally in the dark.

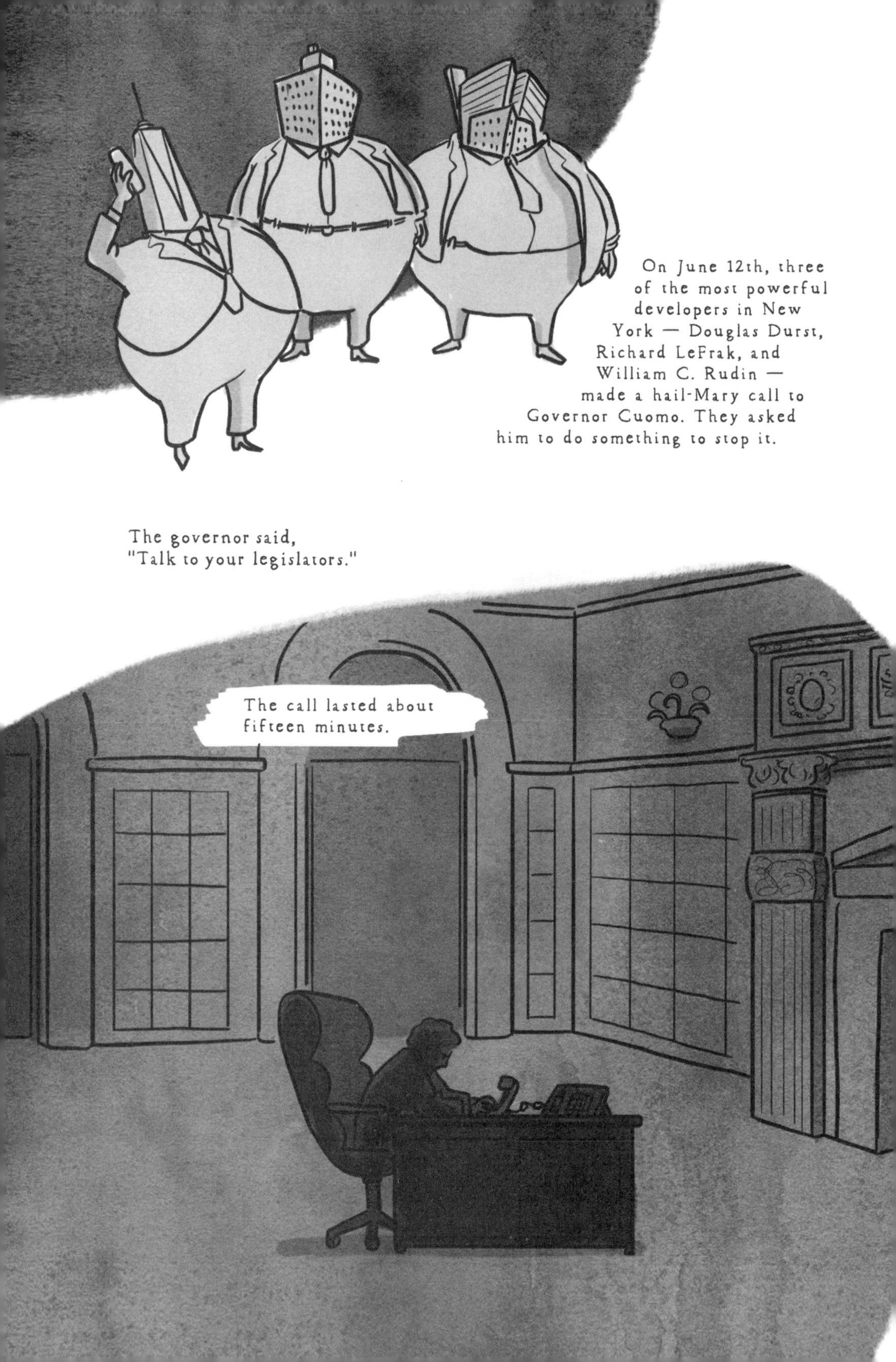
On June 12th, three of the most powerful developers in New York — Douglas Durst, Richard LeFrak, and William C. Rudin — made a hail-Mary call to Governor Cuomo. They asked him to do something to stop it.
The governor said, "Talk to your legislators."
The call lasted about fifteen minutes.

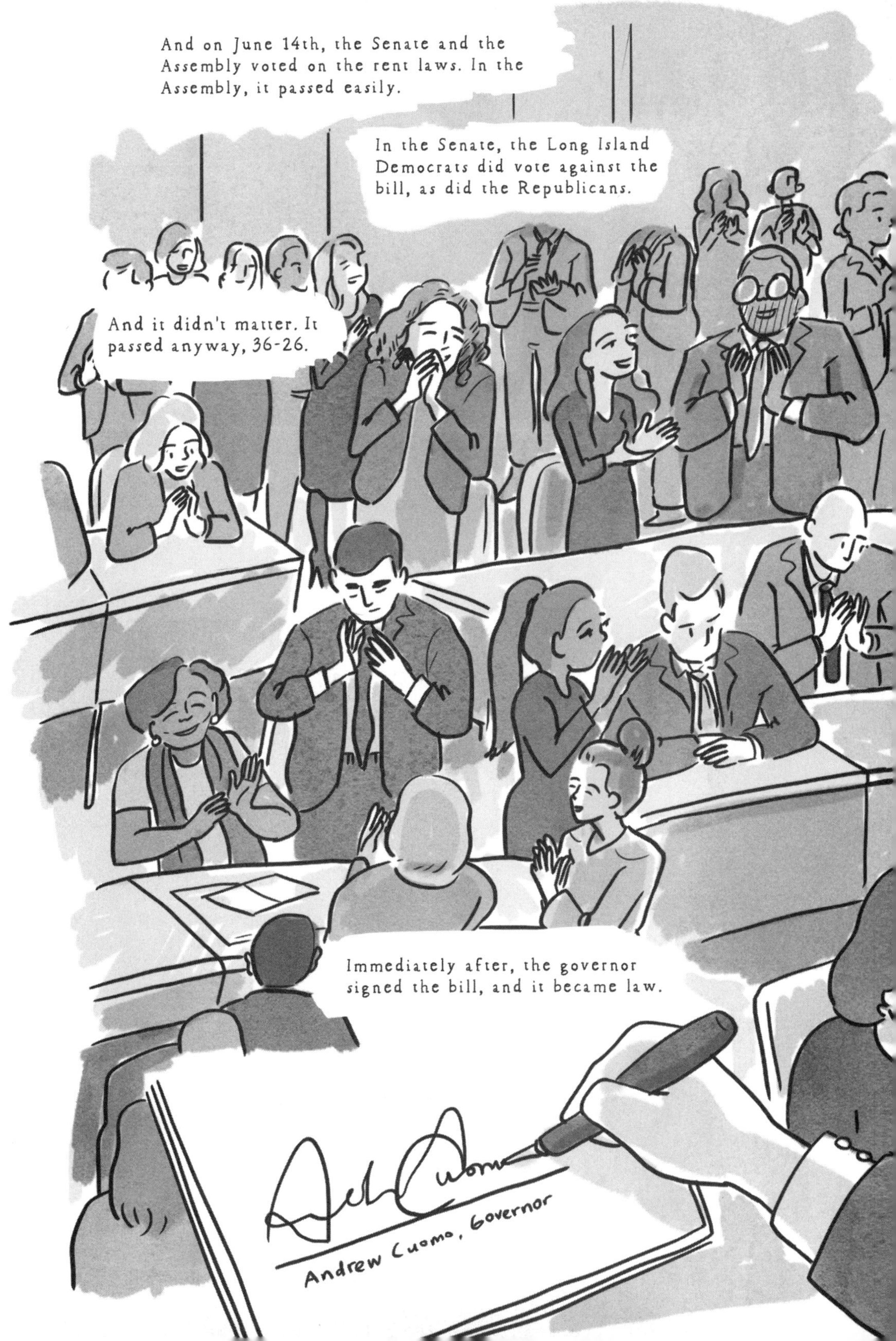
And on June 14th, the Senate and the Assembly voted on the rent laws. In the Assembly, it passed easily.
In the Senate, the Long Island Democrats did vote against the bill, as did the Republicans.
And it didn't matter. It passed anyway, 36-26.
Immediately after, the governor signed the bill, and it became law.
Andrew Cuomo, Governor

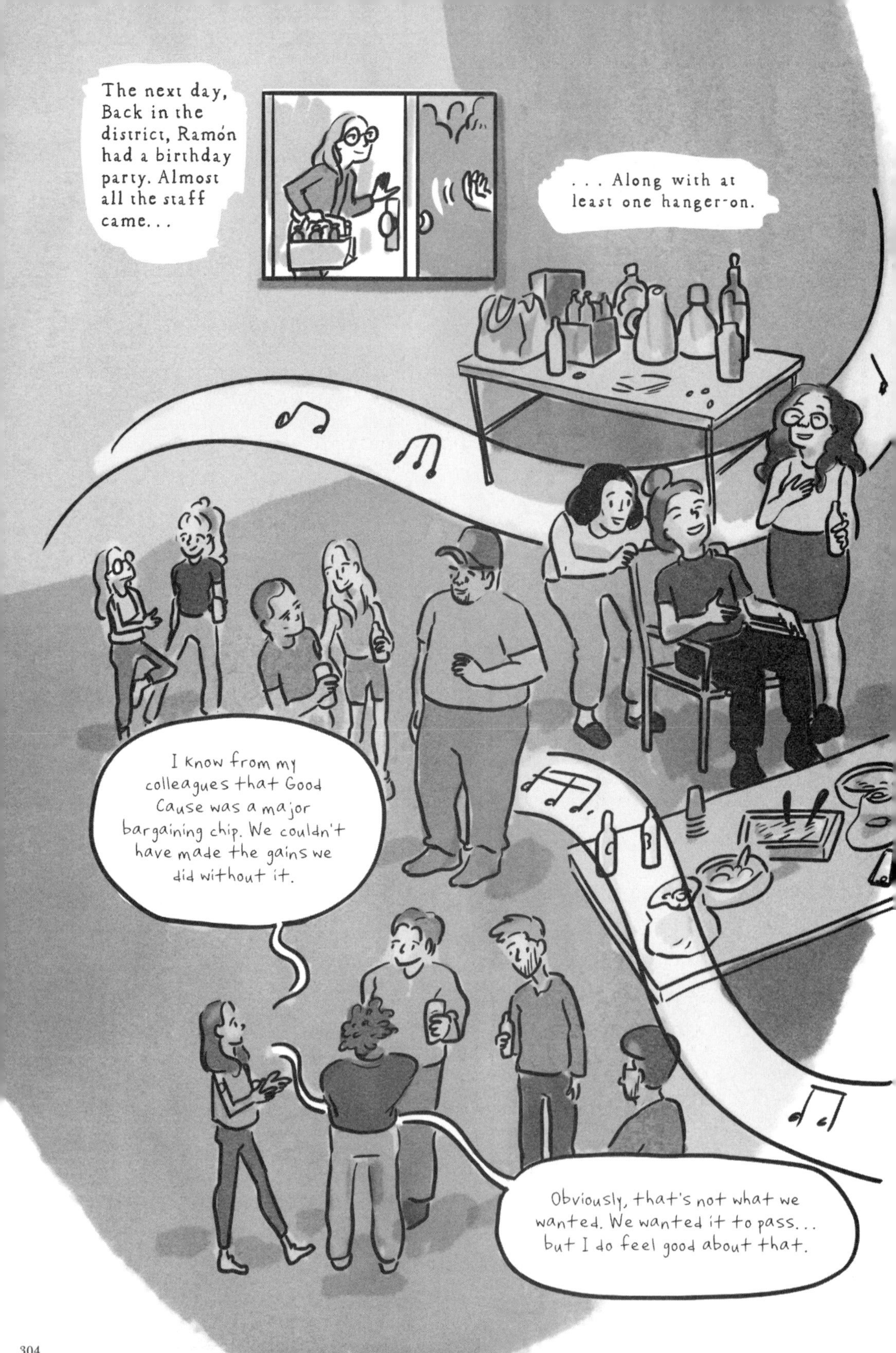
The next day, Back in the district, Ramón had a birthday party. Almost all the staff came...
. . . Along with at least one hanger-on.
I know from my colleagues that Good Cause was a major bargaining chip. We couldn't have made the gains we did without it.
Obviously, that's not what we wanted. We wanted it to pass... but I do feel good about that.

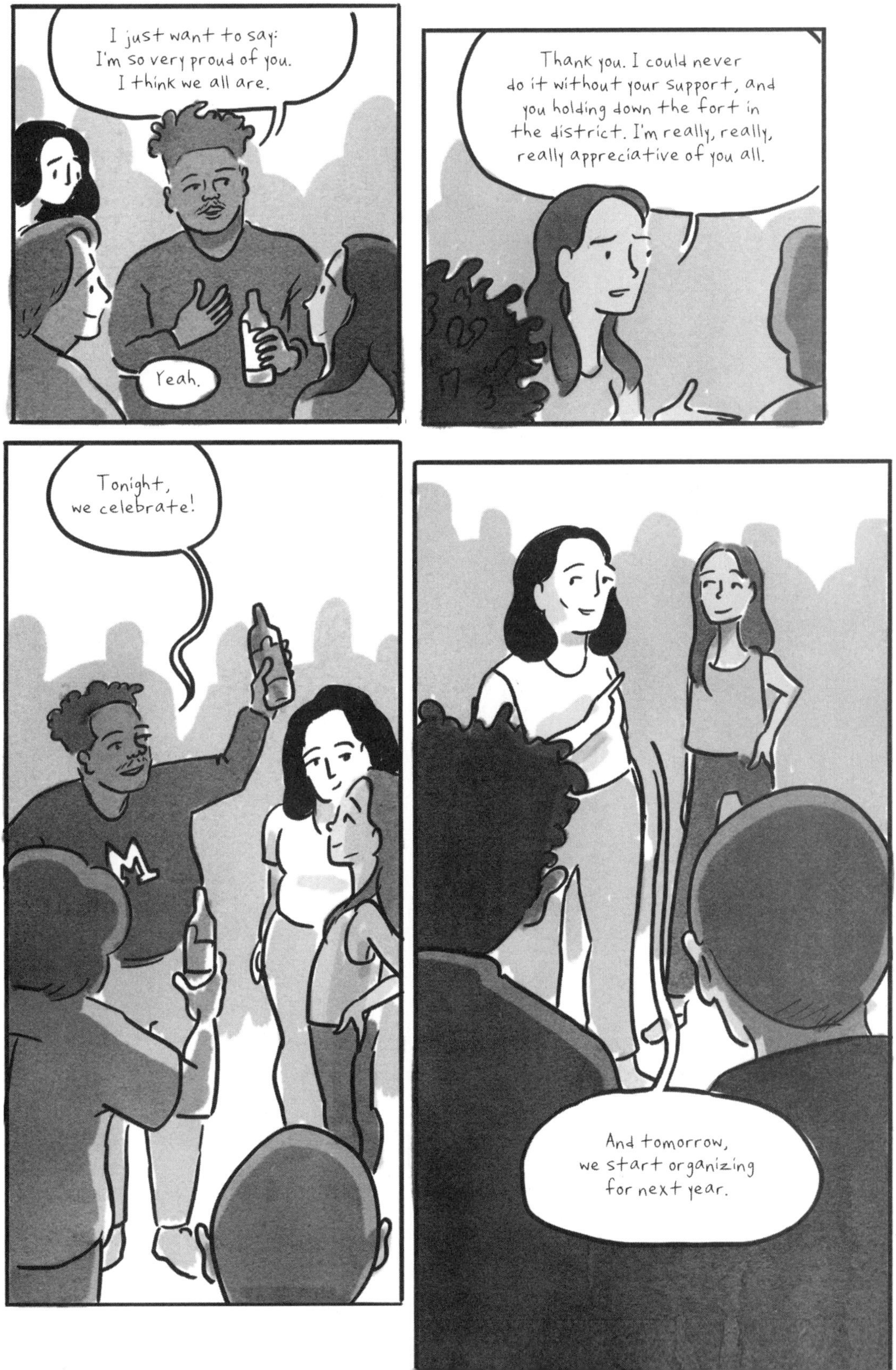
I just want to say: I'm so very proud of you. I think we all are.
Yeah.
Thank you. I could never do it without your support, and you holding down the fort in the district. I'm really, really, really appreciative of you all.
Tonight, we celebrate!
And tomorrow, we start organizing for next year.

Chapter Twelve

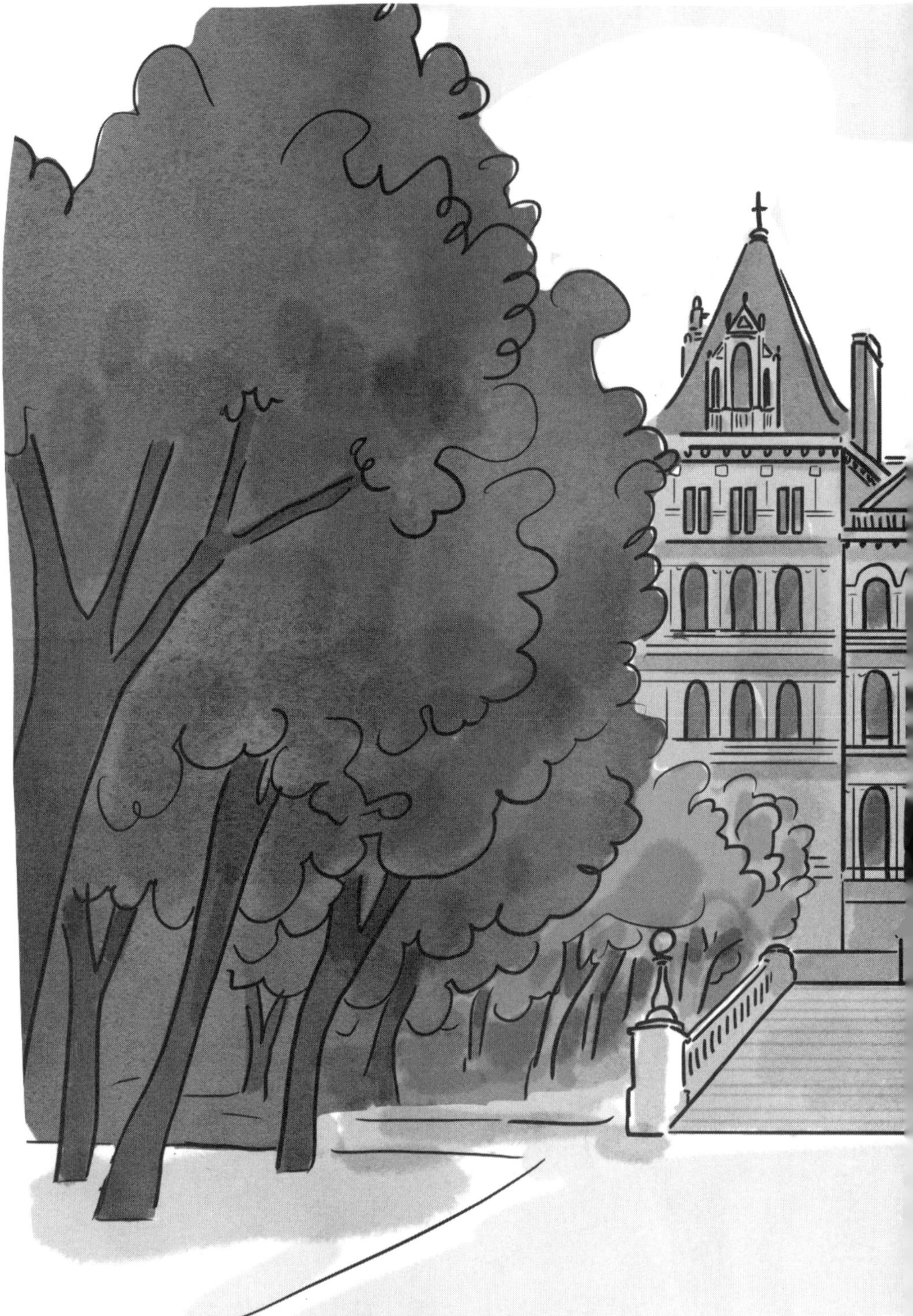

In the few remaining days of the session, the Senate worked into the wee hours, passing as many priority bills as they could. They advanced major reform on climate change, criminal justice, and immigration, to name just a few.

And then, on June 19th, it ended.

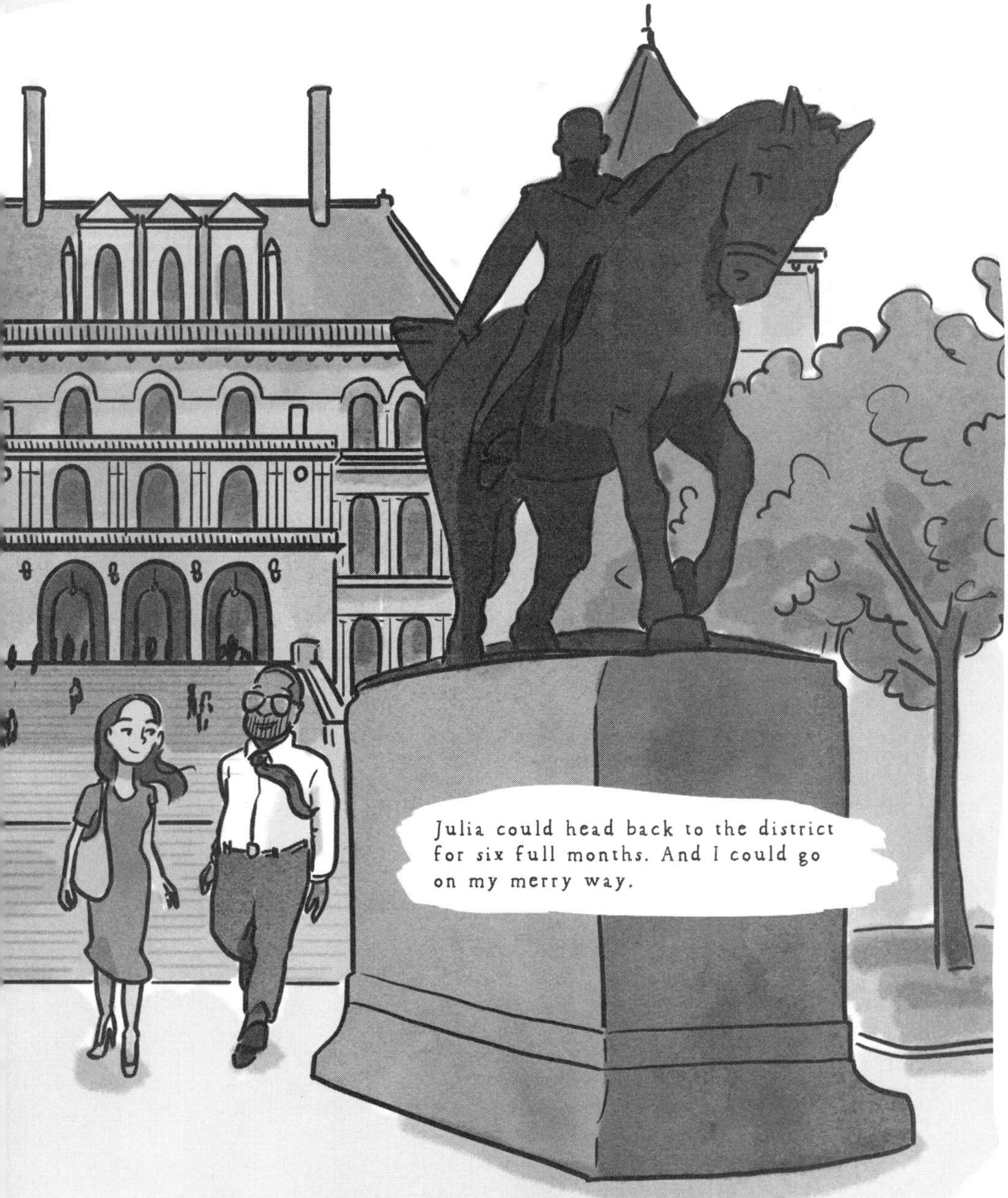
Julia could head back to the district for six full months. And I could go on my merry way.

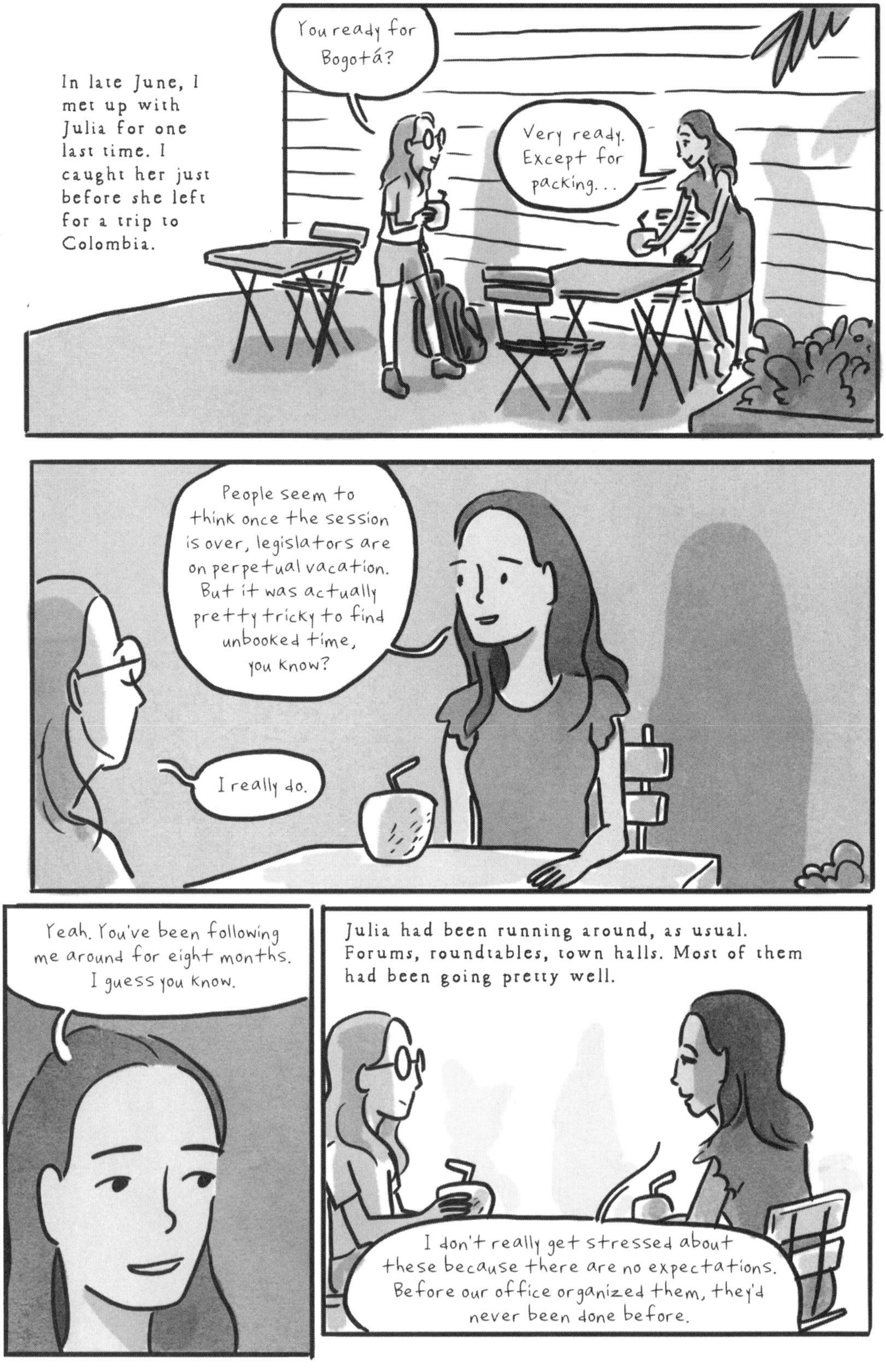
In late June, I met up with Julia for one last time. I caught her just before she left for a trip to Colombia.
You ready for Bogotá?
Very ready. Except for packing...
People seem to think once the session is over, legislators are on perpetual vacation. But it was actually pretty tricky to find unbooked time, you know?
I really do.
Yeah. You've been following me around for eight months. I guess you know.
Julia had been running around, as usual. Forums, roundtables, town halls. Most of them had been going pretty well.
I don't really get stressed about these because there are no expectations. Before our office organized them, they'd never been done before.

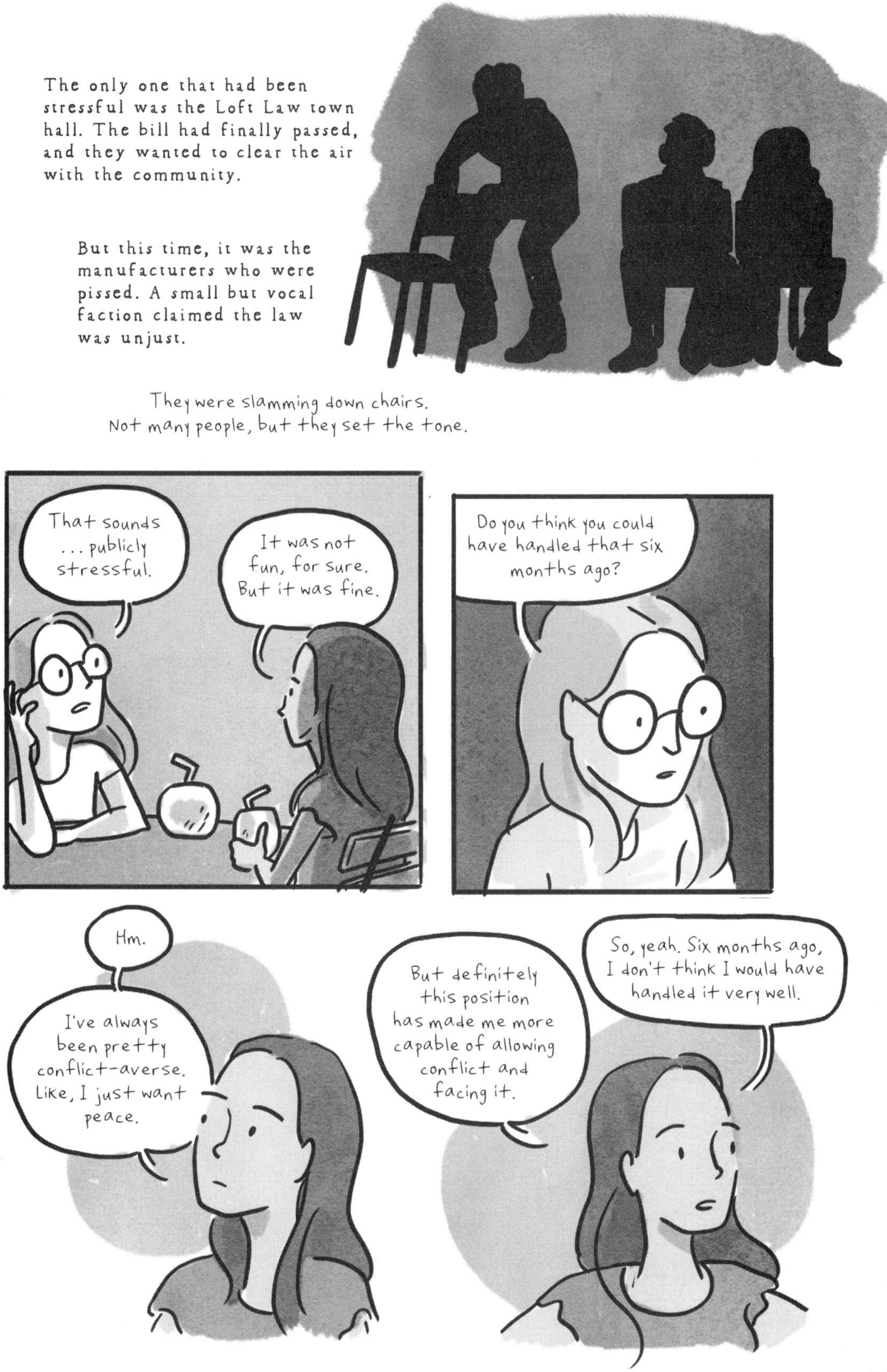
The only one that had been stressful was the Loft Law town hall. The bill had finally passed, and they wanted to clear the air with the community.
But this time, it was the manufacturers who were pissed. A small but vocal faction claimed the law was unjust.
They were slamming down chairs. Not many people, but they set the tone.
That sounds . . . publicly stressful.
It was not fun, for sure. But it was fine.
Do you think you could have handled that six months ago?
Hm.
I've always been pretty conflict-averse. Like, I just want peace.
But definitely this position has made me more capable of allowing conflict and facing it.
So, yeah. Six months ago, I don't think I would have handled it very well.

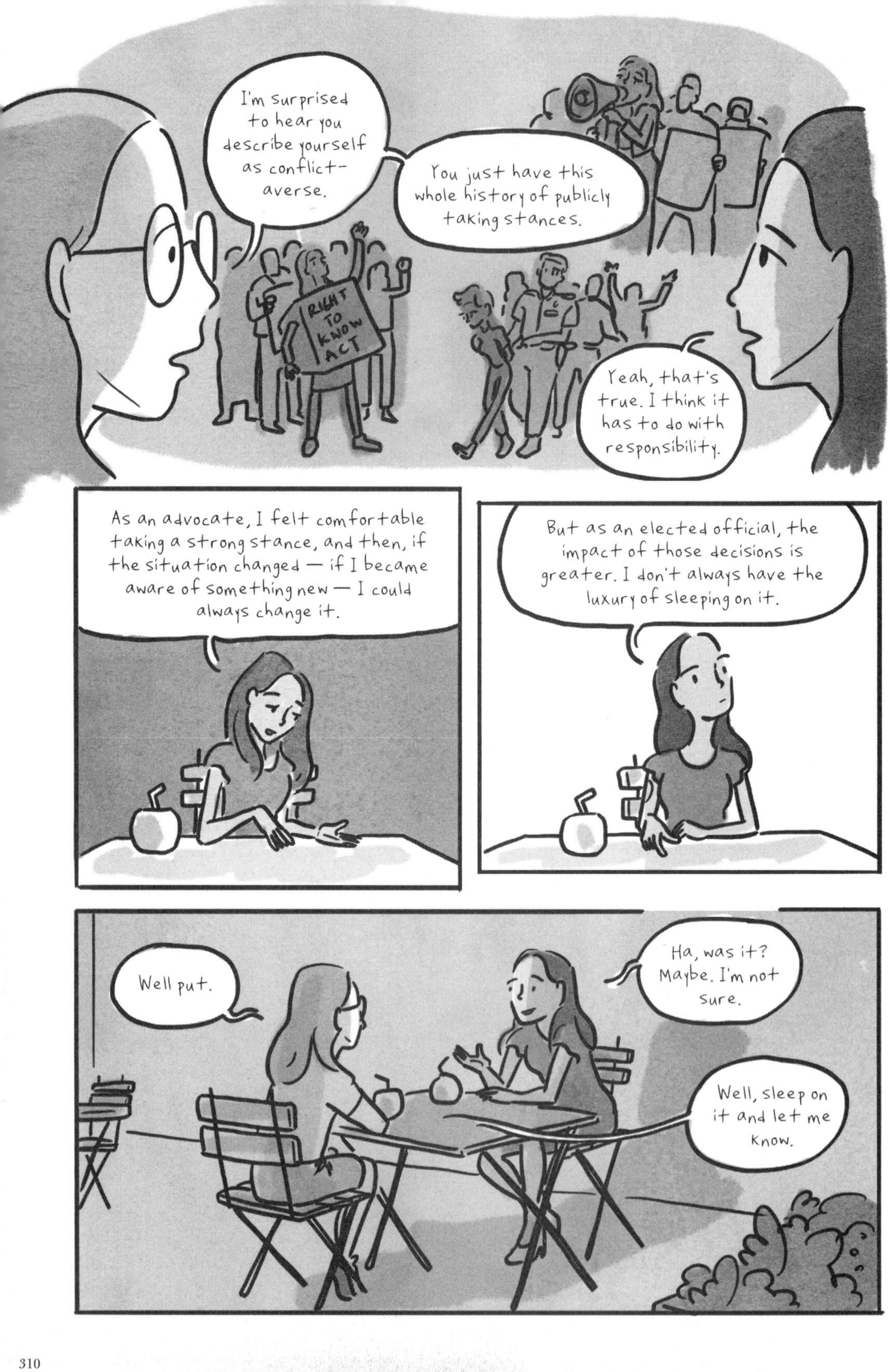
I'm surprised to hear you describe yourself as conflict-averse.
You just have this whole history of publicly taking stances.
RIGHT TO KNOW ACT
Yeah, that's true. I think it has to do with responsibility.
As an advocate, I felt comfortable taking a strong stance, and then, if the situation changed — if I became aware of something new — I could always change it.
But as an elected official, the impact of those decisions is greater. I don't always have the luxury of sleeping on it.
Well put.
Ha, was it? Maybe. I'm not sure.
Well, sleep on it and let me know.

Here I am at the end, and I've barely told you anything about Julia's past.

I haven't told you about how her parents split when she was eight, and her dad, a pilot, was an intermittent presence.

That left her mom a single mother with no college degree and no child support. Things were not always easy, but eventually her mom earned a degree and a stable job in a pharmaceutical company.

On her fourteenth birthday, Julia's mom took her to the grocery store to apply for a job, and she worked in service industry jobs all throughout high school and college. She said it helped her develop class consciousness.

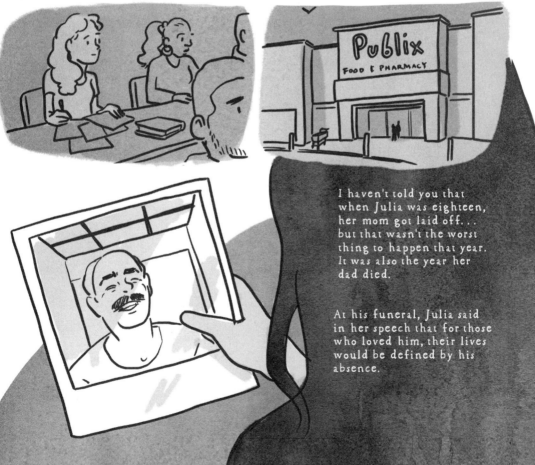

I haven't told you that when Julia was eighteen, her mom got laid off... but that wasn't the worst thing to happen that year. It was also the year her dad died.

At his funeral, Julia said in her speech that for those who loved him, their lives would be defined by his absence.

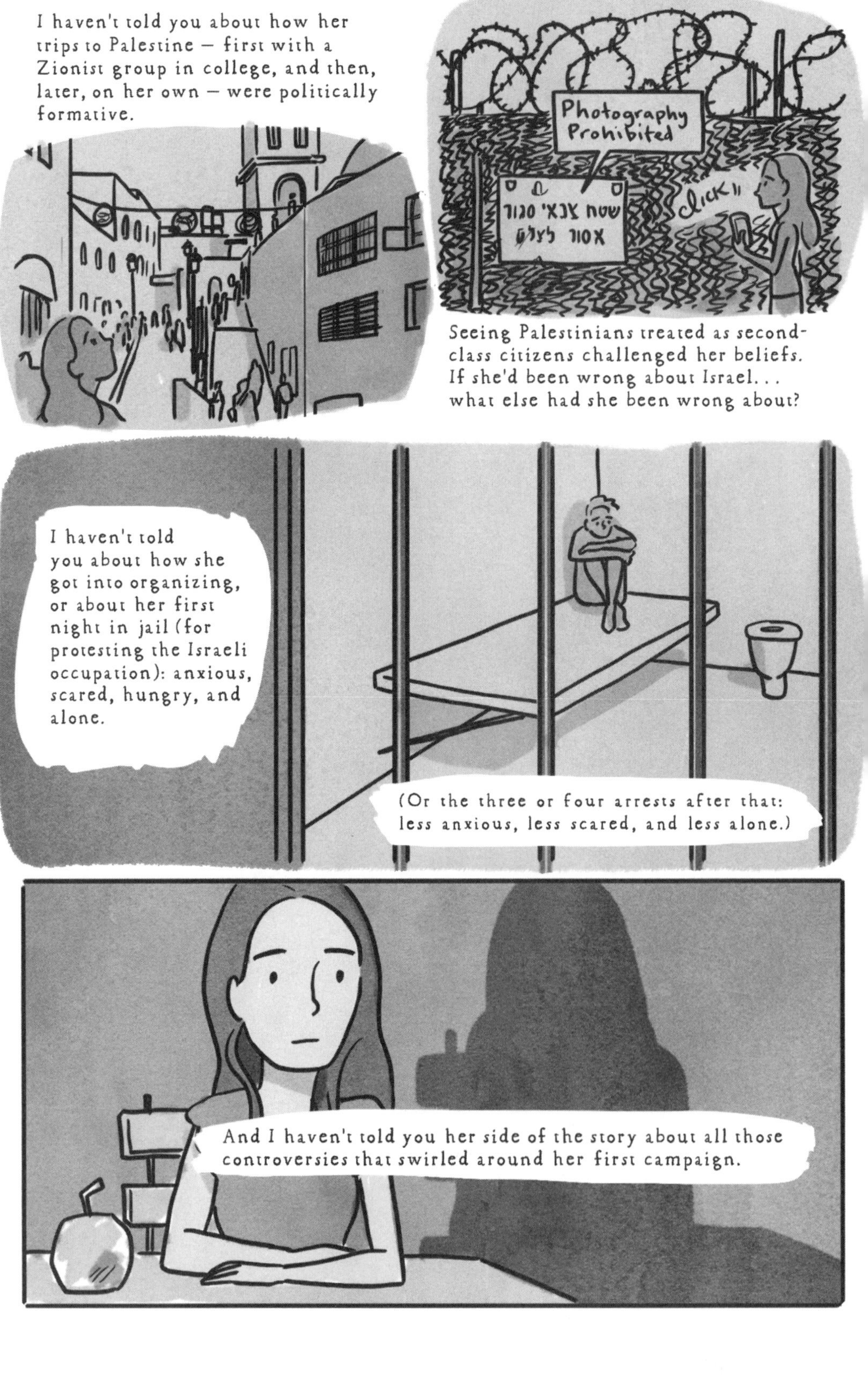
I haven't told you about how her trips to Palestine — first with a Zionist group in college, and then, later, on her own — were politically formative.
Photography Prohibited
שטח צבאי סגור
אסור לצלם
click!!
Seeing Palestinians treated as second-class citizens challenged her beliefs. If she'd been wrong about Israel. . . what else had she been wrong about?
I haven't told you about how she got into organizing, or about her first night in jail (for protesting the Israeli occupation): anxious, scared, hungry, and alone.
(Or the three or four arrests after that: less anxious, less scared, and less alone.)
And I haven't told you her side of the story about all those controversies that swirled around her first campaign.

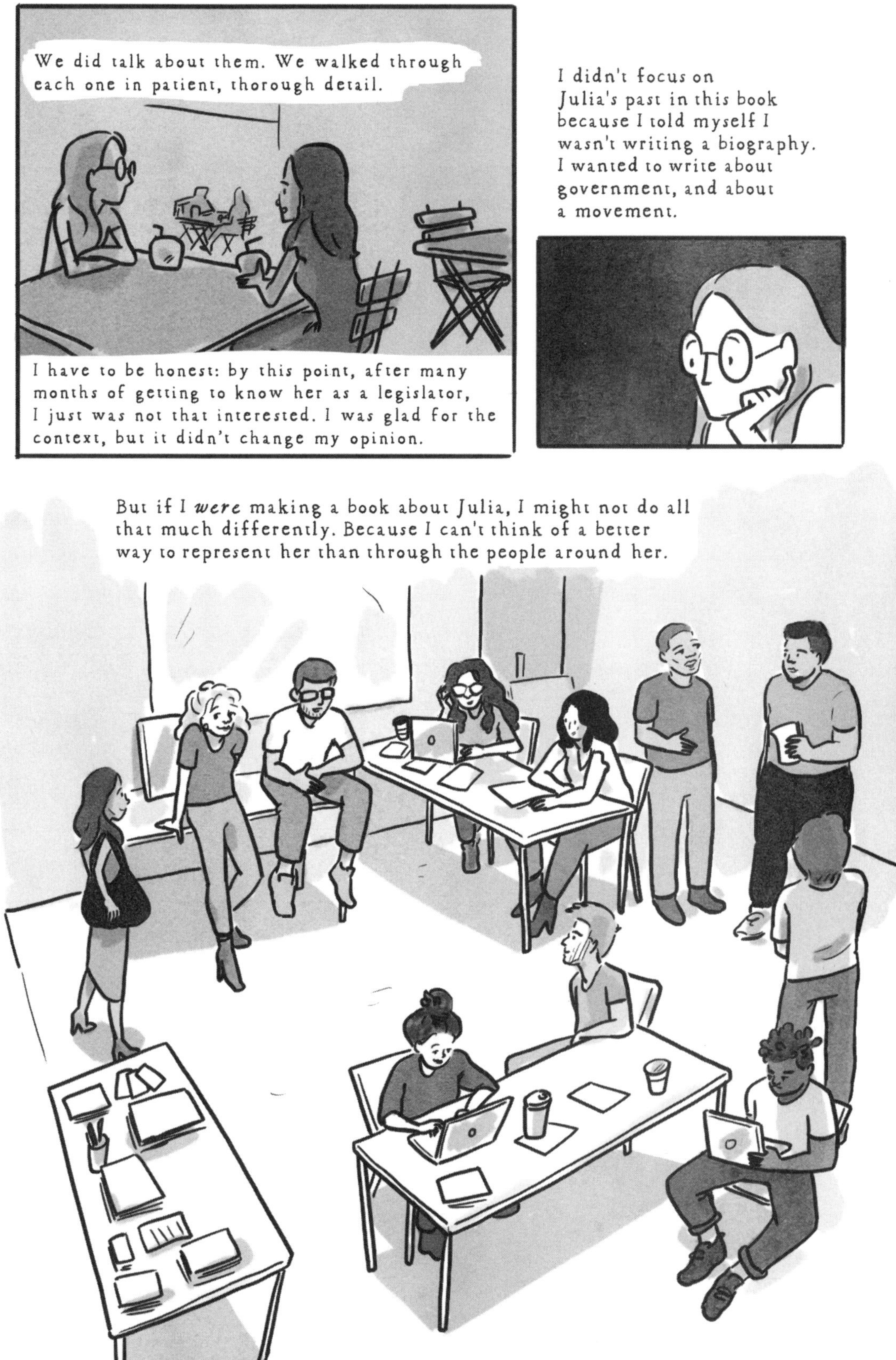

We did talk about them. We walked through each one in patient, thorough detail.
I have to be honest: by this point, after many months of getting to know her as a legislator, I just was not that interested. I was glad for the context, but it didn't change my opinion.
I didn't focus on Julia's past in this book because I told myself I wasn't writing a biography. I wanted to write about government, and about a movement.
But if I *were* making a book about Julia, I might not do all that much differently. Because I can't think of a better way to represent her than through the people around her.

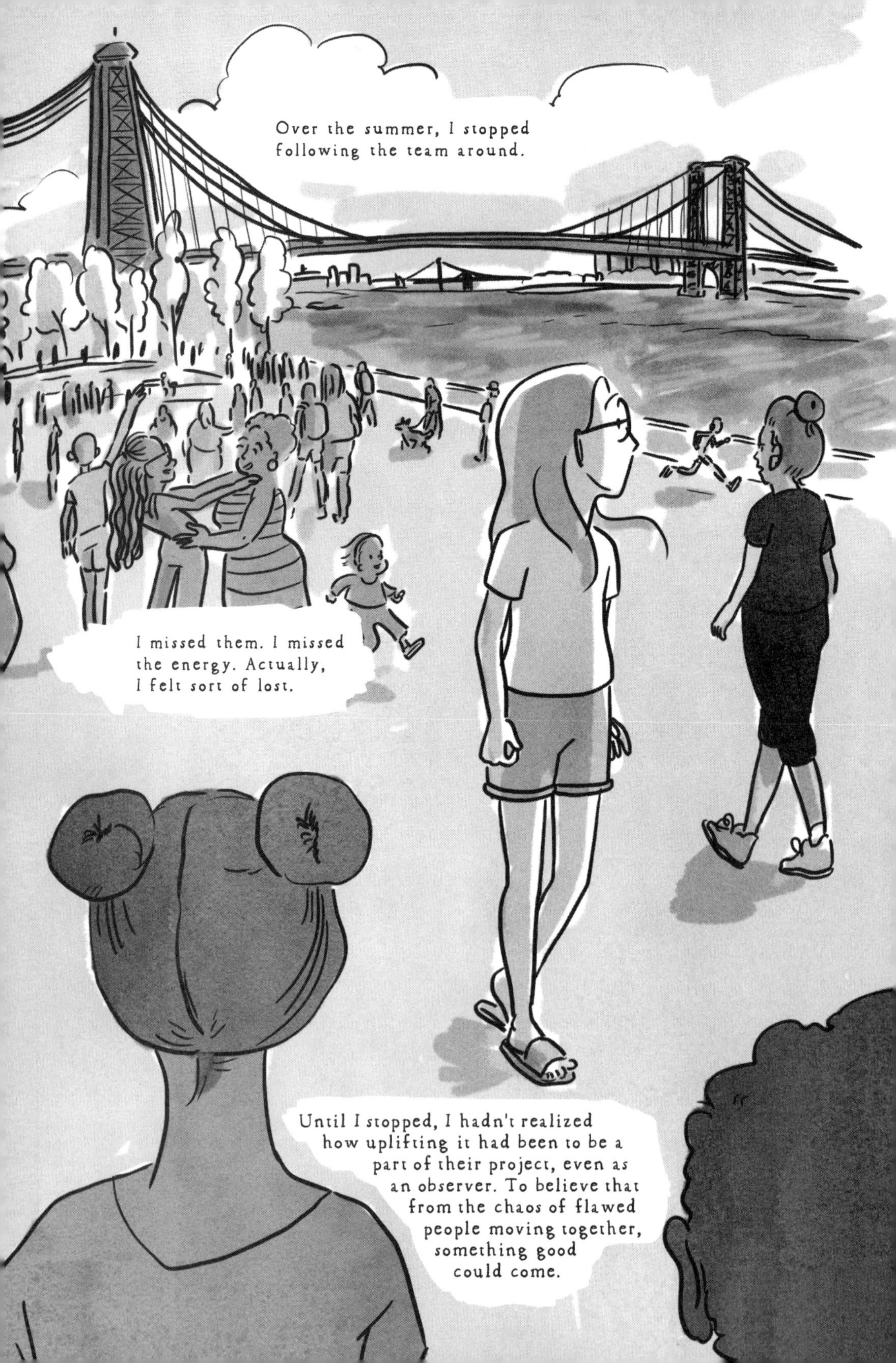

Over the summer, I stopped following the team around.
I missed them. I missed the energy. Actually, I felt sort of lost.
Until I stopped, I hadn't realized how uplifting it had been to be a part of their project, even as an observer. To believe that from the chaos of flawed people moving together, something good could come.

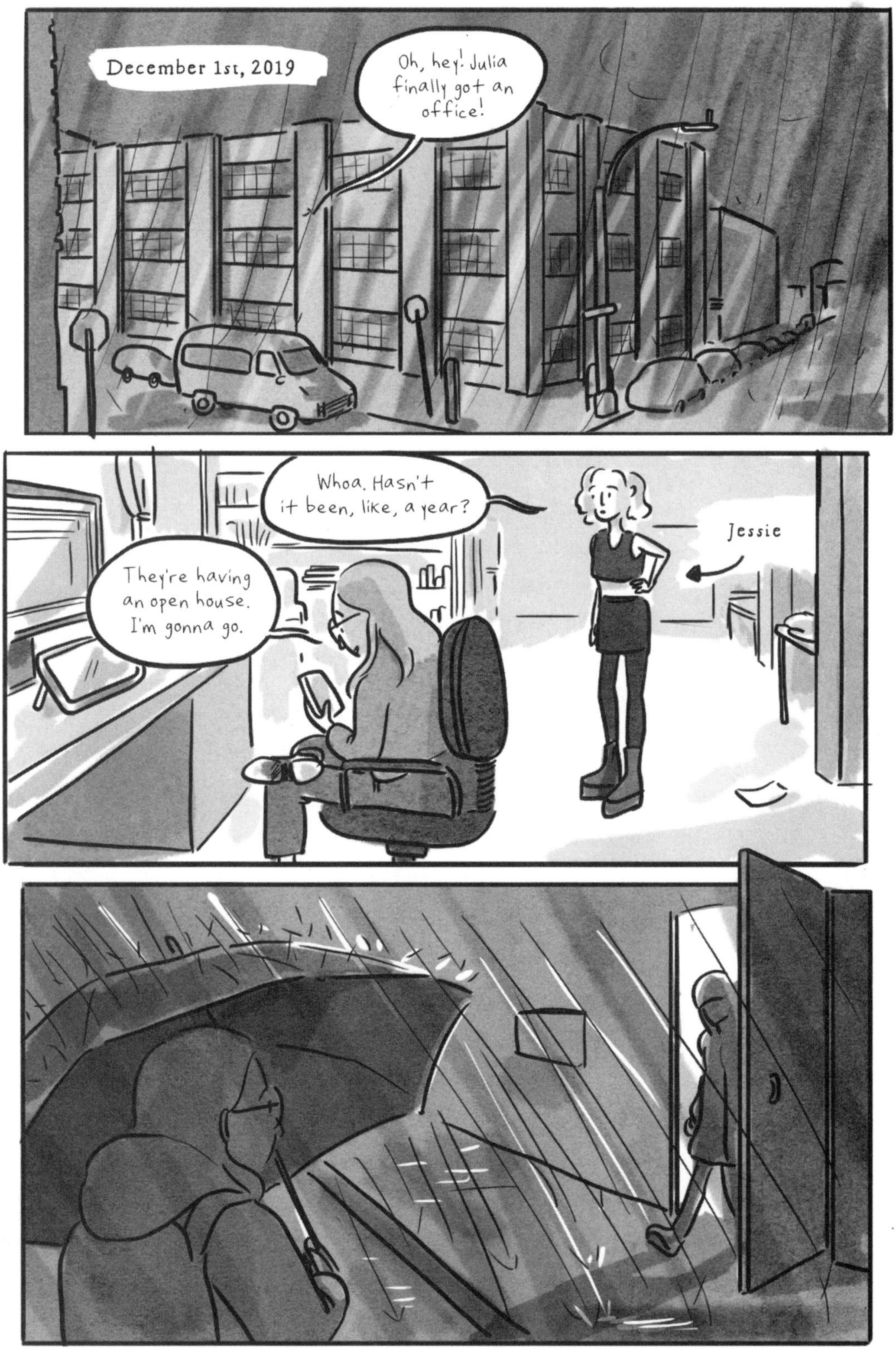
December 1st, 2019
Oh, hey! Julia finally got an office!
Whoa. Hasn't it been, like, a year?
Jessie
They're having an open house. I'm gonna go.

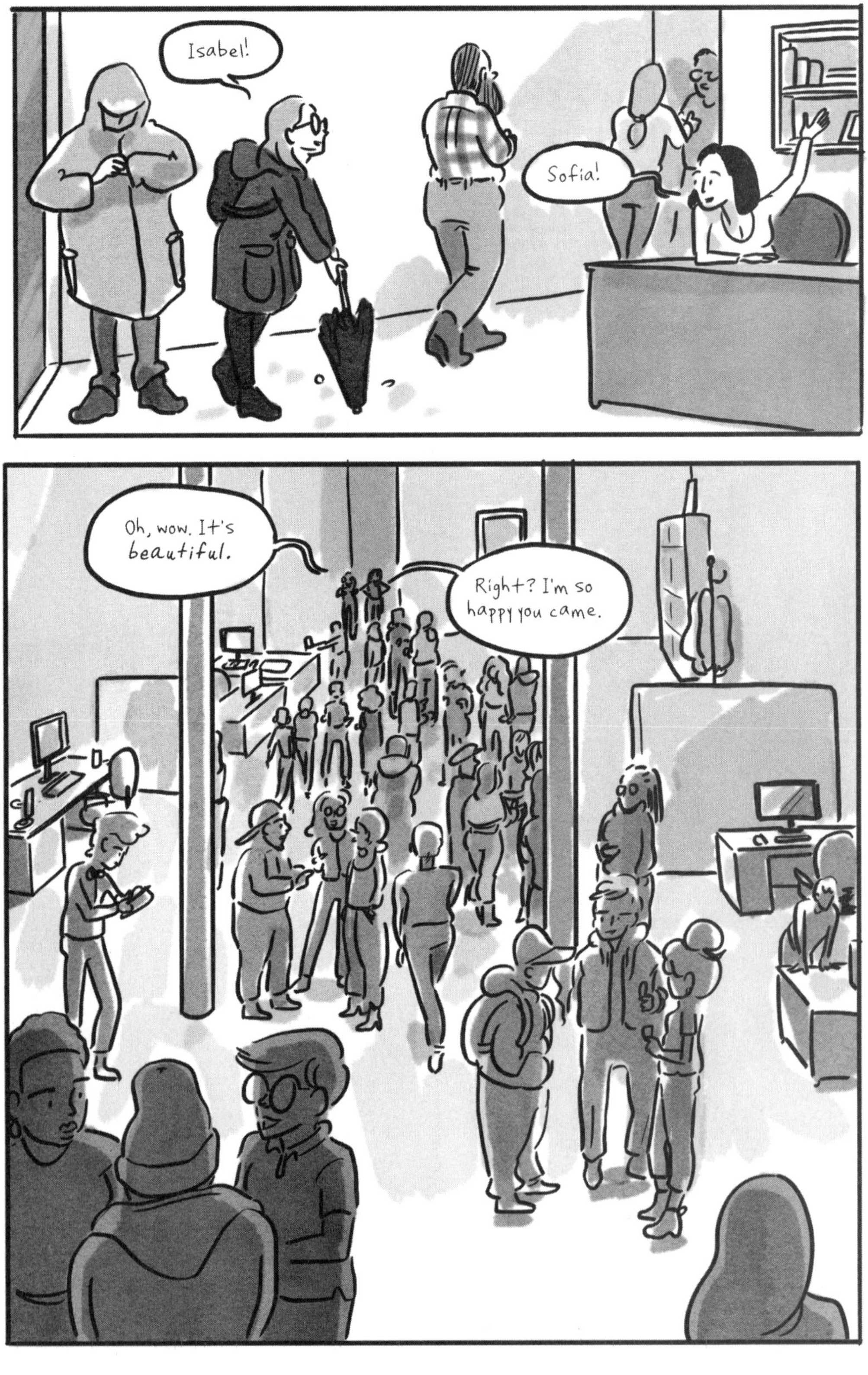

Isabel!
Sofia!
Oh, wow. It's *beautiful.*
Right? I'm so happy you came.

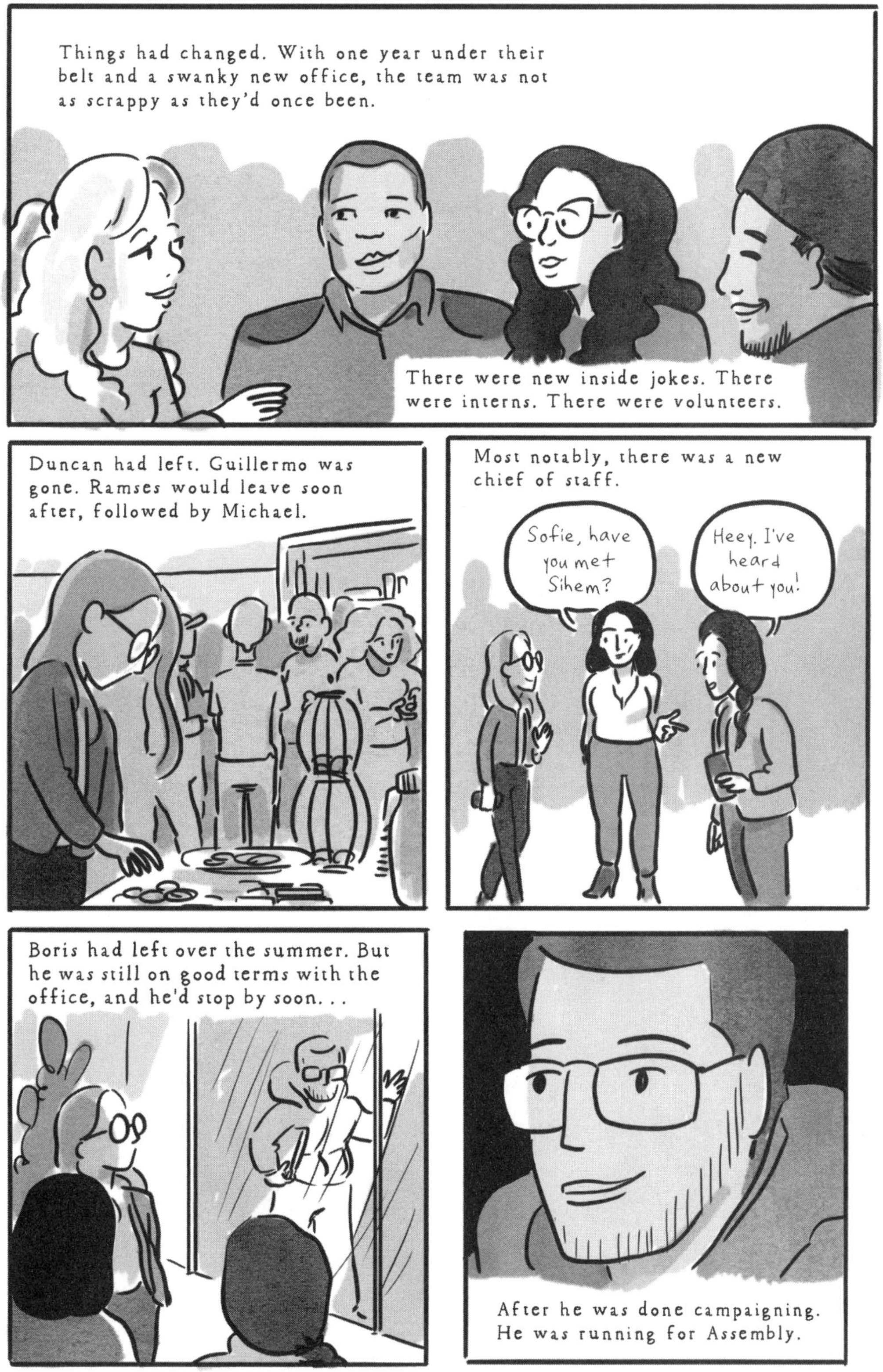
Things had changed. With one year under their belt and a swanky new office, the team was not as scrappy as they'd once been.
There were new inside jokes. There were interns. There were volunteers.
Duncan had left. Guillermo was gone. Ramses would leave soon after, followed by Michael.
Most notably, there was a new chief of staff.
Sofie, have you met Sihem?
Heey. I've heard about you!
Boris had left over the summer. But he was still on good terms with the office, and he'd stop by soon. . .
After he was done campaigning. He was running for Assembly.

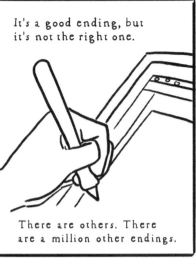

It's a good ending, but it's not the right one.

There are others. There are a million other endings.

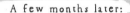

A few months later:

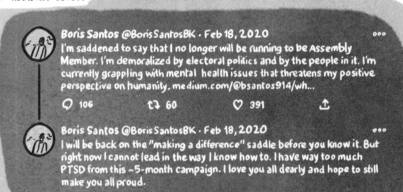

Boris Santos @BorisSantosBK · Feb 18, 2020

I'm saddened to say that I no longer will be running to be Assembly Member. I'm demoralized by electoral politics and by the people in it. I'm currently grappling with mental health issues that threatens my positive perspective on humanity. medium.com/@bsantos914/wh...

106   60   391

Boris Santos @BorisSantosBK · Feb 18, 2020

I will be back on the "making a difference" saddle before you know it. But right now I cannot lead in the way I know how to. I have way too much PTSD from this ~5-month campaign. I love you all dearly and hope to still make you all proud.

11   135

He was broken, he said. But soon, there were bigger things to worry about.

The New York Times

New York City Region Is Now an Epicenter of the Coronavirus Pandemic

The city and its suburbs account for roughly 5 percent of global cases, forcing officials to take urgent steps to stem the outbreak.

New York City to close schools; ba restaurants around U.S. ordered c coronavirus

Gov. Andrew Cuomo ordered schools closed in New York City as Ohio and bars and restaurants in the states to shut down service.

North Brooklyn was devastated by Covid-19. In April 2020, the sirens were nonstop, and the hospitals were overrun. Thousands lost their jobs, went hungry, and couldn't pay rent.

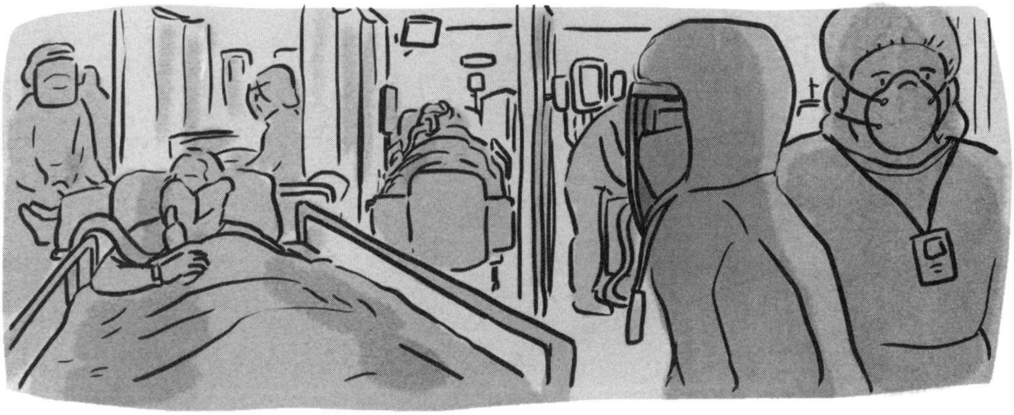

And Julia's office was heroic. Isabel and Gabbi helped people file for unemployment. Alvin and Ramón organized food deliveries and PPE drops. Julia introduced legislation to halt evictions during the pandemic. She got Covid. She recovered. She kept working.

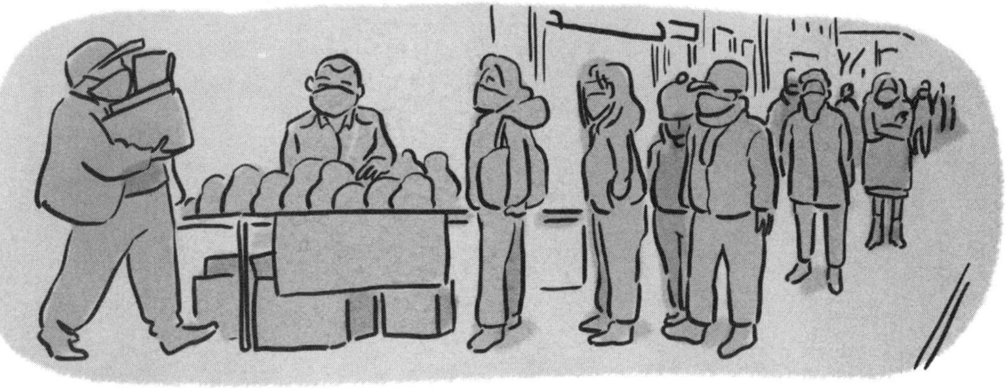

A moderate Democrat challenged her in the primary.

Julia beat him easily, with eighty-six percent of the vote.

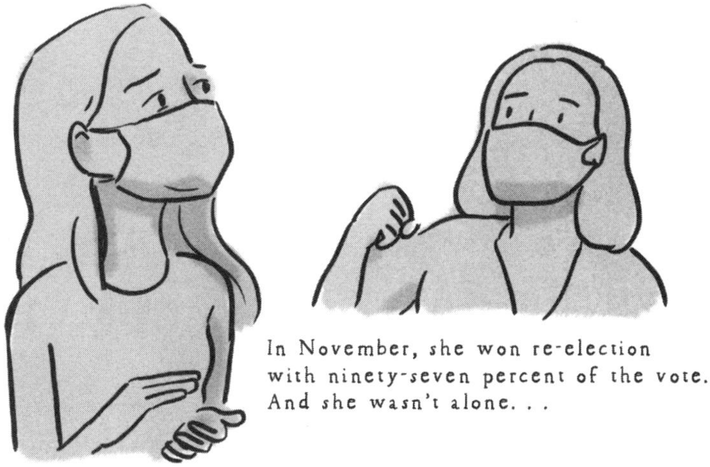

In November, she won re-election with ninety-seven percent of the vote. And she wasn't alone. . .

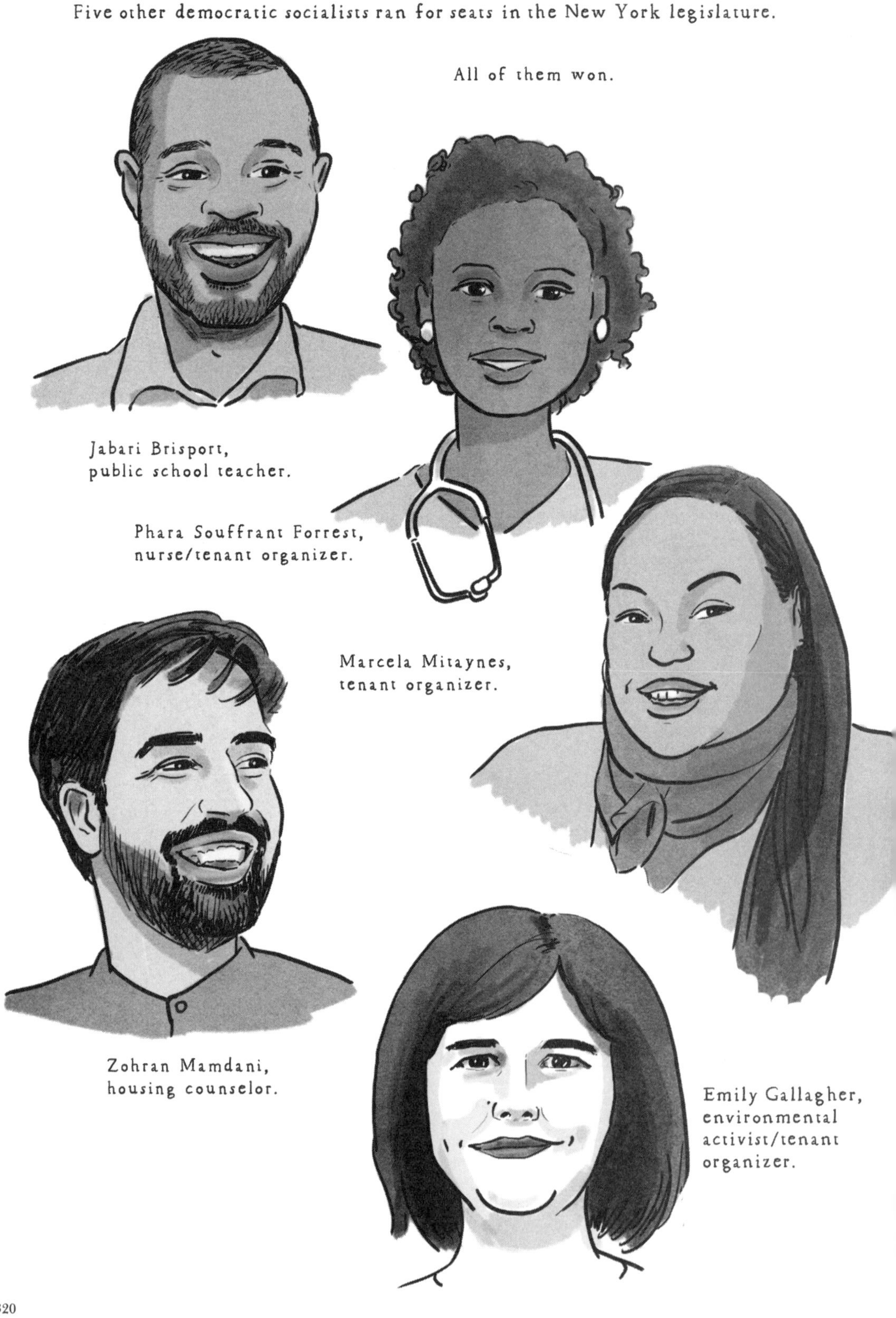
Five other democratic socialists ran for seats in the New York legislature.
All of them won.
Jabari Brisport,
public school teacher.
Phara Souffrant Forrest,
nurse/tenant organizer.
Marcela Mitaynes,
tenant organizer.
Zohran Mamdani,
housing counselor.
Emily Gallagher,
environmental
activist/tenant
organizer.

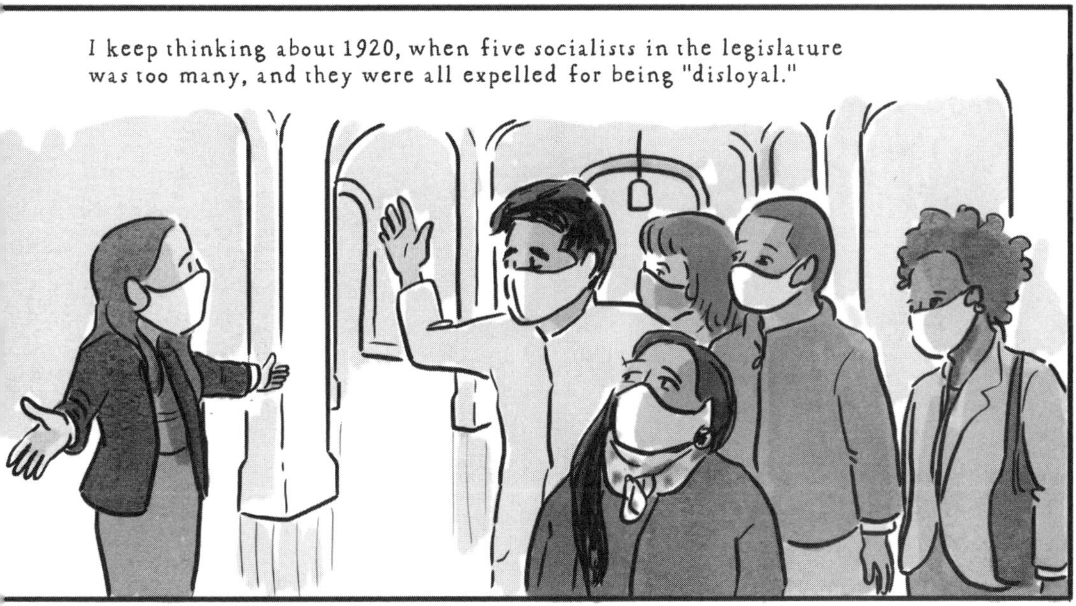
I keep thinking about 1920, when five socialists in the legislature was too many, and they were all expelled for being "disloyal."

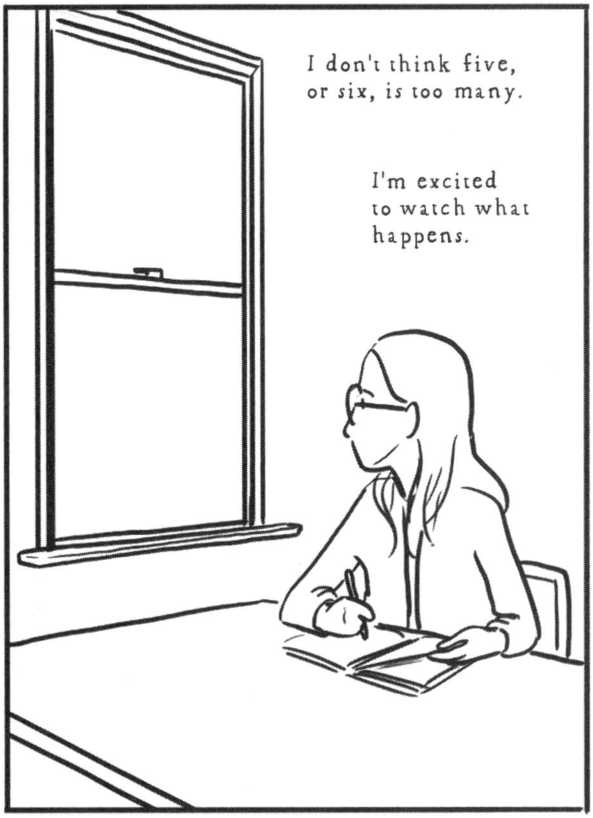
I don't think five, or six, is too many.
I'm excited to watch what happens.

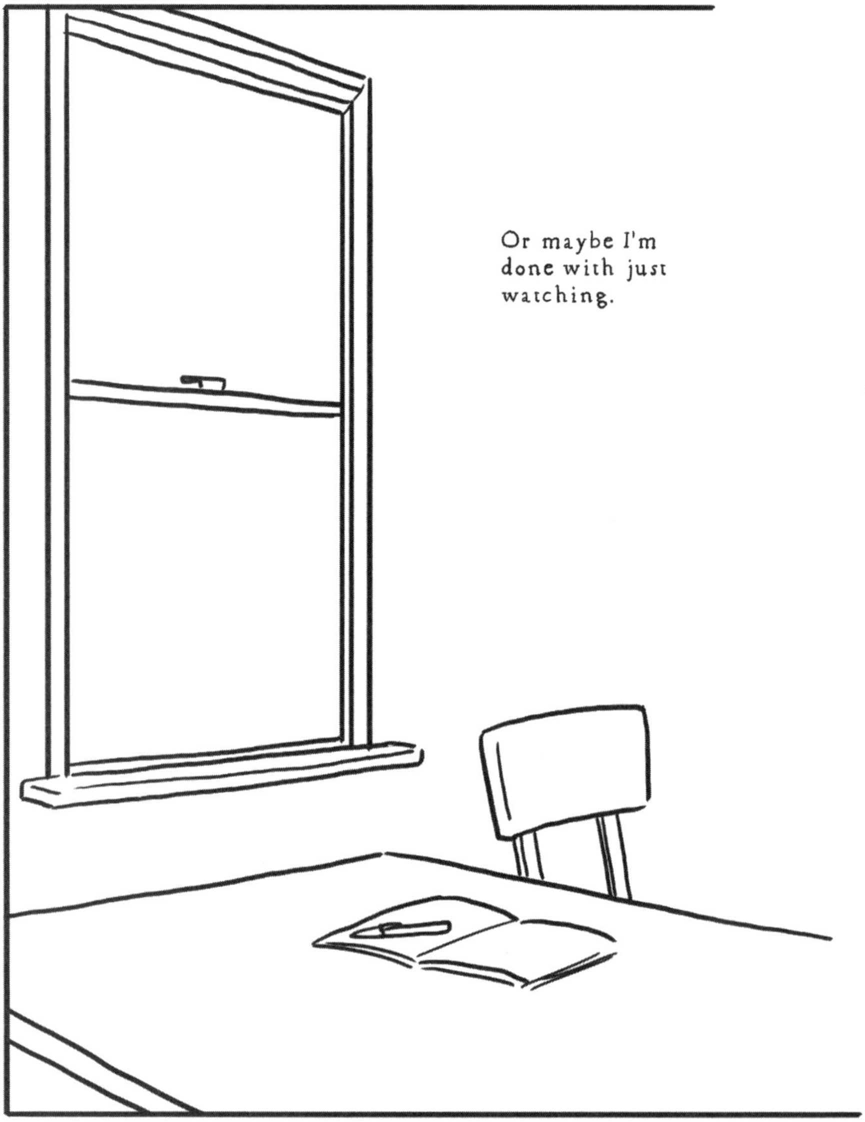
Or maybe I'm done with just watching.

SUPA
WARREN
'21

Acknowledgments

I couldn't have even imagined making this book if not for Jason Katzenstein. When we met a decade ago, his passion for comics reignited my own, and at every stage of this process he patiently offered me reassurance, advice, notes, and jokes. Jason, I'm so grateful for your friendship.

Thank you to the people who helped turn this idea into a reality: to Paul Lucas, my agent, for believing in this project; to Leigh Walton, my editor, for making this a better book in every way; to Chris Staros, Nate Widick, and everyone at Top Shelf Productions, for all your work and magic.

Emma Allen and Colin Stokes: thank you for making me feel like a real cartoonist.

These people read drafts of this book, and I'm deeply grateful for their keen eyes and smart notes: Kendra Allenby, Grace Chou, Will Feinstein, Mort Gerberg, Kerry Klemmer, Matthew Kramer, Amy Kurzweil, Navied Mahdavian, Rebecca Meyer, Jackie Morgan, Ellis Rosen, and Ethan Young. I'm also thankful for Sarah Glidden's valuable insight on turning life into comics, and Liz Frances' early encouragement.

This was an itinerant and pandemicky time. Maison des Auteurs, Peggy Kriss and Cliff Pollan, Mary Gordon, Amy Kurzweil: thank you for giving me places to be.

Thank you to the people who make my life rich and who provided support in many forms, including but not limited to: dancing with me, crying with me, making me dinner, making me laugh, participating in my pranks and/or schemes, lending a pet, and providing an endless supply of commiseration, gossip, and hugs. Marisa Acocella, Emily Berman, Maddie Boucher, Hilary Campbell, Gabe Castanon, Jason Chatfield, Jess Damicis, Johnny DiNapoli, Neil Dvorak, Emilie George, Ivy Haldeman, Neima Jahromi, Christen Kelly, Beck Kitsis, Jenny Kroik, Sam Lee, Maggie Larson, Chris McNabb, Hanna Meltz, Jared Nangle, Scott Pham, Magnus Pind-Bjerre, Jenn Pollan, Leah Roh, Jessica Rovinelli, Lane Sell, Miles Stenhouse, Betsy Tammaro, Rachel Upton, Joe White, and Natalia Winkelman.

To my family, Ana, Gabriel, and Noah: I love you so much.

Boris Santos, Isabel Anreus, Duncan Bryer, Jessica Ramos Franco, Alvin Peña, Ramses Dukes, Ramón Pebenito, Melissa Galeano, Michael Carter, Gabbi Zutrau, Veronica Cruz, Mark Mishler, Guillermo Martinez, Cea Weaver, and everyone in Housing Justice for All: thank you for your generosity, honesty, and patience. I learned so much from you.

Most importantly, to Julia: thank you for trusting me to tell this story.

Resources and Further Reading

 Books

No Shortcuts: Organizing for Power in the New Gilded Age
McAlevey - Oxford University Press - 2016
How can progressives win? Jane McAlevey makes the case for bottom-up organizing by examining a series of labor and union case studies. This is the book Ramón references in Chapter Seven, and it gave me a better sense of the strategy behind successful organizing campaigns.

Failed State: Dysfunction and Corruption in an American Statehouse
Lachman and Polner - Excelsior Editions, an imprint of State University of New York Press - 2017
Seymour Lachman served several terms as a state senator in New York and writes about how even legislators with the best intentions had virtually no choice but to go along with a deeply undemocratic, corrupt system of power. It warns us to pay close attention to our democratic institutions and not to take them for granted.

The Tenant Movement in New York City, 1904-1984
Lawson and Naison - Rutgers University Press - 1986
This book is available in full at tenant.net. It's a fascinating history of New York through the lens of tenant organizing: what brought coalitions together, what strategies were employed, and what led the movement to lose cohesion. One thread I found particularly compelling was the consistent prominence of women in organizing efforts.

Zoned Out!: Race, Displacement, and City Planning in New York City
Angotti and Morse - Terreform/UR - 2016
It was, unfortunately, outside the scope of my project to talk about urban planning, which is one of the major ways policy affects housing. With a focus on racial inequality, Zoned Out discusses how recent zoning policies have impacted communities around New York, including Julia's district.

March (Books One, Two, and Three)
Lewis, Aydin, and Powell - Top Shelf Productions - 2013-2016
This graphic memoir is John Lewis's first-hand account of organizing and activism during the civil rights movement. Personal, gripping, and powerfully drawn, March deepened my understanding of the struggle for racial equality, and it made a book like Radical feel possible.

Studies: Rental policy

It was also outside my scope to discuss rent regulation from a policy angle, which is a shame. These papers explore the impacts of rent regulation and consider the common arguments against such policies through a series of case studies.

- Montojo, Nicole, et al. "Opening the Door for Rent Control: Toward a Comprehensive Approach to Protecting California's Renters." Haas Institute, 2018. https://haasinstitute.berkeley.edu/sites/default/files/haasinstitute_rentcontrol.pdf.

- Mironova, Oksana, and Jeff Jones. "Closing the Loopholes: What Six Rental Histories Tell Us About Fixing Rent Regulation in New York." Community Service Society, May 2019. https://www.cssny.org/publications/entry/closing-loopholes-rental-histories-fixing-rent-regulation.

- Waters, Thomas J. "Rental Housing Affordability in Urban New York: A Statewide Crisis." Community Service Society, May 2019. https://www.cssny.org/publications/entry/rental-housing-affordability-in-urban-new-york-a-statewide-crisis.

- Pastor, Manuel, et al. "Rent Matters: What are the Impacts of Rent Stabilization Measures?" USC Dornsife Program for Environmental and Regional Equity, October 2018. https://dornsife.usc.edu/assets/sites/242/docs/Rent_Matters_PERE_Report_Web.pdf.

- Williams, Barika. "Predatory Equity: Evolution of a Crisis." Association for Neighborhood & Housing Development, November 2009. https://anhd.org/report/predatory-equity-evolution-crisis.

Online Resources

NY

- Housing Justice for All https://housingjusticeforall.org
- Homes Guarantee https://homesguarantee.com
- National Low Income Housing Coalition https://nlihc.org ← national
- Coalition for the Homeless https://www.coalitionforthehomeless.org

NY

Sofia Warren has been a contributing cartoonist to the *New Yorker* since 2017, and her work has been featured in *MoMA Magazine*, *Narrative Magazine*, *Catapult*, and the books *Send Help!* and *Notes from the Bathroom Line*. She was born in Rhode Island and is based in Brooklyn.